THE
BLACK
REVOLT

the civil rights movement,
ghetto uprisings,
and separatism

PRENTICE-HALL, INC., ENGLEWOOD CLIFFS, NEW JERSEY

THE

BLACK

REVOLT

Edited by

James A. Geschwender
State University of New York at Binghamton

Prentice-Hall Sociology Series
Neil J. Smelser, editor

THE BLACK REVOLT:
the civil rights movement,
ghetto uprisings, and separatism,
edited by
James A. Geschwender

13-077339-5 p
13-077347-6 c

Library of Congress Catalog Card Number: 74-149981

Current printing (last digit)
10 9 8 7 6 5 4 3 2 1

PRINTED IN THE UNITED STATES OF AMERICA

Prentice-Hall International, Inc., London
Prentice-Hall of Australia, Pty. Ltd., Sydney
Prentice-Hall of Canada, Ltd., Toronto
Prentice-Hall of India Private Limited, New Delhi
Prentice-Hall of Japan, Inc., Tokyo

CONTENTS

5. Context and Developmental Process 402

part V

SEPARATISM 434

part VI

**THE BLACK REVOLT:
RETROSPECT AND PROSPECTS 460**

*To all those who fought on the front lines
of the black revolt from Montgomery to Newark,
from Selma to Watts, and from Birmingham to Detroit,
and to those who are continuing the struggle
in all of its varied forms.*

PREFACE

This collection is designed to offer a selection of the best social science writing on black protest in America. The selections concern the civil rights movement of the fifties and sixties, separatism, black power, and the ghetto riots of the middle and late sixties. Although numerous books deal with the civil rights movement, riots, or black power, many of them consist of organizational documents and speeches of spokesmen combined with journalistic accounts of the civil rights movement, black power, or separatism. *The Black Revolt* is intended to supplement such volumes by presenting a different treatment of the same subject. It differs in that it consists entirely of writings by social scientists analyzing black protest from varying frames of reference. It also differs because it attempts to analyze the gradual shift from the nonviolence of the civil rights movement, through the militance of black power, to the violence of the ghetto insurrections, with the tangential development of separatism. The reasons for this developmental process are suggested throughout the volume.

It is my hope that this volume contributes to an understanding of the nature and development of the black revolt. If college students and the general public can read these selections and come away with a greater understanding of the societal conditions which made the revolt necessary, and the societal response which made the rejection of nonviolence inevitable, then I have succeeded in my task.

I cannot acknowledge all who have contributed to the ideas presented here, but I will present a partial list. I learned much about the civil rights movement from the members of Liberal Forum at Florida State University and from the members of CORE in Tallahassee between 1962 and 1964. The student body at Wayne State University between 1964 and 1968 included blacks of various degrees of militancy and white radicals who helped to keep me abreast of changing developments in the black revolt. I have received ideas and stimulation, both on the general nature of social movements and the specific nature of the black revolt, from many colleagues. A partial list includes: William H. Form, Carl F. Grindstaff, Lewis M. Killian, James W. Rinehart, William A. Rushing, Benjamin D. Singer, Frederick Waisanen, Henry J. Watts, and Norbert Wiley. I am indebted to all the authors and publishers who allowed me to include the selections in this volume. I wish to thank my wife, Barbara, and my daughter, Laura, for their support and understanding of activities which removed me from "the family scene" at various times.

James A. Geschwender
London, Ontario, Canada
March 25, 1971

part I

AN
INTRODUCTION
TO THE
BLACK REVOLT

Blacks have been unhappy with their status in America and have been revolting against it ever since they first arrived in 1619. Herbert Aptheker has documented the existence of over two hundred Negro slave revolts.[1] Countless Africans committed suicide on the passage to America. Many slaves chose the individual form of revolt of simply running away. Others chose passive resistance. They gave the slave owner the minimum level of cooperation and compliance they could safely get away with. Some free blacks helped to organize and operate the underground railroad. Abolitionists included blacks among their ranks. Blacks fought in the Civil War; they were active participants and leaders in the Southern Populist movement at the end of the nineteenth century.[2] By the early twentieth century they had founded the Niagara Movement, the NAACP, and the Urban League.

The decision as to what to include in a book of this kind is made difficult by the presence of black rebellion throughout American history. I have decided to limit the book to the inclusion of only those aspects of black rebellion which clearly fall within the criteria of a social movement.[3] For this reason, we must pause and examine the nature of a social movement.

A social movement may be defined as a continuing, collective attempt to restructure some basic segment of the social order through means other than institutionalized channels. As such, a social movement encompasses both organized and unorganized elements working toward a common objective. The common objective does not have to be very clearly defined or specific. It may be sufficiently diffuse as to encompass within the same social movement elements which differ sharply from one another. Given agreement on the common goal, there may be considerable disagreement over tactics as well as over specific and secondary objectives. There may be many core associations within the same social movement. These organizations may range from those attempting to reform existing society to those attempting to restructure it completely, from those preferring the use of respectable pressure tactics to those willing to use violence. Unorganized individual participants are likely to differ even more than organizations. Sometimes these differences will be so extreme that the various segments of a movement may expend more time and energy in fighting each other than in contending with the larger society.

African suicides and runaway slaves are clearly examples of revolt but they do not necessarily constitute a part of a social movement as they represent individualistic revolts rather than collective attempts to change the social order. The slave revolts, on the other hand, were collective actions on the part of small numbers of slaves on widely separated plantations. However they do not qualify as part of a social movement because of the relatively small numbers involved in any particular revolt, their lack of continuity over time and space, and the low probability of their being aimed at fundamental changes in the social order. In contrast, the underground railroad and the abolitionist movement were segments of a continuing social movement. They are not included in *The Black Revolt* as they were phenomena primarily controlled by whites. They may have had the interests of blacks in mind and they did include blacks, but they were dominated and controlled by whites. The pre-1955 activities of organizations such as the NAACP, the Niagara Movement, and the Urban League are not included in *The Black Revolt* as they do not possess sufficient collective behavior characteristics to constitute social movements. To a large extent they were formally organized pressure groups with little in the way of active mass support. In addition, there is the question of racial composition and continuity. The Niagara Movement was a black movement but it had a very short life span. The NAACP and the Urban League had continuity over time but, prior to 1955, they were white-dominated and had a primarily white membership.

For these reasons I have chosen to include in this book only selections dealing with the black revolt from the time of the birth of the civil rights movement (around 1955) to the present. During this period the black revolt clearly constituted a social movement. It was a collective attempt to change the social order; it had both organized and unorganized elements within it; it had both mass participation and continuity over time; and it developed both on behalf of and on the part of blacks.

The earlier presocial movement acts of rebellion should not be written off as unimportant. They have great significance in the history and development of black protest in America. These incidents and organizations constitute important bits of evidence that black Americans have always found their circumstances of life in America intolerable and have never passively accepted or been satisfied with them. However, a continuing and fully developed social movement cannot be built upon misery. Despair may produce episodic, rebellious outbursts, but a fully developed revolutionary movement or a continuing reform-oriented social movement requires that dissatisfaction with the present be supplemented by hope and faith. One must have hope in the sense that he must believe that a better world is possible, and he must have faith in the sense that he believes that by joining together with others like himself he may develop sufficient collective power to bring about this better world.

Neither hope nor faith is produced in a vacuum. Both are products of social experience. The one selection reprinted in this chapter analyzes the types of social experience which may produce a combination of discontent with the present plus hope for the future. The selection discusses five such sets of experiences. "The rising expectations hypothesis" describes a set of conditions in which the experience of improvements in life conditions is productive of rising aspirations and hope for further improvements. Aspirations and hopes tend to rise more rapidly than objective conditions, thus producing discontent with the rate of progress. "The relative deprivation hypothesis" is a minor variant of this pattern. A group which is experiencing some improvement compares itself to a significant reference group which is experiencing more rapid progress and comes to define this more rapid rate of progress as desirable and possible for its own members. This is combined with their dissatisfaction with their relatively slower rate of improvement.

"The downward mobility hypothesis" describes a different set of etiological conditions. In this case the perception of the possibility of a better set of conditions is produced by the fact that the group involved has already experienced these better life circumstances in the past. A better life must be possible because they have already had it. The comparison of present with past life conditions produces discontent. "The rise and drop hypothesis" is a combination of two of these sets of experiences. In this case a group which has developed rising aspirations and hope as a result of past improvements in life circumstances then develops discontent when this past progress is not only halted but reversed. This combination may produce a rather intense level of discontent and an extreme response.

"The status inconsistency hypothesis" differs from the preceding hypotheses in that it does not include temporal changes in life circumstances as part of the etiology of hope and discontent. Both hope and discontent are produced by a comparison of one's own status profile with that of others in the larger society. One develops hope by observing that one has some of the status attributes which are normally rewarded in society, while discontent develops because such rewards are not being received despite the possession of the relevant status attributes.

This selection does not discuss the origin of faith. It is possible that the best single source of faith is action, and that faith in collective action can be best developed and confirmed through successful action. The first preliminary, groping, presocial movement attempting to bring about social change may be successful in bringing about some limited change. If it is, this will constitute concrete evidence of the efficacy of collective action. Nor is this selection exhaustive of all circumstances which produce hope and discontent. The government may provide an additional source of hope and discontent. If a government recognizes the injustice of the *status quo*, promises remedial action, and fails to deliver as rapid and sweeping changes as promised, a subject population may simultaneously develop hope and discontent. This may be what happened when the government of the United States enacted the Supreme Court school desegregation decisions and passed the Civil Rights Acts of 1964 and 1965 without making any major alterations in the life situations of most American blacks. A similar pattern emerges when the accomplishments of "The War on Poverty" are compared with early publicity.

NOTES

1. Herbert Aptheker, *American Negro Slave Revolts* (New York: Columbia University Press, 1945); for a brief history of other Negro protest activity see Gunnar Myrdal, *An American Dilemma* (New York: Harper & Row, 1944), pp. 736–937.
2. C. Vann Woodward, *The Strange Career of Jim Crow* (New York: Oxford University Press, 1966), pp. 31–107.
3. The concept of social movement used herein is modeled after that developed in Kurt Lang and Gladys Engel Lang, *Collective Dynamics* (New York: Thomas Y. Crowell, 1961).

Explorations in the Theory of Social Movements and Revolutions

James A. Geschwender

James C. Davies made a first step toward formulating a theory of societal conditions which tend to produce revolutions.[1] His formulation is limited in two ways. First, Davies overly restricted himself by limiting his concern to "progressive" revolutions rather than analyzing the preconditions for revolutions of either a leftist or rightist direction. As a result, he formulated a statement of a set of preconditions which may be a special case of a more general set which would produce revolutions of either type.

The second limitation arises from his failure to distinguish between two separate but related problems. One may attempt to ascertain those factors which dispose specific individuals or types of individuals to take part in revolutionary activity or one may attempt to ascertain those factors which produce a revolution at a particular time and place. These two problems require different types of information. The former requires a theory of motivation which predicts that individuals experiencing certain specified conditions will manifest the behavioral response of revolutionary activity. It would further require the ability to document the existence of instantiations or examples of the classes of preconditions called for in the motivational theory.

The second problem requires an explanation in terms of conditions which disrupt the normal societal or institutional processes operating at a given time. One may tie the two problems together by assuming that revolutions occurring at a particular time and place are the final product of intra- and inter-individual expressions of revolutionary activity of sufficient intensity. If one makes this assumption, it follows that *conditions which produce a revolution are no different in principle from those which produce a smaller or even an unsuccessful protest movement.* The major difference between the two would be in the numbers of individuals aroused to revolutionary activity and in those procesess which develop after the protest movement has begun. The present analysis will parallel Davies as it will be limited to the initial conditions producing a movement.

THE RISE AND DROP HYPOTHESIS

Let us examine the structure of the argument put forth by Davies. He explicitly focused on the problem of specification of conditions that produce a revolution at a particular time and place. But the structure of his reasoning is focused upon the manner in which specific sets of ob-

From *Social Forces* 47 (December 1968): 127–35; reprinted by permission of the publisher.

jective conditions impinge upon individuals or types of individuals and motivate them to take part in revolutionary activities. He states his reasoning as follows:

> Revolutions are most likely to occur when a prolonged period of objective economic and social development is followed by a short period of sharp reversal. The all-important effect on the minds of people in a particular society is to produce, during the former period, an expectation of continued ability to satisfy needs—which continue to rise—and, during the latter, a mental state of anxiety and frustration when manifest reality breaks away from anticipated reality. *The actual state of socioeconomic development is less significant than the expectation that past progress, now blocked, can and must continue in the future.*[2]

The conclusion that actual conditions of deprivation are less important than the development of a particular state of mind wherein one believes that he is unjustly deprived relative to another possible state of affairs is consistent with the earlier writings of L. P. Edwards [3] and Crane Brinton.[4] The suggestion that this state of mind may be produced by a period of progress followed by a sharp reversal is well documented in Davies' analysis of Dorr's Rebellion, the Russian Revolution, the Egyptian Revolution, and numerous other civil disorders. However, Davies' preoccupation with the point at which revolution begins led to overlooking the fact that his own data suggest the existence of other patterns which would also produce this state of mind.

ALTERNATIVE PATTERNS: THE RISING EXPECTATIONS HYPOTHESIS

Davies included a diagram of the period preceding Dorr's Rebellion.[5] This illustrates the fact that the rebellion broke out in 1842 after just such an improvement and decline in socioeconomic conditions as predicted. However, the earlier period is of considerable interest. Davies labeled the period from about 1812 to about 1838 as a period of increased agitation for suffrage. This period of increased agitation represents a period of protest—the beginning of a protest movement—which results from the same state of mind that produces revolutionary activity. The individuals who are engaged in protest and agitation are doing so because they perceive an intolerable gap between a state of affairs believed possible and desirable and a state of affairs actually existing. This perception of an intolerable gap did not result from the curve of economic development proposed by Davies but rather from a simple decline in the rate of social and economic progress. The diagram shows a continued increase in the level of need satisfaction from 1812 to 1835 but at a slower rate of increase than had occurred from 1790 to 1810. In short, the mere decline in the rate of improvement in the level of need satisfaction was sufficient to produce a gap between expectations and experience great enough to be considered intolerable by some.

This pattern of development of a gap between level of need satisfaction and expected level of need satisfaction appears to be a slight variant of the pattern suggested for the French Revolution by Tocqueville,[6] and

also suggested by Edwards,[7] and Crane Brinton [8] in their studies of com-
monalities in the Puritan, French, Russian, and American revolutions.
They stated that the experiencing of a period of improvement yields the
expectation of, and desire for, further improvements. When these come
too slowly, rebellion follows.

It seems that this scheme could be used to account for a portion of
the protest activities on the part of Negroes in American society today.
One could say that the improvement in general social conditions as
evidenced by a certain amount of school integration, improved opportunities to vote, etc., have led many American Negroes to believe that progress
is possible. They have experienced some acceptance into American life
and expect to receive more. Once given this hope of full participation
they become dissatisfied with the rather slow rate of change which may
be observed. They see school integration, but only on a token basis; they
see the loosening of many restrictions, but at such a slow rate that they
become concerned that their shackles will never be completely thrown
off. As they become increasingly impatient with the rate of improvement
in social conditions, they begin to resort more and more to direct action,
to sit-ins, wade-ins, etc.[9]

THE RELATIVE DEPRIVATION HYPOTHESIS

Marx suggested that workers become restless and eventually revolt after
experiencing a similar improvement in the material conditions of their
lives.[10] He suggested that workers develop the standards for their desired
and expected level of need satisfaction from the level that they see prevailing throughout society. Their desired level of need satisfaction rises
at a pace equivalent to the rate of improved living standards for the rest
of society so that, despite an improvement in the objective level of need
satisfactions, there is an increasing gap between what the workers feel
they should get and what they actually receive. This gap grows until the
workers revolt. In this case, the level of expected need satisfaction derives
from perception of the level of need satisfaction experienced by a reference group.

The current Negro revolt has been explained in terms of relative
deprivation.[11] Many Negroes believe that Negroes are improving their
objective position in American society but they are not gaining relative
to whites. They use the metaphor of a train starting from New York to
California and say that while they have reached Chicago they are still
riding in the caboose and maybe the train has grown longer. In other
words, the Negro today is better off than his grandfather but so is the
white, and possibly the gap between Negro and white has increased.
Thus, dissatisfaction results and leads to protest activities.

THE DOWNWARD MOBILITY HYPOTHESIS

While he did not study social revolutions, implications regarding the
nature of the process of development of discrepancies between aspirations

and need satisfactions may be drawn from Durkheim's classic study of suicide.[12] Durkheim's analysis of the development of anomie revolved around the relationship between needs (goals) and means of satisfying these needs. He assumed that satisfaction is a result of balance between needs and means of need satisfaction. Dissatisfaction results whenever needs exceed the means of need satisfaction. These needs may be dichotomized into organic and nonorganic needs. The former are limited in an absolute sense, while the latter are unlimited by nature. One's position in the stratification system places a limit upon aspirations and therefore maintains a balance between needs and need satisfactions.

Durkheim contended that the individual is in trouble whenever anything happens to disrupt this balance between needs and satisfactions. He will be frustrated whenever his desires exceed his achievements. A sudden improvement in wealth or power of the type that is expected to precede revolutions stimulates aspirations causing them to grow beyond means of satisfaction.

But improvements in status were not the only means envisioned by Durkheim whereby the balance between needs (aspirations) and means of satisfaction would be upset. He also stated that economic disasters upset the balance. Disasters declassify individuals, forcing them into a lower state than their previous one. This necessitates the painful process of reducing aspirations or needs to the level of possible need fulfillment. This is just as painful and disorienting a process as that which results from sudden improvement in one's position. It seems that this particular type of imbalance could also be brought about through downward social mobility in either an absolute or a relative sense.

Relative downward mobility refers to the felt loss of status experienced by a group which observes a previously inferior group closing the gap between them. Killian points out that southern whites who have migrated to Chicago feel a loss of status relative to Negroes despite the fact that they have experienced an objective improvement in economic conditions.[13] This type of imbalance between reality and desire is as likely to produce a social movement or revolution as the types discussed above.[14]

There are sufficient empirical data to support the notion that rebelliousness may grow out of a decline in one's objective material position. Lipset's analysis of the rise of the C.C.F. (an agrarian socialist political party) in Saskatchewan is a case in point.[15] Lipset interpreted the C.C.F. as the culmination of a class-conscious movement on the part of Canadian wheat farmers. He suggested that the C.C.F. received its earliest and most consistent support from those groups in the rural population who had the highest social and economic status. By this he meant that they had the largest farms and were least likely to be tenants. The poorer farmers were more difficult to organize during the Thirties. However, once they were organized they turned out to be the movement's staunchest supporters during the war years. The Thirties were times of severe depression and the war years were prosperous times for the wheat farmers.

It is possible to reanalyze Lipset's findings with a view toward determining what happened during the Depression and how this led to the development of the movement. Historically, wheat farmers have an insecure income. They fluctuate between good and bad times depending upon the price of wheat. All farmers are not equally affected by economic fluctuations, as is especially revealed by the Depression. "In the first period, 1929–31, the small farms had a net cash income but increases in the size of the farm were accompanied by a declining income until at 500 acres no Net Cash Income and increasingly larger operating losses resulted for the larger farms." [16]

The wealthier farmers during the Depression experienced a rapid and sharp decline in their economic position in both absolute terms and relative to the poorer farmers. This decline relative to their previous high position (which we may assume they preferred) led to their organization and participation in the C.C.F. The poorer farmers did not become strong supporters until they experienced a rapid improvement in their objective economic status. They engaged in protest activity only after it had been demonstrated that this type of activity could bring about objective improvements. They were responding not only to the improvements, but also to the example set by the wealthier wheat farmers. The wealthier farmers protested in response to a deteriorating objective state and, in turn, acted as agitators in stimulating unrest and protest activities in others.

The American Populist Movement seems to have been produced by the same type of situation that gave rise to the C.C.F. Draper described the Populists as, "property-conscious farmers threatened with debt and bankruptcy." [17] Kornhauser suggests that the Italian Fascist and German Nazi movements drew heavily from individuals who had undergone a decline in their objective economic position. It is not unreasonable to assume that they looked back to their former positions as desirable and proper.[18] Therefore, they perceived themselves as experiencing an "intolerable gap" between their proper level of need satisfaction and their actual level. This experience led them to participate in a revolutionary protest movement.

THE STATUS INCONSISTENCY HYPOTHESIS

All of the patterns of conditions likely to produce protest or revolution discussed above have had temporal change as an essential element. They all analyzed the manner in which changes in one's position over time give rise to a belief in the possibility and justice of an improvement in circumstances. The difference between desired and actual circumstances is what leads to revolutionary or protest activity. The concept of status consistency, developed by Lenski, makes possible the analysis of a nontemporal source of this discrepancy.[19]

Broom agreed that status inconsistents may make up the membership of a social movement and gives the concept special relevance for ethnic minorities.[20] He suggested that an aggregate with a low degree of stratum consistency, i.e., a number of persons having similar patterns of inconsistency, may develop ethnic-consciousness. He predicted that tension will be positively associated with low attribute consistency. This is based on the assumption that an erratic profile will reflect areas of blockage of mobility opportunities. If a group's mobility were strictly determined by the abilities and initiative of its individual members, it would be expected to move up in all status hierarchies at corresponding rates. If their mobility in one dimension lags behind others it indicates the existence of impediments to free mobility. These impediments tend to create tensions which could produce protest activity. Status-inconsistent members of minority groups have been found to participate in social movements, such as the N.A.A.C.P., European Socialist parties, and the C.C.F. in Canada.[21]

Sorokin used the concept of "multibonded stratification" to analyze the relation between status inconsistency and revolutionary behavior.[22] He considered stratification in terms of a number of status dimensions that are bonded or welded together to form affine or disaffine strata. Affine strata are defined as those groups whose multiple bonds are mutually congenial and lead the members of such groups to the same type of behavior or mentality. Disaffine strata are those whose bonds are innerly contradictory. This would include groups who are high occupationally but low racially or ethnically, or high on the racial-ethnic dimension but low in economic status, as well as other combinations. Sorokin emphasized that these disaffine strata are not rare or exotic. They tend to appear quite frequently, though less frequently than affine strata. He further states that the disaffine strata are unstable and tend to decompose rapidly to be replaced by a new affine coalescence of the stratifying bonds.

The simultaneous appearance in a population of two double disaffine groups is a symptom which portends revolutionary change. Sorokin stated that the French Revolution was a perfect example of this. The nobility was a politically powerful group which had little economic wealth, while the third estate was a wealthy group virtually powerless in the political arena. The French Revolution was the decomposition of these two double disaffine strata and the creation of two new affine strata. Sorokin claimed that similar sets of circumstances prevailed in the case of the Russian Revolution of 1905, the Communist Revolution, and numerous other examples.

TOWARD A GENERAL THEORY OF SOCIAL MOVEMENTS

The empirical relationship between status inconsistency and propensity toward revolutionary or protest activities is documented above. However, each of the temporal hypotheses included a rationale which accounted for the development of individual dissatisfaction sufficiently intense to produce protest. This is lacking in the preceding discussion of status consistency. This gap has been filled through an integration of the status consistency literature, Homan's Theory of Distributive Justice,[23] and Festinger's Theory of Cognitive Dissonance,[24] into an expanded theory.[25]

This integrated theory includes seven assumptions. The following are the relevant portions for an analysis of social movements and revolutions:

1. All individuals hold sets of cognitions which include some that are reality-based, some that are definitional, and some that are normative.
2. Any set of cognitions may stand in a relation of dissonance, consonance, or irrelevance, depending upon the internal relations which hold among reality-based and normative cognitions. If the conjunction of a reality-based and a normative cognition implies the negation of another reality-based cognition, then a state of dissonance exists.
3. Reality-based cognitions will include perceptions of one's status in the educational, occupational, income, and ethnic hierarchies. Definitional cognitions will include the definition of ethnicity as an ascribed investment, education as an achieved investment, occupation as a social reward, and income as a material reward. Normative cognitions will include the belief that rewards received should be proportional to investments.
4. Dissonance is an upsetting state and will produce tension for the individual. This tension will lead to an attempt to reduce dissonance by altering cognitions, adding new cognitions, or deleting old ones. Attempts to alter reality-based cognitions will involve attempting to change the real world.
5. Status inconsistents whose rewards received are less than believed to be proper for their investments will feel anger and inconsistents whose rewards exceed investments will feel guilt. Anger is a sharper form of dissonance than guilt. The intensity of dissonance-reducing behavior will be directly proportional to the sharpness of dissonance.
6. Dissonance-reducing attempts will take the form of coping responses, attempts to change the real world, when possible.
7. Dissonance-reducing attempts will move from the simple to the complex. The most complex form of attempting to change reality is attempting to alter society.

These assumptions allow the derivation of predictions of specific behavioral responses to specific profiles of status inconsistency. Included are a number of predictions regarding the manner in which status inconsistency may contribute to the origin of social movements. More will be said on this below. The addition of the following assumptions will permit the derivation of predictions regarding the manner in which temporal changes in socioeconomic conditions may contribute to the origin of social movements:

8. Reality-based cognitions will include perceptions of present socioeconomic circumstances, past socioeconomic circumstances, and time lapse between the two. A higher level of socioeconomic circumstances will be defined as preferable to a lower level of socioeconomic circumstances.
9. Individuals whose present socioeconomic circumstances are at a higher level than past circumstances will be aware of the fact that they have experienced improvement and will define further improvement as

possible and desirable. The discrepancy between anticipated future circumstances and present circumstances will produce dissonance. Anticipation of future rate of progress will be determined by rate of past progress (time lapse cognition).

10. Reality-based cognitions will include perceptions of present and past socioeconomic statuses of relevant reference groups. Comparisons will be made between rates of progress of self and relevant reference groups. Discrepancies between perceived rates of progress will produce dissonance.

11. Individuals whose present socioeconomic circumstances are at a lower level than past circumstances will be aware that they have experienced a worsening of conditions and will be fearful of further deterioration. A comparison of present circumstances and past circumstances will produce dissonance.

12. Attempts to reduce dissonance will take the form of attempting to change society when it is believed that sufficient power is, or can be, harnessed to bring this about. They will take a rightist direction when present circumstances are at a lower level than past circumstances and a leftist direction when present circumstances are at a higher level than past circumstances.

13. The intensity of dissonance experienced will be inversely proportional to the time span during which the discrepancies developed and will be directly proportional to the size of the discrepancies. The intensity of change attempts will be directly proportional to the intensity of dissonance.

14. Change-oriented, dissonance-reducing attempts on the part of status inconsistents will take a rightist orientation when high ethnic status is combined with lower levels of occupation or income; they will take a leftist orientation when high educational status is combined with a lower level of occupation or income.

DISCUSSION

All of the patterns of temporal change which produce revolutionary activities may be explained within dissonance theory. Changes in objective conditions produce a state of mind in which individuals believe that they are unjustly deprived of a better way of life. First, they develop the image of a state of affairs which is possible of attainment. Second, they develop the belief that they are entitled to that state of affairs. Third, they know that they are not enjoying that state of affairs. The simultaneous possession of these three cognitions produces a state of dissonance. Dissonance is not comfortable and it produces pressures toward dissonance reduction. One means of reducing this dissonance is to alter the environment so as to produce the desired state of affairs. Therefore, dissonance-reducing activities often take the form of social protest or revolutionary behavior.

The fact that different individuals may experience different intensities of dissonance (or may have different levels of tolerance for dissonance) would lead to their engaging in protest activities at different points in time. It is conceivable that attempts to reduce dissonance (protest activities) on the part of the earliest and most severely affected will help to create dissonance in others similarly situated. Thus, the former group acts as agitators in helping to stir the latter to revolt.

It is also possible to predict the direction and intensity of the protest response with the aid of dissonance theory. It is reasonable to assume that the intensity of the response will be proportional to the intensity of dissonance experienced. Certain of the patterns would be likely to produce a more intense state of dissonance than others. Davies' "rise and drop" hypothesis describes a set of circumstances which produces a large discrepancy between expected level of need satisfaction and actual level of need satisfaction. This discrepancy should be much smaller for those sets of circumstances described by the "rising expectations" hypothesis. The former might then be expected to produce a more intense form of dissonance, and, consequently, a more intense form of dissonance-reducing behavior (e.g., revolutionary rather than reform movements).

This can be illustrated by two types of Negro protest movements. The relationship between the "rising expectations" hypothesis and civil rights protest has been discussed above. The more extreme reaction to the "rise and drop" hypothesis can be illustrated with the Universal Negro Improvement Association of Marcus Garvey.[26]

Garvey had been actively, but unsuccessfully, attempting to recruit supporters prior to World War I. During the war opportunities for Negroes improved dramatically. As whites went into the armed services and defense needs expanded, many jobs were opened to Negroes for the first time. Other Negroes went into the service, and some went to Europe and saw that conditions prevailing in the United States were not necessarily inevitable. Their accounts were printed in Negro newspapers throughout the country. These circumstances produced an anticipation of, and a desire for, better conditions of life than those prevailing prior to the war. When the war ended, whites returned from the armed services and defense spending was sharply curtailed. Negroes lost jobs gained during the war. Riots occurred all over the country to "put the Negro back in his place." The "rise and drop" circumstances had been experienced and Marcus Garvey found his recruits. The growth of the movement, until it was crushed, is history.

It is conceivable that the growth of the Nation of Islam after World War II and of Black Nationalism after the federal government's recent retreat on civil rights is the result of a similar "rise and drop" experience. This would illustrate the fact that different segments of the Negro community differentially experience the same societal changes. Middle-class Negroes have experienced a continual improvement in life circumstances and may be reacting in terms of the "rising expectations" hypothesis. Lower-class Negroes have had their aspirations raised simply to find the doors closed as tightly as ever. They may be reacting in terms of the "rise and drop" hypothesis.

Similarly, we would expect that those sets of circumstances described by the "relative deprivation" hypothesis and the "downward mobility" hypothesis would vary in the intensity of dissonance created, and in intensity of dissonance-reducing behavior, according to the degree of relative deprivation and the rate of downward mobility. The set of circumstances described by the "status inconsistency" hypothesis would produce varying intensities of dissonance and dissonance-reducing behavior according to the degree of discrepancy between relevant status dimensions.

The "rise and drop" hypothesis, the "rising expectations" hypothesis, and the "relative deprivation" hypothesis all describe sets of circumstances in which dissatisfaction results from a comparison of actual conditions with anticipated conditions. It involves a future orientation on the part of those affected. This future orientation is represented by a desire to bring about a better state of affairs—one which has never existed in reality. Thus, it may be predicted that protest movements and revolutions resulting from these sets of conditions are likely to be "progressive" or leftist in character.

The "downward mobility" hypothesis, whether absolute or relative mobility, describes a set of circumstances in which dissatisfaction is created by comparing present conditions with conditions which existed in the past. Thus, it may be predicted that dissonance reduction would take the form of a "regressive" or rightist protest movement.

The direction taken by movements resulting from circumstances described in the "status inconsistency" hypothesis would depend upon the nature of the inconsistency involved. Individuals who experience status inconsistency resulting from greater educational investments than income and/or occupational rewards will likely attempt to reduce dissonance in one of two ways. They may attempt to bring about consonance through individual mobility. If this is not possible and they shift to protest activities, it is likely to be in the direction of creating an equalitarian society in which rewards are based upon universalistic criteria—a "progressive" or leftist movement.

Those individuals who experience dissonance resulting from their ethnic investment being greater than their income and/or occupational rewards are not likely to select either of these modes of dissonance reduction. Individual mobility is not possible without education, and rewards distributed upon the basis of universalistic criteria will not help. They are much more prone to support a movement emphasizing rewards based upon particularistic criteria—a "regressive" or rightist movement.

Just as not all revolutionary attempts succeed, Festinger acknowledged that not all attempts to reduce dissonance will be successful. If an attempted revolution or protest movement fails, the dissonant individuals will be forced to attempt to reduce dissonance by altering one of their cognitions (such as that of the desired state of affairs or the proper relation between investments and rewards), or by adding new cognitions (such as their lack of ability to bring about the desired state). This could produce the apathetic, disinterested, nonprotesting type of fatalistic behavior that we find among the severely downtrodden.

One of the assumptions presented above stated that social change would be perceived as a means of reducing dissonance if it is believed that sufficient power is, or could be, harnessed. It is also possible that the required intensity of dissonance may be present but the required perception of power absent. This combination cannot be expected to produce social movements or revolutions. However, the dissonance that has been generated will not simply dissipate and may not be reduced by cognitive reorganization. It is possible that this combination may produce hostile outbursts such as the ghetto riots currently occurring throughout the country.

Civil rights legislation, the "war on poverty," VISTA, and other governmental actions may lead ghetto-dwelling Negroes to drastically raise their levels of aspirations and expectations. The failure of these measures to bring about significant improvements may lead to disillusionment. The discrepancy between expectation and reality creates dissonance. No improvement is actually experienced; only hopes are raised. Thus, intense dissonance is combined with feelings of powerlessness that typify the ghetto dweller, and riots or explosions emerge.

CONCLUSIONS

It has been shown that the particular sequence of temporal changes described by Davies is only one of several sequences which produce in individuals the state of mind that tends to be expressed in revolutionary or other protest activities. The experiencing of status inconsistency is a nontemporal condition which also produces this same state of mind. Dissonance theory is capable of explaining the manner in which this state of mind is produced by these diverse sets of conditions and the manner in which it finds its expression in protest activities.

Hypotheses have been derived which predict the particular mode of dissonance reduction that will be attempted under certain sets of conditions, the direction of change attempts (rightist or leftist movements), the intensity of change attempts (revolutionary or reform), and the conditions under which change will not be attempted but hostile outbursts emerge or apathy and hopelessness set in. Research is needed to test these hypotheses and to detail the relationship between these and other possible sets of preconditions of revolutionary activity. Davies has taken a major step in the development of a theory of revolution and the present paper has helped to place this contribution into a more general context.

NOTES

ACKNOWLEDGEMENT: I am indebted to Frederick B. Waisanen for the hours of discussion which gave rise to many of the ideas included herein. I am also indebted to William A. Rushing, Lewis M. Killian, and Leland Axelson for the careful reading of an earlier version and the useful suggestions which they made.

1. James C. Davies, "Toward a Theory of Revolution," *American Sociological Review* 27 (February 1962): 5–18.
2. Ibid., p. 6 (italics added for emphasis).
3. Lyford P. Edwards, *The Natural History of Revolution* (Chicago: University of Chicago Press, 1927).

4. Crane Brinton, *The Anatomy of Revolution* (New York: Norton, 1938).

5. Davies, "Toward a Theory of Revolution," p. 9.

6. Cited in ibid, pp. 5–6.

7. Edwards, *Natural History of Revolution*, pp. 34–35.

8. Brinton, *Anatomy of Revolution*, p. 286 and pp. 78–79.

9. Cf. Dan Wakefield, *Revolt in the South* (New York: Grove Press, 1960).

10. Cited in Davies, "Toward a Theory of Revolution," p. 5.

11. James A. Geschwender, "The Negro Revolt: An Examination of Some Hypotheses," *Social Forces* 43 (December 1964): 248–56.

12. Emile Durkheim, *Suicide* (Glencoe, Illinois: The Free Press, 1951).

13. Lewis M. Killian, "The Adjustment of Southern White Migrants to Northern Urban Norms," *Social Forces*, 32 (October 1953): 61.

14. For a discussion of such countermovements see Ralph H. Turner and Lewis M. Killian, *Collective Behavior* (Englewood Cliffs, N.J.: Prentice-Hall, 1957), pp. 382–84; Lewis M. Killian, "The Purge of an Agitator," *Social Problems*, 7 (Fall 1959: 152–56; and James W. Vander Zanden, "Resistance and Social Movements," *Social Forces*, 37 (May 1959): 212–15.

15. Seymour M. Lipset, *Agrarian Socialism* (Berkeley: University of California Press, 1950).

16. Ibid., p. 91, quoted from William Allen and E. C. Hope, *The Farm Outlook for Saskatchewan* (Saskatchewan: University of Sasketchewan, 1934), p. 2.

17. Theodore Draper, *The Roots of American Communism* (New York: Viking, 1957), p. 37.

18. William Kornhauser, *The Politics of Mass Society* (Glencoe, Illinois: The Free Press, 1959), p. 181. For a similar interpretation see also Emile Benoit-Smullyan, "Status, Status Types, and Status Interrelations," *American Sociological Review*, 9 (April 1944): 353–59.

19. Gerhard Lenski, "Status Crystallization: A Non-Vertical Dimension of Social Status," *American Sociological Review* 19 (August 1954): 405–13. For a summary of some of the literature on the relationship between status inconsistency and participation in social movements see James A. Geschwender, "Continuities in Theories of Status Consistency and Cognitive Dissonance," *Social Forces,* 46 (December 1967): 165–67.

20. Leonard Broom, "Social Differentiation and Stratification," in Robert K. Merton, Leonard Broom, and Leonard S. Cottrell, eds., *Sociology Today* (New York: Basic Books, 1959), pp. 429–41.

21. Cf. E. Franklin Frazier, *Black Bourgeoisie* (Glencoe, Illinois: The Free Press, 1959), pp. 98–104; Robert Michels, *Political Parties* (New York: Dover Publications, 1959), pp. 260–61; and Lipset, *Agrarian Socialism*, p. 191.

22. Pitirim A. Sorokin, *Society, Culture and Personality* (New York: Harper & Row, 1947), pp. 289–94.

23. George C. Homans, *Social Behavior: Its Elementary Forms* (New York: Harcourt, Brace & Jovanovich, 1961).

24. Leon Festinger, *A Theory of Cognitive Dissonance* (Evanston, Illinois: Row, Peterson & Co., 1957).

25. Geschwender, "Continuities . . .," pp. 160–71.

26. Gunnar Myrdal, *An American Dilemma* (New York: Harper & Row, 1962), pp. 745–49.

part II

THE
CIVIL RIGHTS
MOVEMENT

Defining the civil rights movement is no easy task. The exact temporal cutting points as to when it began, when and if it ended, and what falls within its scope between these two points in time all call for rather arbitrary decisions. The NAACP came into being in 1909 replacing the earlier Niagara Movement. The Urban League was founded in 1910. CORE was established in Chicago in 1942 and went national in 1943. All of these organizations undertook programs that could be classified as civil rights activities; their activities and accomplishments were significant and had an impact upon the position of American blacks. But I do not include the activities of these organizations at this time as part of the civil rights movement because of the limited population base which provided active support. The movement at this time tended to draw its major support from middle-class blacks and whites, and was thus necessarily limited in scope.

I also exclude the post World War I Garvey movement from the civil rights movement. Its major impact was one of withdrawal from American society rather than toward fuller participation in it. The Garvey movement would meet the test of massive support but not the test of direction. More will be said about this when we discuss separatism in Part V.

There are two candidate dates for the beginning of the civil rights movement as used herein. One is December 1, 1955, when Mrs. Rosa Parks refused to give up her seat on a Montgomery bus. This touched off the Montgomery Bus Boycott that brought Martin Luther King, Jr., to prominence and eventuated in the formation of the Southern Christian Leadership Conference (SCLC). The other date is in 1960 when four unorganized black college students spontaneously held what is widely considered the first sit-in.[1] This sit-in touched off a wave of sit-ins that led to CORE's moving South and to the formation of the Student Nonviolent Coordinating Committee (SNCC). The choice between these two dates is largely a matter of preference. Either would qualify as the kick-off of the civil rights movement as both marked the inception of widespread, continuing, mass participation in protest activities on the part of American blacks.

It has been argued that the civil rights movement died in 1964 when it was replaced by ghetto riots. Regardless of the orientations toward change of rioters or of the consequences of riots for social change, there is a qualitative difference between the civil rights movement and riots. One of the distinguishing features of the civil rights movement in the popular mind has been its non-violence, and the riots clearly do not qualify as nonviolent. Thus, riots should be classified as outside the traditional civil rights movement. This does not mean that the civil rights movement died in 1964, for nonviolent protest activities continued at a much diminished pace. But certainly it has been upstaged since 1964. Besides excluding the riots from the civil rights movement, we may also exclude any confrontations or activities between 1954 and 1964 which involved violence (other than in self-defense) on the part of blacks. This does not exclude riots or other violent activities from the black revolt, merely from the traditional civil rights movement.

Thus, for the purpose of this book, the civil rights movement will be defined as involving widespread, continuing, mass black protest of a nonviolent nature aimed at bringing about a fuller participation of blacks in American society. This chapter will include sections dealing with the background conditions that produced the civil rights movement, the organizations involved, the leadership, tactics, and participation.

NOTES

1. This was not actually the first sit-in, but it was the one that sparked the wave of sit-ins that swept the nation. See Martin Oppenheimer, "The Southern Student Movement: Year 1," *The Journal of Negro Education* (Fall 1964): 396–403.

1. The Background Circumstances

If we are to understand the civil rights movement, it will be necessary to examine the context from which it emerged. This section includes two selections dealing with the historical period which produced a significant mass black action in the South aimed at bringing about social change. In the first selection, Robin Williams describes the changes that have taken place in race relations in the United States since World War II. The selection is quite valuable in that it demonstrates the folly of attempting to view prejudice or discrimination apart from considerations of social structure. For too long social scientists have been content to explain discrimination simply by saying it is caused by prejudice. This explains nothing. Both social scientists and persons interested in bringing about social change must analyze the existing social structure in order to determine which vested interests are being served by the maintenance of patterns of discrimination. This analysis must precede any effective civil rights campaign. One must be certain that whatever tactics are selected will be those that bring pressure upon those groups that both benefit from existing patterns of discrimination and have the power to alter them.

The second selection is an article in which I attempt to apply the hypotheses described in Part I to the origins of the civil rights movement. Census data on the objective status of blacks in America in 1940 and 1960 are compared temporally and in relation to the objective status of whites. It was found that in these two decades blacks improved their level of educational achievements both absolutely and relative to whites. They experienced absolute improvement in their occupational status but fell further behind whites in terms of representation in professional and semi-professional occupations. They improved their income levels absolutely but fell further behind whites in so doing. Their occupational gains did not keep pace with their educational advances.

All of this adds up to the conclusion that neither "the rise and drop" nor "the downward mobility" hypotheses can be utilized to explain the origins of the civil rights movement. Either "the rising expectations," "the relative deprivation," or "the status consistency" hypotheses might apply, each of these hypotheses involves the component of relative deprivation as one compares oneself to others in society and becomes dissatisfied by such comparisons. Discontent with the fact that past improvements have not reduced the gap between white and black combines with hope stemming from such improvement to account for part of the origin of this protest movement. The fact that the gap has not been closed is illustrated by the finding that the objective level of occupational discrimination against blacks *increased* in the United States between 1940 and 1960.[1]

NOTES

1. See James A. Geschwender, "Negro Education: The False Faith," *Phylon* 29 (Winter 1968): 371–78.

Social Change and Social Conflict:
Race Relations in the United States,
1944-1964

Robin M. Williams, Jr.

THE BASES OF ORGANIZED PROTEST

Organized protest emerges from collectivities that have acquired a sense of common fate, a basis for hope of successful protest, common aspirations, and a "moral" claim to redress of grievances.

Minorities are created, to an important degree, by the action of dominant groupings. If all the members of a population aggregate are identified and treated alike, they will tend to become alike in some interests, values, beliefs, and effective responses. To the extent that the members of such emerging collectivity thus come to be alike, their awareness of commonality tends to increase. As both commonality and the awareness of it grow, the possibility of concerted action for collective objectives is increased. It is in this way, for example, that segregation and discrimination have created and are now creating the basis for a continuing Negro-American collectivity.

Severe relative deprivation plus social humiliation may result in accommodation and outward apathy in a fragmented, weak, and overpowered minority. But the same combination is explosive when conjoined with (1) a high level of intragroup communication, resulting in a widely shared and intense sense of collective rate, (2) a recent history of rapidly rising aspirations, (3) a strong sense of legitimacy of these aspirations, (4) a strong sense of the arbitrary or immoral character of the blockages to these aspirations, (5) awareness of power or potential power of the minority in the political arena, and finally, (6) failure of the dominant grouping to evidence realistic action to remove the basic sources of grievance.

Clearly, it is an easy prediction that conflicts over segregation and group discrimination are certain to emerge as Negroes increase their education, income, and occupational status, without at the same time securing a reduction in barriers to full participation in the society at large.

The situation of the greater part of the American Negro population over the last decade has been that of conspicuous and chronic relative deprivation. Although absolute gains have been made, ". . . in each interrelated realm—health, employment, business, income, housing, voting, and education—the absolute gains of the 1950's pale when contrasted with

Originally published in Vol. 35, No. 1 of *Sociological Inquiry* (Winter 1965): 15–24; reprinted and abridged by permission of the author and publisher.

current white standards . . . The resulting relative deprivation is the fundamental basis of mass Negro American dissatisfaction today." [1]

In spite of increased alienation and despair among some segments of the population, the evidence indicates that on the whole Negroes have become more knowledgeable, assertive, and eager in their orientation to the future; group pride and sense of collective fate and membership have increased, and group rejection and self-hate have decreased.[2] Evidences of desires for social ascent are abundant, ranging from aspirations for promotion among soldiers in World War II [3] to the occupational aspirations of high school students. In an industrial city in upstate New York, Negro high school students had a higher level of aspiration than whites of similar socioeconomic backgrounds.[4]

Gist and Bennett show that among high school youths Negroes and whites did not differ in their educational and occupational aspirations or plans, but on a revised North-Hatt scale, higher mobility aspirations were advanced by Negro students, especially the girls.[5] Many other pieces of evidence corroborate these indications of relatively high ambition.[6]

On the other side, the Negroes meet the massive entrenched interests of whites in the perpetuation of invidious distinctions, forced segregation, discrimination in housing, education, and employment, and white political supremacy. These advantages are not lightly relinquished by whites.[7]

As relative deprivation contributed to *ressentiment,* rising aspirations sharpened a widely shared feeling of injustice. To these potent elements were added, in the large cities, the anomie and hostile despair of the unskilled, poorly educated masses. Many of the latter have only recently left the rural South for the "freedom" and "opportunity" of New York, Philadelphia, Cleveland, Chicago, Detroit, or Los Angeles.[8] It is among the disenchanted urban lower classes that black nationalism and rampaging violence have grown.[9]

It is clear enough that poverty and unemployment by themselves are not enough to account for social protest and militant action. We have known for some time that organized and sustained protest is most likely not when the economic position of a population is continuously low and oppressive but rather when conditions have been improving, especially if advancement is abruptly blocked or reversed. When people have "gained enough to realistically hope for more," barriers to future movement will be felt as severely frustrating. This, obviously, is one kind of relative deprivation. But a sense of relative deprivation is enormously accentuated in the case of Negro Americans by sharp awareness of Negro-white differentials.

In the midst of continuous reminders of rising affluence, Negroes have not increased their income levels relative to whites for over a decade. Median family incomes of nonwhites were 53.4 per cent of median family incomes of whites in 1948; in 1962 the figure still was exactly 53.4 per cent. Meantime, the ratio of nonwhite unemployment rates to white rates has actually shown substantial increase: from a rate hovering around 160 in the late 1940's it has risen to over 200 in the early 1960's.

"In 1962, the unemployment rate of nonwhite teenagers remained near 29 per cent, compared with 12 per cent for white youth of the same ages." [10] Seven times as large a proportion of nonwhites as of whites are employed as private household workers, and an increasing proportion of whites are being employed in other service occupations, such as hospital attendant, barber, and cook.[11] All the handicaps of unemployment and low incomes have borne down most heavily on the less well educated non-whites: nonwhite family income as a per cent of white is 58 for those with only elementary schooling, in comparison with 85 for college graduates.[12]

Meanwhile school desegregation has "crept in its petty pace" from year to year, averaging 1 per cent for the Southern and Border States. Once more, high promise and high hope had brought protracted frustration and an additional measure of disillusionment.

PROTEST MOVEMENTS

In all relationships between organizations and groups, the *internal* dynamics of *each* collectivity is affected by the external relationship and, in turn, the internal processes and relationships affect the inter-collectivity relationship. It follows that adequate predictions of the relationships between two social units are likely to require knowledge of internal processes. Thus, a struggle for power within a fragmented leadership structure in a situation of crisis and flux often results in extreme pressure on leaders to exhibit "quick results" to their constituencies and, in consequence, to be driven toward more and more extreme short-run measures. Or, the white segment of a community relies upon the traditional "leaders" of the Negro sub-community well beyond the point at which a new set of quite different leaders have emerged within the Negro grouping. As Pfautz has reminded us:

> The power structures of Negro sub-communities in American cities are in a process of schism and realignment under the impact of desegregation movements and activities. On the practical side, lack of knowledge of the dramatic changes taking place with regard both to the personnel and tactics of the sub-community leadership on the part of the dominant group power structure invites communication breakdowns which can lead to mutual miscalculations and ultimately to civic violence.[13]

The mass movements within urban Negro communities during the last decade have drawn upon long-deferred hopes, massive frustration, moral indignation and newly-revived aspirations. The Negro minority has been handicapped by subjection to extreme discrimination and by internal problems.[14]

As American Negroes have been drawn increasingly into a tightly-woven network of communication, news of events in any one community quickly spread. High sensitivity develops to new modes of collective action. Disillusionment with the promises of white people has spread to the ordinary processes of law, court action, law-enforcement, and the police. The alienation of the Black Muslims is only an extreme case of a pervasive collective attitude especially among the low-income masses of the large Northern centers. In New York City half of the nonwhite population aged 20 and older has come from the South. These immigrants did not come into an established community of ethnic fellows that could help them; they lacked a special language, culture, religion; they did not have close family ties or strong extended kinship relationships; they lacked urban and business experience and commercial skills. In short, they were altogether "outsiders," without "insiders" to help them.[15]

Under these circumstances, the Negro "leader" is likely to find himself under great pressure to prove that he is not "selling out the race" or "giving in." Leaders are likely to need, or to believe that they need, public evidences of "victories" that are local and tangible and that provide an appeal to the numerous disaffected and suspicious elements of the population on the periphery of established organizations.[16] At the same time, the younger, well-educated population tends to move into action, often by-passing the older leadership. The one simple fact that the sit-in movement (as the spearhead of the direct action following the Montgomery breakthrough) was primarily a movement of college students is of very great importance.

> Socialized to value respectability and achievement, educated to affirm their rights of equal opportunity, legitimized in their expectations by civil rights legislation and an important body of opinion, living in a college environment where freedom from constraints and ease of communication facilitate the development and spread of protest activity, these students have selected non-violent protest as an acceptable means of demonstrating their anger at barriers to first-class citizenship. Far from being alienated, the students appear to be committed to the society and its middle class leaders.[17]

The relatively articulate, educated, young persons feel acutely the gap between aspirations and opportunities. To these young men and women, segregation and discrimination are experienced, as Max Weber might have put it, as "specifically senseless."

A number of studies of Negro protest actions have suggested that militancy represents rising aspirations growing out of a measure of upward socioeconomic mobility and the acceptance of the standards of achievement and reward of white middle-class populations. Increased similarity of Negroes and whites in education, income, and occupations facilitates comparison and the growth of conviction that equality of public rights is deserved. The tenor of major legal changes for more than two decades has increasingly reinforced the legitimacy of Negroes' aspirations.

Probably the most common error of white community officials who deal with racial and ethnic problems is to underestimate the strength of the sentiments and the determination of the interested parties in these questions. A particularly conspicuous variety of this miscalculation or unwitting mistake consists of the prediction by white people that intransigent action will cause Negroes to cease their pressure for desegregation and removal of discriminatory barriers. A mass movement such as the present collective demand for civil rights can be stopped by repression —even temporarily—only if the dominant group is firmly united, willing to accept massive economic loss and social disruption, and supported by law and government policy at all levels. These conditions are only roughly approximated in Alabama and Mississippi, and usually are not found in most Northern and Western states.

It is to be specifically emphasized that the implementing decision of the Supreme Court of May 31, 1955, laid out a procedure that invited litigation—legal contest—as the means for determining and enforcing the terms and timing of desegregation. As Robert A. Leflar says: "Thus the Court not only decided the cases immediately before it, but laid down a pattern for lower courts to follow in handling the mass of anticipated future litigation." [18]

On the other hand, protest tactics that directly inconvenience and irritate large numbers of ordinary white citizens, without bringing decisive pressure immediately to bear upon crucial decision-makers, obviously involve great risk of alienating potential supporters and driving "neutralists" into an unsympathetic or opposing position.

Nonviolent tactics that minimize loss of "by-stander" support are at the same time tactics that are in many ways well suited to the psychological needs of many Negro "protestants" as well as to the basic situation in which the minority group " . . . lacks access to major sources of power within a society and to the instruments of violent coercion." [19]

As many recent examples of demonstrations and white-Negro conflict suggest, token integration and frequent communications between Negro and white "spokesmen" or nominal leaders, often are not enough to resolve the pressing issues. When many Negroes want nothing less than full citizenship rights and complete abolition of discrimination *now*—and many white business proprietors, real estate operators, employers, and public officials refuse or find it technically impossible to grant the claimed rights and privileges—conflict ensues when negotiations fail or are not attempted.

Finally, the growth of deep despair and alienation among the low-income, low-education strata of the urban Negro ghettos has been the prelude to the predictable outbreak of more and more "expressive violence." Unlike the well-disciplined, highly purposive, and remarkably patient behavior of earlier organized protests, the emergence of diffuse terrorism and rioting is non-instrumental and chaotic.

PROCESSES OF CONFLICT AND CONFLICT RESOLUTION

Conflict is, by definition, at least a two-sided relation. In the case of Negro-white relations in recent times, the conflict has been centered upon pressure for change from Negroes, versus the resistance to change from white partisans of the *status quo ante*.[20]

It seems broadly correct to say that changes in Negro-white relations since World War II have been most rapid when the changes worked to the economic or other advantage of established positions of certain white persons (e.g., the case of professional baseball), or when powerful politico-legal considerations led to authoritative change by the exercise of governmental authority (e.g., desegregation in the Armed Services).[21] There is no evidence that the great bulk of the white population has been strongly moved to favor desegregation or the abolition of discrimination. On the other side, actual efforts to bring about the integration of Negroes in educational, occupational, political, religious, and other public spheres of life have often been met with strong resistance.[22]

Resistance to change in an established system of segregation and discrimination is so powerful partly because the structure typically represents, at one and the same time, a set of vested interests, normal expectations, conformity pressures, reinforcing ideologies, and modes of assuaging at least some of the anxiety and guilt the system may create. In short, systems of intergroup relations of dominance and subordination are supported by multiple, inter-supportive motivations and beliefs that greatly overdetermine support of the system by those who are actively committed to it.[23]

In the analysis of conflict, considerable research progress has been made since 1944 in disentangling hostility from militancy. Militancy is the opposite of apathy or resignation and involves the willingness to protest discrimination and to fight for rights. Hostility is a continued condition of resentment and hatred directed toward persons and groups. In the instance of American Negroes, there is much evidence that high militancy tends to be associated with relatively low rejection of white individuals, whereas low militancy often is associated with strong prejudice against whites, and to some extent with "self-hate" as well.[24] It should occasion no surprise, accordingly, to find that highly disciplined, well-organized, purposive protest movements directed toward essentially integrative changes can coexist with separatist movements of alienation and with tactically hazardous outbursts of expressive violence.

Most interracial violence in the past has been initiated by whites as a diffuse reaction to ". . . real or perceived assaults upon the accommodative structure, by Negroes, and not from any policy decisions, conscious or unconscious, by the leadership of either group." [25]

Research during these two decades repeatedly has documented also the pervasiveness of a sense of threat among white people concerning relationships to Negroes. The studies suggest widespread fears. Arnold Rose shows in a Minneapolis sample of white people that 66 per cent believe that the presence of a Negro family in a residential area lowers property values.[26] Bressler describes in detail the reaction of panic—and its violent sequelae—to the move of a single middle-class Negro family into Levittown, Pennsylvania.[27] The strikingly "disproportionate" behaviors are inexplicable if viewed solely as expressions of "individual prejudice." [28]

Thus, as Grimshaw has shown, interracial violence is not a simple expression of prejudice or social tension; in urban race riots (of whites versus Negroes) a primary source of actions leading to violence has been the reaction of the dominant group to real or perceived attacks by the subordinate group upon a stabilized set of accommodative arrangements.[29] The actual occurrence of violence is strongly dependent also upon external social controls, especially the behavior of local governments through police agencies.[30]

Furthermore, new evidence on older hypotheses has been supplied by recent events. Certain long-standing propositions concerning conflict and group militancy appear to be well-supported even if imprecise. E.g.:

40. Mass violence (e.g., race riots) is most likely under the following conditions: (a) prolonged frustration, leading to a high tension level; (b) presence of population elements with a propensity to violence (especially lower class, adolescent males in socially disorganized areas); (c) a highly visible and rapid change in intergroup relations; (d) a precipitating incident of intergroup conflict.[31]

42. Militancy, except for sporadic and short-lived uprisings, is not characteristic of the most deprived and oppressed groups, but rather of those who have gained considerable rights so that they are able realistically to hope for more.

43. A militant reaction from a minority group is most likely when (a) the group's position is rapidly improving, or (b) when it is rapidly deteriorating, especially if this follows a period of improvement.[32]

During the last two decades, new approaches to the study of social conflict have been developed in some detail, and "conflict theory" has attracted considerable attention among social scientists.[33] At the same time, many old insights have been re-examined and refurbished. We have been reminded that conflict sometimes is unavoidable, save at a price few wish to pay, and that processes of opposition and conflict often bring results that are widely accepted as "constructive" or beneficial.

Even while the possible positive values of conflict have been asserted again, some students of the matter have pointed out some of the causes of the uncontrollable ("break-away") character so frequently noted in initially small or seemingly trivial conflicts. Any sizeable conflict quickly comes to involve issues and elements over and above those initially engaged in the struggle. Conflict often becomes a vortex into which diverse interests and impulses are attracted: [34] on occasion what started out as restrained group rivalry becomes transformed into "wanton" aggression and destructiveness.

It is difficult to sustain the nonviolent character of nonviolent social movements intended to substantially change the existing subordination and segregation of a minority group, especially if the movement is successful in initial attacks on limited objectives, and then confronts hardening resistance to broader and more crucial aims.[35] When objectives are limited, the tactics can be such as to clearly show a direct connection between means and ends, e.g., the sit-ins to desegregate lunch counters. Selective pressure on the sensitive "pocketbook nerve" of business enterprises by a highly selected and well-disciplined organization often has brought specific, restricted gains. But as hopes rise, such gains may be seen as illusory by those who fail to benefit and whose problems of employment and status worsen rather than lessen. Cynical alienation gains increased frustration. Hostility is more freely expressed, and the likelihood grows of *expressive* aggression. Actual outbreaks assume a run-away character and release a great variety of hostile and opportunistically predatory forces.

It is partly because of this cumulatively self-transforming nature of conflict that conflicts only rarely, if ever, can be resolved merely by removing the initial causes or occasions that set the process in motion. In the absence of a super-ordinate source of constraint, conflicts often are subject to escalation in severity or ferocity—a tendency for increasingly drastic means to drive out the less drastic, resulting in "the sovereignty of the least moral participant."

As formal equality is attained in the field of civil rights, and as desegregation continues to occur, the focus of protest and pressure will necessarily move ". . . away from an exclusive emphasis upon desegregation and equal opportunity toward a broader demand for a 'fair share' and advantages directly comparable to whites." [36] As this shift occurs it will entail complex considerations of the "readiness" of previously disadvantaged population to utilize new opportunities. It will raise questions, perhaps even more complex and difficult, concerning institutional rearrangements in all major areas of the social system. . . .

NOTES

1. Thomas F. Pettigrew, *A Profile of the Negro American* (Princeton, N.J.: Van Nostrand, 1964), p. 191.
2. Ibid., pp. 44–46.
3. Samuel A. Stouffer et al., *The American Soldier* (Princeton, N.J.: Princeton University Press, 1949).
4. Aaron Antonovaky and Melvin J. Lerner, "Occupational Aspirations of Lower Class Negro and White Youth," *Social Problems* 7 (Fall 1959), pp. 132–38.
5. Noel P. Gist and William Bennett, Jr., "Aspirations of Negro and White Students," *Social Forces* 42 (October 1963): 40–48. Compare the discussion of Patricia Sexton, "Negro Career Expectations," *Merrill-Palmer Quarterly* 9 (October 1963): 303–16.
6. E.g., George Felix Boyd, "The Levels of Aspiration of White and Negro Children in a Non-Segregated Elementary School," *Journal of Social Psychology* 36 (August 1952): 191–96; Albert J. Lott and Bernice E. Lott, *Negro and White Youth: A Psychological Study in a Border-State Community* (New York: Holt, Rinehart & Winston, 1968).
7. "They will not voluntarily sacrifice their status advantage. They will give it up only when confronted with power that threatens other values." Lewis Killian and Charles Grigg, *Racial Crisis in America: Leadership in Conflict* (Englewood Cliffs, N.J.: Prentice-Hall, 1964), p. 132.
8. Cf. Eunice S. Grier, "Factors Hindering Integration in America's Urban Areas," *The Journal of Integroup Relations* 11 (August 1961): 293–301.
9. "Black Nationalism," *The Journal of Intergroup Relations* (Winter 1961–1962): 8. Cf. the data in Basil C. Zimmer, "The Adjustment of Negroes in a Northern Industrial Community," *Social Problems* 9 (Spring 1962): 378–86.
10. Matthew A. Kessler, "Economic Status of Nonwhite Workers, 1955–62," *Monthly Labor Review*, 86 July 1963): 783. See also: Samuel Sabin, "Work Experience of the Population in 1962," *Monthly Labor Review* 87 (January 1964): 18–27.
11. Kessler, "Economic Status . . .," p. 782.

12. Ibid., p. 787.

13. Harold W. Pfautz, "The Power Structure of the Negro Sub-Community: A Case Study and a Comparative View," *Phylon* 23 (Second Quarter, 1962): 156. We need only add that sheer knowledge of the new leadership pattern is not enough to insure avoidance of conflict. Cf. Daniel C. Thompson, *The Negro Leadership Class* Englewood Cliffs, N.J.: Prentice-Hall, 1963).

14. Nathan Glazer and Daniel Patrick Moynihan, *Beyond the Melting Pot: The Negroes, Puerto Ricans, Jews, Italians, and Irish of New York City* (Cambridge: M.I.T. Press, 1964), p. 52: "Migration, uprooting, urbanization always create problems. Even the best organized and the best integrated groups suffer under such circumstances. But when the fundamental core of organization, the family, is already weak, the magnitude of these problems may be staggering."

15. Ibid., p. 39: "Who can become an electrician, a plasterer, a bricklayer, a machinist, unless he has connections? The problem is not just discrimination against an outsider."

16. Cf. Herman Long, "The Challenge to Negro Leadership," *Journal of Intergroup Relations* 1 (Spring 1960); James Q. Wilson, "The Strategy of Protest: Problems of Negro Civic Action," *Journal of Conflict Resolution* 5 (September 1961): 291–303.

17. Ruth Searles and J. Allen Williams, Jr., "Negro College Students' Participation in Sit-Ins," *Social Forces* 40 (March 1962): 219. Active participants in the sit-ins tended to be those who were optimistic, less hostile to white people, of relatively higher status.

18. "Law of the Land," in Don Shoemaker, ed., *With All Deliberate Speed: Segregation-Desegregation in Southern Schools* (New York: Harper & Row, 1957), p. 4.

19. James W. Vander Zanden, "The Non-Violent Resistance Movement Against Segregation," *American Journal of Sociology* 68 (March 1963): 544. [Reprinted in this volume, Part II, Section 4.]

20. Cf. Killian and Grigg, *Racial Crisis in America*, p. 13: "It [communication between whites and Negroes] takes place in the context of a fundamental conflict of values, with neither side being willing to admit that the other is right."

21. H. M. Blalock, Jr., "Occupational Discrimination: Some Theoretical Propositions," *Social Problems* 9 (Winter 1962): 240–47.

22. James Allen Moss, "Currents of Change in American Race Relations," *British Journal of Sociology* 2 (September 1960): 232–43.

23. Cf. Robin Williams, Jr., in collaboration with John P. Dean and Edward A. Suchman, *Strangers Next Door* (Englewood Cliffs, N.J.: Prentice-Hall, 1964), pp. 348–51.

24. Ibid., pp. 280–87.

25. Allen D. Grimshaw, "Negro-White Relations in the Urban North: Two Areas of High Conflict Potential," *The Journal of Intergroup Relations* 3 (Spring 1962): 146.

26. Arnold M. Rose, "Inconsistencies in Attitudes toward Negro Housing," *Social Problems* 8 (Spring 1961): 286–92.

27. Marvin Bressler, "The Myers Case: An Instance of Successful Racial Invasion," *Social Problems* 8 (Fall 1960): 126–42.

28. See also: Joshua A. Fishman, "Some Social and Psychological Determinants of Intergroup Relations in Changing Neighborhoods: An Introduction to the Bridgeport Study," *Social Forces* 40 (October 1961): 42–51.

29. Allen D. Grimshaw, "Relationships among Prejudice, Discrimination, Social Tension and Social Violence," *Journal of Intergroup Relations* 2 (Autumn 1961): 302–10.

30. Allen D. Grimshaw, "Police Agencies and the Prevention of Racial Violence," *Journal of Criminal Law, Criminology, and Police Science* 54 (March 1963): 110–13.

31. "The Reduction of Intergroup Tensions," *Social Science Research Council Bulletin* 57 (1947): 60.

33. Ibid., p. 61.

33. Among many examples we may note: Thomas C. Schelling. *The Strategy of Conflict* (Cambridge: Harvard University Press, 1960); Kenneth Boulding. *Conflict and Defense* (New York: Harper & Row, 1962); Anatol Rapoport, *Fights, Games, and Debates* (Ann Arbor: University of Michigan Press, 1960); James S. Coleman, *Community Conflict* (Glencoe, Illinois: The Free Press, 1957); Jessie Bernard, *American Community Behavior* (New York: Holt, Rinehart & Winston, 1962); Lewis Coser, *The Functions of Social Conflict* (Glencoe, Illinois: The Free Press, 1956); Bernard Berelson and Gary A. Steiner, *Human Behavior: An Inventory of Scientific Findings* (New York: Harcourt, Brace & Jovanovich, 1964), pp. 619–23.

34. Cf. Williams et al., *Strangers Next Door*, pp. 383–84.

35. Although the non-violent movement has its own special advantages and appeals, Cf. Vander Zanden, "The Non-Violent Resistance Movement . . .," pp. 544–50.

36. Pettigrew, *Profile of the Negro American*, p. 187.

SOCIAL STRUCTURE AND THE NEGRO REVOLT: AN EXAMINATION OF SOME HYPOTHESES

James A. Geschwender

THE POSITION OF THE NEGRO IN THE UNITED STATES

. . . It is time to examine the data which permit an evaluation of these hypotheses. Let us examine the position of the Negro in the United States in terms of the categories: education, occupation, and income. These particular categories are chosen for analysis because of the belief that they are most crucial in determining one's life chances and one's style of life.[1]

Unfortunately, direct data on Negroes are not available in most areas one would wish to examine. One is forced to rely upon data for nonwhites and infer to Negroes. This will introduce some distortion into the data. This distortion, however, should not be overestimated. The number of non-Negro nonwhites has been less than ten percent of the nonwhites throughout the time period with which we will be concerned. Furthermore, data are available showing both nonwhite and Negro occupational distributions for 1940 and 1950, and in no occupational category for either year do the two frequencies differ by over seven-tenths of one percent.[2] This lends support to the belief that the position of the nonwhite may be taken as a reasonable approximation of that of the Negro.

Table 1 portrays the changes that have taken place in male level of

From *Social Forces 43* (December 1964): 250–56; reprinted as abridged by permission of the publisher.

education by race between 1940 and 1960. There are two approaches one could take to the analysis of comparative rates of educational improvements of whites and nonwhites. One could compare the proportional distributions of whites and nonwhites by educational categories or one could examine rates based upon nonwhite proportional representation within educational categories. Each technique has its merits and they can be used to supplement one another. The first six columns of Table 1 represent the former and the last three columns represent the latter.

In analyzing the ethnic distributions by educational categories, levels of education may profitably be broken into three broad categories: low—from none to six years of elementary school; middle—seventh grade through eleventh grade; and high—high school graduates through four or more years of college. A much larger percentage of nonwhites than whites (24.3 to 8.5 percent) are moving out of the lower educational category. The middle educational category shows an increase in the proportion of nonwhites (11.6 percent) and a decrease in the proportion of whites (8.7 percent). This suggests that nonwhites are moving in larger numbers than whites out of the lower educational categories; that they are moving into the middle educational categories which the whites are moving out of; and that the nonwhites are moving into the upper educational categories in smaller numbers than whites.

Changes in the proportional representation of nonwhites in each educational category are measured by ratios comparing 1960 proportions to 1940 proportions standardized by numbers reporting education. The standardized ratios give a precise way of measuring the rate of educational improvement of nonwhites relative to that of the society as a whole. A ratio of one represents proportional improvement; less than one, improvement at a slower rate; and more than one, improvement at a more rapid rate. There was a net gain in proportion of nonwhites in all educational levels above the fourth grade. The size of the gain at the two highest levels was less than that for the three middle levels. Thus, it would appear that nonwhites are improving their level of education at a more rapid rate than whites.

The use of census data for comparing changing educational levels over time has one major weakness. Age distributions are not controlled, so it is not possible to know how much of the result is a reflection of different age distributions. Table 2 presents median years of schooling completed by age, sex, and color for 1959 and sheds some light on this difficulty. A comparison of the ratios of the nonwhite median to the white median for each of the age categories reveals that, with the singular exception of the 55 to 64 age category, there is a steady progression toward greater equality in level of education between white and nonwhite as age decreases. This can only reflect a situation in which nonwhites are improving their educational accomplishments relative to whites.

Thus, it may be concluded that the nonwhite is improving his educational level relative to previous generations of nonwhites and also is improving his educational level relative to whites. The data are ambiguous as to proportional gains in the upper educational categories.

TABLE 1. Level of Education by Color, Males, 1940 and 1960*

Level of Education	White			Nonwhite			Nonwhite as Percent of Total		Ratio**
	1940	1960	% change	1940	1960	% change	1940	1960	
No schooling	3.2	2.0	- 1.2	11.7	6.6	- 5.1	26.1	26.3	0.94
Elementary									
1–4 yrs.	8.8	5.5	- 3.3	34.5	21.1	-13.4	27.7	28.9	0.97
5–6 yrs.	11.1	7.1	- 4.0	20.6	14.8	- 5.8	15.3	17.9	1.09
7 yrs.	7.0	6.6	- 0.4	7.5	8.5	+ 1.0	9.5	11.8	1.16
8 yrs.	30.5	18.4	-12.1	11.4	12.3	+ 0.9	3.5	6.6	1.77
High:									
1–3 yrs.	15.1	18.9	+ 3.8	7.4	17.1	+ 9.7	4.6	8.7	1.77
4 yrs.	13.0	22.1	+ 9.1	3.8	11.7	+ 7.9	2.8	5.3	1.77
College:									
1–3 yrs.	5.3	9.0	+ 3.7	1.7	4.4	+ 2.7	3.0	4.9	1.52
4 yrs.	5.9	10.3	+ 4.4	1.4	3.4	+ 2.0	2.3	3.4	1.38
Total reporting	99.9	99.9		99.9	99.9	0.1	8.9	9.5	1.00
	3,359	5,150	-43,157,862	327	9,786	-4,547,539			

*Source: United States Bureau of the Census. *Characteristics of the Population, United States Summary, 1940, 1960.* Alaska and Hawaii excluded.

**Standardized by number reporting education.

TABLE 2. Median Years of Schooling Completed Age 25 Years And Over By Age, Sex, And Color, March 1959*

	Male			Female		
Age	Total	Non-white	Nonwhite as percent of total	Total	Non-white	Nonwhite as percent of total
25-29	12.4	10.9	88	12.3	11.0	89
30-34	12.2	9.5	78	12.2	10.0	82
35-44	12.1	8.1	67	12.1	8.8	73
45-54	10.2	6.7	66	10.8	7.7	71
55-64	8.7	6.7	77	8.9	6.6	74
65 and over	8.2	3.8	46	8.4	5.4	64

*Source: Data taken from Murray Gendell and Hand L. Zetterberg, *A Sociological Almanac for the United States* (New York: Bedminister Press, 1961), Table 68, p. 70.

OCCUPATION

Table 3 presents the changes which have taken place in male occupations by race from 1940 to 1960. It presents the data in the same two ways that were used earlier in the analysis of data on education. The first three columns portray the changes in the distribution of persons into occupational categories by race. It may be noted that nonwhites have increased their representation in all nonfarm occupational categories and that whites have increased their representation in all non-farm occupational categories except labor. This makes it difficult to determine whether the increase in numbers of nonwhite professionals and managers represents occupational upgrading. Nonwhites increased their representation in the highest status non-farm occupations (professional-technical) and (manager-official-proprietor) by 13.8 percent but decreased their representation in the highest status category of farm occupations (farmer and farm manager) by 16.3 percent.

The second three columns present the distribution of persons into occupational categories by race when non-farm occupations only are considered. We now note that there is a decrease in the proportion of nonwhites in the two lowest status occupational categories (service and labor); an increase in representation in the upper blue collar and lower white collar categories (operatives, craftsmen-foremen, clerical-sales); an increase in the professional-technical occupational category; and a negligible decrease in the manager-official-proprietor category.

These figures appear to demonstrate an occupational upgrading of nonwhites. The data are unclear as to relative rates of upgrading. Nonwhites are shifting from farm to non-farm occupations in larger numbers than whites; shifting into the highest status occupations less rapidly than whites; shifting into the middle status occupations more rapidly than whites; and shifting out of the lowest occupations more rapidly than whites, if we consider non-farm occupational data and, less rapidly than whites if we consider data on all occupations.

The seventh and eighth columns in Table 3 present the proportion

TABLE 3. Occupation by Color, United States Males, 1940 and 1960*

Occupation	Color	All Occupations			Non-Farm Only			Nonwhite as Percent of Total		All Occupations Ratio**	Non-Farm Only Ratio***
		1940	1960	Change	1940	1960	Change	1940	1960		
Professional Technical	White	6.0	11.4	+ 5.4	7.6	12.5	+ 4.9	3.0	3.3	1.16	0.82
	Nonwhite	1.9	4.1	+ 2.2	3.2	4.7	+ 1.5				
Farm-Farm Managers	White	14.2	5.9	− 8.3				13.1	7.3	0.59	
	Nonwhite	21.2	4.9	−16.3							
Managers-Prop Officials	White	10.7	12.0	+ 1.3	13.6	13.1	− 0.5	1.5	1.8	1.26	1.01
	Nonwhite	1.7	0.6	+ 0.6	2.9	2.6	− 0.3				
Clerical-Sales	White	14.1	15.2	+ 1.1	17.9	16.5	− 1.4	1.5	4.1	2.87	2.29
	Nonwhite	2.2	6.9	+ 4.7	3.7	7.9	+ 4.2				
Craftsmen-Foremen	White	15.8	21.4	+ 5.6	20.1	23.3	+ 3.2	2.7	4.5	1.76	1.40
	Nonwhite	4.4	10.7	+ 6.3	7.5	12.2	+ 4.7				
Operatives	White	19.1	20.4	+ 1.3	24.3	22.2	− 2.1	6.2	10.7	1.82	1.45
	Nonwhite	12.5	25.9	+13.4	21.3	29.6	+ 8.3				
Service	White	5.4	5.5	+ 0.1	6.9	6.0	− 0.9	22.2	21.5	1.02	0.82
	Nonwhite	15.3	16.0	+ 0.7	26.1	18.3	− 7.8				
Farm Labor	White	7.1	2.4	− 4.7				22.3	23.3	1.09	
	Nonwhite	20.1	7.8	−12.3							
Labor	White	7.6	5.9	− 1.7	9.7	6.4	− 3.3	21.5	25.6	1.25	1.00
	Nonwhite	20.7	21.4	+10.7	35.3	24.5	−10.8				
Total	White	30,480,040	37,846,254		24,000,434	34,620,227		9.1	8.6	1.00	1.00
	Nonwhite	3,072,606	3,558,946		1,801,092	3,107,859					

*Source: United States Bureau of the Census, *Characteristics of the Population, United States Summary, 1940, 1960*, Alaska and Hawaii excluded.

**Standardized by number reporting occupations.

***Standardized by number reporting non-farm occupations.

of nonwhites in each occupational category for 1940 and 1960. The final two columns present ratios of the 1960 proportions to the 1940 proportions standardized by numbers reporting occupations for all occupations and non-farm occupations only. As in the case of education, a ratio of one represents changes at the same rate as the larger society; more than one, increase in proportional representation; less than one, decrease in proportional representation. The ratios computed on the basis of all occupations show a decrease in nonwhite representation in the farmer-farm manager occupational category and an increase in all other occupational categories (but a negligible increase in the service category). The ratios computed on the basis of non-farm occupations show a decrease in nonwhite representation in the occupational categories of professional-technical and service; relative stability in the occupational categories of labor and manager-official-proprietor; and an increase in proportional representation in all other occupational categories.

When considered as a totality, the data on occupational changes indicate that nonwhites are leaving the farms more rapidly than whites, are being occupationally upgraded relative to previous generations of nonwhites; and are experiencing some occupational upgrading relative to whites but possibly not at the highest occupational status levels.

INCOME

It is difficult to examine income changes over extended periods of time because of the large number of different techniques of reporting income that are used, the difficulty in getting data from the same technique for many consecutive years, and the shifting value of the dollar in terms of purchasing power. We will consider the technique of measuring income which was reported over the longest time span, analyzed in both current and constant dollars. Constant dollars are computed by translating the purchasing power of current dollars into the average purchasing power of the dollar from 1947 to 1949.

Table 4 presents median income of males 14 and over having wage or salary income by color for those years in which such data were available from 1939 to 1961. Nonwhite income has shown a relatively steady increase in both current and constant dollars from 1939 to 1961. White income has shown a similar increase in both current and constant dollars. The difference between white and nonwhite median incomes in constant dollars increased from $1,276 in 1939 to $1,776 in 1961. Thus, nonwhite males have improved their income in both current and constant dollars, but have fallen further behind white males in so doing.[3] In other words, nonwhites are raising their standard of living, but less rapidly than whites.

EVALUATION OF HYPOTHESES

Now that the changing position of the Negro (nonwhite) in the United States has been examined, we are in a position to evaluate the hypotheses presented earlier.

TABLE 4. Median Income Males 14 and Over having Wage or Salary Income in Current and Constant Dollars in the United States for 1939 to 1961*

| | White | | Nonwhite | | |
Year	Current dollars	Constant dollars	Current dollars	Constant dollars	White Minus Nonwhite in Constant Dollars
1939	1112	2176	460	900	1276
1947	2357	2468	1279	1339	1189
1948	2711	2637	1615	1571	1066
1949	2735	2686	1367	1342	1344
1950	2982	2901	1828	1779	1122
1951	3345	3014	2060	1856	1158
1952	3507	3090	2038	1795	1295
1953	3760	3286	2833	1826	1460
1954	3754	3270	2131	1856	1414
1955	3986	3480	2342	2045	1435
1961	5287	4134	3015	2358	1776

*Source: *Statistical Abstract of the United States* (Washington, D.C.: United States Department of Commerce, Bureau of the Census, 1962), and earlier editions. 1961 income data from P.60 Series, *Current Population Reports,* 1962.

"The Vulgar Marxist Hypothesis," which predicted rebellion as a result of a worsening of conditions of life, is clearly inconsistent with these data. The position of the Negro is improving educationally, occupationally, and income-wise.

"The Rising Expectations Hypothesis," which predicted rebellion as a result of improvements in conditions of life, is consistent with the data examined. Negroes have improved their level of education; they have better jobs, and they are earning more money with which they may purchase more things. One might assume a more rapid rise in level of aspirations but data are lacking to either substantiate or refute the assumption.

"The Sophisticated Marxist Hypothesis," which gave a relative deprivation basis for its prediction of rebellion, is also consistent with these data. Negroes have improved their level of education and have done so more rapidly than have whites. But education is not a direct measure of living conditions either socially or economically. It is one source of status and, as such, it carries with it certain satisfactions. Occupation may be viewed as a second source of status. The Negro has improved his occupational level, thus improving his status rewards as well as receiving other rewards in terms of better working conditions. The evidence is not clear as to the relative occupational gains or losses experienced by the Negro. He appears to be moving more rapidly than whites into the middle status occupations, but if urban occupations only are considered, he is moving more slowly into the higher status occupations. Whether this situation would produce feelings of relative loss or relative gain is a moot question which could only be settled through further empirical studies.

The area of income most directly affects conditions of life and presents the clearest picture. Negroes are improving their incomes in terms of both current and constant dollars. The gap between white and Negro incomes is also increasing in terms of both current and constant dollars.

Thus, Negroes are improving their material conditions of life but are not doing so at the same rate as whites. This is the perfect situation to create feelings of relative deprivation leading to rebellion.

"The Rise and Drop Hypothesis," which predicted rebellion as a result of the reversal of past progress in conditions of life, is not consistent with the data examined. There appears to be a relatively steady improvement in level of education, level of occupation, and income in both current and constant dollars. No reversal may be observed.

"The Status Inconsistency Hypothesis," which predicted rebellion as a result of an increase in the proportion of status inconsistents, is consistent with the data examined. There has been an increase in the proportion of status inconsistents among Negroes. This is true in both a trivial and a significant sense. Current research in status inconsistency emphasizes the dimensions of occupation, income, education, and ethnicity as the crucial ones for American society. Negroes have retained their low ethnic status, but they have improved their position on each of the other status dimensions. Thus, they have increased their status inconsistency in the trivial sense. They have increased the combination of low ethnic status with higher rankings on other dimensions.

Negroes have also increased their status inconsistency in a more significant sense. These data show that they are not only improving their level of education, but they are doing so at a more rapid rate than whites; while in the area of occupational gains there has not been as significant a gain relative to that of whites. Table 1 shows that nonwhites are increasing their proportional representation in the educational category of one-to-three-years-of-college 1.53 times as rapidly as is the total society, and they are increasing their representation in the four-or-more-years-of-college category 1.38 times as rapidly. When the category of all those with any college is considered, nonwhites are increasing their representation 1.48 times as rapidly as is the general society. Yet Table 3, which covers the same time span, shows that nonwhites are increasing their representation in the occupational category of professional-technical workers only 1.16 times as rapidly as the general society, when all occupations are considered, or 0.82 times as rapidly when only non-farm occupations are considered. They are increasing their representation in the combined managerial and professional categories 1.19 times as rapidly as whites, when all occupations are considered, and 1.00 times as rapidly for non-farm occupations. This shows that nonwhites (and presumably Negroes) are improving their educational qualifications for professional and technical jobs more rapidly than they are receiving these jobs, thus causing an increased disparity between educational qualifications for jobs and level of occupational achievement.[4]

We may observe the same pattern if we consider proportional distributions of whites and nonwhites into educational and occupational categories. Nonwhites increased their representation in the category of some college or college graduate by 4.7 percent. These would presumably be the categories best qualifying them for upper white collar jobs. They increased their representation in the professional-technical occupational category by 2.2 percent (a gain which is 44.7 percent of the educational gain), and they increased their representation in the combined manager and professional-technical categories by 2.8 percent (59.6 percent of the educational gain). The corresponding figures for whites show an increase of 8.1 percent in the some college or college graduate category and an increase of 5.4 percent (66.7 percent of the educational gain) in the professional-technical categories and an increase in the combined professional-technical and manager categories of 6.7 percent (82.7 percent of the educational gain). These data show that whites are making gains in the occupational realm which are much more in proportion to their educational gains than are nonwhites. Data on non-farm occupations reveal the same pattern.[5] Nonwhites are increasing their discrepancy between education and occupation and becoming more status inconsistent.

It was shown in Table 4 that Negroes are not increasing their income level as rapidly as whites. Further evidence that improved educational achievements are not rewarded by increased incomes as rapidly for nonwhites as for whites may be derived from Table 5. Not only do nonwhites receive a lower median income than whites at each level of education, but the dollar gap between medians increases as level of education increases.

Even if we ignore their ethnicity, Negroes are becoming increasingly status inconsistent as a result of the fact that they are raising their level of education but are being denied the occupational mobility or income level which would "normally" be associated with such progress.

DISCUSSION

Only two out of the five proposed hypotheses have been rejected. This leaves the task of either choosing among the remaining hypotheses or somehow reconciling them. It is a relatively simple task to reconcile the "Sophisticated Marxist Hypothesis" with "The Status Inconsistency Hypothesis," as the essence of each is the concept of relative deprivation. The former is explicitly stated in these terms, while the latter's thesis is implied. It is the association between statuses which generally prevails in a society that determines what is status consistency. Deviations from this prevailing association are what constitute status inconsistency. It is the

TABLE 5. Median Income by Level of Education and Color—Males 14 and Over, 1961*

Level of Education	White	Non-white	Difference
Elementary:			
Less than 8 years	2303	1554	749
8 years	3617	2505	1112
High school:			
1-3 years	4090	2427	1663
4 years	5155	3381	1774
Some college	6379	4246	2133
Total	4432	2292	2140

*Source: *Current Population Reports,* P60 Series, United States Bureau of the Census, #39, p. 4.

experiencing of these deviations to one's own detriment which causes the propensity to revolt among status inconsistents.[6]

It is also possible to reconcile "The Rising Expectations Hypothesis" with the "Status Inconsistency Hypothesis." Both Edwards and Brinton see blockages of social mobility as an essential basis for "The Rising Expectations Hypothesis." [7] People feel that they have legitimate aspirations which are blocked, thus interfering with the circulation of the elite, and creating a status inconsistent group. This is very similar to the interpretation that Broom gives to "The Status Inconsistency Hypothesis." [8]

It seems that "relative deprivation" is the essence of all three hypotheses that are consistent with the observed data. It is only by observing the process of social mobility in society that one will develop aspirations for such mobility. Observation of the criteria used to select successful aspirants allows development of feelings that one's aspirations are legitimate. Possession of these characteristics without subsequent mobility creates status inconsistency. Without comparing one's own experiences with those of others in society and subsequently developing feelings of relative deprivation, no rebellion would take place.

CONCLUSIONS

Five hypotheses which purport to account for the current "Negro Revolt" were taken from the literature. Data were examined which resulted in the rejection of two of these. The three which remained were reconciled with each other in terms of their common basis in the concept of relative deprivation. This should not be misinterpreted as a claim that the psychological state of possessing feelings of relative deprivation will, regardless of objective conditions, produce rebellion. In contrast, the suggestion proposed herein is that certain types of objective conditions will produce feelings of relative deprivation, which will, in turn, produce rebellion.

The Negro in the United States has been exposed to just such a set of objective conditions. He is handicapped by blockages in the circulation of the elite, especially in the area of the professions. He is acquiring the education which is normally the key to occupational mobility and economic gain. He is not experiencing as rapid a rate of occupational mobility as he feels he is entitled to. He is not receiving the economic rewards which he feels he has earned. As a result, he is becoming increasingly status inconsistent and he sees himself falling further and further behind the white. He feels relatively deprived and unjustly so. Therefore, he revolts in order to correct the situation.

NOTES

ACKNOWLEDGEMENT: I am indebted to Elwood Guernsey for compiling much of the data upon which Tables 1 and 3 are based and to the Institute for Social Research, Florida State University, for the use of graduate assistants and machines. I have benefited from the critical comments on earlier drafts generously given by William A. Rushing and Henry J. Watts.

1. Gerhard Lenski, "Status Crystallization: A Non-Vertical Dimension of Social Status," *American Sociological Review* 19 (August 1954): 412; Leonard Broom, "Social Differentiation and Stratification," in Robert K. Merton, Leonard Broom and Leonard S. Cottrell, eds., *Sociology Today* (New York: Basic Books, 1959), p. 431.

2. These data were compiled from census data and are available from the present writer upon request.

3. This same general pattern emerges regardless of the choice of income data. It holds for median family income, female income, urban income, as well as the combined individual and family income.

4. I say an increased discrepancy because Turner has already demonstrated the existence of the discrepancy in 1940. He showed that only 39 percent of the nonwhites' lower job status could be attributed to their lesser amount of education. See Ralph H. Turner, "Foci of Discrimination in the Employment of Non-Whites," *American Journal of Sociology* 58 (November 1952): 247–56.

5. Nonwhites: Professional-technical—1.5 percent (31.9 percent of educational gains). Combined Manager and Professional-technical—1.2 percent (25.6 percent of educational gains).

    Whites: Professional-technical—4.9 percent (60.5 percent of educational gains). Combined Manager and Professional-technical—4.4 percent (54.3 percent of educational gains).

6. Cf., George C. Homans, *Social Behavior: Its Elementary Forms* (New York: Harcourt, Brace & Jovanovich, 1961), pp. 232–64. Homans points out that anger leading to rebellion will result from the experiencing of this deviance to one's detriment, while guilt (which is a weaker emotion not calculated to lead to rebellion) will result from the experiencing of this deviance to one's benefit.

7. Lyford P. Edwards, *The Natural History of Revolution* (Chicago: The University of Chicago Press, 1927), p. 30; and Crane Brinton, *The Anatomy of Revolution* (New York: Norton, 1938), pp. 78–79.

8. Broom, "Social Differentiation . . .," p. 439.

2. Organizations

Kurt and Gladys Lang have indicated that the history of any social movement tends often to be written in terms of the history of its organizations and the speeches of its organizational spokesmen.[1] It is equally true that current accounts of a movement presented in the mass media display a similar focus. Thus it is not surprising that the general public comes to see a movement as being coexistensive with its organizations and its leadership.

This is understandable as organizations keep records, have a written history, a table of organization, and official spokesmen, set official objectives, and perhaps most important, issue press releases. Thus it becomes relatively easy to write stories regarding an organization's objectives, ideology, tactics, membership, and rationale or reason-for-being. A reporter or historian can document his sources and be fairly confident about his statements. This is not the case with the unorganized periphery of a movement. Some participants are active today, passive supporters tomorrow, and uninterested the next day. Others follow the opposite path from noninvolved to committed, while still others move in and out of the movement in an irregular and unpredictable fashion. This makes it extremely difficult to arrive at a complete and accurate analysis of the motivations for participation, the objectives, philosophy, or ideology of the nonorganized segments of a social movement.

Although it is clear that we inevitably will have an incomplete and partially inaccurate picture of a social movement if we view it entirely in terms of its core associations, it is equally clear that we would have an even less complete picture of a movement if we failed to describe or analyze its core associations. This section includes three selections designed to provide a treatment of the organizations central to the civil rights movement.

The first selection, by Kenneth B. Clark, traces the origin and development of the major civil rights organizations up to 1964. In so doing it illustrates a number of important points. First, it demonstrates that militance is a function of time and place. The activities of the NAACP in its early days were regarded as extremely militant. They led to the vilification of the organization as communist, irresponsible, and so on. The tactics were, in all probability, as militant as any which then might have had a chance of successfully bringing about social change. Second, the selection illustrates the fact that success is a double-edged blade. The tactics of litigation utilized by the NAACP brought about many changes. This undoubtedly had an impact upon the hopes and faith of American blacks, who saw that it was possible to fight the establishment and win. Protest could bring about change; a better life was possible, and it could be brought about through collective action. The successes of the NAACP helped to spread the black revolt. Yet they also led to the stagnation of a portion of it. It appears that the NAACP became too aware of the fact that litigation brings about changes. They tended to stick with a tactic that worked rather than progressing to new approaches. Times changed, more militant tactics became feasible, but the NAACP stayed with what worked in the past. It thus became necessary for new organizations to take up the battle with newer tactics.

The Clark selection also demonstrates the existence and functional consequences of a division of labor in social movements. From the earliest days the NAACP and the Urban League coexisted and carried out different types of activities. Both types of activities were beneficial to blacks. It is doubtful that a protest organization could have been as successful as the Urban League in carrying out its activities, for it would not have received the type of cooperation it needed from the white establishment. And the threat posed by the existence of the more militant NAACP aided it in gaining this cooperation. This division of labor continues to the present. SNCC, CORE, and SCLC have all taken up the battle where the NAACP left off. They adopted more militant forms of direct action which could attack the status quo in areas where formal litigation could not. This does not mean that the NAACP became outmoded and ceased to play a role. SNCC, CORE, and SCLC filled the jails and generated many court cases, some of which were fought by the experienced legal arm of the NAACP. Any social movement that has a diversity of core associations following a number of different tactical paths has increased strength and an increased likelihood of eventual success.

Elliott Rudwick and August Meier take up the development of the civil rights organizations where Clark leaves off. They attempt to analyze and explain the process by which CORE changed from an assimilationist to a separatist organization. SNCC evolved in a manner similar to that of CORE, while SCLC remained assimilationist despite its direct action orientations. CORE and SNCC differed from the NAACP in that they were more youth-dominated and more oriented toward direct action. They also differed from SCLC in that the latter had always had a more religious orientation. These initial differences may have supplemented the factors analyzed by Rudwick and Meier in leading to the differential evolution of the civil rights organizations. It would seem that persons predisposed to participate in the civil rights movement will tend to affiliate with organizations more similar to their initial orientations. Thus one finds a rolling stone effect. Initial differences in organizations lead to differences in types of members recruited, which in turn leads to an intensification in organizational differences, which leads to further differences in recruitment patterns, and so on.

The third selection, by Harold A. Nelson, describes the emergence of a new type of civil rights movement. Many blacks are unhappy with society and want to participate in attempts to change it, but they simply can't buy the nonviolence of the traditional civil rights movement. The definition of a man in American society usually includes the willingness to fight to defend himself, and always includes the willingness to fight to defend his women. Having been exposed to many of the same socializing agencies as whites, many blacks have developed definitions of masculinity that would prohibit their commiting themselves to courses of action which would force them to allow themselves and their women to be attacked without retaliating. Others have ideological orientations which rule out nonviolence. Thus the traditional nonviolent civil rights organizations are closed to them. But they share their anger and objectives. In fact their anger is intensified by white attacks upon black civil rights activists. Thus the emergence of black defense organizations was inevitable. With them, the civil rights movement began a drift away from a strict commitment to nonviolence.

NOTES

1.   Kurt Lang and Gladys Engel Lang, *Collective Dynamics* (New York: Thomas Y. Crowell, 1963), p. 496.

THE CIVIL RIGHTS MOVEMENT:

MOMENTUM AND ORGANIZATION

Kenneth B. Clark

. . . One could define the civil rights movement in terms of organized and sustained activity directed toward the attainment of specific racial goals or the alleviation or elimination of certain racial problems. Such a definition, with its emphasis upon organization as the basis for changes in the status of Negroes in America, would suggest that the civil rights movement was synonymous with civil rights organizations. But this definition would obscure the important fact that the civil rights movement had its own historic and impersonal momentum, responsive to deep and powerful economic and international events and political and ideological forces beyond the control of individuals, agencies, or perhaps even individual governments. In fact, the uncontrollable power and momentum of the civil rights movement impelled it to create the necessary machinery, organizations, and leaders.[1]

THE HISTORY AND CHARACTER OF THE
CIVIL RIGHTS ORGANIZATIONS

There is an understandable tendency to think of the civil rights movement, organizations, and leaders as if they were interchangeable or as if they were only part of the same historic and social phenomenon. But, while there are similarities and overlaps among them, they are not identical, and their important historical and contemporary dynamic differences need clarification if one is to understand the present nature and force of the civil rights movement, or if one is to assess accurately the role and power of the various civil rights organizations and the actual extent of personal decision-making power held by their recognized leaders. Confusion on these questions can lead only to dangerous miscalculations. Specifically, political and governmental leaders may make demands upon civil rights leaders, demands which they genuinely believe can be fulfilled in the normal course of social bargaining and negotiations. The parties to these discussions may enter into such agreements in good faith only to find themselves unable to fulfill them. Those who view the civil rights movement in terms of the model of the American labor movement, with elected labor leaders holding responsibility for negotiating and bargaining for a disciplined rank and file, misjudge the nature of the movement. One obvious difference is that civil rights leaders have not been elected by any substantial number of Negroes. Either they are essentially hired executives, holding their office at the pleasure of a board of directors, or

Reprinted by permission from *Daedalus: Journal of the American Academy of Arts and Sciences*, Boston, Massachusetts, Vol. 95, No. 1 (Winter 1966): 241–64.

else they emerge as leaders by charismatic power, later creating an organization which, in effect, they control. Whitney Young is an example of the one, Martin Luther King of the other. So far, no machinery exists to enable the masses of Negroes to select a leader, but, if an individual strikes a responsive chord in the masses of Negroes, they will identify with him and "choose" him. So, too, an organizational leader may be accepted as spokesman by default, by the mere fact that he has been able to avoid overt repudiation.

One cannot understand the nature and the problems of contemporary civil rights organizations without understanding some of their individual histories. The *National Association for the Advancement of Colored People* and the *Urban League,* the two oldest, were founded in the first decade of this century, in 1909 and 1910 respectively.

THE NATIONAL ASSOCIATION FOR THE ADVANCEMENT
OF COLORED PEOPLE

The NAACP emerged from the Niagara Movement of W. E. B. Du Bois and other Negro and white liberals during that period when Negroes were moving North.

A meeting of some of the members of the Niagara Movement was held in 1908, and it was agreed that a call should be issued by whites and Negroes for a conference on the centennial of the birth of Abraham Lincoln to discuss the status of the Negro in the United States. Oswald Garrison Villard wrote the Call for the Conference which was held in New York City on February 12 and 13, 1909. It read in part:

> In many states today Lincoln would find justice enforced, if at all, by judges elected by one element in a community to pass upon the liberties and lives of another. He would see the black men and women, for whose freedom a hundred thousand of soldiers gave their lives, set apart in trains, in which they pay first-class fares for third class service, and segregated in railway stations and in places of entertainment; he would observe that State after State declines to do its elementary duty in preparing the Negro through education for the best exercise of citizenship. . . . Added to this, the spread of lawless attacks upon the Negro, North, South, and West—even in Springfield made famous by Lincoln—often accompanied by revolting brutalities, sparing neither sex nor age nor youth, could but shock the author of the sentiment that "government of the people, by the people, for the people, shall not perish from the earth." . . . Silence under these conditions means tacit approval. The indifference of the North is already responsible for more than one assault upon democracy, and every such attack reacts as unfavorably upon the whites as upon the blacks. Discrimination once permitted cannot be bridled; recent history in the South shows that in forging chains for the Negroes the white voters are forging chains for themselves. "A house divided against itself cannot stand;" this government cannot exist half-slave and half-free any better today than it could in 1861. . . . Hence we call upon all the believers in democracy to join in a national conference for the discussion of present evils, the voicing of protests, and the renewal of the struggle for civil and political liberty.[2]

The Call clearly indicates that, at its founding, the NAACP sensed that the status of the Negro in the North would not be significantly better than his status in the South. The founding of the NAACP anticipated the race riots of 1917, following the clues of the New York City riot of 1900. It was an attempt by the more perceptive and sensitive Negroes and whites to recapture the fervor, the purpose, and the concern of the pre-Civil War abolitionists.

The NAACP, from its beginning, took a more direct and militant stance, in spite of the fact that its founders and its Board of Directors were always interracial. The top staff tended to address itself to legislation and litigation. It pioneered in the use of direct action demonstrations. The more militant approach of the NAACP reflected, among other things, the role of W. E. B. Du Bois, paradoxically both a detached scholar and poet and an intense actionist. The direction and approach of the NAACP, to the extent that they can be attributed to a single person, were determined by his power and personality. In the tradition of a nineteenth-century New England aristocratic poet-actionist-crusader, Du Bois was a dignified intellectual, Harvard-educated, detached, aloof, and cold, but also intensely concerned and committed to the attainment of unqualified justice and equality for Negroes. He may well have been the most important figure in the American civil rights movement in the twentieth century. His importance lies not only in his role in setting the direction and the methods of the NAACP, but in his capacity to understand and predict the larger dimensions of the American racial problem. Like Frederick Douglass, he was a prophet and leader of the movement, but, unlike Douglass, he was a founder and leader of an organization within the movement, capable of articulating the purposes of that organization. Du Bois the scholar gave Du Bois the leader of the NAACP a deeper human understanding, and to the NAACP he gave a significance which a mere organization could not have had without him. Yet his temperament, facing the contradictions and the turmoil necessary to organizational struggle, determined that his role in the organization itself would be limited. One could speculate that the ardor, the intensity, the militance of Du Bois, his inability to tolerate anything other than acceptance of his complete humanity were viewed as a handicap to those willing to make the "necessary" compromises for the survival of the institution. He was a proud and uncompromising man.

The essence of the controversy between Du Bois and Booker T. Washington was that Washington could accommodate and adjust, while Du Bois could not. If the NAACP had been run by Washington, it would have been pragmatic and practical, but not militant or crusading. The clash between Washington and Du Bois was a clash of temperament and principle. Washington was willing to accept qualifications of his humanity; Du Bois was not. Du Bois' dignity and his inability to settle for anything less than total human acceptance set the tone for the approach, methods, and early militant stance of the NAACP.

The Du Bois-Washington controversy could be illustrated by their conflicting views on education for Negroes. Washington's support for a special kind of education "appropriate" to the caste status of the Negro —vocational education, the acceptance of separation (in a sense the ac-

ceptance of segregation itself)—was consistent with his pragmatic accommodation. Du Bois' insistence on academic education, his belief that, if
the Negro were to progress in America, he would need to assume the same
stance as whites, his belief that one could not make judgments about a
person's role in terms of his color, his slogan of the "talented tenth," all
were consistent with his refusal to allow color to qualify the rights of persons. He took seriously the American ideology. Washington was the re-
alist, the moderate, yet he never founded a civil rights organization, but
operated from the institutional base of Tuskegee Institute. He had gained
acceptance from the white power controllers without an "organization."
It is indeed doubtful that he could have mobilized a civil rights agency.
It may be that his power and his usefulness to the equally pragmatic white
political and economic structure would have been curtailed by even the
semblance of a functioning civil rights organization. That Washington
was not a particularly significant influence in the movement during its
earliest stages may be due to the fact that his domain by this time was
clearly the Southern Negro. The civil rights movement was then becoming Northern-oriented. One could speculate that the doctrine of accommodation preached by Washington and reinforced by white power effectively curtailed the growth of a Negro civil rights movement in the South
until the mid-twentieth century.

THE NATIONAL URBAN LEAGUE

The Urban League was founded a year later than the NAACP, in
1910, for the specific purpose of easing the transition of the Southern
rural Negro into an urban way of life. It stated clearly that its role was to
help these people, who were essentially rural agrarian serf-peasants, adjust
to Northern city life. Until the termination of Lester Granger's tenure as
director in September 1961, the League announced in its fund-raising appeals and to both business and government that it was essentially a social
service agency with a staff of social workers. Its implicit assumption was
that the problems of the Negro were primarily those of adjustment and
that their need was for training and help. The League summoned whites
to demonstrate their good will, relying upon negotiation and persuasion
to show white business leaders that it was in their "enlightened self interest," to use Lester Granger's term, to ease the movement of Negroes
into middle-class status. The Urban League played down the more primitive and irrational components of racial hostility, depending on the conviction that white leadership, particularly in the North, could be dealt
with in terms of rational economic appeals. The League courted the
white community through its national and local boards, considering itself
an effective bridge between the Negro community and the white decision-
makers; to this end, it recruited a staff skilled not only in social work but
also in negotiation procedure and style. During the early 1950's, one member of the top national staff of the Urban League described the role of
the League as "the State Department of race relations," in contrast to the
NAACP, which was characterized as "the War Department." This was

more than an analogy; the style of speech and dress and manner of the League tended to be a stereotype of the style of the staff of the American State Department.

NAACP AND URBAN LEAGUE: DEMOCRATIC, NONPARTISAN, CONSERVATIVE

These two civil rights organizations, the NAACP and the Urban League, had in common their Northern base and their interracial character. They also shared a basic assumption that major changes in the status of the Negro could be obtained within the framework of the American democratic system. They sought to manipulate the machinery of government and to influence other institutions. The Urban League's primary emphasis was placed upon the economic, industrial, and social-service clusters of power, while the NAACP's primary interest was in political and legal power, with a major emphasis upon propaganda which sought to reach the conscience of the American people, both white and Negro. The League's appeal was to self-interest—employ Negroes, or you will spawn large numbers of dependent people. The NAACP's appeal was to public and judicial conscience; their argument was that America is intended to be a democratic nation with justice for all.

From the very beginning, both organizations were politically nonpartisan and therefore in some measure effective in flexibility of appeal and action. They could not afford identification with a particular political group, for they faced an always imminent prospect of political changes in government and the possibility of retaliation. Their decision, on its face, seemed quite wise; but it limited the extent to which the civil rights organizations could, in any meaningful sense, be politically or socially revolutionary. They could not or did not identify with labor, and their sense of alienation was stimulated by the political immaturity of the American labor movement itself. The rank-and-file members of organized labor, if not its leaders, were contaminated by racism; thus, the civil rights organizations and American labor could not form a political coalition or develop a significant labor party. It would, however, be inaccurate to say these civil rights groups ever "sought" an alliance with a political labor movement. The mere fact that civil rights organizations were necessary made a civil rights-labor coalition impossible since one of the major sources of racial exclusion has been and remains the organized American labor movement.

The civil rights organizations were never revolutionary. Their assumptions and strategy and tactics were essentially conservative, in that they did not seek to change and certainly made no attempt to overthrow the basic political and economic structure. The social changes they sought were limited to the inclusion of the Negro in the existing society; the Negro wanted his own status raised to that of other American citizens. The NAACP and Urban League staked their strategies on a belief in the resilience, flexibility, and eventual inclusiveness of the American democratic system—in an ultimate sense, perhaps in a pathetic sense, upon acceptance and identification with the articulated American concept of democracy. They took literally the ideology and promises of the system and shared unquestioningly American democratic optimism. They believed in the words of Jefferson, the Declaration of Independence, the Constitution, and the Bills of Rights and asked only that these rights—and nothing less —be extended to Negroes. This was their main source of power. They could be considered revolutionary only if one tortures the meaning of the term to imply a demand to include other human beings in a system which promises fulfillment to others. . . .

It may be that the strategies and techniques of the civil rights organizations could have been only more systematic and organizational forms of the very kinds of accommodations that individual Negroes were required to make in the face of the superior power of the white system. As the material economic, political, and military power of the United States increased during the twentieth century, the validity of this strategy of assertive accommodation on the part of the civil rights organizations became even more justifiable, practical, and realistic. It is important, however, to understand that these accommodations were never acquiescence in or acceptance of injustice, but rather tactical maneuvers, strategic retreats, or temporary delays, and the effective timing of demands for specific changes.

NAACP AND URBAN LEAGUE:
LEADERSHIP AND STRATEGY

What were the effects of this strategy? There is no question that the rationale and techniques of the NAACP led to notable successes in the field of legislation and litigation. Civil rights victories in the federal courts, including equalization of salaries for teachers, the Gaines, Sweatt, and McLaurin cases, the restrictive covenant cases, and, finally, the *Brown vs. Board of Education* school-desegregation decision of 1954, are examples of the extent to which the NAACP has removed almost every legal support for racial segregation in all aspects of American life. Probably the only exception to this is the remaining laws dealing with intermarriage, and these laws may soon be declared unconstitutional.

The techniques, methods, and organizational structure of the NAACP in 1965 are essentially the same as they were in the 1920's. If one were to examine the NAACP today and compare it with the NAACP twenty or thirty years ago, the only significant difference one would find is an increase in the number of staff, particularly in the Legal Defense and Education Fund, Inc., staff.

This important legal arm of the NAACP has been officially separated as an independent corporation from the rest of the NAACP since 1939. But by the early 1950's this technical separation had increased in fact. The Legal Defense and Education Fund, Inc., has its own offices, budget, fund-raising program, and Board of Directors and staff. While there has remained a close working relationship with the NAACP itself, this increasing independence of the Legal Defense and Education Fund has made it possible for it to work closely and provide legal services to the newer more activist civil rights organizations such as CORE and SNCC.

The NAACP itself has added some staff for specialized work in such problem areas as labor and housing. The newer and more direct-actionist civil rights groups have forced the NAACP to initiate more concrete measures, but there is reason to believe that this advance was reluctant and that, left to its own devices, the NAACP would have continued to put its major emphasis on its traditional concerns. Ironically, ten, fifteen, or twenty years ago, such concerns seemed to be extreme militance. Today, in the view of the development of more activist civil rights groups, such as the Congress of Racial Equality (CORE), the Southern Christian Leadership Conference (SCLC), and the Student Nonviolent Coordinating Committee (SNCC), the NAACP is seen as a rather moderate, even conservative, organization.

As leaders of the NAACP, Walter White and, later, Roy Wilkins continued the tradition of Du Bois, but they stopped short where he had only begun. There is every reason to believe that Du Bois would have taken the NAACP to the front lines where CORE, SCLC, and SNCC are now. Walter White developed the method of personal contact and friendship with top public officials, and during his administration an effective NAACP lobby was begun and the legal staff strengthened. Nevertheless this program and his predilection for a "first name" approach to power figures necessarily supplanted direct-action confrontation. It approached the methods of the Urban League and transformed the Du Bois style of militance into one of personal diplomacy. On the death of Walter White in 1955, Roy Wilkins became executive director of the NAACP, after serving as editor of *The Crisis*, the NAACP's official journal. His approach differs little from Walter White's, in spite of the counter pressure of the more militant groups and more activist and impatient forces within the Board and staff of the NAACP. His style, manner, background, and personality are not consistent with a mass appeal. He seems more comfortable in rational discussions with key decision-makers in economic and governmental centers of power than before a mass meeting of his "followers." Wilkins is the personification of responsible, statesmanlike leadership. He jealously guards his belief in the rational and intellectual approach to significant social change and refuses to be pushed even temporarily into the stance of the fiery leader. The value of this approach is clear; its dangers are more obscure but nonetheless real. Its chief danger is that a primary and understandable concern of civil rights leaders for a posture of respectability might make them more vulnerable to the shrewd, psychological exploitation of skillful political leaders. The power of civil rights leaders could probably be more effectively controlled by affability than by racial brutality.

The NAACP either was not able or did not desire to modify its program in response to new demands. It believed it should continue its important work by using those techniques it had already perfected. It may, of course, have been impossible for an old-line organization to alter its course dramatically, and thus it may have been inevitable that new programs would have to stem from the apparently more militant, assertive, and aggressive civil rights organizations.

The Urban League, contrary to popular opinion, has by no means been so visibly successful as the NAACP in attaining its stated goals. Certainly its desire and efforts to aid the smooth adjustment of the Southern Negro who moved to Northern cities, while quite laudable, have not prevented the massive pathology which dominates the expanding ghettos of such cities as New York, Chicago, Philadelphia, Detroit, and Cleveland. The fascinating paradox is that the very areas in which the Urban League program has been most active—the blight of segregated housing, segregated and inferior education, and persistent and pernicious discrimination in employment—have been those areas in which the virulence of racism has increased in the North. Obviously, one cannot blame the program and activities of the Urban League for this blight. It remains a fact, however, that the approach used by the Urban League has not effectively stemmed the tide nor obscured the symptoms of Northern racism. The goals of the NAACP, resting on the vision and courage of the federal courts, were far more concrete and limited and hence more easily achieved. The ghettos of Northern cities and the forces which perpetuate such ghettos are clearly beyond the scope of an agency such as the Urban League or indeed any private agency. In response to this, there are indications that the League's present leadership is moving closer to direct involvement with governmental power.

It is clear also that the victories of the NAACP in the federal courts, the victories of all the combined forces of the civil rights organizations, leading to the Civil Rights Act of 1964 and the voting rights act of 1965 do not appear to be relevant to the peculiar cancerous growth of racism in American ghettos now spreading from the North back to more "liberal" Southern cities like Atlanta and New Orleans. The difficult truth civil rights agencies must eventually face is that so far no technique has been developed which seems relevant to this problem which now has emerged as the key civil rights issue. Protest demonstrations, litigation, and legislation do not seem to be specific remedies for this pattern of social pathology.

Within recent years, under the guidance of its new executive director, Whitney Young, the Urban League has indicated its awareness of the complexities of the present civil rights problem. The Urban League has joined with more "militant" civil rights groups, associating itself with mass protest movements, acknowledging that a social-service approach is not adequate to deal with the more flagrant predicaments of Negroes in the North and South. It has joined in demands for effective legislation. Whitney Young, probably by force of his personality, his background as an academician and administrative social worker, and his diplomatic skill, has managed to combine the traditional approach with a more dramatic and seemingly more militant stance without major disruption to the Urban League. He has not alienated white supporters; indeed, he has convinced them to increase their contributions. He has demonstrated beyond question that a more assertive insistence upon the inclusion of Negroes in the main stream of American life (his "fair share" hiring plan) and the willingness of the Urban League to identify itself with more "militant" direct-action dramatization of the plight of the Negro have not been at a financial sacrifice. Whitney Young demonstrated in the Urban League a degree of flexibility not yet so clearly apparent in the NAACP.

THE CONGRESS OF RACIAL EQUALITY

The Congress of Racial Equality (CORE), like the Urban League and NAACP, began in the North. It was founded in Chicago in 1942 and became a national organization in 1943. From its inception it emphasized direct action and the dramatization of special forms of racial segregation. The founders of CORE were associated in some of their activities with a pacifist-oriented group, the Fellowship of Reconciliation, and the organization was interracial. In the initial stages of CORE, the evolution of a civil rights organization with a larger political commitment seemed possible. The pacifist aura and direct-action orientation of early CORE founders and members suggested a significant divergence from the politically nonpartisan policies and programs of the NAACP and the Urban League. In fact, one of the rationales for the founding of CORE was that it felt that legalism alone could not win the war against segregation.[3]

It is significant that CORE did not become a major civil rights organization until the civil rights movement reached a crescendo after the Brown decision of 1954. Before that, CORE seemed to be a rather constricted, dedicated, almost cult-like group of racial protesters who addressed themselves to fairly specific forms of racial abuse which could be dramatized by their particular method of direct action and personal protest. In 1943, they sat-in at a segregated Chicago restaurant, successfully desegregating it; in 1947 they co-sponsored with the Fellowship of Reconciliation a two-week freedom-ride to test discrimination in buses engaged in interstate travel; and through nonviolent stand-ins, they successfully desegregated the Palisades Amusement Park's pool in 1947–48.[4] These techniques could be viewed as the harbingers of the more extensive use of direct action, nonviolent techniques, which, since the Montgomery bus boycott, have become almost the symbol of the civil rights protest movement. Whether or not Martin Luther King, Jr., was aware of his debt to the CORE precedent, CORE set the pattern for Montgomery. The sit-in technique was initially CORE's and CORE was also the first civil rights organization to rely upon nonviolent political pacifism.

James Farmer, executive director of CORE, was formerly a Methodist minister. He combines the appearance of personal calm and tolerant objectivity with a surprising forthrightness and fervent commitment. He makes no diplomatic accommodation to power figures, but demands uncompromising equality. In CORE's loose confederation of militant and seemingly undisciplined local chapters under a permissive national board, Farmer is a stabilizing influence, a convergence point; he holds power by virtue of his personal example of commitment. But while he is a symbol of the integrity of CORE and is generally accepted as such by the public and by CORE members, so far he does not seem able to control the activities of some of the more zealous and activistic CORE chapters.

When local CORE groups in Brooklyn threatened to use a dramatic, but seemingly ineffective tactic—the abortive stall-in to keep people from getting to the New York World's Fair in April of 1964—Farmer was forced to intervene in an unaccustomed show of discipline to save the national organization. He allowed himself to be arrested at the Fair partly to demonstrate his own commitment to the cause but also to divert the spotlight from his unruly locals. Yet, whatever the anarchism of these locals and the inadvisability of demonstrations not directly related to concrete grievances, there is something to be said for the observation that, when multitudes are inconvenienced or threatened with discomfort, the very random quality of the action reflects the desperation of the demonstrators and has some impact, even if only irritation, upon the white majority. To the Negro, white irritation and anger is at least a *response*. And where chaos threatens, more responsible leaders of society intervene. The danger of disruptive demonstration, of course, is that the intervention may be repressive and the repressiveness may seem justifiable in the name of public order. But thus far CORE has not demonstrated that its tactics and methods are relevant to the problems and the pervasive pathology of the Negro in urban ghettos.

THE SOUTHERN CHRISTIAN LEADERSHIP CONFERENCE

The Southern Christian Leadership Conference, which Martin Luther King, Jr., heads, has the distinction of being the first civil rights organization to start in the South. It began in Atlanta in 1957, primarily as an expression of the commitment of nearly one hundred men throughout the South to the idea of a Southern movement to implement through nonviolent means the Supreme Court's decision against bus segregation. This commitment was made concrete by formation of a permanent organization, the SCLC, and Martin Luther King, Jr. was elected its president.

In order to understand SCLC and King, one must understand that this movement would probably not have existed at all were it not for the 1954 Supreme Court school-desegregation decision which provided a tremendous boost to the morale of Negroes by its clear affirmation that color is irrelevant to the rights of American citizens. Until this time, the Southern Negro generally had accommodated himself to the separation of the black from the white society. In spite of the fact that Southern rural Negroes in Clarendon County, South Carolina, were the original plaintiffs in the school-desegregation cases, one could speculate that if the United States Supreme Court had ruled against them, the Southern Negro would probably have retreated into stagnation or inner rebellion or protest by indirection. The leadership of King came immediately, however, as a consequence of a Negro woman's refusal, in 1955, to make the kinds of adjustments to racial humiliation that Negro women had been making in the South throughout the twentieth century. Rosa Parks' defiance was publicized in *The Montgomery Advertiser,* which also revealed the fact that Negroes were organizing. Ironically, the chief boost of the boycott came from the white press. Scores of Negroes, who would not have known about the boycott, learned of it in the Montgomery newspaper and offered help to King and other ministers.

The bus boycott catapulted King first into local leadership as head of the Montgomery Improvement Association, formed for the purpose of coordinating the bus boycott, and then by virtue of the drama and success of that boycott into national leadership. He had responded to forces beyond his control, forces let loose by the early work of the NAACP in clearing away the legal support for segregation, by the urbanization and industrialization of society, and by the pressures of America's role in a predominantly nonwhite world. Here was a man who, by virtue of his personality and his role as minister, did not excite an overt competitive reaction from others. He could and did provide the symbol of unified protest and defiance. As a minister trained not only in theology, but in philosophy and history as well, sensitive and jealous of his understanding of world events and world history, King could develop and articulate a philosophical rationale for the movement, an ideology to support his strategy. Associating his role in Montgomery with the Gandhian philosophy of passive resistance and nonviolence, he emphasized another dimension of the civil rights movement in America, systematically articulating and developing the form of racial protest first used by CORE more than ten years before. The question has been raised whether or not this philosophy and the commitment to love one's oppressor is relevant to the effectiveness of the method itself. What happened in Montgomery was not a consequence of King's philosophy. The Montgomery affair demonstrated rather the ability of King and others to exploit the errors of the whites and to unify the Negroes for an effective boycott. There is no evidence that whites react to philosophy, but they do react to what happens. King's philosophy did not exist before the fact; rather, it was adopted after it was found to be working.

The development of philosophical and religious support for the method did, however, help to gather support for future action by focusing and refining a tactic and by an appeal to the conscience of Negro and white. King effectively turned the main weakness of the Negro, his numerical, economic, and political impotence, into a working strategy. Practically speaking, he could not seek redress by violence, but he did have available resources of nonviolence. Nietzsche said that Christ developed a philosophy of love because the Jews were weak; and that only when Christianity becomes strong can love become powerful. King's philosophy is actually a response to the behavior of others, effective directly in terms of the ferocity of the resistance it meets. It is not only nonviolent; it is also assertive: It depends on the reactions of others for its own strength. King and SCLC sometimes appear, indeed, to be satisfied, as in the case of Birmingham, with negotiations leading to minimal concessions. King does not insist upon total change in the status of Negroes in a community but considers partial change temporarily satisfactory. What he settles for can be questioned in terms of the energy expended and the risks taken.

One cannot understand SCLC solely in terms of its organization, which is amorphous and more symbolic than functional, even though the national headquarters in Atlanta, Georgia has sixty-five affiliates throughout the South. To understand this organization, one has to understand King, because SCLC *is* Martin Luther King, Jr. King is a national hero, a charismatic leader, portrayed in America and through the world as a man of quiet dignity, a personification of courage in the face of racial danger. He has the ability to articulate a philosophy and ideology of race relations clearly acceptable to the larger society. As far as the general public is concerned, the civil rights movement has converged in his personality. His ability to portray selflessness and to understand other civil rights leaders has made him a suitable person for his role. In the complexities, tensions, and frustrations of the civil rights movement, King fills an important function of simplification through personalization.

The presence of King and SCLC indicates something about the inadequacy or the inappropriateness of the methods and techniques used by the NAACP and the Urban League in the South today. If either the NAACP or the Urban League had been sufficient, King could not have been so successful as he is. King moved into a vacuum that existing civil rights groups did not fill. He mobilized people not in protest against the entire system but against specific injustices. Concrete successes, in turn, raised Negro morale. But SCLC's program, as a means to transform society, is more apparently than actually successful. The dramatization of the direct-action, SCLC-King technique over the mass media leads to the impression that the civil rights movement in the South is in fact a mass movement. In those situations in which white police and political officers do not exacerbate the resentment of Negroes by acts of cruelty and hostility, even King's appeal does not actively involve more than a fraction of the Negro population. It can, of course, be said of any "mass" movement that it rarely involves more than a small minority in direct action, at least in its initial stages.

King himself seems to realize the limitations of his method as shown by his unsuccessful attempt to encourage a less concrete strategy, a general boycott of the state of Alabama. In his plans to extend his program into Northern cities he seems likely to be less successful. In the future phase of the civil rights movement where Negroes confront not direct tyranny but pervasive oppression, King's strategy and charisma may be less effective. Furthermore, it would probably be all too easy to abort and to make impotent the whole King-SCLC approach, if white society could control the flagrant idiocy of some of its own leaders, suppress the more vulgar, atavistic tyrants like Sheriff Jim Clark, and create instead a quiet, if not genteel, intransigence. Such intransigence presents a quite different problem to the civil rights movement. A philosophy of love or techniques which seem compatible with such a philosophy would seem effective only in a situation of flagrant hate or cruelty. When love meets either indifference or passive refusal to change, it does not seem to have the power to mobilize the reactions of potential allies. Nor does it seem to affect the enemy—it appears irrelevant to fundamental social change.

Gandhi, of course, whose philosophy was one of nonviolent resistance, was the leader of a *majority* in the fight for Indian independence, King of a *minority;* this fact, important in an analysis of power, may be the decisive one in determining whether King can achieve a transformation of American society as deep and real as the Gandhian victory in India. The willingness of an oppressed people to protest and suffer, passively or assertively, without bitterness or with "love for the oppressors" seems to have influence only where the conscience of the majority of the society can be reached. In Hitler's Germany the Jews suffered nonviolently without stirring Nazi repentance; the early Christians who were eaten by lions seem to have stimulated not guilt but greed in the watching multitudes. King's strategy depends therefore for its success not only upon the presence of flagrant cruelty in a society but also upon the inherent good will, the latent conscience of the majority of the American people, as Gandhi's did upon the British commitment to justice.

In a situation of benign intransigence—like New York City—or a society of gentlemen—North Carolina, for example—a philosophy of love for the oppressor may be less effective than in Alabama. There Negroes do not face overt cruelty but rather the refusal to alter their status. What do you do in a situation in which you have laws on your side, where whites smile and say to you that they are your friends, but where your white "friends" move to the suburbs leaving you confronted with segregation and inferior education in schools, ghetto housing, and a quiet and tacit discrimination in jobs? How can you demonstrate a philosophy of love in response to this? What is the appropriate form of protest? One can "sit-in" in the Board of Education building, and not a single child will come back from the suburbs or from the private and parochial schools. One can link arms with the Mayor of Boston and march on the Commons, but it will not affect the housing conditions of Negroes in Roxbury. One can be hailed justifiably as a Nobel Prize hero by the Mayor of New York City, but this will not in itself change a single aspect of the total pattern of pathology which dominates the lives of the prisoners of the ghettos of New York.

THE STUDENT NONVIOLENT COORDINATING COMMITTEE

The rise of the Student Nonviolent Coordinating Committee intensified and sharpened the dramatic confrontation begun by CORE in the 1940's and developed by Martin Luther King, Jr., in the late 1950's. The restless young students who originally led the movement used direct assertive defiance and resistance, nonviolent in tactic and yet militant in spirit. They had gone beyond the quiet, stubborn, passive resistance of the bus boycott in Montgomery to a new stage of challenge—no less stubborn but considerably less passive. The first demonstrations in Greensboro, North Carolina, and Nashville, Tennessee, were appropriately in college towns. It was as a result of these that the Student Nonviolent Coordinating

Committee was formed.[5] SNCC was organized in April 1960 at a meeting at Shaw University in Raleigh, North Carolina. It took as its original function the coordination of the protest work of the many student groups conducting sit-ins.[6]

This program, representing the impatience of a younger generation, came at a time when more established civil rights groups seemed ready to settle for post-Little Rock tokenism and moderation. During the years since 1954 and up to that time, the letter and spirit of the Brown decision had been effectively eroded. "All deliberate speed" had been translated into "any perceptible movement," or mere verbalization of movement. The presence of a single Negro child in a previously white school was considered a famous victory. But the SNCC "kids" in their worn denims brought new verve, drive, daring, and enthusiasm—as well as the brashness and chaos of youth—to sustain the dynamism of direct-action civil rights tactics. They propelled more orderly and stable groups like the NAACP and Urban League toward increasing acceptance of direct-action methods not only because some of the older leaders found the ardor of youth contagious but also because, after the manner of experienced leaders, they sensed that bolder programs would be necessary if their own role were not to be undermined. The intervention of youth revitalized CORE and sustained the intensity of the direct involvement of King and SCLC. It has helped make possible—indeed it may have played a vital part in —the continuation of King's role as charismatic leader by arousing weary and apathetic Negroes to the imminence of justice, thereby stimulating an atmosphere sympathetic to crusade and sacrifice.

The SNCC uniform of blue denims and the manner of defiance were far removed from the neat white shirt and tie and Ivy League jacket of Urban League workers and the courteous, biblical eloquence of King. After SNCC's initial stage of urban protest, it decided to move into the deep South and consciously attempted to express through dress, manner, and method a direct identification with working-class Southern Negroes. Nonetheless, many of the SNCC leaders were actually even closer than the SCLC, NAACP, and Urban League leadership to sophisticated Northern campuses where militance previously had been less action-oriented than intellectual.

SNCC seems restless with long-term negotiation and the methods of persuasion of the Urban League, and it assumes that the legislative and litigation approach of the NAACP has practically attained its goals. SNCC has not overtly repudiated King's philosophy of nonviolence, but it does not root its own acceptance of this strategy in love of the enemy. Rather SNCC leaders seem almost nationalistic in spirit, in the sense of pride that they hold, not so much in *being* black (an appreciable number of SNCC workers are white) as in their conviction that justice and the future are on their side. SNCC welcomes dedicated whites and others who presumably share its concern for total justice. The style and manner of the SNCC leaders and workers are not consistent with any overt display of gratitude even to those whites who share their dangers and daily risks. The underlying assumption of the SNCC approach appears to be that the struggle for political and social democracy in the South is the responsibility of all Americans. They approach their programs and tasks with pride, courage, and flexibility and with an absence of sentimentality which those seeking gratitude or deference might view as disdain. They do not seem to be so concerned with the careful political screening of co-workers and exclusion of "radicals" as are the more experienced and "respectable" civil rights organizations. But it would be a mistake to interpret the SNCC style and method of challenge to the racial hypocrisies of the South as evidence of "left-wing" or Communist domination. SNCC is flexible and inclusive—not doctrinaire and dogmatic. Being loosely organized, SNCC has practically no hierarchy or clear lines of authority. The discipline of its workers seems to be determined by each individual's identification with the "cause" and the direct confrontation approach rather than by external controls or organizational structure.

Instead of a single leader, SNCC has many "leaders." Nominally, John Lewis is president of the Board of Directors and James Forman is executive director of SNCC. Actually "policy" and "operational" leadership is not only shared by Lewis and Forman but must be shared with others. Robert Moses, who plays a key role in the SNCC leadership team, directed the activities of the Council of Federated Organizations (COFO) in Mississippi during the summer of 1964. The individuals who coordinate SNCC activities for such Southern states as Georgia, Louisiana, and South Carolina also insist upon being heard in the leadership councils of SNCC. So far no single personality has emerged to speak for SNCC. John Lewis and Bob Moses seem deceptively retiring and soft-spoken in manner, but each is doggedly determined, assertive, and courageous in pursuit of the goals of unqualified equality. James Forman and Donald Harris, formerly SNCC coordinator in Georgia, are more overtly assertive and articulate but are no less likely to assume personal risks. The essence of SNCC leadership appears to be this willingness to assume personal risks, to expose oneself to imprisonment and brutality, and thereby to dramatize the nature of American racism before the nation and the world. Its members play the important role of commando raiders on the more dangerous and exposed fronts of the present racial struggle. This is not to be understood as mere adolescent bravado or defiance. It must be understood as an insistence upon total honesty, unwillingness to settle for anything less than uncompromised equality. It is an impatience with the verbalizations and euphemisms of "the accommodations" of more "realistic" or "strategic" leaders and organizations. This stance could be and has been described as "unrealistic" and "radical."

A VARIETY OF METHODS, THE SAME GENERAL GOALS, AND CONTEMPORARY RELEVANCE

There are obvious and subtle problems in any social movement when a variety of organizations with different philosophies, strategies, tactics, organizational structure, and leadership all seek the same broad goals. All civil rights organizations are committed to full inclusion of the Negro in the economic and political life of America, without restrictions based on race or color. But each differs from the other in its conception of how this commitment can best be fulfilled.

There is general agreement that the successes of the civil rights movement and organizations have catapulted the civil rights struggle into a new stage with more complex and difficult problems and goals. . . .

An examination of some of the concrete deficiencies in the organizations themselves shows that the NAACP and Urban League are under the handicap of experience. Committed to a method and a goal, they have not altered either in major ways since their founding. The sweep of the civil rights movement in the past two decades has not significantly affected these two elders of the movement. They still appear to function primarily in terms of personal leadership rather than staff competence. An exception is the expansion of the NAACP's legal and educational fund staff, which still remains largely legal and pays little attention to education. A serious analysis of the way in which the NAACP has attempted to modify its structure to meet the current civil rights struggle would force one to conclude that it has done so to a minimal degree. For example, the staff concerned with the problems of housing is, practically speaking, nonexistent. As of June 1965, and for the previous two years, the position of housing secretary was unfilled. The NAACP staff concerned with labor consists of a director and a secretary. This is true also for education. The staff responsible for public relations, promotion, and propaganda has increased from five to seven persons within the past crucial decade of civil rights activity. These facts suggest that the NAACP has made virtually no organizational response to meet the present increased civil rights demands. The local branches are archaic and generally ineffective, with barely adequate communication and coordination of policy and procedures between the national organization and the local branches. Probably the NAACP's most glaring inadequacy in light of the present and future demands of the civil rights revolution is the lack of a fact-gathering and research staff.

The Urban League seems more modern and efficient in its fund raising, promotion, and public relations and in its relationship with its local groups. It also, however, seems weak in research.

One could speculate that this weakness—which is shared by the newer organizations as well—reflects the difficulty of moving from reliance on personal leadership to the more demanding, less dramatic, less ego-satisfying but imperative staff approach. Now that the maximum gains have been obtained through legislation, litigation, and appeals to conscience, the difficult problem of implementation, of translating these gains into actual changes in the lives of Negroes, remains. This cannot be achieved by charisma alone. It requires adequate and efficient staffs, working, of course, under inspired and creative leadership. . . .

CORE's chief deficiencies are its weak organizational structure, the fact that its executive does not have sufficient power, and the problem that it has seemed at various times to be endangered by lack of discipline. However weak in discipline, it is nevertheless strong in enthusiasm and dedication among its members and its locals. It appears to be weak also in its fiscal arrangements, its fund-raising and systematic promotion.

CORE is in serious financial difficulties. There is a serious question whether CORE's lack of organizational discipline and structure is an asset or liability in terms of the flexibility necessary for it to be relevant to the present civil rights problems.

Behind SCLC's inspiring reality lie some very real difficulties, many of them quite human. Financially, however, it seems strong; it seems relatively easy for SCLC, through King, to attract a majority of the non-selective contributions to the civil rights movement, despite the minimal organization of SCLC itself. It is reasonable to conclude that if King were not its leader there would be no SCLC. Indeed, it is difficult to understand the role of SCLC's Board of Directors. It and the organization seem to be dominated by the magnetic appeal of King, by the personal loyalty and reverence of his top aides and of the masses who respond to his leadership. It is reasonable to assume that most of those who respond most enthusiastically to King's and SCLC's leadership are not members of his organization. The burdens of this special type of personal leadership are great if not intolerable. Probably the most desperate need of King and SCLC is for an effective supporting working staff to provide King with the type of background information and program planning which are necessary if this organization is to be relevant and if the type of leadership held by King is to continue to be effective.

SNCC is probably the least organized of all the civil rights organizations, suggesting that the degree of organization is not necessarily related to effectiveness or to the appearance of effectiveness.

As movements become more structured, they fall prey to the problems that plague most organizations, namely, red tape, bureaucracy, hierarchical discipline restricting spontaneous and imaginative experimentation, fear of change and, therefore, of growth. In large industrial, economic, financial, and governmental bureaucracies, and in political parties, major decisions are not personal, in spite of the existence of a charismatic leader. Similarly in the civil rights movement, major decisions must now reflect painstaking, difficult staff work based on fact-finding, intelligence, continuing critical analyses of data and strategies. Institutions tend to repress the rebel and to elevate the businessman-diplomat, yet the civil rights movement is full of rebels and its goal is independence. It is possible that the vitality of all of the civil rights organizations will depend on sustaining certain respectable organizations like the NAACP and the Urban League while stimulating them to pursue new programs and encouraging the fluid realignment of younger, more restless forces from whom the momentum for change must certainly come.

NOTES

1. For a thoughtful discussion of the Negro revolt, see Lerone Bennett, Jr., *Confrontation: Black and White* (Chicago: Johnson Publishing, 1965).

2. E. Franklin Frazier, *The Negro in the United States,* rev. ed. (New York: Macmillan, 1957), pp. 524–25.

3. Louis Lomax, *The Negro Revolt* (New York: Harper & Row, 1962), p. 145.
4. James Peck, *Freedom Ride* (New York: Simon and Schuster, 1962), passim.
5. For an excellent study of SNCC, see Howard Zinn, *SNCC: The New Abolitionists* (Boston: Beacon Press, 1964).
6. W. Haywood Burns, *The Voices of Negro Protest in America* (London: Oxford University Press, 1963), p. 44.

ORGANIZATIONAL STRUCTURE AND GOAL
SUCCESSION: A COMPARATIVE ANALYSIS
OF THE NAACP AND CORE, 1964–1968

Elliott Rudwick / August Meier

CORE and the NAACP have responded very differently to militancy of the separatist type generally known as Black Power.[1] During the early 1960's, although their tactics differed markedly, both organizations had an identical goal—full participation in an integrated society. While the NAACP changed somewhat in response to internal and external pressures, these shifts have been relatively small, and its commitment to the goal of integration remains intact. In contrast, CORE, faced by similar pressures, experienced a dramatic change in ideology, tactics, and goals, becoming one of the leading advocates of black separatism.[2]

CONTRASTING STRUCTURES OF NAACP AND CORE

It was our initial assumption that these different reactions largely stemmed from the contrasting structures of these two organizations. As is well known, the structure of an organization is an important factor in determining its adaptation to changing internal demands and environmental pressures. The NAACP and CORE respectively correspond to what David Sills has called the "corporate-type" and the "federation-type" of voluntary organization. Sills defines the former as consisting of a national headquarters and local branches, and the latter as consisting of semi-autonomous local affiliates.[3] In this paper, it is our purpose to explore the way in which the sharply contrasting organizational structures of CORE and NAACP affected their response to the black separatist thrust. It is our thesis that the centralized, rather highly bureaucratized structure of the NAACP made the organization relatively stable in ideology and goals.

From the *Social Science Quarterly* 51 (June 1970): 9–24; reprinted by permission.

On the other hand, CORE, a decentralized organization consisting of a weak national body possessing what can be best described as an incipient bureaucracy, and of local chapters possessing a high degree of autonomy and exhibiting strong anti-bureaucratic tendencies, proved extremely unstable and underwent a radical transformation in the last few years.

Actually the situation was both more subtle and more complex than the preceding paragraph suggests. Despite its decentralization and its anti-bureaucratic tendencies, CORE proved to be no more of an exception to Michels' "Iron Law of Oligarchy" than the NAACP. But unlike the NAACP, whose national decision-making elite has been historically a stable one, CORE has been characterized, to use Pareto's phrase, by a rapid "circulation of the elite." It is our thesis that this difference, itself rooted in the diverse organizational structures, is a key factor in explaining the contrasting responses of the two organizations of the black separatist thrust.

Historical origins are important in explaining the structural development of an organization,[4] and this is as true for CORE and the NAACP as it is for other voluntary groups.

The NAACP was founded in 1909–1910 by a group of distinguished Negroes—most notably W.E.B. Du Bois—and reform-minded whites (ranging from Socialists like William English Walling to Moorfield Storey, a distinguished constitutional lawyer and former president of the American Bar Association). Essentially, the NAACP, chartered under the laws of the state of New York, was a self-perpetuating Board of Directors of 30 members which employed a national staff and established local branches over which it possessed strict legal control. In theory the annual meeting of the Association held in New York City, open to all dues-paying members, was the highest policy-making body of the organization, and elected the Board of Directors. In actual fact, only a handful attended the yearly meeting of the corporation, and those present regularly endorsed the slate picked by the Board. The large annual Conference, attended by delegates from branches across the country, was not a policy-making body but essentially an educational forum for the members and the general public.[5]

CORE began in 1942 as the Chicago Committee of Racial Equality, which was composed primarily of students at the University of Chicago. An offshoot of the pacifist Fellowship of Reconciliation, its leaders were middle-class intellectual reformers, less prominent and more alienated from the mainstream of American society than the founders of the NAACP. They regarded the NAACP's legalism as too gradualist and ineffective, and aimed to apply Gandhian techniques of nonviolent direct action to the problem of race relations in the United States. A year later, the Chicago Committee joined with half a dozen other groups that had emerged across the country, mostly under the encouragement of the F.O.R., to form a federation known as the Congress of Racial Equality. Thus, in contrast to the NAACP, which started with a national committee and a national office, CORE began as a federation of local groups, who were jealous of their autonomy. In one respect, it is true, CORE was more elitist in character than the NAACP. For whereas in the

NAACP a simple annual payment of a dollar membership fee entitled one to all the privileges of membership, in CORE, full—and voting— membership went only to those who worked actively in direct-action projects. CORE chapters thus remained small (generally between 20 and 30 members, and seldom over 50). They consisted of a small band of dedicated activists, for whom CORE tended to become a way of life.

From the point of view of internal structure CORE was far more decentralized and democratic than the NAACP. Within local CORE affiliates, decisions tended to be made by the chapter as a whole, rather than as in the NAACP, by the local executive board. Again, in contrast to the NAACP, the CORE National Action Council, the counterpart to the NAACP Board of Directors, was elected directly by the annual conventions. In the early years, the decision to affiliate and disaffiliate CORE chapters was generally made by a vote of the groups rather than by the national body, while the annual convention itself selected such staff as there was: the volunteer or subsistence field representatives, and the unpaid national executive secretary.

In general the CORE groups were extremely reluctant to establish a strong national secretariat. For years the executive secretary worked on a volunteer part-time basis. The affiliates deliberately rejected the idea of financing the national organization through memberships as practiced by the NAACP (where about half the membership fees go to the national organization). Again, unlike the NAACP, where most of the special fund-raising is the responsibility of the branches, the CORE groups refused to make significant contributions of any sort to finance the national organization. As a consequence almost all of national CORE's income has come through special fund raising conducted by the national office. Not until 1957, 15 years after CORE's founding, did a salaried secretariat appear.[6]

The years produced changes in the structure of both organizations, though the basic form of each was not affected. By the 1960's the NAACP structure provided for more influence upward from the branches, while CORE had moved toward developing a bureaucracy.

As a result of both criticism by intellectuals outside the organization during the 1930's, and internal demands for reform, the NAACP had undergone several significant changes. In practice, the Annual Convention had become the highest legislative body, its resolutions establishing the policies and programs for the ensuing year. While the Board and staff have considerable discretionary power in implementing these resolutions, the convention does set the basic policy for the Association. The national Board, which raised its membership from 48 to 60 members at the recommendation of the 1961 convention, was chosen by a complex procedure. Members were elected for three years as previously, with one-third retiring each year. This fact in itself naturally promotes stability. Of the 60, 21 were elected by the seven regions (three from each region), three by the youth division (as the result of pressures from the young activists in 1960 and 1961), 18 by the Board, and 18 at-large. The nominating committee for the at-large candidates consists of three chosen by the Board and four elected by the convention. The nominating committee's slate, and the names of those nominated by petition, are then submitted to a vote of the branches.[7]

Meanwhile, over the years, the NAACP had developed a well organized and specialized bureaucracy. Experienced executives were placed in charge of branch work, youth work, church work, public relations, branch membership drives, and life memberships. Specialists had been added to the staff since the 1930's through the creation of a legal department, and after the second World War, of housing, education, and labor secretaries. At the same time the field staff expanded markedly. Finally, after the NAACP Board consulted a management firm in 1964, the structure was further rationalized, with a strict hierarchical organization, and with much of the authority for internal operations resting in the hands of an assistant executive director, thus freeing the executive director for the larger planning and relationships with outside organizations.[8]

In practice an informal structure has evolved, meshing with this formal structure, making for stability in the organization. Thus in theory the branches and the convention ultimately set policy; in practice the staff and especially the executive director are the main source. In part, this situation is a product of a long tradition of strong executive secretaries, who have worked very closely with the leadership on the Board; in part it is due to the fact that the dynamic nature of the civil rights movement required critical day-to-day decisions by the national secretariat —within the broad framework of NAACP policy, of course. On the other hand, even though legally the NAACP national office and the Board have control over the branches, in practice the branches act autonomously in setting their own specific programs and exercise considerable constraints on the policy of the national staff. In addition to conducting local protest activities, and recommending cases to the national legal staff, the most important function of the branches has been to raise money for the national office through annual memberships and special financial appeals. This fact in itself required the national office to retain the support of its branches. Thus the power over the branches was clearly subject to serious limitations.[9]

Yet there are also ways in which the national office can influence the situation at the local, state, and regional level, and thus ultimately in convention voting and elections. Critics of the NAACP's national administration charge that the field secretaries exercise an informal, but potent influence at the grass roots in the selection of delegates and candidates.[10] Certainly field secretaries can often channel the program and activities of the branches. Suggestions and advice on policy from national leaders are, naturally, considered seriously by state and local leaders.

Thus there is a complex web of relationships—between branches and state and regional conferences, between branches and national staff, between state and regional conferences and national staff, between staff and national Board—a network of mutual obligations and constraints and influences, that serves to promote stability, to prevent any sudden change. The complex system of elections to the Board also prevents sudden change, and this body, while less important than the executive secretary in day-to-day policy decisions, still exercises a constraining role—especially when dissident elements are able to articulate their dissatisfactions through a minority group on the Board. Finally, interlacing and underpinning the whole structure is a deep sense of tradition among NAACP staffers, branch leaders, and Board members. NAACP leaders, especially above the branch level, are almost always people of long experience with the Association, steeped in its traditions and philosophy.[11]

Changes in CORE's structure came about through a series of crises in the organization's history. In the middle 1950's, for a number of reasons which space prevents us from discussing, CORE had declined nearly to the point of extinction. A vigorous fund-raising campaign, followed in 1957 by the creation of a paid full-time executive secretary and field worker paved the way for extensive growth and development. The organization's extraordinary expansion in the early 1960's and the challenge created by the events of the period led to growth in the power of the National Action Council and in the size and functions of the national staff. Nevertheless, CORE's bureaucracy must be regarded essentially as incipient rather than fully developed. For one thing, CORE's method of nonviolent direct action meant that dedication, a long record of activism, arrests and time in jail were often more important as job qualifications, particularly for field staff, than technical knowledge or expertise. Moreover, though new positions were created as CORE expanded, the national staff remained relatively unspecialized,[12] there was a tendency for individuals to shift from one office to another, and there were serious cases of overlapping jurisdictions that sometimes led to conflict. Unlike the NAACP, where growth and specialization of the staff were an orderly process, in CORE there was much instability, frequent reshuffling of positions by the National Action Council, and considerable experimentation in an effort to create a more efficient mechanism to meet the challenges posed by the rapid developments of the 1960's.

Meanwhile the local chapters, which reached about 200 at maximum, remained as autonomous as before, and had, if anything, less to do with the national affairs of the organization. Without any financial responsibility for national interests, the chapters almost entirely pursued local ones. The National Action Council, however, did grow in influence. Constitutionally, it, instead of the convention, now selected the national director; to it had been delegated the major responsibility regarding affiliation of chapters.

Theoretically, of course, the convention remained the highest policy-making body of the organization; but in fact the chief locus of authority rested in the National Action Council. CORE's anti-bureaucratic sentiments, and the weakness of the bureaucracy itself, meant that the National Action Council was far more influential in shaping the ongoing policy of the organization than its counterpart—the NAACP Board of Directors. On the other hand, there were actually fewer constraints from the chapters on national [leadership] than in the case of the NAACP. For example, the failure of the CORE chapters to contribute significantly to the financial support of the national office meant that the latter was less dependent upon the local affiliates. The chapters as such were not consulted in the election of any of the National Council and officers—all of which were elected directly by the convention. This situation was exacerbated by the fact that the convention was less representative of the chapters than the NAACP convention, many CORE chapters not bothering to send delegates and some delegates being seated from essentially inactive chapters without rigorous examination of credentials. Ironically, in fact, the very autonomy of the chapters contributed to the lack of constraints which they exercised upon the national organization.[13]

Thus although both organizations had oligarchic tendencies, various factors combined to make CORE potentially far less stable than the NAACP: the National Action Council, elected annually directly by the convention, and therefore more likely to be swayed by new fashions than the NAACP Board; the weakness of the national bureaucracy; and the lack of mutual constraints between national and the locals. This situation was accompanied by a far more rapid turnover in CORE's leadership—thus many people relatively new to CORE and not steeped in its earlier traditions of interracialism and nonviolence, but attracted because of its militance, moved into positions of leadership in the middle 1960's.[14]

THE BLACK POWER THRUST

In order to understand the change in CORE from interracialism to black separatism, it is necessary to examine developments beginning in 1964, just after the high tide of success in the direct action phase of the civil rights movement. As CORE had moved into the northern cities and begun to articulate the problems of the northern ghettos in the winter of 1963–1964, it had become evident that the millenial expectations of 1962–1963 were premature. Recalcitrant southern resistance to the voter-registration campaigns produced a similar effect. In both areas there was a growing skepticism of the philosophy of nonviolence, and a rising feeling that black Americans would have to depend for their advancement more upon Negro community organization than upon the action of white allies.

The thrust for change in CORE came chiefly from individuals in the northern chapters that had sprouted as the organization turned its attention from public accommodations to the socioeconomic problems of the slumdwellers. Job campaigns had been successful against retail stores, but demonstrations for employment in the building trades, the rent strikes, and the school integration campaigns had failed. The dashing of the high expectations produced first a tendency toward ever more extreme tactics (such as the threatened Brooklyn CORE stall-in at the opening of the New York World's Fair),[15] and, tentatively at first, a tendency toward black nationalist sentiments. These trends in CORE were reflected in the elections to the National Action Council in 1964. At this 1964 convention, many of the more moderate chapters were virtually unrepresented, and the elections to the National Action Council directly reflected the new emerging currents. The number of old-line Negroes and whites on the Council declined, and they were replaced with newer people who had entered CORE in the preceding two or three years.

The ranks of the Council now included individuals with a point of view very different from the traditional CORE orientation.

As already noted, the Council was more influential in shaping policy than the NAACP Board of Directors was in its organization. Furthermore, with CORE increasingly emphasizing militance rather than its tradition of nonviolent interracialism, there was no strong ideological commitment that could act as a brake upon the change. Without effective checks upon the National Action Council from the local chapters, the more moderate views prevailing in many of them were underrepresented. At this juncture, moreover, the Council faced a bureaucracy weakened by a factional dispute which had led to the resignation of several staff members, chiefly black, who, like their opponents were deeply committed to attacking the problems of the ghetto, but who were also firmly dedicated to interracial action and the goal of integration. Under the circumstances, with a national leadership strongly desiring to relate more closely to the problems of the northern ghettos and searching for new and more effective strategies to deal with them; and with the absence of a consensus within the organization as to what these new strategies should be, the nationalists on the Council were able to push their views. This became more dramatically evident in the discussion and actions concerning white officeholders. The number of whites in the national staff declined rapidly in 1965–66. When an important white official who held the second highest post in the national staff resigned at the end of 1964, the race of his successor became an important issue at the meeting of the Council, and a decision was made to employ a Caucasian only on a temporary basis until a suitable Negro could be found. The question of whites holding office in the local chapters was raised vigorously at the 1965 convention, and the new constitution officially declared that most of the officers in the chapter must be black.[16]

Symbolically and practically, this change was of momentous importance—it flew directly in the face of the explicit ideology of CORE's founders that only an interracial, nonviolent direct action movement could achieve racial equality in the United States. As these decisions over white leadership in CORE indicate, the year 1965 was a turning point. Basically the stage had been set for the acceptance of the Black Power slogan in 1966, for the total exclusion of whites from active membership in 1968, and for the adoption of a black separatist program.[17]

The internal challenge of the NAACP in the middle 1960's came from a group known as the Young Turks, and basically the Association handled it as it had handled similar challenges to its program in the past. To some extent it accommodates itself to the pressures; but its basic ideology and goals remain intact. For example, there had been much agitation in the 1930's, especially from younger black intellectuals, to compel the organization to democratize its structure and shift its emphasis from constitutional rights to a program attacking the economic problems of the masses. The NAACP Board did provide for the election of some at-large Board members under procedures described earlier. It adopted in principle an economic thrust as part of the program of the Association, and by the time the United States entered World War II, had cemented a close alliance with the interracial, industrial, CIO unions. Yet the NAACP program retained its former emphasis on attacking franchise restrictions, segregation, and mob violence, and the board, with the staff, still remained in basic control of policy.[18] Again in the early 1960's, pressed by the dramatic direct action campaign of competing civil rights organizations, and by internal pressures, especially from the youth, the Association had endorsed and, especially on the part of the college and youth chapters, often participated in nonviolent direct action projects. Pressed by the younger people it also gave the Youth Councils a degree of autonomy from the adult chapters in their communities, and provided them with representation on the national Board. On the other hand, the leadership—and large segments if not the majority of the adult membership—maintained that the older program and tactics were still vital and important.[19]

The Young Turks were a small group of men, chiefly lawyers, businessmen, and doctors in their thirties and forties,[20] who during the early 1960's were among those challenging the NAACP orientation toward legalism, and urging greater emphasis on direct action. They did not disagree with NAACP goals, but were concerned about tactics. For example, they wanted the executive director to go South and directly challenge the competitive threat posed there by Martin Luther King, who was receiving national publicity while NAACP accomplishments were largely ignored in the press. In this the Young Turks were supported by certain members of the national staff.

Subsequently in the mid-1960's, their emphasis was on combatting the deep-seated social ills of the northern ghettos. At the same time, beginning in 1964 their attacks upon the national leadership grew sharper. They openly advocated the removal of the executive secretary and of the older black and white Board members, including the national Board chairman. They demanded the replacement of the white president with a Negro. They criticized the Association's dependence upon white liberal allies in the national government and in the labor unions, particularly in the United Auto Workers, whose president sat on the NAACP Board of Directors.

While their suspicion of many whites actively associated with the NAACP cause was thus evident as early as 1965, and while they urged community organization in the ghettos to meet the needs of the slum-dwellers, they did not advocate an explicitly separatist program until the convention of 1968. At that time, calling themselves the "National Committee to Revitalize the NAACP," they demanded "a black approach" for the organization rather than old-style interracialism. The Turks insisted that the Association become "relevant to the black community" and denied "the very relevance of racial integration as a prime goal." They proposed the establishment of several convention committees, including one on "the Survival of Black Americans," evidently referring to armed self-defense of black communities. They also urged the creation of convention committees on African-American Culture, Afro-American and Non-White World Affairs, and Building Black Economic and Political Institutions. This proposal was defeated by a vote of 444 to 272, with the majority of northern delegates favoring it, while the Southerners over-whelmingly rejected it.[21]

Thus, while slower to move to a separatist position, the Young Turks paralleled their CORE counterparts in first being advocates of more mili-tant direct action, then becoming disillusioned with the limited results of direct action after emphasis shifted to the ghettos' economic and social problems, and finally, as a consequence of their frustration, turning to a separatist program. Their challenge first took the form of verbal criticism, then, an attempt to dominate the annual convention proceedings,[22] and most dramatically, a campaign to gain control of the national Board of Directors.

The national office used a variety of techniques to repulse the chal-lenge of the Young Turks. Thus for example, when the Turks attempted to eliminate a white labor leader and a black bishop from the Board, the national staff denounced them for an anti-labor and anti-church stance, and union as well as religious groups rallied to the cause of the established NAACP leadership. Again, when the Young Turks, exploiting techni-calities in convention procedures, secured control of the nominating com-mittee in 1964 and 1966, candidates supporting the NAACP administra-tion were nominated by petition and in most cases won election over the Young Turk candidates on the nominating committee's slate.[23]

At their high point in 1966–1967, the number of Young Turks on the Board was not more than 12. The largest number of votes they ever obtained on a particular issue was 17 on a Board of 60.[24] Similarly, at the dramatic 1968 convention, they mustered only about one-third of the votes.[25]

In the aftermath of this convention, both the top leaders of the Young Turks resigned from the Board. Even though the challenge of the Turks and their separatist ideology had been repulsed, the Association had modified its program to some extent. From 1965, in part seizing the opportunity presented by War on Poverty funds and foundation grants, the NAACP encouraged branches to become more actively engaged in organizing community action programs in the ghetto. It paid more at-tention than previously to aspects of black consciousness such as Negro history. It developed a program to help black businessmen—specifically organizing Negro contractors to pool their resources in order to qualify for substantial federal contracts.[26]

Finally, though insisting on retaining a white man in the ceremonial position of president of the Association, the NAACP leadership permitted the proportion of white members of the Board to decline from 22 per cent in 1963 to 12 per cent in 1969.[27] Actually, the decline in white member-ship on the Board came about for two reasons. It was partly due to the fact that many well qualified Negroes who deserved recognition for their long service and many contributions to the Association were anxious to fill the vacancies. However, the pressure from the insurgents was a signifi-cant factor. In any case, it no longer seemed feasible to elect to the Board whites who had national prestige but had not given years of service to the Association. And since the organization had for a long period been overwhelmingly black in its local membership (more than 90 per cent), eligible whites were scarcely likely to rise from the ranks.

CONCLUSIONS

Thus it would seem clear that the strong, bureaucratic, centralized nature of the NAACP, including its complex system of elections, acted as a brake upon the internal and external pressures pushing for a reorientation of goals; while the loose, decentralized nature of CORE with its weak bureaucracy, and relatively simple organizational structure made it easy for such pressures to express themselves successfully. Yet in the course of our investigations two other factors clearly emerged: the character of top leadership in the bureaucracy and the nature of the constituency. By 1964–1966, the CORE leadership, which no longer had a strong ideological commitment to the organization's original philosophy, and which deeply desired to relate to the black masses in the ghettos, tended to move in the direction of the strongest pressures. In contrast, the NAACP leadership stood firmly on its commitment to the organization's traditional ideology,[28] and used all the legitimate instruments at its disposal to oppose the dissidents. Even more important was the striking difference between the two organizations in constituency. The NAACP, with a constituency that has always been overwhelmingly Negro, has been firmly rooted in the black community, with strong ties to the churches and fraternal orders. It represents a better cross section of the Negro community than any other national racial advancement organization, and comes closer than any of the others to representing the majority voice of that community. Certainly the mass of its membership, especially in the South, favored its traditional integrationist position. In contrast, CORE has had a rapidly changing membership. CORE, predominantly white at least until 1963, had become predominantly black by the beginning of 1964. Moreover, there was a rapid turnover among its black members, who were typically activist types and therefore less representative of the total Negro community than the NAACP.

Thus, while the contrasting structures of the two organizations were an important factor in accounting for their differing responses to the pressures of the mid-1960's, clearly leadership and constituency were also important factors. In CORE the loose structure facilitated, and probably made possible a more complete shift than would otherwise have happened; changes in constituency were very rapidly reflected in the National Action Council; neither the Council nor the staff were responsible to the chapters in the way the Board and the secretariat were in the NAACP.

In a situation where the staff leadership was searching for a new direction, and had been weakened by a serious factional fight, the active minority of Black Power-oriented people on the National Action Council were able to rather quickly change the thrust of the organization. In the NAACP, on the other hand, with a constituency that, especially in the South, remained committed to integration; with a complex structure in which the Board, staff, regions, and branches were all mutually responsible to each other in a complex network of relationships; where because of election procedures it was difficult to change the composition of the Board radically; and where the national leadership knew what it wanted and had the constitutional power and informal structural resources to assert itself, change was slower, less radical, and the basic commitment to the original ideology remained.

Viewed in the larger context of social theory the contrasting roles of the policy-making elite in the two organizations is significant. As is evident from the preceding discussion, both the NAACP and CORE, like other voluntary organizations, have exhibited oligarchic tendencies. But these tendencies have taken strikingly different forms in the two racial advancement organizations. In the case of the NAACP, the corporate structure, the complicated elections procedures, the well-developed bureaucracy, and the complex machinery of branch, state, and regional organization have all facilitated the creation of an elite which is highly stabilized in terms of its personnel and ideology. Entrance of new members into this elite is constantly occurring, but only after a lengthy process of acculturation in the NAACP tradition as one climbs the ranks through years of active service. In the case of CORE, on the other hand, the simplicity of its structure and the policy of direct annual elections of members to the National Action Council, as well as its anti-bureaucratic ethos, have all facilitated a rapid circulation of the decision-making elite. It was this fluid and changing membership in its national governing elite which, reflecting changes in the larger society, brought a sharp shift in ideology, program, and goals in the Congress of Racial Equality.[29]

NOTES

ACKNOWLEDGEMENT: This paper was done under a research grant from the Kent State University Center for Urban Regionalism, James G. Coke, Director. We also wish to thank Professors Gary T. Marx of Harvard University and John H. Bracey, Jr., of Northern Illinois University, for their perceptive criticisms of an earlier version of this paper, which was read at the 1969 convention of the American Sociological Association. The paper itself is part of a larger study of the Congress of Racial Equality, which Atheneum will publish in 1971.

  1. Civil rights organizations have loomed in importance during the past decade. The largest ones, with their thousands of members, branches or chapters in hundreds of cities, and a national staff or bureaucracy, can be studied as complex organizations.

  Thus far, there has been little serious sociological study of this type of voluntary organization. The most detailed work on the NAACP has been done by a historian, Charles Flint Kellogg, *NAACP: A History of the National Association for the Advancement of Colored People I, 1909–1920* (Baltimore: Johns Hopkins Press, 1967). The only published sociological analysis of the NAACP is to be found in the work of Wilson Record in his *Race and Radicalism: The NAACP and the Communist Party in Conflict* (Ithaca: Cornell University Press, 1964). See also his "The Sociological Study of Action Organizations," *Journal of Human Relations* (Summer 1959), pp. 451–72.

  An unpublished but perceptive historical work employing many sociological concepts and insights is Barbara Joyce Ross, "Joel Elias Spingarn and the Rise of the National Association for the Advancement of Colored People," (Ph.D dissertation, American University, 1969). Attention should also be called to Ralph Bunche's early examination of the NAACP which formed the basis for Gunnar Myrdal's description of the organization. (Ralph J. Bunche, "Programs, Ideologies, Tactics, and Achievements of Negro Betterment and Interracial Organizations," Memorandum submitted for the Carnegie-Myrdal Study of the Negro in America, 1940). CORE has been the subject of even less study: but one very significant work, based primarily on an examination of several CORE chapters and their leaders, has appeared: Inge Powell Bell, *CORE and the Strategy of Nonviolence* (New York: Random House, 1958).

This paper is an attempt to study the question of goal succession in the NAACP and CORE during the middle 1960's from a broadly sociological perceptive. Works that have been helpful in formulating the approach used in this study include: Philip Selznick, "Foundations of the Theory of Organization," *American Sociological Reveiw* 13 (February 1948): 25–35; Seymour Lipset, "The Political Process in Trade Unions: A Theoretical Statement," in Morroe Berger, Theodore Abel, and Charles H. Page, eds., *Freedom and Control in Modern Society* (New York: D. Van Nostrand Company, 1954), pp. 82–124; Peter M. Blau, *Bureaucracy in Modern Society* (New York: Random House, 1956); Robert Michels, *Political Parties: A Sociological Study of the Oligarchical Tendencies of Modern Democracy* (Glencoe, Ill.: The Free Press, 1949); Philip Selznick, *Leadership in Administration: A Sociological Interpretation* (New York: Harper & Row, 1957); Owen E. Pence, *The YMCA and Social Need: A Study of Institutional Adaptation* (New York: Association Press, 1939); Sheldon L. Messinger, "Organizational Transformation: A Case Study of a Declining Social Movement," *American Sociological Review* 20 (February 1955): 3–10; Joseph R. Gusfield, "Social Structure and Moral Reform: A Study of the Woman's Christian Temperance Union," *American Journal of Sociology* 61 (November 1955): 221–32; and Joseph R. Gusfield, "The Problem of Generations in an Organizational Structure," *Social Forces* 25 (May 1957): 323–30. Our greatest debt is to David L. Sills's classic study of a voluntary organization, *The Volunteers: Means and Ends in a National Organization* (Glencoe, Ill.: The Free Press, 1957).

This paper is part of a long range study of the civil rights movement in the twentieth century. It is based upon research in the following sources: archives of NAACP and CORE; personal manuscript materials; files of *The New York Times,* 1960–1968; and interviews with leaders of the two organizations. Particularly important were these confidential interviews which supplied an intimate knowledge both of the internal workings and informed structure of the two organizations, and of the processes of social change in them.

2. Black Power and black separatism are phrases that embrace a wide variety of ideologies and specific programs. CORE has espoused a reformist rather than a revolutionary version of black separatism. Broadly speaking it has emphasized "community organization," "black consciousness," and all-black educational, political, economic and protest institutions and organizations. While CORE leaders on occasion say that this separatist program is the prerequisite to any long-range integration on a basis of equality, the thrust of their rhetoric is that integration is now an irrelevant issue, and in practice they have substituted for the goal of integration the goal of black community control over local institutions and the maintenance of a separate Negro community.

3. Sills, *The Volunteers*, p. 3.

4. Ibid., pp. 6–7; Lipset, "The Political Process in Trade Unions," p. 105. David B. Truman, *The Government Process* (New York: Knopf, 1951), p. 120.

5. Kellogg, *NAACP*, chaps. 1, 2, and 5; Ross, "J. E. Spingarn," pp. 66–78.

6. This description of early CORE is based upon our personal research in the CORE Archives and the James Farmer Papers, and upon confidential interviews with some of the early leaders. For the founding of CORE see August Meier and Elliott Rudwick, "How CORE Began," *Social Science Quarterly* 49 (March 1969): 789–99. CORE officials were very conscious of the contrasting structures of the two organizations. As one of them put it in 1960: "The structure of CORE is quite different from that of the NAACP. First of all, we are a federation of local semi-autonomous groups. These local groups function through the use of non-violent direct action on local projects. Secondly, instead of having the local groups support the national organization, we operate the other way around. That is, the Congress

of Racial Equality exists primarily to build and aid our local chapters. We do not subsidize them directly but most of our activities are aimed toward aiding their local programs." (Gordon Carey to I. Diane McClure, October 7, 1960, CORE Archives).

7. Confidential interviews; *Constitution of the Natural Association for the Advancement of Colored People* (New York: NAACP, 1968); *Crisis* 70 (February 1963): 107–8; ibid. 73 (February, 1966): 100; ibid. 68 (August–September 1961): 411. See also Record, *Race and Radicalism*, pp. 142–43. In 1968, the Board was increased to 64 members, to permit seven youth representatives, one from each of the seven regions. NAACP Board *Minutes*, June 27, 1968; and NAACP, *Summary Minutes*, 59th Annual Convention, 1968.

8. Ross, "J. E. Spingarn," *passim;* confidential interviews; for administrative reorganization of 1964 see NAACP Board *Minutes*, April 13, September 14, 1964. In 1964 the title of the executive secretary was changed to executive director.

9. Confidential interviews. The autonomy of the branches has led one historian of the organization to state, with some exaggeration, that although the branches were theoretically "subject to the close supervision of the Board, it is obvious that the Board's close control of local affairs was more apparent than real." (Ross, "J. E. Spingarn," pp. 137–38). A report to the Board of Directors in 1966 recommended a campaign to inform the branches of their relationship to the national office, emphasizing that the branches are "a subordinate and constituent unit" of the national organization, according to the constitution for branches. ("Report of Committee on Inter-Relationship of Funds between Branches and National Office," NAACP Board of Directors *Minutes*, January 3, 1966).

10. Louis E. Lomax, *The Negro Revolt* (New York: Harper & Row, 1963), p. 130.

11. Confidential interviews. On awareness of NAACP officials that the system of choosing the Board of Directors was a stabilizing influence, making it "proof against a coup d'etat," see Report of a Special Committee to the Board of Directors entitled "Tenure of National Officers and Directors," NAACP Board of Directors *Minutes*, April 12, 1966.

12. Thus, a community relations director—the most important post after that of national director—handled a broad range of functions, including both public relations and fund raising, and often took on other duties as well.

13. In addition to confidential interviews, the above section was based on an in-depth study of the CORE Archives. See especially, Minutes of National Action Committee, National Council, National Action Council (name varies), and of National Conventions, and reports of major staff officials, as well as CORE constitutions, 1957–1964, *passim,* in addition to correspondence and internal memoranda too voluminous to be cited here.

14. Confidential interviews. In one case, a West Coast leader who figured prominently among the CORE advocates of Black Power and exclusion of whites from office in the organization in 1965, had been elected to the National Action Council in 1964, about two-and-a-half years after he had first become active in CORE.

15. *New York Times*, April 11–14, 18, 22, 26, 1964; National Action Council *Minutes*, May 1–3, 1964.

16. As Gary T. Marx and Michael Useem put it in a forthcoming article in the *Journal of Social Issues*, "Majority Involvement in Minority Movements: Civil Rights, Abolition, Untouchability," there are other factors involved in the rejection of white leadership in the civil rights movement. Tensions between blacks and whites arose from a variety of causes such as differences in education and in verbal organizational skills. As Negroes became more self-confident and more desirous of controlling the struggle for their own freedom, they generally took steps to oust whites from leadership positions. James Farmer has described the process in the case of CORE in *Freedom—When?* (New York: Random House, 1966), chap. 4. We have not included a discussion of this type of internal organizational pressure because a comparable situation did not exist in the NAACP. The NAACP was almost completely black in leadership at both local and national levels,

and the minority of white members on the national board were symbolic public figures rather than wielders of significant influence within the Association. To the extent that this had been an issue in the NAACP—and it never was as serious in the Association as it was in CORE and SNCC—it had been resolved by the end of the 1930's when whites were virtually eliminated from policy-making positions. (See Ross, "J. E. Springarn," *passim*.)

17. These changes are reflected in CORE archival materials: Steering Committee *Minutes*, January 24, 1964; National Action Council *Minutes*, February 21–23, 1964; National Action Council *Minutes*, May 1–3, 1964; Steering Committee *Minutes*, June 19, 1964; National Action Council *Minutes*, June 30–July 2, 1964; National Director's Report, 1964 convention; National Action Council *Minutes*, August 8–9, 1964; Norman Hill to James Farmer, August 14, 1964; National Action Council *Minutes*, October 10–12, 1964; National Action Council *Minutes*, February 6–7, 1965; National Action Council *Minutes*, April 10–11, 1965; National Action Council and Staff Meeting, June 29 and July 6, 1965; National Action Council *Minutes* (closed session), July 6, 1965; National Convention *Minutes*, July 1965; Report of National Director to 1965 convention; James Peck to James Farmer, July 27, 1965; National Action Council *Minutes*, December 31, 1965 to January 2, 1966 (open and closed sessions). See also, "A Brief History of the Congress of Racial Equality," mimeographed pamphlet, February 1969, for general survey of growing nationalism in CORE. For an understanding of the dynamics of the process the confidential interviews were essential. See also *New York Times*, July 4, 5, 1965; July 2, 5, 1966; July 6, 1967; September 17, 1968.

18. Resolutions of the Second Amenia Conference, 1933, NAACP Archives, Library of Congress; Report of the Committee on Future Plan and Program of the NAACP (The Harris Committee), 1935, NAACP Archives; Ross, "J. E. Spingarn," chaps. 8 and 9.

19. On NAACP support for direct action (including direct action on part of NAACP branches in the late 1950's), see, e.g., *Crisis* 67 (March 1960): 162; ibid., 67 (May 1960): 313, 315, 319; ibid., 70 (June–July 1963): 347; ibid., 70 (August–September 1963): 389, 400; *New York Times*, July 6, 1963; and *Summary Minutes* of the 54th NAACP Annual Convention, 1963.

On NAACP youth acquiring greater autonomy see especially *Crisis* 70 (August–September 1963): 399; and Board of Directors *Minutes*, July 3, 1966.

For a typical defense of NAACP legalism see *New York Times* of July 11, 1961, quoting NAACP Board Chairman Bishop Stephen Gill Spottswood as supporting Freedom Rides but calling them a mere "signal flare," compared to the NAACP's "barrage," and adding "We are too old in the ways of the long struggle that has engaged our fathers not to realize that wars are won by using every available military resource and not by the employment of raiding parties." For a discussion of whole matter of changes in NAACP in period 1960–1963 see August Meier, "Negro Protest Movements and Organizations," *Journal of Negro Education* 32 (Fall 1963): 437–50.

20. Confidential interviews; *New York Times*, July 16, 1961. One, a veteran of a generation of civil rights activity, was actually in his sixties.

21. Confidential interviews; *New York Times*, January 4, 1967, and July 16, 1967, for criticism of NAACP's alliance with white liberals, especially the UAW; *New York Times*, July 2, 1968, and NAACP 59th Annual Convention, 1968 (for events at 1968 convention). See also "Statement Presented to National Committee to Revitalize the N.A.A.C.P. at N.A.A.C.P. National Convention. . . . June 23, 1968, from Chester I. Lewis . . ." (courtesy of Chester I. Lewis), and leaflet circulated by Young Turks, "Goals of the NAACP 'Young Turks' " (1968).

22. The Young Turks' attempts to control the annual convention took several forms. In 1964 and 1965, they exploited the unit rule, which was repealed at the 1966 convention. (See NAACP 57th Annual Convention, 1966, *Summary Minutes*.) The unit rule provided that the vote of each region would be cast as a bloc, with the votes of four of the seven regions needed to carry a motion. Strong in three of the regions, the Young Turks by means of astute politicking and horse-trading were

able to gain enough support in other regions to win on critical issues, and, most important, to win a majority of the places on the Nominating Committee. Similarly, by securing a majority of seats on the Committee on Time and Place, they were remarkably successful in arranging to have conventions meet at locations where many of their supporters would attend; and by controlling the Committee on Convention Procedure and Rules they were often able to have their candidates selected as chairmen of the important legislative sessions where the resolutions establishing NAACP's official policy were debated and passed. (Confidential interviews.)

It should also be noted that through their representatives on the "Committee on Evaluation for a Dynamic Program," appointed by the Board of Directors in 1962, the Young Turks also sought to accomplish their goals by a structural reorganization of the NAACP. Some important structural changes were accomplished, but they did not aid the cause of the Young Turks. (Interview materials; "Report of Committee on Evaluation for a Dynamic Program," January 1963, in Board of Directors *Minutes;* "Organizational and Procedural Survey of the National Association for the Advancement of Colored People, Adopted by the Board of Directors at its meeting April 13, 1964;" Board of Directors Meeting *Minutes,* September 14, 1964).

For other evidences of the Young Turks' challenge in the Board Minutes see, e.g., *Minutes* of Executive Committee, December 14, 1965; and *Minutes* of Board of Directors, April 11, 1968.

23. Confidential interviews; *New York Times,* October 5, December 8 and 17, 1964; January 6, 1965; September 20, 1966; *Crisis* 71 (December 1964): 693; ibid., 73 (November 1966): 489; and ibid., 74 (January–February 1967): 17.

24. Usually only one of the three youth members on the Board voted with them. The whole question of the relationship of the youth to the Young Turks is one that deserves research. On the whole the youth did not ally themselves with the Young Turks; their thrust was aimed less at modifying the program of the Association than at achieving more representation and autonomy for youth within the NAACP structure. At the 1966 convention the repeal of the unit rule, which the Young Turks wanted to retain, was initiated by the youth division. However, at the 1968 convention many youth, in a dramatic demonstration, walked out with the Young Turks. Undoubtedly the Turks drew most of their youth support in the North and were weak among the youth in the South.

25. Actually even one-third of the convention delegates is an over-representation of their real strength. Because the key votes concerned non-ideological issues the Turks picked up many more votes than they would have obtained if the ideological issue had been clearly joined. (Confidential interviews.)

26. Confidential interviews; see also Roy Wilkins' speech at Annual Meeting, January 1965, reported in *Crisis* 73 (February 1965): 82.

27. The issue of white dominance in the NAACP has been raised periodically. In 1963 Congressman Adam Clayton Powell mounted the most publicized attack prior to the Young Turks. (See *New York Times,* April 1, 1963; "The NAACP and Adam Clayton Powell," NAACP Pamphlet, April 1963; *Minutes* of NAACP Board of Directors, April 8, 1963; Report of Secretary of the Board of Directors for March 1963, dated April 8, 1963).

28. For reaffirmation of NAACP traditional ideology and goals see keynote address of Roy Wilkins to 1966 NAACP convention, attacking Black Power, *Crisis* 73 (August–September 1966): 353–54, 361; "Time to Speak Up," *Crisis* editorial, November 1968 (reprinted as leaflet); Roy Wilkins, "The State of the NAACP, 1968," Report of the NAACP Executive Director to the Association's Annual Meeting, January 13, 1969 (New York: 1969); and pamphlet, *Common Sense Anyone?* (New York: NAACP, 1969). The Board of Directors, meeting at the time of the 1968 convention, condemned its critics, resolving "that the historic policies of the Association should be and are hereby reaffirmed, the recently encountered pressures to abandon democratic processes are rejected, and sowers of discord and

advocates of threats and terror within our ranks are repudiated" (*New York Times,* June 29, 1968).

29. Throughout CORE's history it has experienced far greater turnover in leadership than the NAACP. As its national officers used to say, CORE has been like a "revolving door." Epitomizing this contrast between the two organizations is the striking difference in tenure of their chief executives. Where the NAACP has had three executive secretaries in the nearly half century since 1921, CORE has had three national directors in the period of less than a decade since 1961.

THE DEFENDERS: A CASE STUDY OF AN INFORMAL POLICE ORGANIZATION

Harold A. Nelson

I. INTRODUCTION

In many Southern communities, the concept of "law and order" has one meaning for whites and another for Negroes. In oversimplified terms, whites tend to equate it with adherence to traditional Southern mores. These mores *are* the law regardless of what judges, federal officials or Congress may have said to the contrary. Order exists when community behavior patterns are in strict compliance with the dictates of the mores. Primary responsibility for maintaining this order rests with local law enforcement agencies. It is their responsibility to protect the "Southern way of life" by crushing any challenge to it which may arise in the community.

Negroes equate this definition of law and order with the determination of whites to maintain a system which operates solely for their own benefit and which is rooted in illegality and brute force. They see themselves confined to a world governed not by law and order but by a vicious white populace which maintains its dominant position because it holds a monopoly of power. Law enforcement agencies are nothing more than the "white man's army" committed to protecting the "white man's society" by any means they choose to employ. These agencies function not for the protection and welfare of all citizens but for that of whites alone. No agency exists for the protection of Negroes from the dominant group and no mechanism is provided within the mores whereby they may challenge the monopoly of power held by whites.[1]

At issue is whether a group which perceives itself thus victimized can alter this situation. If it is denied services normally provided by law

From *Social Problems* 15 (Fall 1967): 127–47; reprinted as abridged by permission of the author and the Society for the Study of Social Problems.

enforcement agencies, can it provide at least some of them for itself? More generally, can such a group develop a mechanism by which it can successfully confront the monopoly of power arrayed against it and effectively challenge the mores which govern the community?

This paper is concerned with the efforts of Negroes in a Southern community to accomplish these goals. It describes the development of an informal police organization which not only provided certain services to Negroes, but also acted as the vehicle whereby traditional mores were challenged and a redistribution of power in the community was effected.[2]

II. ORIGIN OF THE DEFENDERS

Southville is located in a Deep Southern state. Its population of 50,000 persons includes 18,000 Negroes. It is the largest city in a county of 100,000 persons, approximately one-third of whom are Negroes. While the county is heavily agricultural, Southville is sufficiently industrialized to rank as one of the important industrial areas of the state. Prior to 1964, the city maintained the traditional patterns of segregation characteristic of most Southern communities. Local law enforcement agencies employed only white persons and were disliked and distrusted by the city's Negro population. A long-time and widespread dissatisfaction with racial conditions was shared by the community's Negroes, but prior to 1964 no organized attempt was made to change this situation. In that year, a Negro minister was installed in one of the largest Negro churches in Southville with the understanding that he would also act as a civil rights leader. With the aid of several ministers and laymen, he organized the Southville Action Organization, which initiated a series of mass meetings and freedom schools. After several months, S.A.O. drew up a list of demands for changes in the city's segregation practices and presented them to the city commission. The commission rejected the demands, and S.A.O. countered by holding Southville's first protest march. Law officers and S.A.O. leaders agreed in advance on procedures to be followed during the demonstration. Although the marchers adhered to these procedures; police used electric cattle prods and night sticks to harass the protesters.

Response to S.A.O. and the demonstrations by white public officials was predictable. Communist influence was suspected and "outside agitators" were seen as stirring up "a few dissidents" who in no way reflected the dominant mood in the Negro community. Calls were issued for the restoration of "harmony between the races." This could best be accomplished, it was held, by disbanding S.A.O. and removing its minister-leader from his pulpit and from the city. These expressions faithfully reflected the mood of most of Southville's white citizens. While the great majority was passive in its response, the Ku Klux Klan applauded the public pronouncements and publicly dedicated itself to firm opposition to the activities and demands of S.A.O. Civil rights activists interpreted this as confirmation of their belief that there was no important difference between the belief-systems and objectives of public officials and those of the Klan. Law officers were especially distrusted. Many were believed to be Klansmen and the rest were seen as Klan sympathizers.[3] Almost all were believed to be prepared to carry out any orders issued by the Klan. Negro activists were certain that the officers were eagerly awaiting an opportunity to conduct Klan-inspired violence against them.

During the next three months, S.A.O. activity increased. New and stronger demands were made, stores were boycotted, marches were held with increasing frequency, violence against the activists accelerated and tensions in the community increased. Finally, city officials announced a ban on further demonstrations and charged the police with enforcing it. To S.A.O. leaders, this was the same as announcing a ban on change in favor of tradition and charging the Ku Klux Klan with enforcing it. They announced that they would defy the ban, and a date was set for the proposed march.

More than a thousand persons appeared for the demonstration. As the leaders led the marchers out of the church they were confronted by police, sheriff's deputies, firemen and "special deputies," some of whom were suspected of being Klansmen. The leaders were promptly arrested. Immediately thereafter, law officers charged the demonstrators, forcing them back into the church with nightsticks, cattle prods, fists and water hoses. Tear gas was shot into the building, and the officers continued their attack as the demonstrators fled from the gas-filled church. As the protesters dispersed, they were chased into neighboring areas. Homes of those living nearby were invaded, and persons not involved in the demonstration came under indiscriminate attack. Numerous arrests were made, and several of the demonstrators were hospitalized as a result of beatings and gassing. Word of the incident spread rapidly. Stories of police brutality against men, women and children circulated throughout the Negro sections of the city. The police had, in the eyes of the Negroes, confirmed that if they were not Klansmen, they might as well be, and that they would use any measures of force and violence they wished against those who dared defy white Southern racial mores.

When Southville's evening newspaper carried a distorted account of the events together with a justification of the actions of the law officers, Negroes interpreted this as proof that the officers had been carrying out the orders of the "white power structure." This seemed to be the opening shot in an all-out war to kill the civil rights movement in the city. Faith in the effectiveness of the nonviolent posture of S.A.O. was seriously undermined, and most of its leading spokesmen were in jail. That evening, Negroes armed themselves, some waiting for an expected nightride of Klansmen through their neighborhoods, others hoping to ambush police cars, and still others planning to go to the business district of the city and burn it to the ground. In the early evening hours, an unstructured, unorganized violent retaliation seemed certain. While the total number of Negroes planning to take part in offensive violence was not large, it would have been sufficient to destroy much of the downtown area of Southville and to cause widespread injury and death to whites.

At this same time, one of the S.A.O. members began taking steps to thwart the impending riot. He did this not because he feared violence or was opposed to it in principle, nor because he believed massive retaliation was not merited, but because he felt it was futile. He opposed it because it was unstructured, disorganized, lacking in plan or lasting value and because it would result in death and injury to a great many innocent persons. It was his desire to translate the prevailing mood into something which could permanently restrict the activities of police and Klan, and which would provide a forceful mechanism for changing the community's power distribution. He called together several close friends, convinced them that a disorganized riot would serve no useful purpose, and together, they set out to find the rioters-in-waiting to convince them also. One by one they were found and the case was argued. The message was simple: "If we're going to do this thing, let's do it right"; and "right" meant organization and planning. One by one, the potential rioters were persuaded to surrender their arms on the promise that the weapons would be returned at a meeting which would be held that night. So great was the respect commanded by this small group, and especially by its leader, that the riot was averted.

The meeting held that night centered on proposed retaliation for the day's events. A major source of bitterness was the abject failure of law officers to perform their duties in even a minimally acceptable manner. Under prodding by the meeting's chairman, immediate retaliation became less important in the minds of those in attendance than a basic alteration in the power distribution in Southville. The chairman argued that if the police failed to perform their duties, either they would have to be forced to do so, or someone else would have to perform them. If the Klan was determined to run rampant, someone would have to control it. If men, women and children were to be beaten, someone would have to prevent it. The meeting ended with the agreement that the "someone" would have to be a new organization dedicated to bringing about a basic redistribution of power in the city. A meeting was called for the following night to establish such an organization.

The second meeting was attended by some 300 persons. They included gang leaders and members, white collar and blue collar workers, the highly educated and the uneducated. Chairing this meeting, as he had the first, was William Smith, who had led the effort to thwart the riot. Almost immediately, the question arose as to who should be the leader of the new organization. Smith's name was suggested and there was no dissent. At this point, Smith advised the meeting that he would accept only on condition that he be allowed to choose a small executive board which would devise a series of qualifications for membership and evaluate the candidacy of each applicant. His and the board's decisions would be final. Further, he stated that all decisions regarding policy would be set by the board and would be binding on all members. Finally, he said that all members would be required to pledge their lives to him and the organization. He asked for a formal vote on whether those in attendance still wished him to head the organization. He was unanimously elected. He then announced that the organization would be called the Defenders.

III. ORGANIZATIONAL STRUCTURE

Smith patterned the organization along the lines of a military combat unit. Four levels were established: the leader, his executive board, a cadre of lieutenants, and the rank and file membership. The leader and his executive board were designated as policy makers, strategists and final authority for tasks to be undertaken by the organization. The lieutenants were assigned some limited authority, primarily in conducting investigations, and the rank and file were to carry out assignments handed down from the executive board.

From the 300 persons attending the organizational meeting, 100 were selected for membership, and the organization has remained approximately at that number since then. Roughly one-half the membership may be described as "hard-core" and is distributed throughout all four levels. The remaining 50 members are utilized for special assignments, usually when large numbers of persons are needed for some task. At any time, the leader can mobilize 50 members and have them prepared for a task in less than two hours.

Membership in the Defenders is conferred only after a thorough investigation. Final authority for acceptance or rejection of a candidate rests with the executive board. Individual board members may veto any potential member and are not hesitant to do so. (In one instance, a board member vetoed his brother's candidacy.) The board imposes various criteria for membership, some of which are clearly objective and which serve as preliminary filtering devices, and others which demand a more subjective evaluation. No one is admitted to candidacy unless he has served at least six weeks under active war combat conditions. This experience is considered of crucial importance in familiarizing the individual with extreme crisis situations and the imminent possibility of death, conditions which he must be prepared to face in the performance of his organizational duties. This is an effective device for eliminating those persons who see crisis and possible death as "romantic episodes" through lack of experience with such events. It seeks to insure that those admitted to membership realize the seriousness of the commitment they are making. A second requirement is that the potential candidate be married and, preferably, have a family. Meeting this requirement indicates to the organization a willingness to assume responsibility. It indicates, further, the belief that a married man is a more stable member of the community than a single person, and that he will have a stronger dedication to correcting community injustices because of their effects upon his family. The candidate must be judged to be "head of his household." Any person likely to place his wife's opposing wishes above organizational demands is a threat to the operations of the organization. Any wife who would constantly raise counter demands is a threat to the commitment all members must give to the Defenders. Such threats are not tolerated, and persons likely to come under them are disqualified.

The organization believes its work may be carried out most effectively without general publicity or public attention. Therefore, the candidate is expected to be discreet and "close-mouthed." He must be judged capable of keeping classified information secret and must be able to restrict knowledge of his activities to those persons deemed appropriate by his organization. This may include restricting knowledge of his membership to the organization executive board and hard-core members alone. Any person who is known to drink immoderately is automatically excluded. The heavy drinker is seen as "a talker" and therefore not trustworthy. In addition, his drinking may cause him to be unavailable at some time when the organization needs him. In this regard, Smith has set the standard. He drinks very rarely, and never has more than one drink at any social gathering.

The candidate's personal conduct must be above reproach. A rigid code of personal morality is applied as a standard, and any deviation from it effectively eliminates him from consideration. Of necessity, the candidate's background is submitted to searching scrutiny. If he is found acceptable to this point, he is submitted to final tests. Various persons, both men and women, are assigned to interact with him socially and to observe his conduct, under as many conditions as possible. For example, he may be told "confidential" information and asked not to reveal it, and then deliberately encouraged to do so by persons working secretly for the organization. He is, in effect, given an extensive final opportunity to disqualify himself by some act deemed unacceptable to the organization. If he passes this test he is then accepted into membership, with the understanding that any time he violates the code of the Defenders, he is subject to its punishment up to and including expulsion. This has occurred only once in the organization's history. He is then administered an oath in which he swears to be "his brother's keeper," even at the cost of his own life.

Membership in the organization is drawn from a wide range of occupations, educational backgrounds, ages and areas of residence. By maintaining a heterogeneous membership, as representative as possible of the Negro population, the information network nurtured and maintained by the organization is made as inclusive as possible. As a result, status within the organization is not determined by amount of formal education, occupational prestige or income level. Rather, it is allotted on the basis of performance of assigned duties and degree of responsibility conferred within the organization. Each member, because of his particular socioeconomic position in the community, is seen as being able to make a unique contribution to the organization. He is valued because he holds a particular social position regardless of whether the general community would so value that position. For example, neighborhood and route salesmen are occupationally valuable, since their work allows them a flexibility of movement and puts them in wide contact with the community, placing them in a position to gain valuable information. Historically, the Klan has used such occupations to gather information in Negro neighborhoods. Members of the Defenders, acting unofficially, were able to convince several companies that Negroes were more likely to buy from Negro salesmen than from white, and then supplied several of their own members to fill these positions. This had the effect of reducing the Klan information network at the same time it increased their own.

The organization functions in a semi-secret manner. It operates on the principle that those who need to know of its existence do know or will be informed of it. The efficiency of the Defenders' information network guarantees that anyone who may not know will be informed should the occasion arise. However, it sees no value in general publicity, and consciously avoids it. One reason for this is because of the kinds of investigations it conducts and data which it gathers. Another reason is the belief that the whites will be more amenable to pressure and compromise if they are assured that the general public is not aware they are yielding to such pressure.

IV. ORGANIZATIONAL ACTIVITIES

The tasks which the organization has undertaken include protection, investigation, intelligence, and a form of "crime" prevention.

The immediate impetus for the creation of the Defenders was provided by the perceived failure of law officers to perform their role adequately for Negro citizens. While this failure was most obvious in conjunction with civil rights activities, it was not limited to them. A long-standing complaint against the police was that *no* Negro could be certain he would receive the same treatment, concern or respect as would a white person. The organization conceives of its duty, therefore, as more encompassing than concern with massive civil rights demonstrations alone. Rather, it holds the prerogative to choose to assume responsibility in any situation in which a person has suffered some injustice for which law officers would normally be expected to take some action but where it is not expected that they will perform their role adequately. The organization may become involved either at the request of an individual or without such request if the situation seems to have important implications for other persons in the community. (In one instance, dynamite was set off near a group of homes. Without waiting for a specific request for aid, the organization concerned itself with the situation.) Should an individual request the aid of the Defenders, it may or may not be given. Representatives of the organization must be satisfied that the party requesting aid has suffered some injustice and that he was not the instigator. It must also be satisfied that the complainant is willing to give his full cooperation to the organization, including providing all information which he possesses. Should the organization conclude that the complainant is withholding information, it may refuse to enter the case. Should it enter and then conclude that he is the offending party, it may withdraw. At this point, the Defenders must act in a supra-police function. Differing from the police, the organization has no court system to determine ultimate guilt or innocence, hence it must accept some responsibility in this area. Since it must do so, it is important that the Defenders obtain all available information. If it is convinced that some of this information is being withheld by the complainant, the most "responsible" decision it can make is that some presumption of guilt thereby exists and on this basis it withdraws. Since most of its activities center about allegation of Negroes against whites, it seeks to be absolutely certain of its "legal" (i.e. moral) position before it moves against offending whites.

At the organization's inception, it was faced with two immediate problems. To that time, segregation and its attendant patterns of white supremacy had been enforced formally by law enforcement agencies and informally by the Ku Klux Klan. When law was not sufficient to do so, extra-legal methods were employed to establish and maintain an atmosphere of fear and intimidation. No effective counterforce or neutralizing agent existed; the test of the Defenders' viability was whether it could establish itself as such a force. Smith saw the organization's first task as eliminating the Klan as a force in Negro life and the second as restricting the police to their normal duties. If the police could not be forced to fulfill their legal role, they *could* be blocked from performing an extra-legal one. Klan and police, then, had to be confronted with sufficient power to limit effectively their sphere of influence. The mere announcement to these agencies of the formation of a "protective organization" was not sufficient, nor was it expected to be. The dominant stereotype of Negroes held by these groups as docile, fearful, cowardly and deathly afraid of police and Klan necessitated direct confrontation to disprove the stereotype.

Two incidents were of major importance in limiting Klan activities. From the inception of S.A.O., it had been the practice of the Klan leader to be near the scene of any movement activity. At any time a meeting was held he would "patrol" the area in his car. This gesture expressed his contempt for S.A.O. and his stated conviction that the Klan, not S.A.O., would be the dominant force in Negro life. One evening as he began his vigil, armed Defenders appeared in front of the meeting place. As the Klansman began to drive by, he saw that they were prepared to fire at him and he quickly maneuvered his car so that a truck was between him and the church and immediately left the area. Not only did he "run," but he never again appeared at the site of S.A.O. activity.

By this single act, the organization had demonstrated publicly to its own members, civil rights activists, Negro townspeople and the Klan leader and fellow Klansmen that the old order had changed, at least partially. If the organization was prepared to confront the Klan leader, it was obvious that it was equally prepared to confront lesser Klansmen. From the date of this incident, the number of Klan cars seen in Negro neighborhoods decreased considerably, and those which did appear passed through quickly. The Klan relinquished its control over these areas, but sought to limit the Defenders to these same neighborhoods. On another evening, in a peripheral area of the city, a car loaded with Klansmen opened fire on a car holding Defenders. One of the members noted later that "they shot too soon," and when the Defenders' car pulled closer, its passengers returned the fire and the Klansmen fled. These two incidents demonstrated to the Klan the determination of the Defenders to eliminate Klan influence among Negroes and to insert itself into the power structure of the community. Although other incidents did occur, for all intents and purposes, large scale organized semi-public Klan activity against Negroes ended with these incidents. Negro neighborhoods were now effectively closed to Klansmen. Neither did they attempt to intimidate the Defenders again.

While the police officially recognized the organization's formation, they opposed its existence and sought to discredit and destroy it. Official recognition came in the form of a meeting between Smith and a high ranking police officer. The official told him the organization could gain no power, would accomplish nothing, and would not be tolerated by the police. His statements, on the surface, constituted a dismissal of the organization as inconsequential, but carried the deeper message that the police would not permit their own power to be challenged or restricted. The police set out to do what the Klan had failed to do—to frighten the Defenders into submission. Individual members were subjected to various forms of harassment. When this failed, the police increased their pressure. A critical point was reached early one morning when a number of police cars appeared at Smith's home. Crouched behind their cars with weapons drawn and spotlights directed at the front door, the police ordered "the occupant" of the house to come out. When he did, they demanded his name and he pointed to a sign on the lawn which carried his name and house number. Again they demanded his name and he told them to look at the sign. The question was repeated several times, always with the same answer. The incident ended with the police finally asking him if he were a "John Greene" for whom they were allegedly looking. He replied that his name was on the sign and that, further, they knew full well who he was. At this, the police claimed a case of mistaken identity and left. Smith is convinced that the police had so acted in the hope of frightening him into running or making some other move which would have given them a "justification" for killing him. When he did not, they lost their nerve and, in some confusion, withdrew. Failing to frighten and thereby to discredit the leader, they arrested a number of his members. Smith countered by informing the Chief that unless his men were released, he would "turn loose" the remaining members of the organization. The arrested men were immediately released. Smith then met with the Chief and told him that the organization would remain in existence, that its members could not be frightened, and that if any harm came to them or their families, "blood would flow." He stated his intention to see that extra-legal activities carried out by police against Negroes were stopped by any means necessary. Subsequent to this meeting, not only did harassment of the Defenders cease, but reports of police brutality against Negroes in general declined rapidly.

The first task of the organization had been accomplished. The Klan had been defeated and its effectiveness as a social control mechanism among Negroes severely diminished. No longer could it operate openly as a public, unofficial arm of the police. Secondly, the police had been confronted and their extra-legal power to a great extent stripped from them. The organization had inserted itself into the power structure of the city and had to be considered by any group planning activity against Negroes. In effect, a "war of fear" had been waged to determine the order of power not only in the Negro sections of the city but over the lives of Negroes in general. The Defenders had clearly won.[4]

With their failure to destroy the Defenders, the police resorted to a different strategy. Rather than actively opposing those connected with civil rights activities, they passively refused to perform any meaningful functions whatsoever regarding them. Apparently, it was assumed that by so doing, mobs of whites would control the activities of the activists. This was a miscalculation which inserted the Defenders directly into the role of policemen and thereby increased the organization's role and broadened its sphere of influence and power. Adoption of this passive role coincided with the "testing" of a restaurant to determine if it would comply with the newly passed Civil Rights Act of 1964. The owner did comply by serving the testers. However, in the process, a group of whites began to gather in front of the business. Although some police were present, they made no attempt to disperse those gathering. In a short period of time, approximately 600 whites appeared, and the crowd began defacing the business. Still the police took no action, nor did they threaten any arrests. As the crowd developed into a mob challenging the testers to come out, the police informed the testers that they could not control the mob nor guarantee the safety of those inside the building, thus washing their hands of the whole affair. Smith was notified of the situation and immediately dispatched several cars to the scene. Defenders spirited the testers to the cars and they drove off. The cars went immediately to a pre-arranged location which had been "staked out" by other members of the organization. Had the mob followed, which it did not, it would have been caught in a trap. The Defenders had not only provided the police function of protection but had also constructed its own form of "crowd control."

Protection quickly became a major function of the organization. A great many civil rights activists had received anonymous threats of violence and death. Law enforcement agencies were unwilling to provide protection for the persons involved, their families or their homes, therefore the Defenders assumed this responsibility.[5]

The organization's protective role extends to whites as well as Negroes. A few white persons had acted in concert with S.A.O. and hence were no more assured of police protection than were Negro activists. Streets on which they lived were patrolled by car, they were guarded when they were in places of potential danger, and, in general, were given the same services provided Negro activists. Smith pointed out on several occasions that when a member swore to "be his brother's keeper" this meant "his brother regardless of race." [6]

Organizational protection also extends to visitors to the city who might be in danger because of their support of the civil rights movement. On these occasions, the Defenders have supplanted the police in providing escort and protective services. On one such occasion, aides to the white person involved were put in contact with the leader. Smith shared their doubts as to the probable dedication of the police to protecting the person in question. When asked whether he would provide the protection he agreed, but only under certain conditions. Smith and the aides were to agree upon a detailed timetable of the activities of the visitor while he was in Southville. Once he arrived, he and his associates were to be subject to any orders Smith gave them. When this was agreed to, Smith took the schedule of events to an organizational staff meeting. There decisions were made as to the number of Defenders needed, which members would be used, and what the specific duties of each would be. Late one evening, a "dry run" was held to determine the adequacy of the plan. Alternate plans were worked out in the event of a crisis, and plans were made for the disposition of any persons attempting to disrupt the activities. Some three hours before the visitor arrived in the city, each member was in his assigned position and various buildings had been inspected to assure that they were secure. Occasionally, police appeared near scenes of the activities, but at no time did they attempt to assert a special prerogative to be present. The members, in turn, regarded them with the same degree of watchfulness they reserved for any suspicious white persons. At no time were weapons displayed, but in the words of one member, "A man *might* get one shot at . . . but he'd never get the second one off." Only when the visitor had been escorted out of Southville did the organization cease its alert.

At times, the organization goes beyond normal protective duties. In one case, a family in a community some twenty miles from Southville was being subjected to a serious form of harassment. Both husband and wife had been physically assaulted by whites, and the husband had been hospitalized as a result of the attack. His wife contacted members of S.A.O. who in turn contacted Smith. He met with her and it was agreed that neither she nor her children were safe in the community, therefore it was decided to bring them to Southville. The Defenders assumed responsibility for moving her and her family to the city, securing a house and assuring financial support of the family until a job was found for her eldest son. When doubts arose as to whether her husband was receiving proper medical treatment, a Southville doctor was contacted who agreed to treat the man if he were transferred to the city's hospital. Smith then contacted a local ambulance service and received assurance that it would transfer the man at any time it was deemed necessary.[7]

A second broad task of the organization, closely related to protection, is that of investigation. The purpose is to insure as complete knowledge as possible of plans and activities of anyone or any group having any relation to Negroes, civil rights advocates or their opponents. This includes any information which could conceivably relate to potential organizational duties and tasks. The insistence of the leader that the organization have as complete and accurate data as possible regarding any incident *before* the Defenders enter a case makes investigation of great importance and places great responsibility upon the men selected to do the investigating. The men charged with this task constitute the organization's intelligence unit.

As soon as Smith is informed of an incident with which the Defenders might become involved, he dispatches investigators to interview witnesses and to gather any other pertinent information. Seldom do investigators make public their duties. Rather, interviewing and data gathering are carried on without revealing that an investigation is under way or that the organization is in any way involved in the situation. Not infrequently, Defenders are present with the police and both agencies collect information at the same time.[8]

In addition to the mechanism for specific investigations, the organization maintains a highly efficient and effective permanent data gathering system. This system has provided sufficient information to permit quick identification of automobile ownership from license numbers and, in many cases, from description of the car when the license is not available. Dossiers are maintained on all persons with whom the organization has had dealings or with whom it is felt it might come in contact at some later date. These dossiers include not only addresses, descriptions and information on current activities, but also rather extensive background data including past behavior and activities. The organization has demonstrated the ability to obtain data which is kept in locked files in public and private offices and which is, supposedly, unavailable to the public.

Historical records are also maintained and investigations of incidents which occurred long before the organization's creation have been carried out. In one case, a record has been compiled of a lynching which occurred in Southville 30 years ago. Included in the record are the names of persons, including many still alive, who took part in the planning and actual lynching of the victims and who went unpunished at the time. Included is information on the present whereabouts of several key figures who left Southville shortly after the murders. Only when the last of the major figures in the case has died will it be marked "closed." Records are also maintained on important public figures who have had some connection with Southville. These include information not only on current activities but on activities in which they participated as much as 30 and 40 years ago. These current and historical records are maintained because of the possibility that they may, at some time, be of value in providing information regarding some incident or event of interest to the Defenders. Hence, they might provide important data regarding the decision to enter a case and the type of action to be taken.

The "crime prevention" phase of the Defenders' duties also illustrates the high degree of organization of the group. Smith was aware from the outset that at times the organization would have "no choice" but to act, to commit its resources and the lives of its members to some task. However, he wanted to insure that this would occur only when absolutely necessary and when he could be satisfied that no other method for handling the situation was available. Investigation makes it possible for him to determine if there is just cause for action. Intelligence makes it possible for him to become aware of developing, potentially dangerous situations. With this knowledge, he may act to prevent an incident from occurring, rather than being limited to acting only after some incident has occurred which demands a form of retribution. A critical component of this prevention function is the Defenders' surveillance team which is maintained in all Negro sections of the city. This team is comprised of members, each of whom has been assigned responsibility for a particular Negro neighborhood. These persons are to keep fully informed about the activities of residents of the neighborhoods, especially those activities which might result in some kind of racial incident. Primarily, members of the team are to identify potential "trouble-makers" and observe their activities. Should these persons become a "threat to the peace," a report is made to Smith, and representatives of the organization talk to the person involved, explaining to him that his activities may cause a serious situation if continued. So great is the respect for the Defenders that this action has been sufficient to control such persons. This form of prevention seeks to assure, insofar as possible, that Negroes will not be the cause of racial incidents and that the organization will not have to become involved in situations which could have been avoided or handled in a peaceful way.[9]

V. CONCLUSION

Although the Defenders does not seek publicity, it is well known among Negroes in Southville. It enjoys great respect and is a source of considerable pride, primarily because it is proof that white Southern mores can be successfully challenged and that a change in the distribution of power can be effected. Violence, so often employed by whites, is revealed as a two-edged sword. With considerable pleasure, Negroes note that "white men are not as tough as they thought they were," and that Negroes, in the person of the Defenders, have proved themselves more than a match for violent white power. They are aware that it is now much less likely that they will be the victims of arbitrarily administered white violence. They know also that they have a champion which will extract a heavy price from the perpetrators of any such violence. For Negroes in Southville, this represents a most important and valued kind of social change.

The nonviolent S.A.O. also welcomes the Defenders, whose existence has strengthened their bargaining position. Prior to the creation of the Defenders, white officials were confronted solely by the alternatives of accepting or rejecting S.A.O. demands. Subsequent to its creation, additional variables had to be considered. The alternative to S.A.O. demands no longer is the maintenance of the status quo but the possibility that the city may be transformed into a battlefield which will destroy Southville. Formerly, acquiescence to S.A.O. demands had been the less attractive alternative. The Defenders has served to make the nonviolent S.A.O. considerably more attractive to white officials than it once was.

Ridicule has replaced fear as the dominant reaction of Negroes to the Ku Klux Klan. While the Klan continues to issue pronouncements reaffirming its dedication to Southern white mores and predicting victory in the struggle to maintain them, Negroes view these statements with contempt. Occasional pronouncements by the Klan leader that the Klan is nonviolent are viewed with amusement. Considering the Defenders' existence and the Klan's unwillingness to confront that organization, there is no other choice. While the Klan still inspires hatred, its power to control the action of Negroes is rapidly vanishing. In Southville, the Klan has become little more than a social club, without the power to enforce its desires. It is now much more concerned with national politics than with local racial conditions. Its failure to control these conditions has forced it to look elsewhere if it is to *seem* an active organization.

The role played by law enforcement agencies has undergone considerable change. These agencies are much less a "white man's army" and much more in conformity with the normal police role. While individual officers may continue as Klansmen, the quasi-public relationship between the Klan and law agencies has ceased. On occasion, officers do overstep the boundaries of their role, but when this occurs, they are much more likely to be censured by their superiors. In one instance, an officer made a racial slur against Smith. Immediately, Smith registered a complaint with the officer's superiors. The issue was resolved when both the officer and the police chief apologized for the remark. In the main, white officers maintain a distant and "correct" attitude toward the Defenders. However, two newly employed Negro officers have reacted somewhat differently. They have talked with Smith and have asked for any assistance the Defenders would be willing to give in maintaining peace and order in Negro sections of the city.

The vast majority of white persons remain unaware of the Defenders' existence. They speak of the recent past as a time of "racial unrest" and are pleased that this is no longer the case. They tend to attribute this change to the "inherent good will between the races" which exists in the city. They accept the desegregation which has occurred as proof of the good will of whites, and attribute the impetus for this change to the basic decency of white persons rather than to efforts by Negroes. S.A.O. is viewed not only as unnecessary but as having introduced conflict where none should have been. Change has been accomplished more despite that organization than because of it. Whites are proud of their law enforcement agencies, reject any allegations of brutality against Negroes and credit much of the return of peace to the "professionalism" of law enforcement agencies. These agencies are praised for their impartiality, good sense and good will toward all citizens. Neither the newspaper nor white officials have sought to advance any other explanation for the changes which have occurred in Southville.

The Defenders was organized to alter the distribution of certain types of power in the community. It removed the threat of fear, intimidation and violence from the lives of Negroes. As a result, it became a kind of referee enforcing a set of rules by which S.A.O. and white officialdom would confront each other on the subject of social change. So long as organized violence was the sole prerogative of the white population, S.A.O. was overmatched in the struggle. The presence of the Defenders removed the threat of violence and permitted S.A.O.'s nonviolent methodology to confront a Defenders-insured nonviolent white opposition. This permitted the issues of racial change to be debated and settled within the framework of peaceful coexistence. The Defenders' continued existence acts to insure that violence will remain neutralized in the struggle.

Members of the Defenders believe that Southville is a microcosm of the total society. Throughout the nation, they see the commitment to nonviolence among Negroes diminishing rapidly. No longer is it possible to rely upon a nonviolent response to white violence and police brutality. They see the issue not as whether there will be violence but the form that violence will take. Unless organizations such as their own which lend support to the more broadly based nonviolent movement become the rule, there will be an ever increasing random violence. This random, goalless and widespread violence will be the result of the abandoning of hope that a redistribution of power is possible in the American society.

It is the Defenders' belief that their organization has prevented this kind of desperate violence because it has proved to Negroes in Southville that it is possible to challenge successfully the monopoly of power held by whites. The organization is firm in its belief that it has accomplished this because it speaks the only kind of language many persons in power understand.

NOTES

ACKNOWLEDGEMENT: I wish to acknowledge the many contributions of "William Smith" to my understanding of the Defenders. Not only did he spend long hours educating me in the general area of racial problems in the South, but he gave extended assistance in the preparation of this paper. I am deeply indebted to him, for without his aid, this paper could not have been written.

1. There is considerable evidence to justify this belief, evidence with which white Americans in general have only recently become acquainted. As the nation watched the televised brutality of Southern law officers, what Negroes had long known became general knowledge. This was one of the major goals of civil rights demonstrators. They sought to dramatize the fact that they were subject to the most brutal forms of violence employed to enforce white Southern mores, many of which ran counter to law. However, television cameras and reporters could present the situation in only a few communities, and eventually the public seemed to grow accustomed to such displays and demanded more to gain its attention. Many communities quietly maintained their commitment to tradition regardless of law. In much of the South today this continues the rule rather than the exception. (In one such community in 1966, a city judge said from the bench during a civil rights trial that "custom takes precedence over law").

2. Data for this paper were gathered over a four year period. Included is material obtained both prior to the inception of the Southville Action Organization and the Defenders and following their creation. (Data gathered prior to their inception were intended for a paper, as yet unwritten, on various phases of Southville's racial situation.)

   The data were gathered in several ways. Material collected on various facets of the Southville Action Organization were gained as a result of my participation in that organization from its inception. Additional data were accumulated throught. many long conversations held with both S.A.O. leaders and members. Data on the attitudes and opinions of Negroes not affiliated with S.A.O. were acquirea primarily in two ways. Certain of the organization's programs were directed toward Negroes who were not involved in the movement. My participation in these activities allowed me extensive contact with some of these persons. In addition, a formal research project was carried out in which a cross section of the city's Negro population was sampled to determine attitudes on such issues as the racial situation in the community, methods of initiating social change, violence and opinions of S.A.O. and its activities. (I hope to present the complete results of this research in a future paper.) Additional information on the perspectives of movement and non-movement Negroes resulted from my participation in meetings held in Southville and throughout the state.

My assessment of white attitudes in the city was derived from several sources. My own association with a segment of the white population allowed me to ascertain their reactions to S.A.O., the changing racial scene and race relations in general. Access to various segments of white opinion and action was closed to me, however. This included first-hand knowledge of such agencies as the city commission and the Ku Klux Klan. In these instances, I have relied upon information provided me by persons who did have access and who I believed could provide accurate data. I also made use of newspaper reports and editorials and radio coverage of various facets of the racial situation in the city as well as certain historical documents. Finally, my participation in S.A.O. activities permitted me to assess the direct reaction of some whites to these activities as they were being carried out.

Material on the Defenders was obtained in several ways. Participation in S.A.O. resulted in my friendship with William Smith before he assumed leadership of the Defenders. When he founded that organization, this relationship allowed me access to it which might have been impossible otherwise. This included not only contact with Smith but with other members or the organization as well. Smith was willing to discuss the Defenders in detail with me and to permit the presentation of this material in written form. He did so because he believed it important that others understand the necessity of organizations such as the Defenders, given the racial conditions of the South. He also felt that there was a widespread misunderstanding of the purposes of such organizations, and he hoped to see this corrected. Because of this, not only did I have the opportunity to observe the Defenders in the performance of their more obvious duties, but was permitted to be present during some of their less public activities as well.

Various persons who provided information for this paper did so with the understanding that, insofar as possible anonymity would be preserved. Therefore, the names of persons and places appearing herein are fictitious.

3. This was hardly an unfounded belief. The police chief had told his officers that he wanted no Klansman on his force, but he possessed neither complete knowledge of Klan membership nor sufficient power to compel resignation. Many Negroes believed that he also lacked the desire and that his statement was merely a subterfuge to "cool them out."

4. The vast majority of the white population was not aware of the Defenders' existence. The news media published no stories and no public officials made mention of it during the conflict. After the Defenders' victories over Klan and police, it is doubtful that those whites who knew of the battles wished to publicize their results. One candidate for public office did try to make the organization an issue. The reaction of the white community in general was disbelief that such an organization existed. One might hypothesize that the thought of such a militant organization of indigenous Negroes was so at variance with their stereotype of Negroes as docile, fearful and "content with their lot" as to prohibit its acceptance even as a possibility.

5. Had the police assumed this role, it is still likely that the organization would have provided protection, since one of the agency's activists believed that what they needed protection *from* was the police. Teams of guards assigned to homes under the threat of violence, and a number of "squad cars" toured Negro sections of the city each night watching for suspicious persons. Any who were found were ordered out of the area. The presence of this force acted as a deterrent to violence although on one occasion it became necessary to use force to stop a group intent upon assassinating the leader of S.A.O.

6. In order to carry out this protective function efficiently, the organization utilizes not only weapons of various kinds but walkie-talkies, two-way radio equipped cars, and a number of other devices. It is safe to say that most equipment which is employed by the standard police department is also present in the Defenders' arsenal.

7. This illustrates a major canon of the organization: "Once we agree to take some-

thing on, we go all the way with it." Members of the organization scorn no one so much as the person who accepts responsibility and then fails to carry it through to completion. Smith is firm in his insistence that the Defenders not commit itself to any project unless it is prepared to do anything and everything to bring it to successful conclusion. Once committed, the organization is completely committed up to and including the lives of its members.

8. This is possible since the police know only part of the Defenders' membership list and are generally not aware of the investigators who may be present in such guises as "curious neighbors" or "helpful friends."

9. It is true that the Defenders could refuse to enter a situation which had been provoked by a Negro. However, if the situation had resulted in an overly severe response by the police, for example, their serious mistreatment of the offender, the organization might be forced to act to remind the police that their extra-legal activity was restricted.

3. Leadership

Whites have always expressed considerable interest in black leadership. We constantly see references in the mass media to Rev. X or Dr. Y, the national Negro leader, or to Mr. Z, the local Negro leader. Distinctions are drawn between moderate and militant leaders, between integrationist and separatist leaders, and between responsible and extremist leaders. Much of this discussion is based upon an inadequate conceptualization of the term leader and upon an incomplete analysis of the role of a leader.

I will not attempt a precise definition of "leader" at this point. However, it would seem that the minimal requirement for any person to be recognized as a leader is that he have a following. A person must be able to influence and give direction to the behavior of others before he can be said to lead in any meaningful sense. There are many types of leaders that meet this minimal requirement. They range all the way from persons holding policy-making positions of authority in formal organizations to persons who lead by example in collective behavior situations.[1]

It is interesting to note that while the media refer to Negro leaders they never refer to white leaders. Whites are referred to as prominant businessmen, community officials, or local civic leaders, but never as white leaders. This is a tacit reflection of the media's awareness of the fact that American whites do not constitute a corporate body with unity of purpose and a central recognized leadership. It appears that the implicit assumption is often made that blacks have a more highly organized community and a single unified leadership structure. This assumption is patently false.

There is no single person or group of persons who may validly be said to represent black Americans. There are persons who may be called black leaders in the sense that they are black and hold positions of authority in formal organizations such as the NAACP, CORE, or similar organizations, or in the sense that they can influence segments of local, state, or national black communities. This is what is sometimes meant by references to Negro leaders. It is also the case that the term "Negro Leader" is often used to refer to celebrities, politicians, or other persons whom whites believe to have influence among blacks but who may not in fact have any such influence or whose influence may be limited to segments of regional and national communities. The stoning of Martin Luther King's brother in Birmingham, the shooting of Dick Gregory, the shouting down of Martin Luther King in Watts, and the total futility of the attempt to cool down Twelfth Street in Detroit by black congressman John Conyers, Jr. and black Assistant to the Commissioner of Police Hubert G. Locke are only a few of the many examples which illustrate this point. It is also sometimes the case that persons give the appearance of having influence among blacks because they are "leading" in the direction in which the community is moving. If these "leaders" attempt to shift directions, or if they fail to shift directions when the community is ready to do so, they often lose their following. An example would be the inability of Martin Luther King to prevent the 1967 march into Cicero in conformity with his agreement with Chicago's Mayor Daley.

The term black leader will be used in the selections in this section to refer to blacks who have influence, or appear to have influence, with some segment of a local black community at a given point in time. No assumption is made that the influence is either real, national, with the total black community, or transferable from one specific situation to another.

In the first selection Lewis M. Killian and Charles U. Smith compare those persons reputed to be black leaders in Tallahassee prior to a major conflict (the bus boycott) and those reputed to be leaders after the conflict. They find an almost total turnover of top leadership. It would appear that persons suited to the leadership role in accommodative situations are not likely to be suited to the leadership role in conflict situations. Thus, as the need for black accommodation diminishes and the need for a conflict or power orientation increases, there may be a major reshuffling of reputed black leaders.

Cothran and Phillips (in an article not included in this volume) found this same type of leadership shift.[2] They also found that there is a demonstrated need for financial independence if blacks are to play a leadership role in a crisis situation. If an individual is dependent upon whites for his livelihood, he will generally have to restrict the degree of his militance. Financial independence need not mean private wealth, but simply independence from whites. Cothran and Phillips also found that crises effect the nature of internal disagreements. There may be a considerable amount of privately held reservations about the conduct of various spokesmen during a crisis, but the expression of these reservations will be inhibited and there will be no public attacks upon reputed leaders. Any expressions of criticism will be strictly limited to small groups of intimate associates. One cannot afford to weaken a cause by showing the enemy anything other than a united front.

In another article not included in this volume, Walker found that it is sometimes the case that the older, more conservative black leadership regains dominance after the crisis situation has run its course.[3] This finding sets the stage for the McWorter and Crain analysis of civil rights leadership as a competitive process. They find that competition for leadership functions to make leaders more militant, to place leaders under greater pressure to achieve results, and to make negotiations with whites more complex. Thus tightly planned campaigns for specific goals may best be carried out in the absence of leadership competition. Organized leadership competition appears to maximize the amount and intensity of civil rights activity while individual leadership competition may provide the pool of potential leaders that makes sustained activity over a number of years more likely.

NOTES

1. For a discussion of types of leadership, see Neil J. Smelser, *Theory of Collective Behavior* (New York: Free Press, 1963), pp. 254–55.
2. Tilman C. Cothran and William Phillips, Jr., "Negro Leadership in a Crisis Situation," *Phylon* 22 (Summer 1961) 107–18.
3. Jack Walker, "The Functions of Disunity: Negro Leadership in a Southern City," *Journal of Negro Education* 32 (Summer 1963) 227–36.

Negro Protest Leaders in a Southern Community

Lewis M. Killian / Charles U. Smith

One of the significant features of race relations in the past five years has been the emergence of new patterns of Negro leadership in southern communities. Prior to the various court decisions which withdrew legal support from the traditional framework of segregation, Negro leadership gave the appearance of conforming to the pattern of "accommodating" or "compromise" leadership. Analyses of leadership in southern Negro communities, such as the treatment found in Myrdal's *American Dilemma,*[1] suggest that the compromise leaders held their positions primarily because they were acceptable to white leaders. They were also accepted by Negroes because accommodation was regarded as the most practical and effective mode of adjustment in the existing power situation.

The desegregation decisions of the U.S. Supreme Court, even without extensive implementation, redefined this power situation. In the years following 1954 militant leaders, reflecting the protest motive instead of the theme of patience and accommodation, have moved into the focus of attention of both whites and Negroes. Whereas the accommodating leaders had not been widely known to the white public, largely because they operated in a noncontroversial and often clandestine manner, the new leaders quickly rocketed to fame or notoriety, depending upon the observer's point of view. Martin Luther King, defying the white power structure of his community and being featured on the cover of *Time* magazine, symbolizes this new leadership. Many white leaders have reacted by bewailing the "breakdown of communication" between the races, denouncing the militant Negro leaders as reckless, radical parvenues, and attempting to isolate them by parleys with hand-picked, "responsible" leaders. Both practical and theoretical considerations dictate the need for a new appraisal of Negro leadership in the South.

The north Florida community of Tallahassee is one of the southern communities in which a change in the pattern of Negro leadership seemed to accompany a crisis in race relations. The critical situation arose from a challenge to segregation on city buses, culminating in a boycott. Here, too, news media featured daily the names of militant Negroes who previously had been anonymous ciphers in the Negro community as far as most whites were concerned. There were allegations to the effect that "newcomers" had come into the community and stirred up the erstwhile contented population, and that the Negro leadership had "split" with the result that white leaders did not know with whom to deal. Hence this community was well suited for a case study of Negro leadership in crisis.

The situation proved an opportunity to get the answers, for this

From *Social Forces* 38 (March 1960): 253–57; reprinted by permission of the authors and publisher.

community, to certain questions. Was the leadership in this Protest Movement actually new to the Negro community, or were the new leaders merely people who had suddenly become known to the white community because of a change of strategy? If they were new to the higher levels of the power structure in the Negro community, had they actually displaced the old group of leaders or was the community split between two competing sets of leaders? A corollary is the question whether these "new leaders" drew their strength from popular support or simply from a tightly organized, activist minority.

METHOD OF STUDY

The study, executed shortly after the end of the bus boycott, consisted of two related parts. The first was an assessment of the structure of Negro leadership through interviews with a panel of 21 Negroes tentatively designated as "leaders" by social scientists familiar with the community. This list subsequently proved to include what came to be defined as "old" and "new" leaders in almost equal proportions.

A panel of 21 white leaders was also selected. This panel included all of the white leaders who had dealt with the Negro community in connection with the bus protest, in either an official or unofficial capacity. It also included white functionaries who were known to have worked directly with the Negro community in connection with other matters, such as fund drives, civic projects, and community problems, both before and after the boycott. They are the white leaders who most often speak to the Negro community in behalf of the white community. Some of them are high in the power structure. That this group represents fairly the position of the white leadership in Tallahassee is indicated by the absence of opposition to their representations to the Negro community.

The names of the 21 Negroes tentatively listed as "leaders" were placed on a card which was handed to the subject during the interview. Then he was asked a series of questions about Negro leadership *before* and *after* the bus boycott, and told to respond by giving names from the list. The questions which are of interest here were:

1. As best you can recall, which would you have identified as "leaders" among Tallahassee Negroes 2 years ago?
2. At that time, which do you feel were able to influence large numbers of Negroes on important public issues?
3. Which ones were able to express most accurately the feelings of most Negroes in Tallahassee on important public issues?
4. Which ones were able to deal most effectively with white leaders as representatives of the Negro group?
5. Now, at the present time, which do you feel are most able to influence large numbers of Negroes on important public issues?
6. Which are able to express most accurately the feelings of most Negroes, etc.?
7. Which are able to deal most effectively with white leaders, etc.?

Subjects were allowed to give as few or as many responses to each question as they wished, and Negro subjects were encouraged to include their own names if they felt they should.

After the data had been collected, the answers of white and Negro informants were tabulated separately. Each of the 21 potential Negro leaders was given a score and a rank on each question, according to the number of times his name was mentioned in response to the question. Hence each Negro had, for each question, a rank assigned him by the Negro informants and a rank assigned by the white leaders.

The second portion of the study was an attitude survey of a sample of the adult Negro population of Tallahassee. Every fifth address was taken from a list of all the households in blocks occupied only by Negroes. Any adult available at the address was interviewed. A total of 196 usable interviews were obtained. A Likert-type scale of questions concerning attitudes toward segregation in general, the bus boycott, and the leadership of the Bus Protest Movement was used. Key questions for purposes of this study were:

1. The Negro should not boycott to achieve his goals. (Agreement with this statement would represent a repudiation of the militant leaders.)
2. The old, established leaders in Tallahassee were more effective than the ones leading the bus protest.
3. The leadership in the Tallahassee Bus Protest is very good.

Subjects were grouped into three categories on the basis of whether their answers to these three questions reflected approval or disapproval of the leaders who had called for the bus boycott. Those who answered all three of the questions favorably were classified as "Highly favorable," those who answered two favorably were classified as "Favorable," and those who answered only one or none in this manner were placed in the "Unfavorable" category.

FINDINGS

The interviews with the panel of potential Negro leaders revealed that a real change in leadership had indeed taken place between the "Pre-Boycott" and "Post-Boycott" periods. On the basis of high rankings on the answers to the questions "Who were the leaders?" "Who were influential?" and "Who were representative?" two years previously, six individuals were classified as "Pre-Boycott Leaders." Of these six, not one was found in the first five ranked on "influence" and "representativeness" in the Post-Boycott period. None of them were ranked even in the first ten on "influence," although two did remain in the first ten on "representativeness." An indication of how complete the turnover of leadership personnel was is the fact that of the first five ranked as both "influential" and "representative" in the Post-Boycott period, not one was among the first ten named as "leaders" in the Pre-Boycott period.

This change of leadership was also found to involve, as had been postulated, a replacement of Accommodating Leaders by Protest Leaders. Of the six Pre-Boycott leaders, five were ranked by Negroes as being most able to deal effectively with white leaders during this period. Five of the six were also ranked by whites as most able to deal effectively with white leaders. Four, including the three ranked highest by Negroes as "leaders," were ranked in the first five as "emissaries" by both Negroes and whites. This finding bears out the theory that, in the era of accommodation in race relations, leadership in the Negro community was based primarily on acceptability to white leaders and ability to gain concessions from them.

In contrast, none of the five "new leaders" were ranked by either Negroes or whites as among the five Negroes able to deal most effectively with white leaders in the Post-Boycott Period. In fact, none of them ranked in the first ten on acceptability to white leaders as it was perceived by Negroes. Clearly these new leaders were not seen by other prominent Negroes as "Compromise Leaders."

The panel of Negroes interviewed included both the "old leaders" and the "new leaders," plus some individuals who did not receive high rankings for either period. The Negro panel was divided, for purposes of further analysis, into an "old group" of subjects who had ranked in the first ten on the question concerning Pre-Boycott leadership, and a new group. The new group identified as the five most influential leaders in the Post-Boycott period the same five men who had been ranked as "new leaders" by the entire panel. The "old group" ranked four of these five men as the five most influential leaders in this same period, indicating that their perception of the change in leadership was almost the same as that of the "new group." Moreover, none of the "old group," including the "old leaders," gave their own names in response to the question on ability to influence large numbers of Negroes. Although during the course of the boycott some of the old leaders had openly challenged the influence of the the new leaders, by the time of this study they seemed to have accepted the fact that they had been displaced. It is accurate, therefore, to say that a change, not a split, in leadership had occurred.

Although no intensive study of the individual characteristics of the old and new leaders was made, certain ones were evident. Even though at the time of the study, the boycott had ended and had obviously failed of its purpose to force desegregation of city buses, all of the New Leaders were strongly identified with it. All were officers of the organization which had led the boycott and all had been arrested and fined for "operating an illegal transportation system" (a car pool). In contrast, not one of the Old Leaders had been active in promoting the boycott, and at least two of them had opposed it as a tactic. Of the six Old Leaders, three were employed in the state-supported school system; none of the five New Leaders were state employees. There were three ministers among the New Leaders, none among the old. Although the Old Leaders had, as a group, indeed lived in the community a longer time than their successors, the shortest time that any of the New Leaders had lived in Tallahassee was three years. One of them had lived there over thiry years. It was only in a limited and relative sense that they could be described as "new-comers."

Since the New Leaders had been identified as synonymous with the leaders of the Bus Boycott, the questions asked in the opinion poll were suited to serve as a measure of their popular support. Were they leaders not only in the eyes of the small panel of prominent Negroes but also in the eyes of the Negro community? The results of the survey indicate that they were. When asked if the leadership in the Bus Protest was very good, 84 percent of the sample agreed that it was. Some inconsistency was found between the answers to this question and the question, "The old established leaders in Tallahassee were more effective than the ones leading the Bus Protest," since only 62 percent of the sample disagreed with this statement. But, to the extent that this sample can be taken as representative, it appears that the New Leaders did have majority support in the Negro community. Subjects were also asked to agree or disagree with the statement, "Should the Negro population of Tallahassee need to develop united action to obtain rights or services not connected with the Bus Protest, the people leading the Protest would probably be selected to lead such action." Again, strong majority support of the New Leaders was indicated, 82 percent of the sample agreeing with this statement.

Using the categories "Highly Favorable," "Favorable," and "Unfavorable," established earlier, an analysis was made of certain differences between Negroes showing greater or lesser support for the boycott and its leaders. The Chi-square test of independence was used. Differences significant beyond the .01 level were found in age and education, the more favorably disposed subjects being younger and better educated. Those who were favorably disposed toward the boycott were more likely to own automobiles than those who were not, this difference also being significant beyond the .01 level. This difference may have reflected the fact that the boycott caused less personal inconvenience for car owners than it did for others, or it may have been that car ownership was an indirect measure of socio-economic status. No significant difference in ownership of real property was found between supporters and nonsupporters, however, so the former explanation seems the more likely. This is also suggested by the fact that differences in occupation were not significant at the .05 level.

SUMMARY AND CONCLUSIONS

In the community studied, the impression that there has been a change in the quality of race relations is borne out. The clearest indication of this change is the replacement of the Old Leaders by New Leaders who clearly reflect the protest motive rather than any spirit of accommodation. These New Leaders have widespread popular support, and the extent of their influence is conceded by the Old Leaders whom they displaced.

Additional findings lend added significance to this shift in Negro leadership. The panel of white leaders were found to perceive Negro leadership in the Post-Boycott period in almost the same way that the Negro leaders did. Of the six men ranked highest by whites as "most influential" in the Post-Boycott period, four were among the Negroes' New Leaders. At the same time, most of these white leaders indicated that they were unwilling to deal with these New Leaders because the militant spokesmen were uncompromising in their opposition to segregation. It is only in this sense that communication has broken down between the races. The New Leaders are unwilling to communicate and negotiate with whites in the circumscribed, accommodating fashion of yesterday. The Old Leaders can no longer claim the support of the Negro population, no matter how acceptable they might be to the whites. As long as this situation prevails, the structure of the situation seems to permit only one kind of communication between the Negro community and the white power structure: formal, peremptory demands, backed by the threat of legal action, political reprisal, or economic boycott. So long as the New Leaders are not accepted as bona fide, albeit antagonistic, emissaries of the Negro community in the same way that the Old Leaders were, this would seem to be the only way in which they can get the attention of the white leaders.

While the present study was principally concerned with a description of the changes in Negro leadership in Tallahassee during the Bus Protest, there is evidence which indicates that the new leaders and new leadership are permanent in this community. Although they may have been "issue leaders" at first, they have continued to maintain their position of leadership as the sample of the Negro population predicted they would.

In the first place some of the "old" leaders were called upon by the Tallahassee City Commission to get the Negroes to agree to a compromise settlement in the early days of the bus protest. The efforts of the "old" leaders to do this failed completely and ever since they have made no overt efforts to regain the following they had prior to the bus protest. This is apparently due to their belief that neither the Negro population nor the city officials have confidence in them. The Negroes do not trust them because of what they regard as underhanded dealing with the City Commission. The city officials apparently feel that these erstwhile leaders cannot be trusted to gauge Negro sentiment accurately or to deliver results when called upon, because they lack following.

Secondly, the "New" leaders have continued to enjoy reasonable support for their undertakings. Some of them have moved into other areas of leadership, such as the NAACP, the Southern Christian Leadership Conference, and the Florida Council of Human Relations. One of them is president of the Tallahassee Chapter of the NAACP. Another is on the State NAACP Board and on the Board of Directors of the Southern Christian Leadership Conference.

Finally these "new" leaders have sought to keep the Negro community of Tallahassee militant and dynamic by continuing weekly meetings of the ICC, the organization formed to promote the bus protest, conducting institutes on nonviolence, taking preliminary steps toward school integration, working to get more Negroes registered and voting, and making many local and nonlocal public appearances in connection with the uplift of Negroes. Furthermore, the press has done much to contribute to their status as permanent leaders by seeking their opinions and comments on various matters affecting the Negro community in Tallahassee (e.g., the recent rape case).

The writers feel that the "new" leaders are becoming permanent leaders not because of the attractiveness of their personalities or their skill at organizing, but rather because they adhere rigorously to the *form* of militant leadership which is becoming the trend for Negroes throughout the United States. This new leadership is not of the accommodating type. It seeks gains for the Negro community through formal demands and requests, boycotts, lawsuits, and voting. The protest leaders are not concerned with whether or not the whites high in the power structure know, like, or want to deal with them. Until the "old" leaders are willing or able to translate their mode of leadership into a form similar to this, it appears that they will not again rise to prominence as leaders in Tallahassee.

NOTES

ACKNOWLEDGEMENT: The authors are indebted to the Society for the Psychological Study of Social Issues for a Grant-in-Aid which helped make this study possible. This is a revised version of a paper read at the twenty-second annual meeting of the Southern Sociological Society, Gatlinburg, Tennessee, April 17, 1959.

1. Gunnar Myrdal, *An American Dilemma* (New York: Harper & Row, 1944) pp. 768–80.

SUBCOMMUNITY GLADIATORIAL
COMPETITION: CIVIL RIGHTS LEADERSHIP
AS A COMPETITIVE PROCESS

Gerald A. McWorter / Robert L. Crain

As is often the case, the folklore of American politics contains two conflicting statements about the value of competition for political leadership. On the one hand, competition for political office is assumed to be

From *Social Forces* 46 (September 1967): 8–21; reprinted by permission of the authors and publisher.

the measure of a thriving democracy. On the other hand, we tend to think of intensely competitive politics as the breeding ground for the spectacular demagogue. In particular, the American Negro civil rights movement is seen as an example of a situation in which high levels of competition have promoted "irresponsible" leadership.[1] In this paper we will examine the civil rights movement in 14 cities, and present an analysis of the factors which cause variations in the degree and character of leadership competition and the way in which this competition has affected these movements.

THE PROBLEM

Much of the literature on the social bases of competition for leadership centers around the word "pluralism." One position is that stated by Kornhauser:

> A plurality of independent and limited-function groups supports liberal democracy by providing social bases of free and open competition for leadership, widespread participation in the selection of leaders, restraint in the application of pressures on leaders, and self-government in widespread areas of social life. Therefore, where social pluralism is strong, liberty and democracy tend to be strong; conversely, forces which weaken social pluralism also weaken liberty and democracy.[2]

Here, the competition referred to is clearly functional to a democracy. While the mass society theorists claim that severe social conflict is prevented by these same forces which produce moderate competition, Gusfield has described ways in which pluralism can encourage such conflicts.[3] This is clarified by James S. Coleman, who distinguishes between participation in voluntary organizations which tend to integrate a community by weaving community-wide patterns of communication and influence, and attachments to ethnic and other subcommunity organizations which encourage a division of the community.[4] William A. Gamson's study of 16 middle-sized and small New England cities presented evidence to support this distinction, showing that rancorous conflict was more likely to occur in communities which had isolated subcommunities within their boundaries.[5] By either argument, we might expect the pluralistic community, with a more elaborate network of voluntary organizations, and a larger supply of potential leaders, to provide the greatest degree of leadership competition, although whether such competition sustains or weakens democratic values is left an open question.

However, one apparent difficulty with the pluralism argument is that it would lead us to expect a fairly low level of leadership competition. There is no reason to expect a more elaborate structure of voluntary associations within the generally low socioeconomic status Negro community than in a white community of similar status.[6] And there is little basis for severe ideological cleavage on civil rights as major civil rights leaders command the overwhelming endorsement of the Negro community.[7]

There is another approach to the question which provides a somewhat different set of hypotheses; Ralf Dahrendorf has noted that one can contrast an "integration" theory of society—stressing equilibrium and continuity—with a coercion theory which emphasizes strains and changes.[8] He accepts these as compatible viewpoints reflecting the "two faces" of society, but focuses on the coercion theory and writes:

> I shall try to show how, on the assumption of the coercive nature of social structure, relations of authority became productive of clashes of role interest which under certain conditions lead to the formulation of organized antagonistic groups within limited social organizations as well as within total societies.[9]

This suggests that in analyzing groups such as those of the civil rights movement, we should keep in mind the possibility that a seemingly stable status hierarchy within the Negro community can itself create competition and conflict. Dahrendorf's remarks lead us back to a traditional viewpoint which says that conflict in politics is to be expected as long as there are bases of power available to competitors.

Much of the existing discussion of the consequences of competition is irrelevant to our concern because it assumes a competition between stable two-party systems. Local studies of competition in nonpartisan or one-party political systems would be more relevant, but there is little material. V. O. Key and others have pointed out the way in which "every man for himself" politics in southern states rewards ideological extremists,[10] and several writers have noted that in Louisiana, where stable party factions have persisted for several decades, racism did not play a major role in electoral contests.[11] James Q. Wilson has noted that the structured politics of Chicago has produced Congressman William Dawson, while the unstructured (and probably more competitive) politics of New York City has recruited Adam Clayton Powell.[12] Following this line of reasoning, Wilson has hypothesized that the growth of amateur political clubs in both major political parties has caused ideology to become more important in electoral campaigns and has tended to restrict the freedom of elected officials by binding them to more detailed party platforms.[13] Whether introducing ideology and platform loyalty are good or bad depends not only on one's point of view, but also on the particular community studied. Hunter, for example, suggests that the limiting of competition by the influentials of Atlanta has tended to discourage innovation and prevent the masses from winning new programs.[14]

There does seem to be one consistent finding: political party competition results in increased political participation. Milbrath found a high correlation between party competition and general turnout for senatorial and gubernatorial elections,[15] and Agger *et al.,* in a comparative study of four cities, demonstrate how elite competition stimulates mass participation in politics.[16] This is especially true if the bases of the competition is ideological. Lane,[17] and Matthews and Prothro [18] have presented similar findings about contested primary elections and rates of voter turnout.

Similar themes have emerged from studies of leadership in the Negro subcommunity. Hunter found the Negro subcommunity of Atlanta had managed to sustain a monolithic leadership structure despite considerable competition for leadership.[19] Studies of Providence, Rhode Island [20] and "Pacific City" [21] suggest the same pattern. More recently, Ladd has found similar monolithic patterns in Greenville, South Carolina, and Winston-Salem, North Carolina.[22] However, Ladd notes that Winston-Salem does have considerable competition for leadership, and suggests that this is the pattern for the Negro communities of the "new South."

One study found that during periods of intense racial controversy new leaders appeared; [23] another study noted that during a similar controversial period, the opposing factions within the Negro subcommunity merged during the crisis.[24]

Both Glick [26] and Walker [26] hypothesize that competition within the civil rights movement has unanticipated consequences which benefit the Negro subcommunity. Walker concludes that "disputes among the leadership tend to increase, not decrease, the effectiveness of the Negro community's battle against the institution of segregation." [27]

In general, our analysis follows the essential questions being raised in this literature. After clarifying the concept of leadership competition in the civil rights movement, we will investigate: (1) What are the social bases which generate and sustain competition? and (2) What are the social consequences of competition?

THE DATA

The research reported here is part of a larger study conducted by the National Opinion Research Center on decision-making with regard to school integration.[28] Fifteen cities were studied by teams of graduate student interviewers who spent from ten to 15 man-days in each city during the winter of 1964–65. Techniques employed included (a) formal questionnaire interviews with decision-makers, (b) unstructured interviews (up to eight hours in length) with decision-makers and informants, and (c) collecting documentary materials. An average of 20 respondents were interviewed in each city, including an average of four civil rights leaders. In general, there was no difficulty in obtaining interviews with the leading civil rights leaders. The civil rights leaders interviewed included those with important formal positions (e.g., the NAACP president) and those identified as important actors in the school segregation issue. The sample is thus biased (partly, but not completely) toward those persons concerned with education.

The 15 cities included eight in the North, drawn from a sampling frame including all cites between 250,000 and 1,000,000 which were at least ten percent Negro in population. The cities were selected randomly, with substitutions then made for cities which had not faced demands for school integration. The seven southern cities were selected to maximize the range of behavior on school integration, and include three cities which are the largest in their state, three smaller cities from the same states for comparison, and a fourth small city; the smallest city contained

158,623 people. One small southern city is deleted from this analysis because of insufficient direct interviews.

VARIATIONS IN LEVELS OF COMPETITION

As the word is used here, competition for leadership includes competition for formal offices in the government and in voluntary organizations such as the NAACP; but also (and more importantly) competition for status, influence, and power, for the loyalty of masses of civil rights activists, and for control over the policy and the program of the civil rights movement. A civil rights leader may be one who has the reputation for leadership, has the loyalty of a following, holds a formal office, or who is able to use other sources of prestige and status to influence the white subcommunity regarding civil rights. A civil rights leader, by our definition, may be either white or Negro. While it follows that competition can occur in several different ways, the most important distinction is between organized and individual competition. By organized competition we refer to competition between competing organizations or groups, each committed more or less permanently to a program or ideological stance. By individual competition, we refer to the competition between individuals for leadership in such a way that a majority of the civil rights leaders are not permanently committed to one side of a conflict. While in principle it would be useful to distinguish competition for leadership from conflict over ideology, in practice the two go hand in hand.

The variables were constructed primarily from the interviews with civil rights leaders. Our judgment of the leader and types of competition is based largely upon three factors—the response to sociometric questions about other leaders; the attitudes expressed by leaders about different civil rights organizations; and a detailed history of the relationships between the groups during the course of the school desegregation issue, which in the North was usually the most important civil rights issue. While the result is a largely impressionistic judgment, we are more confident about its reliability than we might otherwise be because of the great variance among the cities. The differences among cities are quite large, as will be shown when some of the cases are described.

In all 14 cities there is some degree of competition and conflict among civil rights leaders. However, in five of the cities the level of competition is so low that for present purposes we describe them as having minimal competition. These five cities are Baltimore and Miami, where most civil rights activity is handled by the NAACP and competition within the NAACP is light; Columbus, Georgia, where a "ruling elite" of five men work as a close-knit unit; and Pittsburgh and Buffalo, where various groups work in reasonable harmony, again with only a small number of highly active leaders. In all five of these cities, there are no civil rights leaders who were willing to criticize other leaders, and no case when a civil rights group opposed or criticized publicly a program advanced by another.

Four cities—St. Louis, Newark, Atlanta, and Jacksonville—fit our model of having intense organized competition. In all four cases, the

TABLE 1.   Level and Intensity of Civil Rights Leadership Competition in 14 Cities, by Region

Level of Competition	Region of Cities	
	North	South
Individual competition:		
Intense	San Francisco	Montgomery
Moderate	Oakland	New Orleans
	Boston	
Minimal competition	Baltimore	Miami
	Pittsburgh	Columbus
	Buffalo	
Organized competition	St. Louis	Jacksonville
	Newark	Atlanta

conflict can be briefly described as between the establishment and the outsiders. The conflict tends to polarize the entire movement; even the leaders who try to think of themselves as nonaligned can only be understood by their relationships to one of the opposing factions. In each case, most leaders interviewed were critical, not merely of other leaders, but of other particular civil rights groups as well.

The remaining five cities have individual competition for leadership. In two, San Francisco and Montgomery, the competition can be described as intense and persisting over long periods of time without clear factional alignments. In the other three—Oakland, Boston, and New Orleans—competition and conflict tend to come and go, and are often pushed into the background. Because, as we shall see, the cities without competition are in some ways intermediate between those which have organized competition and those which have individual competition, it is useful to present them graphically in the center of the typology. The civil rights leaders in these cities often qualified their criticism of other leaders in terms of how much support was offered or available for their own program. Since each actor appeared to be a free agent, everyone was considered a possible ally, as well as a potential enemy.

The five cities with individual competition have in common a volatile style of civil rights activity. In all five, since the temporary withdrawal of one or another leader can alter the picture considerably, it is difficult to predict the level and style of civil rights activity. This is especially true of Montgomery, whose leaders have been consistently drafted into the national civil rights movement. As new leaders appear, the pattern of competition changes, and civil rights programs change with them.

THE SOCIAL BASES OF ORGANIZED COMPETITION

Let us first consider the roots of organized competition; later we will consider the causes of individual competition. In all four cities in this category, it is possible to locate sources of structural competition in the different bases of power available to competing factions. In the two northern cities the conflict is between the political "establishment" and militant neighborhood-based groups. In St. Louis, the demands for school integration were first made by the West End Community Council with the support of CORE. At first, the NAACP lent its support to the campaign, but later they began to withdraw. After some important victories, an open split between the militant grass-roots groups and the NAACP brought about the collapse of the school integration drive. The militants generally accused the NAACP of being conservative and tied to the Democratic party organization in the Negro wards, though one of the militants used his civil rights activity to win control of one ward.[29]

In Newark the pattern was nearly identical. The most militant leader in the NAACP was also a leader of the community organization in a middle-income integrated neighborhood. Under the stress of the school integration campaign, he left the NAACP and the community group continued to battle the school system without the NAACP branch's support. Again, the militants accused the NAACP of being too close to the ruling faction of the Democratic party.

The only other city in the sample with a strong patronage-based Negro political machine is Jacksonville, and here again the result has been organized competition for leadership. However, the cast is a bit different, since the NAACP is militant and anti-machine, and the machine leadership does not have a civil rights organization. In part, this is the effect of Jacksonville being a southern city; the NAACP is not legitimate enough to be accepted by white politicians, and Negro political leaders without autonomous bases of power cannot afford to be active in it. In addition, there is less distinction in the South between generalized community leadership and civil rights leadership, so that the Negro political leader does not need to be a representative of a civil rights group in order to claim status as a civil rights leader.[30]

The fourth city with organized competition is Atlanta. The competition here is between the generations, older and less militant leaders being attacked by young upwardly-mobile militants.[31]

A general but simple proposition fitting all four cities is that organized competition will occur if and only if one faction has access to status independent of an appeal to mass support, and the other faction can successfully appeal to the masses for its power. In the first three cities the political machine can supply patronage and other material incentives maintaining Negro political leaders without requiring that they make a mass appeal on ideological grounds. The competing group is a neighborhood-based mass organization in St. Louis and Newark, and a traditional civil rights group in Jacksonville. Since their claim to leadership is based upon the loyalty of a visible group of followers, all three cities have engaged in considerable direct action. Neighborhood-based groups are more successful competitors to the NAACP than city-wide groups such as CORE, probably because they have a more committed following. Thus in all four cities the contest is between militant direct-action groups and moderates.

In Atlanta the same proposition seems to hold. One faction draws its power from its association with the elites of Atlanta's Negro business and academic communities. Of all the cities, Atlanta has the greatest amount of resources for such an elite; the second largest Negro-owned life insurance company and the second largest Negro-owned bank are in Atlanta,[32] in addition to seven Negro colleges and universities. These same resources (especially the colleges) have produced the following for the mass-oriented activists.[33]

To put it another way, the machine city makes it possible for the white leadership to offer resources to particular Negro leaders in exchange for conservative behavior on civil rights. It was probably once true that most cities were able to maintain a conservative group of leaders in this way by offering money or various symbols of honor and prestige. Indeed, the threat of physical violence in some cases might have made such an offering unnecessary. But in the eleven nonmachine cities in our sample, we found little evidence of this today. One reason is that the civil rights revolution has placed these Negro leaders under attack, and the white community has usually been unwilling or unable to counter by inflating their payments to them.

The white leadership also has a negative sanction; it can withhold recognition from civil rights leaders by simply refusing to deal with them. While we have no example of a city which was able to suppress an issue in this fashion, it seems probable that this tactic has increased the turnover of leadership as unrecognized leaders drop into the background. Actually, this is not an "effective" device; as we shall see, an increase in competition tends to increase militancy, so that the whites may find the new leadership more difficult to deal with.

At first it would seem that almost any city could provide a basis for power independent of a mass following, and hence have organized competition, but this is apparently not the case. In Boston there is only one Negro elected official and very few in appointed posts. In the other northern cities the absence of a machine vote requires that ambitious political leaders take militant positions, or at least give public support to the militant leaders. Of the northern cities, none has the elaborate Negro economy of Atlanta; furthermore, the Negro economic leaders are sometimes either politically active or are newspaper publishers and therefore still dependent upon a mass following. Similarly, in the South, Jacksonville is represented as a home office of one of the large Negro-owned insurance firms but is otherwise not an important Negro economic center, and the other cities have even less Negro-owned business.[34] Outside of Atlanta, there are so few Negroes holding political positions that they can hardly constitute a faction. One might expect competition on general ideological grounds between militants and conservatives, but there has been a constantly accelerating rise of militancy in the Negro community since World War II. Conservative ideologies no longer offer a competitive alternative to this increased militancy. Unless the "Uncle Tom" is propped up with a considerable number of favors from white sources, it seems he is fast becoming a mere anachronism.[35]

The general hypothesis predicts that one other type of city will not have organized competition; this is the city where there is no basis for a grass-roots movement. A city with a low-status population, without (for example) the resources of a Negro college, might fall into this class. But even here this is unlikely because of a strong general endorsement of civil rights activity by the Negro masses. If any city in our sample can be described this way it is Columbus, Georgia, where the "ruling elite" has up to now been able to handle civil rights activity with little competition from direct-action groups. Columbus has the lowest status Negro population of the cities in our sample; with a higher status population, there might be a conflict between the generations here as in Atlanta (but it is also possible that the elite might become more militant).

It would also be possible for a city to be led by a group of elites who have enough prestige to be "above criticism." This may have been the case in Montgomery during the early days of the Montgomery Improvement Association, when the MIA leadership combined their prestige as nationally recognized civil rights leaders with their local prestige as ministers of the church.[36] And of course this would have been more often the case before the current thrust of civil rights activities. But in most cities, the holders of traditional status can be attacked (with or without justification) as being conservative. Even when the traditional prestige hierarchy retains its importance, an increase in civil rights activity may encourage competition among elites for the leadership of the movement.

THE BASES FOR INDIVIDUAL COMPETITION

If by individual competition we refer to competition between individuals without permanent factional coalitions or stable ideological differences, we can choose between two seemingly contradictory hypotheses. First, competition will be most present in the "mass society" since there will be few loyalties or agreements binding people into "follower" roles; anyone who wants to be a leader is free to do so. This is a special case of Coleman's hypothesis that a person without an elaborate network of social attachments is free to take controversial positions.[37] However the more commonly accepted opposing hypothesis is that the pluralistic society, with its complex network of associations, is the training ground for potential leaders. The arguments are not really contradictory, and taken together suggest that we should find greatest competition in (a) the community with many leadership roles and many people in high-status positions, but with little in the way of interdependent relations and a weak internal prestige structure, and less competition in either, (b) the community with a large number of roles for training potential leaders, but with a stable prestige hierarchy and interdependence, or (c) the community with few leadership roles, which will not have competition even if it has an inadequate prestige hierarchy.[38]

We would expect a city of type (a) to have a fast growing middle-class Negro community which is partially assimilated. In such a situation, many persons with leadership skills will be holding "white" jobs, some of the civil rights leaders will be white, and there will not be a traditional prestige structure. All three of the northern cities with individual competition seem to fit this description. In Boston, San Francisco, and Oakland, a large number of civil rights leaders are either white, hold "white" jobs, or live in predominantly white areas. Thus they are autonomous vis-à-vis the Negro economic structure, and have ambiguous status in the Negro prestige hierarchy. Table 2a suggests the lack of autonomy of the Negro community in these cities compared to the less competitive Pittsburgh and Baltimore. In all three individual competition cities, Negroes are less segregated, and the lack of autonomy of the Negro community is reflected in the unimportance of the Negro press. The table also suggests that if it were not for the political organization of St. Louis and Newark, these two cities would have little competition—St. Louis because it has a Negro elite which would maintain considerable power, Newark because it has almost no basis for a grass-roots movement. In general, Table 2a indicates that in the non-machine cities of the North, the higher the status of the Negro community, the greater the individual competition. This pattern does not hold in the four southern cities which do not have organized competition.

In the South, Negro subcommunities are somewhat more self-sufficient, have more visible prestige structures, and have lower status populations. There is little variation in the degree of autonomy of these highly segregated subcommunities. Hence, we would expect them to have less individual competition. Two cities, New Orleans and Montgomery,

TABLE 2a. Selected Social Factors Influencing Competition (North)

Level of Competition	Socioeconomic Status		Size	Level of Segregation	
	Percent white collar	Percent high school graduates	Percent population negro	Index of residential segregation*	Importance of Negro Newspapers†
Individual competition					
Intense:					
San Francisco	27	40	9.0	69.3	Low
Moderate:					
Boston	17	37	9.8	83.9	Low
Oakland	18	32	26.4	73.1	Low
Minimal competition					
Baltimore	15	19	35.0	89.6	High
Pittsburgh	14	25	16.7	84.6	High
Buffalo	11	22	13.8	86.5	Low
Organized competition					
St. Louis	15	24	28.8	90.6	Medium
Newark	11	22	34.4	71.6	Medium

*Data compiled from Karl E. Tacuber and Alma F. Tacuber, *Negroes in Cities* (Chicago: Aldine Publishing Co. 1965).

†Data compiled from *Negro Newspapers in the United States* (Jefferson City, Missouri: Lincoln University, Dept. of Journalism, 1964). The Baltimore *Afro-American* and the Pittsburgh *Courier* are well-known: the St. Louis *Argus* and the Newark *Afro-American* are weeklies with circulations of 9,000 and 7,000 respectively.

TABLE 2b. Factors Influencing Competition (South)*

	Socioeconomic Status		Size	
Level of Competition	Percent white collar	Percent high school	Percent population negro	*Number of Negro Colleges†*
Individual competition				
Intense:				
Montgomery	14.3	17.8	38.1	1
Moderate:				
New Orleans	11.6	14.5	30.8	2
Minimal competition				
Miami	8.5	18.1	14.7	0
Columbus	11.9	12.7	29.0	0
Organized competition				
Atlanta	12.7	21.1	38.2	6
Jacksonville	10.7	18.2	23.2	1

*Importance of Negro Newspapers and the Index of Residential Segregation are not relevant to the study of southern Negro leadership: see text.
†Data compiled from Earl J. McGrath, *The Predominantly Negro Colleges and Universities in Transition* (New York: Columbia University, Teachers College, 1965).

do have a limited amount of individual competition, but this may be the result of unique historical factors in each case. A pioneering thrust of civil rights activity in 1955 established the MIA as the model for a mass-based organization in the South. However, several key leaders moved to regional and national levels of leadership, notably Dr. Martin Luther King and Rev. Ralph Abernathy (successive presidents of the MIA). At the time of our interviews, several leaders in the MIA were struggling to organize activity, and thus were competing for power. But our proposition holds that if a direct-action program was organized successfully, the level of competition would decline considerably. Similarly, this appears to be the case for New Orleans which has always had a relatively weak civil rights movement.[39] The cities without competition do have in common a lower supply of "troops" for mass demonstrations; neither has a Negro college whose student body could be used for demonstrations.

SOCIAL SOURCES OF COMPETITION: A SUMMARY

There seems to be some evidence in these data to support several propositions about the causes of competition.

1. A necessary condition for competition is an adequate supply of social resources.
2. A necessary condition for competition to be organized or factional is that there be distinctly different ways to mobilize resources. In our case, this means a choice between appealing for mass support and obtaining

resources in other ways; in another context it would include appealing to different sectors of the population for support.

3. Individual competition is facilitated by a weak or ambiguous prestige structure. Social control over potential leaders and loyalty to factions can exist only to the extent that the Negro subcommunity is in fact a subcommunity with binding integrative attachment mechanisms.

TABLE 3. Social Characteristics of Civil Rights Leaders, by Type of Leadership, Competition and Region

	Competition	Median Age		Percent With Professional Education		Percent Income Over $10,000	
North	Individual	33	(8)	67	(9)	50	(8)
	Minimal	41	(12)	42	(12)	67	(9)
	Organized	34	(6)	58	(12)	20	(5)
South	Individual	53	(7)	43	(7)	50	(4)
	Minimal	46	(7)	50	(8)	0	(6)
	Organized	49	(9)	44	(9)	67	(9)

SOCIAL CONSEQUENCES OF LEADERSHIP COMPETITION

In a competitive environment, prospective leaders must make appeals for support. It is commonly assumed that this produces a more militant movement, and our data support this assumption. Without competition, leadership remains in traditional hands, which suggests that the leadership in noncompetitive cities will be older and have higher statüs. Our data indicate that this is also the case, at least partially. Table 3 gives the age, educational attainment, and income of the civil rights leaders interviewed in each class of city; the data suggest that the noncompetitive cities have older leaders who have high incomes, but without especially high educational attainment. However, the South presents a reverse pattern with the noncompetitive cities having younger leaders who are better educated with lower incomes. In both of the noncompetitive southern cities, the leadership was occupied by upwardly-mobile professionals. The Negro professional holds an indisputable status in the Negro subcommunity functionally similar to that of a member of a traditional elite.[40]

Militancy is measured by a four-item scale from a longer agree-disagree questionnaire.[41] The meaning of this militancy scale is perhaps best captured by one of these items which asks the respondent to agree or disagree that "Too many times Negroes have compromised when they could have made more progress if they had held out a little longer." But another component of militancy is the willingness to disagree that "The average white man really wants the Negro to have his rights." Apparently the militant feels there is little to be gained from appealing to the better nature of whites, and therefore the only hope is to make discrimination so unpleasant or costly that whites will give in out of self-interest. In

Table 4, we see that the cities with competition, both organized and individual, have more militant leaders. It is understandable that the southern leaders would generally be more militant than those in the North.

Thus far, we have observed that leadership in competitive cities differs in means orientations. Let us now consider two other factors, differences in goal orientation, and differences in the actual amount of civil rights activity. Here we will draw upon the 15 case studies without attempting to present the data in each case. The reader is referred to the parent monograph for a more complete story.

One might suppose that under conditions of intense competition, the goals of the local civil rights movement might become more attuned to the national civil rights climate as competing leaders draw upon the idioms of the national movement for legitimation. This is partly true in cities where competition is individualized. In these cities the leadership goals have been set in an effort to bid for the support of the entire Negro community, hence the goals have been stated in the most diffuse way. In all three cities, the goals have stressed the elimination of *de facto* segregation and have been highly symbolic.[42] In the two cities with organized competition, the goals have been determined (it seems) by the need of the anti-establishment leaders to build a specific base in one sector of the community from which to wage war on the establishment. The result is that the stated goals have been set to meet the particular needs of only one part of the subcommunity. In both cases, the base was a racially changing neighborhood which developed a mixture of city-wide and local goals (and a mixture of symbolic and welfare goals) designed to encourage whites to stay in the area and to meet the most salient needs of the incoming Negroes. The two southern cities with organized competition have also shown a tendency toward a mixture of "symbolic" and "welfare" goals; this is particularly true in Jacksonville. The three cities without internal competition developed a set of goals which are in some ways more traditional. Although they were generally city-wide in orientation,

TABLE 4. Militancy of Civil Rights Leaders, by Competition Level of City and Region*

Level of Competition	Region of Cities		Total†	
	North	South		
Individual competition	2.14 (7)	2.74 (9)	1.78	(16)
Minimal competition	1.30 (10)	2.00 (7)	1.07	(17)
Organized competition	2.00 (9)	2.50 (10)	1.72	(19)
Mean	1.77 (26)	2.42 (26)	1.77	(52)

*Each civil rights leader interviewed was given a militancy score, the average number of militant responses to four statements. The possible range of scores is from very militant (score=4) to not militant at all (score=0).

†The total column is derived after reducing the southern militancy scores by .65 so that the North-South differences will not influence the result. In the total column the level of militancy in the two competitive cases are each significantly higher than the militancy in the minimal competition case (at the .05 level, one-tailed test).

they tended to be more specific; in Baltimore and Pittsburgh, focus was upon techniques for eliminating overcrowding by an integration plan; in Buffalo, the movement stressed integration of particular schools.

In the South, there is a narrower range of alternative goals available since the elimination of *de jure* segregation has been the main target. In the one city where there is competition between civil rights groups and a Negro political "establishment," the movement has adopted a heavy welfare orientation which led to a three-day boycott aimed at forcing the upgrading of Negro schools. As in the North, the movements with individual competition for leadership (New Orleans and Montgomery) have stated their goals in abstract terms, and have not paid much attention to specific goals or goals designed to benefit any particular sector or neighborhood of the Negro community. Thus, the data suggest that individualized competition leads to diffuse goals stressing symbolic issues, that cities with organized competition become welfare-oriented, while the cities with low competition tend to stress general and symbolic goals phrasing them in specific terms.

This is only a general tendency, and the data are confounded by three factors. First, the high-status city can be expected to develop more symbolic and diffuse goals since it tends to have an audience for mass-media exhortations, and (we assume) weaker neighborhood orientations. But, as we have discussed above, the high-status cities have individualized competition. Thus our correlation of individualized competition and diffuse goal orientation may be spurious. Secondly, the movements with low competition for leadership are better able to negotiate (since the school board knows who it has to negotiate with), a factor which probably affects the kinds of demands developed and made. And third, the willingness of the school system to meet the particular demands affects the goals of the movement. Since these extraneous factors are important, it is probably wisest to conclude that competition is not necessarily the most important factor in determining the goal orientation of the movement.

Competition also places great pressure on leaders to achieve results. However, in the case of northern school desegregation, the movement has relatively little impact on the degree to which the school board will acquiesce to the demands made.[43] Therefore there is some tendency for the movement to become means-oriented and evaluate its leaders by their ability to put together a good demonstration or boycott. Again, it is easy to exaggerate the importance of competition in determining level of activity. Much depends upon the amount of resources—especially man-power—available to the movement; and much depends upon whether the school system chooses to be resistant and invite demonstrations. However, with these two qualifications, we can suggest such a pattern. Within the northern sample, both cities with organized competition tend to have aggressive demonstrations, although they tend not to be able to sustain civil rights activity over a long period of time. There is almost an element of desperation in the style of militant groups in these cities. In St. Louis, for example, a blockade of school buses was agreed upon late the preceding evening, and final plans were not developed until a few hours before the blockade. However, it is difficult to sustain civil rights activity without complete support of the Negro community, and in both cities the presence of an organized opposition group eventually crippled the movement.[44] In the three cities with individualized competition, demonstrations have been sporadic, but have continued over a long period of time. In the noncompetitive cities, as expected, the decision to demonstrate is a purely tactical one; the demonstration is regarded as the ultimate weapon and is infrequently used.

The same general pattern seems to hold in the South, even though activity in connection with court-ordered desegregation is quite different from activity generated within a northern context. In the cities with organized competition (Atlanta and Jacksonville), there has been direct action in connection with the schools; there has not been such action in the other four cities. Accordingly, in these four cities, it is difficult to establish a relationship between competition and activity, although the civil rights action does seem more predictable when there is little competition.

The most important effect of competition in the civil rights movement has been to make negotiation with white leadership much more complex. In all northern cities, the movements with individualized competition have been more unpredictable. The San Francisco school superintendent has had to deal with nine civil rights groups. In another city the civil rights movement virtually forced the board to break off negotiations so that a boycott could be held. In the third city, the demands were so vague as to be perceived as merely antagonistic slogans.[45] In the two cities with organized competition, the main difficulty with negotiations is that the school board could not know how large an element of the Negro community was "represented" by a group of civil rights leaders vis-à-vis their opponents or competitors.[46] In contrast, the three cities with minimal competition have had much more orderly processes of negotiation—although in one case, the school board was so disorganized that the civil rights leaders didn't quite know with whom *they* should be talking.

SOCIAL CONSEQUENCES OF COMPETITION: A SUMMARY

Table 5 summarizes the data presented above. From this summary table we can clarify Walker's contention that competitive movements are more successful in achieving their goals.[47] It is probably true that organized competition is beneficial to a civil rights movement in that it stimulates the most intense (though sometimes short-lived) activity. On the other hand, individual competition, which produces a constant circulation of leaders, probably equips the movement best for sustained activity over a period of years. However, the city without competition is probably best able to carry out a tightly planned campaign to achieve specific goals, although in the process its small leadership may become stolid and lose the initiative to raise new issues or the courage to use ultimate sanctions.

TABLE 5. Style of Civil Rights Activity, by City Competition Level and Region

| Region | Level of Competition | Style of Civil Rights Activity | | |
		Goals	Action	Militancy
North	Individual	Symbolic, diffuse, city-wide	Demonstration (sporadic)	Medium
	Minimal	Symbolic, specific, city-wide	Bargain-table negotiation (extensive)	Low
	Organized	Welfare and symbolic, specific, local and city-wide	Demonstration (intense, but short-lived)	Medium
South	Individual	Symbolic, city-wide	Court action (limited)	High
	Minimal	Symbolic, city-wide	Court action (extensive)	Medium
	Organized	Welfare and symbolic, diffuse, city-wide	Court action and demonstration (short-lived)	High

NOTES

1. As an example of this diagnosis, see Daniel Bell, "Plea for a 'New Phase in Negro Leadership,'" *The New York Times Magazine,* May 31, 1964.
2. William Kornhauser, *The Politics of Mass Socety* (New York: Free Press, 1959), pp. 230–31.
3. Joseph Gusfield, *Symbolic Crusade: Status Politics and the American Temperance Movement* (Urbana: The University of Illinois Press, 1963). See especially "A Dramatistic Theory of Status Politics," chap. 7, pp. 166–88. See also "Mass Society and Extremist Politics," *American Sociological Review* 27 (February 1962): 19–30.
4. James S. Coleman, *Community Conflict* (Glencoe, Illinois: The Free Press, 1957).
5. William A. Gamson, "Rancorous Conflict in Community Politics," *American Sociological Review* 31 (February 1966): 71–81.
6. See Anthony M. Orum, "A Reappraisal of the Social and Political Participation of Negroes," *American Journal of Sociology* 72 (July 1966): 32–46.
7. For national data see William Brink and Louis Harris, *The Negro Revolution in America* (New York: Simon & Schuster, 1964), and for a local example (Durham, North Carolina) see M. Elaine Burgess, *Negro Leadership in a Southern City* (Chapel Hill: The University of North Carolina Press, 1962).
8. Ralf Dahrendorf, *Class and Class Conflict in Industrial Society* (Stanford: Stanford University Press, 1959). See Part II, "Toward a Sociological Theory of Conflict in Industrial Society," pp. 157–318. He writes that the integration theory of society "conceives of social structure in terms of a functionally integrated system held in equilibrium by certain patterned and recurrent processes; the other one, the *coercion theory* of society, views social structure as a form of organizaton held together by force and constraint and reacting continuously beyond itself in the sense of producing within itself the forces that maintain it in an unending process of change" (p. 159).
9. Ibid., p. 165.

10. V. O. Key, *Southern Politics in State and Nation* (New York: Knopf, 1949); Hugh D. Price, *The Negro and Southern Politics* (New York: New York University Press, 1957).

11. For a comprehensive analysis of the data see Robert Crain, Morton Inger, and Gerald A. McWorter, *School Desegregation in New Orleans: A Comparative Study of the Failure of Social Control* (Chicago: National Opinion Research Center, 1966), pp. 15–106.

12. James Q. Wilson, *Negro Politics: The Search for Leadership* (New York: Free Press, 1960); and "Two Negro Politicians: An Interpretation," *Midwest Journal of Political Science* 4 (November 1960): 346–69.

13. James Q. Wilson, *The Amateur Democrat* (Chicago: University of Chicago Press, 1962).

14. Floyd Hunter, *Community Power Structure: A Study of Decision-Makers* (Chapel Hill: The University of North Carolina Press, 1954).

15. Lester W. Milbrath, "Political Participation in the States," in Herbert Jacob and Kenneth Vines, eds., *Comparative State Politics* (Boston: Little, Brown, 1965).

16. Robert E. Agger, Daniel Goldrich, and Bert Swanson, *The Rulers and the Ruled: Political Power and Impotence in American Communities* (New York: John Wiley, 1964).

17. Robert E. Lane, *Political Life: Why People Get Involved in Politics* (Glencoe, Illinois: The Free Press, 1959).

18. Donald R. Matthews and James W. Prothro, "Political Factors and Negro Voter Registration in the South," *American Political Science Review* 57 (June 1963): 355–67.

19. Hunter, *Community Power Structure.*

20. Harold Pfautz, "The Power Structure of the Negro Sub-Community: A Case Study and Comparative View," *Phylon* 23 (Summer 1962): 156–66.

21. Ernest Barth and Baha Abu-Laban, "Power Structure and the Negro Sub-Community," *American Sociological Review* 24 (February 1959): 69–76.

22. Everett C. Ladd, *Negro Political Leadership in the South* (Ithaca: Cornell University Press, 1966).

23. Lewis M. Killian and Charles U. Smith, "Negro Protest Leaders in a Southern Community," *Social Forces* 38 (March 1960): 253–57. [Reprinted in this volume, Part II, Section 3.] Also see Tillman Cothran and William Phillips, "Negro Leadership in a Crisis Stuation," *Phylon* 22 (1961): 107–18.

24. Jacquelyn Johnson Clarke, "Standard Operating Procedures in Tragic Situations," *Phylon* 22 (Winter 1961): 318–28.

25. Clarence E. Glick, "Collective Behavior in Race Relations," *American Sociological Review* 13 (June 1948): 287–94.

26. Jack Walker, "The Functions of Disunity: Negro Leadership in a Southern City," *Journal of Negro Education* 32 (1963): 227–36.

27. Ibid., p. 228.

28. For the case studies and an analysis of the data, see Robert Crain, with Morton Inger, Gerald A. McWorter, and James J. Vanecko, *School Desegregation in the North: Eight Comparative Case Studies of Community Structure and Policy Making* (Chicago: National Opinion Research Center, 1966), and Crain, Inger, and McWorter, *School Desegregation in New Orleans.*

29. A key actor in St. Louis described this pattern: "Traditionally there have been certain Negroes who are recognized as leaders and they start off as militant, but somewhere along the line they become part of the establishment. They first become militant, and this is caused by being anti-establishment, and then they become part of the establishment—they shift from one position to another. Of course, you can't remain a revolutionary as part of the establishment."

30. A clear example of this in Jacksonville occurred during a recent three-day school

boycott run by a militant NAACP-oriented leadership. On the second day of the boycott, a major establishment Negro politician appeared on television to appeal to the Negro community to return to normal and send the children back to school. However, his appeal was not legitimated by his political role, but by his "leadership in many areas, such as civil rights, etc." Further, while appearing on television a NAACP sign was visible in front of him. He warded off charges of fraudulent representation made by NAACP, local and national officials, by declaring that his life membership allowed him such prerogative.

31. The data were collected prior to significant changes in the political involvement of Negroes in the South, particularly Atlanta. Our findings are essentially similar to those presented by Walker (see Walker, "The Functions of Disunity"). After reapportionment in Georgia, the summer primary and general elections added up to two Negro state senators, and five Negro state representatives including Attorney Ben Brown and Julian Bond, both former leaders of the Atlanta Student Movement during 1960–1961 sit-ins. What seems to have subsequently developed is the abdication of leadership by the two key figures (one died, one moved to New York), which in effect has turned over the power to the younger more militant cadre of leaders.

32. Andrew F. Brimmer, "The Negro in the National Economy," in John P. Davis, ed., *The American Negro Reference Book* (Englewood Cliffs, N.J.: Prentice-Hall, 1966); see especially the section titled "Negroes as Entrepreneurs," pp. 291–321.

33. The largest Negro-owned bank and insurance firm are both in Durham along with a large Ph.D.-granting Negro university. At times, Durham seems to have a pattern of civil rights competition resembling Atlanta's. For a detailed analysis of Durham see Burgess, *Negro Leadership in a Southern City;* E. Franklin Frazier, "Durham: Capital of the Black Middle Class," in Alain Locke, ed., *The New Negro* (New York: A. and C. Boni, 1925); and on the early development of Atlanta see August Meier and David Lewis, "History of Negro Upper Class in Atlanta, Georgia, 1890–1958," *Journal of Negro Education* (Spring 1959): 128–39.

34. Brimmer, "The Negro in the National Economy."

35. For a more detailed analysis of this pattern of increasing militancy see Louis Lomax, *The Negro Revolt* (New York: Harper & Row, 1962); August Meier, "New Currents in the Civil Rights Movement," *New Politics* (Summer 1963): 7–31; and August Meier and Francis L. Broderick, ed., *Negro Protest Thought in the Twentieth Century* (Indianapolis: Bobbs-Merrill, 1965).

36. For a general interpretive discussion see Martin Luther King's *Stride Toward Freedom* (New York: Ballantine, 1960).

37. Coleman, *Community Conflict,* p. 26.

38. A possible fourth type, the community which maintains a stable elite but has no leadership roles, is almost an internal contradiction, and seems to be rare; but as we noted earlier Columbus, Georgia, comes close to this type.

39. Detailed analysis can be found in Crain, Inger, McWorter, *Social Desegregation in New Orleans;* and Daniel Thompson, *The Negro Leadership Class* (Englewood Cliffs, N.J.: Prentice-Hall, 1963).

40. One can interpret leadership competition of the minority community as mechanisms of mobility. The northern pattern differs from the South in part because protest leadership is a functional alternative to established routes of leadership mobility, whereas in the South it is ofttimes the same as the total minority leadership. This is particularly true in cities without established political leadership; thus, the one Negro attorney in Columbus being elected to the Georgia House of Representatives following reapportionment was predicated on both his station in the Negro community and moderate acceptability to whites.

41. The two items not cited above are (a) "Unless you dramatize an issue through mass protests and demonstrations it seems that there is scarcely any progress made," and (b) "It is sometimes better to have white resistance to Negro requests, because then you have a basis for bringing the overall problem to the public's

attention." Yules Q was used as a measure of association and produced the following matrix:

	2	3	4
1	.45	.73	.89
2	—	.62	.69
3	—	—	.54

42. In this discussion of civil rights goals we have employed two axes of differentiation, status (symbolic) to welfare, and diffuse to specific. Wilson clearly states that the first basis of distinction is between tangible *things* (welfare) and intangible *principles* (status or symbolic). See Wilson, *Negro Politics: The Search for Leadership*, esp. pp. 185–99. The second dimension concerns the level of specificity of the goals, the extent to which the goals reflect a limited set of concrete propositions as compared to an ever expanding set of general claims.

43. The major analysis of the parent study revealed that characteristics of the school board and its members so explained acquiescence that adding the effect of civil rights activity did not appreciably add to the predictability. Moreover, the explanatory relationship is opposite this, i.e., the initial reaction or acquiescence of the school board is a cause of civil rights activity rather than being caused by it.

44. Related to a movement's resource needs for sustaining activity, there is probably an inverse relationship between the number of "troops" needed and the intensity/quality of commitment. But an opposition group affects both factors by drawing off some troops and immobilizing others, and providing alternative gratification which depletes the urgency of the initial controversy.

45. Killian poses one explanation for cases when ". . . the Negro leader-agent takes the white agent's arguments as the rationalizations of a prejudiced person rather than the tactics of a bargaining agent. When he reiterates his demands, almost as slogans, rather than countering the tactics, he appears either unintelligent or unreasonable. This leads the white agent, in turn, into the psychodynamic fallacy, and he breaks off the negotiations on the ground that the Negro is simply an agitator who makes impossible demands for the sake of 'stirring up trouble.'" See Lewis Killian, "Community Structure and the Role of the Negro Leader-Agent," *Sociological Inquiry* 35 (Winter 1965): 69–79.

46. School boards have normally faced the representation question with regard to teachers' unions and parent groups. But civil rights leaders face different problems because the above two are more easily defined constituencies, with longer traditions of negotiating with school boards, and are working within the context of a clearer uncontroversial set of legal guidelines.

47. Walker, "The Functions of Disunity."

4. Tactics

Having organization and leadership will not in themselves bring about desired societal change. One must also have a set of strategies and tactics. Merely convincing established power groups of the justice of your cause will rarely be sufficient to get them to make concessions. The enticement to retain the advantages of the status quo are too strong. One must also convince the established power bloc that the retention of their advantages will be more expensive than the advantages are worth. In other words, no meaningful changes are ever brought about unless tactics are devised and power is brought to bear. Of course, there are no universal tactics that work at all times in all situations. Tactics have to be situation-specific. They tend to undergo an evolution over time as some prove less effective than desired, as goals change, as participants change, or as situations become altered for other reasons.

The four selections included in this section discuss the various tactics used by the civil rights movement. Harry A. Bailey, Jr., discusses the general problem of strategies and tactics and their evolution. This selection illustrates the fact that specific types of tactics have tended to be linked to particular organizations. It also demonstrates the manner in which new tactics have evolved as established tactics fail to bring about changes as rapidly as desired. Legal equality may be achieved through litigation, pressures upon legislators, and pressures upon executives. However, legal equality on paper is not always equality in practice. The translation of legal rights to operative equality demands direct action. Certain situations call for the combination of respectable middle-class and less respectable direct action tactics.

James W. Vander Zanden provides an analysis of nonviolent resistance. The tactic of nonviolent resistance appears to be ideally suited to a group with relatively little power. If a powerless group attempted to bring about change through violence, they would be totally and ruthlessly crushed. However, the cloak of nonviolence and loving one's oppressors places morality clearly on the side of the insurgents. Any overt and violent attempt to crush nonviolent demonstrators attracts the support and sympathy of the neutrals. Many observers would not be reached by the simple justice of a plea by oppressed persons but they become aroused at the sight of defenseless and nonaggressing persons being set upon by dogs, firehoses, clubs, cattle prods, and violent police. Indeed, riotous police are the best allies of nonviolent demonstrators. Thus nonviolent resistance provides a means by which a weak, oppressed group may express their hostility toward their oppressors in a morally acceptable manner which has the potential of bringing about limited social change.

One of the most commonly used tactics of nonviolent resistance is the sit-in. Martin Oppenheimer provides us with an analysis of the sit-in movement. Sit-ins have been highly successful. To achieve this success, they needed a considerable amount of discipline. This discipline has generally been produced by extensive advance preparation and training through workshops. A disciplined group of sit-inners who have the staying power to withstand harassment and continue with their activities over a long period of time can have a major impact upon their target. First of all, they disrupt ongoing activities and bring an immediate economic loss to their target. If their target is part of a national chain, they may touch off sympathetic national boycotts of the chain which will have an even greater economic impact. It is this continuing economic impact that contributes most to their eventual successes.

Closely allied to the sit-in in its economic impact is the boycott. William Phillips, Jr., provides an analysis of one usage of this tactic. Boycotts have often been successful in desegregating facilities and in creating new jobs for blacks. The particular one Phillips examines was not similarly successful. However, it cannot be viewed as a failure. It served to unify the black community through action, to give a sense of sacrifice and contribution to the civil rights movement to individual blacks, and quite probably made the task of future organization for concerted action simpler and more likely to be successful. Nothing gives a sense of commitment to a cause like the act of having sacrificed for that cause. This sense of sacrifice can have long-range consequences even if the degree of sacrifice is minimal. Boycotting one variety store while another is available for shopping is a minimal sacrifice, but it is still perceived as a positive act on behalf of the cause.

NEGRO INTEREST GROUP STRATEGIES

Harry A. Bailey, Jr.

Negroes are organized around their communality, and have developed strategies to change the distribution of social and economic values consistent with their needs and aspirations. This paper attempts to make plain the strategies of some of the major Negro interest groups which pursue race goals, and to explain why some strategies are used by some participants in the struggle and other strategies by others. Throughout, we hope to show something of the impact of the various strategies on the political system. In this way, we hope to elucidate a significant area of our common political life.

ORGANIZATION AND POWER

Political organization and political power are inextricably intertwined. An unorganized mass of people can have little impact on the governmental allocation of social and economic values. However, power has bases other than political organization. Votes, money, prestige, and knowledge constitute additional significant resources which can be translated into political power.[1] Any cursory survey of the Negro's environment will reveal that Negroes have all these resources in varying amounts; but relatively speaking, their greatest assets are political organization and the ballot.

Negroes in the North can use the political parties to further race goals. But even in the North this option is limited. The existence of other interests to be considered makes it difficult for either of the parties to move directly on Negro demands. In the South, Negroes can rarely use existing political organizations to promote their own interests.[2] The political parties in the South, at both the state and local levels, are controlled by whites who are primarily concerned with winning elections in a region where to be identified as pro-Negro is to court political defeat. The result, in both North and South, has been the necessity for Negroes to create their own political organizations.

Two sorts of political action groups have grown to primacy in the Negro sub-community:[3] those relying on the middle-class politics strategy[4] and those relying on the nonviolent direct action strategy. The middle-class politics model assumes the pursuance of goals within the framework of traditional processes such as lobbying, electioneering, and litigation. The nonviolent direct action strategy assumes the pursuance of goals through peaceful public protests and confrontations with the political establishment or with the obstacles to one's goals. Each of these will be discussed in turn.

Reprinted from *Urban Affairs Quarterly 4*, no. 1 (September 1969): 26–38, by permission of the Publisher, Sage Publications, Inc.

The middle-class politics strategy

The best example of a Negro interest group which has utilized the middle-class politics strategy is the National Association for the Advancement of Colored People. The NAACP, the largest and oldest of the Negro political interest groups, emphasizes the legal approach, lobbying, and education. The organization operates on the assumption that the traditional channels of judicial appeals, of legislative and executive lobbying, and of informing the public are the means through which desired social change can come about.

The NAACP has utilized litigation in the federal courts to achieve race policy, in the absence of action by legislative bodies. It has made the test case the foundation of its legal strategy to bring issues to the courts "at the appropriate time and under the most propitious circumstances." [5] Moreover, the NAACP has relied upon the use of class action rather than individual action to achieve race goals. Its strategy is designed "to secure decisions, rulings, and public opinion on the broad principle instead of being devoted to merely miscellaneous cases." [6]

In recent years, the NAACP has won almost every Supreme Court case in which it has been involved.[7] Since 1941, NAACP lawyers have successfully argued at least 43 of the 47 cases in which they have appeared before the Supreme Court.[8] Among the cases they have won were those outlawing the white primary in the South, the abolition of judicial enforcement of racially restrictive covenants in housing,[9] and the barring of racial discrimination in the public schools.

At the legislative level, NAACP lobbyists have been instrumental in the enactment of fair employment practices acts in at least fifteen states and twenty-six cities,[10] the passage of the Civil Rights Acts of 1957, 1960, and 1964,[11] the Voting Rights Act of 1965, and the Civil Rights Act of 1968.

The NAACP, through its program of education and information, also claims to have brought about a greater recognition of Negro achievement, though this claim is less easy to assess.

A fourth, but usually little-noted tactic of the NAACP has been the use of pressure on the Chief Executive.[12] President Truman's Executive Order of July 26, 1948, banning racial discrimination in the armed forces, is said to have come about as a result of pressure from the NAACP and other groups.[13] The NAACP was also instrumental in getting President Kennedy to issue an Executive Order in 1961 establishing a Presidential Committee on Equal Employment Opportunity,[14] and an Executive Order in 1962 requiring equal opportunity in federally supported housing.[15]

Finally, it should be noted that implicit in the NAACP's efforts to remove obstacles from Negro voting is the belief that the ballot can pave the way for all other political and social rights. Such, at least, seems to have been the reasoning behind the Civil Rights Acts of 1957 and 1960 and the Voting Rights Act of 1965. All three of these deal primarily with the right to vote. While historically identified with judicial attacks on segregation, the NAACP is also committed to a "battle of the ballot." [16]

Whether or not the success of the NAACP alone increased the expectations of Negroes is difficult to determine. There is considerable belief, though, that the Supreme Court's decision of 1954 (in which the NAACP participated), outlawing racial segregation in the public schools, broadened the margin of Negro freedom and aspirations and thus led to increasing demands for "freedom now" in all areas of American life.[17] In response to those unhappy with the slow pace of change came individuals and groups devoted to the use of strategies designed to redistribute values more quickly. The doctrine of change through the use of the middle-class politics strategy had reached its zenith.

The nonviolent direct action strategy

Those groups utilizing the nonviolent direct action strategy are represented by the Southern Christian Leadership Conference, the Congress of Racial Equality, and the Student Nonviolent Coordinating Committee. The nonviolent direct action strategy assumes a variety of open protests and confrontations with the obstacles to integration and full citizenship, in order "to create a situation so crisis-packed that it will inevitably lead to negotiation." [18]

The first spectacular success of nonviolent direct action came in the boycott of the public transportation system in Montgomery, Alabama, under the leadership of Dr. Martin Luther King. The organization formed to coordinate the boycott was the Montgomery Improvement Association. Since Negroes constituted a majority of the regular bus users, the economic impact was effective, although the city of Montgomery steadfastly refused to change its policy of discrimination. However, on November 13, 1956, almost a year after the boycott had started, the United States Supreme Court affirmed a lower federal court's decision declaring Alabama's state and local bus segregation laws unconstitutional.[19] The strategy of direct action combined with litigation had won an important victory.

Out of the Montgomery Improvement Association grew Martin Luther King's Southern Christian Leadership Conference. Founded in 1957, the organization of Negro clergymen set as its goals the immediate achievement of full citizenship rights for Negroes and the integration of the Negro into all areas of American life. Its methods were those set out initially by Dr. King in the Montgomery bus boycott. In addition, voter registration drives were to be made to get additional Negro voting power, to augment the direct action strategy.

The general strategy of direct action, utilizing a wide variety of tactics, was taken up in a number of situations with increasingly greater results. Important impetus to the strategy was provided by a group of Negro high school and college students who, in February, 1960, inaugurated the "sit-in" tactic at lunch counters in the stores of Greensboro, North Carolina. A significant element of the strategy was the selection of stores—usually parts of nationwide corporations, thus enabling demonstrators to bring to bear important economic sanctions through sympathizers in other cities, including Northern ones. By the end of 1960, the "sit-inners" were dizzy with success; 126 cities had desegregated facilities at their lunch counters. In January, 1962, the number of "success cities" was in the neighborhood of 200.[20] The 1964 Civil Rights Bill has since opened up all public accommodations.

Interestingly enough as Louis Lomax has said: "Greensboro happened by itself; nobody planned it, nobody pulled any strings. Negro students simply got tired and sat down." [21] However, once the sit-ins began, Southern white opposition mounted and national civil rights organizations joined the fray. One of the first was the Congress of Racial Equality.

Although founded in 1943, the Congress of Racial Equality was a relatively little-known organization until the 1960 sit-ins. However, CORE has from its inception advocated the strategy of nonviolent direct action. It assumes that legalism is not a sufficient means to win race goals. After entry into the sit-in efforts, CORE played an important role in organizing, coordinating, and advising protest demonstrators. Since the sit-ins, CORE has used the tactic of "freedom rides" to achieve desegregation of interstate transportation terminal facilities. The freedom rides initiated by CORE began in the spring of 1961 and continued through the summer, after which the Interstate Commerce Commission issued a nondiscrimination order to bus companies and terminals throughout the country. The order went into effect November 1, 1961.[22] The important difference in strategy between the sit-ins and the freedom rides was that the former depended largely on the effort of *local* Negro students, whereas the latter relied mainly on "outside" help.

Despite the fact that CORE and a number of other civil rights organizations came in to assist the sit-inners, the students decided to form an organization of their own. It was their feeling that they could accomplish more if students on each college campus set up their own nonviolent protest movement under the guidance of a South-wide group. Thus, in April, 1960, the Student Nonviolent Coordinating Committee was formed.

Like CORE, SNCC feels that legalism is insufficient for the accomplishment of race goals.[23] SNCC argues that "They who would be free themselves must strike the first blow." [24] Since its beginning as a *coordinator* of protest work of student groups, SNCC has moved to *initiating* protests and has carried out voter registration projects in Mississippi. SNCC's efforts in Mississippi are seen as having brought considerably stronger federal action to protect prospective Negro voters,[25] and increasing the number of registered Negro voters.

As legal barriers to Negro participation in the South have fallen, the direct action groups have moved from a position of dealing primarily with Negro problems in the South to that of dramatizing the economic and social difficulties of Negroes everywhere in the United States. As this is written, the Southern Christian Leadership Conference is preparing a "poor folks" march on Washington, with the ambitious goal of "camping in" near the Capitol until Congress passes legislation to meet the needs of the poor, both black and white, in the country. In the case of some direct action groups, notably SNCC, the strategy of nonviolence is espoused no longer, at least by its leadership. Moreover, the use of violence to achieve race goals has been openly advocated by Stokely Carmichael, the former head of the Student Nonviolent Coordinating Committee, and H. Rap Brown, the present head of the organization. What this new turn of events may mean is yet to be decided.

The significance of the strategies

We began this paper by asserting that Negroes have developed interest groups and strategies to help win race goals. It is now important for us to show why the need for different strategies: why the middle-class politics strategy in some cases and the nonviolent direct action strategy in others. It seems appropriate, however, before we do this, to make a brief statement of how policy outcomes are achieved in the American political system.[26]

In the American scheme, powers and opportunities to act effectively on public policy, at any level of government, are parceled out to the chief executive, to the legislature, to the courts, to independent regulatory agencies, to various of the administrative bureaucracies, to the political parties, and to interest groups. In the major areas of public policy determination, they share powers.[27] Because this is so, they can achieve their ends only by cooperating with other participants in the system. To get something, participants must be able to give something. In addition, the actual ability of participants to influence policy outcomes depends not only on their resources, but the skill to use these resources as well. Values are thus allocated to those individuals and groups who are skilled in using their resources to best advantage.

Racial inequalities in political resources have long been documented.[28] The vote, however, is perhaps the largest political resource that Negroes have. The importance of this resource for Negro politics, however, assumes the viability of the middle-class politics model for the achievement of race goals.

Many observers of the American political system, most of whom accept the middle-class model of politics, have assumed that the vote will automatically give Negroes influence over public policy commensurate with their numbers in the population. Once Negroes vote in substantial numbers, they say, public officials will either respond to Negro demands or suffer at the polls. But as the plight of Northern Negroes who have long had the vote attests, the vote alone can hardly achieve race goals. The linkages between votes cast in elections and public policy outcomes are exceedingly complex, precisely because of the pluralistic nature of power and decision-making discussed above. As William R. Keech has said, "Candidates for public office will have reasons other than their own values to be reluctant to concede to Negro demands. Negroes are not the only important group of voters in the electoral environment. Candidates for office are no freer to ignore the demands and concerns of these non-Negro voters than they are to ignore those of Negroes. . . ."[29] Thus Negroes will have less influence over policy than their proportionate share of the electorate would indicate.

This is not to argue that the vote is of little or no value to Negroes. It is to say that the vote is not a guarantee *per se* for any policy output.

Negro voting does increase the probability that certain race goals will be realized, without being a sufficient condition for this to occur.

An important consideration for Negro voting strategy is how evenly divided white voters are. Where white voters are almost evenly divided, as they were in the presidential elections of 1948 [30] and 1960,[31] Negroes can hold the balance of power. To the extent that the election of candidates constitutes some sort of influence over public policy, Negro voting can be meaningful in these instances.

Another important consideration for Negro voting strategy is the formal electoral system and the residential configuration of the Negro population. Are elections at-large or by wards? Are Negroes residentially concentrated or dispersed? The former is usually an important question; the latter is not. Negro voters will have the greatest chance of influencing a candidate's election if elections are by ward. Where this is the case, Negroes are likely to slate and elect their own to public office. This is so because where there has been a poverty of Negro representation in the political system, as has been the case almost everywhere in the United States, the presence of an "ethnically relevant" candidate does not suffice; [32] only an ethnic candidate of one's own group satisfies.[33]

The election to public office of whites who are sympathetic to Negro needs, as a result of Negroes holding a balance of power, or the election of Negroes to public office as a result of Negroes having a majority in a given constituency, is only part of the vote goal. A more important question for Negro voting strategy is: Are votes translatable into public policy once elections are over? Are the elected officials and parties able devices for the redistribution of values?

Obviously, in a government of shared powers, the allocation of values according to the absolute needs of any one group is very near impossible. This is not to say that no race goals can be achieved. It is to say that goals on which there is a modicum of consensus by both whites and Negroes have a greater prospect for success than those that do not.

To be sure, the election of Negroes to the federal Congress, to state legislatures, to city councils, and, more recently, to the mayor's post in several Northern and Midwestern cities, is a significant development for the obvious reason that it places the Negro representative in the formal political framework where he can maneuver, report, and press for action. But however important formal penetration into the strategic political decision centers may be, the Negro politician's relative success in attaining race goals depends in part upon the extent of party strength among the general electorate and the amount of party control in the legislature. When the party is extremely strong in either or both cases, the Negro politician is less able to use his influence to effect civil rights policies; where the party is relatively weak, the Negro politician has a better chance. In Chicago, for example, where the Democratic party is strong and there is little interparty competition, Negro politicians have relatively little success in the pursuance of race goals; whereas in New York, where the party is weak and a great deal of interparty competition exists, Negroes have a relatively greater amount of success.[34]

While strong interparty competition is critical for Negro achievement of race goals, so is the existence of party discipline. Duane Lockard has shown that state legislation furthering Negro goals is affected by party alignments.[35] When the roll is called on key issues, such as civil rights, state legislators tend to line up by party. The extent to which party members will line up behind civil rights legislation will depend upon the degree of party discipline and accepted party position on key issues. Where there is tight party discipline, Negro politicians have only to persuade the key party leaders and the battle is almost won. In states with relatively less party discipline, party membership continues to be significant, although the lack of party discipline precludes leadership control over votes. However, party control over legislative offices and legislative schedules, plus a similarity of attitudes among party members around key issues, tends to influence policy outcomes.

Another major question for Negro voting strategy is which of the major parties serves the Negro interest best. Are both parties equally responsive to Negro aspirations? The record clearly shows that Negroes "feel" the Democratic party best serves their interest.[36] With the exception of minor defections to the Republican party in the Presidential elections of 1952 and 1956, Negroes have been solidly in the Democratic camp since 1932. Moreover, there is ample evidence to show that the Democratic party best serves the Negro interest. Duane Lockard, in a review of 30 roll calls of partisan differences in voting for civil rights legislation in eight Northern states between 1944 and 1963, "found that Democratic delegations voted 90% or more for the bills most of the time, whereas Republicans infrequently achieved high unity even where they favored the issue." [37]

A final question for Negro voting strategy is: Should Negroes place all their voting eggs in one basket or should they keep their vote "free-floating"? For the present, the answer is to be found more in the behavior of the political parties and less in the Negro voting strategy. So long as the Republican party policy offers less in the way of race needs, symbolic and material and social and economic, the "free-floating" vote strategy could not work anyway. Thus the bloc vote. On the other hand, although the Negro vote has not shown any great flexibility to date, there does seem to be some indication that it is growing more sophisticated and is prepared to move to whichever parties and candidates offer the best policies and programs commensurate with Negro needs.[38]

Precisely because the Negro vote remains largely a one-party vote and because Negroes are registered in proportionately smaller numbers than whites, due mainly to socioeconomic conditions, and because Negroes are without a considerable number of additional political resources necessary to make the voting strategy pay off, they will have a better chance of achieving some types of racial objectives by modes of attack other than the ballot box.

At present, the legal status of the Negro in the United States is almost equal to that of whites.[39] After almost a century of litigation, the Supreme Court has struck down virtually every state action segregating Negroes or discriminating against them. The actions of the United States Congress between 1957 and 1968 have legitimized and extended the governmental judgment of Negro equality. But the formal status of equality can be empty if opportunity is not fully equalized. Social inclusion of the Negro is the more difficult task remaining.

The Negro in America continues to suffer considerable cumulative disadvantage. The first problem is mainly financial. For an individual to be able to take advantage of available opportunities, he must have not only the capacity but also the financial means to do so. With about 43% of America's Negro population living in poverty, and a considerable additional number living only slightly above that level, it goes without saying that many opportunities available to Negroes will go untaken. Nothing short of a radical new economic policy can alter this fact.

The second problem concerns the underlying capacity of people, especially families, to function effectively in the environment in which they are placed. The Moynihan report of the Negro family in the ghetto makes it clear that the fabric of family relationships there has all but disintegrated, and that without family stability a large proportion of Negro youth can never learn even the basic human interaction skills necessary to cope with the environment. This problem is related to the first, in that without a radical redistribution of wealth the basis for family unity can hardly be achieved.

The third problem concerns the social exclusion of the Negro on the basis of alleged inherent inferiority. The extension of full membership to the Negro in the American community still awaits considerably more evaporation of the notion that Negroes are inherently inferior and that the American community will deteriorate if Negroes are admitted under the standards of full citizenship.

The resolution of these problems is likely to be less responsive to the middle-class politics strategy than to the nonviolent direct action strategy. Quite clearly, the middle-class politics model assumes a matrix of competing pressures, all of which must receive relatively equal recognition. It appears at this time that only the nonviolent direct action strategy can have the power to override those pressures which stand in the way of the achievement of future race goals. As James Q. Wilson has said in a comparable context, "This is not a counsel of despair but only a sobering reminder that political activity can only produce political gains and that other—and far more difficult—remedies must be sought for most problems of race relations in America." [40]

NOTES

1. For a detailed list and discussion of resources which can be translated into political power, see Robert A. Dahl, *Who Governs?: Democracy and Power in an American City* (New Haven: Yale University Press, 1961), p. 266.

2. Donald R. Matthews and James W. Prothro, *Negroes and the New Southern Politics* (New York: Harcourt, Brace & Jovanovich, 1966), p. 203.

3. The use of the term *sub-community* to refer to the Negro community is spelled out in Harry A. Bailey, Jr., ed., *Negro Politics in America* (Columbus, Ohio: Charles E. Merrill, 1967), p. 1.

4. See Everett C. Ladd, Jr., *Negro Political Leadership in the South* (Ithaca, N.Y.: Cornell University Press, 1966), pp. 164–65. The middle-class politics model is implicit in any textbook on American politics which describes how competition for scarce values goes on.

5. Abraham Haltzman, *Interest Groups and Lobbying* (New York: Macmillan, 1966), p. 137.

6. Herbert Hill and Jack Greenberg, *Citizen's Guide to Desegregation* (Boston: Beacon Press, 1955), pp. 56–57.

7. W. Haywood Burns, *The Voices of Negro Protest in America* (New York: Oxford University Press, 1963), p. 23.

8. Ibid.

9. For an interesting account of NAACP strategy in this effort, see Clement E. Vose, "NAACP Strategy in the Covenant Cases," *Western Reserve Law Review* 6 (Winter 1955): 101–45.

10. R. Joseph Monsen, Jr., and Mark W. Cannon, *The Makers of Public Policy* (New York: McGraw-Hill, 1965), p. 142.

11. For a list of backers of the 1964 Civil Rights Act, see *Legislators and the Lobbyists* (Washington: Congressional Quarterly Service, undated), p. 65.

12. See, however, Clement E. Vose, "Presidential Activism and Restraint in Orders and Proclamations on Race," paper delivered at the 52nd Annual Meeting of the Association for the Study of Negro Life and History, Greensboro, N.C., October 13, 1967. For an earlier study of pressure on the Chief Executive by a Negro political organization, see Herbert Garfinkel, *When Negroes March: The March on Washington Movement in the Organizational Politics of the FEPC* (Glencoe, Ill.: Free Press, 1959).

13. Burns, *The Voice of Negro Protest,* p. 25.

14. Executive Order No. 10925. 26 *Fed. Reg.* 1977 (1961).

15. Executive Order No. 11063. 27 *Fed. Reg.* 11527 (1962).

16. Donald R. Matthews and James W. Prothro, "Negro Registration in the South," in Allan P. Sindler, ed., *Change in the Contemporary South* (Durham, N.C.: Duke University Press, 1963), p. 121.

17. See Harmon Ziegler, *Interest Groups in American Society* (Englewood Cliffs, N. J.: Prentice-Hall, 1964), p. 224.

18. Martin Luther King, Jr., "Letter From Birmingham Jail," *Christian Century,* June 12, 1963, p. 768.

19. *Gayle* v. *Browder,* 142 F. Supp. 707 (M. D. Ala. 1956), affirmed, 352 U. S. 903 (1956).

20. Burns, *The Voice of Negro Protest,* p. 43.

21. Louis E. Lomax, *The Negro Revolt* (New York: New American Library, 1963), p. 134.

22. Constance Baker Motley, "The Legal Status of the Negro in the United States," in John P. Davis, ed., *The American Negro Reference Book* (Englewood Cliffs, N. J.: Prentice-Hall, 1966), p. 500.

23. Monsen and Cannon, *The Makers of Public Policy,* p. 145.

24. Burns, *The Voice of Negro Protest,* p. 46.

25. Ibid., pp. 58–59.

26. Our discussion of policy outcomes follows Nelson W. Polsby and Aaron B. Wildavsky, *Presidential Elections: Strategies of American Electoral Politics* (New York: Scribner's, 1964), pp. 189–90.

27. Richard E. Neustadt, *Presidential Power: The Politics of Leadership* (New York: John Wiley, 1960), pp. 33–34, remains the best statement on this point.

28. Perhaps the best and most recent documentation is that of Matthews and Prothro, *Negroes and the New Southern Politics,* esp. p. 478.

29. William R. Keech, "Some Conditions of Negro Influence over Voting Policy through

Voting," paper delivered at the 1966 Annual Meeting of the American Political Science Association, New York City, September 6–10, 1966, p. 16.

30. See R. H. Brisbane, "The Negro's Growing Political Power," *Nation* (September 27, 1952), pp. 248–49; and Oscar Glantz, "The Negro Voter in Northern Industrial Cities," in Bailey, ed., *Negro Politics in America*, pp. 338–52.

31. See Theodore H. White, *The Making of the President 1960* (New York: Pocket Books, 1961), p. 283.

32. An "ethnically relevant" candidate is a member of another ethnic group sympathetic to the aspirations of the Negro, or a white liberal who is seen not as one of his own, but in opposition to his own. See Harry Holloway and David Olson, "Electoral Participation by White and Negro in a Southern City," *Midwest Journal of Political Science* 10 (February 1966): 115.

33. James Q. Wilson, "How the Northern Negro Uses His Vote," *The Reporter,* March 31, 1960, p. 20.

34. See James W. Wilson, "Two Negro Politicians: An Interpretation," in Bailey, ed., *Negro Politics in America*, pp. 144–62.

35. Our discussion of the place of party in the achievement of race goals relies heavily on Duane Lockard, *Toward Equal Opportunity: A Study of State and Local Antidiscrimination Laws* (New York: Macmillan, 1968), pp. 46–49.

36. For a summary of some of the evidence, see Glantz in Bailey, ed., *Negro Politics in America*, pp. 338–52. The only qualification to this argument is that Southern Negroes are not as firmly committed as are Northern Negroes to the Democratic Party. See James Q. Wilson, "The Negro in American Politics: The Present," in Davis, ed., *The American Negro Reference Book*, p. 441.

37. Lockard, *Toward Equal Opportunity*, p. 47. The "Northern" states are California, Connecticut, Massachusetts, Minnesota, New York, Ohio, Pennsylvania, and Rhode Island.

38. A case in point is Henry Lee Moon's analysis of the Negro vote in the 1956 Presidential election. See his "The Negro Vote in Presidential Election of 1956," in Bailey, ed., *Negro Politics in America*, pp. 353–65.

39. For a review of the evidence, see Motley, "The Legal Status of the Negro . . .," pp. 484–521.

40. James Q. Wilson, "The Negro in American Politics," p. 457. To be sure, Wilson limits "political activity" to what we have called the middle-class politics model. For the evidence, see his "The Negro in Politics" in *Daedalus* 44 (Fall 1965): 949. We, however, place the direct action model within the pale of politics, since politics is, for us, any activity by which conflict over goals is carried on. The "far more difficult remedy" is, for us, then, the nonviolent direct action model.

THE NON-VIOLENT RESISTANCE MOVEMENT
AGAINST SEGREGATION

James W. Vander Zanden

"Passive" or "non-violent resistance" has become a major weapon in the arsenal of the Negro movement against segregation.[1] A dramatic and spectacular tactic, it found its first large-scale employment in a movement launched in late 1955 against segregation on city buses by Negroes in Montgomery, Alabama. The success of the Montgomery movement established passive resistance as a key weapon in desegregation efforts, and projected upon the national horizon a new group of militant Negro leaders represented by Rev. Martin Luther King, Jr. The movement places great stress upon non-violent means such as boycotts and sit-ins, and non-violent reactions in the face of attack.

Non-violent resistance is a tactic well suited to struggles in which a minority lacks access to major sources of power within a society and to the instruments of violent coercion. The stratification structure and the functional division of labor of a society are so constituted that a minority group undertaking "non-co-operation," the withholding of its participation from certain essential areas of life, can exert considerable pressure upon the dominant group and extract concessions from them. By the same token, non-violent resistance is less likely to bring direct retaliation from the dominant group than are tactics employing more directly aggressive forms of expression. Moreover, within the South, the mass character of the movement has posed particular difficulties to whites who would undertake to punish the participants, for example, the relative infeasibility of mass imprisonments. During the past two decades vast social changes within the South have contributed to a redefinition of lynching as illegitimate. Simultaneously, within the larger American society, the Negroes' tactic of non-violent resistance has gained a considerable degree of legitimacy.

Prior to 1954, the predominant response of southern Negroes to their minority status was that of accommodation. Within the past decade, however, a number of forces have made southern Negroes susceptible to a protest or militant approach to racial segregation. A number of factors played an especially important role. First, a new definition of the Negro's position within the United States, especially within the South, has come sharply and forcefully to the foreground. The net effect of the 1954 Supreme Court decision against mandatory school segregation was that it advanced, in an authoritative, formal, and official fashion, a definition of the Negro as a first-class citizen. This decision overturned the "separate but equal" doctrine formulated in 1896 in *Plessy v. Ferguson,* which relegated the Negro to second-class citizenship and which, within the

From the *American Journal of Sociology* 68 (March 1963): 544–50; reprinted by permission of the author and publisher; copyright © 1963 by the University of Chicago.

South, gave legal sanction to the Negro's castelike position of stigmatized inferiority, subordination, and segregation.

The Supreme Court's action was closely associated with another factor, the emergence of the new nations of Africa. With the breakup of the old colonial empires, the world was no longer "a white man's world." On the international scene, the new Negro nations were defined, at least in theory, as the equals of the white nations (for example, within the United Nations). The Supreme Court's antisegregation decisions and the emergence of the African nations created a new self-image for many Negroes in which accommodation to Jim Crow no longer could be an acceptable response to the enduring and aggravated frustrations of the racial order.

Accompanying these developments is the growing awareness among southern Negroes that the Jim Crow structure is not a final and inevitable reality, and that antisegregation efforts offer the promise of success. Although the nation had for decades been more or less willing to allow the South a measure of sovereignty on the race issue, it has become increasingly unwilling to do so since World War II. There has been a growing insistence, reinforced by international pressures, that the racial norms of the South give way to the democratic norms of the American Creed. The Supreme Court's antisegregation rulings have been both a factor contributing to, and a product of, this sentiment. Even more important, the decisions of the Supreme Court reversed the racial situation within the United States: where segregation had previously enjoyed the highest legal sanction, mandatory segregation was now declared unconstitutional. Hence, the machinery and resources of the federal government became decisively committed for the first time since Reconstruction to an antisegregation program. Where previously there had been widespread despair and hopelessness among southern Negroes and resignation to the Jim Crow order, now the situation was progressively defined as one that could be altered. Where the "road to a better life" had appeared as an endless maze, with a mammoth white wall at every turn, now the Negro enjoyed potent white allies in any antisegregation movement. Sentiments and attitudes that had reinforced a pattern of accommodation have been increasingly undermined, contributing to the emergence of a protest pattern.

These changes have caused the great masses of southern Negroes to be caught up between two contradictory ways of life, the old one of second-class, the new one of first-class citizenship. Negro status is in a state of flux, lacking clarity and precise definition. The normative guideposts defining the Negro's position are in conflict between traditional patterns and the new patterns of racial equality. The white South itself is uncertain as to the "Negro's place." Where once there was a well-defined definition of the Negro's role, now that definition is in transition.

Although responses of overt, unaggressive accommodation to the racial structure generally prevailed among southern Negroes prior to 1954, various investigators noted that southern Negroes harbored considerable covert or latent aggressive impulses toward whites.[2] These feelings of latent hostility and aggression were not always manifest or conscious. From her psychiatric treatment of Negroes, McLean observed: "The intense fear of the white man with its consequent hostility and guilt may not be conscious in the Negro, but from my own psycho-analytic experience in treating Negro men and women, *I have yet to see a Negro who did not unconsciously have a deep fear of and hostility toward white people.*" [3] Karon, in a study of Negro personality characteristics in a northern and a southern city, concluded that Negroes in the South develop strong mechanisms of denial with respect to aggression, not only with respect to the race situation but to the whole of life. Compared with the Negroes in the northern city, the southern Negroes were characterized by a higher incidence in the number of people whose whole emotional life was colored by the struggle not to be angry.[4]

Within this setting, a program of non-violent resistance to segregation offered a strong psychological appeal (in addition to its already-noted suitability as a tactic). On the one hand, there exist among Negroes considerable undercurrents of resentment toward whites and the southern racial structure. On the other hand, Negroes have been socialized generally in a tradition calling for the suppression of hostility and aggression toward whites, and also in a religious tradition stressing Christian love and tabooing hatred. Many Negroes have taken very literally the Christian doctrine that it is sinful to hate. Yet, they are placed in race situations in which hostility is an inevitable product; life confronts Negroes with circumstances that constantly stimulate aggressive thoughts and fantasies that are defined as sinful.[5]

The matter is compounded by widespread Negro feelings of self-hatred.[6] Within many minority groups there exist strong tendencies to accept the dominant group's evaluations and conceptions of the minority.[7] By virtue of his membership in the Negro group, the Negro suffers considerably in terms of self-esteem and has every incentive for self-hatred. In many respects, even good performance is irrelevant insofar as the Negro frequently gets a poor reflection of himself in the behavior of whites, regardless of what he does or what his merits are. Identified by society as a Negro, he, of necessity, so identifies himself. To compensate for this low self-esteem, the Negro identifies in part with whites and white values; for example, the success of the Negro cosmetic industry rests, in large measure, upon the considerable demand for skin bleaches and hair straighteners.[8] Hostility toward whites and simultaneous self-hatred and identification with whites are likely to intensify the internal turbulence which seeks for resolution.

Rev. Martin Luther King, Jr., has given articulate and forceful expression to these crosscurrents (the feelings of hostility toward whites on the one hand, and the dictates requiring suppression of these impulses on the other), and has posed a solution to the dilemma. He has told Negroes that they have long been abused, insulted, and mistreated, that they have been "kicked about by the brutal feet of oppression." In essence, he has repeatedly told his Negro audiences, using such veiled euphemisms as "protest," that it is permissible and legitimate for them to feel hostility and to engage in aggressive activities against the existing racial order.[9] In fact, an important theme in his speeches has been that Negroes have "a moral obligation" to fight segregation: "To accept passively an unjust system is to cooperate with that system; thereby the oppressed become as evil as the oppressor. Noncooperation with evil is as much a moral obligation as is cooperation with good." [10] He has thus defined the traditional pattern of acceptance and resignation as immoral.

Simultaneously, King and his followers have paid extensive homage to non-hatred, to Christian love: "Love must be our regulating ideal. Once again we must hear the words of Jesus echoing across the centuries: 'Love your enemies, bless them that curse you, and pray for them that despitefully use you.' " [11] In essence, King's message to Negroes has been that they can have their cake and eat it too; that they can "hate," but that really it is not animosity but "love." He has aided Negroes to redefine as moral and acceptable what otherwise would be defined as immoral and unacceptable. This is not to suggest hypocrisy; rather, it is an example of the facility with which humans can rationalize and legitimatize feelings, attitudes, and behavior that might otherwise be a source of emotional distress to them.

An incident at a Knoxville rally in support of the "Stay Away from Downtown" movement (part of the campaign to win the desegregation of that city's lunch counters) is illustrative. After a number of bitter, biting, and militant speeches, the chairman of the meeting came back to the microphone and reassuringly indicated, "We're making a lot of noise, but that doesn't mean we're angry at anybody. If you have no love in your heart, stay at home. Why, even Jack Leflore's got it now, a little bit!" [12] The assembled Negroes were permitted to vent their hostility but then, fittingly enough, were comforted, "We're really not angry." Further relief from the tension was provided by the good-natured ribbing of one of the community's Negroes.

The King appeal attempts to mediate between the conflicting traditions, of the accommodating Negro and the militant Negro. Ambiguously immersed within conflicting roles, the appeal looks in both directions, toward the suppression of hostility (the traditional approach), and toward its expression in a militantly aggressive social movement. Although such activities may be labeled "passive resistance," in reality they constitute what psychologists refer to as "passive aggression." Their net result is to challenge, to aggress against, existing patterns (and by implication the people who adhere to such patterns, e.g., the boycotted white merchants).

Yet as is so frequently the case rationalizations are not always completely successful in handling impulses defined as unacceptable. Bitterness, resentment, and hostility cannot be dispensed with so simply; protestations of love cannot totally veil aggressive impulses. The consequence is a wide prevalence of deep and disturbing guilt feelings. King has noted this in his own experience. Referring to his encounters with bus and city officials, he writes: "I was weighted down by a terrible sense of guilt, remembering that on two or three occasions I had allowed myself to become angry and indignant. I had spoken hastily and resentfully, yet I knew that this was no way to solve a problem. 'You must not harbor anger,' I admonished myself. 'You must be willing to suffer the anger of the opponent, and yet not return anger. You must not become bitter. . . .' " [13]

Prevailing guilt feelings caused by aggressive and hostile impulses seek satisfaction in the need for punishment. This probably accounts, in part, for the considerable premium assigned by the non-violent resistance movement to suffering. In fact, the endurance of suffering and the "turn the other cheek" orientation have become exalted in their own right. King declares: "We will match your capacity [referring to whites] to inflict suffering with our capacity to endure suffering. We will meet your physical force with soul force. . . . Do to us what you will and we will still love you. . . . But we will soon wear you down by our capacity to suffer." [14] And "The non-violent say that suffering becomes a powerful social force when you willingly accept that violence on yourself, so that *self-suffering stands at the center* of the non-violent movement and the individuals involved are able to suffer in a creative manner, feeling that unearned suffering is redemptive, and that suffering may serve to transform the social situation." [15]

Similarly, it is not unusual to hear the movement's activists express their willingness to die for their cause, to suffer the severest form of punishment, a martyr's death. King, indicating his "personal sense of guilt for everything that was happening" as a result of the bus boycott (e.g., the violence that had ensued), explains that he "broke down" in a public meeting and then "in the grip of an emotion I could not control," exclaimed, "Lord, I hope no one will have to die as a result of our struggle for freedom in Montgomery. Certainly I don't want to die. But if anyone has to die, let it be me." [16] At times it appears that some members of the movement engage in subtle provocations, in a masochistic-like fashion, whereby they expect to bring about pain and degradation; they offer their "cheek" with the prospect of receiving a slap.

The emphasis upon suffering has still another source. Christianity teaches that voluntary submission to sacrifice, privation, and the renunciation of gratification are preconditions for the attainment of the prospective goal, eternal happiness. Life is viewed as a brief period of affliction, to be replaced by eternal bliss for the righteous. The death of Christ upon the cross, the Savior's suffering, was the means by which the gates of paradise were opened.[17] Within this religious heritage, it is not difficult to make the attainment of an improved earthly future also contingent upon suffering. Suffering, and often merely its anticipation, clears the path to the fulfilment of otherwise forbidden values, the good life in which Negroes will enjoy a better future on earth. It is the Gandhian mandate that "Things of fundamental importance to people are not secured by reason alone, but have to be *purchased* with their *suffering.*" The principle is seen in this illustration:

> Once a pool driver [Montgomery Negroes established a car pool during the period of the bus boycott] stopped beside an elderly woman who was trudging along with obvious difficulty.
> "Jump in, grandmother," he said. "You don't need to walk."
> She waved him on. "I'm not walking for myself," she explained. "I'm walking for my children and my grandchildren." And she continued toward home on foot.[18]

Developments on the national and international scene have sharply posed the issue of the Negro's status within America. Within the context of these many crosscurrents, suffering provides a source by which Negroes may increase their self-esteem: First, one can appear uncommonly noble, gentle, and heroic through suffering and sacrificing one's own comfort and well-being for a cause. Second, suffering enables the Negro to feel that "we are after all the better men," "better" in the moral and spiritual sense. Christianity teaches that "He that humbleth himself shall be exalted" and "Blessed are the meek for they shall inherit the earth." Negroes can find a considerable sense of self-worth in these teachings, for "after all, we are the better Christians; in God's eyes we are honored." King indicates: "Since the white man's personality is greatly distorted by segregation, and his soul is greatly scarred, he needs the love of the Negro. The Negro must love the white man, because the white man needs his love to remove his tensions, insecurities, and fears." [19] Third, Negroes can enjoy the idea that they will finally triumph, that they will conquer their enemies. They can gain considerable satisfaction in the fantasy that the very society that neglects and rejects them now will see its sinful ways and repent. There is an inner expectancy and foreknowledge of coming victory.[20] Then "the last shall be first." Here again this sentiment finds frequent expression in King's speeches: "Before the victory is won some may have to get scarred up, but we shall overcome. Before the victory of brotherhood is achieved, some will maybe face physical death, but we shall overcome . . . behind the dim unknown standeth God within the shadows, keeping watch above His own. With this faith in the future, with this determined struggle, we will be able to emerge from the bleak and desolate midnight of man's inhumanity to man, into the bright and glittering daybreak of freedom and justice." [21]

A social movement as such offers certain rewards to a people weighed down by a sense of inferiority, powerlessness, and insignificance. In fusing oneself with a social movement external to the self, one can acquire the strength which the individual self lacks by becoming part of a bigger and more powerful whole. In so doing the individual may lose some of his personal integrity as well as some of his freedom, but he can also gain a new sense of strength and significance.[22] In this connection, one is struck by the intense exaltation and glorification of the leadership of the non-violent movement by the rank and file, by its messianic character. Although mass meetings are frequently held during which the audience votes on various matters, their action is little more than a rubber stamp for the decisions made by the leadership and presented for perfunctory approval.[23] By the same token, a social movement helps to answer the question, "Who am I?" for a people whose social role is ambiguous and undergoing change.

The non-violent resistance to segregation has an assimilationist orientation in which Negroes aim to gain total acceptance and equality within American society. Should the movement fail to make what its members perceive and define to be satisfactory progress toward this goal, it is conceivable that movements of black nationalism, such as the "Black

Muslims" (the Nation of Islam led by Elijah Muhammad), may gain ascendency among southern Negroes. At present these separatist movements operate primarily among the Negro lower classes of northern cities. E. U. Essien-Udom suggests that these Negroes are estranged from the larger society that they seek to enter, a society that rejects them, while simultaneously they are estranged from their own group which they despise. Black nationalism provides a response to this dual alienation, rootlessness, and restlessness.[24]

Whereas the South, until recently, rather formally and rigorously defined the position of the Negro within the region, the North did not do likewise. Within northern cities, Negroes, at least in theory, were the equals of whites, although in practice this was frequently not the case. Accordingly, it is understandable that many northern Negroes, especially among the lower socioeconomic groups, should become disillusioned and that they should turn their backs on integration for separatism. However, southern Negroes generally have not lost faith in the feasibility of the assimilationist approach; it has still to be tried. Furthermore, there is evidence that within the North the Negro church has lost its significance for many urban Negroes who seek to define their situation within religious terms.[25] This has not been the case within the South. A new group of Negro religious leaders, as represented by Rev. Martin Luther King, Jr., have undertaken to help the southern Negro define his situation within the terms of the church.

NOTES

1. From 1954 to 1956 the author taught at an accredited Negro college with an interracial faculty in a Deep South state. By virtue of this position he was able to move rather freely within the Negro community. The interpretation advanced within this paper in large measure rests upon the observations made from this vantage point.

2. John Dollard, *Caste and Class in a Southern Town* (3d ed.; New York: Doubleday, 1957), p. 252; Abram Kardiner and Lionel Ovesey, *The Mark of Oppression* (New York: Norton, 1951), p. 342; Guy B. Johnson, "Patterns of Race Conflict," in Edgar T. Thompson, ed., *Race Relations and the Race Problem* (Durham, N.C.: Duke University Press, 1939), p. 126; Bertram P. Karon, *The Negro Personality* (New York: Springer Publishing Co., 1958), pp. 165–67; Helen V. McLean, "The Emotional Health of Negroes," *Journal of Negro Education* 18 (1949): 286; and Hortense Powdermaker, "The Channeling of Negro Aggression by the Cultural Process," in Clyde Kluckhohn and Henry A. Murray, eds., *Personality* (2d ed.; New York: Knopf, 1956), pp. 602–3.

3. McLean, "The Emotional Health of Negroes," p. 286. My italics.

4. Karon, *The Negro Personality*, pp. 165–67.

5. Powdermaker "The Channeling of Negro Aggression . . .," pp. 602–3.

6. See Kardiner and Ovesey, *The Mark of Oppression*, p. 297; Kenneth B. Clark and Mamie P. Clark, "Racial Identification and Preference in Negro Children," in Theodore M. Newcomb and E. L. Hartley, eds., *Readings in Social Psychology* (New York: Holt, 1947), pp. 169–78; Robert Johnson, "Negro Reactions to Minority Group Status," in Milton L. Barron, ed., *American Minorities* (New York: Knopf,

1957), p. 205; Charles S. Johnson, *Growing Up in the Black Belt* (Washington, D.C.: American Council on Education, 1941), p. 259; and E. Franklin Frazier, *Negro Youth at the Crossways* (Washington, D.C.: American Council on Education, 1940), p. 180.

7. Kurt Lewin, *Resolving Social Conflicts* (New York: Harper & Row, 1948), pp. 186–200.

8. For a discussion on Negro incorporation and distortion of white middle-class values see E. Franklin Frazier, *Black Bourgeoisie* (Glencoe, Ill.: Free Press, 1957).

9. There is reason to believe that Rev. Martin Luther King, Jr., himself, harbors considerable animosity toward whites; see Martin Luther King, Jr., *Stride toward Freedom* (New York: Ballantine Books, 1958), pp. 71, 97, and 112.

10. Ibid., p. 173.

11. Ibid., p. 51.

12. Merrill Proudfoot, *Diary of a Sit-In* (Chapel Hill: University of North Carolina Press, 1962), p. 118.

13. King, *Stride Toward Freedom*, p. 97.

14. Ibid., p. 117.

15. King, "Love, Law and Civil Disobedience," *New South* 16 (December 1961): 6. My italics.

16. King, *Stride toward Freedom*, p. 143.

17. In this connection see Theodor Reik, *Masochism in Modern Man* (New York: Grove Press, 1941), pp. 319, 341–42, 428, 430–33.

18. King, *Stride toward Freedom*, p. 61.

19. Ibid., p. 84.

20. See Reik, *Masochism in Modern Man*, pp. 319–22, 430–33.

21. King, "Love, Law and Civil Disobedience," pp. 10–11.

22. See Erich Fromm, *Escape from Freedom* (New York: Rinehart & Co., 1941), pp. 141, 151–56.

23. See Jacqueline Mary Johnson Clarke, "Goals and Techniques in Three Negro Civil-Rights Organizations in Alabama" (Doctoral dissertation, Ohio State University, 1960).

24. E. U. Essien-Udom, *Black Nationalism: A Search for an Identity in America* (Chicago: University of Chicago Press, 1962).

25. Ibid., pp. 331–32.

THE SOUTHERN STUDENT SIT-INS: INTRA-GROUP RELATIONS AND COMMUNITY CONFLICT

Martin Oppenheimer

The sociology of conflict encompasses several traditions. There are those who have been interested primarily in intra-group conflict from the angle of control, or power;[1] others have put their emphasis on the field of community relations and inter-group conflict;[2] and overlapping both is the field of sociometry and the study of small groups.[3] While much of the historical background in this field comes from the work of German sociologists such as Georg Simmel,[4] it was only recently that an American sociologist, Lewis Coser, managed to bring these emphases together. Coser, in *The Functions of Social Conflict*,[5] brought in also the work of psychologists, including Freud, and derived from this synthesis a series of propositions which analyze social conflict from a functional standpoint.

From the works of Coser and others, it would appear that there are some rules which enable groups following them, even though not consciously, to succeed in attaining their goals. In other words, some activities by groups engaged in community conflict are functional to the attainment of goals, while others are dysfunctional.

It should be possible, therefore, to identify these rules from the existing literature, and, in the light of a specific community conflict situation, see if they are pragmatically useful in making predictions and in working out solutions. The conflict situation which has been chosen as a test is the Southern Student Sit-In Movement of 1960.[6] The paper will be divided into a general discussion of the internal relationships of parties involved in conflict situations, and the interactive relationships of contending groups in conflict situations and the conditions of conducting and settling a conflict.

INTERNAL RELATIONSHIPS

It has long been an axiom in the field of race and ethnic minority relations that the internal cohesion (or ingroup identification, or morale) of a group is heightened by hostility from the outside. Coser and other recent writers suggest, in addition, that for successful conduct of a conflict, there must also be a consensus within the group as to how to carry out that conflict. In addition, the morale of participants can be heightened by conducting the conflict in terms of some super-individual goals, such as an appeal to religion or other values. But while on the one hand a consensus, a sense of group identification, and an ideology are needed,

From *Phylon: The Atlanta University Review of Race and Culture*, 27 (Spring 1966): 20–26; reprinted by permission of the author and publisher.

on the other hand the more totally an individual participates in a group (in terms of involving his personality and dedicating himself to the purposes of the group) the more tensions tend to arise; hence mechanisms must be supplied to get rid of these tensions in a constructive rather than a destructive way if the group is to survive.

A sit-in protest group, and for that matter any group confronting great physical danger in a subordinate status in the society, in fact involves a good deal of an individual's personality. To be successful, the group must be cohesive and well-organized. The "self-image" of the participant is involved in everything the group does. Within the social context, which to begin with is one of frustration, a great deal of aggressive energy, or hostility, accumulates. This frustration is increased by the negative response of the dominant power structure—in the form of refusal of service at a lunch counter, etc., and is accompanied by great hostility by white persons in the area; the participant cannot give way to his pent-up frustrations, hostilities, and aggressions in physical or vocal acts of violence, because his tactics and strategy are based on nonviolence. The result is that hostility tends to turn inward, either upon the participant himself, and/or upon his group. Unless measures are taken to provide a channel for this aggression, the individual may be rendered useless rapidly by his feelings in the situation (a kind of battle-fatigue which has been observed in the race relations field) and the group broken up under the strain.

Three devices have been observed which to one degree or another appear to release just such tensions: singing, joking, and the workshop. What cannot be said in words is said in music, not only to the white opponents, but to other persons within the group, or to institutions and ideas which must be criticized, but without creating the appearance of division. Song inspires morale and group identification by expressing the group's ideology as it is universally perceived by the participants. It unifies the group in a stressful situation and permits release of emotions which have been pent up in circumstances of conflict where emotions, particularly of the violent kind, cannot be permitted. Thus the songs of the sit-in movement have become an integral part of the image of civil rights in this country.

Joking, or humor, has long been recognized as an indirect way of expressing hostility towards an object. Political jokes in totalitarian countries are only one example of this, for jokes, like song, permit one to drain off hostilities without the danger of direct confrontation. There are now dozens of jokes which had their origin in the sit-in demonstrations, altogether aside from the more standard jokes of the Negro community. And a series of Negro comedians has risen to fame because of a certain brand of humor that pokes fun at Negroes and white liberals alike. The sociological and psychological function of this kind of humor is not hard to uncover if one has any close acquaintance with the Negro community and its behavior patterns.

The workshop is probably the most formal device associated with tension-releasing mechanisms. This was initially associated with the Congress of Racial Equality, which has been experimenting with it since the early 1940's, and is now inseparable from nonviolent direct action campaigns. The workshop is essentially a socio-drama in which the participants, Negro students planning an action, play a variety of roles, including white parts. On the surface this merely serves to prepare the students emotionally for what to expect—and, in the case of violence, how to react. It is seen, in the main, as simply practice in the perfection of control of oneself in stress situations. One latent function of the workshop is as a morale-builder. The students who go into a conflict situation after the socio-drama are not only better prepared emotionally to deal with violence in nonviolent ways, but also know each other, hence trust each other, and know what the group's code of behavior is. They tend to be loyal to the buddies with whom they have been trained, and to their values. As *The American Soldier* series pointed out, in a combat situation loyalty to one's buddies is often more important to success than hatred of the opponent or knowledge of the reason for the battle.[7]

In the workshop itself, intense feeling is invested in the roles being played, and much latent hostility is released. Negro students play roles of white policemen, store managers, university administrators, etc., with quite a depth of understanding. They imitate the actions of hoodlums with a vehemence which actually calls forth violent reaction from Negroes playing the roles of Negro students, even though the actors are their own peer-group associates. Words are thrown about as if the actor had been waiting all his life for a chance to use the words as others have used them in relation to himself. But, solidified by the exclusiveness of membership in a group which has undergone treatment somewhat akin, one supposes, to fraternity hazing, and having drained off latent hostility through play-acting, the group goes forth to function more positively in terms of its goals.

INTERACTIVE RELATIONSHIPS

Conflict between groups is frequently unrecognized. That is, the absence of conflict does not mean there is an absence of hostility. In fact, the longer hostility remains suppressed, the more violent it tends to be once it does break out into the open, as in the case of civil rights. But before hostility can come out, a channel of relationship between the conflicting groups must be present. In a sense, therefore, the act of conflict already presupposes progress towards communication between the contending groups, because, at the very minimum, a common field of action is created, underneath which there sometimes lie common values or goals.

Once conflict has broken out, new relationships are constantly being created between the groups involved. Conflict not only presupposes some agreement as to the rules, but is in addition often a necessary prerequisite to finding out, realistically, what the opponent's strength is, which in turn is a prerequisite to realistic negotiations. Hence conflict can perform a positive function on the road to settlement of a dispute.

A problem, however, is generated by the fact that as the group under attack becomes aware of itself as a group (self-identification) and takes countermeasures, the opposing group also enhances its self-image, takes countermeasures, and so on. Thus the organization of counteractive moves (specifically the founding of the Citizens Councils) on the part of segregationist elements immediately after the Supreme Court decision of 1954 served to make Negroes more aware of their identity, which in turn served to increase the resistance of some white groups, which in turn increased the militancy of Negro groups, etc.

These two elements in the conflict situation are of different weights, depending on circumstances, and play varying roles, which can be decisive in whether or not a settlement takes place. Obviously, "reconciliation will presumably be easier if reconciliation itself is highly valued as a process by the contending parties." [8] The key to an understanding of these two elements in the conflict situation is the degree of reality with which the contending forces approach each other. Realistic perception of the strength of the opposing party is difficult if that perception is clouded by preconceptions inherited from the past. In case after case, the white community leadership in the South has been unable to recognize the seriousness of civil rights movement efforts. Only when students demonstrated their staying power after the initial, and sometimes following, rounds of negotiations had failed, did merchants and city officials begin to realize the real strength of the opposition, and, in the light of a new and realistic appraisal, come to terms.

A significant factor determining the degree of resistance to a realistic appraisal—one might say the reality-testing level—in any community seems to be the relative sizes of the dominant and subordinate groups.[9] Where the white group is dominant and the Negro group is large (say, 35 percent of the population or more) but subordinate, the white group tends to regard the protest activity of Negroes as endangering the white status quo altogether and tends to resist despite risks to business and commercial activity. Where the Negro group is small, protests by Negroes are not a real threat to the total white status, power, and leadership structures. Since such communities historically also tend to be more commercially oriented, it becomes far more probable that a common acceptance of aims can be reached, aims which will stop trouble and which will give some measure of relief to the Negro group. In the former case, compromise is emotionally impossible; in the latter, it is acceptable. Willingness to create a normal situation, one in which business can be conducted as usual, or nearly so, is more likely when compromise is emotionally acceptable, and when some mechanism for negotiation such as a bi-racial committee is available in addition. As Boulding points out,

> . . . when there are no institutions for procedural conflict, violence is likely to result . . . violence in itself prevents the conflicts from being resolved and indeed perpetuates them. . . . [Violence] creates an atmosphere in which reconciliation is difficult. . . . It likewise makes compromise difficult.[10]

Once the hostility between groups on the community level has come to the surface and conflict has broken out, a series of unfolding stages can be identified, varying somewhat with some of the conditions described above. First, there is an incipient stage, characterized by a good deal of spontaneity and lack of formal mechanisms of control or organization on either side. Both the attacking and defending groups are unorganized and unfamiliar with the strengths and weaknesses of the other. Reactions tend to be swift and uncontrolled, unplanned, and not thought through. This is the stage of the first demonstration, the early growth of the protest organization, and the relatively unplanned reaction to it by the police, by managers of stores and by other officials and vigilante groups.

Then comes a counteractive phase, which is characterized by the formation of a consensus by the white power structure on tactics of dealing with the demonstrations. Here patterns begin to develop for both sides, and the Negroes become formalized and structured in their organizations. Further training to cope with the counteraction of the whites takes place in the ranks of the Negroes. Store managers move to end the dispute without changing existing patterns of segregation. At the close of this phase, in part due to a failure of the contending forces to come to full-scale grips with each other, the dominant power structure offers to negotiate, or accepts student offers to negotiate, at the price of calling a halt to demonstrations.

Third is a stage of detente, stoppage of action, or "cooling-off period," during which there is no action but the opponents engage in negotiations and size up each other. The student movement gradually comes to the realization that it has misapprehended the purpose of the negotiation and underestimated the staying power of the local power structure. Some become impatient and call for immediate resumption of direct action; others advocate this also, but for a different reason—they realize that further delay will undermine the faith of the rank-and-file in themselves and in their leaders. The end of this phase is often marked by handing to the store managers a deadline or ultimatum naming a date for the resumption of action.

There are situations, however, where no detente ever takes place. Sometimes the dominant group is so prepared to use violence, despite its consequences to the community, that no common ground for negotiation can be reached. In fact, it appears that the greater the amount of violence utilized by the dominant group, the less likely it is that any subsequent stage will take place at all. Where, for various historical reasons, resistance to integration is small, the conflict will tend to follow through a normal series of stages until an agreement is achieved; where there is greater resistance (usually in areas with high proportions of Negro population) the movement for integration will bog down in earlier stages, possibly even being totally suppressed during the incipient stage.

Assuming a normal development, a reorganizational stage follows the detente. Both sides retrench for a long struggle. Negro students enlist new numbers in their campaign, train them, obtain legal assistance, sit-in and picket, make liaison with the Negro community, whose aid is obtained for auxiliary action such as boycotts and selective buying campaigns. White merchants and city officials make arrests, obtain anti-picketing ordinances and injunctions, and urge various compromises at the negotiating table. The economic boycott becomes a serious factor during this stage.

A show-down phase concludes the development. Basically, this is the final test of nerve for both sides in the controversy. If the white community is prepared to utilize violence on a large scale, it can still dominate the situation and crush the civil rights organizations at this point. Or, the white leadership may split, enabling the students to settle with some, who obtain a competitive advantage commercially. More commonly, merchants await the coming of summer in the hope that the departure of local college students will take the steam out of the campaign. Meanwhile, however, as a side effect of the detente stage, there now exists a mechanism for settlement: the negotiating group, or the interracial commission. The merchants, weakened by a continuing boycott by the adult Negro community which does not stop during the summer, finally surrender to the interracial committee, which quietly and without publicity arranges a truce with Negro leaders and provides tests on a predetermined date for the newly integrated facilities.

These stages can be seen functionally as performing two tasks: (1) they create a changing and new set of relationships among the contending forces, including the centralization of command on both sides so that negotiation and mediation can take place if white resistance is not too severe; and (2) they enable the parties to gauge the strengths of each other as a prerequisite to realistic negotiations.

Thus a sociological and historical investigation of contemporary protest activities on the community level illustrates a host of concepts which have been in literature for some years. The positive functions of conflict, the functioning of a group for survival, how ecology affects social action, and the life cycles of local movements are only a few of the many phenomena illuminated by the events of the day. The civil rights movement is a veritable mine for sociological investigation, one which remains relatively unexplored some six years after the outbreak of the sit-ins in Greensboro, North Carolina.[11]

NOTES

1. For example, the work of Pareto, Mosca, Michels, Selznick.
2. Robin M. Williams, Jr., *The Reduction of Intergroup Tensions* (New York, 1947) and other studies in the field of prejudice analysis.
3. K. Lewin, Bales, Borgatta, Hare, Homans, Moreno, Mayo and many others. See especially the recent work by Kenneth E. Boulding, *Conflict and Defense* (New York, 1962).
4. Georg Simmel, *Conflict* (Glencoe, Illinois, 1955) and Theodore Abel, *Systematic Sociology in Germany,* (New York, 1929).
5. (Glencoe, Illinois, 1956). Lewis Killian and Charles Grigg, *Racial Crisis in America* (Englewood Cliffs, N.J., 1964), closely follow this orientation.
6. See also Martin Oppenheimer, *The Genesis of the Southern Negro Student Movement (Sit-In Movement): A Study in Contemporary Negro Protest* (Doctoral dis-

sertation, University of Pennsylvania, 1963). Data are based on study of some 70 communities involved in sit-in activity during 1960 and 1961.

7. S. A. Stouffer et al., *The American Soldier: Adjustment during Army Life* (Princeton, N.J.: Princeton University Press, 1949).

8. Boulding, *Conflict and Defense,* p. 312.

9. An exception to this rule is large urban centers. See Oppenheimer, *The Genesis of the Southern Negro Student Movement.*

10. Boulding, *Conflict and Defense,* p. 323.

11. A revised version of this paper was read at the meeting of the American Sociological Association, Chicago, August 31, 1965. For a more detailed discussion of the "Workshop" and of specific tactics used in conflict situations by both nonviolent civil rights groups and law enforcement agencies, see Martin Oppenheimer and George Lakey, *A Manual for Direct Action* (Chicago, 1965).

THE BOYCOTT: A NEGRO COMMUNITY IN CONFLICT

William M. Phillips, Jr.

On Thursday evening, March 24, 1960, the following bulletin was carried on the front page of the only city daily newspaper:

> The Pine Bluff branch of the National Association for the Advancement of Colored People has announced a boycott of all chain variety stores operating segregated lunch counters.

This announced policy and proposed action by an organization purporting to represent the Negro community was considered to be inseparable from the all-pervasive attempt of the Negro in America to diminish intergroup antipathy, discrimination, segregation, and prejudice. Moreover, it was viewed specifically as part and parcel of the attempt, particularly for the Negro of the South, to accelerate the attainment of a more democratic way of life in the United States.

Thus, the announced boycott of the two variety stores which operated segregated lunch counters was viewed as being linked with continued litigation on educational desegregation, efforts to increase Negro suffrage, desegregation of transportation and other public facilities, increase in employment and occupational opportunities, housing and urban redevelopment trends, and the dramatic sit-in demonstrations. Also, this

From *Phylon: The Atlanta University Review of Race and Culture,* 22 (Spring 1961): 24–30; reprinted by permission of the author and publisher.

policy was assumed to be directed at the fundamental but more intangible ethos of the entire community: the ethical, valuational, and morality systems.

This study is concerned with the organization and participation of members of a minority group in conflict relations with the members of a dominant group.[1] The major question raised was to what extent did the members of the Negro community agree with and support the public policy of economic aggression as announced by the NAACP.

From measurement of the amount of support to, and cooperation with, this policy, inferences may be made as to the legitimacy of the leadership role of the NAACP among Negroes; the cohesion and solidarity of Negroes in the Pine Bluff area; and the effectiveness of the techniques utilized by the NAACP to enhance support and cooperation within the Negro community. Stated differently, if the effectiveness of the withdrawal of Negro trade from the selected variety stores and correspondingly the redirection of Negro trade to the non-boycotted variety store is measured, inferences may be made with respect to: (1) the social cohesion and solidarity of the Negro community; (2) the recognition and acceptance of the leadership role of the NAACP by Negroes; and (3) the effectiveness of the communicational and organizational techniques utilized by the NAACP in this specific instance of group conflict.

The phrase "members of the Negro community" demands definitional precision. Jefferson County, consisting of 890 square miles, is located south and slightly east of the geographical center of the state. This county constitutes a hinterland served by Pine Bluff. Thus, for this study the phrase, "members of the Negro community," is defined as representing those Negroes of both Pine Bluff and Jefferson County who possibly utilize the services and facilities of the city.

Preliminary statistics for the 1960 census show that Jefferson County has a population of 80,546 and that Pine Bluff has a population of 43,807. No color breakdown of these preliminary 1960 statistics has been released. However, a special census was conducted by the United States Bureau of the Census in August, 1956, which indicated that the Negro population was 39 percent of the total city population. Assuming that this proportional relationship remained constant from 1956 to 1960, the Negro population of Pine Bluff in 1960 may be estimated at 17,085.

The Negro proportion of the Jefferson County population commonly has been larger than the Negro proportion of the Pine Bluff population. (In 1950, 49.8 percent of the county population was non-white.) This fact leads to the utilization in this study of the assumption that the members of the Negro community ranged, at the least, between 17,085 and 31,413 (39 percent of the 1960 county total population).

The task of this study was to ascertain or measure the extent of economic withdrawal on the part of the Negro community from trade relations with the selected variety stores. This task involved many difficulties. There existed no prior information about the usual or customary utilization pattern of Pine Bluff variety stores by Negroes. Granting the diversity of goods and the price pattern of variety stores in general, and the relatively low economic level of the members of the Negro community, it may be assumed that rather extensive utilization of the three local variety stores was common.

The strategic location of all these variety stores in proximity to the traditionally defined "Negro area" of the business district would likewise support the notion of extensive and relatively equal utilization of these outlets by Negroes.

With these difficulties at hand, the plan devised to measure the extent of economic pressure applied to the selected variety stores by Negroes was as follows: An actual count was to be made of all persons visually identifiable as Negro who entered the three variety stores between the opening and closing hours on a Saturday, which is the peak shopping day of the week for these stores. Underlying this procedure of observing the pattern of behavior was the assumption that Negroes entering these variety stores did so for the purpose of shopping. All Negro customers, age and sex characteristics ignored, were enumerated regardless of repeated entries. While it is recognized that observations on one business day would not justify inferences about utilization on other days of the business week, for the purposes and within the means of this study a Saturday could be considered as the most suitable period for observation.

One variety store—Kress—was not included as a target in the announcement of the economic policy of the NAACP. This permitted a comparison of Negro customers entering the two "target" stores with Negro customers entering a store which served as a "control." Observed variation in entry of Negro customers between the control and target stores would permit, assuming a prior equality of Negro utilization of all three variety stores, some inferences as to the questions raised in this study.

In addition to the utilization of observational methods to ascertain the degree of economic withdrawal of the Negro community from the target stores, an attempt was made to contact directly each Negro customer observed to emerge from the target stores. This contact took the form of a brief interview after the customer emerged from the store. Inquiry was made as to whether the person was aware of the announced policy of the NAACP. If an affirmative reply was given, an attempt was made to determine the reason for non-conformity with this policy.

The objective of this portion of the research plan was to obtain information concerning the attitudes of Negroes toward the leadership role of the local NAACP, especially with regard to this particular policy, and to obtain an estimate of the effectiveness of the techniques and methods used by the NAACP to disseminate its policy throughout the Negro community.

In implementing this design, interviewers were systematically stationed at observation posts covering all business entrances of all three variety stores. Tallies were run on each store by entrance. Other interviewers mingled with the shoppers on the street so as to observe and personally interview each Negro adult seen to emerge from the two target stores. The field work was done on April 9, 1960, which was the third Saturday, or a little over two weeks after the announcement of the policy by the NAACP.

The data presented in Table 1 show that a definite pattern was ex-

TABLE 1.   Number and Percentage Distribution of Negro Customers Entering
Variety Stores in Pine Bluff, Saturday, April 9, 1960

| | Total | *Target Stores* | | *Control Store* |
		Woolworth	Newberry	Kress
Number	4,818	28	128	4,662
Percent	100.0	0.5	2.7	96.8
(round numbers)				

Source: Field data.

hibited in the utilization of the three variety stores by the members of
the Negro community.

Over 96 percent of the Negroes entering variety stores, presumably
for business purposes, entered Kress. This particular store was not identified in the announced policy as one to be avoided. The two target stores,
Woolworth and Newberry, had less than 4 percent of the Negro customers
entering their premises on this date. The NAACP specifically identified
these variety stores as ones to be avoided by Negroes. This unmistakable
pattern of selective behavior on the part of Negroes leads to the deduc-
tion that definite forces were operating to produce this mass behavior.

Assuming that the customary utilization of variety stores by members of the Negro community was on an individualized and largely unstructured basis, and that the ecological locations of the three stores were
not such as to produce the distinct pattern as indicated above,[2] the interpretation may be made that the great bulk of the Negroes had knowledge of, agreed to, and behaved in conformity with the policy announced
by the local branch of the NAACP.

Of the 4,818 Negro customers entering the three variety stores, 156
were observed to enter the target stores. These persons were interviewed
on the street after they had merged from either of the two target stores.
Of this number 132, or 84.6 percent, indicated that they were unaware
of the policy of avoiding the target stores. Thus, the bulk of the Negro
customers entering the target stores did not know of the community policy
sponsored by the NAACP.

Among the 156 Negro customers entering the target stores, 24 stated
that they knew of the announced policy. On inquiry, four of these customers indicated that they had forgotten about the policy and had entered the target store unintentionally, and three stated that they entered
these stores out of curiosity to see whether other Negroes were shopping
there.

Seventeen Negroes, or less than 1 percent of the 4,818 Negroes who
shopped in variety stores on this date, stated that they knew of the
NAACP announcement but disagreed with the policy of boycott and
would not conform to it because of their dislike of the general program
of the organization. Their diverse comments about the local branch of
the NAACP were pungent, and some resentment and hostility were
vented. Nevertheless, a relatively minute segment of the Negro shoppers
in variety stores on this date were antagonistic to the announced policy.

The techniques used by the local NAACP to publicize and secure the cooperation of the members of the Negro community were numerous. It should be pointed out that the time of announcement coincided with similar protests and mass actions throughout the South, and to some extent, throughout the nation. Thus, the local branch timed the announcement of its policy of economic aggression so as to benefit from the more general publicity given to similar protest actions through all of the mass media of communication in the Pine Bluff community. Negroes of this community could therefore participate in carrying out the local policy and simultaneously secure a sense of identification with a larger and more diffuse social protest movement.

Moreover, a slogan was adopted and used by the local NAACP. The slogan, "We No Longer Pay to Be Segregated," was conspicuously placed on mimeographed materials and announcements distributed at mass meetings and stacked for general circulation in Negro business places. It was printed also by the *Pine Bluff Daily* in news items about this policy of the Negro community.

At least two large public mass meetings were announced and conducted by the NAACP in local churches on Sunday afternoons to publicize and solicit support of this policy. Judicious selection of community leaders to participate in these mass meetings was made, and representatives of the local press were always invited and cordially welcomed.

In the earlier stages of this community action the only daily newspaper, unwittingly perhaps, aided the organization of the Negro community by treating as extremely newsworthy the apparent results of the economic policy. After about three weeks, however, the newsworthy character of this boycott disappeared and no further mention of it was made by the local daily newspaper.

The various leaders and voluntary associations of the Negro community were sent a letter by the president of the local NAACP notifying them of the policy and requesting their support. No appeal was made for financial assistance.

Finally, the local NAACP conducted a tabulation each Saturday of the numbers of Negroes observed utilizing the three variety stores. These tabulations were carried out by officers and members of the NAACP and other interested Negro citizens. Out of these activities there seemed to develop in the participants a feeling of personal contribution to the success of the policy and thereby a feeling of group responsibility. The participants, in turn, by word of mouth and by action, signalized the continued need of support from the entire Negro community.

Briefly, the local branch of the NAACP displayed a workable knowledge of its community and some skill in utilizing the available resources in publicizing and encouraging community support for its announced policy. The evidence suggests that a considerable degree of compliance with the NAACP policy was secured from Negroes and that the techniques of communicating to them used by the NAACP were effective.

In conclusion, the tasks of this study were to ascertain the degree of cohesion and solidarity of the members of a Negro community in carrying out a policy of economic aggression against two local variety stores. The acceptance or rejection of the leadership role of the local NAACP, which sponsored this policy, was to be investigated, and an assessment of the effectiveness of the organizational and persuasive techniques utilized by the NAACP in carrying out this policy was to be attempted.

It should be noted first that the primary and manifest objective of this policy has not been achieved. The two variety stores, Woolworth's and Newberry's, have shown no inclination to change their traditional and customary pattern of differential customer service. Negro customers are still not served at the lunch counter. In this sense the policy and action of the Negro community, under the leadership of the NAACP, can be said to be a failure.

On the other hand, the evidence collected clearly permits the conclusion that a considerable amount of cohesion and solidarity characterizes the members of the Negro community. In no other way can the definite pattern of utilization of the variety stores by Negro shoppers be reasonably explained.

Likewise, this evidence and the significantly minute overt reaction against the leadership role of the NAACP suggest that an influential role of leadership is accorded the NAACP within the Negro community. It is noteworthy that no Negro organization or prominent Negro leader publicly voiced objections to the economic action initiated by the NAACP. Little doubt exists as to the general acceptability among Negroes of the NAACP as an indigenous and representative leadership organization.

The evidence suggests, also, that the local branch of the NAACP skillfully utilized the leadership and organizational structures of the Negro community to inform, educate, and compel observance of its announced policy of action. It seems significant that the NAACP studiously phrased its community appeal and program so as to ask for assistance only from "Negro" citizens.

Thus, this demonstration of community action may be described as a success. Especially may this engagement in conflict be described as a success in view of the broader implications of the continuous struggle of the minority for complete acceptance into the full life of the community. This exercise of power, inducing controlled change in behavior pattern, strategic and tactical deliberations and actions, use of techniques of persuasion and coercion, augurs favorably for the future of these citizens and their posterity.

NOTES

This report is based upon data collected by students in an undergraduate sociology class at A. M. and N. College in Pine Bluff, Arkansas.

1. For a general statement on the theoretical and conceptual attributes of group conflict and intergroup relations, see George E. Simpson and J. Milton Yinger, *Racial and Cultural Minorities* (rev. ed., New York, 1958).

2. Two of the stores were located in the same block and two were corner stores directly across the street from each other.

5. Characteristics
of Participants

So far we have discussed the nature of the civil rights movement, its leadership, organizations, and tactics. Now we shift to a consideration of what really makes it go—the rank-and-file participants. Because the central focus of this book is on the black revolt, this analysis is primarily limited to the black participants of the movement. Although whites have contributed greatly to the revolt during its civil rights stage, white and black participants differ in type, in social background, in motivations for participaton, and in level of ultimate commitment. Thus, the inclusion of analyses of white participants would obscure more than it would clarify in the present context.

Two of the three selections included in this section deal with college students. The third includes college students as well as others. This is a reflection of the fact that college students dominated the black revolt during its direct-action, civil rights phase.

John M. Orbell studied the participation of college students in the civil rights movement in 1962. Highest participation rates were found among students from high socioeconomic origins, attending private universities and high quality colleges (which draw their students from upper status families). Participation was positively related to urban background and negatively related to the percentage of Negroes in the college county.

Anthony and Amy Orum, utilizing data gathered in 1964 analyzed the participation of college seniors. They concluded that there is no relationship between socioeconomic status and participation. It would be possible to conclude that during the two-year period between the studies by Orbell and the Orums, more and more students of lower-class origins were drawn into the movement so that by 1964 there were no longer any class differences in participation rates. However, the data in Tables 2 and 3 deserve closer examination. Table 2 reveals a 5 percent difference in participation rates between those whose family income is less than $5000 and those whose family income is over $5000. Table 3 indicates that participation rates in low SES schools are 14 to 15 percent lower than those in medium and high SES schools. What is more to the point, the increase in participation rates from low to high SES schools is

16 percent for low SES students and only 10 percent for high SES students. This would suggest that socioeconomic status still did make a difference in participation rates but that it exerted its greatest influence in terms of the social milieu which it created. In predominantly low SES schools, high SES students partially took on the participation characteristics of low SES students. Low SES students in high SES schools even exceeded the participation rates of high SES students.

Maurice Pinard, Jerome Kirk, and Donald Von Eschen conducted their study earlier (1961) and included all participants in sit-ins. They studied both students and nonstudents. They found participation to be related to high socioeconomic status although the most active participants were of low status. The most deprived absolutely were generally the latest to join, but left-oriented ideology could lead to early joining patterns among the deprived. The relatively deprived (status inconsistents) were more likely to participate than those who were not relatively deprived (status consistents).

PROTEST PARTICIPATION AMONG SOUTHERN NEGRO COLLEGE STUDENTS

John M. Orbell

A recent article in [*The American Political Science*] *Review* has drawn attention to the inadequacies in our knowledge of how great social movements arise.[1] On the Negro protest movement there are many hypotheses but few attempts to relate them to differences in individual behavior. Considerable confusion also exists in the variety of explanatory terms involved. James A. Geschwender lists five hypotheses that focus variously on economic conditions and the psychological meaning given them. They are the *Vulgar Marxist* hypothesis—that Negro dissatisfaction results from a progressive deterioration in the social and economic position of the race; the *Rising Expectations* hypothesis—that Negro expectations are rising more rapidly than their fulfillment; the *Sophisticated Marxist* hypothesis or the *Relative Deprivation* hypothesis—that Negro perceptions of white life have led to dissatisfaction with their own rate of improvement; the *Rise and Drop* hypothesis—that improvement in conditions followed by a sharp drop is responsible; and the *Status Inconsistency* hypothesis—that a group possessing status attributes ranked differently on various status hierarchies of a society will be dissatisfied and prone to rebellion.[2]

This paper will suggest that theory based on variations in the structure of intergroup relations can go some way toward integrating the different kinds of explanation that have been advanced. A more general aspiration is to draw attention to one set of terms that might be useful in the long overdue development of a genuinely comparative study of social movements such as the Negro movement. The broad hypothesis arising from—but by no means fully tested by—an examination of several individual and contextual variables is that *proximity to the dominant white culture increases the likelihood of protest involvement*. The analysis will give a priority to structural considerations, but will also suggest something about intervening psychological variables.

Most of the existing knowledge about this and other social movements comes from case studies of one, or at best very few, cities or districts.[3] Consequently, we know little about the variation in participation *among* such areas. The data on which the present study is based are drawn from a survey of Negro college students conducted in 1962, about two years after the sit-in movement began, by Professors Donald R. Matthews and James W. Prothro as part of their wider study of Southern attitudes and behavior.[4] Included were 264 Negro students who attended, in all, thirty colleges of various kinds in all eleven former Confederate states. Although there were never enough students interviewed in any one college to treat them as a separate sample, the breadth of the survey

From *The American Political Science Review* 61 (June 1967): 446–56; reprinted and abridged by permission of the author and publisher.

lets us test a variety of ecological and institutional variables as well as many individual variables.

The dependent variable of this study is participation in the Negro college student protest movement. Presumably this should be conceptualized, in the manner of more general political participation, as stretching on a continuum of related activities.[5] A number of different kinds of behavior suggest themselves. Students belonged to protest organizations, marched, picketed, took part in sit-ins and freedom rides. Simply giving support to the protest movement was nearly universal among the students and of little use in differentiating them. In this case, however, the various kinds of protest behaviors reported by the students could not be related acceptably as a Guttman scale [6] and instead a simple index was adopted. In what follows, the term "participants" refers to those students who had either taken part in a sit-in or a freedom ride or belonged to one of several kinds of protest organizations.[7] Although these two variables are strongly associated, in several instances it will be appropriate to examine them separately. Table 1 gives the distribution of students according to these categories.

TABLE 1. The Dimensions of Protest Participation

Membership in Protest Organizations	Participation in Freedom Rides or Sit-ins		
	Yes	No	Totals
Yes	42	41	83
No	23	158	181
Totals	65	199	264

I. COLLEGE VARIABLES

Not all protest activities that Negro college students get involved in have their origin in the colleges they attend, but the data suggest that at least two college variables have a significant impact on protest, independent of all other factors.[8] These are the manner in which the college is supported—by state or private finance—and its quality.

Control of the college

The reasons for believing that college control may have an impact on protest are straightforward: state-run institutions are open to many kinds of pressures from which private colleges are free. Undoubtedly the willingness and ability of college administrators to resist such pressures vary from college to college and state to state, but there is ample evidence that they can be most compelling. At Southern University, Baton Rouge, students became involved in demonstrations shortly after the sit-in movement began in North Carolina. On March 29, 1960, a large number of Southern's students were arrested following sit-ins at S. H. Kress and Co.

and the Greyhound Bus Station. As had already happened elsewhere, the all-white State Board of Education immediately warned that "stern disciplinary action" would be taken against any future demonstrators. The president of the University, Dr. Felton Clark, was reported as saying he had "no alternatives," and further demonstrations resulted in eighteen students being expelled from the University.[9] In a speech to the students he said, "Like Lincoln who sought to preserve the Union, my dominant concern is to save Southern University." [10]

Colleges not run by state governments can be divided according to whether their administration is formally secular or denominational. Participation was about equally likely among students attending these two kinds of colleges: 55 percent in the former and 53 percent in the latter participated. However, only 33 percent of the students attending state colleges were participants. Table 2 shows that both organizational mem-

TABLE 2.   Percent of Students Participating in Different Forms of Protest by College Control [a]

| | Type of Participation | |
Control of College	Sitting-in	Membership
State	19%	23%
	(169)	(169)
Denominational, private	37%	57%
	(62)	(62)
Secular, private	30%	55%
	(33)	(33)

[a]The entry in each cell is the percent of respondents in colleges of a given kind who reported participation of the type indicated. In this table and those following, the figures in parentheses are the base from which the percentages were calculated.

bership and participation in demonstrations were less probable among state college students—although it also suggests that the difference between the two modes of participation at state colleges was less than at either of the two kinds of private colleges. All plausible situational or individual control variables failed to eliminate this relationship.

Some further data support the conclusion that more restrictive circumstances do exist at the state colleges and also suggest something about sub-culture tensions accompanying the development of protest. Louis Lomax has commented on such tensions between Negro teachers and their students:

> "Intellectual Uncle Tom—" that's the phrase one hears throughout the South nowadays. It is uttered by college students and their supporters, and it is used in the open, at public meetings and rallies. It is the students' way of talking about the "failure" of Southern Negro intellectuals—school teachers, for the most part—to support the revolt in clear, open terms.
> This is excruciatingly painful.[11]

TABLE 3. Sit-Inners' Perceptions of Support
from Professors and Administrators in State
and Private Colleges

Perceived Attitudes	Type of College	
	Private	State
Professors	46%	50%
Administrators	46%	15%

The interview schedule included two questions asking sit-inners for their perceptions of what their college administrators and professors thought about what they were doing. Although such perceptual data should not necessarily be taken as recording an *actual* state of affairs, the responses were different between state and private colleges. For each sit-inner who perceived neutrality from a given group, a score of zero was recorded; "strong approval" and "strong disapproval" were scored +2 and −2 respectively; while "approval" and "disapproval" were scored +1 and −1 respectively. The resulting figures were then normalized in percentage terms. The final scores, shown in Table 3, suggest plenty of scope for the development of the hostilities Lomax writes about: no matter where the students attended college, their perceived support from both professors and college administrators fell far below the possible 100 percent. On the other hand, the striking thing about these data is the similarity of all the scores except that recording the attitudes of state college administrators. Private college sit-inners saw little difference in the attitudes of their professors and administrators; but at state colleges, while support from professors is seen at about the same level as at private colleges, support from administrators is seen far less frequently than from their private counterparts. Perhaps evidence can also be found in these perceptual data that points to differences of opinion between professors and administrators at state colleges. At any rate, the conclusion seems justified that sub-culture tension arising from the student movement is most acute in state colleges, and that it centers on those roles which mediate between the sub-culture and the dominant white culture.

Quality of the college

College quality was measured in essentially the manner developed by Lazarsfeld and Thielens in *The Academic Mind*.[12] Five indicators of quality were selected, the appropriate data on the thirty colleges included in the sample were collected from a number of standard sources, and an acceptable Guttman scale was developed.[13] Four categories of quality were used. The resulting data show quite clearly that protest participation—both organizational membership and participation in demonstrations—increased as the quality of the college increased. Only 22 percent of the students in the lowest category colleges claimed participation, 41 percent did so in the second lowest, while in the highest two participation was nearly equal—around 54 percent. In each category of colleges organizational membership was more frequent than activism, but both increased as the quality of college increased.

Several explanations are available for this association between college quality and protest participation. On the one hand, high-quality colleges may selectively recruit students whose participation can adequately be accounted for by certain individual variables; on the other hand, high quality in Negro colleges may be associated with some other situational factor which itself explains the levels of protest. Perhaps the distribution reflects the spatial spread of protest throughout the South; perhaps protest spread first to the comparatively few high quality colleges in the South, and only later to the poorer institutions. Without a panel design surveys are poorly suited to treat such longitudinal processes as the spread of a social movement through time, but even if this spread were systematically associated with college quality we would still be left with the original question unanswered.[14]

As might be expected, the data leave no doubt that the higher quality colleges recruit from the higher status part of the Negro population, but they also show that such high status is strongly associated with protest participation. Only 35 percent of students from households where the head was classed as semi-skilled or unskilled were participants, while 53 percent of the skilled or professional group could be similarly classed. There is a nearly linear association between participation and family income from the under-$2,000 bracket in which only 13 percent were participants to the above-$6,000 bracket in which 53 percent participated.

However, the data given in Table 4 show that quality of college has an effect even when family income is held constant, although the *strength* of the quality-participation relationship varies between income categories.

There are signs here of what Hubert M. Blalock and others have called a "multiplicative effect." In one kind of situation—called "additive"—there is no evidence that independent variables $X_1, X_2 \ldots X_n$

TABLE 4. Percent of Students Participating by Quality of College and Income of Student's Family

Quality of College:	Income of Student's Family[a]	
	High	Low
High	57%	50%
	(44)	(34)
Low	46%	25%
	(63)	(102)
Difference	11	25

[a]The cut-off point between the "high" and "low" income categories was $4,999.

interact with each other in their impact on the dependent variable Y; their effect remains the same regardless of empirical juxtapositions with each other. In a multiplicative situation the combined impact of two or more independent variables is greater than expectations based on knowledge of each acting in isolation from the others. "In a fairly common kind of theoretical situation," says Blalock, "one assumes that a given phenomenon is most likely when two (or more) factors are *both* present, but that it is unlikely whenever either of these factors is absent." [15]

This crude dichotomization of income and quality modifies the conclusions that can be drawn from examination of both variables acting in isolation from each other, while failing to eliminate the original association in either case. Adopting the method used by Blalock to infer interaction, we can observe a 14 percentage point difference between the two difference scores in Table 4. If low family income and low college quality are both present the depressing effect on participation is substantially greater than additive expectations.

The data also confirm the suspicion that most high-quality Negro colleges in the South are private and that most low-quality ones are state-run. But again that fact is not sufficient to eliminate the original association between college quality and participation. Holding control of college constant and varying quality produces an eight percentage point difference in participation among state college students—31 and 39 percent at the high and low quality state colleges respectively—and a twenty percentage point difference among private college students—41 and 61 percent respectively. As in the previous case, the relation between the three variables appears to be multiplicative. When quality and control are acting together to boost participation, their impact is greater than the sum of each acting in isolation.

II. SOCIAL CHARACTERISTICS OF THE COUNTY

County-level social variables have been shown to relate importantly to many aspects of Southern politics. Two in particular should be tested in the present case: the urban-rural character of the county and the Negro proportion of the population.

Urbanism

Matthews and Prothro find that urbanism and industrialization ". . . are vastly overrated as facilitators of Negro registration. Urbanization and industrialization may provide necessary conditions for high levels of Negro participation but, by themselves, they are not sufficient to ensure them." [16] Protest participation is markedly different from Negro voter registration in this respect, but the relation is a threshold rather than a linear one. Variation in the proportion of the population that is rural-farm in the county where the college is situated makes very little difference in protest until the least rural category is reached. At that point (0–4.9% rural-farm), there is a jump of 23 percentage points—from 29

TABLE 5. Percent of Students Participating by
Percent of County Population
Rural-Farm and Quality of College

	Percent of County Population Rural-Farm*	
Quality of College	Low	High
High	71%	38%
	(44)	(45)
Low	43%	24%
	(84)	(91)
Difference	28	14

*The cut-off point between the "high" and "low" categories was 4.9% rural-farm.

percent participating to 52 percent. Student protest, unlike other forms of Negro political activity, is characteristically an urban phenomenon.

The addition of further variables to the analysis elaborates on this association. Table 5 shows percent rural-farm and quality of college have an independent impact on participation, but it also suggests that when they are acting together their impact goes considerably beyond simple additive expectations. The difference between the differences in this case is 14 percentage points. Interestingly, a comparable finding does not appear when control of colleges and percent rural-farm are considered together; the data confirm that each variable has an impact independent of the other, but the difference-of-differences score is almost zero. When income and percent rural-farm are considered together in relation to participation, however, there is once again evidence of interaction. The data are given in Table 6.

The presence of two interaction effects such as these raises the possibility of what Blalock calls a "second-order" interaction—that all three variables may interact to produce levels of participation beyond additive expectations for the three individually.[17] Unfortunately, testing this possibility involves frequencies too small to use with any confidence. The data

TABLE 6. Percent of Students Participating
by Percent of County Rural-Farm
and Income of Family[a]

	Percent of County Population Rural-farm	
Income of Family	Low	High
High	54%	44%
	(62)	(45)
Low	46%	20%
	(55)	(81)
Difference	8	24

[a]The cut-off point between "high" and "low" categories of income was $4,000.

do suggest, however, that such a higher level of interaction also exists.[18] When urban living, high college quality and high income all occur together, participation is boosted beyond what would be the case if all three variables were acting independently. In other words, although the generalization does not include variations in the control of colleges, adding successive favorable conditions to attending college in an urban county produces an accelerating curve of participation.

Percent negro in the college county

The power of the percent Negro in a Southern county to predict many aspects of its social and political life has been repeatedly documented.[19] Matthews and Prothro conclude that the variable is "more strongly associated with the county's rate of Negro registration than any other social and economic attribute on which we have data." [20] There are, however, good reasons for expecting its impact on student protest participation to be somewhat muted. H. D. Price has argued that the percent Negro should not be seen as working in some mechanical way on the behavior in question, but as representing in a summary way the history and cultural traditions of race relations in the area.[21] Thus, where Negroes are a large part of the population there is also likely to be a history of a particular kind of race relations often dating to slavery times. A student population, however, is often a distinct community with its own mores and traditions that may run quite counter to those of the locality. Even in colleges where no such community exists—possibly a majority of those included in this study—the population is distinct in age, socio-economic status, education, and usually the frequency of social roots outside the area itself. The history and cultural traditions of the area seem likely to have less impact on participation in the student protest movement than on other kinds of political participation among the general Negro population in the county.

Despite these expectations student protest participation seems to be inversely related to percent Negro, in line with other kinds of behavior. Participation increases in a linear fashion from about 22 percent among those students attending college in areas with more than 40 percent Negroes to about 62 percent among those where there is less than 20 percent Negroes. The association is maintained when all other individual and contextual factors are held constant, and there is little evidence of interaction between percent Negro and any of the other variables tested. The data also show only a very slight and probably insignificant association between the percent Negro in the students' home counties and protest participation of any kind.

Matthews and Prothro have demonstrated that areas where Negroes are a high proportion of the population have whites with considerably less permissive attitudes toward Negro political participation,[22] and James W. Vander Zanden has pointed out the general role that resistance to social movements can have in shaping the course of a movement.[23] Perhaps this opposition is an important factor in explaining the varying rates of student protest participation by percent Negro, just as the opposition of state college administrators seems to be important in explaining the power of variations in college control.

But the question of motivation is also relevant here. Matthews and Prothro have demonstrated that "Negro commitment to voting declines as white disapproval of Negro voting increases. Not only are fewer Negroes registered where white attitudes are less permissive, but fewer Negroes express a desire to vote." This lack of desire, they suggest, represents in part, "a realistic adjustment to the environment and in part the psychological mechanism of rationalization. Some Negroes will realistically calculate that they do not want to vote if the costs in terms of possible social, economic, or physical reprisals are too great." [24] Quite possibly such a lowering of motivation extends across the barriers that separate the college from the population at large and is responsible, in turn, for lowering rates of student protest participation.

If overt pressures are involved, however, there is no sign of it in the reports from demonstrators of the white hostility they encountered as a consequence of their participation. There was no difference in the number or character of the incidents reported by students in areas with a high proportion of Negroes and those with only few—although the n's involved are admittedly very small. While it seems quite likely that differences in Negro assertiveness are associated with differences in the percent Negro in the area, how much of this is a "mechanical" result of white attitudes in the area and how much is due to other properties of the social structure must remain an open question. . . .

III. PROTEST AND THE SOCIAL STRUCTURE

A full explanation of the variance in protest would require consideration of such things as the role of initiators and accidents of leadership in certain places, underlying economic conditions, the role of resistance from groups opposing the movement, geographic spread and many other factors. Nothing so ambitious has been attempted here. Rather, the suggestion is made that by focusing on one factor—the structure of intergroup relations—some advance can be made toward integrating various theoretical propositions about the origin of the Negro protest movement. In a nutshell, the argument runs as follows: Certain structural positions in Negro society are characterized by higher awareness of the wider society and, as a consequence, individuals occupying these positions are more prone to develop the particular set of attitudes and perceptions that lead to protest. Resistance from the white community, particularly as it is channeled through state college administrators and, possibly, as it occurs in certain kinds of areas, plays a role in modifying and shaping the particular patterns of protest that arise.

Unfortunately, it is necessary to rely on a rather small amount of data and a rather large amount of inference in arguing that such structural factors as high quality in colleges, high socio-economic background, and urban residence all involve high levels of interaction with the wider society. The inferences, however, are not too strained. All the respondents in the survey were students and therefore more likely to have higher levels of general awareness than the rest of the Negro population; high quality colleges might not unreasonably be expected to increase that awareness. In fact the data show that students attending these colleges were more able to answer correctly a series of factual questions about politics than were the others.

In his large study of intergroup relations in several communities, Robin Williams finds support for the basic proposition that

> exposure to intergroup situations available in a community depends to a large extent upon the individual's daily living patterns—which in turn are strongly influenced by his position and function (or status and role) in the community.[25]

He also shows that in these communities, ". . . the more educated Negro has more opportunity for contact with whites than the less well-educated," and that higher occupational status works the same way.[26] Data from the present study show that students attending high-quality colleges do have considerably higher levels of social interaction across the race barrier— particularly with white students and teachers, although the generalization extends to a wide variety of contacts. The same applies to students from high socio-economic backgrounds.

Attending college in an urban county is likewise associated with a higher frequency of intergroup contact than doing so in a rural county. The presence of such contact seems to make the urban environment a particularly fertile ground for protest. When urban living is considered in conjunction with several indicators of intergroup contact, a marked multiplicative effect appears. Matthews and Prothro comment that urban living appears to provide the necessary conditions for high levels of Negro voter registration.

> The urban-industrial life is more rational, impersonal and less tradition-bound; both Negroes and whites enjoy more wealth and education; the Negroes benefit from a concentration of potential leaders and politically relevant organizations in the cities. The urban ghetto may provide social reinforcement to individual motivations for political action.[27]

When intergroup social fluidity is added to these conditions, the data suggest that such individual motivations are particularly high.

Intergroup communication is, of course, a most difficult concept to operationalize; social contact across the race barrier is only one indicator of a complex process that can go on in a great variety of informal and formal ways. There are, nevertheless, several reasons why it is congenial to focus theory building in the present case on such communication and the structural conditions that promote it. First, it provides a firm basis for what Sherif and Sherif call a "clear functional picture" of the factors that lead to protest participation.

> . . . Social psychological theories of intergroup relations which base the whole edifice primarily on a universal instinct (e.g., aggression), on displacements of aggressions always as the product of frustrations in personal life history, on a leadership principle, on situational factors, on culture, on national character, or, in a direct and mechanical way, on economic

considerations result in one-sided pictures. . . . Compilations of these factors side by side in the form of a syllabus have not led to a clear functional picture.[28]

Economic and psychological variables are, from this perspective, placed in a theoretical context from which their importance in the whole structure of explanation can be assessed. Data have been indicating that feelings of discontent about *personal* prospects in a bi-racial world are not associated with particularly high levels of protest. On the other hand, there is a marked association between protest and feelings about the general position of the *whole Negro race:* among students who recorded "high" on a measure of satisfaction with the present racial situation 28 percent were participants; among those recording "low" 52 percent were participants.[29] Evidently, explanation that focuses on feelings of personal relative deprivation must be modified to emphasize perceived deprivation of the *group* with which the individual identifies.[30] The present data do not detail just what objective social and economic conditions might lead to such feelings, but it is clear that such feelings would be particularly likely to develop in situations that constantly emphasize the differences between the races. The objective conditions are there for the whole group; but only some individuals are constantly exposed to the fact that there are differences. It is among this population that protest is most likely to develop.

A further advantage is that such a theoretical position also provokes useful speculation about why the Negro protest developed at this particular point in American history and about its likely future course. Arguing that protest can be explained adequately in terms of the economic fortunes of the Negro group as a whole fails to explain why the movement did not develop when—as seems quite possible—comparable conditions existed in the past. By emphasizing that other structural changes have a priority over purely economic ones, we are led to search for factors that can increase the visibility of whatever objective situations may lead a group to revolt. They are readily available in the increased mobility of all groups in United States society, the development of modern mass communications, and major wars that have at once increased mobility and brought different groups into close proximity with each other. So long as the objective conditions exist, we can expect that increased communication between the races will bring a furtherance of protest, not a quieting. Conservative Southern claims that the progress of integration will only bring an increase of Negro assertiveness seem quite plausible from the present theoretical position.

Much significant contemporary history concerns massive demands from various groups for large-scale adjustments in their social, economic and political positions, but there has been little systematic theory-building about such phenomena. Existing knowledge about the conditions that give rise to various kinds of social movements is generally couched in terms unique to the movement being considered and meaningless to the analysis of others. The structural perspective on the Negro movement suggested here does point to one direction in which research might be fruitful. If analysis were to concentrate, first, on the objective economic, social and political differences between groups, and then on the processes by which such differences are communicated and given meaning to the individuals concerned, major advances might be made. A large literature on the relation between communication and national integration has appeared in recent years. Analysis of the structure of communication between groups might lead to a better understanding of why some groups—such as the American Negroes—produce integrative movements, while others—such as the French Canadians—produce disintegrative ones. It would at least cast the analysis of broadly comparable phenomena in comparable terms.

NOTES

1. See Jack Walker, "A Critique of the Elitist Theory of Democracy," *American Political Science Review*, 60 (June 1966): 293–95.

2. James A. Geschwender, "Social Structure and the Negro Revolt: An Examination of Some Hypotheses," *Social Forces* 43 (December 1964): 248–49. [A selection from this essay is reprinted in this volume, Part II, Section 1.]

3. See for example, Lewis Killian and Charles Grigg, *Racial Crisis in America* (Englewood Cliffs, N.J.: Prentice-Hall, 1964); Daniel C. Thompson, *The Negro Leadership Class* (Englewood Cliffs, N.J.: Prentice-Hall, 1963); Jack Walker, "Protest and Negotiation: A Case Study of Negro Leadership in Atlanta, Georgia," *Midwest Journal of Political Science* 7 (May 1963): 99–124.

4. See Donald R. Matthews and James W. Prothro, *Negroes and the New Southern Politics* (New York: Harcourt, Brace & Jovanovich, 1966). The present survey was made in addition to their surveys of the adult Negro and white populations in the South. The author is most grateful for their permission to use these data and their helpful suggestions at several stages of the research.

5. See, for example, Campbell et al., *The American Voter* (New York: John Wiley, 1960), p. 92; and Matthews and Prothro, *Negroes and the New Southern Politics*, pp. 53–58. The latter uses a cumulative scale of political participation stretching from talking politics, voting, taking part in campaigns, belonging to political organizations and holding party or public office, and demonstrates that these factors ". . . are not only related to one another but are, in fact, different forms of the same phenomenon" (p. 53).

6. See R. N. Ford, "A Rapid Scoring Procedure for Scaling Attitude Questions," *Public Opinion Quarterly* 14 (Fall 1950): 507.

7. The protest organizations included were: The National Association for the Advancement of Colored People (NAACP), The Congress of Racial Equality (CORE), The Student Non-Violent Co-odinating Committee (SNCC), the Southern Christian Leadership Conference (SCLC), The Urban League and any other Negro Voters' League. No students claimed membership in the black Muslims.

8. In *Organizational Measurement and Its Bearing on the Study of College Environments* (New York: College Entrance Examination Board, 1961), Alan H. Barton gives useful guidance to the dimensions of colleges that may be measured and may have an impact on the behavior of individuals in them.

9. *The New York Times,* April 11, 1960, p. 25.

10. Quoted in Louis E. Lomax, *The Negro Revolt* (New York: Harper & Row, 1962), p. 209.

11. Ibid., p. 207.

12. P. F. Lazarsfeld and Wagner Theilens, Jr., *The Academic Mind* (Glencoe: The Free Press, 1958), p. 412.

13. Lazarsfeld and Thielens developed an index rather than a scale. In this case the scale was preferred because it gave the added assumption of uni-dimensionality in the indicators selected. The index, however, did have some advantages. It was not necessary for Lazarsfeld and Thielens to dichotomize their indicators, and as a result the index could take into account disproportionate "contributions" of quality by one of the indicators. An index was also developed in the present case and findings based on it were found to compare closely with those derived from the scale method. As it resulted, the scale findings were the more conservative of the two in terms of fulfilling expectations of an association between college quality and protest participation.

Obviously no single indicator of quality would do justice to variations in such a heterogeneous collection of colleges; agriculture and technical colleges, teachers' colleges, and some of the most outstanding of southern Negro colleges concentrating on the humanities were all included. The indicators adopted were as follows:

The number of books in the college library;
The ratio of books in the library to students;
The proportion of Ph.D.'s on the faculty;
Dollars in the college budget per student;
The faculty-student ratio.

The last mentioned indicator was not used by Lazarsfeld and Thielens, despite the fact that it is one of the most frequently used "rules of thumb" about the quality of the education a college offers. Two indicators used by them were not used in the present case. They were tuition fees paid and the Knapp and Greenblaum index of scholar productivity. Lazarsfeld and Thielens argued that higher tuition fees gave a college greater financial resources with which to provide education, and also that "tuition to some extent indicates the demand for a college's educational 'product' " (p. 412). However appropriate this indicator might have been for the population of colleges they studied, for the present state and private colleges it does not seem likely to make valid distinctions of quality. The Knapp and Greenblaum index of scholar productivity, used by Lazarsfeld and Thielens, was not used here for the very good reason that the data on which it was based were not available for the colleges under consideration. It is also true that scholar productivity might not be a particularly good indicator of quality in a mechanical or agricultural college.

The variables were dichotomized in the following ways:

Student-faculty ratio: better than 1:11.8
Ph.D.'s on faculty: better than 22.5%
Books in library: better than 38,000
Books per student: better than 25
Dollars per student: better than $800.00

The decision was made by inspection in each case. The coefficient of reproducibility for the scale was .889.

The sources from which the college data were collected were: *The College Blue Book,* 1962 (10th ed.; New York: The College Blue Book, 1962); *American Universities and Colleges* (8th ed.; Washington: American Council on Education, 1960); *American Junior Colleges,* 5th ed.; Washington: American Council on Education, 1960); *The World Almanac 1961.* In addition, use was made of G. W. Jones, "Negro Colleges in Alabama," *Journal of Negro Education* 31 (Summer 1962): 354–61.

14. Newspaper reports of student demonstrations give reasonably good grounds for believing that geographic patterns were well established by the time the survey was taken in the early months of 1962. Examination of *The New York Times* for the two years between that date and February 1960, when the movement started in Greensboro, N.C., suggests that it took only a matter of two or three months

for sit-ins to spread to other states outside the Deep South and then to penetrate the Deep South itself. It would be extremely hard to demonstrate from historical data that protest had still to reach the large number of low-quality colleges scattered throughout the whole South two years after the movement had begun, although the possibility must be admitted.

15. Hubert M. Blalock, "Theory Building and the Statistical Concept of Interaction," *American Sociological Review* 30 (June 1965): 375.

16. Donald R. Matthews and James W. Prothro, "Social and Economic Factors and Negro Voter Registration in the South," *American Political Science Review* 52 (March 1963): 28.

17. Blalock, "Theory Building and the Statistical Concept of Interaction."

18. Testing for such a second-order interaction involves relating college quality and percent rural-farm to participation with income held constant. It is thus possible to arrive at a difference between the two difference-of-differences scores. In this case the difference of difference-of-differences scores was 11 percentage points. The data are as follows:

| | High Income | | | Low Income | |
Quality	Percent rural-farm Low	High	Quality	Percent rural-farm Low	High
High	67% (24)	45% (20)	High	67% (15)	37% (19)
Low	47% (38)	44% (25)	Low	38% (40)	16% (62)
Difference	20	1	Difference	29	21

$(20-1) - (29-21) = 11$

19. For example, see V. O. Key, *Southern Politics* (New York: Knopf, 1949); John H. Fenton and K. N. Vines, "Negro Registration in Louisiana," *American Political Science Review* 51 (September 1957): 704–13; and H. D. Price, *The Negro in Southern Politics* (New York: New York University Press, 1957).

20. "Social and Economic Factors. . . ."

21. H. D. Price, "The Negro and Florida Politics, 1944–1954," *The Journal of Politics* 17 (May 1955): 198–200.

22. Matthews and Prothro, *Negroes and the New Southern Politics,* p. 118.

23. James W. Vander Zanden, "Resistance and Social Movements," *Social Forces* 37 (May 1959): 312–15.

24. "Social and Economic Factors. . . ."

25. *Strangers Next Door* (Englewood Cliffs, N.J.: Prentice-Hall, 1964), p. 146.

26. Ibid.

27. Matthews and Prothro, "Social Factors . . . ," p. 34.

28. M. Sherif and C. W. Sherif, *Groups in Harmony and Tension* (New York: Harper & Row, 1953), p. 136.

29. The students were given a self-anchoring scale and asked to indicate where on a continuum between the "very worst" and the "very best" possible race situations they would place the South at the present time.

30. For example, see Ruth Searles and J. A. Williams, "Negro College Students' Participation in Sit-Ins," *Social Forces* 10 (March 1962): 215–20. The authors argue that reference groups have changed for a large part of the Negro middle class that now identifies with the middle-class standards of the wider society. The result is feelings of relative deprivation that have led to the protest movement.

THE CLASS AND STATUS BASES OF
NEGRO STUDENT PROTEST

Anthony M. Orum / Amy M. Orum

Most contemporary analysts of social and political movements subscribe to the view that such movements originate from a number of different circumstances. Smelser, for instance, argues that social movements may emerge in response to conditions as diverse as economic depressions, wars, and actions of agencies like the police force.[1] Others assign the major impetus for social movements to economic and status-related deprivations.[2] Threats to the maintenance or improvement of a group's economic resources and status accoutrements, they argue, eventually can produce sufficient discontent to permit social movements to arise.

In the case of the present Negro protest movement in the United States, observers frequently trace its roots to barriers to Negroes' economic and status-related achievements.[3] With few exceptions, however, the connection between protest activity and economic or status-related deprivation among Negroes has been based on insufficient evidence.[4] By examining data on Negro college students, the present study seeks to shed light on this matter. Specifically, we ask: To what extent is the participation of Negro college students in the Negro protest movement a response to economic or status-related deprivation?

PERSPECTIVES AND RESEARCH ON THE NEGRO PROTEST MOVEMENT

The literature about economic or status-related conditions and the Negro protest movement can best be viewed in terms of three explanations outlined by Geschwender.[5] In this section we shall examine the evidence for each explanation. The first interpretation, the "vulgar Marxist" orientation, claims that fundamental economic impoverishment may create the dissatisfaction required for a social movement to emerge.[6] Meier and other social scientists as well as Negro political leaders emphasize the importance of such basic economic motivations for the present Negro protest efforts.[7] For instance, in 1963, Whitney Young, Jr., a moderate Negro spokesman, dramatized the economic plight of Negroes by calling for a domestic "Marshall Plan" to help offset unemployment and poverty among Negroes.[8] Miller argues that "usually the long-term economically depressed are unlikely candidates for a dynamic political movement, but the race ethnic dimension, as well as the economic factor, is propelling the poor, whether Negro, Mexican-American, or Puerto Rican." [9] In addition, organizations engaged in the Negro protest movement, like the Student Nonviolent Coordinating Committee (SNCC), focus their campaigns on basic economic issues and problems. Such organizations often have demanded increased job opportunities for Negroes, sometimes in prefer-

From the *Social Science Quarterly* 49 (December 1968): 521–33; reprinted by permission.

ence to voting rights or benefits in housing, frequently have employed economic boycotts to secure fair treatment for Negroes by white-owned or operated businesses, and, most recently, have urged the full-scale development of business enterprises in the ghettos.[10]

The second explanation, the "rising expectations" view, argues that if people of longstanding impoverishment are subject to heightened aspirations, due to partial fulfillment of certain goals, then they may become dissatisfied with gradual improvement of their situation and seek to channel their energies into a social movement. A number of writers accept this point of view as an interpretation of the present Negro protest efforts.[11] Kristol, for instance, remarks that "American Negroes . . . feel . . . that they have a special claim upon American society: they have had some centuries of resignation and now would like to see tangible benefits, quickly." [12] Evidence from public opinion polls conducted in the 1950's and 1960's indicates that Negroes had comparatively high expectations regarding their future. A 1954 nationwide study revealed that 64 per cent of the Negroes felt life would become better as compared with only 53 per cent of a matched group of whites who had this feeling.[13] Approximately 10 years later Brink and Harris found somewhat larger proportions of Negro respondents answering positively to similar questions.[14] However, such high aspirations of Negroes may quickly be transformed into anger and frustration when confronted with insurmountable barriers to their fulfillment. Along these lines, the discovery that the Negro-white income gap increases with additional education prompted Siegel to comment: "We might speak of the motivation provided the civil rights movement by the discovery on the part of thousands of young Negroes that their coveted education wasn't worth much on the open market." [15]

The third thesis, the "relative deprivation" perspective, states that discontent, and subsequently, social rebellion, may occur among people who evaluate their achievements by reference to the standards and accomplishments of some similarly situated persons who differ only in terms of having different or more numerous advantages. Karl Marx provided the essence of this notion by observing:

> A house may be large or small; as long as the surrounding houses are equally small it satisfies all social demands for a dwelling. But let a palace arise beside the little house, and it shrinks from a little house to a hut.[16]

In the case of the Negro protest activities, many observers claim that certain segments of the Negro community, especially the middle class, experience dissatisfaction as a result of comparing their achievements with those of their white counterparts.[17] The evidence for this argument certainly appears convincing. While Negro unemployment, for example, seems to have declined over the past 20 years, it has increased relative to that of whites.[18] In addition, the few studies of Negro participation in the Negro protest movement indicate that the more socially advantaged persons are over-represented in the protest activities. A recent study by G. Marx, for instance, demonstrates that Negroes who have more educational, occupational, and social privileges were more apt to be militant about the need for Negroes to gain equal rights.[19] After finding that middle-class Negro college students were over-represented among student participants, Searles and Williams suggest that many student participants adopted their white middle-class counterparts as a reference group.[20] Similar evidence on the background of Negro student protesters also is presented by Matthews and Prothro and Orbell.[21]

Each of the above interpretations attempts in a somewhat different manner to account for the current momentum of Negro protest efforts by virtue of economic or status-related deprivations among Negroes. In the analysis which follows, an attempt is made to determine whether the phenomenon of fundamental poverty, relative deprivation, or rising expectations is more characteristic of protest participants than of nonparticipants among Negro students.

DATA

The data upon which this study is based are part of a nationwide sample survey conducted in 1964 by the National Opinion Research Center (NORC). The purpose of the survey was to collect information on the graduate plans of seniors at colleges and universities throughout the nation. In April and May of 1964 a questionnaire was sent to a representative group of seniors at these institutions. In addition, a sample was chosen of seniors at predominantly Negro senior colleges and universities, designed to represent all students who received their bachelor's degrees in the spring of 1964.[22] Members of the NORC staff, together with personnel from the Department of Labor, identified 77 schools primarily attended by Negroes.[23] This list was comparable with one compiled independently and, for all practical purposes, exhausted the population of four-year predominantly Negro colleges and universities in the United States.[24] A two-stage probability design was employed in choosing the sample of students. Altogether, a total of 50 schools and roughly 7,000 students were included in the original sample.

Although respondents represent about one-third of all Negro college seniors who graduated in the spring of 1964, about 3,500 students, the response rate was only 49 per cent. In contrast, the response rate to the nationwide 1964 study was 74 per cent. No conclusive evidence was obtained to explain this low rate among Negroes, but one investigation suggests that a major factor was the greater length of the Negro college student questionnaire.[25] The low response rate probably accounts for certain biased characteristics of respondents. Those students who responded were more likely to be women, to have higher grade-point averages, and to have majors in areas such as the physical sciences and humanities. These biases, however, were similar in type and magnitude to those in the nationwide study. Hence, there appears to be no reason for anticipating that the biases affected the representatives of this sample.

FINDINGS

The information on the participation of students in the protest activities comes from two separate questions. Students were asked, first of all, what

TABLE 1. Proportion of Students Reporting Major Types of Protest
Activities on Their Campus

	Per Cent	N
Holding rallies	36	1,244
Public addresses by civil rights leaders	40	1,378
Participation in "freedom rides"	19	655
Participation in boycott moves against segregated businesses	64	2,170
Sit-ins in segregated public places	61	2,098
Fund raising for civil rights movement	35	1,185
Voter registration campaigns	48	1,652
Marches on city hall	42	1,441
Participation in March on Washington	23	802
None of these	12	405
No answer	—	125
Total	380	13,155
Total N		3,423[a]

[a]Variations in total sample size from table to table are due to
rounding off to nearest whole number.

major protest events had occurred on their campuses. As can be seen in
Table 1, most students claimed that economic boycotts were the major
activity at their school, an answer that confirms other evidence on the
popularity of economic boycotts among Negro college students.[26] In addition, students were questioned about their own roles in these efforts.
Approximately 70 per cent of the students reported participation and, of
this group, 32 per cent claimed to be active participants or leaders. A comprehensive measure of participation probably should account for both the
degree and type of involvement, but the ambiguity of the question on type
of activity prevented our creating such a measure. Instead we chose to
distinguish between students who said that they were nonparticipants and
those who reported taking an inactive, active, or leadership role.[27]

Socioeconomic status and participation

Most evidence concerning the link between economic or status factors and involvement in the Negro protest movement is based on the
background characteristics of participants and nonparticipants. Without
exception, such evidence indicates that Negroes from middle-class, or in
general, more privileged background were more apt to be protest participants. In Table 2 we have assembled information on fathers' education, family income, and protest participation that allow us to re-examine
these results. The education of students' fathers shows no association with
participation, whereas the income of students' families has a slight positive relationship with participation. Students from high SES backgrounds
were slightly more apt to participate in protest activities. The "relatively
deprived" students, those from families with high education but low income, were no more likely to be protest participants than were their economic peers from families with less education.

TABLE 2. Father's Education, Family Income, and Protest Participation
(per cent participating)

Father's Education	Family Income	
	Less than $5,000/yr.	$5,000 or more/yr.
Some high school or less	69	74
N	(1,389)	(471)
High school graduate or more	69	74
N	(456)	(617)
Total N		3,424[a]

[a]Variations in total sample size due to rounding.

It will be recalled from our earlier discussion that one interpretation of the Negro protest movement concerns the relative deprivation of Negroes as compared with their white counterparts. Although the data do not permit systematic exploration of this hypothesis, we can examine the relative deprivation of Negro students in their college settings. Table 3 presents data on the SES composition of the school, the SES background of students, and protest participation.[28] If the relative-deprivation argument is correct, then we would anticipate more extensive participation among students whose SES background is lower than that of their fellow students. Specifically, students from homes of low SES should be more likely to participate in schools in which there is a medium or high proportion of students from high SES *backgrounds*. An examination of data in Table 3, however, reveals virtually no difference in participation among students from low- and high-SES families in the different settings.[29]

TABLE 3. Socioeconomic Status Composition of Schools,
Socioeconomic Status Background of Students, and Protest
Participation (per cent participating)

School SES (Proportion of students from high SES families)	Students' SES		Participating
	Low	High	Total Per Cent
Low	61	65	61
N	(850)	(99)	(949)
Medium	76	73	75
N	(677)	(175)	(852)
High	77	75	76
N	(634)	(498)	(1,132)
Total N			3,423[a]

[a]Variations in total sample size due to rounding.

Student occupational aspirations and participation

Some additional depth to our analysis of SES factors and participation in the protest activities is provided by examining students' choices of occupational careers. In order to make this analysis, we first examined the relationship between students' career preferences as freshmen and participation. Using freshman career preferences, the preference in 1960, rather than senior preferences, acts as a control for the possibility that protest participation from 1960 through 1964 might have had either beneficial or adverse consequences for students' aspirations.[30] Among both men and women we found that students with high career aspirations as freshmen were somewhat more apt to participate in the protest events.[31] Among 1,028 male students, 79 per cent of those with high aspirations were participants as compared to 76 per cent of those with low aspirations. Among 1,859 females, the percentages were 72 and 66, respectively. The relationship was stronger for women, but was not very strong in either case.

Let us suppose, however, that a shift in students' career aspirations from their freshman through senior year accompanied differential involvement in the protest movement. For example, some students may have shifted their aspirations from "high" to "low" during their college years because of their dissatisfaction with prospects for occupational success. And, as a consequence, they might have been more likely than other students to participate in the protest movement. Examination of the data in Table 4, however, indicates that such an argument is unwarranted.

Perception of employment opportunities and participation

Both the "rising expectations" and, to a lesser degree, the relative-deprivation explanations suggest that protest activity may arise among Negroes who confront unanticipated limits on their opportunities. Negro

TABLE 4. Sex, Freshman Career Preference, Senior Career Preference, and Protest Participation (per cent participating)

Sex	Freshman Career Preference	Senior Career Preference	
		Low	High
Male	Low	74	78
	N	(392)	(109)
	High	77	81
	N	(167)	(340)
Female	Low	65	69
	N	(1,123)	(127)
	High	72	72
	N	(27)	(283)
Total N			3,423[a]

[a]Variations in total sample size due to rounding.

students tend, as a group, to be one of the more upwardly mobile segments of the Negro community. Yet their earnings are not commensurate with their educational attainment.[32] For that matter, their opportunities for employment in the professions and in business also may not be commensurate with their education.[33] Consequently, those Negro students who recognize the existence of such barriers might turn to the Negro protest movement to relieve their discontent.

Such arguments are examined here by looking at the association between students' perception of employment opportunities and protest participation. Students were asked the following question about job opportunities in the nation: "In your view, when will Negroes have equal job opportunities as compared with whites of the same educational level?" Students' responses to this question, together with the extent of their participation, are presented in Table 5. Among both male and female stu-

TABLE 5. Sex, Perception of Employment Opportunities in the Nation, and Protest Participation (per cent participating)

	Perception of Opportunities	
Sex	Equal now/ten years	Equal twenty years or more
Male	77	77
N	(510)	(501)
Female	66	67
N	(1,032)	(780)
Total N		3,422[a]

[a]Variations in total sample size due to rounding.

dents, perception of opportunities for employment in the nation bore no relationship to the extent of participation. A similar absence of association is found between participation and the perception of employment opportunities in both the North and South.

The analysis above assumes that many students thought that the expansion of employment opportunities for Negroes was an important goal of the Negro protest movement and, thus, joined the movement when confronted with limits on their own mobility. Undoubtedly, some dissatisfied students did not regard the protest movement as a vehicle for such purposes and therefore did not choose to participate in the protest. In order to take account of this possibility, let us examine the relationship between perception of employment opportunities and participation among students who did think that expanded opportunities were the most important goal. As the data in Table 6 indicate, even among the students who believed expanded job opportunities were the most significant aim of the Negro protest movement, the perception of employment opportunities had neither a consistent nor a strong association with participation.

TABLE 6. Gamma Coefficients for Association between Perception of
Employment Opportunities and Participation, Controlling
for Most Important Goal of Protest Movement and Sex

| | *Most Important Goal* | | | |
| | Employment opportunities | | All others | |
Type of Opportunity	male	female	male	female
Employment opportunities in the nation[a]	+.06	−.01	−.02	−.04
Employment opportunities in the South	+.08	−.03	−.05	−.06
Employment opportunities in the North	+.05	−.06	+.01	−.03

[a]In each case, participation is counted as positive, (+), and nonparticipation as negative (−). Thus, a gamma coefficient with a plus sign, (+), means that students who thought equal employment opportunities for Negroes would be obtained in twenty years or more were more likely to be participants than students who thought such opportunities would be achieved more rapidly.

Occupational aspirations, perception of opportunities and participation

Although this investigation has provided less than convincing evidence for the connection between economic or status-related factors and protest participation, one additional hypothesis [will be examined]. It is plausible to argue that the occupational aspirations of students would, in Lazarsfeld's terms, specify the relationship between perception of opportunities and participation.[34] More precisely, we might anticipate that only among the Negro students with high aspirations will the perception of limited employment opportunities lead to protest participation. Table 7 presents data necessary to test this hypothesis. Although freshman career preference continues to be slightly related to participation, students' perception of employment opportunities has no association with participation, even among students with high aspirations.

DISCUSSION

There are three traditional explanations which have been used to account for the growth of the Negro protest movement in terms of economic and status-related deprivations. The "vulgar Marxist" explanation argues that fundamental economic impoverishment of Negroes produces the necessary conditions for the spread of Negro protest efforts. This argument received no confirmation from our evidence on the participation of Negro college students. Students from poor families—lower socioeconomic status—were about equally likely to participate in protest activities as were students from wealthy backgrounds, higher sES.

The "rising expectations" thesis claims that many Negroes are un-

TABLE 7. Sex, Perception of Employment Opportunities in the
Nation, Freshman Career Preference and Protest Participation
(per cent participating)

		Freshman Career Preference	
Sex	Opportunities	Low	High
Male	Equal now/ten years	77	80
	N	(250)	(208)
	Twenty years or more	78	82
	N	(199)	(263)
Female	Equal now/ten years	66	73
	N	(672)	(271)
	Twenty years or more	66	71
	N	(474)	(235)
Total N			3,424[a]

[a]Variations in total sample size due to rounding.

happy with the pace of their recent achievements and, consequently, have
channeled their frustrations into the protest activities. In order to test this
argument, we looked at relationships among students' career aspirations,
perception of employment opportunities, and protest participation. If
this argument were correct, the perception of limited opportunities should
have been associated with participation. However, this hypothesis received no support. We also found that there was no association between
the perception of employment opportunities and participation even among
students with high aspirations, who might be most dissatisfied with limited
opportunities. Finally, we expected that many students who had lowered
their career aims during college were unhappy with their occupational
prospects and, therefore, would be most prone to participate. Instead, we
discovered that students with high career aspirations throughout college
were most likely to participate.

The third interpretation claims that the Negro protest movement
arose largely as a means for expressing the discontent of many Negroes,
especially middle-class Negroes, who feel "relatively deprived" compared
with their Negro or white peers. In order to assess the effect of individual
"deprivation" we examined the SES characteristics of student participants
and nonparticipants, in general, and in different college settings. We
found that students from relatively deprived backgrounds, homes in
which the father's education was high and family income low, had no
greater likelihood of participation than any other group. We also anticipated that students whose parents' SES was lower than that of the majority
of their fellow students would feel relatively deprived and would be most
likely to participate. There was no confirmation of this hypothesis. Of
course, none of this evidence provides a basis for dismissing the importance of the relative deprivation that Negro students might feel toward
their white counterparts.

By and large, all these results contradict those of previous research. Matthews and Prothro as well as Orbell discovered that students from higher SES homes were more likely to be participants than were students from lower SES homes.[35] Searles and Williams also uncovered a similar finding.[36] The present study, however, differs in several respects from earlier research. First, it is based on a much larger and somewhat more representative sample of Negro students and therefore may furnish more reliable evidence of the link between economic and status-related factors and participation. In addition, it was conducted two years after the other studies and reveals about twice as much overall participation. During the intervening two years, it seems likely that many students of lower-class origins became involved in the protest movement. Consequently, the earlier class differences between participants and nonparticipants would tend to disappear.

The different results also could be associated with the fact that the earlier studies used samples of students from all college classes, i.e., freshman through senior, whereas the present research dealt with seniors only. This analysis might indirectly confirm what Newcomb and other social scientists have observed about college students' political behavior: namely, that the impact of background factors such as parents' SES is gradually muted by salient dimensions of the college environment.[37] Along these lines, Matthews and Prothro's research demonstrates that characteristics of the college setting are much better predictors of students' participation in the protest movement than are economic or status-related background variables.[38]

In summary, we have found that several major interpretations of the growth of the Negro protest movement fail to explain student participation in these activities. The inadequacy of these interpretations might be due to the type of group analyzed in this study, or to their limited applicability as explanations of the Negro protest. In either case, the evidence from this research indicates that a re-evaluation should be made of these interpretations. Such a reassessment, moreover, should be conducted not only in light of the results from this study, which deals with Negro protest efforts of the past, but also with an eye to changes occurring in the character of the movement, especially in the strategies of protest organizations.

NOTES

1. Neil Smelser, *A Theory of Collective Behavior* (New York: Free Press, 1963), Chs. 10 and 11.

2. See especially the studies by Richard Hofstadter, "The Pseudo-Conservative Revolt," and "Pseudo-Conservatism Revisited: A Postscript," and by Seymour M. Lipset; "The Sources of the Radical Right," and "Three Decades of the Radical Right: Coughlinites, McCarthyites, and Birchers," in Daniel Bell, ed., *The Radical Right* (Garden City, N.Y.: Doubleday, 1963), pp. 63–86, 259–377.

3. See, for instance, William F. Soskin, "Riots, Ghettos, and the 'Negro Revolt,'" in

182 The civil rights movement

Arthur M. Ross and Herbert Hill, ed., *Employment, Race and Poverty* (New York: Harcourt, Brace & Jovanovich, 1967), p. 209.

4. Studies of participation in the Negro protest movement mainly deal with the participation of students. These studies only briefly consider the relationship between economic and status-related factors and participation. See J. R. Fishman and F. Solomon, "Youth and Social Action: I. Perspective on the Student Sit-In Movement," *The American Journal of Orthopsychiatry* 33 (October, 1963): 872–82; Donald R. Matthews and James W. Prothro, *Negroes and the New Southern Politics* (New York: Harourt, Brace & Jovanovich, 1966); John M. Orbell, "Protest Participation among Southern Negro College Students," *American Political Science Review* 61 (June, 1967): 446–56; and Ruth Searles and J. Allen Williams, Jr., "Negro College Students' Participation in Sit-Ins," *Social Forces* 40 (March 1962); 215–20; F. Solomon and J. R. Fishman, "Youth and Social Action: II. Action and Identity Formation in the First Student Sit-In Demonstration," *The Journal of Social Issues* 20 (April 1964); 36–45; and Howard Zinn, *SNCC: The New Abolitionists* (Boston: Beacon Press, 1964). The only reported research on this topic among adults is in Gary T. Marx, *Protest and Prejudice: A Study of Belief in the Black Community* (New York: Harper & Row, 1967).

5. Geschwender provides a very interesting explication of five hypotheses about the relation between certain social and economic conditions and the rise of the Negro protest movement. James A. Geschwender, "Social Structure and the Negro Revolt: An Examination of Some Hypotheses," *Social Forces* 43 (December 1964); 248–56 [reprinted in this volume, Part II, Section 1].

6. The type of evidence that supports this point of view can be found in: Leonard Broom and Norval Glenn, *Transformation of the Negro American* (New York: Harper & Row, 1965), Chs. 5 and 6; Rashi Fein, "An Economic and Social Profile of the Negro American," in Talcott Parsons and Kenneth B. Clark, eds., *The Negro American* (Boston: Houghton-Mifflin, 1966), pp. 102–33; Dale W. Hiestand, *Economic Growth and Employment Opportunities for Minorities* (New York: Columbia University Press, 1964); Herbert Hill, "Racial Inequality in Employment: The Patterns of Discrimination," in Arnold Rose, ed., *Annals of the American Academy of Political and Social Science*, Special Issue on The Negro Protest, 357 (January 1965), pp. 30–47; Thomas Pettigrew, *A Profile of the Negro American* (Princeton, N.J.: D. Van Nostrand, 1964), esp. p. 189; and U.S. Department of Labor, "The Employment of Negroes: Some Demographic Considerations," in Raymond J. Murphy and Howard Elinson, eds., *Problems and Prospects of the Negro Movement* (Belmont, Calif.: Wadsworth, 1966), pp. 116–24.

7. August Meier, "Civil Rights Strategies for Negro Employment," in Ross and Hill, eds., *Employment, Race and Poverty*, pp. 175–204.

8. Whitney M. Young, Jr., "Domestic Marshall Plan," in *New York Times Magazine*, October 6, 1963, cited in Murphy and Elinson, eds., *Problems and Prospects*, pp. 45–49.

9. S. M. Miller, "Poverty and Politics," in Irving Louis Horowitz, ed., *The New Sociology* (New York: Oxford University Press, 1964), p. 297, quoted in Michael Harrington, "The Economics of Protest," in Ross and Hill, eds., *Employment, Race and Poverty*, p. 236.

10. Broom and Glenn, *Transformation*, pp. 69–72; Jack L. Walker, "Protest and Negotiation: A Case Study of Negro Leadership in Atlanta," *Midwest Journal of Political Science* 7 (May 1963); 99–124.

11. Broom and Glenn, *Transformation*, p. 59; Pettigrew, *A Profile*, pp. 170–91; and Everett Carl Ladd, Jr., *Negro Political Leadership in the South* (Ithaca, N.Y.: Cornell University Press, 1966), p. 24.

12. Irving Kristol, "It's Not a Bad Crisis To Live In," *New York Times Magazine*, January 22, 1967, p. 70.

13. Cited in Pettigrew, *A Profile*, pp. 184–85.

14. William Brink and Louis Harris, *The Negro Revolution in America* (New York: Simon & Schuster, 1964), p. 238.

15. Paul M. Siegel, "On the Cost of Being a Negro," *Sociological Inquiry* 35 (Winter 1965); 57. Siegel's results are also pertinent to the discussion on "relative deprivation."

16. Karl Marx, "Wage-Labor and Capital," in Karl Marx and Friederich Engels, *Selected Works* (Moscow, 1958), I, 93, quoted in Ladd, *Negro Political Leadership*, p. 24.

17. This explanation is found in many discussions of the Negro protest movement. For illustrations: see Broom and Glenn, *Transformation*, p. 106; Joseph Gusfield, *Symbolic Crusade: Status Politics and the American Temperance Movement* (Urbana: University of Illinois Press, 1963), p. 22; Lewis M. Killian and Charles Grigg, *Racial Crisis in America: Leadership in Conflict* (Englewood Cliffs, N.J.: Prentice-Hall, 1964), pp. 133–34; Pettigrew, *A Profile*, pp. 178–79; and Daniel Thompson, "The Rise of the Negro Protest," in Rose, ed., *Annals of American Academy*, pp. 19–20.

18. U.S. Department of Labor Report in Murphy and Elinson, eds., *Problems and Prospects*, p. 121.

19. Gary T. Marx, *Protest and Prejudice*, pp. 55–70.

20. Searles and Williams, "Negro College Students' Participation," p. 219.

21. Matthews and Prothro, *Negroes and the New Southern Politics*, p. 419; and Orbell, "Protest Participation," p. 448. Orbell, incidentally, used the same data as Matthews and Prothro.

22. The result of this study of Negro seniors' career plans are reported in Joseph H. Fichter, "Neglected Talents: Background and Prospects of Negro College Graduates," National Opinion Research Center, February 1966, multilithed.

23. This group of schools does not include the fairly large number of predominantly Negro junior colleges in the United States.

24. The other list was assembled by McGrath. See Earl J. McGrath, *The Predominantly Negro Colleges and Universities in Transition* (New York: Bureau of Publications, Teachers College, Columbia University, 1965).

25. Fichter, "Neglected Talents," App. 1.

26. Broom and Glenn, *Transformation*.

27. Also examined were the correlates of activism by distinguishing between activists, leaders or very active participants, and nonactivists, inactive participants. The characteristics of the activists did not differ much from those who were inactive participants. As a consequence, results were presented only on the dimension of participation.

28. An index of socioeconomic status was created by combining responses to questions on father's education, family income, and occupation of the chief wage earner. In terms of this index, a family of high socioeconomic status would be comprised of a man whose education included at least some college training, whose head—most often a man—held a professional, managerial, or clerical position, and whose annual income was at least $7,500. Of course such families appear to be more prevalent among the parents of the Negro student population than among the Negro population in general.

29. The careful reader will note that the class composition of the school is related to the rate of participation. Specifically, the greater the proportion of students from high socioeconomic status (SES) homes, the greater is the rate of participation. This association can be explained by other variables that are related to the proportion of high SES *students*. For instance, schools of high quality generally have a greater proportion of students from high SES backgrounds and also have higher rates of student participation. See Matthews and Prothro, *Negroes and the New Southern Politics*, pp. 424–29; Orbell, "Protest Participation," pp. 448–50; and Anthony M. Orum, "Negro College Students and the Civil Rights Movement" (unpublished Ph.D. dissertation, University of Chicago, 1967), Ch. 6. The measures of school quality employed in these studies are based upon such indexes as the proportion

of Ph.D.'s on the faculty, student-faculty ratio, ratio of library books per student, and number of books in the library.

30. Pettigrew, for instance, claims that involvement in the protest might have advantageous effects for the self-respect and esteem of Negroes. He states that "the remedial powers of the movements themselves alter their followers in the process. . . . Negro Americans are learning how to be first-class citizens at the same time they are winning first-class citizenship." (Pettigrew, *A Profile*, p. 167).

31. In order to measure the level of students' career aspirations, an index developed by James Davis was employed. It is based upon the number of years of postgraduate education required for a particular occupation. The careers tend to be ranked by skill level or loosely speaking, occupational status. See James A. Davis, *Great Aspirations* (Chicago: Aldine Press, 1964). Sex was used as a control variable in this and subsequent analyses. There were two reasons for this procedure. First, the anticipated associations between economic or status-related factors and participation might have been stronger for men, since occupational data often demonstrate that Negro males seem to face a greater inequality of opportunity than Negro females, particularly in the white-collar occupations. Second, Negro college men were more likely to participate in the protest than Negro women. This difference might have confounded other differences in the association between economic or status-related factors and participation.

32. Siegel, "On the Cost."

33. For instance, see Hill, "Racial Inequality," pp. 30–47.

34. Patricia L. Kendall and Paul L. Lazarsfeld, "Problems of Survey Analysis," in Robert K. Merton and Paul F. Lazarsfeld, eds., *Continuities in Social Research: Studies in the Scope and Method of "The American Soldier"* (New York: Free Press, 1950), pp. 154–65.

35. Matthews and Prothro, *Negroes and the New Southern Politics*.

36. Searles and Williams, "Negro College Students' Participation."

37. Theodore M. Newcomb, *Personality and Social Change* (New York: The Dryden Press, 1943).

38. Matthews and Prothro, *Negroes and the New Southern Politics*, esp. p. 429.

PROCESS OF RECRUITMENT IN THE SIT-IN MOVEMENT

Maurice Pinard | Jerome Kirk | Donald Von Eschen

The purpose of this paper is to examine the role of strain in the growth of social movements. Though it is generally taken for granted that behind any episode of collective behavior lie some form of strains, little is known about the processes through which these strains affect the recruitment of people into a social movement.

From *The Public Opinion Quarterly* 33 (Fall 1969): 355–69; reprinted by permission of the authors and publishers.

STRAINS AND SOCIAL MOVEMENT PARTICIPATION

Since the argument of this paper contains some paradoxes, let us present it briefly at the beginning. Our central argument is that contrary to frequent assumptions, one should not necessarily expect a monotonically positive relationship between strains [1] and the various modalities of participation in a social movement. Students in this field have usually failed to make appropriate distinctions between these modalities. As will be seen below, it seems important to distinguish between *recruitment to* (or *attraction* to) a social movement, and *intensity of activity* in that social movement once it has been joined. On the basis of these distinctions, the following propositions are offered.

On the one hand, we hypothesize a positive relationship between amount of strain and *intensity of activity* in a social movement. Most of the literature on collective behavior—though, as noted, it fails to make the distinction we are introducing—is consonant with the suggestion that the most deprived will always tend to be the most active participants in a social movement, once they have joined it. The only directly relevant finding, however, is reported by Lipset, who found that poor farmers, once aroused, became stronger supporters of the socialist C.C.F. party than well-to-do farmers.[2]

On the other hand, as we have suggested elsewhere,[3] only certain types of strain bear a direct linear relationship to *attraction* to a social movement. The most important strains of this type probably consist of *changes* for the worse in one's condition. But long-endured strains, which are relatively *stable* and *permanent*—poverty being probably the best example—present a handicap for the early recruitment of participants. The most deprived, in this latter sense, are *not* generally the early recruits of social movements. For instance, one's probability of joining a social movement may increase when, during a recession, one's economic hardships keep piling up, but this probability does not generally increase with one's degree of (stable) poverty. Again, most of the literature on the effects of social unrest, deprivation, frustration, etc., is consistent with the idea that *increasing* deprivations are directly related to recruitment to a social movement: the appearance of social movements is indeed generally explained by such conditions of strain, and one could cite an endless list of movements following, for instance, economic or political reverses. We shall not in fact try to test this last proposition again here.[4] At the same time, many observers have noted that the poor—the permanently deprived —do not spur revolts; the reader is referred to a summary of the literature and to empirical data presented elsewhere.[5] Rarely, however, have these various propositions been brought together, and hard data presented to test them within the context of the same movement.

Moreover, we know little about the mechanisms that initially inhibit the recruitment of those permanently deprived. It is suggested here that such steady strains render unlikely the presence of the sophisticated "generalized beliefs" that are essential for translating grievances into political action. Only at later stages, when these beliefs have developed because of the early successes of the movement, do the most deprived become candidates for recruitment.[6]

These hypotheses can be tested with data collected from participants in a sit-in demonstration. On December 16, 1961, some 500 to 600 members of CORE and other civil rights organizations staged a demonstration at eating places along U. S. Route 40 between Baltimore and Wilmington. We distributed questionnaires to the participants at the Baltimore central meeting place, and the questionnaires were filled out by 386 of them (i.e. by about 60 to 80 per cent of the demonstrators).[7]

STRAINS AND ACTIVITY IN THE MOVEMENT

Participation in a social movement is generally first a response to strains that the movement tries to correct. In this sense, racial strains must certainly have been an important determinant of activity in the sit-in movement.[8] But participation can also be a response to strains less clearly related to the goals of that movement; for example, it may represent a partial displacement of protest against targets more easily accessible than those which are the immediate source of one's tensions.[9]

In this instance, racial strains were not the only ones to find their expression among participants; socioeconomic deprivations were also involved.[10] If we take as our indicator of participation in the movement the amount of *activity* the participants engaged in since joining the movement, we find that the lower one's socioeconomic status (the higher one's deprivation), the more active one has been in the movement (Table 1, first panel); notice moreover that this its true for both Negroes and white participants independently.[11]

Similarly, an experience of downward intergenerational occupational mobility can obviously be taken as an indicator of at least status, if not economic, deprivation. Again the data indicate that among non-students, both Negro and white participants who had experienced downward mobility had been more active than the others (Table 1, second panel). Finally, since it has been argued that status inconsistency is a source of stress,[12] we should find the same type of relationship with this indicator. This is once more borne out by the data (Table 1, third section). Those whose status was inconsistent were generally more active than those enjoying a consistent status.[13] Other data from the study (not presented here) also reveal that those whose income was lower than that of their friends, or who expected a discrepancy between their occupational expectations and their aspirations (the latter being higher), or who were unhappy in their jobs tended to be more active participants than the others. In short, the data so far convincingly demonstrate the existence of a direct linear relationship between *strains* and *intensity of activity* in the sit-in demonstrations.

Yet, and this is paradoxical, though deprivations led to active participation, the movement we studied was still a predominantly white and upper-middle-class movement. As indicated above, the denial to American Negroes of so many of the privileges enjoyed by whites should be a signifi-

TABLE 1. The Most Deprived were the Most Active Participants

	Per cent More Active[a]					
	Negroes		Whites		Both	
Status Measures	%	N	%	N	%	N
Socioeconomic Status[b] (all R's)						
High	32	(28)	49	(76)	44	(104)
Medium	44	(63)	59	(108)	54	(171)
Low	67	(27)	83	(18)	73	(45)
Social Mobility[c] (non-students only)						
Upward	42	(12)	61	(23)	54	(35)
Stable	46	(11)	67	(12)	56	(23)
Downward	100	(2)	80	(15)	82	(17)
Status Consistency[d] (non-students only)						
Consistent	35	(23)	64	(14)	46	(37)
Inconsistent I	88	(8)	64	(25)	70	(33)
Inconsistent iI	67	(12)	100	(15)	85	(27)

[a]Per cent who reported having been out on demonstrations 3 times or more, in answer to the question: "How many times have you been out on demonstrations before today?"
  [b]Socioeconomic status: determined by North-Hatt scores for occupations given in response to the question: "What job are you training for in school?" (students), or "What is your job?" (non-students). A high status corresponds to a score of 85 or above; a low status, to a score of 71 or below. (Notice that many low-status participants had at most a lower-middle-class occupational level, i.e. below, approximately, the status of an undertaker, a grade school teacher, or a reporter). The relationships remain the same for Negro students and non-students, and for white students and non-students.
  [c]Social mobility: comparison, for non-students, of their socioeconomic score with that of their father ("What is your father's main occupation?"). The scores were broken into four classes (less than 72; 72-74; 75-84; 85 or more).
  [d]Status consistency: based on a comparison of socioeconomic scores (see above) and educational levels. The educational levels used were: high — finished college or more; medium — some college; low — finished high school or less. The "inconsistent I" group comprises participants with a combination of high and medium statuses; group II, participants with medium-low or high-low status combinations.

cant source of strain prompting Negroes to participate in this movement. And indeed, while Negroes formed only 8.6 per cent of the population in the census regions from which the participants were recruited (New England, Middle Atlantic, East North Central, and South Atlantic), they constituted 36.4 per cent of our sample, that is, a proportion more than four times what one would have expected on the basis of chance alone. Nevertheless, one may still wonder why this overrepresentation was not much larger, indeed why Negroes were not at least a majority in a movement devoted to the redress of Negro grievances.

Similarly, few of the movement's recruits came from the most deprived segments of the population. Although we found in Table 1 that those of a *relatively* [14] lower socioeconomic status were more active, it is nevertheless true that few participants were from the working classes proper. If we shift for a moment from a measure of relative position on the North-Hatt status scale to the more traditional census categories, we find that the vast majority of the participants (89 per cent; $N = 311$) were either training for, or engaged in, jobs which are usually considered to be of an upper-middle-class status, that is, professional or managerial

jobs; only a very small minority (4 per cent) were workers. The high proportion coming from the upper middle class held pretty well in all
subgroups of the sample: the corresponding figures were, for Negro non-
students, 60 per cent, for Negro students, 92 per cent, for white non-
students, 81 per cent, and for white students, 100 per cent. At the other
extreme, the proportions from the working classes (skilled workers and
below) in each of these four groups were, respectively, 21, 2, 2, and 0 per
cent ($N = 43$, 75, 62, and 131). In short, while deprivations led to active
involvement, Negroes were still a minority in the movement, and the
most deprived Negro and white strata of the population were strongly
underrepresented. How can we account for these apparently contradictory
observations?

STRAINS AND ATTRACTION TO THE MOVEMENT

To answer this question, we must turn to the role of relatively permanent
strains as a determinant of attraction to an incipient movement. If our
argument about the role of this type of strain is correct, it should show
up in the data. When considering as the dependent variable the *length
of participation* in the movement, rather than the amount of activity engaged in since joining it, we should observe that those suffering from
relatively stable deprivations, though the most active, were not the early
recruits of the movement.

The reader should note first that the three indicators of deprivation
we have used so far are all indicators of relatively stable, permanent
deprivations: people's position in terms of socioeconomic status, or intergenerational mobility, or status consistency does not generally represent a
sudden change in their share of society's rewards. If we turn again to
these independent variables, we find first, assuming similar patterns of
attrition,[15] that those of a relatively lower socioeconomic status tended to
have been relatively late joiners, even though we found them to have
been *the most active of all*. This is true for the sample as a whole, as well
as for Negro students and non-students, and white non-students (Table
2a). Similarly, among non-students, those who had been downwardly

TABLE 2a. The Most Deprived, in Terms of Socioeconomic Status,
Were among the Latest Recruits (per cent early joiners[a])

	Socioeconomic Status[b]					
	High		Medium		Low	
	%	N	%	N	%	N
Negro non-students	43	(7)	44	(18)	18	(17)
Negro students	35	(20)	40	(42)	30	(10)
White non-students	40	(5)	42	(40)	33	(18)
White students	22	(65)	26	(61)	–	(0)
Total sample	27	(97)	36	(161)	27	(45)

[a]Per cent who joined the movement one year or more ago.
[b]Socioeconomic status: as in Table 1.

TABLE 2b. The Most Deprived, in Terms of Social Mobility and Status Consistency, Were among the Latest Recruits

	Percent Early Joiners [a]					
	Negroes		Whites		Both	
Status Measures	%	N	%	N	%	N
Social Mobility[b] (non-students only)						
Upward	25	(12)	41	(22)	35	(34)
Stable	50	(10)	33	(12)	41	(22)
Downward	0	(2)	29	(14)	25	(16)
Status Consistency[b] (non-students only)						
Consistent	39	(21)	36	(14)	37	(35)
Inconsistent I	62	(8)	44	(25)	48	(33)
Inconsistent II	8	(12)	40	(15)	26	(27)

[a] As in Table 2a.
[b] As in Table 1.

mobile, or whose status was inconsistent (with some low components—group II), albeit the most active participants, as seen in Table 1, are now found to have been the latest joiners of the movement (Table 2b). And, though the number of cases becomes very small, the over-all pattern seems to hold for Negroes and whites separately. Thus, while those most deprived were the most active participants, *once they had joined,* they were nevertheless relatively late joiners.

In short, while the relationship between steady deprivation and activity is positive and linear, the relationship between these deprivations and length of participation is curvilinear: the early joiners of this incipient movement tended to be people who were only moderately deprived. Neither the least deprived nor the most deprived tended to be early recruits.[16] Among the first, the presence of strains as a condition was lacking—and notice that they were not very active, once they had joined; among the second, though strains were present, something else was lacking: the ability to translate their grievances in political terms.

This process in part accounts for the fact that Negroes were a minority even in "their" movement and for the fact that the movement was so clearly a middle-class movement. The recruitment process just described meant that the bulk of the Negro population did not form the recruiting base of the movement, at least in its early stages. Hence, the movement had to rely on the relatively small Negro middle class and on that part of the white middle class which, as we shall see, was largely marginal.

POLITICAL TRANSLATION OF GRIEVANCES

But what is it that prevents those affected by permanent deprivations from being the early participants of a new movement? As suggested before, it may be that they do not possess the ability to translate their grievances in political terms; there are presumably many facets to this factor, but we will examine only two.[17]

Ideology

First, to engage in any social movement, one must develop, as suggested before, a "generalized belief" that not only identifies the sources
of one's strains but envisages an effective cure through some sort of specific
program.[18] A particularly sophisticated generalized belief is necessary to
compensate for the inherent weakness of a new movement.[19] The inability
of those under permanent strains to develop such a sophisticated belief
would be one of the reasons for their slow recruitment in the early phases
of a movement.

A radical ideology, as a set of articulated beliefs together with moral
commitment to a cause and a deep conviction that historical forces are
on one's side, represents such a sophisticated belief. An indication of how
important this element was in the early phases of the movement we are
studying is afforded by the marginals of the data: only 7 per cent of the
participants said they would vote Republican in a presidential election,
and while 56 per cent mentioned the Democrats, no less than 37 per cent
answered Socialist or Independent (18 and 19 per cent respectively; $N =$
322).[20] More strikingly, about 4 out of every 10 participants (42 per cent)
had political preferences to the *left* of their mother's political preferences
($N = 286$).[21] This hardly compares with the general population.[22]

The crucial role of ideology is particularly revealed by the strength
of the relationship it bears to activity within the movement. While 26
per cent of the Republicans and 47 per cent of the Democrats had been
among the more active participants, 62 per cent of the Independents and
76 per cent of the Socialists had been so ($N = 23$, 180, 60, and 59 respectively). Moreover, the data indicate that in the early phases of the movement at least, ideology was not just an intervening psychological process
between deprivations and participation, since it exerted a strong effect
of its own, as shown in Table 3. Indeed, ideology is almost as strong a
predictor of activity as deprivation.[23]

That the lack of a sophisticated generalized belief was one of the
factors preventing the most deprived from being early joiners is indicated
in Table 4. When ideology is introduced as a control variable in the relationship between socioeconomic status and length of participation, the

TABLE 3.   Ideology and Deprivations are Independently Related to Activity

	Per Cent More Active[a]					
	Democratic or Republican		Independent		Socialist	
Socioeconomic Status	%	N	%	N	%	N
High	42	(55)	33	(12)	69	(16)
Medium	45	(91)	67	(33)	80	(25)
Low	67	(27)	86	(7)	100	(5)

[a]As in Table 1. Ns are reduced because of nonresponse.

TABLE 4.   Ideology Permits a Lower-Status Person to Join Early

| | Per Cent Early Joiners[a] | | | |
| | Left of Mother[b] (ideologues) | | Not Left of Mother (non-ideologues) | |
Socioeconomic Status	%	N	%	N
High	29	(28)	29	(49)
Medium	38	(61)	34	(71)
Low	43	(14)	18	(22)

[a]As in Table 2a. Ns are reduced because of nonresponse.
[b]Based on a comparison of respondent's and his mother's party preference; see footnote 21.

data suggest that, when *low-status participants were also ideologues,* far from being late joiners, *they tended to be the earliest joiners.*

Political alienation

Apart from a radical ideology, which represents the positive side of a strong generalized belief, there is a closely related cluster of factors, such as resignation, withdrawal, hopelessness, and retreatist alienation, which belongs to the negative side of the belief—the loss of faith in present arrangements and the potentialities of action. These could also help to account for the early resistance of the most deprived to the appeals of a new movement; such attitudes would grow out of long-endured deprivations and would lead to a wait-and-see attitude until the new movement has proved itself. One measure of such feelings of hopelessness is political alienation, the belief that routine political action can yield no results. That political alienation is more common among low-status people is revealed both by our data and by many other studies.

Alienation did not seem to bear any clear-cut set of relationships to participation as measured by either of our two indicators.[24] But this is partly because strains are not the only source of alienation. A radical ideology, as a fully developed generalized belief, can itself be an important factor leading one to lose faith in present political arrangements.

TABLE 5.   The Two Sources of Political Alienation

| | Per Cent Politically Alienated[a] | | | |
| | Left of mother (ideologues) | | Not left of mother (non-ideologues) | |
Socioeconomic Status	%	N	%	N
High	78	(25)	45	(47)
Medium	56	(59)	52	(66)
Low	64	(14)	77	(17)

[a]Per cent agreeing with the statement: "Most politicians are corrupt." Ns are reduced because of nonresponse.

Indeed, ideology and deprivation seem to be alternative sources of political alienation (Table 5). But while alienation rooted in deprivation leads to retreatism,[25] one might expect that alienation rooted in ideology will produce rebellious tendencies,[26] for in this case it is associated with a belief that radical political action can yield results.

That these two variants of alienation can be identified and that they lead to opposite responses is suggested by the results presented in Table 6. Though we use only a one-item indicator of political alienation and though the number of cases is very small in some cells, it seems that among non-ideologues, alienation *prevents* one from being an early joiner, while, on the contrary, among ideologues, alienation *increases* one's probability of being an early joiner.[27]

It is important to notice, moreover, that among ideologues, whether alienated or not, the previous curvilinear relationship between deprivation (social status) and length of participation disappears again, as in Table 5. Alienation, when rooted in ideology, is neither a restraining factor in general, nor among the low-status group in particular. On the other hand, among non-ideologues, the curvilinear relationship becomes particularly strong for the alienated subgroup, while it almost disappears for their nonalienated counterparts. Retreatist alienation, therefore, seems really part of the cluster of factors that retard the low-status group in its participation.[28] Obviously, the small number of cases in many cells of Table 6 prevents us from holding the findings above as firm conclusions, but we think they are suggestive enough to warrant consideration.

TABLE 6.   The Opposite Responses Produced by Two Variants of Alienation

	Per Cent Early Joiners[a]							
	Ideologues				Non-ideologues			
	alienated		not alienated		alienated		not alienated	
Socioeconomic Status	%	N	%	N	%	N	%	N
Total Sample	39	(71)	30	(43)	28	(79)	30	(70)
High	28	(18)	29	(7)	20	(20)	31	(26)
Medium	39	(33)	32	(25)	31	(32)	36	(31)
Low	44	(9)	40	(5)	15	(13)	33	(6)

[a]As in Table 2A. N's are reduced because of nonresponse.

SUMMARY AND IMPLICATIONS

Our analysis revealed that various forms of strain, whether directly related to the civil rights movement or not, accounted in part for the degree of activity of members already recruited into the movement. Yet we found that Negroes were not even a majority in the movement we studied, and that the most deprived segments of the population were practically absent from its ranks. The key to these paradoxes seems to be that those most deprived, though having greater motives to participate and being in fact the most active, once involved, tend to be late joiners.

A complex of factors probably accounts for this inability of the steadily deprived to translate their grievances into political terms. We have suggested that the lack of a sophisticated generalized belief, indexed here by a radical ideology, and alienation, more specifically alienation rooted in deprivations, were two of the factors involved. The possession of a radical ideology, in particular, was shown to be a crucial factor in the early phases of the movement, a factor almost as important as deprivation. Moreover, ideology wiped out the negative portion of the relationship between early joining and social status, while retreatist alienation reinforced it. The lack of a sophisticated belief and the presence of retreatist alienation therefore both contributed to the processes uncovered here.

These findings have important implications, both for understanding the failure of the civil rights movement of the early 1960's to exhibit a strong Negro working-class base, and for the strategies such movements must use to maximize their numerical strength in the long run.[29]

Some writers have argued that civil rights leaders were tactically incorrect in attacking status rather than welfare goals; that had the movement stressed job and housing opportunities rather than public accommodations and voting, massive recruitment would have resulted. Our data suggest there are serious problems with this argument. If a sense of efficacy is important, not only would the movement have failed to recruit a larger base, it would have precluded the emergence of whatever level of mass mobilization (in the form of riots) now exists. By stressing welfare goals, it would have directed itself to a population which is very difficult to recruit, while failing at the same time to attract middle-class elements, thus missing *both* the moderately and the severely deprived. Furthermore, because welfare goals are harder to obtain—whites resist more in this area and the locus of power is more diffuse—the efforts of the movement would probably have resulted in failure, creating an image of weakness and thus further inhibiting recruitment. The concentration on status goals may thus have been tactically sound. It permitted the movement to give an image of strength, necessary for long-run recruitment.

That the movement was having this impact is suggested, although not proved, by some of our data. Its successes clearly created a feeling of optimism about political action. The participants, interviewed after substantial gains had already been made, indicated that their assessment of the possibilities of action had changed greatly. Fully 79 per cent of the Negro participants reported that, since they had joined the movement, their expectations of desegregation had increased.[30] That this creation of an image of strength was important in recruiting working-class people is suggested by the successes the movement subsequently had in recruiting working-class participants in demonstrations on Maryland's Eastern Shore.

Thus, it may be functional at times for movements to select as initial targets goals that are only dimly related to the core problems faced by the deprived population, if in this way they develop faith in the movement's power to change things and thus maximize long-run recruitment.

NOTES

ACKNOWLEDGMENT: We are grateful to the organizers of the "Route 40 Freedom Ride," and in particular to James Farmer, former president of CORE, who allowed us to change our role from that of participants to that of systematic observers. We are also indebted to Raymond Breton, James Coleman, Robert Peabody, and Arthur Stinchcombe for their comments on an earlier draft of this paper, although, since they disagreed with some of our arguments, they cannot be held responsible for its contents.

1. The concept of strain is borrowed from Smelser, who devotes a full chapter to its elaboration in his *Theory of Collective Behavior* (New York, Free Press, 1963), ch. 3. We use this concept as the most satisfactory generic term to refer to any impairment in people's life conditions. Though in Smelser's typology, the concept of deprivation refers to only one subtype of strains—in particular the loss of social rewards (wealth, power, prestige, esteem)—the two concepts of strain and deprivation are used here interchangeably, since most of our indicators of strain are of this latter type.

2. S. M. Lipset, *Agrarian Socialism* (Berkeley and Los Angeles: University of California Press, 1950), p. 167.

3. Maurice Pinard, *The Rise of a Third Party: A Study in Crisis Politics* (Englewood Cliffs, N.J.: Prentice-Hall, 1971; and Pinard, "Poverty and Political Movements," *Social Problems* 15 (Fall 1967): 250–63.

4. See, for instance, Smelser, *Theory of Collective Behavior,* pp. 267 ff.; Pinard, *The Rise of a Third Party,* ch. 6.

5. Pinard, "Poverty and Political Movements," pp. 250–56.

6. This is akin to Lipset's idea that because of "the lack of a rich, complex frame of reference," low-status people will always choose the least complex form of politics. Wherever the Communist party is small, he observed, it tends to be supported by the better-off segments of the working-class, while where it is strong, as in France and Italy, for instance, the contrary is true; see his *Political Man* (Garden City, N.Y.: Doubleday, 1960), pp. 122 ff.

7. For a brief history of the sit-ins and freedom rides in the United States, see Donald R. Matthews and James W. Prothro, *Negroes and the New Southern Politics* (New York: Harcourt, Brace & Jovanovich, 1966), pp. 407 ff. The authors date the beginning of the sit-ins to February 1960, in Greensboro, North Carolina, though they report other sporadic instances in 1958 and 1959. In Maryland, the first activities of the sit-in movement took place in early 1960. The "Route 40 Freedom Ride," at which we distributed our questionnaires, was organized after African diplomats complained that they were refused service at eating places along the main artery from Washington to New York. The reason some participants did not fill out the questionnaire is that they either did not arrive at the Baltimore terminal or, more often, were organized in groups leaving for a demonstration before they could complete it. While the sample is not random, so that confidence or significance methods cannot be applied, we have been unable to discern any source of systematic non-response bias and we feel satisfied that these data present an undistorted picture of the group.

8. Though Matthews and Prothro do not carry out a separate analysis of recruitment to and activity in the sit-in movement, their data clearly indicate that dissatisfaction with race relations was monotonically related to participation in the sit-in movement; see *ibid.,* pp. 419–24.

9. According to Smelser (*Theory of Collective Behavior,* pp. 48–49), "any kind of strain may be a determinant of any kind of collective behavior," and the same kinds of strain lay behind a vast array of religious and political movements. See also, from a psychological perspective, John Dollard *et al., Frustration and Ag-*

gression (New Haven: Yale University Press, 1939); Neal E. Miller, "The Frustration-Aggression Hypothesis," in M. H. Marx, *Psychological Theory* (New York: Macmillan, 1951).

10. Most studies have indicated that lower-status people tend to have more complaints about their conditions, to be more dissatisfied, and to be less happy than others. See for instance Geneviève Knupfer, "Portrait of the Underdog," in R. Bendix and S. M. Lipset, eds., *Class, Status, and Power* (New York: Free Press, 1953), pp. 255–63; Alex Inkeles, "Industrial Man: The Relation of Status to Experience, Perception, and Value," *American Journal of Sociology* 66 (1960): 1–31; Norman M. Bradburn and David Caplovitz, *Reports on Happiness: A Pilot Study of Behavior Related to Mental Health* (Chicago: Aldine, 1965), ch. 2. One study which is partly in exception is that of W. G. Runciman, *Relative Deprivation and Social Justice* (Berkeley and Los Angeles: University of California Press, 1966), ch. 10. This study, moreover, along with others cited in Hyman and Singer, indicates that low socioeconomic status is not necessarily accompanied by perceived deprivation unless certain kinds of comparisons are made. See Herbert H. Hyman and Eleanor Singer, eds., *Readings in Reference Group Theory and Research* (New York: Free Press, 1968), pp. 166–221.

11. In the case of white participants, the relationship suggests the "displacement" hypothesis, if we assume that segregation does not account for the strains they suffered. A slightly different interpretation of these relations is that feelings of unjust treatment lead one to help others in similar conditions and/or to desire to change a system in which one has no vested interests.

12. See, for instance, Gerhard E. Lenski, *Power and Privilege* (New York: McGraw-Hill, 1966), pp. 86–88. Lenski suggests that status inconsistency can lead people to support liberal and radical movements.

13. We are aware of the problems involved in measuring the effects of status inconsistency; see, for instance, the papers by Martin D. Hyman, "Determining the Effects of Status Inconsistency," *Public Opinion Quarterly* 30 (1966): 120–29, and H. M. Blalock, "Comment: Status Inconsistency and the Identification Problem," *ibid.*, pp. 130–32. But even if we hold constant status to obviate these difficulties, our results remain: among the consistent subgroup, 44, 50, and 44 per cent of the high, medium, and low status participants were more active ($N = 16$, 12 and 9 respectively); this is much lower than the 70 and 85 per cent of the two inconsistent subgroups (see Table 1; they are differentiated on the basis of their status components).

14. Notice that with the North-Hatt measure used before, we classified as of low socioeconomic status people who were from the lower-middle-class or below; see note to Table 1.

15. A different, and more costly, kind of data would yield a more definitive demonstration of this point. In the absence of longitudinal data, it is impossible to discriminate conclusively between the effects of differential recruitment and the artifact of differential retention.

16. Matthews and Prothro also found that Negro students from lower social classes were less likely to participate in the sit-in movement than others. They did not find, however, a lower rate of participation among the higher classes (i.e., their relationships do not appear to be curvilinear); this may be due to the use of less refined categories of status. See *Negroes and the New Southern Politics*, pp. 418–19. It is interesting to note, however, that in their adult Negro sample, they found that the relationship between political participation and satisfaction with the community's race relations was curvilinear: both those who evaluated these relations as of the very best or as of the very worst kind were less likely to participate than those between these extremes; *ibid.*, pp. 288–92.

17. For other aspects of this factor, see Pinard, "Poverty and Political Movements," pp. 256–62.

18. Smelser, *Theory of Collective Behavior*, ch. 5.

19. Moreover, the more complex the forms of participation—demonstrating is more complex than voting—the stronger and the more sophisticated the belief must be. This certainly accounts in part for the fact that the early voters of new political movements often have a lower status than the early supporters of this movement, though in both cases the most deprived are not the early joiners; compare with the data presented in Pinard, "Poverty and Political Movements."

20. The question asked was: "If you were to register in the presidential election, how would you vote?" (This was followed by "How would your parents [father, mother] vote," the data from which are used below.) The independent subgroup (61) includes 18 "others." In the present data, Independent empirically fits best not between Democrat and Republican, but between Socialist and Democrat, since people placing themselves in this category considered both major parties too conservative. It may be necessary to point out that when we refer to Socialists as ideologues, we do not mean totalitarian revolutionary socialists. Those who called themselves "socialists" were libertarian in their beliefs.

21. Among the 42 per cent classified as "left of mother," about half (20 per cent) were Socialists (including five cases of Socialist sons of Socialist mothers); the others were either Independents (13 per cent) or Democrats (9 per cent) ($N = 286$). We assume here that any adopted preference to the left of one's parents' party preference is indicative of at least a moderately radical ideology, and that the Socialist sons of Socialist mothers similarly fit our nominal concept of "ideologue." And indeed we find that among those classified as left of mother, 39 per cent of the Socialists and 34 per cent of the others were early joiners, while the comparable proportion is 28 per cent among those who were not to the left of their mother ($N = 56$, 65, and 165 respectively).

22. The party identification of most people resembles that of their parents and, it seems, primarily that of their mother; see, for instance, Robert E. Lane and David O. Sears, *Public Opinion* (Englewood Cliffs, N.J.: Prentice-Hall, 1964), pp. 20–21; Eleanor E. Maccoby, Richard E. Matthews, and Alton S. Morton, "Youth and Political Change," in Heinz Eulau, *et al.*, eds., *Political Behavior* (New York: Free Press, 1956), p 301. In general, the proportion of young voters shifting their party preference seems to be about one out of four, and the proportion of them shifting left, less than 15 per cent. This is suggested on the basis of data recomputed from Bernard R. Berelson, Paul F. Lazarsfeld, and William N. McPhee, *Voting* (Chicago: University of Chicago Press, 1954), pp. 88–89; also Herbert H. Hyman, *Political Socialization* (New York: Free Press, 1959), pp. 74 ff., and the other two sources cited above.

23. The average effect of socioeconomic status (i.e. the average percentage difference) is .36, while the average effect of party preferences (ideology) is .27. (This follows James A. Coleman, *Introduction to Mathematical Sociology* [New York: Free Press, 1964], ch. 6.) These findings contrast with those reported by Surace and Seeman, who found ideology, as measured by a version of McClosky's liberal-conservative scale, to be "a weak interpreter of personal engagement in the civil rights movement." See Samuel J. Surace and M. Seeman, "Some Correlates of Civil Rights Activism," *Social Forces* 46 (1967): 204.

24. Surace and Seeman also report no zero-order relationship between generalized powerlessness and civil rights activism; see "Some Correlates of Civil Rights Activism," pp. 204–5.

25. See, for instance, the literature cited in William Erbe, "Social Involvement and Political Activity: A Replication and Elaboration," *American Sociological Review* 29 (1964): 198–215. Erbe reports, however, that there is doubt whether alienation exerts any effect independently of socioeconomic status and organizational involvement.

26. Erbe has called attention to these two variants of alienation, without, however, indicating their respective sources. See *ibid.*, p. 206.

27. Here, an almost identical set of relationships emerges when activity in the movement rather than length of participation is considered. All these factors—low status,

ideology, and rebellious alienation—explain no less than 56 per cent of the variation in activity.

28. This strongly challenges the claims of mass society theorists that the isolated and the alienated are the prime recruits of mass movements. For other qualifications of this theory, see Maurice Pinard, "Mass Society and Political Movements: A New Formulation," *American Journal of Sociology* 73 (1968): 682–90; also Pinard, *The Rise of a Third Party*, chs. 10–12.

29. Additional implications of our findings on recruitment are discussed in Donald von Eschen, Jerome Kirk, and Maurice Pinard, "The Conditions of Direct Action in a Democratic Society," *Western Political Quarterly* 22 (1969): 309–25.

30. Only 19 per cent said their expectations had remained about the same and, more strikingly, only 1 per cent said they had decreased ($N = 139$); the changes were smaller among whites: the comparable proportions are, respectively, 57, 40, and 4 per cent ($N = 239$).

part III

BLACK
POWER

"Black Power" is a development logically, if not temporally, intermediate between the old civil rights movement and ghetto uprisings. There may be no consensus on exactly what "Black Power" means, but the meaning of the lack of black power is clear. The lack of black power meant slavery. During the period of slavery, it meant that black women were property to be used whenever and however white men chose. It meant that black slaves could have no conception of stable family relations, private property, or control over themselves and their destinies. The lack of black power meant that slavery was not ended until whites decided that it should be ended. Since the abolition of slavery, the lack of black power has meant continued economic exploitation of blacks, continued sexual exploitation of black women, psychological castration of black men (sometimes physical castration for those who were not sufficiently castrated psychologically), humiliation, lynchings, and police brutality.

"Black Power," then, is whatever will bring an end to this situation. "Black Power" is anything that will place blacks in such a position that they can make it too expensive to whites to continue exploiting blacks. Thus, there are many roads to black power. One road may be through the development of a political bloc of black voters who may constitute the balance of power between rival groups of whites. A second road may be through a drive to make blacks economically self-sufficient and independent of white capital. A third may be through the development of a black coercive force sufficiently powerful as to intimidate whites from engaging in lynchings (legal or otherwise) and/or police brutality. These are only three of many possible roads, any number of which may be traveled at the same time.

A case could be made then for including the chapter on ghetto uprisings under the title of "Black Power." Ghetto uprisings may be viewed as a tactic used to increase the cost to whites of exploiting blacks, and therefore as a road to greater black self-determination. I have arbitrarily decided to treat them in separate chapters. I am using a rationale based upon the distinction between an intellectual statement of an ideology and a behavioral act which may or may not follow from that ideology. Black Power, as I am using it here, is a philosophical position with considerable breadth while ghetto uprisings are relatively narrow tactical acts.

Three selections will be included in this part. The selection by Joyce Ladner discusses the meaning of "Black Power" for Mississippi Negroes around the summer of 1966. This selection does an excellent job of analyzing the differential attractiveness and impact of an idea for persons of differing backgrounds and orientations. For many, "Black Power" was a slogan and tactic deliberately used to increase morale and esprit de corps. It aids in the development of a sense of worth and value and contributes strongly to the emergence of faith. The philosophy makes it possible for one to see the manner in which unity and solidarity can provide sufficient power to change society. While there were differences in the manner in which the philosophy and slogan were perceived and used, the differences were mainly in the level of abstraction—that is, in the extent to which it was related to long-run objectives and organizational goals or to immediate short-run problems of organizing to achieve specific aims.

Raymond S. Franklin's selection focuses on the interrelationship between the economic system of the society at large and the ideology of "Black Power." The ideology is discussed in terms of its philosophy, ethic, strategies, and conception of the black as a man. The ideology and operation of American capitalism are discussed in relation to the emergence of the Black Power ideology. This selection is especially valuable because of the degree of structural analysis it contains. The position of the American black is clearly a consequence of the operation of the free enterprise system—a system which provides realistic motivation to engage in discrimination. Thus it becomes inevitable that a revolt against discrimination will also take on overtones of a revolt against capitalism as well. Franklin doesn't carry his analysis quite this far, but a strong case could be made for the proposition that any realistic solution to the position of the American black necessarily presupposes the elimination of capitalism.

The selection by Robert Blauner continues the organizational trend from the specific to the general. Both Blauner and Franklin focus their analysis upon broad variables in the social system. Blauner differs from Franklin in that he places primary emphasis upon the experience of the black community as an internal colony rather than as a victim of capitalism. To the extent that it is possible for colonialism to exist without capitalism, Blauner's is a more general approach; to the extent that this is not possible, then both approaches are equally general and tend to reinforce one another. This selection provides an excellent lead into Part Four as it interprets the ghetto riots as insurrections against a colonial system of oppression, thereby revealing the similarities between the ghetto uprisings and other colonial uprisings throughout the world. The "black power" movement, then, is both anticapitalist and antiimperialist.

What "black power" means to Negroes in Mississippi

Joyce Ladner

For three months during the summer of last year, I conducted a study aimed at finding out how Mississippi Negroes who endorsed "black power" interpreted this new concept. I learned that even those civil-rights activists who welcomed the concept attached curiously different meanings to it. My research also helped me understand why the black-power slogan proved so welcome to these activists—and why its acceptance was accompanied by the expulsion of whites from positions of leadership. Finally, my investigation provided some hints on the usefulness of the black-power slogan in helping Mississippi Negroes achieve their goals.

The black-power concept that emerged during the past year created fierce controversy, not only among white liberals but among Negro activists and conservatives. Most of the nation's top civil-rights leaders denounced the slogan—or vigorously embraced it. Instead of "black power," Martin Luther King, Jr., advocated the acquisition of "power for all people." The N.A.A.C.P.'s Roy Wilkins, in condemning the slogan, used such terms as "anti-white power . . . a reverse Hitler . . . a reverse Ku Klux Klan and . . . can only mean black death." On the other hand, Stokely Carmichael, former head of SNCC, was the chief advocate of the slogan, which he defined as "the ability of black people to politically get together and organize themselves so that they can speak from a position of strength rather than a position of weakness." CORE's Floyd McKissick agreed.

But though Negro civil-rights leaders were divided about black power, the slogan was welcomed by many disenchanted Negroes living in Northern ghettos. These Negroes tended to view black power as a tangible goal that, when acquired, would lift them from their inferior positions in the social structure. Still, despite the positive identification that Negroes in the Northern ghettos had with the rhetoric of black power, SNCC and CORE made no massive attempts to involve these Negroes in black-power programs.

But what about the South? How did Negroes in Mississippi, and civil-rights organizations in Mississippi, interpret the new slogan? This was what I wanted to find out.

I used two methods of study. The first was *participant-observation* —in informal, small meetings of civil-rights activists; in civil-rights rallies; and in protest demonstrations, including the historic Meredith march. The second was the *focused interview*. I chose to interview 30 Negroes who, I had found, were in favor of black power. All were friends or acquaintances of mine, and all had had long experience in Southern civil-rights work. They represented about two-thirds of the black-power leaders in the state. (My personal involvement with the civil-rights movement

From TRANS-action 5 (November 1967): 7–15. Copyright © by TRANS-action Magazine, New Brunswick, New Jersey; reprinted by permission of the author and publisher.

helped provide the rapport needed to acquire the observational data, as well as the interview data.)

Among other things, I learned that many Negro activists in Mississippi had immediately embraced the black-power slogan—because of the already widely-held belief that power *was* an effective tool for obtaining demands from the ruling elite in Mississippi. Since 1960, civil-rights organizations have been playing a major role in involving Mississippi Negroes in the fight for equality. As a result these Negroes became more and more dissatisfied with their impoverished, powerless positions in the social structure. The 1960 census reports that the median family income for Mississippi Negroes (who constitute 42.3 percent of Mississippi's population) was $1168, as opposed to $3565 for whites. Until fewer than five years ago, only 6 percent of the eligible Negroes were registered to vote. Today, the traditional all-white primary still exists—in almost the same form as it did 25 years ago. Since many of the efforts Mississippi Negroes made to change the social structure—through integration—were futile, they began to reconceptualize their fight for equality from a different perspective, one designed to acquire long-sought goals through building bases of power.

The black-power concept was, then, successfully communicated to Mississippi Negroes because of the failure of integration. But it was also communicated to them by the shooting of James Meredith on his march through Mississippi. This act of violence made Negro activists feel justified in calling for "audacious black power." For only with black power, they contended, would black people be able to prevent events like the shooting.

LOCALS AND COSMOPOLITANS

But there were varying degrees of acceptance of the slogan among Mississippi Negroes. Some, of course, did not accept the slogan at all—those who were never part of the civil-rights movement. Despite the fact that Mississippi has been one of the centers of civil-rights activity in the United States for the past six or seven years, no more than half the Negro population (I would surmise) has ever been actively involved in the movement. In such areas as Sunflower County, a very high percentage of Negroes have participated; but in many other areas, like Laurel, only a small percentage of the Negroes has taken part.

As for those Negroes active in the movement, they can be broadly classified into two groups. The first: the traditional, moderate, N.A.A.C.P.-style activists, who boast of having been "freedom fighters" before the "new movement" came into existence. They include ministers; small-businessmen; professionals; a sizable following of middle-class people; and a small number of the rank and file. Frequently the white ruling elite calls these activists the "responsible" leaders. The primary activities of this group include selling N.A.A.C.P. memberships; initiating legal action against segregation and discriminatory practices; negotiating with the ruling elite; and conducting limited boycotts and voter-registration campaigns.

The second group of activists are the less economically advantaged. Although a small number were once members of the N.A.A.C.P., most of them joined the movement only since 1960. They are readily identified with such organizations as the Freedom Democratic Party, CORE, SNCC, the Delta Ministry, and the Southern Christian Leadership Conference. Members of this group include plantation workers, students, the average lower-class Negro, and a small number of ministers, professionals, and businessmen. More militant than the first group, these activists conduct mass marches, large-scale boycotts, sit-ins, dramatic voter-registration campaigns, and so forth.

Members of the traditional organizations, in sum, are still committed to working for integration. It is the militants who are oriented toward a black-power ideology, who consider integration irrelevant to what they see as the major task at hand—uniting black people to build black institutions. I suspect that a larger number of activists identify with traditional organizations like the N.A.A.C.P. than with the more militant ones.

The 30 black-power advocates I interviewed were, of course, the militant activists. Even so, I found that even these 30 could be further classified—into categories that Robert K. Merton has called *local* and *cosmopolitan:*

> The localite largely confines his interest to his [town of Rovere] community. Devoting little thought or energy to the Great Society he is preoccupied with local problems, to the virtual exclusion of the national and international science. He is, strictly speaking, parochial.
>
> Contrariwise with the cosmopolitan type. He has some interest in Rovere and must of course maintain a minimum of relations within the community since he, too, exerts influence there. But he is also oriented significantly to the world outside Rovere and regards himself as an integral part of that world. . . . The cosmopolitan is ecumenical.

In this paper, I shall use "local" to refer to those long-term residents of Mississippi—usually uneducated, unskilled adults—whose strong commitment to civil-rights activity stemmed primarily from their desire to produce massive changes in the "home-front," the area they call home.

I shall use "cosmopolitan" to refer to the urbane, educated, highly skilled young civil-rights activists who are usually newcomers to Mississippi. Because they went to the state to work in the civil-rights movement only temporarily, their identification with the area tends to be weak.

THE MOVEMENT'S PHILOSOPHERS

One-third of my respondents, I found, hold the cosmopolitan view. The majority are Negro men, but there are a small group of Negro women and a very small group of white sympathizers. The mean age is about 23 or 24. About half are from the North; the remainder are from Mississippi and other Southern states. Most of the cosmopolitans are formally educated and many have come from middle-class Northern families and gone to the better universities. They are widely read and widely traveled. They are also artistic: Writers, painters, photographers, musicians, and the like are often found in the cosmopolitan group. Their general orientation toward life is an intellectual one. They are associated with SNCC, the Freedom Democratic Party, and CORE. Although a few are actively engaged in organizing black people in the various counties, much of their work in the state is centered on philosophical discussions, writing, and so forth. All of the cosmopolitans have had wide associations with white people. Some grew up and attended school with whites; other had contact with whites in the civil-rights movement. The cosmopolitans maintain that black people in American society must redefine the term "black" and all that it symbolizes, and that black pride and dignity must be implanted in all Negro Americans. The cosmopolitan position embraces the belief that the plight of Negro Americans is comparable to neocolonialized "colored peoples" of the world..

The cosmopolitans' participation in the Southern civil-rights scene, by and large, dates back to 1960 and the beginning of the student movement in the South. Their present ideology has to be viewed in the framework of the history of their involvement in the movement, with special emphasis on the negative experiences they encountered.

Some six years ago, black Americans began to seek their long-desired civil rights with a new sense of urgency. The N.A.A.C.P.'s painstaking effort to obtain legal, theoretical rights for Negroes was challenged. Groups of Negro college students in the South decided to fight the gradualism that had become traditional and to substitute radical action aimed at bringing about rapid social change. These students began their drive for equal rights with lunch-counter demonstrations. After much immediate success, they spread their drive to the political arena. Their only hope for the future, they felt, lay in the ballot. Much to their disappointment, acquiring political power was not so easy as integrating lunch counters. The students met their strongest resistance from whites in full possession of the sought-after political power. To deal with this resistance, the Federal Government passed two civil-rights laws: public accommodation and voting rights. But the Government did little to implement these laws. Still, in the early 1960s, student civil-rights workers had an almost unrelenting faith in the Federal Government and believed that changes in the laws would rapidly pave the way for sweeping changes in the social structure. This was the era when students were much involved in hard-core organizing. They paid little attention to abstract philosophizing. Instead they occupied themselves with such pressing problems as the mass arrests of Negroes in Greenwood, Miss.

As time went on, the cosmopolitans became more and more discouraged about their organizing efforts. They began to seriously question the feasibility of their strategies and tactics. By the end of 1964, after the historic Mississippi Summer Project, the cosmopolitans began to feel that their organizational methods were just not effective. For roughly a year and a half, they groped and searched for more effective strategies. Frequently they felt frustrated; sometimes they despaired. A number of them returned to the North and got well-paying jobs or went to graduate and professional schools. Others were alienated from some of the basic values of American society. Some students developed a strong interest in Africa and began to look to various African states as possible havens. Still others, after deciding that they had accomplished all that was possible through organizations such as SNCC, associated themselves with radical leftist groups.

It was during the tail end of this six-year period that two position papers were written by the cosmopolitans. One was by a group that insisted that Negroes expel whites from leadership roles in civil-rights organizations, and that Negroes develop "black consciousness" and "black nationalism." "Black consciousness" refers to a set of ideas and behavior patterns affirming the beauty of blackness and dispelling any negative images that black people may have incorporated about blackness. "Black nationalism" is a kind of patriotic devotion to the development of the Negro's own political, economic, and social institutions. Black nationalism is *not* a racist ideology with separatist overtones, however, but simply a move toward independence from the dominant group, the whites. This paper states:

> If we are to proceed toward true liberation, we must cut ourselves off from white people. We must form our own institutions, credit unions, co-ops, political parties, write our own histories. . . . SNCC, by allowing whites to remain in the organization, can have its efforts subverted. . . . Indigenous leadership cannot be built with whites in the positions they now hold. They [whites] can participate on a voluntary basis . . . but in no way can they participate on a policy-making level.

In response, one white civil-rights worker—Pat McGauley—wrote a paper acceding to the demands of the black-consciousness group:

> The time has indeed come for blacks and whites in the movement to separate; however, it must always be kept in mind that the final goal of the revolution we are all working for is a multi-racial society.

The cosmopolitans I interviewed conceived of black power in highly philosophical terms—as an ideology that would unite black people as never before. To most of them, black power was intricately bound up with black consciousness. To a long-time SNCC worker, black consciousness was:

> . . . an awareness of oneself as a removed nation of black people who are capable of running and developing their own governments and who have pride in their blackness to the extent that they won't sell out. . . . To the extent that he can say, "I'm no longer ashamed of my blackness." The individual redefines the society's rules in terms of his own being. There is a new kind of awakening of the individual, a new kind of realization of self, a type of security, and a type of self-confidence.

Another cosmopolitan equated black consciousness with community loyalty:

Black consciousness is not the question but rather [the question is] from which community one comes from. If you know that, you can identify with black people anywhere in the world then. That is all that is necessary.

These young people firmly believe that even the term "black" has to be redefined. To one of them, "Black has never had any favorable expression in the English language." To another, "American society has characterized black as the symbol for strength, evil, potency and malignancy. . . . People are afraid of the night, of blackness."

Most cosmopolitans feel that black people must acquire black consciousness before they can successfully develop the tools and techniques for acquiring black power. As one of them put it:

Black consciousness is the developmental stage of black power. Black power will be incomplete without black consciousness. Black consciousness is basically the search for identity; or working out one's own identity. . . . There must be a long process of learning and unlearning in between and a period of self-questing.

In short, by developing black consciousness, a Negro can appreciate his blackness and thus develop a kind of community loyalty to other colored peoples of the world.

Most of the cosmopolitans felt that the redefinition of blackness must take place in the black community *on the black man's terms*. When such a redefinition has taken place, black men who feel psychologically castrated because of their blackness will be able to compete with whites as psychological equals. ("Psychologically castrated" is a popular term among cosmopolitans, and refers to Negroes whose beliefs and behavior have become so warped by the values of white American society that they have come to regard themselves as inferior.)

HEROES OF THE BLACK REVOLUTION

Cosmopolitans are familiar with the works of Marcus Garvey, Malcolm X, Frantz Fanon, Kwame Nkrumah, and other revolutionary nationalists. Some can quote passages from their works. To the cosmopolitans, Marcus Garvey (1887–1940), who tried to instill racial pride in Negroes, was a pioneer of black nationalism and black consciousness in America. The greatest impact on the cosmopolitans, however, comes from the contemporary Malcolm X, whose philosophy—toward the latter period of his life —reflected a revolutionary spirit and a total dissatisfaction with the plight of Negroes in this country. One of the cosmopolitans had this to say about Malcolm X:

Malcolm was very much together. . . . He was a man who knew what he was doing and would have eventually showed everyone what he was capable of doing. . . . Malcolm had history behind him and was with the cat on the block.

To another:

> Malcolm X . . . was able to relate to people and to the press. The press
> is your right arm. . . . In order to be a real militant, you have to use the
> man [press] and that is what Malcolm did. They [the press] didn't create
> Malcolm. . . . The press was attuned to Malcolm. . . . Malcolm was not
> attuned to the press.

Some cosmopolitans call themselves students of Malcolm X and express
the hope that another such leader will soon emerge.

Another symbolic leader is the late Algerian revolutionary, Frantz
Fanon, whose *The Wretched of the Earth* has become a veritable Bible
to the cosmopolitans. Fanon tried to justify the use of violence by the
oppressed against the oppressor, and to relate the neocolonialization of
the black man in Algeria to the plight of colored peoples everywhere.
Similarly, the cosmopolitans have great admiration for Stokeley Carmichael, one of their associates, whose philosophy is highlighted in this
passage:

> The colonies of the United States—and this includes the black ghettos
> within its borders, north and south—must be liberated. For a century this
> nation has been like an octopus of exploitation, its tentacles stretching
> from Mississippi and Harlem to South America, the Middle East, southern
> Africa, and Vietnam; the form of exploitation varies from area to area
> but the essential result has been the same—a powerful few have been main-
> tained and enriched at the expense of the poor and voiceless colored masses.
> This pattern must be broken. As its grip loosens here and there around
> the world, the hopes of black Americans become more realistic. For racism
> to die, a totally different America must be born.

Embodied within the philosophy of the cosmopolitans is an essential proposition that American society is inherently racist, that the majority of
white Americans harbor prejudice against black people. Few make any
distinction between whites—for example, the white Southerner as opposed
to the Northern liberal. Whites are considered symbolic of the black
man's oppression, and therefore one should not differentiate between
sympathetic whites and unsympathetic whites. The conclusion of the
cosmopolitans is that any sweeping structural changes in American society can come about only through the black man's taking an aggressive
role in organizing his political, economic, and social institutions. The
black man must control his destiny.

THE PRACTICAL ORIENTATION

I have categorized the remaining two-thirds of my 30 respondents as
locals. (Of what significance these ratios are, by the way, I am not sure.)
The locals are almost as committed to solving the pressing problems of
inadequate income, education, housing, and second-class citizenship *practically* as the cosmopolitans are committed to solving them *philosophically*.

Most of the locals are life-long residents of their communities or other Mississippi communities. Most of them, like the cosmopolitans, have been drawn into the movement only since 1960. Unlike the generally youthful cosmopolitans, the age range of the locals is from young adult to elderly. Many locals are indigenous leaders in their communities and in statewide organizations. Whereas cosmopolitans tend to be middle-class, locals are members of the lower-class black communities and they range from plantation workers to a few who have acquired modest homes and a somewhat comfortable style of life. Many are leaders in the Mississippi Freedom Democratic Party, which in 1964 challenged the legality of the all-white Mississippi delegation to the national Democratic convention and in 1965 challenged the constitutionality of the elected white Representatives to serve in the U.S. House of Representatives. (Both challenges were based upon the fact that Negroes did not participate in the election of the delegates and Representatives.)

Although most of the locals are native Mississippians who have always been victimized by segregation and discrimination, I have also placed a number of middle-class students in this category—because of their very practical orientation to black power. The backgrounds of these students are somewhat similar to those of the cosmopolitans, except that the majority come from the South and are perhaps from lower-status families than the cosmopolitans are. These students are deeply involved in attempts to organize black-power programs.

Because of segregation and discrimination, the locals are largely uneducated; they subsist on a totally inadequate income; and they are denied the privileges of first-class citizenship. They have had a lot of experience with the usual forms of harassment and intimidation from local whites. Their entire existence can be perceived in terms of their constant groping for a better way of life. Because of many factors—like their low level of income and education and their Southern, rural, small-town mentality (which to some extent prevents one from acquiring an intellectualized world view)—the definition they have given to black power is a very practical one.

The black-power locals can be considered militants to much the same degree as the cosmopolitans, but on a different level. In essence, the nature and kind of activities in which they are willing to participate (voter registration, running for political office, boycotts, etc.) are indeed militant and are not surpassed by the nature and kind to which the cosmopolitans orient themselves. Indeed, in some cases the locals are deeply involved in realizing black-power programs: In certain counties, women have organized leathercraft and dress-making cooperatives. And in Senator Eastland's home county of Sunflower, an unsuccessful effort was even made to elect an all-black slate of public officials.

The great difference between cosmopolitans and locals is that the locals are committed to concrete economic and political programs, while the cosmopolitans—to varying degrees—endorse such programs but actually have made little effort to realize them.

Most locals perceived black power as a more effective, alternate method of organizing and acquiring those rights they had been seeking.

In the past they had been committed to integration. Power had not originally been considered important in and of itself, for it was hoped that America would voluntary give Negroes civil rights. Therefore the locals sought coalition politics—they aligned themselves with Northern labor groups, liberals, national church groups, and so forth. During their several years of involvement, they—like the cosmopolitans—suffered many defeats. For example, many were involved with the Mississippi Summer Project, which brought hundreds of Northerners into the state in 1964. At that time the locals were convinced that such a program would bring about the wide structural changes they desired. But, to their disappointment, once the volunteers returned to the North the old patterns of segregation and discrimination returned. Some of the locals had gone to the Democratic Convention in Atlantic City, N.J., in 1964 hoping to unseat the all-white slate of delegates from Mississippi. When this failed, they invested further moral and physical resources into challenging the legality of the all-white slate of Mississippi Representatives in the U.S. House. Another set-back came when a large contingent pitched their tents on the White House lawn in a last-ditch effort to obtain poverty funds to aid in building adequate housing. All were sharecroppers, evicted because their participation in voter-registration programs was contrary to the desires of their plantation landlords. These evicted sharecroppers later set up residence in the buildings of the inactive Air Force base in Greenville, Miss. They were deeply depressed when officials of the Air Force ordered military police to remove them. One of the leaders of this group remarked, "If the United States Government cares so little about its citizens that it will not allow them to live in its abandoned buildings rather than in unheated tents [this occurred during winter], then that government can't be for real."

I submit that the events outlined above, among many others, caused a large number of the locals—like the cosmopolitans—to pause and question the effectiveness of their traditional organizational tactics and goals. Indeed, many even came to seriously question the Federal Government's sincerity about alleviating the problems of the Negro. A number of the participants in these events stopped being active in the movement. Others began to express strong anti-white sentiments.

THE ATTRACTIONS OF BLACK POWER

Black power was embraced by many of the locals from the very beginning, and they began to reconceptualize their activities within the new framework. To the locals, black power was defined in various ways, some of which follow:

> Voter registration is black power. Power is invested in the ballot and that's why the white man worked like hell to keep you away from it. . . . We were even taught that it was not right to register [to vote]. The civil-rights movement in this state started around the issue of voting—we shouldn't forget that.
> Black power is political power held by Negroes. It means political

control in places where they comprise a majority. . . . Black power is legitimate because any time people are in a majority, they should be able to decide what will and will not happen to them.

Black power was further viewed as a means of combining Negroes into a bond of solidarity. It was seen as a rallying cry, a symbol of identification, and a very concrete tool for action. Many said that former slogans and concepts such as "Freedom Now" were ambiguous. One could easily ask, "Freedom for what and from what?" One local said:

> First we wanted Freedom Now. I ran around for six years trying to get my freedom. I really didn't know what it was.

Black power, they felt, was more concrete, for it had as its central thesis the question of power. (Actually, the locals have also defined black power in various ways, and to some the slogan is as ambiguous as "Freedom Now.") The locals felt that Negroes would be able to acquire certain rights only through the control of their economic and political institutions, which—in some cases—also involves the eventual control of the black community. One black-power advocate put it succinctly when he said:

> Black power means controlling the Negro community. It means that if the Negro community doesn't want white cops coming in, they can't come in. It means political, economic, and social control.

Asked how this control could be obtained, he replied:

> We will have to start putting our money together to organize cooperatives, and other kinds of business. We can get political power by putting Negroes into public offices. . . . We will have to tell them to vote only for Negro candidates.

To others, control over the black community was not the goal, but rather a *share* in the existing power:

> All we're saying to the white man is we want some power. Black power is just plain power. . . . It just means that Negroes are tired of being without power and want to share in it.

Thus, we can observe that there are several variations of the concept, all revolving around a central theme: the acquisition of power by Negroes for their own use, both offensively and defensively.

Despite the obvious practical orientation of the locals, there can also be found traces of black consciousness and black nationalism in their thought patterns. Most have never read Garvey, Fanon, Malcolm X, and other nationalists, but they tend to readily identify with the content of speeches made by Stokely Carmichael bearing the message of black nationalism. They are prone to agree with the cosmopolitans who speak to them about ridding themselves of their "oppressors." When the chairman of the Mississippi Freedom Democratic Party speaks of overthrowing neo-colonialism in Mississippi, shouts of "Amen!" can be heard from the audience. There is also a tendency in this group to oppose the current war in Vietnam on the grounds that America should first concentrate on liberating Negroes within the United States' borders. The locals also believe that the war is indeed an unjust one. Perhaps the following statement is typical:

> Black men have been stripped of everything. If it takes black power to do something about this, let us have it. Black power has got the country moving and white people don't like it. We marched into Dominica [the Dominican Republic], we marched into Vietnam. Now if we [black people] can conquer this country, we will conquer the world.

There is a growing feeling among both locals and cosmopolitans of kinship with the colored peoples of the world, including the Vietnamese. To engage in warfare against other colored people is regarded as a contradiction of this bond of solidarity.

For both the Mississippi cosmopolitans and locals, then, it was mainly frustration that drew them to the concept of black power.

WHY WHITES WERE EXPELLED

The black-power slogan should be viewed in the perspective of the overall civil-rights movement, one of the most popular social movements in the history of this country. Now, there are some scholars who maintain that, by viewing a particular social movement over a period of time, one can discern a typical sequence: the movement's crystallization of social unrest; its phase of active agitation and proselytism; its organized phase; and the achievement of its objectives. The civil-rights movement, with much success, achieved each of these phases—except the final one, the achievement of objectives. Despite the great amount of effort and resources expended by black people and their allies to obtain civil rights, there was a disproportionate lack of gains. Indeed, in much of Mississippi and the South, conditions have barely changed from 10 or even 20 years ago. Many black people are still earning their livelihood from sharecropping and tenant farming; many household heads are still unable to earn more than $500 a year; many black children are still deprived of adequate education because of the lack of facilities and adequately trained teachers. To date, only 42.1 percent of Negroes of voting age are registered as opposed to 78.9 percent of whites. We still hear of lynchings and other forms of violence of which Negroes are the victims.

The black-power thrust is thus an inevitable outgrowth of the disillusionment that black people have experienced in their intense efforts to become integrated into the mainstream of American society. Thwarted by traditional formulas and organizational restrictions, some Mississippi Negroes have responded to the black-power concept in a sometimes semirational, emotionally charged manner—because it seemed the only available resource with which they could confront white American society.

How was the black-power concept related to the expulsion of whites from leadership positions in the movement? The fact is that the alienation and disaffection found throughout the entire black-power group also resulted from strained interpersonal relations with white civil-rights workers. During the past two years, there has been a growing belief among black people in Mississippi that white civil-rights workers should go into the *white* communities of that state to work. Only then, they contended, could the "inherent racism" in American society, with particular reference to the "Southern racist," begin to be dealt with. Even the seriousness of white civil-rights workers was questioned. Many Negroes felt that a sizable number of them had come South mainly to resolve their very personal emotional difficulties, and not to help impoverished black Mississippians. Rather, they were considered rebellious youth who wanted only to act out their rebellion in the most unconventional ways. Stokely Carmichael stated:

> Too many young, middle-class Americans, like some sort of Pepsi generation, have wanted to come alive through the black community; they've wanted to be where the action was—and the action has been in the black community. . . .
> It's important to note that those white people who feel alienated from white society and run into the black society are capable of confronting the white society with its racism where it really does exist.

Much strain also resulted from the inability of many black civil-rights activists—skilled organizers but lacking the formal education and other technical skills white workers possessed—to deal with the increased bureaucratization of the civil-rights movement (writing proposals for foundation grants, for example). Black activists, in addition, constantly complained about the focus of the mass media on white "all-American" volunteers who had come South to work in the movement. The media never paid attention to the thousands of black people who frequently took far greater risks. These factors played a major role in destroying the bond of solidarity that had once existed between whites and blacks in the movement. Before the emergence of the black-power concept, it is true, many young black civil-rights workers had cast white civil-rights workers in the same category as all other white people. The new slogan was, to some extent, a form of justification for their own prejudice against whites.

In terms of practical considerations, however, urging the white volunteers to leave the black communities has had negative effects. SNCC and CORE, which at one time directed most of the grass-roots organizing, have always depended upon the economic and volunteer resources of liberal white individuals and groups. These resources are scarce nowadays.

On another level, there have been positive results from removing whites from black communities. Black activists—all cosmopolitans and some locals—contend that, now that the whites have gone, they feel more self-confident and capable of running their own programs. They tend to view the earlier period of the movement, when whites played active roles in executing the programs, as having been a necessary phase; but they maintain that the time has arrived when black people must launch and execute their own programs.

COSMOPOLITANS vs. LOCALS

Clearly, the long-range aims of the locals and cosmopolitans are basically the same. Unlike Negroes in such traditional organizations as the N.A.A.C.P., locals and cosmopolitans have turned away from integration. Both groups want to unite black people and build political, economic, and social institutions that will render a certain amount of control to the black community. For some time, however, the two groups have been operating on different levels. The cosmopolitans focus on developing black consciousness among black people, which they consider a necessary step to developing black power; the locals concentrate on solving the immediate problems resulting from segregation and discrimination.

While it may seem that the locals are more prudent and realistic than the cosmopolitans, it should be said that there are many positive features to black nationalism and black consciousness. It *is* important to establish a positive black identity in a great many sectors of the black communities, both North and South, rural and urban, lower and middle class. Indeed, it is both important and legitimate to teach black people (or any other ethnic minority) about their history, placing special emphasis upon the positive contributions of other black people. Thus black consciousness has the potential to create unity and solidarity among black people and to give them hope and self-confidence. Perhaps it fulfills certain needs in black people that society, on the whole, cannot. Martin Luther King has made the following statement about black consciousness:

> One must not overlook the positive value in calling the Negro to a new sense of manhood, to a deep feeling of racial pride and to an audacious appreciation of his heritage. The Negro must be grasped by a new realization of his dignity and worth. He must stand up amid a system that still oppresses him and develop an unassailable and majestic sense of his own value. *He must no longer be ashamed of being black.* (Emphasis mine.)

Moreover, the task of getting blacks to act *as blacks, by* themselves and *for* themselves, is necessary for developing black consciousness, or psychological equality. Thus one is led to the conclusion that black consciousness does *necessarily* call for the expulsion of whites from leadership roles in the black communities.

The locals, on the other hand, have adopted concrete strategies that, in reality, involve the same kind of techniques that existed in the integration era. Specifically, when they refer to developing black-power programs, they speak of registering to vote, running for political office, and building independent political parties. As for the economic situation, they have begun to concentrate on building cooperatives and small businesses, and on almost-exclusively patronizing black merchants in an effort to "keep the money in the black community." If we turn back two years, however, we find that the same strategies, though somewhat modified, were being used then. In the past, the locals concentrated on registering large numbers of black people to vote, in an effort to be able to have a voice in the decision-making apparatus. The emphasis is now on registering to vote so that the Negro can have control over his community and eventual control over his political destiny. Cooperatives were organized at least a year before the black-power concept emerged, but—ever since emphasis was put on economic control—there has been an expansion and intensification in certain sectors of this area. At present, cooperatives are still operating on a small-scale, though, considering the masses of people whose lives could be immensely improved by cooperatives.

The differences in the emphasis on priorities of achieving black power between locals and cosmopolitans can be viewed as complementary rather than oppositional, because each level of emphasis is vital for the achievement of their goals. This is becoming increasingly true since, within the last year, black-power advocates have taken a far more aggressive and militant stance toward the realization of such aims. Locals who a year ago might have questioned the importance and feasibility of "Black Liberation" schools, which teach black history and culture, are less likely to do so now. This is an indication that there is a trend toward unity between the groups. Because of the strong emphasis among some sectors of the black-power movement on drawing the parallels of the plight of black Americans with that of the inhabitants of the Third World, locals are quite likely to become more cosmopolitan through time.

Through the development of such unity, there is a great possibility that black-power advocates in Mississippi will again turn to creative, large-scale organizing that would incorporate the major emphases of each group: black consciousness and immediate gains.

THE FUTURE OF BLACK POWER

The key question, of course, is, what are the prospects for Mississippi Negroes' developing black-power institutions in the near future? Clearly, this will depend to a great extent upon the number of organizers in the field, on adequate economic resources, and on commitments from major civil-rights organizations to the Mississippi scene. Certainly the presence of a local charismatic leader also would aid in the development of pervasive black-power institutions. Indeed, a black-power "prophet" whose task was to keep the message before all the advocates would give them immeasurable support and strength for their undertakings.

Where black-power institutions have a good chance of developing at present is in the small number of Mississippi counties where there are strong black-power organizations with large Negro voting populations. Since the cosmopolitans are reentering the field and beginning to organize (and some of the most skilled organizers are in this group), the prospects—here at least—seem favorable. On the other hand, it seems highly doubtful at this point that the needed resources can be obtained from the traditional sources (Northern students, white liberals, church and labor organizations). So these resources (inadequate as they may be) may have to be obtained from the black community. CORE and SNCC have already begun to establish financial bases in the black communities throughout the country. Should this tactic fail, perhaps there will be a revaluation of the strategies employed in the acquisition of black power.

THE POLITICAL ECONOMY OF BLACK POWER

Raymond S. Franklin

The objective of this essay is to examine Black Power as an ideology capable of challenging some of the basic tenets of American capitalism. This requires understanding the notion of Black Power within the context of the broader forces which determine the fate of the Negro community as a whole. Because Black Power has been cast in opposition to the notion of white power, the discussion must also deal with the rhetoric and ideological components of the white power structure. Finally, the prospects of Black Power as a political movement will be assessed.

THE IDEOLOGY OF BLACK POWER

Paraphrasing the *Communist Manifesto,* Jerry Talmer of the *New York Post* began a series of bad articles on Black Power with the following sentence: "A specter is haunting America—the specter is Black Power." A few lines further on, he declared that everyone lives in fear of Black Power, even "a good share of black America," but that nobody seems to know precisely what Black Power means.[1] Roy Wilkins confirmed this in a witty rejection of the 210 Black Power definitions which have come to his attention in the past year.[2] In a book almost totally devoted to explaining Black Power, Nathan Wright, Jr., a clergyman from Newark, and one of the reported organizers of the 1967 Black Power conference, gives it a variety of innocuous meanings, e.g., group solidarity, power to respect self, and power to guarantee all Americans a good life.[3] Floyd B. McKissick described Black Power in terms of black people determining their own actions, black leadership, black consumer activity, and the development of a positive self-image.[4] The task of Black Power, wrote the late Martin Luther King, Jr., is the development of a "situation in which

From *Social Problems* 16 (Winter 1969): 286–301; reprinted by permission of the author and The Society for the Study of Social Problems.

the government finds it wise and prudent to collaborate with us." [5] In an article titled "What We Want," Stokely Carmichael suggested that Black Power's significance as a slogan involved "[speaking] in the tone of the [black] community, not as somebody else's buffer zone." [6] On a different level, Black Power has been linked to sex conflicts,[7] and ultimately, "to the barrel of a gun." [8]

Much of what is called Black Power by whites, and even much of what is called Black Power by blacks, is often a militant extension of race politics, a form of Black Nationalism (separatism), or a use of revolutionary tactics. As a consequence of these varied definitions and specific applications of the term, the meaning of Black Power in its totality has been either misunderstood or completely lost.

Black Power is an ideology which contains a number of elements.[9] First, it is a philosophy in which "certain institutions and practices are justified and others are attacked." [10] Second, it is an ethic used to judge men and decide goals. Third, "it contains strategies and programs that embody both ends and means." [11] And fourth, it is concerned with the nature of the Negro as a Man and his relationship to the broad contours of the society in which his historic fate has been and is being determined. Each of these elements will be considered in turn.

A philosophy

Black Power is aimed at the white power structure in general and at Negro-white liberal coalitions in particular. With regard to the former, Black Power ideologues express disdain for *all* organizations which practice racial discrimination in any form, regardless of whether the organization represents the working class or the property-owning class. This point is seen in the contrasting views of King and Malcolm X with respect to labor unions:

> As co-workers [within the ranks of organized labor] there is a basic community of interest that transcends many of the ugly divisive elements of traditional prejudice. There are undeniably points of friction. . . . But the severity of the abrasions is minimized by the more commanding need for cohesion in union organization. . . . Negroes, who are almost wholly a working people, cannot be casual toward the union movement.[12]

Malcolm X, on the other hand, argued that the Negro revolution did not require cooperation

> with working class whites. The history of America is that working class whites have been just as much against not only working class Negroes, but all Negroes. . . . There can be no working solidarity until there's first black solidarity. . . . I think one of the mistakes Negroes make is this worker solidarity thing.[13]

Black Power advocates stand against the policy of coalition politics but not necessarily against the possibility of co-racial politics.[14] The distinction here is subtle but unmistakably clear. Coalition politics involve

an arrangement whereby the white liberal segments of the power structure act as proxy representatives of Negroes with the purpose of extract-
ing from a hostile society whatever tokens the balance of larger forces
permits the Negroes to have. In return the Negroes provide the liberal
with electoral support to keep him an influential part of the general
power structure. It is an arrangement by which, in the words of Stokely
Carmichael, "blacks will [inevitably] . . . be absorbed and betrayed." [15]
There is no point, states SNCC's original Black Power proclamation, "to
talk about coalition . . . unless black people organize whites. If these
conditions are met . . . and we are going in the same direction . . . al-
liances can be discussed." [16] In other words, among groups separately
organized and controlled by the different races, bilateral arrangements
around specific issues of common interest are conceivable.[17] This is co-
racial or co-determining politics in contrast to the coalition variety involving indirect representation of black interests.

An ethic

As an ethical norm, Black Power is directed against certain types of
Negro leaders specifically, and against the goal of integration in general.
To take the latter point first:

> Integration today means the man who "makes it," leaving his black broth-
> ers behind in the ghetto as fast as his new sports car will take him. . . .
> Integration, moreover, speaks to the problem of blackness in a despicable
> way. As a goal, it has been based on complete acceptance of the fact that
> in order to have a decent house or education, blacks must move into a
> white neighborhood or send their children to a white school. This rein-
> forces, among both black and white, the idea that "white" is automatically
> better and "black" is by definition inferior. This is why integration is a
> subterfuge for the maintenance of white supremacy. It allows the nation
> to focus on a handful of Southern children who get into white schools, at
> a great price, and to ignore the 94 percent who are left behind in unim-
> proved all black schools.[18]

On the question of Negro leadership, Black Power is not only against
accommodationists or moderate integrationists, it is in principle against
issue-oriented or pressure-group leaders as types. That is to say, Black
Power is against the practical men of the Negro struggle whose actions,
even when they are militant, are guided by no ultimate objectives other
than *de facto* objectives of the society at the moment. Such leaders tend
to define issues and adopt policies which are within the purview established by the white power structure or by some part of it.

A Black Power leader, in contrast, is lesson-oriented, a teacher, an
ideologue. This point was developed by John Illo in an analysis of the
speeches, writings, and general style of Malcolm X. The *action* of Malcolm
X consisted mainly of providing his audience with

> relevant ideas and theses, not dignity and amplitude. . . . He was pri-
> marily a teacher, his oratory of the demonstrative kind . . . and filled with

significant matter. [He] moved in the arena of words and ideas, and . . .
usually described a condition . . . rather than urged a . . . response.
. . . In the rhetoric of Malcolm X . . . figures correspond to the critical
imagination restoring the original idea and to conscience protesting the
desecration of the idea.[19]

In somewhat more political terms, the *action* of Malcolm X consisted
of imbuing the Negro masses with ideas about their condition in relation
to the system, and the system in relation to the Negro's own history. Consciousness of the condition in relation to the system was not assumed to
emerge spontaneously from the Negro's day-to-day experiences. The experiences and issues of the moment, although not ignored, were used
mainly as illustrations of the system's mode of exploitation and injustice
in general. Malcolm X, unlike many Negro leaders, did not coddle his
followers; to the contrary, he often ridiculed them without being contemp-
tuous of their limitations. A single but representative illustration will
suffice. As important as the 1963 Birmingham crisis was, to Malcolm X it
was simply another event to develop a general thought:

> As long as the white man sent you to Korea, you bled. He sent you to
> Germany, you bled. He sent you to the South Pacific to fight the Japanese,
> you bled. You bleed for white people, but when it comes to seeing your
> own church bombed and little black girls murdered, you haven't got any
> blood. You bleed when the white man says bleed; you bite when the white
> man says bite; and you bark when the white man says bark.[20]

In essence, the ideological role of Black Power on the question of
Negro leadership is twofold: (a) to fight "pure and simple" issue-oriented
leaders, and (b) to bring home to the Negro the relevance of present
circumstances shaping his life in order to develop his commitment to
confront the system more decisively.

Strategy and tactics

Strategically, Black Power advocates stress self-direction, self-support,
and self-ownership of the wealth of the ghetto. Self-direction and self-
support are the fight against the historically conditioned role of not thinking and acting for yourself. Blacks need to forge their own programs,
create their own ideas, and raise their own money in order to expunge
from their souls the psychological atavisms that still persist from the slave
system.[21] "If we are to proceed toward true liberation," to quote again
from SNCC's original Black Power position paper, "we must . . . form
our own institutions, credit unions, co-ops, and political parties, [and]
write our own histories." [22] If money is sought from the federal government, "we must," in King's words, "have compelling power so that government cannot elude our demands." [23] On the point of owning the
ghetto, Malcolm X raises the following string of rhetorical questions:
"Why should white people be running all the stores in our community?
Why should white people be running the banks of our community? Why

should the economy of our community be in the hands of the white man? Why?" [24]

Black Power, unlike other Negro ideologies, views the Negro working class as *the* instrument of power in the effort to change society. This has far-reaching implications, especially in view of the fact that a significant portion of the total Negro working class is young and unemployed, under-employed, or menially employed. Workers in this condition do not have a vested interest in their place of employment; their salvation is not on the job but in the neighborhood in which they live and roam.[25] The situation is conducive to the development of weapons of protest characteristic of crisis-ridden, company-owned mining towns in which militant labor tactics are applied to the community in general, e.g., the community strike, the obstruction of community routines, and outright violence against symbols of oppression. The importance of such tactics was made clear in a statement by Rev. Albert B. Cleage, Jr., a militant Negro clergyman from Detroit:

> In terms of the realities of the situation, we have got to evolve a strategy of chaos. Deliberately we have got to tear up everything that doesn't give us an equal shake. They say that Negroes have always had a genius for tearing up things. I'm not talking about the natural ability that we have to tear up things. I'm talking about a deliberately conceived plan to tear up those things from which we are excluded, those things that do not give us equality of opportunity, anything that exists in these United States—either accept us in it, or—we'll do everything possible to tear it up.[26]

Violence in the form of the small guerrilla band is one mode of action consistent with a ghetto in which an "underclass" or lumpenproletarians flounder about. The effectiveness of the use or threat of violence as an instrument to increase ghetto outlays from the city or federal government is self-evident. What is less self-evident is that violence may also have a psychological function, i.e., the existential realization of freedom and manhood that comes from striking at the oppressor. In the words of one Negro psychiatrist:

> [the black man, following the necessity of a] severe psychological burden of suppressing and repressing [his] rage and aggression [in order to survive began to seek] a sense of inner psychological emancipation from racism through self-assertion and release of aggressive angry feelings. . . . It . . . appears that old-style attempts to destroy the natural aggressor of the black man and to fail to give him his full rights can only provoke further outbreaks of violence and inspire a revolutionary zeal among Negro Americans.[27]

If this is true, large-scale violence in the form of arson, pilfering, looting, and wrecking is not necessarily nihilistic as some have suggested, and therefore it need not in the long run inevitably lead to consequences detrimental to the Negro's liberation. Continued violence in ten major cities similar in scale to what Detroit experienced in the summer of 1967 is likely to be met in one of two ways: (1) a total repression of the Negro community specifically and a general repression of dissent and agitation groups concerned with fundamental changes in our society, or (2) a more constructive response in the form of larger programs to rehabilitate the ghetto. The former would lead to more violence on a scale even greater than that witnessed to date; it would essentially polarize the American society in ways that would terminate completely the pluralistic order. It would stimulate larger numbers and more layers of the population to go to the right or to join in a struggle to change the social order. In short the outcome would be a garrison state within the old social context or a reconstructed civil society within a new one. The latter response (larger programs to rehabilitate the ghetto) would also justify violence as a rational instrument within the present framework, by making it "respectable" to even the moderate social logicians of the Negro struggle. In either case, violence, incidental to the gradual accretion of organized Negro power, cannot be axiomatically viewed as suicidal or ineffective.[28]

Identity

Finally, the ideology of Black Power gives supreme importance to the problem of the Negro's image of himself. In one sense, Black Power advocates are professional image-makers. This is not for the NAACP or Urban League's purpose of giving Negroes an appearance which makes them more acceptable to whites, but for the purpose of developing an identity—historical, social, and group—which is felt by the Negro to be his own property. The development of identity—ultimately capable of giving the Negro direction in his fight for cultural freedom and economic equality—takes a variety of forms. (1) The meaning of blackness as viewed by whites is turned into its opposite—beauty and strength rather than ugliness and submissiveness. For example, talking about the Lowndes County Freedom Organization, Carmichael states:

> When [it] chose the black panther as its symbol, it was christened by the press "The Black Panther Party"—but the Alabama Democratic Party, whose symbol is a rooster, has never been called the White Cock Party. . . . [Besides], a black panther is a bold, beautiful animal, representing the strength and dignity of black demands today. A man needs a black panther on his side when he and his family must endure—as hundreds of Alabamians have endured—loss of job, eviction, starvation, and sometimes death, for political activity.[29]

(2) Furthering the identification process, Black Power makes the nations of Africa part of the Negro's consciousness. This is done by either pointing to the rich heritage of Africa's past or to the current fact that Black Africans achieved independence through their own efforts. Addressing a Negro audience, Malcolm X reminds it that "the Mau Mau was also a minority, microscopic minority, but it was the Mau Mau who . . . brought independence to Kenya." [30] (3) Finally, and most important, there is the ongoing effort to imbue the individual Negro with an ethos of power and self-respect that grows from self-discipline, commitment to

a great cause, and being part of and identified with a movement that is engaged in a history-shaking journey. The Negro's sense of identity and self-respect can come only in part from the past or from Africa; the essence of it must be created in a vision of the present as history.[31]

In sum, Black Power in its totality is neither a separatist nor an integrationist doctrine, and therefore it is not directly related to either narrow nationalist formulations of the past nor civil rights ones of the present. *It is an answer to the Negro dilemma of neither being able to separate nor integrate.* In the realm of tactics and goals, moreover, Black Power is becoming increasingly revolutionary, employing both legal and extra-legal tactics. Ultimately, it seeks to resolve the Negro problem in co-racial terms, a proposition which warrants serious attention and elaboration.

THE INNER AND OUTER CITY

Giving force to the ideology of Black Power are new urban conditions derived from the migration of the Negro during and following World War II—from rural to non-rural areas and from Southern to non-Southern cities—to an extent previously unknown. This has led Hans Morgenthau to observe that the Negro problem can no longer be viewed as "geographically localized. . . . In consequence, [the Negro problem] cannot be contained or sealed off. . . . [It] is a metastasized cancer." [32]

Of more importance than this general inter-regional migratory pattern, however, is the one that has developed within the metropolitan area itself. As the Negro movement into the cities increased, it was matched by white movement out of the cities. The results are startling increases in Negro population trends in all our major cities and many of our secondary ones. By 1970, it has been estimated that such cities as Washington, D.C.; Richmond, Virginia; Gary, Indiana; Baltimore, Maryland; Detroit, Michigan; Newark, New Jersey; and Birmingham, Alabama will have Negro populations of over 40 percent. Many more cities will have populations that fall between the range of 30 to 40 percent. In general, it is expected that "there will be fifty American cities with total populations over 100,000 . . . having Negro populations of twenty-five percent or more. . . . By 1980, [a number] of our largest cities, Detroit, Baltimore, Cleveland, St. Louis, and New Orleans, will probably have Negro majorities." [33]

The race division between the inner and outer city is accentuated by a residential division by income, tending "to sever all contact between the slum dwellers and the middle and upper-income classes." [34] Since wealth is white and poverty is black, residential segregation by income is obviously residential segregation by race. These economic facts are, of course, the institutional parents of *de facto* social segregation in general and segregation in education specifically.

An examination of the social statistics of white families residing in the central city reveals that a significant portion are of the lower-middle class, older (on the average) than Negroes, and without children or having children who fall under the category of young adults.[35] Age as well as income prevents many whites in this group from having the residential mobility characteristic of younger and wealthier families. They constitute an important component of the white backlash in every major city.[36]

What is important to note about this lower-middle class group is that it feels directly threatened by the compressed Negro community that is forever seeking new areas in which to reside.[37] This insecure layer of whites sees their salvation in terms of keeping the Negro from confiscating "their" neighborhoods, "their" public parks, "their" public schools, and "their" city funds which go to support blacks existing off welfare payments. The situation is blatantly ripe for perpetual strife, conflict, and violence.

Beyond the lower-middle class buffer zones of the central city reside the white families, the suburbanites, who are wealthier and younger than central city whites. In age, white suburbanites come close to matching the median age of Negroes inhabiting the ghetto. As a result, white children live considerable distances from Negro children of the same generation, a demographic fact which makes integrated schooling on a meaningful scale spatially impractical and sociologically difficult because of extreme class differences.[38]

While the above facts about the urban profile have been reiterated often, they have not often received serious political attention. The average liberal's reactions (aside from increasing federal spending) to white fears and Negro miseries are in ethical terms; they point to horrifying dangers and immoral conditions. When the liberal is astute, like Charles E. Silberman, he warns the rest of us

> there is no large city . . . which does not have a large and potentially explosive Negro problem. . . . [And] unless the Negro position improves very quickly, Negroes of whatever class may come to regard their separation from American life as permanent, and so consider themselves outside the constraints and allegiance of American society. The Negro district of every large city could come to constitute an American Casbah, with its own values and controls and implacable hatred of everything white, that would poison American life.[39]

Observing the Negro population trends and segregation patterns, the liberal fails to see that no large city is without a serious white political problem; that is, the problem of containing the Negro's aspirations to shape his own political destiny. In those urban areas in which the Negro constitutes a near or actual majority, the patronizing courtship (both in its vulgar and its subtle forms) between the white liberal and his Negro "friends" is rapidly coming to an end as a practical arrangement. The growth of the Negro population within the political limits of the central city is not only a "problem" of fears and miseries, it is also an event of hope—the hope of building political power by blacks who have deep and permanent vested interests in solving the city problems. These interests, moreover, are unlikely to change, since the Negro population within each locale is unlikely to undergo any consequential spatial dispersion which would tend to alter its long run sociopolitical needs. The importance of this fact can hardly be overemphasized.

When the Negro majority was rural, it was basically impossible for the Negro middle class to interlock politically with the Negro lower class. There were, of course, isolated cries from lonely members of the Negro intelligentsia; but the Negro middle class, however small its size, was isolated from the Negro population as a whole. The reaching upward by the middle-class Negro for a higher station in life necessarily required that he look to the white establishment for political favors, patronage, approval, or economic opportunity. This was accomplished in general by demonstrating "worthiness," by "proving" that he was not like the rest of the race, or by denying blackness and "appearing" white. Acquiescence was rationalized into a belief that the whole race would be helped if a small upper crust "made it" and "proved" to whites that not all Negroes were "bad." It was hoped that the benefits would trickle down to the Negro majority in the lower class. The ridicule which E. Franklin Frazier directed at the black bourgeoisie was not without cause nor is it presently without relevance.[40]

However, as the Negro middle and lower class increasingly became part of the same urban matrix, as the Negro middle class became more numerous and educated, and as the fact of Negroness stubbornly prevailed over the fact of class, the grosser illusions of the Negro middle class faded, or at least changed in complexion. Moreover, from the growing layer of mainly clerical and professional middle-class Negroes, a segment has fallen out to adopt the traditional role of revolutionary intelligentsia. The ideology of Black Power represents the most advanced articulation of the middle-class Negro's awareness that any salvation worthy of its name must begin with developing a revolutionary consciousness and organization among the Negro working class.

As long as the Negro was rural, any movement representing his liberation could be readily isolated, forcefully repressed, or safely ignored. All these social options have disappeared. In the city, Black Power has an objective potential. The realization of the potential depends upon Negro leaders and their ability to develop Black Power in a viable way. Suffice it to say that this latter fact depends in no small degree on the ability of fully committed Black Power leaders to forge an organizing vehicle—if you will, a political party—that can survive and grow in the vacillating currents of the American environment.

BLACK DISCONTENT AND AMERICAN CAPITALISM

Having defined Black Power and examined some of the urban conditions from which Black Power derives its current impetus, it is now necessary to discuss the general sources of the Negro's socioeconomic discontent in relation to the ideology of capitalism which is the ideology of the white power structure. If Black Power is against "the system," it is important to know why the system cannot readily do away with the discontent which gives Black Power its vitality. The starting point of the analysis involves understanding the connection between race and class on the one hand, and the ideology of capitalism on the other.

The over-representation of the Negro mass in the lower class is ideologically intertwined with racial associations which reinforce the white rationalization that the Negro is unfit for equal treatment—be it for reasons of biological endowment or (which is more fashionable nowadays) "cultural deprivation." A significant part of the white man's view of the Negro is related to the Negro's class position. This is true even with regard to such seemingly unrelated but alleged character traits as sexual potency.[41] It should be noted that relating class position to character traits is not a practice that has been applied only to Negroes.

Prior to the integration of the bulk of the American working class into the economy (as consumers under the protection of the union and the legal system in general), even the white working class was periodically described by its enemies in terms similar to those applied now to the Negro. The early chronicles about labor are replete with statements justifying the worker's lowly position in terms of inborn deficiencies of some kind. The early agitators of labor sought not only to improve the worker's immediate economic conditions, but also to rectify the worker's image as a man. This was necessary because of capitalism's view of labor as an ordinary commodity. However, labor is not a natural commodity, and labor power, writes Karl Polanyi,

> cannot be shoved about, used indiscriminately, or even left unused, without affecting the human individual who happens to be the bearer of this peculiar commodity. In dispensing of a man's labor power the system would, incidentally, dispose of his physical, psychological, and moral entity "man" attached to that tag.[42]

Capitalism has long had a propensity to socially castrate the worker as a person and to capitalize upon this castration ideologically. This propensity, when operating on the Negro before and after the formal demise of slavery, was compounded and reinforced by the factor of race. The Negro, because of his color, was readily portrayed as the perennially uncouth, unskilled, ill-mannered foreigner in his own country. In addition to all the normal burdens of a worker in a system that tended to subdue his manhood to the fetish of commodity production, the Negro carried a color burden that involved his representation to and by the white population as evil, ugly, unreliable, and inferior. For this reason, exploitation and segregation of Negroes represented no serious moral dilemma to most whites, Gunnar Myrdal's views (as expressed in *An American Dilemma*) notwithstanding. White society as a whole established the conditions which nourished and perpetuated a style of life for the Negro majority that buttressed the stereotypes. Moreover, these stereotypes were the lens through which whites viewed even those few Negroes who managed to climb into the middle class. Thus, the total Negro population, regardless of its own intra-class differences, is looked upon by whites as one inferior status group.[43]

While the racism of the employing class was clearly related to the need for cheap unorganized labor, the same system tended to generate a worker's mentality that was conducive to the exclusion of black "foreigners." American capitalism has imbued its workers with a primitive scarcity mentality partially derived from their historical experience of period unemployment.[44] This scarcity mentality operating in a competitive context stimulated a tendency to exclude Negroes from trade and industry.[45] Both in the realm of concepts and in the realm of reality, actual and contrived scarcity are essential to the functioning of the private enterprise system. The scarcity principle is central to its mode of rationality and is employed to justify the existing structure of prices, distribution of income, and composition of output. To the Negro, the economics of scarcity has generally meant a paucity of desirable jobs and an abundance of undesirable ones.

The Negro's inferior socioeconomic status is generally viewed by liberals as being determined by discrimination in terms of housing and educational opportunities on the one hand, and in terms of income differences for like jobs and occupational and industrial exclusion practices on the other. More sophisticated establishment formulations of the Negro problem view it as a complex set of interrelated self-fulfilling processes involving innumerable variables.[46] The former view leads to anti-discriminatory programs which are directed at changing white attitudes and behavior. However, a white liberal awareness has grown, possibly through introspection, that changing whites is a hopeless goal and, in any event, not a sufficient one *per se*.[47] This has led to a shift to the later analysis with a programmatic emphasis on ways to "uplift" the Negro. The aim is to enable Negroes to compete more effectively with whites within a private enterprise system, that is, within the very system in which the Negro has been rejected. While both of these views have some relevance, they do not represent the whole truth or even most of it.

The Negro's problem must always be seen in terms of its causes, otherwise what is needed to fundamentally alter his underprivileged status will not be comprehended. The typical white man's view of the Negro operates under a cultural overhead originating from a slave system in which the American Negro was not only physically enslaved but (more important for present purposes) was (a) systematically brainwashed into believing a myth about his own mental and spiritual inferiority,[48] and (b) forced to repress the normal degrees of self-assertiveness.[49] Forced enslavement obliterated the Negro's indigenous history and culture, one source of his pride and his identity. Persuaded that he was essentially endowed with an inferior mental capacity and forced to inhibit his personal will in relation to the white majority, the American Negro was unable to develop a new identity and sense of achievement following his formal emancipation. In a state of disarray and helplessness, a propertyless Negro had to compete in an economy in which the institutions of private property and unfettered individualism reached unfathomable proportions. Given a legacy that denied him an ego and freedom to choose, he had to survive in a society propelled by egomaniacal types whose freedom to choose was more important than the substance of choice. Private enterprise and freedom to accumulate wealth *ad infinitum* conspired against the social protection of those who needed it most. The principles of minimum government and competitive enterprise were welded together by a secular expectation that each man, if he worked hard, could, in the words of Lincoln, "be a hired laborer this year and the next, work for himself afterwards, and finally hire men to work for him. That is the free system." [50] The whole conglomeration (enterprise, laissez-faire, and the psychological expectation that hard work would bring material, if not spiritual, rewards) was nourished by an environment characterized by white class mobility, white frontier egalitarianism, mechanical inventiveness, and an abundance of natural resources. The historic panorama which the Negro witnessed entailed the success of everyone but himself. While the Great Depression and the New Deal may have ushered in some modifications of the acquisitive society in its rawest manifestations, these did not sufficiently alter the relative position or conditions of the Negro.

In the abstract world of competitive ideology—which still reinforces the private enterprise system and underlies much of the rhetoric in the pluralistic vision of society—consumers need freedom to choose among alternatives in order to be satisfied, producers need freedom to choose how to combine factors and harness technology so as to maximize their profits, and employees need freedom to choose jobs so that society can get the necessary allocation of skills. The freedom of choice for everyone in the market place, however necessary it appears to whites, turns into its opposite in relation to Negroes.

In a capitalist society, discrimination against Negroes takes place under the banner of freedom to choose.[51] The freedom of choice to the white consumer means freedom to avoid living next door to a Negro. Freedom to organize an association around your job or trade means freedom to dissociate from Negroes by keeping them out of your trade or industry. The employer's freedom to combine labor and capital in production means freedom not to hire or to promote black labor relative to white labor, or freedom to avoid the social costs of technological unemployment, or those connected with the movement of a plant from the central city.[52]

To the Negro, market freedom and the privacy of wealth have meant the negation of his own freedom—if not to exist—at least to live. Thus, salvation to the Negro, when working and not working, has been outside of the market—either in the form of secure but low paying civil service jobs or in the form of dependence on dole from the government in the welfare state.

Hence, it requires no great powers of reason to understand why the Negro is not a natural ally of the capitalist system. This is not to say that capitalism cannot *logically* incorporate the Negro into the market fold. But it is not a question of logic alone. Given the values of the decision-makers in the market, the objectives of the dominant whites are in fact realized by their freedom to exclude Negroes from jobs, from industries, from neighborhoods, and from integrated educational opportunities. Black Power's castigation in racial terms of the white power structure in general, rather than in some specific Marxian or socialist terms like "the ruling class" or "vested interest groups," is not a vagary obscuring reality. Nor is it a sign, as some white liberals and Negro moderates have maintained, of racism in reverse.[53] The simple truth is that many white interests in discrimination tend to coalesce in the market. A restaurant owner who decides to serve Negroes, or an airline company that decides to employ Negro stewardesses less attractive than Lena Horne, or a motel owner who decides to provide sleeping accommodations to Negroes may, in fact, lose customers and profits.[54]

In a similar vein, an employer who decides to promote a number of Negroes to positions of supervision over whites may, in fact, disturb his labor force and disrupt his production plans. A union which excludes Negroes in order to maintain the scarcity of its numbers is acting in a way consistent with maintaining higher white wages. It is not irrational for an employer to disemploy the Negro first and hire him last in a market in which white labor is scarce and black labor is redundant. The Negro laborer is always available for rehire without cost; this is not the case in a tight market for white labor. And finally, it should be noted that the costs (running into billions of dollars) of fundamentally changing the Negro's position in our society must basically be met by the corporate community in the form of higher taxes, a fact which explains, I believe, why the corporate community has been void of any serious schemes concerning the Negro's salvation.

Because the Negro's fate now is basically at the mercy of the private sector, a sector in which persons whose freedom to discriminate in the use of their wealth and income is viewed by them as an inalienable market right, the Negro can hardly expect the spontaneous forces of the market to function in his behalf. But once Black salvation is viewed as existing outside the market, it is automatically seen to fall inside the domain of political action. Because, however, of the organic separation of our political institutions from our economic ones, white political responses to black pressures tend to take the form of an appeal to the merciful "instincts" of private decision-makers to be fair-minded against, perhaps, their own interests. This means that the realistic enforcement of anti-discriminatory decrees and the development of serious programs, even under the dubious assumption of good intentions on the part of state administrators and politicians, are extremely difficult if not impossible. Thus, important segments of the Negro population are beginning to view the course of Negro salvation as existing not only outside the market process, but also outside the established political routines and organizations.

We see that the ideology of Black Power, whatever its deficiencies, is irreversibly taking the Negro outside the market and outside the political framework which complements that market. Although a minority representing only 11 percent of the total population, the Negro is strategically concentrated in all our major metropolitan areas. This not only establishes a base to launch on the local level an independent political movement that is primarily black, but it also gives the Negro population, properly organized, leverage to deal with the federal government directly, and thus by-pass the state and suburban political machines which are becoming bastions of reaction.[55] Before this can occur, however, Black

Power advocates must forge a sufficient number of independent local political movements in order to bring about the disintegration of the Democratic Party or a radical alteration of its present characteristics. This latter dissolution is a prerequisite to the formation of a new national party ultimately capable of initiating new programs and reordering our national objectives. In essence, the process envisioned is not the creation of a third party, but the development of a new second party.

The break-up or fundamental alteration of the Democratic Party will free a consequential portion of the labor movement, professional class, and other non-propertied segments of the white population from the Party's patronage system and established routines. These groups will be, in turn, more amenable to the formation of a new national party capable of establishing the institutional links connecting the inner city to the central government. Black Power—by its struggle against coalition politics in the current context and its effort to build independent local political movements—offers the only possible hope of stimulating the construction of a new political edifice in which the Negro will be a decisive participant.

The break-up of the Democratic Party is not as remote a possibility as one might presently conjecture. The Democratic colossus has come to be supported by a large number of suburban, tax-paying, proper, middle-class white folks whose loyalty to the Party is increasingly becoming more and more tenuous. As the Northern Negro proceeds to exert pressure—both from within the Democratic Party and by independent action from without—the Party will find it impossible to meet simultaneously the accelerated demands of its Negro supporters and the growing containment sentiments of its white suburban ones. Moreover, as the Black Power movement grows outside the existing political framework, Negro militant integrationists and moderates inside the Democratic Party will have to intensify their actions in order to retain their followers. This will serve to further enhance the fears of white, middle-class suburbanites who, at their very best, might tolerate tokenism, but are not predisposed to any degree to yield to the general needs and aspirations of the Negro middle class—to say nothing about meeting the demands of the total Negro population.

Viewed from the recent, futile efforts of Democratic chieftains to hold together their variegated elements, the Negro activists inside the Democratic Party and the Black Power advocates outside it jointly operate to pull the Party in opposing directions, i.e., in the direction of token reformism on the one hand, and cryptically conservative assurances about maintaining law and order to its white supporters preparing to bolt the Party on the other. As these inconsistent tendencies accumulate momentum in a situation in which even the radical right is learning the art of moderate rhetoric, the Democratic apparatus will become unable to satisfy its incongruous constituencies or resolve any major problem. The Party will gradually drift to a complete standstill and incoherence, and eventually, disintegrate from consequential losses of support from all sides of the loose mosaic that presently constitutes its political surface.[56]

The complete and total severance of the Negro from his slave legacy requires the Negro's control of the inner city and the launching of a vast program—not for more welfare, make-work jobs, or integration—but for cultural, political, social, and economic development. The Negro's control of the central city would stimulate the development of a new national party which would ultimately develop the means to politically overhaul the prevailing relations between federal, state, and city governments in general, and the infra-structure of city life and politics specifically. Such a vast internal development program involves motion in two directions: (a) making public or cooperative much that is presently private in the realm of housing and enterprise, and (b) opposing our present imperial course which has entered a new and costly stage and is forging a reactionary alliance in the domestic political arena. The old reactionary alliance of Southern Democrats and Northern Republicans may bring racial equality to the Negro men prepared to die in the jungles of some underdeveloped country seeking national liberation, but it cannot bring the developmental resources needed to eliminate the inner city jungles in which the vast majority of Negro civilians are prepared to live. Priority for development not only leads to questions about how and for what purpose we use our national wealth—but it leads also to developmental planning and the question as to who is to sit on the emergent developmental planning boards.[57] Developmental planning involves viewing ghettoes as underdeveloped areas that need to undergo a total rebirth in all spheres of life. More specifically, it involves a "policy of import substitution, to be pursued in conjunction with export development . . ."[58] in order to remove the ghetto's "foreign" deficit in the form of a cultural drain, brain drain, political drain, and last but not least, financial drain.

The Negro population is propertyless, poverty-stricken, and disoriented. It is alienated from the established instrumentalities employed by whites for their own ends. It is surrounded by an affluent capitalism ostentatiously representing itself in the form of waste, trivia, and destruction. It is being called upon to support a government engaged in fighting other non-whites whose struggle for social progress is increasingly appearing similar to the Negro's own fight at home. A Black Power movement which reflects the needs of a population living under such conditions cannot but raise some fundamental questions about the way the system operates and provide some revolutionary answers. The specter that haunts the white power structure is that the Negro struggle generally, and Black Power specifically, push the contradictions of capitalism's rhetoric about freedom, equality, and its use of "scarce" resources to the limit, and thereby prepare all of us, black and white, to grapple with the contradictions in the system's reality.

NOTES

1. New York *Post,* June 19, 1967, p. 33.
2. Ibid., p. 33.
3. *Black Power and Urban Unrest* (New York: Hawthorn, 1967), pp. 8, 9, 99.
4. *New York Times,* June 20, 1967, p. 9.

5. "Martin Luther King Defines Black Power," *The New York Times Magazine*, June 11, 1967, p. 26.

6. *The New York Review of Books*, September 22, 1966, p. 5.

7. Jane E. Brody, *New York Times*, May 13, 1967, p. 21.

8. Wallace Turner, *New York Times*, May 21, 1967, p. 66.

9. The elements of an ideology are discussed by C. Wright Mills, *The Marxists* (New York: Dell, 1962), pp. 12–13.

10. Ibid.

11. Ibid.

12. "Martin Luther King Defines Black Power," pp. 27, 99.

13. Quoted by A. B. Spellman, "Interview with Malcolm X," *Monthly Review* 16 (May 1964): 24.

14. For a discussion of the coalition position, see Bayard Rustin, "Black Power and Coalition Politics," *Commentary* 42 (September 1966): 35–40.

15. Carmichael, "What We Want," p. 6.

16. Quoted from an original position paper on Black Power by members of the Student Nonviolent Coordinating Committee, *New York Times*, August 5, 1966, p. 10.

17. Carmichael, "What We want," p. 6.

18. Ibid.

19. "The Rhetoric of Malcolm X," *Columbia University Forum* 9 (Spring 1966): 6–9.

20. As quoted by Illo, "The Rhetoric of Malcolm X," p. 6.

21. The atavisms of slavery are essentially derived from the prescriptions to be followed by the "good" slave as designated by the master. They are: (1) the nonexercise of will or judgment in relation to demands made by the master, (2) the incorporation of feelings of inferiority, (3) the fear of the master's sense of power, (4) the acceptance of the master's judgment as to what constitutes good conduct and sense, and (5) the habit of helplessness and dependence. See Martin Luther King, Jr., *Where Do We Go From Here: Chaos or Community?* (New York: Harper & Row, 1967), p. 39.

22. *New York Times*, August 5, 1966, p. 10.

23. "Martin Luther King Defines Black Power," p. 26.

24. As quoted by Illo, "The Rhetoric of Malcolm X," p. 9.

25. For the development of this idea in general terms, see James O'Conner, "Towards a Theory of Community Unions," *Studies on the Left* 4 (Spring 1964): 143–48.

26. As quoted in Spellman, "Interview with Malcolm X," p. 4.

27. Alvin F. Poussaint, "A Negro Psychiatrist Explains the Negro Psyche," *The New York Times Magazine*, August 20, 1967, pp. 56, 76, 80.

28. One might further add that violence may also function to drive out white owners of business from the ghetto.

29. "What We Want," pp. 5–6.

30. As quoted by Illo, "The Rhetoric of Malcolm X," pp. 10–11.

31. On the Negro identity problem, see Charles E. Silberman, *Crisis in Black and White* (New York: Random House, 1964), chapter 4.

32. "The Coming Test of American Democracy," *Commentary* 37 (January 1964): 61.

33. Social Dynamics Corporation, *The Negro Population: 1965 Estimates and 1970 Projections* (New York, 1966), Table IX, p. 1.

34. Wilbur R. Thompson, *A Preface to Urban Economics* (Baltimore: Johns Hopkins University Press, 1965), p. 6.

35. U.S. Department of Labor, Bureau of Labor Statistics, *Income, Education and Unemployment in Neighborhoods*, January 1963; also, *U.S. Census of Population: 1960. Selected Area Reports. Standard Metropolitan Statistical Areas. Final Report PC (3)-10* (Washington, D.C.: U.S. Government Printing Office, 1963).

36. For an excellent article concerned with the backlash question, see David Danzig, "Rightists, Racists, and Separatists: A White Power Bloc in the Making," *Commentary* 38 (August 1964): 32.

37. See Morganthau, "The Coming Test of American Democracy," p. 62.

38. Whether integration between Negro and white children with extreme class differences is desirable is a moot question. Viewed from the psychological and academic needs of Negro children, it is doubtful that integrated education in the present context is either pedagogically or ideologically in the right direction. Moreover, it has been pointed out that integrated education is mainly a Negro middle-class goal without general support from the Negro majority. See Silberman, *Crisis in Black and White*, p. 205; also A. James Gregor, "Black Nationalism: A Preliminary Analysis of Negro Radicalism," *Science and Society* 27 (Fall 1963): 429–30.

39. Silberman, *Crisis in Black and White*, pp. 17, 35.

40. *Black Bourgeoisie* (New York: Collier, 1962).

41. See Bruno Bettelheim, "Class, Color and Prejudice," *The Nation*, October 19, 1963, p. 233.

42. *The Great Transformation* (New York: Rinehart, 1944), p. 73.

43. This point was developed succinctly by Benjamin Payton in *New University Thought*, Special Issue (1966/67), p. 40. "The Negro community consists . . . of economic and social classes but in the context of a racist society the Negro community forms more in the nature of a status group than a collection of classes. And whether a Negro is middle class, or lower class, or upper class, he is still treated as a Negro."

44. A whole theory of the American labor movement, well-known and widely discussed by labor economists, has been constructed around the point by Selig Perlman, *A Theory of the Labor Movement* (New York: Macmillan, 1928).

45. An official of the Federal Department of Housing and Urban Development made the point in the following terms: "You're whistling in the dark if one thinks that you're going to solve [the problem of the] entrance of Negroes into the construction trades unless you increase the work [opportunities]. You won't get new members until the current members have enough work." *New York Times*, June 4, 1967, p. 42. For a statistical study of the extensiveness of exclusion practices by white workers against minority workers immediately below in occupational rank, see Robert W. and Patricia Hodge, "Occupational Assimilation as a Competitive Process," *American Journal of Sociology* 71 (November 1965): 249–64.

46. For a brief discussion of this point, see Silberman, *Crisis in Black and White*, p. 352.

47. See Eli Ginsberg's review of Vivian Henderson's book, *The Economic Status of Negroes: In the Nation and in the South*, in *The New Republic*, October 12, 1963, p. 26.

48. See Silberman, *Crisis in Black and White*, pp. 79–93; also Harold Isaacs, "Blackness and Whiteness," *Encounter* 21 (August 1963): 8–21.

49. Poussaint, "A Negro Psychiatrist Explains the Negro Psyche," p. 56.

50. Abraham Lincoln, quoted by Vernon Louis Parrington, *Main Currents in American Thought* (New York: Harcourt, 1930), II, 154.

51. See Gary Becker, *The Economics of Discrimination* (Chicago: University of Chicago Press, 1957), p. 5. Here Becker defines discrimination as being similar to the general problem of making choices derived from personal tastes.

52. "In the mid-50's," writes Herbert Bienstock, Regional Director of the United States Bureau of Labor Statistics, "advanced technology hit the factories, making the semi-skilled superfluous. Negroes lost their jobs. Plants moved from the central cities to the suburbs. New York lost 200,000 factory jobs in a decade. Unskilled and semi-skilled jobs disappeared. A million youths from the postwar baby boom

came on the labor market. Many found jobs only in the slum's rackets, such as policy runners." Quoted in *The New York Times,* July 14, 1967, p. 10.

53. See statement by Dr. Samuel DuBois, quoted by Fred Powledge, *Black Power— White Resistance* (Cleveland: World, 1967), pp. 243–44.

54. Such reasoning was explicitly employed, for example, by Dr. Alvine, an owner of the Robin Dee Day Camp, in a testimony before the New Jersey State Supreme Court. While admitting that he refused admittance to Negro children on the grounds of race, he adamantly denied he was prejudiced. Dr. Alvine simply stated that the "admission of Negroes would injure his business." The testimony, incidentally, was not disputed by the Civil Rights Commission. Reported in *The New York Times,* May 18, 1965, p. 41.

55. The growing preoccupation of many political pundits with the proper power balance between the federal, state, and local government is partly, if not wholly, a subterfuge for the growing imbalance created by the potential power of the Negro to "go-it-alone" on the local level and use his strategic position on the federal one at the expense of suburban and state levers of power. In other words, behind the recent semantics of "federalism revisited" is the substance of race politics and power.

56. The strains that the Negro struggle are putting on the Democratic Party's capacity to maintain national consensus have been recognized in somewhat different terms by Samuel Lubell: "For the Democratic coalition the political danger posed by the swelling Negro vote is not that the Negroes will bolt to the Republicans, but rather that the Negro demands may drive white Democratic voters out." See "The Negro and the Democratic Coalition," *Commentary* 38 (August 1964): 23. This process, it should be noted, will make it increasingly difficult for the Democratic Party to meet Negro demands, and therefore, it will automatically feed into Black Power's drive toward independent politics.

57. This question has already been raised in its incipient form around whether the poor (euphemism for black people) should determine the use of the meager anti-poverty funds made available by the federal government.

58. Bennet Harrison, "Economic Development Planning for American Urban Slums: Pilot Project—Harlem," Center for Economic Planning, The New School for Social Research, December, 1967, p. 4.

INTERNAL COLONIALISM AND GHETTO REVOLT

Robert Blauner

It is becoming almost fashionable to analyze American racial conflict today in terms of the colonial analogy. I shall argue in this paper that the utility of this perspective depends upon a distinction between colonization as a process and colonialism as a social, economic, and political

From *Social Problems* 16 (Spring 1969): 393–408; reprinted by permission of the author and The Society for the Study of Social Problems.

system. It is the experience of colonization that Afro-Americans share with many of the non-white people of the world. But this subjugation has taken place in a societal context that differs in important respects from the situation of "classical colonialism." In the body of this essay I shall look at some major developments in Black protest—the urban riots, cultural nationalism, and the movement for ghetto control—as collective responses to colonized status. Viewing our domestic situation as a special form of colonization outside a context of a colonial system will help explain some of the dilemmas and ambiguities within these movements.

The present crisis in American life has brought about changes in social perspectives and the questioning of long accepted frameworks. Intellectuals and social scientists have been forced by the pressure of events to look at old definitions of the character of our society, the role of racism, and the workings of basic institutions. The depth and volatility of contemporary racial conflict challenge sociologists in particular to question the adequacy of theoretical models by which we have explained American race relations in the past.

For a long time the distinctiveness of the Negro situation among the ethnic minorities was placed in terms of color, and the systematic discrimination that follows from our deep-seated racial prejudices. This was sometimes called the caste theory, and while provocative, it missed essential and dynamic features of American race relations. In the past ten years there has been a tendency to view Afro-Americans as another ethnic group not basically different in experience from previous ethnics and whose "immigration" condition in the North would in time follow their upward course. The inadequacy of this model is now clear—even the Kerner Report devotes a chapter to criticizing this analogy. A more recent (though hardly new) approach views the essence of racial subordination in economic class terms: Black people as an underclass are to a degree specially exploited and to a degree economically dispensable in an automating society. Important as are economic factors, the power of race and racism in America cannot be sufficiently explained through class analysis. Into this theory vacuum steps the model of internal colonialism. Problematic and imprecise as it is, it gives hope of becoming a framework that can integrate the insights of caste and racism, ethnicity, culture, and economic exploitation into an overall conceptual scheme. At the same time, the danger of the colonial model is the imposition of an artificial analogy which might keep us from facing up to the fact (to quote Harold Cruse) that "the American black and white social phenomenon is a uniquely new world thing." [1]

During the late 1950's, identification with African nations and other colonial or formerly colonized peoples grew in importance among Black militants.[2] As a result the U. S. was increasingly seen as a colonial power and the concept of domestic colonialism was introduced into the political analysis and rhetoric of militant nationalists. During the same period Black social theorists began developing this frame of reference for explaining American realities. As early as 1962, Cruse characterized race relations in this country as "domestic colonialism." [3] Three years later in *Dark Ghetto*, Kenneth Clark demonstrated how the political, economic, and social structure of Harlem was essentially that of a colony.[4] Finally in 1967, a full-blown elaboration of "internal colonialism" provided the theoretical framework for Carmichael and Hamilton's widely read *Black Power*.[5] The following year the colonial analogy gained currency and new "respectability" when Senator McCarthy habitually referred to Black Americans as a colonized people during his campaign. While the rhetoric of internal colonialism was catching on, other social scientists began to raise questions about its appropriateness as a scheme of analysis.

The colonial analysis has been rejected as obscurantist and misleading by scholars who point to the significant differences in history and social-political conditions between our domestic patterns and what took place in Africa and India. Colonialism traditionally refers to the establishment of domination over a geographically external political unit, most often inhabited by people of a different race and culture, where this domination is political and economic and the colony exists subordinated to and dependent upon the mother country. Typically the colonizers exploit the land, the raw materials, the labor, and other resources of the colonized nation; in addition a formal recognition is given to the difference in power, autonomy, and political status, and various agencies are set up to maintain this subordination. Seemingly the analogy must be stretched beyond usefulness if the American version is to be forced into this model. For here we are talking about group relations within a society; the mother country-colony separation in geography is absent. Though whites certainly colonized the territory of the original Americans, internal colonization of Afro-Americans did not involve the settlement of whites in any land that was unequivocally black. And unlike the colonial situation, there has been no formal recognition of differing power since slavery was abolished outside the South. Classic colonialism involved the control and exploitation of the majority of a nation by a minority of outsiders. Whereas in America the people who are oppresesd were themselves originally outsiders and are a numerical minority.

This conventional critique of "internal colonialism" is useful in pointing to the differences between our domestic patterns and the overseas situation. But in its bold attack it tends to lose sight of common experiences that have been historically shared by the most subjugated racial minorities in America and non-white peoples in some other parts of the world. For understanding the most dramatic recent developments on the race scene, this common core element—which I shall call colonization—may be more important than the undeniable divergences between the two contexts.

The common features ultimately relate to the fact that the classical colonialism of the imperialist era and American racism developed out of the same historical situation and reflected a common world economic and power stratification. The slave trade for the most part preceded the imperialist partition and economic exploitation of Africa, and in fact may have been a necessary prerequisite for colonial conquest—since it helped deplete and pacify Africa, undermining the resistance to direct occupation. Slavery contributed one of the basic raw materials for the textile industry which provided much of the capital for the West's industrial development and need for economic expansionism. The essential condition for both American slavery and European colonialism was the power domination and the technological superiority of the Western world in its relation to peoples of non-Western and non-white origins. This objective supremacy in technology and military power buttressed the West's sense of cultural superiority, laying the basis for racist ideologies that were elaborated to justify control and exploitation of non-white people. Thus because classical colonialism and America's internal version developed out of a similar balance of technological, cultural, and power relations, a common *process* of social oppression characterized the racial patterns in the two contexts—despite the variation in political and social structure.

There appear to be four basic components of the colonization complex. The first refers to how the racial group enters into the dominant society (whether colonial power or not). Colonization begins with a forced, involuntary entry. Second, there is an impact on the culture and social organization of the colonized people which is more than just a result of such "natural" processes as contact and acculturation. The colonizing power carries out a policy which constrains, transforms, or destroys indigenous values, orientations, and ways of life. Third, colonization involves a relationship by which members of the colonized group tend to be administered by representatives of the dominant power. There is an experience of being managed and manipulated by outsiders in terms of ethnic status.

A final fundament of colonization is racism. Racism is a principle of social domination by which a group seen as inferior or different in terms of alleged biological characteristics is exploited, controlled, and oppressed socially and psychically by a superordinate group. Except for the marginal case of Japanese imperialism, the major examples of colonialism have involved the subjugation of non-white Asian, African, and Latin American peoples by white European powers. Thus rascism has generally accompanied colonialism. Race prejudice can exist without colonization —the experience of Asian-American minorities is a case in point—but racism as a system of domination is part of the complex of colonization.

The concept of colonization stresses the enormous fatefulness of the historical factor, namely the manner in which a minority group becomes a part of the dominant society.[6] The crucial difference between the colonized Americans and the ethnic immigrant minorities is that the latter have always been able to operate fairly competitively within that relatively open section of the social and economic order because these groups came voluntarily in search of a better life, because their movements in society were not administratively controlled, and because they transformed their culture at their own pace—giving up ethnic values and institutions when it was seen as a desirable exchange for improvements in social position.

In present-day America, a major device of Black colonization is the powerless ghetto. As Kenneth Clark describes the situation:

> Ghettoes are the consequence of the imposition of external power and the institutionalization of powerlessness. In this respect, they are in fact

social, political, educational, and above all—economic colonies. Those confined within the ghetto walls are subject peoples. They are victims of the
greed, cruelty, insensitivity, guilt and fear of their masters. . . .

The community can best be described in terms of the analogy of a
powerless colony. Its political leadership is divided, and all but one or
two of its political leaders are shortsighted and dependent upon the larger
political power structure. Its social agencies are financially precarious and
dependent upon sources of support outside the community. Its economy
is dominated by small businesses which are largely owned by absentee
owners, and its tenements and other real property are also owned by absentee landlords.

Under a system of centralization, Harlem's schools are controlled by
forces outside of the community. Programs and policies are supervised and
determined by individuals who do not live in the community. . . .[7]

Of course many ethnic groups in America have lived in ghettoes.
What make the Black ghettoes an expression of colonized status are three
special features. First, the ethnic ghettoes arose more from voluntary
choice, both in the sense of the choice to immigrate to America and the
decision to live among one's fellow ethnics. Second, the immigrant ghettoes tended to be a one and two generation phenomenon; they were
actually way-stations in the process of acculturation and assimilation.
When they continue to persist as in the case of San Francisco's China-
town, it is because they are big business for the ethnics themselves and
there is a new stream of immigrants. The Black ghetto on the other hand
has been a more permanent phenomenon, although some individuals do
escape it. But most relevant is the third point. European ethnic groups
like the Poles, Italians, and Jews generally only experienced a brief period,
often less than a generation, during which their residential buildings,
commercial stores, and other enterprises were owned by outsiders. The
Chinese and Japanese faced handicaps of color prejudice that were almost
as strong as the Blacks faced, but very soon gained control of their internal communities, because their traditional ethnic culture and social
organization had not been destroyed by slavery and internal colonization.
But Afro-Americans are distinct in the extent to which their segregated
communities have remained controlled economically, politically, and administratively from the outside. One indicator of this difference is the
estimate that the "income of Chinese-Americans from Chinese-owned
businesses is in proportion to their numbers 45 times as great as the income of Negroes from Negro-owned businesses."[8] But what is true of
business is also true for the other social institutions that operate within
the ghetto. The educators, policemen, social workers, politicians, and
others who administer the affairs of ghetto residents are typically whites
who live outside the Black community. Thus the ghetto plays a strategic
role as the focus for the administration by outsiders which is also essential
to the structure of overseas colonialism.[9]

The colonial status of the Negro community goes beyond the issue
of ownership and decision-making within Black neighborhoods. The
Afro-America population in most cities has very little influence on
the power structure and institutions of the larger metropolis, despite the

fact that in numerical terms, Blacks tend to be the most sizeable of the various interest groups. A recent analysis of policy-making in Chicago estimates that "Negroes really hold less than 1 percent of the effective power in the Chicago metropolitan area. [Negroes are 20 percent of Cook County's population.] Realistically the power structure of Chicago is hardly less white than that of Mississippi." [10]

Colonization outside of a traditional colonial structure has its own special conditions. The group culture and social structure of the colonized in America is less developed; it is also less autonomous. In addition, the colonized are a numerical minority, and furthermore they are ghettoized more totally and are more dispersed than people under classic colonialism. Though these realities affect the magnitude and direction of response, it is my basic thesis that the most important expressions of protest in the Black community during the recent years reflect the colonized status of Afro-America. Riots, programs of separation, politics of community control, the Black revolutionary movements, and cultural nationalism each represent a different strategy of attack on domestic colonialism in America. Let us now examine some of these movements.

RIOT OR REVOLT?

The so-called riots are being increasingly recognized as a preliminary if primitive form of mass rebellion against a colonial status. There is still a tendency to absorb their meaning within the conventional scope of assimilation-integration politics: some commentators stress the material motives involved in looting as a sign that the rioters want to join America's middle-class affluence just like everyone else. That motives are mixed and often unconscious, that Black people want good furniture and television sets like whites is beside the point. The guiding impulse in most major outbreaks has not been integration with American society, but an attempt to stake out a sphere of control by moving against that society and destroying the symbols of its oppression.

In my critique of the McCone report I observed that the rioters were asserting a claim to territoriality, an unorganized and rather inchoate attempt to gain control over their community or "turf." [11] In succeeding disorders also the thrust of the action has been the attempt to clear out an alien presence, white men and officials, rather than a drive to kill whites as in a conventional race riot. The main attacks have been directed at the property of white businessmen and at the police who operate in the Black community "like an army of occupation" protecting the interests of outside exploiters and maintaining the domination over the ghetto by the central metropolitan power structure.[12] The Kerner report misleads when it attempts to explain riots in terms of integration: "What the rioters appear to be seeking was fuller participation in the social order and the material benefits enjoyed by the majority of American citizens. Rather than rejecting the American system, they were anxious to obtain a place for themselves in it." [13] More accurately, the revolts pointed to alienation from this system on the part of many poor and also not-so-poor

Blacks. The sacredness of private property, that unconsciously accepted bulwark of our social arrangements, was rejected; people who looted apparently without guilt generally remarked that they were taking things that "really belonged" to them anyway.[14] Obviously the society's bases of legitimacy and authority have been attacked. Law and order has long been viewed as the white man's law and order by Afro-Americans; but now this perspective characteristic of a colonized people is out in the open. And the Kerner Report's own data question how well ghetto rebels are buying the system: In Newark only 33 percent of self-reported rioters said they thought this country was worth fighting for in the event of a major war; in the Detroit sample the figure was 55 percent.[15]

One of the most significant consequences of the process of colonization is a weakening of the colonized's individual and collective will to resist his oppression. It has been easier to contain and control Black ghettoes because communal bonds and group solidarity have been weakened through divisions among leadership, failures of organization, and a general disspiritment that accompanies social oppression. The riots are a signal that the will to resist has broken the mold of accommodation. In some cities as in Watts they also represented nascent movements toward community identity. In several riot-torn ghettoes the outbursts have stimulated new organizations and movements. If it is true that the riot phenomenon of 1964–68 has passed its peak, its historical import may be more for the "internal" organizing momentum generated than for any profound "external" response of the larger society facing up to underlying causes.

Despite the appeal of Frantz Fanon to young Black revolutionaries, America is not Algeria. It is difficult to foresee how riots in our cities can play a role equivalent to rioting in the colonial situation as an integral phase in a movement for national liberation. In 1968 some militant groups (for example, the Black Panther Party in Oakland) had concluded that ghetto riots were self-defeating of the lives and interests of Black people in the present balance of organization and gunpower, though they had served a role to stimulate both Black consciousness and white awareness of the depths of racial crisis. Such militants have been influential in "cooling" their communities during periods of high riot potential. Theoretically oriented Black radicals see riots as spontaneous mass behavior which must be replaced by a revolutionary organization and consciousness. But despite the differences in objective conditions, the violence of the 1960's seems to serve the same psychic function, assertions of dignity and manhood for young Blacks in urban ghettoes, as it did for the colonized of North Africa described by Fanon and Memmi.[16]

CULTURAL NATIONALISM

Cultural conflict is generic to the colonial relation because colonization involves the domination of Western technological values over the more communal cultures of non-Western peoples. Colonialism played havoc with the national integrity of the peoples it brought under its sway. Of course, all traditional cultures are threatened by industrialism, the city, and modernization in communication, transportation, health, and education. What is special are the political and administrative decisions of colonizers in managing and controlling colonized peoples. The boundaries of African colonies, for example, were drawn to suit the political conveniences of the European nations without regard to the social organization and cultures of African tribes and kingdoms. Thus Nigeria as blocked out by the British included the Yorubas and the Ibos, whose civil war today is a residuum of the colonialist's disrespect for the integrity of indigenous cultures.

The most total destruction of culture in the colonization process took place not in traditional colonialism but in America. As Frazier stressed, the integral cultures of the diverse African peoples who furnished the slave trade were destroyed because slaves from different tribes, kingdoms, and linguistic groups were purposely separated to maximize domination and control. Thus language, religion, and national loyalties were lost in North America much more completely than in the Caribbean and Brazil where slavery developed somewhat differently. Thus on this key point America's internal colonization has been more total and extreme than situations of classic colonialism. For the British in India and the European powers in Africa were not able—as outnumbered minorities—to destroy the national and tribal cultures of the colonized. Recall that American slavery lasted 250 years and its racist aftermath another 100. Colonial dependency in the case of British Kenya and French Algeria lasted only 77 and 125 years respectively. In the wake of this more drastic uprooting and destruction of culture and social organization, much more powerful agencies of social, political, and psychological domination developed in the American case.

> Colonial control of many peoples inhabiting the colonies was more a goal than a fact, and at Independence there were undoubtedly fairly large numbers of Africans who had never seen a colonial administrator. The gradual process of extension of control from the administrative center on the African coast contrasts sharply with the total uprooting involved in the slave trade and the totalitarian aspects of slavery in the United States. Whether or not Elkins is correct in treating slavery as a total institution, it undoubtedly had a far more radical and pervasive impact on American slaves than did colonialism on the vast majority of Africans.[17]

Yet a similar cultural process unfolds in both contexts of colonialism. To the extent that they are involved in the larger society and economy, the colonized are caught up in a conflict between two cultures. Fanon has described how the assimilation-oriented schools of Martinique taught him to reject his own culture and Blackness in favor of Westernized, French, and white values.[18] Both the colonized elites under traditional colonialism and perhaps the majority of Afro-Americans today experience a parallel split in identity, cultural loyalty, and political orientation.[19]

The colonizers use their culture to socialize the colonized elites (intellectuals, politicians, and middle class) into an identification with the colonial system. Because Western culture has the prestige, the power, and the key to open the limited opportunity that a minority of the colonized may achieve, the first reaction seems to be an acceptance of the dominant values. Call it brainwashing as the Black Muslims put it; call it identifying with the aggressor if you prefer Freudian terminology; call it a natural response to the hope and belief that integration and democratization can really take place if you favor a more commonsense explanation, this initial acceptance in time crumbles on the realities of racism and colonialism. The colonized, seeing that his success within colonialism is at the expense of his group and his own inner identity, moves radically toward a rejection of the Western culture and develops a nationalist outlook that celebrates his people and their traditions. As Memmi describes it:

> Assimilation being abandoned, the colonized's liberation must be carried out through a recovery of self and of autonomous dignity. Attempts at imitating the colonizer required self-denial; the colonizer's rejection is the indispensable prelude to self-discovery. That accusing and annihilating image must be shaken off; oppression must be attacked boldly since it is impossible to go around it. After having been rejected for so long by the colonizer, the day has come when it is the colonized who must refuse the colonizer.[20]

Memmi's book, *The Colonizer and the Colonized,* is based on his experience as a Tunisian Jew in a marginal position between the French and the colonized Arab majority. The uncanny parallels between the North African situation he describes and the course of Black-white relations in our society is the best impressionist argument I know for the thesis that we have a colonized group and a colonizing system in America. His discussion of why even the most radical French anti-colonialist cannot participate in the struggle of the colonized is directly applicable to the situation of the white liberal and radical vis-à-vis the Black movement. His portrait of the colonized is as good an analysis of the psychology behind Black Power and Black nationalism as anything that has been written in the U.S. Consider for example:

> Considered *en bloc* as *them, they,* or *those,* different from every point of view, homogeneous in a radical heterogeneity, the colonized reacts by rejecting all the colonizers *en bloc.* The distinction between deed and intent has no great significance in the colonial situation. In the eyes of the colonized, all Europeans in the colonies are de facto colonizers, and whether they want to be or not, they are colonizers in some ways. By their privileged economic position, by belonging to the political system of oppression, or by participating in an effectively negative complex toward the colonized, they are colonizers. . . . They are supporters or at least unconscious accomplices of that great collective aggression of Europe.[21]

> The same passion which made him admire and absorb Europe shall make him assert his differences; since those differences, after all, are within him and correctly constitute his true self.[22]

The important thing now is to rebuild his people, whatever be their authentic nature; to reforge their unity, communicate with it, and to feel that they belong.[23]

Cultural revitalization movements play a key role in anti-colonial movements. They follow an inner necessity and logic of their own that comes from the consequences of colonialism on groups and personal identities; they are also essential to provide the solidarity which the political or military phase of the anti-colonial revolution requires. In the U.S. an Afro-American culture has been developing since slavery out of the ingredients of African world-views, the experience of bondage, Southern values and customs, migration and the Northern lower-class ghettoes, and most importantly, the political history of the Black population in its struggle against racism.[24] That Afro-Americans are moving toward cultural nationalism in a period when ethnic loyalties tend to be weak (and perhaps on the decline) in this country is another confirmation of the unique colonized position of the Black group. (A similar nationalism seems to be growing among American Indians and Mexican-Americans.)

THE MOVEMENT FOR GHETTO CONTROL

The call for Black Power unites a number of varied movements and tendencies.[25] Though no clear-cut program has yet emerged, the most important emphasis seems to be the movement for control of the ghetto. Black leaders and organizations are increasingly concerned with owning and controlling those institutions that exist within or impinge upon their community. The colonial model provides a key to the understanding of this movement, and indeed ghetto control advocates have increasingly invoked the language of colonialism in pressing for local home rule. The framework of anti-colonialism explains why the struggle for poor people's or community control of poverty programs has been more central in many cities than the content of these programs and why it has been crucial to exclude whites from leadership positions in Black organizations.

The key institutions that anti-colonialists want to take over or control are business, social services, schools, and the police. Though many spokesmen have advocated the exclusion of white landlords and small businessmen from the ghetto, this program has evidently not struck fire with the Black population and little concrete movement toward economic expropriation has yet developed. Welfare recipients have organized in many cities to protect their rights and gain a greater voice in the decisions that affect them, but whole communities have not yet been able to mount direct action against welfare colonialism. Thus schools and the police seem now to be the burning issues of ghetto control politics.

During the past few years there has been a dramatic shift from educational integration as the primary goal to that of community control of the schools. Afro-Americans are demanding their own school boards, with the power to hire and fire principals and teachers and to construct a curriculum which would be relevant to the special needs and culture style of ghetto youth. Especially active in high schools and colleges have been Black students, whose protests have centered on the incorporation of Black Power and Black culture into the educational system. Consider how similar is the spirit behind these developments to the attitude of the colonized North African toward European education:

> He will prefer a long period of educational mistakes to the continuance of the colonizer's school organization. He will choose institutional disorder in order to destroy the institutions built by the colonizer as soon as possible. There we will see, indeed a reactive drive of profound protest. He will no longer owe anything to the colonizer and will have definitely broken with him.[26]

Protest and institutional disorder over the issue of school control came to a head in 1968 in New York City. The procrastination in the Albany State legislature, the several crippling strikes called by the teachers union, and the almost frenzied response of Jewish organizations makes it clear that decolonization of education faces the resistance of powerful vested interests.[27] The situation is too dynamic at present to assess probable future results. However, it can be safely predicted that some form of school decentralization will be institutionalized in New York, and the movement for community control of education will spread to more cities.

This movement reflects some of the problems and ambiguities that stem from the situation of colonialization outside an immediate colonial context. The Afro-American community is not parallel in structure to the communities of colonized nations under traditional colonialism. The significant difference here is the lack of fully developed indigenous institutions besides the church. Outside of some areas of the South there is really no Black economy, and most Afro-Americans are inevitably caught up in the larger society's structure of occupations, education, and mass communication. Thus the ethnic nationalist orientation which reflects the reality of colonization exists alongside an integrationist orientation which corresponds to the reality that the institutions of the larger society are much more developed than those of the incipient nation.[28] As would be expected the movement for school control reflects both tendencies. The militant leaders who spearhead such local movements may be primarily motivated by the desire to gain control over the community's institutions—they are anti-colonialists first and foremost. Many parents who support them may share this goal also, but the majority are probably more concerned about creating a new education that will enable their children to "make it" in the society and the economy as a whole—they know that the present school system fails ghetto children and does not prepare them for participation in American life.

There is a growing recognition that the police are the most crucial institution maintaining the colonized status of Black Americans. And of all establishment institutions, police departments probably include the highest proportion of individual racists. This is no accident since central to the workings of racism (an essential component of colonization) are attacks on the humanity and dignity of the subject group. Through their normal routines the police constrict Afro-Americans to Black neighborhoods by harassing and questioning them when found outside the ghetto; they break up groups of youth congregating on corners or in cars without any provocation; and they continue to use offensive and racist language no matter how many intergroup understanding seminars have been built into the police academy. They also shoot to kill ghetto residents for alleged crimes such as car thefts and running from police officers.[29]

Police are key agents in the power equation as well as the drama of dehumanization. In the final analysis they do the dirty work for the larger system by restricting the striking back of Black rebels to skirmishes inside the ghetto, thus deflecting energies and attacks from the communities and institutions of the larger power structure. In a historical review, Gary Marx notes that since the French revolution, police and other authorities have killed larger numbers of demonstrators and rioters; the rebellious "rabble" rarely destroys human life. The same pattern has been repeated in America's recent revolts.[30] Journalistic accounts appearing in the press recently suggest that police see themselves as defending the interests of white people against a tide of Black insurgence; furthermore the majority of whites appear to view "blue power" in this light. There is probably no other opinion on which the races are as far apart today as they are on the question of attitudes toward the police.

In many cases set off by a confrontation between a policeman and a Black citizen, the ghetto uprisings have dramatized the role of law enforcement and the issue of police brutality. In their aftermath, movements have arisen to contain police activity. One of the first was the Community Alert Patrol in Los Angeles, a method of policing the police in order to keep them honest and constrain their violations of personal dignity. This was the first tactic of the Black Panther Party which originated in Oakland, perhaps the most significant group to challenge the police role in maintaining the ghetto as a colony. The Panther's later policy of openly carrying guns (a legally protected right) and their intention of defending themselves against police aggression has brought on a series of confrontations with the Oakland police department. All indications are that the authorities intend to destroy the Panthers by shooting, framing up, or legally harassing their leadership—diverting the group's energies away from its primary purpose of self-defense and organization of the Black community to that of legal defense and gaining support in the white community.

There are three major approaches to "police colonialism" that correspond to reformist and revolutionary readings of the situation. The most elementary and also superficial sees colonialism in the fact that ghettoes are overwhelmingly patrolled by white rather than by Black officers. The proposal—supported today by many police departments—to increase the number of Blacks on local forces to something like their distribution in the city would then make it possible to reduce the use of white cops in the ghetto. This reform should be supported, for a variety of obvious reasons, but it does not get to the heart of the police role as agents of colonization.

The Kerner Report documents the fact that in some cases Black policemen can be as brutal as their white counterparts. The Report does not tell us who polices the ghetto, but they have compiled the proportion of Negroes on the forces of the major cities. In some cities the disparity is so striking that white police inevitably dominate ghetto patrols. (In Oakland 31 percent of the population and only 4 percent of the police are Black; in Detroit the figures are 39 percent and 5 percent; and in New Orleans 41 and 4.) In other cities, however, the proportion of Black cops is approaching the distribution in the city: Philadelphia 29 percent and 20 percent; Chicago 27 percent and 17 percent.[31] These figures also suggest that both the extent and the pattern of colonization may vary from one city to another. It would be useful to study how Black communities differ in degree of control over internal institutions as well as in economic and political power in the metropolitan area.

A second demand which gets more to the issue is that police should live in the communities they patrol. The idea here is that Black cops who lived in the ghetto would have to be accountable to the community; if they came on like white cops then "the brothers would take care of business" and make their lives miserable. The third or maximalist position is based on the premise that the police play no positive role in the ghettoes. It calls for the withdrawal of metropolitan officers from Black communities and the substitution of an autonomous indigenous force that would maintain order without oppressing the population. The precise relationship between such an independent police, the city and county law enforcement agencies, a ghetto governing body that would supervise and finance it, and especially the law itself is yet unclear. It is unlikely that we will soon face these problems directly as they have arisen in the case of New York's schools. Of all the programs of decolonization, police autonomy will be most resisted. It gets to the heart of how the state functions to control and contain the Black community through delegating the legitimate use of violence to police authority.

The various "Black Power" programs that are aimed at gaining control of individual ghettoes—buying up property and businesses, running the schools through community boards, taking over anti-poverty programs and other social agencies, diminishing the arbitrary power of the police—can serve to revitalize the institutions of the ghetto and build up an economic, professional, and political power base. These programs seem limited; we do not know at present if they are enough in themselves to end colonized status.[32] But they are certainly a necessary first step.

THE ROLE OF WHITES

What makes the Kerner Report a less-than-radical document is its superficial treatment of racism and its reluctance to confront the colonized relationship between Black people and the larger society. The Report emphasizes the attitudes and feelings that make up white racism, rather than the system of privilege and control which is the heart of the matter.[33]

With all its discussion of the ghetto and its problems, it never faces the question of the stake that white Americans have in racism and ghettoization.

This is not a simple question, but this paper should not end with the impression that police are the major villains. All white Americans gain some privileges and advantages from the colonization of Black communities.[34] The majority of whites also lose something from this oppression and division in society. Serious research should be directed to the ways in which white individuals and institutions are tied into the ghetto. In closing let me suggest some possible parameters.

1. It is my guess that only a small minority of whites make a direct economic profit from ghetto colonization. This is hopeful in that the ouster of white businessmen may become politically feasible. Much more significant, however, are the private and corporate interests in the land and residential property of the Black community; their holdings and influence on urban decision-making must be exposed and combated.

2. A much larger minority have occupational and professional interests in the present arrangements. The Kerner Commission reports that 1.3 million non-white men would have to be upgraded occupationally in order to make the Black job distribution roughly similar to the white. They advocate this without mentioning that 1.3 million specially privileged white workers would lose in the bargain.[35] In addition there are those professionals who carry out what Lee Rainwater has called the "dirty work" of administering the lives of the ghetto poor: the social workers, the school teachers, the urban development people, and of course the police.[36] The social problems of the Black community will ultimately be solved only by people and organizations from that community; thus the emphasis within these professions must shift toward training such a cadre of minority personnel. Social scientists who teach and study problems of race and poverty likewise have an obligation to replace themselves by bringing into the graduate schools and college faculties men of color who will become the future experts in these areas. For cultural and intellectual imperialism is as real as welfare colonialism, though it is currently screened behind such unassailable shibboleths as universalism and the objectivity of scientific inquiry.

3. Without downgrading the vested interests of profit and profession, the real nitty-gritty elements of the white stake are political power and bureaucratic security. Whereas few whites have much understanding of the realities of race relations and ghetto life, I think most give tacit or at least subconscious support for the containment and control of the Black population. Whereas most whites have extremely distorted images of Black Power, many—if not most—would still be frightened by actual Black political power. Racial groups and identities are real in American life; white Americans sense they are on top, and they fear possible reprisals or disruptions were power to be more equalized. There seems to be a paranoid fear in the white psyche of Black dominance; the belief that Black autonomy would mean unbridled license is so ingrained that such reasonable outcomes as Black political majorities and independent Black police forces will be bitterly resisted.

On this level the major mass bulwark of colonization is the administrative need for bureaucratic security so that the middle classes can go about their life and business in peace and quiet. The Black militant movement is a threat to the orderly procedures by which bureaucracies and suburbs manage their existence, and I think today there are more people who feel a stake in conventional procedures than there are those who gain directly from racism. For in their fight for institutional control, the colonized will not play by the white rules of the game. These administrative rules have kept them down and out of the system; therefore they have no necessary intention of running institutions in the image of the white middle class.

The liberal, humanist value that violence is the worst sin cannot be defended today if one is committed squarely against racism and for self-determination. For some violence is almost inevitable in the decolonization process; unfortunately racism in America has been so effective that the greatest power Afro-Americans (and perhaps also Mexican-Americans) wield today is the power to disrupt. If we are going to swing with these revolutionary times and at least respond positively to the anti-colonial movement, we will have to learn to live with conflict, confrontation, constant change, and what may be real or apparent chaos and disorder.

A positive response from the white majority needs to be in two major directions at the same time. First, community liberation movements should be supported in every way by pulling out white instruments of direct control and exploitation and substituting technical assistance to the community when this is asked for. But it is not enough to relate affirmatively to the nationalist movement for ghetto control without at the same time radically opening doors for full participation in the institutions of the mainstream. Otherwise the liberal and radical position is little different than the traditional segregationist. Freedom in the special conditions of American colonization means that the colonized must have the choice between participation in the larger society and in their own independent structures.

NOTES

ACKNOWLEDGEMENT: This is a revised version of a paper delivered at the University of California Centennial Program, "Studies in Violence," Los Angeles, June 1, 1968. For criticisms and ideas that have improved an earlier draft, I am indebted to Robert Wood, Lincoln Bergman, and Gary Marx. As a good colonialist I have probably restated (read: stolen) more ideas from the writings of Kenneth Clark, Stokely Carmichael, Frantz Fanon, and especially such contributors to the Black Panther Party (Oakland) newspaper as Huey Newton, Bobby Seale, Eldridge Cleaver, and Kathleen Cleaver than I have appropriately credited or generated myself. In self-defense I should state that I began working somewhat independently on a colonial analysis of American race relations in the fall of 1965; see my "White-wash Over Watts: The Failure of the McCone Report," *Trans-action* 3 (March-April 1966): 3–9, 54.

1. Harold Cruse, *Rebellion or Revolution* (New York: 1968), p. 214.
2. Nationalism, including an orientation toward Africa, is no new development. It

has been a constant tendency within Afro-American politics. See *ibid.,* esp. chaps. 5–7.

3. This was six years before the publication of *The Crisis of the Negro Intellectual* (New York: Morrow 1968), which brought Cruse into prominence. Thus the 1962 article was not widely read until its reprinting in Cruse's essays, *Rebellion or Revolution.*

4. Kenneth Clark, *Dark Ghetto* (New York: Harper & Row, 1965). Clark's analysis first appeared a year earlier in *Youth in the Ghetto* (New York: Haryou Associates, 1964).

5. Stokely Carmichael and Charles Hamilton, *Black Power* (New York: Random House, 1967).

6. As Eldridge Cleaver reminds us, "Black people are a stolen people held in a colonial status on stolen land, and any analysis which does not acknowledge the colonial status of black people cannot hope to deal with the real problem." "The Land Question," *Ramparts* 6 (May 1968): 51.

7. *Youth in the Ghetto,* pp. 10–11; 79–80.

8. N. Glazer and D. P. Moynihan, *Beyond the Melting Pot* (Cambridge, Mass.: M.I.T. Press, 1963), p. 37.

9. "When we speak of Negro social disabilities under capitalism, . . . we refer to the fact that he does not own anything—*even what is ownable in his own community.* Thus to fight for black liberation *is to fight for his right to own.* The Negro is politically compromised today because he owns nothing. He has little voice in the affairs of state because he owns nothing. The fundamental reason why the Negro bourgeois-democratic revolution has been aborted is because American capitalism has prevented the development of a black class of capitalist owners of institutions and economic tools. To take one crucial example, Negro radicals today are severely hampered in their tasks of educating the black masses on political issues because Negroes do not own any of the necessary means of propaganda and communication. The Negro owns no printing presses, he has no stake in the networks of the means of communication. Inside his own communities he does not own the house he lives in, the property he lives on, nor the wholesale and retail sources from which he buys his commodities. He does not own the edifices in which he enjoys culture and entertainment or in which he socializes. In capitalist society, an individual or group that does not own anything is powerless." H. Cruse, "Behind the Black Power Slogan," in Cruse, *Rebellion or Revolution,* pp. 238–39.

10. Harold M. Baron, "Black Powerlessness in Chicago," *Trans-action* 6 (November 1968): 27–33.

11. R. Blauner, "Whitewash Over Watts."

12. "The police function to support and enforce the interests of the dominant political, social, and economic interests of the town" is a statement made by a former police scholar and official, according to A. Neiderhoffer, *Behind the Shield* (New York: Doubleday, 1967), as cited by Gary T. Marx, "Civil Disorder and the Agents of Control," *Journal of Social Issues* 26 (Winter 1970): 19–58.

13. *Report of the National Advisory Commission on Civil Disorders* (New York: Bantam, March 1968), p. 7.

14. This kind of attitude has a long history among American Negroes. During slavery, Blacks used the same rationalization to justify stealing from their masters. Appropriating things from the master was viewed as "*taking* part of his property for the benefit of another part; whereas *stealing* referred to appropriating something from another slave, an offense that was not condoned." Kenneth Stampp, *The Peculiar Institution* (New York: Random House, 1956), p. 127.

15. *Report of the National Advisory Commission on Civil Disorders,* p. 178.

16. Frantz Fanon, *Wretched of the Earth* (New York: Grove Press, 1963); Albert Memmi, *The Colonizer and the Colonized* (Boston: Beacon Press, 1967).

17. Robert Wood, "Colonialism in Africa and America: Some Conceptual Considerations," December 1967, unpublished paper.

18. F. Fanon, *Black Skins, White Masks* (New York: Grove Press, 1967).

19. Harold Cruse has described how these two themes of integration with the larger society and identification with ethnic nationality have struggled within the political and cultural movements of Negro Americans. *The Crisis of the Negro Intellectual.*

20. Memmi, *The Colonizer and the Colonized,* p. 128.

21. Ibid., p. 130.

22. Ibid., p. 132

23. Ibid., p. 134

24. In another essay, I argue against the standard sociological position that denies the existence of an ethnic Afro-American culture and I expand on the above themes. The concept of "Soul" is astonishingly parallel in content to the mystique of "Negritude" in Africa; the Pan-African culture movement has its parallel in the burgeoning Black culture mood in Afro-American communities. See "Black Culture: Myth or Reality" in Peter Rose, ed., *Americans From Africa* (New York: Atherton, 1969).

25. Scholars and social commentators, Black and white alike, disagree in interpreting the contemporary Black Power movement. The issues concern whether this is a new development in Black protest or an old tendency revised; whether the movement is radical, revolutionary, reformist, or conservative; and whether this orientation is unique to Afro-Americans or essentially a Black parallel to other ethnic group strategies for collective mobility. For an interesting discussion of Black Power, as a modernized version of Booker T. Washington's separatism and economism, see Harold Cruse, *Rebellion or Revolution,* pp. 193–258.

26. Memmi, *The Colonizer and the Colonized,* pp. 137–38.

27. For the New York school conflict see Jason Epstein, "The Politics of School Decentralization," *New York Review of Books,* June 6, 1968, pp. 26–32; and "The New York City School Revolt," *ibid.,* October 10, 1968, pp. 37–41.

28. This dual split in the politics and psyche of the Black American was poetically described by Du Bois in his *Souls of Black Folk,* and more recently has been insightfully analyzed by Harold Cruse in *The Crisis of the Negro Intellectual.* Cruse has also characterized the problem of the Black community as that of underdevelopment.

29. A recent survey of police finds "that in the predominantly Negro areas of several large cities, many of the police perceive the residents as basically hostile, especially the youth and adolescents. A lack of public support—from citizens, from courts, and from laws—is the policeman's major complaint. But some of the public criticism can be traced to the activities in which he engages day by day, and perhaps to the tone in which he enforces the 'law' in the Negro neighborhoods. Most frequently he is 'called upon' to intervene in domestic quarrels and break up loitering groups. He stops and frisks two or three times as many people as are carrying dangerous weapons or are actual criminals, and almost half of these don't wish to cooperate with the policeman's efforts." Peter Rossi *et al.,* "Between Black and White—The Faces of American Institutions and the Ghetto," in *Supplemental Studies for The National Advisory Commission on Civil Disorders,* July 1968, p. 114.

30. "In the Gordon Riots of 1780 demonstrators destroyed property and freed prisoners, but did not seem to kill anyone, while authorities killed several hundred rioters and hung an additional 25. In the Rebellion Riots of the French Revolution, though several hundred rioters were killed, they killed no one. Up to the end of the Summer of 1967, this pattern had clearly been repeated, as police, not rioters, were responsible for most of the more than 100 deaths that have occurred. Similarly, in a related context, the more than 100 civil rights murders of recent years have been matched by almost no murders of racist whites." G. Marx, "Civil Disorders and the Agents of Social Control."

31. *Report of the National Advisory Commission on Civil Disorders,* 321. That Black officers nevertheless would make a difference is suggested by data from one of the supplemental studies to the Kerner Report. They found Negro policemen working in the ghettoes considerably more sympathetic to the community and its social problems than their white counterparts. Peter Rossi *et al.,* "Between Black and White—The Faces of American Institutions in the Ghetto," chap. 6.

32. Eldridge Cleaver has called this first stage of the anti-colonial movement *community* liberation in contrast to a more long-range goal of *national* liberation. E. Cleaver, "Community Imperialism," Black Panther Party newspaper, 2 (May 18, 1968).

33. For a discussion of this failure to deal with racism, see Gary T. Marx, "Report of the National Commission: The Analysis of Disorder or Disorderly Analysis," 1968, unpublished paper.

34. Such a statement is easier to assert than to document but I am attempting the latter in a forthcoming book tentatively titled *White Racism, Black Culture,* to be published by Little Brown.

35. *Report of the National Advisory Commission on Civil Disorders,* pp. 253–56.

36. Lee Rainwater, "The Revolt of the Dirty-Workers," *Trans-action* 5 (November 1967): 2, 64.

part IV

GHETTO
UPRISINGS

There is a qualitative difference between the nonviolent civil right movement discussed in Part II and the ghetto riots discussed here in Part IV. They differ in at least five ways: degree of organization, degree of planning, type of leadership, explicitness of objectives, mode of behavior of participants, and societal response. I wish briefly to explore these differences.

The nonviolent civil rights movement, like all social movements, included both organized and unorganized elements. At the center of the movement were national organizations such as the Urban League, CORE, NAACP, SNCC, and SCLC, as well as a host of local associations. These organizations functioned to give general direction and continuity to the movement. Surrounding these organizations were a multitude of persons who may have been members of some, all, or none of the organizations. These are the individuals who were attracted to a particular demonstration or confrontation. These persons functioned to give life, dynamism, and power to the movement at a given time and place but lacked the necessary organizational commitments to provide continuity between confrontation situations. The organizations provided leaders who could act as spokesmen for the organizations. For the most part, these leaders held official positions in one or more of the organizations. The leaders formulated objectives and developed the strategy and tactics appropriate to specific confrontations. The degree of planning and organization made it possible to control the behavior of participants, which for the most part remained nonviolent and nondestructive of property. This tended to give the movement an aura of respectability which attracted the support of white liberals across the nation.

There is no reason to believe that any such organizations were involved in the ghetto riots. The riots were not planned or deliberately instigated. They appear to have developed spontaneously and fortuitously. The leadership appeared to be primarily leadership by example. The behavior of the participants was violent and destructive of property and appeared to develop independent of any pre-set strategy. Explicit demands were rare and either of a broad and diffuse, or of a quite limited, nature. The riots were surrounded by an aura of nonrespectability and they drew strong condemnation from most white liberals.

The riots, of course, were not entirely free of organization or objectives, but I must emphasize the fact that the organization and objectives of the riots are of a qualitatively different nature from the organization and objectives of the nonviolent civil rights movement. It would appear that ghetto rioters were seeking the end of white exploitation in the ghetto and the right of black men to control their own destinies. These are rather broad, diffuse goals in contrast to the demands for jobs, voting rights, open housing, or desegregation of lunch counters and public facilities which characterized the earlier civil rights movement. The ghetto riots did develop a type of temporary, emergent organization which came forth during the course of a riot and disappeared when it was over. This contrasts with the more permanent, formally enacted organization found in the earlier civil rights movement.

One final difference which may be observed is a temporal one. The non-violent civil rights movement appears to have declined in vitality and activity as the ghetto riots emerged and became increasingly frequent occurrences. Although riots have not completely replaced the nonviolent civil rights movement, they certainly have usurped center stage for a time. It is probable that the riots constitute a portion of episodic action in the black revolt while the civil rights organizations provides continuity and a negotiating link to white society. Rioters cannot effectively negotiate but civil rights organizations can; on the other hand, civil rights organizations are compromised if they resort to violent coercion but they can use the violence of ghetto uprisings as a weapon and a threat. This is a true division of labor.

There are a number of questions to answer about riots: what are they? in what type of cities do they occur? who participates in them? what attitudes do most blacks hold toward them? and how do they develop and spread?

1. Types of Interpretation

Social scientists, like all Americans, have been struck by the urban ghetto disorders. They did not predict them, although they issued many warnings that the civil rights movement would not remain nonviolent indefinitely. Despite these warnings, they were surprised by the depth, intensity, and breadth of violence which finally blossomed forth. The "riot research industry" sprang into being and social scientists everywhere began studying the ghetto disorders. Perhaps we shouldn't be surprised at the fact that social scientists could not agree even as to what the disorders were, let alone what caused them. Over the course of time some sort of consensus may have emerged, but there is still considerable disagreement. This disagreement reflects, to a certain extent, discipline and sub-discipline differences. This section will present a cross section of the various attempts to classify the disorders.

The selection by Kurt and Gladys Lang recognizes the protest nature of riots. The nature of riot targets and riot participants dictates this type of orientation. Ghetto disorders appear to be closely tied to the militance of the traditional civil rights organizations and participants. Yet the Langs view the riots as a type of prepolitical activity rather than as political activity *per se;* that is, they view the disorders as anomic outbursts on the part of isolated masses in the ghetto community. Thus, they have an interesting and unique view which interprets the riots as a combination of protest with anomic behavior on the part of alienated masses. They do not view riots as consciously conceived attempts to bring pressure to bear upon the white establishment in order to coerce social change.

Anthony Oberschall does not go as far as the Langs in perceiving the disorders as protests and attempts at change. This selection begins by examining the characteristics of the participants. It rejects the "riffraff" and criminal hoodlum thesis and concludes that there is widespread participation of persons from all class levels. This conclusion is drawn despite the data, presented in the article, which clearly reveal the riot participants to be a deprived portion of the lower class. The selection, which applies a collective behavior model to the Watts riot, continues with an analysis of long-term grievances, the precipitating incident, the development of the riot as a hostile outburst. Oberschall concludes that the riot was neither a revolt nor a collective attempt to bring about social change. He bases this conclusion on the relative lack of organization, leadership, demands, and attempts to bring about social change. More will be said about this in connection with later selections.

The collective behavior model is highly useful for viewing the ghetto insurrections. However, Oberschall has a rather naive view of collective behavior. The content of his analysis implies an underlying view of collective behavior as irrational. Actually, participants in collective behavior situations are acting in terms of their perception of their own self-interests, so that there is far more in the way of emergent organization and rational action than is implied in the Oberschall selection.

The analysis of looting by E. L. Quarantelli and Russell R. Dynes provides added support to the above comments. Looting is the form of participation adopted by most riot participants. The popular view perceives looting as an individualistic form of criminal behavior carried out for motivations of personal gain when and wherever there is a breakdown in law enforcement. Quarantelli and Dynes demonstrate that looting does not normally occur in natural disasters which are accompanied by a breakdown of law and order. The selection further demonstrates that looting is not individualistic criminal behavior. Looting in ghetto disorders is a form of normative, group behavior in which the prime motivation is not personal enrichment. The selectivity with which targets are picked clearly indicates a protest motivation for looting.

My own article continues the trend toward viewing ghetto riots as insurrections which are carried out with the manifest motivation and intent of bringing about social change. They are seen as being part of the evolving social movement which we call the black revolt. This interpretation is based on a number of different factors. It utilizes the Quarantelli-Dynes analysis of looting. The selection rejects the Oberschall contention that the disorders were unorganized and leaderless. It is true that the riots were neither planned nor deliberately instigated. However, that is not the same as saying that they were disorganized and leaderless. There appears to be good evidence that once the disorders were under way, a primitive form of leadership and organization emerged. There is solid evidence that riots are generally accompanied by demands and attempts at negotiations on the part of blacks. All of these factors combine with the observed characteristics of riot participants to indicate that riots are a tactic utilized to bring about social change. Thus one must conclude that ghetto riots and nonviolent protest are two different manifestations of the same social movement. The black revolt grows, changes, expands, and contracts over time. As some tactics prove to be failures in terms of the objectives of some segments of the black community, they come to be replaced by new tactics. Other segments of the community find their objectives are being met by the older tactics, so they retain them. The movement becomes increasingly complex and involves more and more obvious manifestations of a division of labor.

The analysis provided by Jules J. Wanderer tends to support the interpretation of ghetto disorders as insurrections. The very fact that it is possible to construct an eight item scale of riot severity with a coefficient of reproducibility of .92 demonstrates the fact that riots are not random unpredictable occurrences.

It would appear that after a preliminary period of confusion caused by lack of data and systematic analysis, a consensus gradually developed among social scientists as to the nature of ghetto disorders. Differences remain as to the extent to which academics perceive the disorders to have revolutionary overtones and to be a part of a continuing social movement. Nevertheless, there does appear to be agreement on the fact that the ghetto riots are protest activities carried on in an attempt to punish oppressors and to coerce social change.

RACIAL DISTURBANCES AS COLLECTIVE
PROTEST

Kurt Lang / Gladys Engel Lang

To overlook the purposive meaning of acts which comprise a collective disturbance implies an acceptance of the official perspective of the law enforcement agency, whose judgment of what is or is not a riot is simply a matter of the degree to which it is felt to be a menace to public order, a judgment apt to depend on the time and place it occurs. A relatively minor disturbance in closed quarters such as a dance, a rally, or a sporting event becomes a riot if it attracts the attention of police. Or in a tense racial situation, even a small incident will be suppressed as if it were a riot, as in some gang friction in East New York in the summer of 1966. Similarly, many diverse incidents—vandalism, looting, and brawling—are together declared a riot when they are so concentrated in time and space that to cope with them requires an unusual show of force. Thus, the term *riot*—especially in the present political climate—is often used indiscriminately to refer to rather different events which constitute a single category only because they evoke a similar official response.

In other words, the kind of disturbance that has become almost commonplace in the United States cannot be adequately explained or dealt with simply as a pathological manifestation or as an inevitable product (and symptom) of social change. In what follows, we present a brief outline of what we see as the underlying dynamics of these disturbances. This includes, first of all, the face-to-face confrontations that precipitate the polarization of a collectivity to a point where violence functions as a spontaneously shared defense against anxieties that individuals experience; second, the epidemic spread of disruptive behavior to nearby areas, and mutations in the pattern of rioting; and third, the ways in which direct action in the form of violence or other illegal acts becomes accepted as a technique of protest, so that the pattern is repeated in other cities even without deliberate organization, the movement being carried along by the myth of the violent uprising.

THE PRECIPITATING EVENT

The collective disturbances discussed here can be fruitfully viewed as a spontaneously shared collective defense, i.e., a collectively sanctioned defense against demoralization through the spontaneous coalescence of individual reactions in a distressing situation. In such a situation, the members of an aggrieved population act directly and coercively to assert certain norms against established authority, or to impose their conception of

Reprinted from *Riots and Rebellion: Civil Violence in the Urban Community* (1968), pp. 121–30, ed. Louis H. Masotti and Don R. Bowen, by permission of the authors and the Publisher, Sage Publications, Inc.

justice against deviants defined as a threat. Though such action may involve a deliberate defiance of authorities, the willful violation of laws, and savage acts of intimidation, violence, and destructiveness, it nevertheless represents at the same time a method of social control, no matter how unconventional.

The basic postulate here is that the standard practices by which any society or group defends itself against demoralizing tendencies are in some sense analogous to the characterological defenses of individuals. They mobilize sentiment and affect to support and maintain social solidarity. This mobilization of sentiments to uphold a threatened norm is evident in loyalty parades or propaganda rallies to counteract "heresies."

The probability that violence in some form will emerge as the spontaneously sanctioned collective form of defense is increased when institutionalized channels for the expression of grievances are ineffective or when they are, or seem to be, lacking. The potential for violence furthermore depends on the degree to which (1) there is a threat and (2) the threat touches on common moral sentiments. The greater the perceived threat, the stronger will be the response and the greater the need for action with visible consequences, to allay any sense of outrage. Accordingly, any population is capable of violent reactions.

Wherein lies the special potential of arrests (which in most instances appeared to be a legitimate exercise of police functions) to evoke moral outrage? First of all, there is a disposition *common to all segments of the population* to view the use of force by police as provocative and offensive, especially when the suspect's protests and policeman's reactions are highly visible, while the reasons for the arrest are obscure.

Second, this reaction is all the more likely among a population where many persons have suffered severe damage to their sense of self-esteem at the hands of the impersonal authorities; welfare, police, and other agents of what is often seen as an alien "occupying force."

Third, the residents of the Negro ghettoes constitute in a very special sense an "isolated mass," segregated together by color and with little sense of participation in the larger community. This facilitates the generalization of sentiment, even if the grievance is, to begin with, minor.

Finally, there are the latent effects of civil disobedience as a political tactic to force compliance with nationally proclaimed politics for eliminating discriminatory practices. Often such action has been met by one-sided law enforcement clearly directed against the demonstrators. Publicity has centered as much on police against demonstrator as on demonstrator against police. Thus the image of its struggle for equality that does disseminate into the Negro community can be invoked to justify acts of overt resistance, even in the instance of legitimate arrests.

The disposition of groups of slum-dwellers to view the use of force in any given situation as threatening accounts for the special potential of certain incidents to evoke a spontaneous collective defense. Sentiment quickly rallies behind the victim of an apparent outrage, as some of the bystanders begin to assert a non-debatable demand. *The polarization with the victim and against the police hinges on the presence of a "critical mass" of susceptible individuals ready to go into action at what they per-*

ceive to be provocation. How many susceptible people must be on the scene for a collective outburst to occur depends on the level of existing grievances and on the amount of counter-force at hand. The time and place at which these incidents have typically occurred contributes to the likelihood that people are ready to act against authority from whatever mixture of reasons would be present in large numbers of people.[1] The volatile among them help polarize action against the police, and even though the mass of bystanders may be passive and themselves indisposed to commit any violent acts, their mere presence lends tacit support to those who initiate action. Very few dare to intervene decisively in the interest of law and order.

EPIDEMIOLOGY: THE RIOTING SPREADS

During the first phase, hostile action has usually been directed primarily against the police equipment immediately involved in the incident. Thereafter, as reinforcements arrive, "rioting" quickly extends to all law enforcement personnel. Then, in a third phase, any visible representatives of the "white power structure"—the press, autoists, curiosity seekers —and their property become targets of attack. This pattern may change and is, in fact, beginning to change already. However, if the initial eruption of violence depends on the formation of a physical-contact group, the spread of a local disturbance no longer does. Once order breaks down, people begin to experience a sense of their power. For a time at least, there is general immunity from punishment. Destructiveness then becomes less discriminating, and looting for personal gain begins to proliferate.

From all evidence, only a minority of the residents of Negro ghettoes have participated in the various kinds of "riotous" behavior, and in all likelihood most will continue to remain immune to its contagious appeal. However, given the widespread sense of grievance, it has been extremely difficult to organize an active opposition once the rampage has begun. Civil rights leaders who have attempted to intervene on the side of order have not been able to make themselves heard.

Press reports on the predominance of unemployed youths among the "rioters" are not substantiated by the few statistics available. Thus, the *typical* Negro male rioter arrested in Rochester in 1964 and in Watts in 1965 was in his upper twenties: only one-fourth under twenty-one. Likewise, the majority were employed—albeit usually in an unskilled job.[2] Similarly, self-reports on riot activity obtained by Murphy and Watson in their post-riot survey, while revealing a slight concentration of activity among the 15- to 24-year-old group and among the unemployed, still show these two categories to have been in a minority.[3] All indications are that those active in the riots approximate in certain respects a cross section of the younger male population in the ghetto areas.

It is nevertheless most unlikely that any incident can expand into a pattern of rioting without the prior existence of groups that become the nuclei of trouble from which other incidents develop. These groups are of two kinds: sectarian agitators ready to foment trouble and/or to exploit any incident for their own purpose, and those who normally participate in all sorts of illegal activities and are therefore prepared to take advantage of any disorder as a cover for their usual pursuits.

The part played by agitators is undeniable when it comes to creating a climate and spreading the initial incident. However, the extent of their responsibility for keeping the rioting going, once it becomes widespread, is difficult to fix.

As regards the presence of so-called criminal elements, police and court statistics on arrests, despite their inherent biases, continue to be the major source of evidence. Of adults arrested in the Watts riot, one-third had no previous arrest records, another third had "minor" and the remainder "major" criminal records. Given the slim chances young, poor Negroes have to avoid arrest for 20-odd years, the following statement by the California Bureau of Criminal Identification and Investigation is significant: "A review of their prior criminal history fails to show a record as serious as that generally present in many non-riot felony bookings usually handled by urban police and courts." [4]

One cannot conclude, nevertheless, that looters are "amateurs" who cannot resist taking things that are there to be had. Ponder the fact that more of those arrested for burglary and theft had records of previous arrests or imprisonment than those charged with assault and homicide. The degree to which conflict with law enforcement agencies becomes generalized and leads to arrests may be gleaned from the case of the Rochester woman who, after having saved the life of the police chief, was herself arrested while helping conduct people out of the riot area. The tendency on the part of the police to overreact and to be undiscriminating in their counter-violence certainly fans the fires of conflict until they are put out.

THE REPLICATION OF A RIOT PATTERN

It is usually considered axiomatic that racial outbreaks of the kind that have rocked our major cities can be prevented by dealing with the basic structural deficiencies at the root of unrest in the slums. Direct action has typically been an avenue by which suppressed groups gain recognition and lend force to their demands. In the United States, for example, violence in the labor field has generally accompanied those disputes in which management refused to treat the union as a responsible bargaining agent. The machine-wrecking actions of Luddites had elements of what Hobsbawn has called "collective bargaining by riot." [5] Historical research has shown that attacks on mills and places of storage likewise served to reduce prices and levy money from the wealthy.

To what extent, then, are we dealing in these recent riots with the use of violence as an instrument of politics? The evidence bearing on this question is to be found largely in the pattern of replication throughout the country. That there should have been so many similar incidents of large-scale rioting within a short time span implies that, however spontaneous the elements that underlie any incident and its particular pattern of expansion, the rioting reflects at the same time the stirrings of a major social-political movement.

Two observations seem at first glance to contradict this depiction of the activity as a means to articulate some particular interest. First, most of the recent outbreaks have coincided with unusually hot weather and not with politically significant events. (Chicago 1966 and Newark 1967 are among the exceptions.) The diffuse nature of the outbreak gives it the appearance of an occasion for collective license, i.e., an occasion where normal restraints are no longer binding. Yet the political climate lends implicit sanction to this disposition to cast off certain restraints while channeling it into intergroup conflict. The evidence suggests that Negro rioters, far from going on a binge, were in fact highly discriminating with regard to their targets, venting their destructiveness primarily on stores of white property owners, while Negro-owned stores went largely un-scratched. One finds that the majority of stores ransacked and burned were indeed owned by whites, and that some store owners were able to secure a measure of protection by exhibiting in thin show windows a dec-laration of their Negro ownership. But then it is generally true that most supermarkets, appliance, liquor, clothing and other stores favored by Negro rioters are owned by whites. In spite of the fact that they brought some personal gain and satisfied some feelings of revenge, one cannot view these attacks as a deliberately planned tactic of intergroup conflict. They also abolished many jobs held by Negroes, without offering alternative job opportunities. Even where they closed down white businesses, they made it possible only in a few instances for Negroes to come in. They brought about neither an extension of credit and/or a reduction of retail prices. The protest was primitive and anomic because most participants lacked any clear perception of how to advance the collective interests of the Negro community.

Our second observation refers to the militant rank and file of the civil rights movement. Except for a small number of persons on its ex-treme wing, they have dissociated themselves from the violence. Never-theless, increasing militancy reflects the growing expectation among Ne-groes of all walks of life that they should be enjoying full equality and their fear that these claims are being denied. The appeal of mass civil disobedience was certainly the product of such a pairing of frustration with hope. Yet, mass civil disobedience was more than a tactic for drama-tizing especially irritating Negro grievances. Participation in sit-ins and demonstrations carried with it the mystique of direct action. It often at-tracted recruits who may not have grasped the significance of the new tactic but nevertheless caught the new spirit. This then sets the context within which militant collective protests can spill over to become collec-tive license.

The white power structure often responds to outbursts, or to threats of violence, by focusing on troublemakers while avoiding serious nego-tiations over an issue that touches the entire Negro community. Negro accommodationist leaders are then caught on the horns of a clear-cut di-lemma. On the one side, they need dramatic successes in order to maintain their tenuous hold over their following. On the other side, their ability to gain a hearing within the power structure depends on their ability to restrain their constituencies. The prospect of violence reinforces their claim that legitimate Negro demands be met, and they can therefore exploit disorder to present themselves as the better of two alternatives.

The ambivalence of many Negro leaders about civil disobedience and extremes of militancy as tactics, coupled with a tendency on the part of the mass media to give a disproportionate amount of attention to violent incidents and to would-be leaders advocating violence, however limited their following, causes such acts to attain some legitimacy as a means of conflict. It comes to be expected more and more.

A society with a mature civic culture is not prone to counter violence with physical repression. In such cultures, the use of force to suppress rioting is apt to come in for very strong criticism. The forces for law and order are committed only with the utmost hesitancy, and any misapplication of force by any of its members undermines the legitimacy of its use.

The emergence in these circumstances of personalities bent on stirring up the potential for disorder—always so close to the surface in depressed communities—expresses only the ambivalences and structural maladjustment of the society at large.

IMPLICATIONS

Recent racial disturbances, despite the presence of irrational factors, do not develop as automatic responses to frustration. They are complex social phenomena involving many different kinds of actions by different kinds of participants. They are part and parcel of a new pattern of Negro militancy developing among depressed masses alienated together, whose political skills are as yet poorly developed and whose level of political organization is low. Among the main carriers of movements of radical protest in their early phase are persons who, because of their poor adjustment, exhibit many facets of pathology. Such persons were, undoubtedly, among the arrestees in these recent riots. But as efforts at reasonable negotiations are frustrated, and alternative collective solutions to problems disappear, even psychologically adjusted persons will be prone to tactics that include or invite violence. The resort to violence is indicative of social, and not an individual, pathology. The riots come more and more to fit the model of the anomic movement.[6]

Explanations of the origin of the recent disturbances must take the following into account:

(1) the prevalence within the urban ghettoes of a *subculture* that sanctions illegitimate means, including violence; (2) the presence there of large numbers of youths to whom *limited opportunity structures* for achieving status are available; (3) the *remoteness and impersonality of the "power structure"* and its apparent inertia when it comes to improving conditions in the ghettoes; (4) the *low level of political skill and of organization* among poor people which reduces the capacity for effective negotiations and stymies many self-help programs; (5) the high visibility of police, storeowners, and other "privileged" groups, with the inevitabil-

ity of *frictions on the interpersonal level;* (6) the *apparent effectiveness of a disturbance* in forcing official cognizance of conditions in the urban slums; (7) *tacit legitimation* by other extralegal forms of civil rights protest; (8) the *sanctioning "by default"* of collective license due to the reluctance in the present climate to employ counter-force; (9) the *presence of core groups* whose agitation provides counter-norm sanction.

It may seem obvious that an integrated society is the best deterrent to rioting. If our analysis is valid, then rioting will continue for a time, and perhaps even increase, despite the crash efforts to upgrade the conditions of life in depressed areas of our cities. Rioting evolves as a form of collective pressure or protest where large numbers of people are crowded and alienated together, sharing a common fate that they no longer accept as necessary, though it may seem inevitable to them.

Even small incidents are likely to precipitate larger disturbances. Whatever their underlying cause, civil society cannot tolerate physical violence and destruction as a means of pressure without changing its character, but neither can it suppress them by force alone. Conflict needs to be rechanneled into more effective day-to-day negotiations with visible results. The main result of efforts toward the political organization of slum dwellers is to provide organizational alternatives to "collective bargaining by riot." Until this happens, the "isolated mass" within the Negro community is apt to continue to produce its own forms of anomic protest that can, at best, be contained.

NOTES

This is a slightly revised version of a paper presented before a joint session of the American Sociological Association and the Society for the Study of Social Problems, San Francisco, September 1, 1967.

1. Raymond J. Murphy and James M. Watson, *The Structure of Discontent: The Relationship Between Social Structure, Grievance, and Support for the Los Angeles Riot* (Institute of Government and Public Affairs, U.C.L.A., 1967).
2. By "typical," understand "median."
3. Murphy and Watson, *The Structure of Discontent.*
4. Statistical report on the Watts riot supplied to the authors by the State of California Department of Justice.
5. E. J. Hobsbawm, *Primitive Rebels* (New York: Norton, 1965).
6. G. A. Almond and J. S. Coleman, eds., *The Politics of the Developing Areas* (Princeton: Princeton University Press, 1960); George Rudé, *The Crowd in History* (New York: John Wiley, 1964).

THE LOS ANGELES RIOT OF AUGUST 1965

Anthony Oberschall

While the Watts-Los Angeles [1] riot is now more than two years past, it has not yet received the scholarly attention it deserves. Most newspapers and national magazines reported it at some length since it was an eminently newsworthy event. Four months after the riot, the Commission which Governor Brown appointed to make an objective and dispassionate study of the riot handed in the report of its findings.[2] The *McCone Report* was a mere 88 pages in length, and in it the actual description of riot events received no more than 15 pages of space. The Report concentrated mainly on cataloguing the social, economic, and psychological conditions which prevailed in the South Los Angeles area prior to the riot (which were well known to students of the Negro, poverty, and urban problems), and on suggesting changes designed to prevent a future riot. No attempt was made to provide anything but a superficial explanation of the motivation of the rioters and the patterns of their actions. In this paper, an attempt will be made to use existing social science knowledge on collective behavior and riots to provide a fuller explanation for the riot. Because the socioeconomic conditions which acted as a backdrop to the riot are generally well-known they will receive only limited attention in this paper. An account of the natural history of the riot and other statistics on the duration, number of victims, extent of the property damage, and magnitude of the law enforcement effort will not be provided here since they have been widely publicized and are readily available.[3]

The sociological analysis of the riot undertaken below relies on Smelser's analytic framework in accounting for the causes of collective behavior and the forms which it takes.[4] The strength of this approach consists in the emphasis on a number of determinants of social action which must all be present at the same time for a riot to occur. In addition to socioeconomic factors, such as high unemployment, low income, well defined racial cleavages, and authorities inaccessible and unsympathetic to grievances, this approach emphasizes the importance of a generalized belief in the population as a necessary determinant of collective action. It refers to a state of mind, formed over a period of time, which provides a shared explanation for the undesirable state of affairs and pinpoints blame upon specific agents or groups who become the targets of hostility. Incidents, such as the police arrest or shooting of a suspect, that normally receive but passing attention and are considered the private business of the parties involved, can become the precipitants of a riot when that state of mind is present and when it provides a symbolic interpretation of the incident in terms of shared cleavages, grievances, and hostilities. Another useful feature of the scheme is the emphasis on the operation of social

From *Social Problems* 15 (Winter 1967): 322–41; reprinted by permission of the author and The Society for the Study of Social Problems.

control as a crucial variable in explaining the magnitude and course which the collective outburst takes.

A methodological difficulty in applying the scheme should, however, be pointed out and is indeed typical of many instances where the social scientist is confronted with an event whose causes have to be reconstructed after it has already occurred. Evidence for the amount of deprivation in the population and for the presence of a generalized belief to the collective outbreak is usually hard to come by. There is the temptation to take the outbreak itself as an indication of the prior presence of a state of mind conducive to the outbreak. Yet if this is done, there does not exist the possibility of disproving the view that an outbreak might have occurred even in the absence of such a state of mind. Evidence for the existence and extent of the generalized belief has to be established independently of the subsequent events upon which it is meant to shed some light. Fortunately, in the case of the Los Angeles riot, there exists some information on the state of police-Negro relations and Negro grievances prior to the riot itself. But before a sociological explanation of the riot is presented, it will be useful to review briefly the views about the riot which have been propagated in the press and by official circles.

POPULAR AND OFFICIAL VIEWS OF THE RIOT AND THE EVIDENCE

Important questions about the riot need be answered before one can explain what the riot was all about. How many individuals actually participated in the looting, the burning, fighting the police, obstructing the firemen? Who were they? Was the riot spontaneous or planned, and if spontaneous, did certain groups subsequently provide the riot with leadership and organization? To what extent were youth gangs and adult criminal groups involved in the riot and the looting? Just what did the rioters and inhabitants do during the riot week? What levels of participation were there, and by whom? How widespread was the use of firearms and where did these weapons come from? How did the ecology of the area and the riot events themselves establish covert or tacit communication links among the rioters? Did the news media coverage of the riots contribute to its intensity and duration? Was the aggression of the rioters directed at the police and the white absentee owners as such, or were they conveniently available targets symbolizing the white man and white domination in general? Was the riot an irrational outburst directed against all authority, stemming from the life-long accumulation of frustrations which found release in generalized aggression and violence? Is there evidence for norms operating among the rioters? Were specific targets selected and bounds to action recognized? Because of lack of information, or inaccurate and biased information, definitive answers cannot be given to all of these questions. Nevertheless, enough information is now available from many sources to rule out some characterizations of the riot, and to permit a plausible reconstruction of the character of the 1965 Los Angeles riot.

Immediate public reaction was a mixture of shock, fear, and belief that the riots were organized and led by some radical and disaffected groups in league with gangs and hoodlums; that quite possibly a conspiracy was at work; that it was a typical manifestation of irrational crowd behavior, unpredictable and similar to an animal stampede; that the rioters were well armed after they had systematically looted gun stores, hardware stores and pawn shops; and that the riot consequently was an armed uprising by Negroes against the police, the political authorities, and the white man in general.

This initial climate of opinion was a result of the news coverage and the pronouncements of officials. They focused selective attention upon those events that did in fact fit the above loose conception of what the riot was all about. The irrational aspect of the riot was highlighted in Police Chief Parker's widely quoted phrase describing the rioters as behaving like "monkeys in the zoo." The insurrectionary aspect was stressed by *Time* and by the *Los Angeles Times* coverage, both of which reported extensively on the weapons allegedly used by the rioters and seized from them.[5] The conspiratorial and organized aspects of the riot, after its start, were stressed by Mayor Yorty [6] and other officials such as Police Chief Parker in his testimony on the use of bullhorns during the riot and the "expertly made" Molotov cocktails used by the rioters.[7] Indirect evidence for police belief in riot organization is the August 18th police siege, storming and subsequent destructive search of a Black Muslim Temple which was "deliberately provoked by false telephone calls to police that Negroes were carrying guns into the building." [8] The police did not question the veracity of the anonymous callers because the information fitted their belief of some formal riot leadership and organization. The reaction of fear by the white population of Los Angeles is illustrated by the run on gun stores, which took place far beyond the residential areas adjoining the curfew area.[9]

While the conspiracy theory was popular with some officials and could be used as a political alibi, the McCone Commission found no evidence for a conspiracy in setting off the Los Angeles riot. The Commission wrote that "there is no reliable evidence of outside or pre-established plans for rioting," although it pointed to some evidence of the promotion of the riot by gangs and other groups within the curfew area after the riot had started, such as the "sudden appearance of Molotov cocktails in quantity" and of "inflammatory handbills." [10] The Commission did not elaborate a comprehensive theory of its own, yet it nevertheless hinted at another theory that has often been invoked in the explanation of violent collective outbursts, namely the "criminal riff-raff" theory of rioting. According to this view, every large urban ghetto contains a disproportionate number of criminals, delinquents, unemployed, school dropouts, and other social misfits who on the slightest pretext are ready to riot, loot, and exploit an explosive social situation for their private gain and for satisfying their aggressive anti-social instincts.[11] Thus the Commission emphasized that many Negroes were caught in a frustrating "spiral of failure," that they had been encouraged "to take the worst extreme and even illegal remedies to right a wide variety of wrongs, real and supposed," that nonetheless only a small minority of Negroes were involved in the disorder, and that a majority of those arrested had a prior criminal record.[12]

But as Blauner has pointed out in a perceptive analysis, the Report is, in the main, silent about who the participants were and what their motivations were. It did not attempt to explain how in the absence of planning and formal leadership a collective action on the scale and duration of the riot could be sustained in the face of a major show of force by over 1000 police and eventually 13,000 National Guardsmen.[13] Indeed, if the Commission's figure of a maximum of 10,000 Negroes taking to the streets is accepted,[14] this represents about 10 percent of the age cohorts 15 to 44, male and female, of the Negro population living in the South Los Angeles area, which roughly corresponds to the curfew area. Moreover, one should distinguish between several levels or degrees of participation. There are some who participated to the extent of physically fighting the police, of obstructing the firemen, of beating white motorists, and of breaking into stores and setting them on fire, in short, the activists. There are others who helped themselves to the merchandise in the stores already broken into. Still others, far more numerous, simply milled about in the streets, jeered at police, and openly encouraged the activists. Finally there were those who were not involved beyond being curious observers, or just went about the business of survival at a time of disaster. Among active participants in a riot, adolescents and young adult males can be expected to predominate. But if a substantial proportion of the remaining population overtly manifests sympathy and support for the active participants, the riot can only be interpreted as a broad group response to shared grievances, and not as the expression of an unrepresentative, lawless minority. An examination of the characteristics of those arrested during the riot can bring us a step closer to resolving this controversy.

Almost 4,000 people were arrested on riot-related charges during the Los Angeles riot, and a considerable amount of information about many of them has been collected and tabulated in two separate studies conducted by government agencies. The first of these, entitled *Riot Participation Study*,[15] concerns juvenile arrests only and rests ultimately on information assembled by Deputy Probation Officers from questioning the arrested youths and other family members, and consulting the police and other official records, for the purpose of presenting the Juvenile Court with a "social report" on each youth. The second of these reports, entitled *Watts Riot Arrests*,[16] is ultimately based on police and court records, and for a large sub-set, on data secured by the Los Angeles Probation Department during a pre-sentence investigation demanded by the courts. These data should therefore be treated with caution, but in my opinion can lead to fairly definite conclusions on whether the riot participants were disproportionately composed of criminals, school dropouts, hoodlums, youths from broken homes, the unemployed, recent migrants, in short the rootless and drifting element which according to some is a characteristic of all the large urban ghettos in the United States.

A question that has to be answered first, however, is whether those arrested can reasonably be considered a typical cross-section of the unknown total of persons who participated in some way in the riot. It could well be that those arrested are more likely to be representative of the groups which were milling about or looting than of the activists.

Several facts suggest that this may indeed be the case. Available eye-witness reports indicate that on the first three days and nights, Wednesday to Saturday morning before the National Guard was fully deployed, police officers were seldom in a position to make arrests among the rioters who were physically fighting them, assaulting white motorists, preventing the effective operation of firemen, and breaking into stores and looting. Many arrests were of course made, but the bulk of them took place after the curfew had been declared, and the police and National Guard had begun to control the riot. For the juveniles 30 percent were arrested on Wednesday, Thursday, and Friday, and the rest on Saturday and later.[17] The figures for adults probably do not differ much but are unfortunately not available. Thus the bulk of those arrested were arrested at a time when the pattern of rioting had shifted from mass confrontation to small scale looting and more isolated incidents of confrontation with the authorities. Furthermore, since roughly 8 percent of the adults arrested were later released by the police, and another 32 percent not convicted by the courts, it is evident that a substantial proportion of the arrests were in fact of people who were not riot participants in the legal sense. It remains therefore an open question whether the activists of the first three nights differed significantly from those arrested for whom data are available.

A total of 3,371 adults and 556 juveniles were arrested, of whom about 60 percent were convicted. The most common booking offense for adults was for burglary yet the most common conviction was for trespassing. It would seem that many individuals who happened to be in or near stores that were broken into were arrested without positive proof that they had stolen any merchandise. The booking offenses in most cases are more serious than the final dispositions, which resulted primarily in misdemeanors, ranging from simple assault and petty theft to trespassing, curfew violation, disturbing the peace, drunkenness and drunken driving, and the like. All in all, only 63 cases, or less than 3 percent of those arrested, received sentences of 6 months or more.[18]

Examining the prior criminal record of adults arrested—and the distribution is the same for those not convicted and those convicted—one finds that 26 percent had no prior record whatsoever, 29 percent had an arrest record but no conviction, 7 percent had convictions of less than 90 days, 18 percent had one or two convictions of 90 days and over, 4 percent had 3 or more convictions of 90 days and over, and 11 percent had a prior prison record, with no information available on the remaining 5 percent.[19] These facts about convictions and prior criminal record prompted the following concluding comment by the compilers of these statistics:

> The relatively minor types of offenses for which the great majority of riot participants were convicted would seem to indicate that this group of individuals was not the same type of persons usually booked on similar felony charges. A review of their prior criminal history fails to show a record as

serious as that generally present in many of the nonriot felony bookings usually handled in urban areas by the police and courts.[20]

The criminal riff-raff and hoodlum theory of riot participation does not receive any support from these data.

It is difficult to establish to what extent those arrested were representative of the South Los Angeles population, because census categories and breaking points often differ from those reported in the riot statistics and the potential reservoir for riot participants is mainly the male 14 to 50 year old group. Nevertheless, since 41 percent of those arrested were in the 25 to 39 age category, and a further 17 percent 40 years old and over, it is inaccurate to describe the rioters as mainly composed of irresponsible youth and young hoodlums. Unlike gang incidents and other outbursts that are confined to a particular age cohort, the Los Angeles riot drew its participants from young and old alike.

Socioeconomic information about adults arrested is available for the 1057 convicted cases that were referred to the Los Angeles Probation Department for a pre-sentence investigation and report. This figure is 31 percent of all adults originally arrested in the riot, and 52 percent of the adults convicted. These cases therefore represent slightly over a half of those arrested against whom proof of criminal participation was sustained in the courts. Of these 75 percent have lived in Los Angeles County 5 or more years, and only 6 percent less than a year. The rioters were therefore not "recent migrants" to Los Angeles. Furthermore their educational achievements compare favorably with that of the population. The median years of education of the 1057 convicted adult participants is slightly over ten completed years, which is about the same as that of the South Los Angeles area. The information on labor force characteristics of the rioters is unfortunately not comparable to the census breakdowns for Watts and the South Los Angeles area. Among the arrested rioters, only about 10 percent were in the non-manual category, and of the remaining proportion only 9.4 percent are classified as skilled workers. Moreover, 22.6 percent of the arrested rioters were unemployed, compared with 13.2 percent for the Watts labor force in November 1965, and 10.1 percent for South Los Angeles.[21] The lower-class character of riot participation clearly emerges from these figures.

The detailed information on the juveniles arrested during the riot, incomplete as it is, confirms the picture which emerges from the adult data. There were 556 juvenile arrests, resulting in 338 cases referred to formal probation supervision. The vast majority of them were placed under probation supervision in their own home. 82.5 percent of the youths were in school, as opposed to 14.8 percent who were dropouts, not a high figure in an area where two-thirds of the students do not finish high school. The youths arrested cannot be accurately called "dropouts." They appear to have come in disproportionate numbers from the poor and broken homes of the ghetto, but were not typical "delinquents." Thus 81 percent of the cases are described as having "acceptable" to "good" relations with their families, 57 percent have never been on probation before, and a further 26 percent only once. On the other hand 34 percent of their families were currently receiving their major economic contribution from the Bureau of Public Assistance (compared to 24 percent for the Watts population), only 26 percent were living in homes with both parents present (compared to 53 percent of persons under 18 years old in Watts living with both parents, and 62 percent for the South Los Angeles Area), and a little over 50 percent lived in families classified as having a "major family problem" by the Probation Department, the most frequent one being a major economic problem such as unemployment and poverty.[22]

All in all, piecing together the above information for adults and juveniles, what strikes one is the extent to which the riot drew participants from all social strata within the predominantly lower-class Negro area in which it took place. The riot cannot be attributed to the lawless and rootless minority which inhabits the ghetto, though, no doubt, these were active in it as well. The riot is best seen as a large scale collective action, with a wide, representative base in the lower-class Negro communities, which, however much it gained the sympathy of the more economically well-off Negroes, remained a violent lower-class outburst throughout. If there were numerous jobless among the participants and many youths from families with problems, it is precisely because such cases abound in the neighborhoods in which the riot occurred.

POLICE-NEGRO RELATIONS

The conspiracy and criminal riff-raff theories of the riot are not supported by the evidence on arrests. The key to a sociological explanation is the state of police-Negro relations before the riot, for it was a major source of Negro frustrations and accounts for the presence of a generalized belief which is a necessary ingredient in producing collective action. The objective factors producing strain among Negroes in the South Los Angeles area, such as high unemployment rate and stationary (even declining) incomes at a time of increasing prosperity in the rest of Los Angeles and the country at large, have been well documented and noted.[23] The increases in racial tensions due to other than economic factors have also received the attention they deserve. In the November 1964 election, California voters repealed the Rumford Fair Housing Act in a constitutional referendum by a 2:1 margin. Repeal was particularly high in Southern California and even higher among the white population surrounding the Negro neighborhoods in Los Angeles County. White areas there were in favor of the repeal in the 80 percent to the 90 percent range, whereas Negro precincts voted against it in the 90 percent range. The vote was widely interpreted as a hardening of white public opinion with respect to integrated housing. While most major U.S. cities had come up with acceptable organizational structures within the War on Poverty Program by the summer of 1965, events took a different turn in Los Angeles:

> Advance billing with respect to federal programs had created the false impression that more job opportunities would be available than actually

developed. The endless bickering between city, state and federal government officials over the administration of the authorized programs—most particularly the Poverty Program—has disappointed many.[24]

There were no compensating factors in Los Angeles such that Negroes would be conscious of progress in some matters directly affecting them. The civil rights movement has not been very active in Los Angeles, and its crowning achievement, the passage of the Civil Rights Act of 1964, has not had any impact on the city's Negro population since segregation did not exist in Los Angeles, and California has had, for many years, laws against discrimination in employment, political participation, and other activities.

The charge of police malpractice and of police "brutality" is of course not confined to Los Angeles, but has been a problem in most large U.S. cities and a precipitant in the 1964 and later riots in the U.S. The situation in Los Angeles had been the subject of hearings held in Los Angeles in September 1962 by the California Advisory Committee of the U.S. Commission on Civil Rights, headed by Bishop Pike of San Francisco. The purpose of the hearings was to ascertain the state of police-minority group relations after an April 1962 incident involving Los Angeles police officers and Black Muslims became a focal point of organized Negro protest against alleged discriminatory treatment by Los Angeles police.[25] According to the Committee,

> Most of the Negro and civil rights organization spokesmen who testified believe that there is discriminatory law enforcement in Los Angeles. The types of discrimination most referred to was excessive violence at the time of the arrest, greater surveillance and arrest in areas of minority group concentration, the arrest of Negroes and Mexican-Americans for conduct for which Caucasians are not arrested, discourteous and uncivil police language, conduct and other behavior directed against Negroes and Mexican-Americans, unjustified harassment of Negroes and Mexican-Americans, and an unwillingness and inability to distinguish between law-abiding and potentially law-breaking minority group members. These charges, with one exception, were directed against the Los Angeles Police Department (as opposed to the Sheriff's Department).[26]

Police Chief Parker's testimony stated however that

> He did not think that the Department had a "bad image among the Negro community, the majority of them," and that "basically I do not believe that there is any difficult problem existing in the relationship between the Los Angeles Police Department and the Negro Community." The Chief did allude however to elements who are trying to inflame the Negro community with false charges of police brutality.[27]

Already in 1962, therefore, the lines of cleavage were sharply drawn. On the one side a generalized belief in police brutality and discriminatory law enforcement was widespread and gaining strength within the Negro community. On the other side there was a denial of these charges by the police and the elected city officials, with the added insinuation that the belief itself was being spread by agitators who were trying to exploit certain racial tensions for their own political ends.[28]

There can be little doubt that the cleavage itself contributed to bring about the very situation both parties were trying to avoid. In the words of John Buggs, Chairman of the Los Angeles County Human Relations Commission, who testified before the Committee,

> A situation is being created in which the claim by minority group persons of police brutality and the counterclaim by police of minority group resistance to police authority are beginning to be a self-fulfilling prophecy.[29]

In concrete terms, a belief on the part of a Negro about to be arrested that the arrest is going to involve the use of force has the consequence of an attempt to avoid or resist arrest, thus increasing the probability that force will in fact have to be used to implement the arrest; whereas a belief on the part of police that an arrest is going to be resisted might produce a behavior in which force is in fact used. Thus the ground is prepared for the fulfillment of the prophecy.

One of the most controversial issues was and still is the existing procedure for handling citizen complaints against police conduct. The Police Department has an Internal Affairs Division (IAD) which has the responsibility of investigating and evaluating serious charges of misconduct made against police officers by citizens and by other police or public officials. Other charges are investigated by the operating divisions themselves, subject to review through the IAD.

The minority groups contend that the existing machinery for registering complaints and disciplining police is such that the police department is able to and in fact does whitewash police conduct, and by pressures and intimidations even prevents many complaints from being filed in the first place. Consequently, the Negroes demand a civilian police review board, independent of the police department. Chief Parker opposed a civilian police review board on the ground that the wrong kind of people would get on it, and that police discipline and morale would be harmed.[30]

The whole matter of police-Negro relations in Los Angeles is a complicated one. Police brutality refers to more than the excessive use of physical force during an arrest, the manhandling of suspects in the police station and in jail, and other physical acts usually associated with the term brutality. It means arrests, questionings and searches of Negroes by police without apparent provocation, the use of abusive and derogatory language in addressing Negroes, such as the word "nigger," and a general attitude toward the minority groups which represents an affront to their sense of dignity.[31] Police brutality in this sense is a reality to be reckoned with in the Negro ghetto, no matter how exaggerated some incidents turn out to be and regardless of whether political or criminal groups try to exploit the issue. The presence of the police in the South Los Angeles area was a constant source of irritation and left behind a legacy of bitterness and hostility. Two years before the riot, a study conducted by the Youth Opportunities Board with 220 people in Watts, Avalon, and Willowbrook on their attitudes toward several agencies operating in the community found that a majority of both adults and children felt that "the behavior of the police aggravated the problems of growing up in the Negro community rather than contributed to their solution" in marked contrast to the respondents' attitudes towards schools, probation officers, and health agencies.[32] It is important to note, however, that the tension-filled relations between police and Negroes have a structural and situational, as well as a personal origin. The police as the daily visible representative of a white-dominated world bears the full brunt of the accumulated frustrations and hostility of the ghetto. Negro attitudes towards the police are not merely a reaction to police behavior and attitudes, but to their total situation in the society. The role of the police in this situation is as unrewarding as it is dangerous.

One reason for the deterioration of Negro-police relations in Watts can be attributed to Parker's "reforms." Whereas before Parker, policemen patrolled city blocks on foot, thereby getting to know personally the people living in an area, and therefore able to use selective judgment in making an arrest (i.e., they would be able to tell a professional gambling game from an improvised neighborhood crap game, or know which drunks were trouble makers, which ones cared for by family and friends), Parker took the police off the beat and put them into police cars. In a matter of months, police lost the special knowledge and contacts with neighborhoods which alone makes law enforcement bearable especially in lower-class neighborhoods. When police enforced the law strictly and without exception, it was violating previous practices that had become part of the social structure, and thence caused hostility and resentment. These, in turn, led to resistance to arrests, with local groups helping the victim evade arrest, which in turn led the police to intensify its law enforcement practices in this "lawless" community. Thus, a dangerous spiral of suspicion and antagonism was allowed to develop.

Negro objections to the pro-police bias in the existing system of reviewing citizen complaints against police malpractice are borne out by the record. In 1961, 540 complaints were filed against police officials, 64 percent of these by ordinary citizens. Of 121 citizen complaints alleging the excessive use of force, only 5 were sustained, as opposed to 243 complaints sustained of the remaining 419 complaints (mainly drunkenness on duty, bad debts, etc.).[33] In 1964, of 412 complaints alleging police misconduct received from citizens, 42 complaints were sustained, a higher proportion than in 1961, but still only slightly above ten percent.[34] These figures strongly suggest that in the overwhelming majority of cases of alleged police misconduct in dealing with citizens, the existing review machinery ruled in favor of the police. Moreover the recommendations of the Pike Commission with respect to a civilian police review board, a police community program, and increase in the proportion of Negro police, have still not been acted upon.[35] Furthermore, neither the Pike nor the McCone Commission has done anything beyond looking at dozens of case histories of police malpractice on file with various civil rights and Negro organization. Both Commissions have felt that any action based on these complaints was outside their jurisdiction.

THE PRECIPITATING INCIDENT AND MOBILIZATION FOR ACTION

Prior to the start of the riot, therefore, Negroes in South Los Angeles were subjected to considerable strain due to unemployment, low income, police-Negro relations, frustrated hopes about the war on poverty, and similar factors. The normal channels for voicing Negro grievances had been ineffective in bringing about a change in the conditions producing these strains. A widespread belief in police brutality had existed for some time and was coupled with deep hostility against police. The Frye arrest on the evening of August 11 provided the spark which ignited the accumulated frustrations of the South Los Angeles population. In order to explain how a simple traffic arrest could escalate in a short time into a full-fledged riot of the magnitude and duration of the subsequent events, one has to examine the characteristics of the precipitating incident, the communications processes within the riot-prone population, the ecology of the South Los Angeles area, and the nature of the police effort to control it.

Marquette Frye, a 21-year-old Negro, driving his mother's car, with his brother as a passenger, was stopped by a California Highway Patrolman after he failed to stop at a red light, about 7 p.m. near, but not in Watts. Marquette Frye had been drinking and was unable to produce a driver's license. The officer, soon joined by two more, was getting ready to arrest him. The evening this occurred was the hottest one so far of the summer, a lot of people were simply hanging about on the sidewalks outside their homes. A small crowd quickly gathered to observe the arrest. Everything went without incident until Frye's mother, living nearby, arrived on the scene. What happened after that is still not clear since the police, the Fryes, and witnesses have sworn to contradictory testimony.[36] Apparently, while at first Mrs. Frye turned against her son to discipline him, eventually the three Fryes, with encouragement from the onlookers, turned upon the policemen and had to be forcefully subdued and arrested. Meanwhile the Highway Patrolmen had radioed for reinforcements, and Los Angeles police officers arrived for help. By 7:25 p.m. the patrol car with the Fryes under arrest and a tow truck pulling the Frye car left the scene.[37] As the patrolmen were about to leave, a woman in the menacing crowd spat on one of them, and an officer did go into the hostile crowd to arrest her. She was wearing a shirt outside her skirt. The rumor immediately spread that the police were beating and arresting a "pregnant" woman—which she was not—just as the crowd had earlier "seen" the policemen use excessive force to subdue the Fryes. By the time the last police car left the arrest location, it was stoned by the crowd and the riot had begun.[38]

Regardless of what actually happened, the events surrounding the arrest fitted in with preconceptions and the generalized belief about police brutality. In a confusing context such as an arrest in the evening with lots of people milling about and a high noise level it is plausible that apart from a few Negroes who actually eyewitnessed most of the arrest-events, many others pieced out an incomplete perceptual record of these events according to their preconceptions and predispositions.[39] It is particularly important to note the belief and the rumors about the police beating of a pregnant woman, for such action is one of the clearest violations of a basic norm of human conduct and arouses everywhere condemnation and revulsion. Person-to-person communication in a neighborhood on a hot night, with many individuals hanging around in the streets or in their houses but with windows open, can spread a message rapidly over a large area, and subsequent movement of people reinforced by the sound of police sirens further revealed where the focal point of the action was.[40] It seems plausible then that the original "witnesses" to the Frye arrest interpreted what they perceived as an act of police brutality, which fitted in with a long prior history of similar behavior that was expected from the police. Later arrivals had no particular reason to question this interpretation of the precipitating event and, sharing the beliefs and emotions of those already present, reacted to it similarly.

The original incident was widely reported in the news media, and in all probability a majority of the entire Los Angeles population knew the next day that a riot had taken place in a particular location in Watts during the previous evening and night. This piece of information in turn acted as a significant clue for the collection of crowds in the vicinity of the original arrest location the following day in the absence of any explicit coordination. Anybody, whether merely curious or wishing to settle an old score with the police, had but the same piece of information to go on, namely the location of the incident of the night before, and knew that everybody else, too, had the same clue to act upon. Hence the original location acted as a magnet and as the focal point for the collection of similarly disposed crowds on Thursday evening and Friday morning before the riot eventually spread throughout the South Los Angeles area.

During the entire riot a common thread was the aggression against the police. Yet from the start the riot was more than just a police riot. The Los Angeles riot did not exhibit the character of the classic race-riot in which crowds of one race systematically seek out and assault isolated individuals and smaller groups of another race. Nevertheless the first two nights witnessed many incidents which fit the classic pattern as unsuspecting (and later curious) white motorists driving through the riot area were pelted with bricks and bottles, pulled out of their cars and beaten up, and news reporters and TV crews were assaulted. It is difficult to document how the subsequent major pattern of breaking into stores, looting, and burning them down became established. The fickleness of hostile crowds as they move from one object to another has been well established in other instances of rioting and collective behavior. People with frustrations and grievances other than the specific grievance against the police witness and join in the riot. The situation becomes defined as one in which a broad class of race-related grievances can be translated into direct aggressive behavior, and targets other than the one involved in the precipitating incident become the objects of aggression.[41] The pattern of store breaking and arson was not totally devoid of some leadership, apparently provided by gangs, though it is impossible to establish the magnitude of this factor.

One of my informants stated that the big time, professional criminals in anticipation of a police dragnet took the first opportunity after the riot started to get out of the riot area and even out of Los Angeles. Many petty thieves and other small time professional crooks came individually or in small groups into the riot area to seize this opportunity of breaking into stores while the police were busy with the rioters. These groups were not, however, interested in leading the riot crowds to loot and destroy the white owned stores since that would have interfered with the efficiency of their operations. Another informant who has been close to some of the gangs in the South Los Angeles area reported, however, that gang members, in an effort to prove their claims upon leadership in a certain territory and in competition with each other, were vying for leadership over the crowds during the riot, and this meant among other things actively participating in the skirmishes against the police, breaking into the stores, and setting them on fire.

The success of the store breakers, arsonists, and looters in eluding the police can in part be put down to the role of the mass media during the riot week. The Los Angeles riot was the first one in which rioters were able to watch their actions on television. The concentration and movements of the police in the area were well reported on the air, better than that of the rioters themselves. By listening to the continuous radio and TV coverage, it was possible to deduce that the police were moving towards or away from a particular neighborhood. Those who were active in raiding stores could choose when and where to strike, and still have ample time for retreat. The entire curfew area is a very extended one. It was not possible to seal off several blocks and trap rioters, as could be done in cities where apartment houses are built side to side. People could move from street to street through gardens, driveways, and alleys.

The magnitude of the riot measured in terms of its duration, the area affected, and the casualties and injuries sustained, can in part be accounted for by the measures taken to bring it under control. Officials at all levels underestimated the riot at the start. Deputy Police Chief Murdock stated on Thursday morning that "Wednesday was just a night to throw rocks at policemen." [42] Friday at dawn the police department felt that they had the situation under control, and Mayor Yorty flew to San Francisco later in the morning to keep a speaking engagement before the Commonwealth Club under the impression that the riot had mostly spent itself.[43] Police Chief Parker requested formally on Friday at 10:50 a.m. that National Guardsmen be brought into South Los Angeles, yet because of the conflicting reports he received about the seriousness of the situation, Lt. Governor Anderson, who was acting in the absence of Governor Brown vacationing in Greece, did not sign the papers until 5 p.m. on Friday. While some Guardsmen were deployed in the riot area by Friday night, it was not until after three nights of rioting had taken place that the 8 p.m. curfew was imposed on Saturday and the National Guard fully deployed.[44]

The police were of course outnumbered and undermanned, given the size of the riot area and the number of riot participants. Its efforts to disperse rock throwing crowds proved singularly ineffective. Motorcycle officers who penetrated through the thick of the crowd in an effort to disperse it and arrest the rock throwers were vulnerable to physical assault. The crowds afforded a convenient shield for hit and run tactics.[45] Much of the police effort on the first two nights of the rioting consisted of protecting itself, motorists, firemen, and news reporters from physical assault. Realizing that it often acted as a stimulant and focal point for the rioting, the police periodically withdrew from physical proximity to the rioters. In retrospect it would appear that the proposal of John Buggs of the Los Angeles County Human Relations Commission and of Reverend Brooking on Thursday afternoon to Deputy Police Chief Murdock to withdraw white uniformed police, and let community leaders control the crowds with the help of Negro officers in civilian clothes, which was turned down, might have been a more effective way of limiting the riot.[46] As it turned out, the partial show of force happened to be a demonstration of vulnerability and weakness, and acted more as an incitement than a deterrent to the riot.

RIOT BEHAVIOR AND MOTIVATION

No one would deny the extensive property damage perpetrated by the rioters in looting and burning the stores, the physical assault upon police, white motorists, firemen, and others. One can however question whether this behavior is essentially an irrational stampede and orgy of destruction, and hence void of collective social significance and personal meaning. Nothing is gained by defining riot behavior as irrational *a priori.* There is considerable evidence that the rioters observed certain *bounds,* that they directed their aggression at *specific targets,* and that they selected *appropriate means* for the ends they intended to obtain.

The fact that no deaths resulted from the direct action of the rioters is evidence that they observed certain bounds and limits. The first two nights when white motorists were dragged out of their cars and beaten, and when newsmen were severely roughed up, none were beaten to death or killed as might easily have happened since the police were unable to offer protection at the time. Furthermore, the sniper fire directed at police and firemen did not result in any fatalities either, despite reports that it was widespread and lasted throughout the riot week and the fact that police and firemen were easy targets. It seems that sniping was aimed towards obstructing law enforcement and fire fighting and not towards killing officials.

The riot crowds gave evidence of being able to pick specific targets for their aggression. Negro business establishments, many of them carrying signs such as "Blood Brother" or "Soul Brother," were for the most part spared. Private houses, post offices, churches, schools, libraries, and other public buildings in the riot area were not broken into and burned down, vandalized, or otherwise purposely damaged. Some white-owned stores also were spared. While the McCone Commission states that "Our study of the patterns of burning and looting does not indicate any significant correlation between alleged consumer exploitation and the destruction [of stores]" [47] insufficient evidence is cited to back up this conclusion which would require a careful and controlled study of all stores and their practices in the riot area. Some informed observers have disagreed with the Commission's conclusions on this point. Moreover, the Los Angeles Police, the main target of pre-riot hostility, was also the main target of riot aggression. Only ten National Guardsmen out of a maximum of 13,900 were reported injured, as compared to 90 Los Angeles policemen out of a combined total of 1653 police at the time of maximum deployment.[48] The evidence, meager as it is, supports the view that there was a systematic relationship between the specific targets of aggression and the sources of the rioters' grievances.

The destructive and violent behavior of the rioters was confined to specific kinds of events within the riot situation. Eyewitnesses reported that rioters and looters in cars were observing traffic laws in the riot area —stopping for red lights, stopping for pedestrians at cross walks—even when carrying away stolen goods. Firemen were obstructed in putting out fires set to business establishments, yet one incident is reported where "people beseeched firemen to save a house which had caught fire when embers skipped to it from a torched commercial building," [49] and during which firemen were not hindered in any way from carrying out their job. These and similar incidents testify to the ability of riot participants to choose appropriate means for their ends. While riot behavior cannot be called "rational" in the everyday common meaning of that term, it did contain normative and rational elements and was much more situationally determined than the popular view would have it.

Looting is furthermore quite common in disaster situations other than riots and need not be interpreted as expressions of specifically racial hostility. Its attraction to people lacking the consumer goods others take for granted needs no complex explanation beyond the simple desire to obtain them when the opportunity to do so involves a low risk of apprehension by the police. Such action is facilitated by low commitment to the norms of private property expressed in the propensity of "the poor to seek a degree of elementary social justice at the expense of the rich," [50] the fact that others were doing the same thing, and the fact that the stores sacked in this case belonged to "Whitey." These observations can be illustrated by an eyewitness account of one such incident:

> One booty-laden youth said defiantly: "That don't look like stealing to me. That's just picking up what you need and going." Gesturing at a fashionable hilltop area where many well-to-do Negroes live, he said: "Them living up in View Park don't need it. But we down here, we do need it." [51]

Looting was a predominantly neighborhood activity, often uncoordinated, and carried out by small groups. Between 50 and 65 percent of the minors were arrested less than a mile from their home, and a little over 63 percent were arrested in the company of others, mainly for "burglary," that is they were apprehended in or near stores broken into.[52] The casual process through which individuals would get involved in looting, and the group and neighborhood aspects of it, are illustrated in the following statement of an arrested minor to a Probation Officer:

> [Minor] states that he was at home when his brother came home and said there was a riot going on in the streets. Minor states that he went out on the streets to watch and met a friend who said that people were going into a store on Broadway and "taking stuff out." Minor states that he and the companion went to observe and after arriving there and seeing everyone taking stuff from the store, he decided that he would take something also. . . . The only reason Minor offers for his behavior is that "everybody else was taking stuff, so I decided to take some too." [53]

While the actions of some looters were described in some accounts as that of a savage mob bent on plunder and fighting each other for the spoils, other descriptions and material, such as a photograph showing two women and one man rolling a fully loaded shopping cart past firemen, suggest a much more relaxed and calm mood.

Looting as well as other riot activity were essentially group activities during which participants and onlookers experienced a sense of solidarity, pride, and exhilaration. They were bound together by shared emotions, symbols, and experiences which a black man inevitably acquires in white America and which makes him address another one as "Brother." [54] They were also bound together by the common enemy, "Whitey," and struck out against Whitey's representatives in the flesh, the police, the firemen, the merchants, the news reporters, and the motorists, and they felt good about striking out. Bystanders were swept along in this tide of we-feeling. One such Negro who was attracted out of curiosity into the riot area on Thursday night and immediately afterwards recorded his impressions and feelings into a tape recorder, described what he experienced in the following words:

> A brick came out of nowhere and smashed through the window of a hot dog stand across the street. Someone yelled: "That's Whitey's, tear it down." A number of people from both sides of the street converged on the stand and began breaking all the windows. Several men climbed into this stand and began passing out Cokes and other beverages to the people outside. . . . As they passed a small gas station, several people wanted to set it afire. One of the people standing nearby the station told them: "Let it stand. Blood owns it." A liquor store and a grocery store were the next targets. . . . Next to the liquor store was a meat market. These windows were also smashed and people in cars drove up and began loading meat into the trunks of their cars. Two young boys . . . came running out of the store . . . carrying a side of beef. The crowd roared its approval and greeted the boys with laughter and cheers. Several men came walking towards me laden down with liquor. One of them paused in front of me and asked: "What do you drink, brother?" He and the other stopped right here on the street to have a drink. My reply was: "Whiskey." They opened a bottle of whiskey and handed it to me. I drank a large swallow and handed it back. Twice around and the bottle was empty. We laughed and they continued down the street. . . . A cry went up the street: "One-Oh-

Three. Hit the Third!" It referred to 103rd Street, the business center of
Watts (a mile to the east and the north). The people piled into cars and
headed for 103rd Street. Others followed on foot. As I was getting back into
my car to drive to "One-Oh-Three," several men jumped into my car and
said: "Let's make it, baby." [55]

The narrator adds at the end of his impressions: "I did not feel like
an outsider at any time during the night. While my involvement was
passive and some of the sights I witnessed appalling and saddening, I
felt a strong bond with these people."

The rioters did not form an amorphous mass, a collection of individuals acting out private frustrations and hostility. Rioting was a group
activity in the course of which strangers were bound together by common
sentiments, activities, and goals, and supported each other in the manner
typical of primary groups. The riot was a collective celebration in the
manner of a carnival, during which about 40 liquor stores were broken
into and much liquor consumed. It was also a collective contest similar
to that between two high school or college athletic teams, with the supporters cheering and egging on the contestants. One could settle old scores
with the police, show them who really controlled the territory, humiliate
them and teach them a lesson. Just as a rioting youth was quoted by two
Negro newsmen as saying: "This is what the police wanted—always messin'
with niggers. We'll show them. I'm ready to die if I have to." [56] Police
Chief Parker mistakenly boasted, "We are on top and they are on the
bottom." [57] Both sides in this tragic and deadly contest had a high emotional stake in the outcome. While the riot was put down eventually,
many Negroes saw it as a victory for their side and derived a sense of pride
and accomplishment from this public demonstration of their collective
power.

In assaulting the police and breaking into business establishments,
some rioters were not only responding to the long standing frustrations
and humiliations suffered at the hands of the police and the exploitative
practices of merchants, but were reacting along racial lines which can only
be understood in the wider social context of the Negro in the U.S. Rioters
were pelting motorists and firemen with rocks while shouting: "This is
for Bogalusa! This is for Selma!" The riot situation became defined in
global, dichotomous, we-they terms, where we and they stood for the two
races and the long history of conflict associated with them. In such a situation, when one status (racial membership) becomes predominant and one's
other statuses and role obligations irrelevant, mediation becomes impossible because one cannot remain sitting on a fence. When Negro Assemblyman Marvin Dymally tried to calm some rioters a boy asked him:
"Who you with?" Dymally answered: "I'm with you, man," to which the
boy retorted: "Then here's a rock, baby, throw it!" [58] Those who bridge
the dichotomy by siding with the opponent are perceived as traitors, and
will be singled out for special abuse as was the case with a Negro National
Guardsman who was called a "white nigger" by the crowd.[59]

CONCLUSION

These considerations about the actions and motivations of the rioters enable one to come closer to a characterization of the Watts riot. Was it a police riot, a race riot, an insurrection, a revolt, a rebellion, a nationalist uprising, or a revolution? A lot depends upon how these terms are defined, and they are often used loosely and interchangeably. There is no point in engaging a definitional exercise with which many will take issue. It can however be pointed out that in all of the above manifestations of collective behavior, common grievances, sentiments, emotions, and we-feeling bind the actors together, common targets become the object of aggression, and violent physical means are used by the participants. These cannot therefore be used to distinguish a riot from a revolt or a rebellion. One must examine what collective goals and demands are voiced by the actors. If their actions are directed at overthrowing the constituted authorities, if political demands are voiced such as the resignation of certain leaders and officials, if an attempt is made to achieve physical control in an area or territory by forcing out the existing authorities and substituting for them other authorities, then one is dealing with a revolt, rebellion, insurrection, or uprising. If, on the other hand, the main purpose of the action is to inflict damage and/or injury upon certain groups or a category of persons, such as police, merchants, or whites in general, then one is dealing with a riot.[60] The Los Angeles events therefore constituted a riot rather than anything else.

The riot was remarkable for the lack of any leadership and organized effort to express collective demands of the rioters and the Negro population in South Los Angeles. However many persons in that area may have wished to see the resignation of Police Chief Parker, or the establishment of a Civilian Police Review Board, no banners proclaiming these demands were raised.[61] No attempts were made to address the crowds to spell out collective aims. No spokesmen emerged from the ranks of the rioters to make a statement to the authorities or the press.[62] No effort was made to hold an area after the police were forced out of it and to coordinate action designed to prevent its comeback. No barricades were thrown up. Single individuals sniped at police and firemen from different locations and on numerous occasions, but there was no attempt to create a more organized form of armed resistance. While the precipitating incident touched off a police riot, which soon thereafter widened into a riot during which the targets of aggression became other whites besides police, subsequent days and nights produced a repetition of the same sort of behavior over an ever wider area and involving greater numbers of participants, but did not produce a change towards a more insurrectionary or revolutionary pattern of action.

It is the magnitude of the Los Angeles riot, both in duration, participation, amount of damage and casualties, and the forces needed to control it, which led many to characterize it as more than just a riot. But aside from magnitude, the Los Angeles riot was structurally and behaviorally similar to the Negro riots in other cities during the Summers of 1964, 1965, and 1966. The collective significance of these events, however, is that the civil rights gains made by the Negro movement in the last few years, which have benefited the Southern Negro and middle-class Negroes, have not altered the situation of the lower-class urban Negroes outside of the South and have not removed the fundamental sources of grievances of a large proportion of the Negro population in the U.S.

NOTES

ACKNOWLEDGEMENT: I wish to thank Mr. Borden Olive for helpful comments and assistance in locating some of the data on which this account is based.

1. While the riot engulfed a far wider area of South Los Angeles than the Watts district, it has come to be known as the Los Angeles or the Watts riot, and I use both these terms interchangeably. The question of whether the events that took place are best characterized as a "riot" or something else will be dealt with below.

2. Governor's Commission on the Los Angeles Riots, *Violence in the City—An End or a Beginning,* December 2, 1965, popularly known as the *McCone Report* after the Commission chairman's name.

3. For the relevant statistics, see the *McCone Report,* p. 1 and pp. 23–25; for a natural history of events, see Jerry Cohen and William S. Murphy, *Burn, Baby, Burn* (New York: Dutton, 1966), and *McCone Report,* pp. 10–23.

4. Neil J. Smelser, *Theory of Collective Behavior* (New York: Free Press, 1962), chapter 8.

5. *Time,* August 20, 1965, p. 16: "After looting pawn shops, hardware and war supply stores for weapons, the Negroes brandished thousands of rifles, shotguns, pistols, and machetes." See also the *Los Angeles Times,* August 17 and 18, 1965.

6. *Los Angeles Times,* August 15, 1965.

7. Ibid., September 20, 1965.

8. Ibid., September 16, 1965.

9. While the immediate reaction about what the riot was all about is to my mind distorted, the news media, statements by many officials, especially Negroes, as well as the later *McCone Report,* did reveal at least a moderate amount of sophistication and acceptance of ideas current in social science when it came to a description of the broader social and economic conditions that made the riot possible and even likely.

10. *McCone Report,* pp. 22–23.

11. On how both the conspiracy and criminal riff-raff explanations have been traditionally invoked by contemporaries to explain riots and rebellions in the 18th and 19th centuries see George Rudé, *The Crowd in History* (New York: John Wiley, 1964), esp. chapter 14.

12. *McCone Report,* pp. 1, 4–6, 24.

13. Robert Blauner, "Whitewash over Watts," *Trans-action* 3 (March-April 1966). Blauner himself concluded from published statements of Negro leaders and the reports of his informants that the McCone Commission had underestimated the widespread support for and participation in the riot, and explicitly rejects the view that the riot was primarily a rising of the lawless.

14. *McCone Report,* p. 1: "perhaps as many as 10,000 Negroes took to the streets in marauding bands."

15. Los Angeles County Probation Department, *Riot Participation Study,* Research Report No. 26 (November 1965), hereafter referred to as *RPS.*

16. Bureau of Criminal Records, Department of Justice, State of California, *Watts Riot Arrests* (Sacramento, California, June 30, 1966), hereafter referred to as *WRA.*

17. *RPS,* p. 21.

18. *WRA,* Tables 25 and 2.

19. *WRA* , Table 6.

20. *WRA,* p. 37.

21. Figures above taken from or recalculated from *WRA, RPS, McCone Report,* and "Special Census Survey of the South and East Los Angeles Areas: November 1965," *Current Population Report,* Technical Studies, Series P–23, 17 (March 23, 1967).

22. Figures cited above were taken from or recalculated from *WRA, RPS,* "Special Census Survey . . . ," and the *McCone Report.*

23. See "Special Census Survey . . . ," which contains up to date figures and allows a comparison to be made between the separate districts making up the South Los Angeles area. Other pertinent information is contained in the *McCone Report.*

24. *McCone Report,* p. 40.

25. U.S. Commission on Civil Rights, California Advisory Committee, *Police Minority Group Relations in Los Angeles and the San Francisco Bay Area* (hereafter referred to as the *Pike Report*), August 1963, p. 1.

26. *Pike Report,* p. 9.

27. Ibid., p. 8.

28. Mayor Yorty's campaign flyer (*Mayor Yorty Reports*) distributed in March 1966 at the start of the 1966 Democratic gubernatorial primary contest linked the Communist Party and other left-wing organizations with the anti-police campaign. *The Los Angeles Times,* August 18, 1965, Part I, page 3, quotes Yorty as saying that "for some time now there has existed a world-wide campaign to stigmatize all police as brutal. . . . The cry of 'police brutality' has been shouted in cities all over the world by the Communists, dupes, and demagogues irrespective of the facts. Such a campaign has been pushed here in Los Angeles."

29. *Pike Report,* p. 8.

30. *Pike Report,* pp. 14–15.

31. On these points, see Ray Murphy and Howard Elinson, ed., *Problems and Prospects of the Negro Movement* (Belmont, Cal.: Wadsworth, 1966), p. 232; Blauner, "Whitewash over Watts," p. 8; and Cohen and Murphy, *Burn, Baby Burn,* p. 210.

32. Blauner, "Whitewash over Watts," p. 6.

33. *Pike Report,* p. 12.

34. *McCone Report,* p. 32.

35. In 1962 the Los Angeles police department had apparently about 150 Negro police officers out of a total force of 4700. The reason given by police officials for the low proportion of Negroes on the force was their inability to meet eligibility standards and the scarcity of applications (*Pike Report,* p. 34).

36. The most plausible reconstruction of the incident is presented in great detail in Chaps. 2–4 of Cohen and Murphy, *Burn, Baby, Burn.*

37. *McCone Report,* p. 11.

38. Ibid., p. 12.

39. Evidence for these psychological processes can be found in Bernard Berelson and Gary Steiner, *Human Behavior* (New York: Harcourt, Brace & Jovanovich, 1964), pp. 101, 115.

40. The fact that August 11 was one of the hottest days in the entire summer has been regarded by some as the precipitating factor. Actually it was important insofar as more people than usual do hang around on the streets near their homes in the

slums on hot nights, so that an incident immediately attracts a larger number of spectators than usual and news of events travels faster and uninterruptedly by word of mouth. To the extent that people tend to be more irritable and "on edge" at the end of a day with high levels of heat, smog, and humidity, these factors in themselves were also contributory causes after the precipitating incident had occurred.

41. On these processes, see Neil Smelser, *Theory of Collective Behavior*, pp. 258–60.
42. Cohen and Murphy, *Burn, Baby, Burn*, p. 74.
43. Ibid., pp. 121, 126.
44. *McCone Report*, pp. 17–19.
45. Cohen and Murphy, *Burn, Baby, Burn*, pp. 69–70.
46. Ibid., p. 88.
47. *McCone Report*, p. 62.
48. Ibid., p. 20.
49. Cohen and Murphy, *Burn, Baby, Burn*, p. 157.
50. See Rudé, *The Crowd in History*, p. 244, and *passim* for historical instances of this.
51. *Time*, August 20, 1965, p. 17.
52. *RPS*, pp. 16, 18. Comparable data on adults arrested are not available.
53. *RPS*, p. 19.
54. A Negro student recalls driving his run-down automobile during the riot outside of the curfew area, and stopping at a red light next to a late-model car driven by a middle-aged, prosperous looking Negro. The other driver, a total stranger and probably mistaking the student for one of the active rioters, smiled broadly and told him before driving off: "Where are you going to strike next, Brother?"
55. Quoted in Cohen and Murphy, *Burn, Baby, Burn*, pp. 111–12.
56. *Time*, August 20, 1965, p. 17.
57. *Time*, August 27, 1965, p. 11.
58. Cohen and Murphy, *Burn, Baby, Burn*, p. 119.
59. Ibid., p. 195.
60. "A riot is an outbreak of temporary but violent mass disorder. It may be directed at a particular individual as well as against public authorities. But it involves no intention to overthrow the government itself. In this respect riot stops short of insurrection or rebellion, although it may often be only a preliminary to the latter" is the definition of Smellie in the *Encyclopedia of the Social Sciences*.
61. Although some handbills from an unidentified source denouncing Parker were passed out during the riot.
62. Negro leaders and influentials did of course speak out during the riot on television and through other means. They expressed Negro demands such as Assemblyman Dymally's call for Parker's removal. But the leaders were reiterating views that they had long held and publicly voiced. They were not asked by the rioters to be spokesmen for riot goals or terms of negotiation with the authorities.

PROPERTY NORMS AND LOOTING:
THEIR PATTERNS IN COMMUNITY CRISES

E. L. Quarantelli / Russell R. Dynes

Massive civil disturbances are not new in American society. And since the turn of the century at least, blacks as well as white citizens have participated on a large scale in intermittent street disorders that peaked in 1919 in the famous Chicago riot, and again in 1943 in the equally well known Detroit racial clash. However, starting about five years ago, a somewhat new pattern involving the conflict of blacks and community law enforcement agencies appeared.

From 1964 through September 1969 these disturbances have numbered in the high hundreds. At least 189 of them can be considered major incidents. At a very minimum, looting occurred in 122 of these events. Looters have perhaps struck 10,000 different stores, buildings and other places in both the major and minor incidents. The dollar cost of the loot taken—difficult to estimate because it is impossible to distinguish from losses stemming from vandalism and burning, has probably been over $55 million. Just by late spring of 1968, about 60,000 persons had been arrested for looting and directly related activities.[1]

Scholarly, ideological, political and other explanations of the civil disturbances as a whole abound in the literature. There have been somewhat fewer systematic attempts to account for looting behavior, which is not only recognized as a major feature of such events but also as a basic change from patterns in pre-1960 disturbances. The explanations advanced tend to be predominately variations upon one theme. Looters are viewed as manifesting personal desocialization under stress. Looting is seen as deviant behavior of individuals and is interpreted as primarily being expressive in function. Our position is that a rather different perception of this phenomena in civil disturbances is required than is currently held by many social scientists as well as most laymen.

We develop this point of view in what follows by: (1) contrasting two different perspectives on massive looting behavior; (2) noting differences in patterns of looting in dissensus and in consensus situations (i.e., between civil disturbances and natural disasters); (3) advancing an explanation of looting in terms of the emergence of new group norms, particularly those pertaining to property, at times of major crises; (4) suggesting that massive looting has become a semi-institutionalized response pattern even though a less prominent feature of civil disturbances since mid-1968; and, (5) indicating what accounts for the failure of contemporary social scientists to see looting as normative behavior.

From *Phylon:* The Atlanta University Review of Race and Culture, 31 (Summer 1970): 168–72; reprinted by permission of the author and the publisher.

THE INDIVIDUAL PERSPECTIVE ON LOOTING

Most people—governmental and other organizational officials who have to deal with the problem, as well as many academicians—essentially have an invalid overall perspective about the looting behavior seen in recent ghetto disturbances in American cities. They seek the explanation for looting in the psychological makeup or characteristics of the individual. We believe that the evidence at hand does not support such a view.

Although the basic theme is the same, this perspective on looting takes variant forms depending upon the sophistication of the explainer. At the simpler end of a continuum are explanations that rest on the assumption that behind the civilized facade of man lurks a savage animal that will surface especially under stress circumstances. Looting, from this viewpoint, represents a breakdown of the thin "cultural veneer" that overlays human behavior. Although the imagery can be traced back to Le Bon, this model of man is still used today, as can be noted in a current social psychology text in its discussion of different kinds of community emergencies.

> Under unusual conditions, the socialization process may be more or less reversed, so that individuals are "disassimilated" from the social system. For example, under conditions of catastrophe, war, or natural disasters . . . the effects of socialization and social control appear to be generally undone. . . . Frequently, in times of natural disaster such as fires, floods, or hurricanes, mobs of plunderers raid the broken shopwindows, scooping up displayed goods.[2]

In a later passing reference to the disturbances in Watts, California, these same authors note "that many ordinarily law-abiding citizens took part because of their inability to resist the seductive pressures of mob action" and relate this to "the temporary suspension of organized social controls that normally inhibit impulsive eruptions of hostile feelings."[3] In short, the baser part of man will come to the fore given the opportunity.

Outside of scholarly circles, this conception of course also fits in well with widely held racial notions about Negroes. Less diplomatic police officials have been known to talk of "animals in the zoo" in connection with civil disorders. Some of the earlier mass media accounts of looting likewise have tended to imply a breaking loose of "mad dogs" in such situations.

A somewhat more complex but related explanation of looting behavior is one popularly used several decades ago to explain war between nations as well as individual violence, i.e., the frustration-aggression thesis. More recent versions of this formulation have discarded some of the simpler notions in the earlier statements, but the basic model remains the same.[4] Insofar as looting is concerned, it is seen as an expression of object-focused aggression that surfaces as a result of long-lasting frustrations among ghetto dwellers. The looter deviates from the norms because he has reached the limits of his endurance and in giving vent to his normally suppressed rage strikes out indiscriminately.

Since the frustration-aggression notion has slowly permeated much popular thinking, it is not surprising to see it applied to this aspect of current civil disturbances. However, unlike the previous explanation which seems to be most popular among lawmen, this explanation of looting appears to be more prevalent among community officials and political figures. Furthermore, instead of talking in academic terms of "grievance banks" or "relative deprivation," the layman is more likely to say that the looting was a way of "blowing off steam," that the tension built up had to be released in some way.

The most sophisticated of the versions of the individual approach to looting behavior tend to use two closely related notions frequently associated with mass societies, i.e., alienation and anomie. Thus, one very recent study concretely applied the concept of alienation in analyzing the behavior of participants in civil disturbances. It is treated as perceived isolation from the larger society giving such persons a feeling of being unable to control events in their world, and consequently increasing their readiness to engage in extreme behavior.[5] If this is valid, presumably looting would most likely be undertaken by the most alienated of the ghetto dwellers. Other writers talk of the social isolation of the ghetto inhabitant instead of his alienation or anomic neighborhoods, but the logic appears to be the same.

At a more lay level, particularly in the early days of the disturbances, recent urban migrants were frequently seen as being the core of the participants. Implicitly at least the more deviant actions in disturbances, such as looting, were thought more likely to be undertaken by those without local social ties. For example, such a view is implied in part in the McCone Commission report on the Watts disturbance.[6]

All of the preceding explanations of looting rest basically on the notion of shallow, incomplete or faulty socialization. Given the opportunity, the animal in man comes forth. Given enough stress, the frustrated creature strikes out. Given a feeling of isolation and powerlessness, extreme violent actions are undertaken. In this logic, looters of course are seen as deviating from accepted patterns, not behaving as fully socialized human beings.

This is one general perspective on looting. It is quite congenial to the individualistic and nominalistic view of social reality that prevails in American society. It also fits in well with the idea that no major structural changes are necessary if deviants can be taught to change their outward behavior. Whether it is police chiefs, politicians or social scientists who are talking, in this approach the "evil" of looting is seen as rooted in man and not in his social conditions. Of course it can be noted that Tolstoy in his *To the Working People* declared that nothing does more harm to man than attributing misery to circumstances rather than to man himself, so this general point of view is neither particularly new or specially American.

Conceptions of looting primarily as a form of regressive or desocialized behavior lend themselves to functional interpretations in expressive terms. That is, the behavior is viewed as an overt manifestation or symptom of some underlying psychological state. Since the expressed behavior however is illegal and thus publically deviant, the problem then essentially is thought of as one of formal social control. Such ideas are more implied than stated and appear more in popular thought than academic discussions, but nevertheless are part of the individual perspective on looting behavior.

Occasionally this interpretation is set forth in very explicit terms. For example, Wilson very recently stated: The Negro riots are in fact *expressive* acts—that is, actions which are either intrinsically satisfying ("play") or satisfying because they give expression to a state of mind.[7] Some public officials and police use rather different language, but frequently the general idea is roughly equivalent. They see looting as an expression of criminal tendencies, as opportunistic stealing by individuals already inclined in such directions and who use civil strife as a cover for their everyday deviant personal proclivities.

The general public recognizes that the police generally have no expertise in dealing with psychic states, but still feel that law enforcement agencies have the responsibility for preventing at least this outward manifestation of deviancy. Thus, the Campbell and Schuman survey found that about one-third of the white population sampled thought the racial civil disturbances criminal in character and felt that tougher police measures were the prime answer to the problem. (Another third of the sample believed that perhaps some real grievances were involved, but still supported repressive police measures.) [8] In essence, the matter is defined as one of law enforcement. In general, this means the application of formal control measures of a repressive nature. Looting is to be treated in such a way so that prone individuals will hesitate to give overt expression to their attitudes and tendencies. If the police cannot do anything about the *covert* psychic states responsible, it is assumed that they can at least suppress the *overt* symptom.

Popular as the individual approach to looting behavior may be, it does not square with a number of empirical observations and studies. Thus, the Jekyll and Hyde image of man implied in some of the previous discussion is not supported. For example, it is true that natural disaster contexts also present extensive "opportunities" for widespread looting. However, as we shall detail later, almost all of the potentials for much deviant behavior of this kind are never realized in such emergency situations. To assert that looting is widespread in disasters and then to attempt in part to account for similar behavior in civil disturbance on the same basis as Oberschall did recently, for example, is to make an incorrect assumption.[9]

Similarly, frustration-aggression formulations with regard to disturbances and looting within them, also have to ignore certain observations. For example, study after study has shown it is not the most downtrodden, the Marxian lumpenproletariat, the "down and outer" who participates and who loots in civil disturbances. In fact, if arrest records can be taken seriously, the vast majority of looters are regularly employed.

Some studies that have attempted to work with more sophisticated versions of frustration such as "relative deprivation" have likewise produced disappointing results. Thus, one study of civil disturbances concluded that the relationship with regard to "relative deprivation and participation [was] less than expected and in many cases [there was] no consistent pattern of relationship between activity and either level of aspiration or extent of discontent." [10] Another study of 14 cities found that "the relative deprivation explanation as tested in this paper is apparently in need of amplification if we are to be able to explain and predict ghetto riots." [11] Furthermore, few persons would claim that blacks as a whole are less frustrated today than say four years ago, yet there are far fewer massive street disorders.

With regard to social isolation as the explanatory factor the picture is somewhat the same. Looters do not see themselves as particularly isolated, and objectively have many social ties in that arrestees are typically employed, married and long-time residents of their cities. Warren, in an intensive study of Detroit, found that "in neighborhoods with a high degree of withdrawal from the riot, informal social ties and both attitudinal and behavioral linkage to the larger white and black communities were lacking." [12] Geschwender, although believing the social isolation conception is of some value, perhaps best expresses the major criticism of this view in his statement that "this model is too simplistic. It ignores the effect of emergent norms in attracting individuals other than social isolates with severe grievances into the riot." [13]

We believe looting behavior cannot be understood as simply a failure of persons to incorporate or maintain surrounding societal values nor can it be interpreted primarily as expressive behavior. The evidence does not seem to support such an approach. Looting has to be seen in more than individual psychological terms or as primarily a problem in social control.

THE GROUP PERSPECTIVE ON LOOTING

Another perspective on massive looting is possible. It is to think of looting in urban areas as normative behavior of a particular segment of American society, i.e., as a sub-cultural pattern that becomes manifest under certain appropriate stress circumstances and no different in this respect from other normative behavior. Thus, looting in this formulation is viewed as a characteristic of a group, not actions of individuals. It can consequently be thought of as conforming rather than deviant behavior, and as a problem in social change rather than in social control.

We will document this by looking not only at civil disorders but also at the pattern that looting behavior assumes in another kind of major community stress, i.e., natural disasters. The most parsimonious common explanation for the looting behavior in these emergency situations is that the usual group norms which govern property in both instances change. Because one of these community crises is a consensus type and the other is a dissensus type situation, the resulting pattern of looting behavior is different, but nevertheless the major explanatory factor is to be found in emergent norms of groups, not in expressions of individual characteristics.

TWO PATTERNS OF LOOTING

There are two major types of community crises, some reflecting consensus, others mirroring dissensus. The best example of these two are natural disasters in the former instance, and civil disturbances in the latter case. Contrary to the image presented in most news accounts as well as fictional stories of emergencies, there is not total social chaos and anarchy in such situations. Behavior in both kinds of crises shows definite patterns being neither random nor idiosyncratic for each specific case. Furthermore, while there is a pattern to the behavior, it differs in the two kinds of crises. This is as true of looting behavior as it is of many other emergency behaviors.

There are at least three major differences between the looting that occurs in civil disorders and in natural disasters.

1. In civil disorders looting is very widespread whereas in natural disasters actual looting incidents are quite rare. The behavior is widespread in at least three senses. One, it occurs in almost all major disorders and many of the less serious ones. Two, looters come from all segments of the population, females as well as males, oldsters as well as youngsters, middle-class as well as lower-class persons, and so on. Looting is not the behavior solely of a delimited or distinctive part of black communities. Third, if we extrapolate figures from some studies made by other researchers, in at least the major disturbances it seems possible that as many as a fifth of the total ghetto residents may participate in the activity.[14] This contrasts sharply with natural disaster situations. In those, looting often does not occur at all, and in the infrequent cases where it does take place, is apparently undertaken by a handful of individuals in the general population.

Furthermore, looting in civil disorders is almost always, if not exclusively, engaged in by local residents, whereas in natural disasters it is undertaken by "outsiders." It is the local ghetto dweller who participates in urban civil disturbances. Arrest records for all offenses show that those involved overwhelmingly reside in the city experiencing the disorder.[15] There is in fact reason to suspect, when the high percentage of women who engage in massive looting is taken into account, that the great majority of looters are from the local neighborhoods around the places looted. In natural disasters on the contrary, such looting as there is, in general, is done by non-local persons who venture into the impacted community. Sometimes they are part of the very security forces often sent in from outside the area to prevent such behavior (as was recently reported to be the case regarding some National Guardsmen dispatched to the Gulf Coast of Mississippi after Hurricane Camille).

2. One of the most striking aspects about looting in civil disturbances

is its collective character. This is dramatically depicted in many television and movie films of such incidents. Looters often work together in pairs, as family units or small groups. This is a marked contrast to natural disasters where such looting as occurs is carried out by solitary individuals. In the civil disturbances, the collective nature of the act sometimes reaches the point where the availability of potential loot is called to the attention of bystanders, or in extreme instances where spectators are handed goods by looters coming out of stores.

The collective nature of massive looting is also manifest in its selective nature in civil disorders compared with its situational nature in disasters. Press reports to the contrary, ghetto dwellers have been far from indiscriminate in their looting. Grocery, furniture, apparel and liquor stores have been the prime objects of attack. In Newark they made up 49 percent of those attacked; in Watts they made up a majority. Many other kinds of establishments such as plants, offices, schools and private residences have been generally ignored. Furthermore, within the general category of stores and places selected for attack, there has been even finer discrimination. One chain store in Washington, D.C., had 19 of its 50 stores looted while supermarkets of other companies located in the same neighborhoods were left untouched. Obviously, such massive action is not a matter of individual but of collective definition of "good" and "bad" stores from the viewpoint of ghetto dwellers. In contrast to this focus in civil disorders on commercial enterprises, in natural disasters such early looting as there is often seems to center on personal effects and goods. It likewise appears to depend on the opportunity presented by the availability of discarded clothing of victims, open doors into residences, spilled items on sidewalks from storefronts and the like. In other words, the looting in natural disasters is highly influenced by situational factors that present themselves to looters rather than any conscious selection and choice of places to loot, as is the case in civil disturbances. (However, even in natural disasters, there are far more situational opportunities for looting that could be taken advantage of, but are not.)

3. The public nature of the looting behavior in civil disorders is also striking. It is not a private act as it is in natural disasters. Goods are taken openly and in full view of others, bystanders as well as co-participants, and often even policemen. In natural disasters, such looting as occurs is very covert and secret with care being taken not to be observed by others. The open dashing into stores or the carrying of stolen goods through the streets in broad daylight as is common in the urban disturbances just does not occur in the wake of such catastrophes as hurricanes and earthquakes.

Furthermore, in natural disaster, acts which are defined as looting are condemned very severely. In civil disturbances instead, both during and after the event there is little local community sanction for such behavior. In fact, while the disturbances are going on, and looting is at its peak, there is actually strong local social support for the activity. The so-called "carnival spirit" observed in the major civil disturbances, rather than being a manifestation of anarchy, is actually an indication of the open collective support of a local nature for looting. Even after the disturbances are over, as different studies and surveys show, the disorders are justified by most blacks and judged as helpful in bringing about change.[16] In contrast, looting is considered a very serious crime in natural disasters, spoken of in highly condemnatory tones by residents of the area, and is never seen as justifiable behavior.

To summarize: looting in civil disorders is widespread, collective and public, and is undertaken by local people who are selective in their activity and who receive community support for their actions. In contrast, looting in natural disasters is very limited, individual and private, being engaged in by outsiders to the community taking advantage of certain situations they find themselves in but who are strongly condemned for their actions.

EMERGENT PROPERTY NORMS

In order to explain the looting patterns in the two kinds of community crises just considered, it is necessary to examine the nature of property. In this we may be misled by the term looting. In the military context from which it is derived, looting implies the taking of goods and possessions.

However, property has reference not to any concrete thing or material object, but to a right. "Property consists of the *rights* held by an individual . . . to certain valuable things, whether material or immaterial." [17] But if we talk of rights we are talking of shared expectations about what can or cannot be done with respect to something. Property can therefore be viewed as a set of cultural norms that regulate the relation of persons to items with economic value. In effect, property is a shared understanding about who can do what with the valued resources within a community.

Normally, these understandings or expectations are widely shared and accepted. There are all kinds of norms, the legal ones in particular, which specify the legitimate forms of use, control and disposal of economically valued resources within a community. It is these expectations which change in both kinds of community crises we are talking about.

In natural disasters, in American society at least, there quickly develops a consensus that all private property rights are temporarily suspended for the common good. In one way, all goods become "community property" and can be used as needed for the general welfare. Thus, warehouses can be broken into without the owner's permission to obtain generators necessary to keep hospitals functioning, and the act is seen as legitimate if undertaken for this purpose even though the participants might agree that it was technically an act of burglary. However, the parties involved, the local legal authorities and the general public in the area at the time of the crisis do not define such actions as looting and would react very negatively to attempts to impose such a definition.

On the other hand, there is very powerful social pressure against the use of goods for purely personal use while major community emergency needs exist. In a way, the individual who uses anything for himself alone is seen as taking from the common store. The new norm as to property is that the affected group, as long as it has emergency needs, has priority.

It is this community expectation or consensus that develops which explains the characteristic pattern of looting in natural disasters outlined earlier. Thus, it is understandable why such looting as occurs is typically undertaken by someone from outside the impacted area. Such persons not having undergone the experience are not part of the new although temporary community consensus regarding property. They can act as individuals toward strangers, pursuing highly personal goals and appropriating whatever resources opportunities provide them.

In civil disturbances there is also a redefinition of property rights. The looting undertaken is likewise a temporary manifestation of a new group norm. The "current" right to use of available resources becomes problematical. If property is thought of as the shared understanding of who can do what with the valued resources within a community, in civil disorders we see a breakdown in that understanding. What was previously taken for granted and widely shared becomes a matter of dispute among certain segments of the general population.

Viewed in this way much of the pattern of looting in civil disturbances discussed earlier also makes sense. At the height of such situations, plundering becomes the normative, the socially accepted thing to do. Far from being deviant, it becomes the conforming behavior in the situation. As in natural disasters, the legal right does not change, but there is local group consensus on the massive use and appropriation of certain public and private goods, be these police cars or items on grocery store shelves. In many ways, a new property norm has emerged.

As most sociologists have argued, social behavior is always guided by norms, traditional or emergent.[18] Looting does not constitute actions in the absence of norms. Even situations of civil disorder are not that unstructured. The observed cases of looters continuing to pay attention to traffic lights should be seen as more than humorous anecdotes; they are simple indications of the continuous operations of traditional norms even in situations that seem highly confused. The parties involved in massive looting are simply acting on the basis of new, emergent norms in the ghetto group with regard to some categories of property. They are not behaving in a situation devoid of social structuring.

Of course, there is differential distribution of the frequency of looting in different civil disorders, and even where there is maximization of the behavior, not everyone loots. Civil disturbances are not of one kind, as the various typologies of them that have been developed clearly indicate. Looting, for example, is more likely in a disorder that is explicitly focused on protest than one not involving such a kind of focus. Furthermore, neither black ghettoes nor the neighborhoods within them are of one piece, as both Warren and Hill and Larson have documented.[19] Warren, in his studies, for example, has shown that degree of participation in disorders (and therefore presumably looting) is related to the kind of prevailing social organization in the local neighborhood area.

SEMI-INSTITUTIONALIZATION OF LOOTING BEHAVIOR

Looting may not be engaged in by everyone and there is no doubt an illusion of greater unanimity regarding public support of the behavior among the actual participants than is the case. Nevertheless, it seems fairly clear that in the period from 1964 through 1969 this kind of response on the part of ghetto dwellers became partly institutionalized, i.e., it seems to be the immediate behavioral response if a disorder grows beyond a very minimal point. Massive looting can start almost immediately in a community as it did in many ghettos in the very widespread disturbances that occurred after the King assassination. There are also other indirect signs of the probable institutionalization of the behavior. After the disorders are over, there seems to be far less returning or turning in of looted goods by repentant looters than was the case several years ago. Furthermore, in the more recent ghetto disturbances there are no reports of looters destroying the goods they have taken. Yet, in the earlier disorders, for example, in Plainfield, New Jersey in 1964 and even in Watts in 1965, some of the liquor taken was destroyed rather than consumed.[20]

The semi-institutionalization of looting behavior as a group response pattern under certain circumstances has been facilitated by a number of factors. For one, the police have generally been unable, and perhaps even unwilling for a variety of complex reasons that cannot be discussed here, to stop attempts at massive looting. This of course contributes to recidivism. Probably, however, the mass communication system has been more important in this respect by providing role models and even a degree of legitimation. As Janowitz and Mattick have noted, television in particular has inadvertently taught ghetto dwellers all around the country the details of the disturbances, how people participate in them, and the tactics to be used and gratifications to be obtained in looting goods.[21] The overall definition of the situation and its general acceptance has also been reinforced by some radio and television stations, who at the height of disturbances repeatedly point out that the police are standing by while looting is pursued with impunity.

Since early 1968 the number of large-scale civil disturbances has dropped considerably compared with the prior four years. As such, massive looting behavior on the Newark scale occurs less frequently. In this sense the behavior is less prominent. Noticeable, however, is the fact that when disturbances do occur currently, even on a small scale, looting almost inevitably takes place, usually developing quickly and without any build up. This argues for the present semi-institutionalized nature of the action—it is the expected and accepted normative action and almost automatically appears in certain stress situations.

If looting is seen as a form of normative group behavior, it lends itself quite readily to interpretations in instrumental terms. It can be visualized as communicating a message from the ghetto areas to the larger society. In other words, massive looting can be defined as a form of group protest about certain aspects of interracial relationships in American society. The looters themselves may or may not be conscious of such a message, but the motives of actors need not necessarily correspond to the functions of their actions. Looting can have a communication function and in a way serve as a kind of primitive political protest mechanism.

This would not be a new pattern in history. Subordinate groups in the past have developed subcultural traditions of violent protest with regard to property. This has been well documented by European historians who have analyzed many instances where groups of workers and shop-keepers—incidentally, not the unemployed or criminal elements—in the 18th and 19th centuries in different communities protested in the streets to communicate discontent about their economic positions in their societies.

As Hobsbawm has noted of the "pre-industrial city mob," its actions were guided partly by the expectation of achieving something by its disruptive actions.[22] Groups who undertake such activities are not necessarily incorrect in this assumption. Instructive in this respect was the behavior of the Luddites, the so-called machine breakers who, as recent historical analysis shows, were far less indiscriminate in their destructive acts than is generally supposed. Perhaps more important, it has been said of their behavior that "collective bargaining by rioting was at least as effective as any other means of bringing trade union pressure, and probably *more* effective than any other means available before the era of national trade unions." [23] In other words, the recurrent violent behavior of the Luddites and similar groups was instrumental in bringing about a change in their relative socioeconomic position in the society.

Could anything similar be said of the looting behavior that seems to have established itself in American ghettos over the last few years? Certainly there has been increasing recognition that the civil disturbances as a whole are more than a matter of breakdown of law and order. One of the last studies sponsored by the National Advisory Commission on Civil Disorders took the position that the ghetto disorders are a form of social protest engaged in by non-criminal elements and justified as such by a majority of black people.[24] In fact, the Campbell and Schuman survey showed that a consistent majority of from 51 to 60 percent of all Negro respondents, varying somewhat with age, interpreted the urban disturbances as protest activities.[25]

Many scholars are also beginning to interpret the civil disorders in similar terms. Paige observes that "rioting can profitably be considered a form of disorganized political protest engaged in by those who have become highly distrustful of existing political institutions." [26] Boesel has said that "when violence erupts in the ghetto, it ordinarily constitutes a violent protest without ideology which focuses on certain key institutional points of contact between the ghetto and white society—such as the police and the stores—without developing a comprehensive collective rationality." [27] This is similar to our more delimited theme. Massive looting can be interpreted as a form of violent group protest, and not merely individualistic expressive acts. The protest is focused on existing property rights in American society.

Furthermore, if looting is seen not as expressive reactions on the part of individuals but as instrumental behavior by a group, it suggests thinking of it not as absolute *deviation* from existing norms, but as relative *conformity* to new norms or expectations. If that is the case, social control by the larger society can only be achieved by creating new institutional patterns that will be the functional equivalent in the group of the existing pattern of looting. In other words, instead of thinking about the repression of unsocialized or aggressive impulses of individuals, it is necessary to think of the institutionalization of new social structures. The problem viewed in this way thus becomes one of bringing about social change rather than suppressing deviant behavior. The issue therefore is one that goes far beyond law enforcement, although the actions of the police are not irrelevant to what will occur in certain kinds of community emergencies.

RESISTANCE TO THE NORMATIVE VIEW OF LOOTING

Many persons, scholars, political figures and others, have failed to note or to accept the view of looting as normative behavior and its interpretation in instrumental terms. Illustrative of the more general societal reaction is that taken by the Mayor's Special Task Force in Pittsburgh in its examination of the disorders in the city after the King assassination. It very correctly notes, for example, that the looting was highly selective, but attributes this to advance planning and preparation.[28] The conspiracy theory of history is of course an ancient one, and is a particular favorite of public authorities. It is certainly not peculiar to American society. Jones and Molnar in a wide-ranging examination of civil disorders in a variety of places and at different historical times note:

> Those in power have usually assumed that the rioters had no worthwhile aspirations and could be motivated to activity only by the promise of reward from outside agitators or conspirators. Until the deeper aspirations of the poor began to be investigated their periodic rebellions and riots were often attributed to the manipulation of a political opponent or a "hidden hand." This attitude has been so popular in history that it has been shared by all authority, regardless of whether the governing elite was aristocratic, middle class, conservative, liberal, or revolutionary.[29]

Along with playing up the conspiracy theory, there is also a tendency to downplay the massive nature of the disturbances or their acceptability among ghetto dwellers. Thus, the mistaken position is taken that only a tiny fraction of black people participate. As earlier indicated also, another general reaction is to attribute the disorders to malcontents or individuals without ties to the social system. There seems to be an unwillingness to face up to the fact that looters, for example, are not persons without jobs. In particular there is a great reluctance to believe that if there is a protest involved, it is by a group with any sense of power or hope of achievement through street tactics. Yet the evidence is that there is a "genuine protest temper" among the participants in disturbances. Discussing the development of European trade unionism, Rimilinger notes that this temper demands that those involved "be convinced of the righteousness not only of their demands but also of the novel means proposed to enforce them." [30] Substantial numbers of black people in American urban areas seem convinced about both aspects.

The inability or unwillingness to see massive looting as a normative group protest undoubtedly stems from many factors, some of which have already been implied. There is one additional element, however, which should be noted for it seems to affect both social scientists and laymen in their approaches to looting in urban disturbances. This is their difficulty in accepting violence as something more than incidental in social behavior. To conceive of "the Negro problem largely as an issue in deviant behavior" minimizes the possible use of mass violence in many situations as a tactical tool for affecting social change.[31]

It has been frequently observed that almost all theoretical models in American sociology have consistently ignored social conflict and its relation to social change. The consensus and equilibrium frameworks generally used by sociologists have led them to focus attention on social order. It is an easy step with such an orientation to see collective violence as a deviant if not pathological phenomena and as not intrinsic to the basic character of social structures and processes. As Feldman has observed:

> Social theory has remarkably little to say about the occurrence of large-scale violence. . . . The study of social violence is typically viewed as an area of social pathology. . . . In this sense violence is conceived as being *incidental* to the basic character of social structures and processes.[32]

But as we have tried to suggest, any approach to massive looting behavior with such a conception seems to be rather unrealistic. The phenomena instead must be recognized as normative group behavior focused on property rights and as such interpretable as an attempt to alter intergroup relationships in American society.

Coser has noted that:

> The often violent forms of rebellion of the laboring poor, the destructiveness of the city mobs, and other forms of popular disturbances which mark English social history from the 1960's to the middle of the nineteenth century, helped to educate the governing elite of England, Whig and Tory alike, to the recognition that they could ignore the plight of the poor only at their own peril. These social movements constituted among other things an effective signaling device which sensitized the upper classes to the need for social reconstruction in defense of a social edifice over which they wished to continue to have over-all command.[33]

Will American society read the massive looting in urban disturbances for a similar protest message and will it respond accordingly in an appropriate adaptive manner? We believe we have documented the question involved. The answer will have to come from elsewhere.

CONCLUSION

In what preceded, we have not attempted to analyze or to account for all phases of the civil disturbances that have wracked urban American society from 1964 through 1969. On the contrary, if we have learned anything from our studies of these situations, it is that the behaviors and participants involved are far more heterogeneous than is implied in a statement that "violence" broke out in this ghetto or that the Negroes in a particular community "rioted." Sniping and looting, arson and vandalism and other behaviors are not the same kinds of acts; different participants take part in these activities, the action takes place at different locations and at different time periods of the disturbances. To treat such varying activities separated in time and space and undertaken by different persons and groups as only one kind of phenomenon is to blur vital empirical as well as analytical distinctions, and to make homogeneous that which is not. Our focus in this paper was almost exclusively on massive looting behavior. We have not pretended to explain outbreaks, when and where they occur, but mostly have focused on attempting to identify the nature of and to account for one of their most prominent features, i.e., massive looting.

NOTES

This is a substantially revised version of a paper presented at the 1968 annual meeting of the American Sociological Association in Boston, Massachusetts. Some parts of the original paper are included in an article by the authors published in a 1969 issue of the Italian journal, *Il Politico*. Work on this version was supported in part by the Center for Studies of Mental Health and Social Problems, Applied Research Branch, U.S. Public Health Service National Institute of Mental Health Grant 5–RO1–MN15399–02.

1. Figures given in this paragraph, while estimates, are probably on the low side. They were compiled from a variety of sources including unpublished data from a number of insurance companies and associations, records kept by the Lemberg Center for the Study of Violence at Brandeis University and the Ohio State University Disaster Research Center, as well as several Congressional committees. All later discussions not otherwise documented are based on field research conducted in over 120 emergency situations by the Disaster Research Center. For a discussion of the early work of the Center see Russell R. Dynes, J. Eugene Haas, and E. L. Quarantelli, "Administrative, Methodological and Theoretical Problems of Disaster Research," *Indian Sociological Bulletin* 4 (July 1967): 215–27.

2. John W. McDavid and Herbert Harari, *Social Psychology: Individuals, Group, Societies* (New York: Harper & Row, 1968), pp. 120–21, 388.

3. Ibid., pp. 390–91.

4. Earlier versions are discussed in John Dollard et al., *Frustration and Aggression* (New Haven: Yale University Press, 1939). Later versions are set forth in Leonard Berkowitz, "The Study of Urban Violence: Some Implications of Laboratory Studies of Frustration and Aggression," *The American Behavioral Scientist* 2 (March-April 1968): 14–17, and Ted Gurr, "Psychological Factors in Civil Violence," *World Politics* 20 (January 1968): 245–78.

5. H. Edward Ransford, "Isolation, Powerlessness and Violence: A Study of Attitudes and Participation in the Watts Riot," *American Journal of Sociology* 73 (March 1968): 581–91.

6. Governor's Commission on the Los Angeles Riots, *Violence in the City—An End or a Beginning?* (Los Angeles: College Book Store, 1965).

7. Quoted from James Q. Wilson, a professor of government at Harvard in an article

in the May 19, 1968 issue of the *New York Times Magazine* entitled, "Why We Are Having a Wave of Violence."

8. Angus Campbell and Howard Schuman, "Racial Attitudes in Fifteen American Cities" in *Supplementary Report of the National Advisory Commission on Civil Disorders* (Washington: Government Printing Office, 1968), p. 47.

9. Anthony Oberschall, "The Los Angeles Riot," *Social Problems* 15 (Winter 1968): 335–38 [reprinted in this volume].

10. Raymond Murphy and James Watson, "Levels of Aspiration, Discontent, and Support for Violence: A Test of the Expectation Hypothesis," paper presented at the 1969 annual meeting of the American Sociological Association in San Francisco, California, p. 12 [reprinted in this volume].

11. R. K. Newsom, "Relative Deprivation and Ghetto Riots," paper presented at the 1969 annual meeting of the Southwestern Social Science Association in Houston, Texas, p. 30.

12. Donald I. Warren, "Neighborhood Structure and Riot Behavior in Detroit," *Social Problems* 16 (Spring 1969): 483.

13. James Geschwender, Benjamin Singer, and Richard Osborn, "Social Isolation and Riot Participation," paper presented at the 1969 annual meeting of the American Sociological Association in San Francisco, California, p. 15.

14. Robert Fogelson and Robert Hill, "Who Riots? A Study of Participation in the 1967 Riots" in *Supplementary Report of the National Advisory Commission on Civil Disorders* (Washington, Government Printing Office, 1968), pp. 229–31.

15. Ibid., p. 235.

16. Joseph Boskin, "The Revolt of the Urban Ghettos, 1964–1967," *Annals of the American Academy Political and Social Science* 382 (March 1969): 1–14.

17. Alvin and Helen Gouldner, *Modern Sociology* (New York: Harcourt, Brace & Jovanovich, 1963), p. 218. A more comprehensive statement is that "property is the name for a concept that refers to the rights and obligations and the privileges and restrictions that govern the behavior of man in any society toward the scarce objects of value in that society." This definition and a general discussion of property is presented in David Sills, ed., *International Encyclopedia of the Social Sciences* (New York: MacMillan, 1968), Vol. 12, p. 590.

18. See Ralph Turner, "Collective Behavior" in Robert E. Faris, ed., *Handbook of Modern Sociology* (Chicago: Rand McNally, 1964); Russell R. Dynes and E. L. Quarantelli, "Group Behavior Under Stress: A Required Convergence of Organizational and Collective Behavior Perspectives," *Sociology and Social Research* 52 (July 1968): 416–29; and E. L. Quarantelli and Russell R. Dynes, "Looting in Civil Disorders: An Index of Social Change," *The American Behavioral Scientist* 2 (March-April 1968): 7–10.

19. Richard Hill and Calvin Larson, "Differential Ghetto Organization," paper presented at the 1969 annual meeting of the American Sociological Association in San Francisco, California, and Warren, "Neighborhood Structure and Riot Behavior in Detroit."

20. David Boesel, "Negro Youth and Ghetto Riots," paper presented at the 1968 annual meeting of the American Sociological Association in Boston, Massachusetts, and Bayard Rustin, "The Watts 'Manifesto' and the McCone Report," *Commentary*, March 1966.

21. Morris Janowitz, *Social Control of Escalated Riots* (Chicago: University of Chicago Center for Policy Study, 1968), pp. 32–33; and Hans W. Mattick, "The Form and Content of Recent Riots," *Midway* 9 (Summer 1968).

22. Eric Hobsbawm, *Primitive Rebels* (New York: Norton, 1959).

23. Eric Hobsbawm, *Labouring Men: Studies in the History of Labor* (New York: Basic Books, 1964), p. 21.

24. See Fogelson and Hill, "Who Riots?" and also Peter Rossi et al., "Between Black and White: The Faces of American Institutions in the Ghetto," in *Supplementary*

Report of the National Advisory Commission on Civil Disorders (Washington: Government Printing Office, 1968).

25. Campbell and Schuman, "Racial Attitudes in Fifteen American Cities," p. 50.
26. Jeffery Paige, "Political Orientation and Riot Participation," paper presented at the 1969 annual meeting of the American Sociological Association in San Francisco, California, p. 23.
27. Boesel, "Negro Youth and Ghetto Riots," p. 12.
28. "Progress report" of the Mayor's Special Task Force, Pittsburgh, Pennsylvania, 1968 which discusses the April 5–12 disturbances in the city. Similarly, when looting developed in St. Petersburg, Florida, on August 17, 1968, the police said the behavior was the result of a "planned program of harassment." *Columbus Dispatch,* August 17, 1968, p. 1.
29. Adrian Jones and Andrew Molnar, *Combating Subversively Manipulated Civil Disturbances* (Washington: Center for Research in Social Systems, 1966), p. 14
30. Gaston Rimilinger, "The Legitimation of Protest: A Comparative Study in Labor History," *Comparative Studies in Society and History* 2 (April 1960): 343.
31. Irving Horowitz, "Black Sociology," *Trans-action* 4 (September 1967); 8.
32. Arnold Feldman, "Violence and Volatility: The Likelihood of Revolution," in Harry Ekstein, ed., *Internal War* (New York: Free Press, 1964), p. 111.
33. Lewis A. Coser, "Some Social Functions of Violence," *Annals of the American Academy Political and Social Science* 364 (March 1966): 14–15.

CIVIL RIGHTS PROTEST AND RIOTS:
A DISAPPEARING DISTINCTION

James A. Geschwender

The civil rights movement has dominated much of the American scene from 1954 to the present, with urban disorders pretty well taking over center stage since 1963. The liberal segment of white America has generally had a positive image of the civil rights movement but has viewed big city riots with a mixture of fear and disgust. A number of social scientists also view civil rights activities and riots as two different and contradictory types of phenomena. This paper will take the assumption of difference as a hypothesis rather than as a postulate. In this discussion sociologists' conceptualizations of social movements and riots will be examined, characteristics of recent urban disorders will be evaluated, and conclusions will be drawn.

It must be emphasized that the problem to be examined is not one of mere labeling. This paper is concerned with the proper label for recent urban disorders, but only because the question has broader implications.

From the *Social Science Quarterly* 49 (December 1968): 474–84; reprinted by permission.

First, there are important theoretical considerations. The nature of the concepts used, the theories invoked, and the hypotheses drawn all will be influenced by the correct classification of the disorders as riots or as parts of a developing social movement, for the problem cannot be understood accurately by using an invalid classificatory scheme. If predictions of the future are to be accurate, we must start with a valid base.

The second implication—the application of sociological principles—is closely related to the need for accurate prediction. Social scientists cannot make useful recommendations for action to politicians or segments of society unless they have a correct image of the current expressions of black unrest, a correct image of the depth and intensity of unrest, a perception of the extent to which this unrest has crystallized into a prerevolutionary movement, and some reasonably accurate predictions for the future. The types of societal changes that will ameliorate conditions producing hostile outbursts will not be sufficient to change the direction of a social movement which is developing along potentially revolutionary lines.

HOSTILE OUTBURSTS AND SOCIAL MOVEMENTS

Neil J. Smelser has developed a highly elaborate conceptual framework for the analysis of collective behavior.[1] He uses a value-added approach in which six determinants (necessary conditions) of collective behavior combine to specify the nature and characteristics of any particular collective episode. The six determinants are structural conduciveness, structural strain, growth and spread of a generalized belief, precipitating factors, mobilization of participants for action, and the operation of social control.[2] Any particular form of collective behavior produced by these determinants may be analyzed in terms of four basic components of social action: values, norms, mobilization of motivation for organized action, and situational facilities.[3] Each component of social action is categorized into seven levels of specificity, but present purposes do not require a detailed exposition of the theory.

For Smelser, the crucial distinction between hostile outbursts (riots) and norm-oriented movements (that category of social movements which includes the civil rights movement) lies in the area of growth and spread of generalized beliefs. The value-added analysis of the development of hostile outbursts begins by examining ambiguity and anxiety. Anxiety is fused with the mobilization series to produce a generalized belief that some agent, or agents, is responsible for the anxiety-producing situation. This suspicion of agents is short-circuited to the selection of a particular kind of agent. A desire to punish, restrict, damage, or remove the agent then emerges, and wish-fulfillment beliefs of two types manifest themselves. They take the form of an exaggerated belief in the ability to punish agents of evil and to remove the evils ascribed to the agents. This belief is basically a generalized sense of omnipotence which is short-circuited to specific results.[4]

The early stages of the development of a norm-oriented movement are identical to those in the development of a hostile outburst. The norm-oriented movement, too, begins with ambiguity, anxiety, the attachment of the anxiety to some agent, and the exaggeration of the threatening nature of that agent. At this point, however, its development diverges. A belief develops that the normative control of the agent is inadequate and this belief becomes directed toward a particular set of laws or customs. Thus it comes to be accepted that the problem can be solved by changing the normative structure. This expectation becomes channeled into a decision about the particular type of normative change that would be expected to immobilize or destroy the agent, eliminating the source of the problem.[5]

The distinction between hostile outbursts and social movements focuses attention on the belief system. If the episode of collective behavior is seen as a direct attempt to attack or punish the agents of evil (in this case, police and white businessmen), then it is classed as an hostile outburst (a riot). However, if the episode of collective behavior is seen as a means of bringing about normative change to prevent the agents from working their evil, then it is termed a social movement. The presence or absence of scapegoating and/or violence does not determine the classification of a particular episode, because violence and scapegoating are elements of both hostile outbursts and norm-oriented movements. Smelser states that

> hostile outbursts are frequently adjuncts of larger-scale social movements. On certain occasions reform movements . . . may erupt into violence. Revolutionary movements . . . are frequently accompanied by violence. The primary difference among terms such as "riot," "revolt," "rebellion," "insurrection," and "revolution"—all of which involve hostile outbursts—stems from the scope of their associated social movements.[6]

The task, then, is to determine whether the recent urban disorders are isolated outbursts of pent-up hostility directed against perceived oppressors, such as police and white businessmen in the black ghetto, or part of a larger movement aimed at bringing about fundamental alterations in the normative order of American society. Probably a majority of white liberals and many social scientists have decided on the former alternative.[7]

CHARACTERISTICS OF THE DISORDERS

Research reports suggest that three aspects of the disorders contribute most to the labeling of the disorders as riots. First, the prime activity of most participants was looting.[8] Second, the disorders were spontaneous, relatively unorganized, and leaderless.[9] Third, the participants apparently did not attempt to seize permanent control of an area or specify political demands.[10] These objections will be examined one at a time.

Looting

First, the existence of looting, per se, should be investigated. Oberschall makes two points with regard to looting. He suggests that many petty thieves and small-time professional crooks came into the Watts area to engage in looting but left prior to the major waves of arrests. He indicates further that looting is a frequent occurrence in all disasters, natural or otherwise.[11] Both of these points may be well taken. Fires, floods, tornadoes, and riots all represent periods of upheaval. At such times, the burden upon police and other agents of social control is greatly increased. They are not in a position to enforce all aspects of the law and many persons take this opportunity to improve their lot temporarily by acquiring a ham, a television set, furniture, or liquor. Looting during a riot may be, as Lee Rainwater describes it, "a kind of primitive attempt at an income redistribution."[12] In other words, the "have-nots" temporarily increase their possessions without seriously attacking the distributive system.

This view must be balanced with an alternative one, for theft of any sort may be considered an act of rebellion. Hobsbawm has documented the fact that banditry in peasant societies has often been a form of social protest and represents an archaic form of social movement.[13] In such a case, the bandit who followed the Robin Hood model of stealing from the privileged and redistributing a portion of his gains to the underprivileged often had the support and affection of the peasantry. American history has its counterparts. Jesse James, Pretty Boy Floyd, and Babyface Nelson are only a few of the many American bandits who have been renowned in song and legend for their fights against the propertied and their generosity toward the needy. Theft, when directed against the right targets, may be seen as a direct attack upon the exploiter and upon the whole system of exploitation.

There is evidence that looting during the recent urban disorders was so directed. Rustin indicates that in the Watts riot the victims of looting and arson were whites rather than blacks.[14] He further points out that not all whites were victims; the white-owned businesses that had reputations for fair dealing and nondiscriminatory practices were spared. In Detroit some black-owned businesses were also targets.[15] These, however, were black merchants who had the same reputation for exploitation as did many whites.[16] There is, incidentally, some indication that in Detroit a group of individuals provided leadership in looting without participating in it themselves.[17]

A more basic criticism of the Oberschall interpretation of looting must be made, however. Dynes and Quarantelli state that looting rarely occurs in natural disasters and the little that does occur differs in many significant respects from that which occurs in urban disorders.[18] They cite one example of major looting in a natural disaster (the Chicago snowstorms of January and February, 1967) but suggest that the similarity in area of incidence may mean that this looting was a continuation of the looting during the disorder of 1966.[19]

If looting is characteristic of the current urban disorders but rarely occurs in natural disasters, it cannot be explained in the same terms in both cases. It is doubtful that the Dynes-Quarantelli interpretation in terms of property redefinition is adequate.[20] Looting appears to be more than simply a protest against the prevailing definition of property rights. The selection of white and black exploiters as targets of looting and arson suggests that it is an attack upon the system of distribution of property and that it also provides an opportunity to acquire property. In short, looting constitutes an attack upon exploitation rather than upon exploiters—an act more characteristic of social movements than of hostile outbursts.

Organization

Second, the fact that the disorders were spontaneous rather than the result of conspiracy is informative. The Kerner Commission saw no evidence of conspiracy, of deliberate incitement, or of organization in the disorders.[21] This is, however, no reason to conclude that they are not part of a social movement. To make such a statement is to misunderstand the nature of a social movement.

The treatment of social movements by Lang and Lang provides instructive insights.[22] They define a social movement as a "large-scale, widespread, and continuing, elementary collective action in pursuit of an objective that affects and shapes the social order in some fundamental aspect." [23] A social movement is seen as having organized associations at its core that provide general direction and focus; but it also includes large, unorganized segments pushing in the same direction but not integrated with the core associations. Lang and Lang specifically state that "unless we are able to distinguish between the core group and a larger mass of supporters not formally joined, we are not dealing with a social movement." [24]

Not all participants in every social movement need to have identical definitions of goals, strategy, and tactics; it is only necessary that they share the same general objectives. The degree of mutual cooperation and coordination of activities is, in fact, problematic in any given social movement. Lang and Lang state:

> One group working for a cause . . . may appear to be so involved in its quarrels with another group sharing its objective that members of both groups hardly seem to be participants in the same movement. Yet, however riddled by factional disputes a movement may be, the knowledge that other groups are working toward the same ends gives each unit a sense of participation in it. They compete to see which is the purest representative of the doctrine.[25]

Thus it would seem that any definition of the civil rights movement must be broad enough to include such disparate organizations as the Urban League, National Association for the Advancement of Colored People, Southern Christian Leadership Conference, Student Nonviolent Coordinating Committee, and the Congress of Racial Equality, provided they are all working for the same general objectives, such as the furthering of the position and rights of the black American. The definition must also be broad enough to include the unorganized participants of demonstrations, boycotts, and even urban disorders, provided, again, that the participants have the same general goals.[26] The lack of organization does not, *ipso facto*, exclude looters, snipers, and arsonists from the civil rights movement. Their motives must be examined. This will be done later in this paper.

Tactics

Third, does the absence of stated political demands and/or any attempt to seize permanent control of a geographic area exclude urban disorders from the category of social movements? The answer to this question requires a comprehensive analysis of the nature and role of tactics in a social movement.

The reluctance to treat urban disorders as a segment of the civil rights movement very likely stems from the tendency to define the movement in terms of its organized core associations and to define its tactics in terms of the more respectable ones of court suits, nonviolent direct action, and voter registration drives. Killian and Grigg note, however, that each of the above tactics emerged when previous modes of behavior proved inadequate in bringing about sufficiently broad results as rapidly as desired.[27] It is plausible to assume that segments of the black community have become dissatisfied with the slow, token changes brought about by the respectable tactics and are developing more drastic ones to increase the speed and scope of change. Oberschall lends support to this interpretation when he states:

> The collective significance of these events, however, is that the civil rights gains made by the Negro movement in the last few years, which have benefitted the Southern Negro and middle-class Negroes, have not altered the situation of the lower-class urban Negroes outside of the South and have not removed the fundamental sources of grievances of a large proportion of the Negro population in the U.S.[28]

The historical role of urban mobs in controlling ruling elites and in attempting to bring about changes is well documented. Hobsbawm states:

> Provided the ruler did his duty, the populace was prepared to defend him with enthusiasm. But if he did not, it rioted until he did. . . . The treatment of perennial rioting kept rulers ready to control prices and to distribute work or largess, or indeed to listen to their faithful commons on other matters.[29]

> Nevertheless, such a symbiosis of the "mob" and the people against whom it rioted was not necessarily the fundamental factor about its politics. The "mob" rioted, but it also sometimes made revolutions. . . , It was poor; "they" were rich; life was fundamentally unjust for the poor. These were the foundations of its attitude. . . . The implicit revolutionism of the "mob" was primitive; in its way it was the metropolitan equivalent of the stage of political consciousness represented by social banditry in the countryside.[30]

Thus, a plausible assumption is that the civil rights movement has undergone an evolution of tactics. As one tactic proves inadequate to the task it is replaced by another seen as more adequate. In the recent past, accommodation gave way to court suits. The orderly tactics gave way to the less orderly tactics of direct action, which Waskow analyzes under the concept of "creative disorder." [31] "Creative disorder" may now be giving way to "creative rioting." [32] Ghetto riots may be an attempt to use violent disorder creatively to bring about change. This does not mean that all individuals involved in the civil rights movement are now, or will be, participating in riots. There always has been a tactical division of labor: some civil rights adherents use court suits; others engage in nonviolent direct action; others, however, may have moved on to creative rioting.[33]

The stating of political demands and the attempts to permanently occupy and control a given territory are tactics which are likely to appear in a fully developed insurrection or revolution. The tactic of creative rioting represents a move in this direction developing from creative disorder. It is an intermediate tactic which does not go as far as revolution. That is, it may appear in prerevolutionary situations—situations which have the potential for developing into revolutions but which will not necessarily do so.

Oberschall may not be entirely accurate when he states that political demands are missing in the current urban disorders. The Kerner Commission report states:

> In 21 of the 24 disturbances surveyed, discussion or negotiation occurred during the disturbances. These took the form of relatively formal meetings between government officials and Negroes during which grievances and issues were discussed and means were sought to restore order.[34]

These meetings usually were with "established leaders" but youths were involved in 13 discussions. The combination of discussion of grievances and the presence of the more militant youths indicates the presence of some sort of political demands even though no attempt to occupy territory permanently may have been made. Urban disorders, therefore, may be a new civil rights tactic which stops short of revolution.

The case for creative rioting—ghetto riots as an integral part of the civil rights movement—has not yet been fully demonstrated. The nature and pattern of looting lend more support to this interpretation than they do to the alternative interpretation of urban disorders as hostile outbursts. The lack of deliberate instigation or organization in the disorders is neutral, as it is equally consistent with either interpretation. The lack of an attempt to assume permanent control of a given territory does not prevent the current ghetto riots from being a step in the evolution of tactics within the civil rights movement just short of full-blown insurrection. Due to the inconclusive nature of the foregoing, one must analyze the characteristics of riot participants prior to drawing final conclusions. The prime source of data will be the recent surveys of riot participation conducted in Detroit and Newark.

CHARACTERISTICS OF RIOT PARTICIPANTS

A number of characteristics of self-identified rioters or riot supporters correspond to those noted in the sociological literature as characterizing individuals who are prone to participate in social movements or revolutions. Both Lyford P. Edwards and Crane Brinton state that individuals who perceive their legitimate aspirations for mobility to be blocked are especially prone to engage in revolutionary behavior.[35] The Kerner Commission report notes that the self-identified rioters in Newark were significantly (p<.05) more likely than the self-reported noninvolved individuals to believe that their level of education entitled them to a job with more income and responsibility than the one they presently possessed.[36] The Newark rioters were also less likely than the noninvolved to perceive that there was an opportunity for them to acquire their desired job (p<.06) and significantly more likely (p<.025) to believe that discrimination was the factor preventing them from so doing.[37] No comparable data from Detroit are available. Taken jointly, these characteristics indicate the existence of the blocked-mobility syndrome that Edwards and Brinton find typical of potential revolutionaries.

Status inconsistency also has been interpreted as a characteristic that predisposes individuals toward participation in social movements or revolutions.[38] Evidence suggests that rioters tend to be status-inconsistent. The Detroit rioters were significantly *better educated* than the noninvolved (p.<.05) and the Newark rioters, too, tended to be better educated than the noninvolved (p<.06).[39] Both Newark and Detroit rioters tended to have *lower incomes* than the noninvolved, although neither difference is statistically significant.[40] The Newark rioters also tended to have lower job status than the noninvolved (p<.06).[41] No data on occupational status are available from Detroit. While there is no difference between rioters and the noninvolved in terms of current rate of unemployment, the Newark rioters were significantly more likely to have been unemployed for a month or longer within the past year (p<.05).[42] No comparable data are available from Detroit.

These data together indicate that rioters were considerably less likely to be able to bring their occupational status, income, or employment status up to a level comparable to their level of education. When this observation is combined with the fact that Negroes are more likely than whites to have their levels of occupation and income lag behind their educational level, then there can be no doubt that active rioters are status inconsistent —and inconsistent to a greater degree than the noninvolved.[43] More important, the rioters' "profiles" are inconsistent with high education—low income or high education-low occupation profiles, which are precisely the ones most likely to produce participation in extremist social movements of leftist inclinations.[44]

The fact that rioters exhibit status inconsistency and possess thwarted aspirations does not in itself demonstrate that riots are part of a social movement. One additional factor, however, lends credence to this interpretation. Ransford found that Watts Negroes who were socially isolated from whites were significantly more willing to use violence than were those with greater contact with whites.[45] This conclusion agrees with the suggestion by Marx that the isolation of an aggrieved category of persons into an interacting collectivity is likely to produce a conflict group with a high degree of group consciousness and an awareness of a common enemy.[46] The likelihood that racially isolated blacks may develop "black consciousness" and a hostility toward whites which could manifest itself in rioting as revolutionary activity gains support from data on the Detroit and Newark rioters. Both Newark and Detroit rioters were significantly more likely than the noninvolved to believe that Negroes are more dependable than whites ($p<.05$ and $<.001$, respectively) and that Negroes are "nicer" than whites ($p<.025$ and $<.001$, respectively).[47] Newark rioters were significantly more likely than the noninvolved to describe themselves as "black" ($p<.025$) and were more prone to believe that all Negroes should study African history and languages ($p<.06$).[48] No comparable data are available from Detroit. Newark rioters were significantly more likely than the noninvolved to believe that presently integrated civil rights groups would be more effective without whites ($p<.005$) and to admit that sometimes they hated whites ($p<.001$).[49] While there are no data on the likelihood that Detroit rioters hated whites, they, also, were more likely than the noninvolved to say that integrated civil rights groups would be more effective without whites ($p<.10$).[50]

These data strongly suggest that rioters are individuals largely isolated from whites, that they interact with blacks who share common grievances, that they develop a high level of hostility toward whites, combined with a high level of black consciousness, and that they subsequently participate in riots as a means of attacking the "system." In short, they are participating in a social movement that may or may not reach revolutionary proportions.

The suggestion presented above—that urban riots may represent an evolution of tactics from the more respectable to the more violent—gains support from the following facts. Newark rioters were significantly more likely than the noninvolved to participate in discussions of Negro rights ($p<.025$), to participate in activities of civil rights groups ($p<.05$), to identify political figures ($p<.025$), to be politically knowledgeable ($p<.025$), and to not trust the Newark government to do what is right ($p<.10$).[51] While there are no directly comparable data from Detroit, the rioters there were significantly more likely than the noninvolved to feel that anger toward politicians ($p<.05$) and toward the police ($p<.05$) had much to do with causing the riots.[52]

CONCLUSION

The rioters discussed above are not the normally apathetic, noninvolved individuals who participate in hostile outbursts. They tend to be politically knowledgeable and active in civil rights activities. Many of them have apparently come to the conclusion that traditional political and civil rights tactics cannot bring about desired results and thus they have shifted to newer tactics. This interpretation is supported by the desire of a large number of rioters to exclude whites from civil rights organizations. The theoretically relevant characteristics of thwarted aspirations and status inconsistency suggest, but do not demonstrate, this conclusion. The factor of racial isolation, though, pushes further in the direction indicated. Political knowledgeability, civil rights activities, black consciousness, hostility toward whites, and mistrust of government "put the icing on the cake" and make the conclusion emphatic.

The earlier discussion of looting strongly suggested that current urban disorders were a developing part of the civil rights movement. The discussions of degree of organization of riots and of tactics were consistent with the interpretation of urban disorders as either hostile outbursts or segments of a social movement. The discussion of the characteristics of rioters, however, removed remaining doubts. The present author no longer questions that the urban disorders are, in fact, creative rioting. Creative rioting falls clearly within the evolutionary pattern of the civil rights movement, a social movement which may or may not eventually become revolutionary.

This thesis should not be misconstrued; this paper does not contend that all urban disorders were creative rioting. The outbreaks of 1964 in Harlem, Rochester, Jersey City, and Philadelphia may have been simple hostile outbursts, although they did bring about a response on the community, state, and national levels. As subsequent riots continued to bring about real, if limited, results, individuals may have become aware of riots as a potentially successful tactic. This is not to say that the riots were deliberately instigated. Rather, a potential riot situation may have made some individuals aware of the utility of rioting, which in turn stimulated riot behavior. Once a riot was underway, other individuals were motivated to continue and direct it. Thus, rioting shifts from the category of a hostile outburst to that of a creative force in the civil rights movement.

NOTES

1. Neil J. Smelser, *Theory of Collective Behavior* (New York: Free Press, 1963).
2. Ibid., pp. 14–17.
3. Ibid., pp. 23–28.
4. Ibid., pp. 101–3.
5. Ibid., pp. 111–12.
6. Ibid., p. 227.
7. See, for example, Allen D. Grimshaw, "Civil Disturbance, Racial Revolt, Class Assault: Three Views of Urban Violence," paper presented before the American Association for the Advancement of Science, New York, December 28, 1967; and Anthony Oberschall, "The Los Angeles Riot," *Social Problems* 15 (Winter 1968): 322–41 [reprinted in this volume]. For examples of sociologists taking positions similar to the one presented herein, see Lewis M. Killian, *The Impossible Revolution* (New York: Random House, 1968); and Robert Blauner, "Whitewash over Watts," *Trans-action* 3 (March-April 1966): 9.

8. See, for example, Tom Parmenter, "Breakdown of Law and Order," *Trans-action* 9 (September 1967): 13–21; Oberschall, "Los Angeles Riot," p. 327; and *Report of the National Advisory Commission on Civil Disorders* (New York: Bantam Books, 1968), p. 93.

9. See, for example, Oberschall, "Los Angeles Riot," p. 341; *Report on Civil Disorders*, pp. 201–2; and Arthur I. Waskow, *From Race Riot to Sit-In* (Garden City, N.Y.: Doubleday, 1967), p. 260.

10. Oberschall, "Los Angeles Riot," p. 340.

11. Ibid., pp. 335–38.

12. Lee Rainwater, "Open Letter on White Justice and the Riots," *Trans-action* 9 (September 1967): 25.

13. E. J. Hobsbawm, *Primitive Rebels* (New York: Norton, 1959), esp. Ch. 2.

14. Bayard Rustin, "The Watts 'Manifesto' and the McCone Report," *Commentary* 41 (March 1966): 29–35.

15. *Report on Civil Disorders*, p. 88.

16. Private interviews with observers of the disorder.

17. Louis E. Lomax, "Seeds of Riot Planted Here by Salesmen," Detroit *News*, August 6, 1967, pp. 1–2.

18. Russell Dynes and E. L. Quarantelli, "What Looting in Civil Disturbances Really Means," *Trans-action* 5 (May 1968): 9–14.

19. Ibid., p. 12.

20. Ibid., pp. 13–14.

21. *Report on Civil Disorders*, pp. 201–2.

22. Kurt Lang and Gladys Engel Lang, *Collective Dynamics* (New York: Crowell, 1961), pp. 489–544.

23. Ibid., p. 490.

24. Ibid., p. 497.

25. Ibid., p. 496.

26. Although probably clear from the context, the term "civil rights movement" is not here used in the narrow sense of attempts to acquire legal rights and legal equality through normative means. It is used in the broader sense of all attempts to gain legal rights and legal equality as well as those attempts to translate legal rights into actual functioning rights and equality.

27. Lewis Killian and Charles Grigg, *Racial Crisis in America* (Englewood Cliffs, N.J.: Prentice-Hall, 1964), pp. 18–23.

28. Oberschall, "Los Angeles Riot," p. 341.

29. Hobsbawm, *Primitive Rebels*, p. 116.

30. Ibid., p. 118.

31. Waskow, *From Race Riot to Sit-In*, pp. 225–90.

32. "Creative rioting" as used herein refers to a particular tactical type of behavior aimed at bringing about societal change. It involves the conscious and deliberate use of violent attacks against property and/or persons. The violence against property may be either of a destructive or of a confiscatory (theft) nature. Violence against persons usually is not directed randomly against persons as individuals or members of a group; rather, it is frequently directed against persons as symbols of authority or oppression. It tends to be incidental to attacks upon property or the system of exploitation.

   Thus, creative rioting differs from creative disorder in that the latter is nonviolent and, while disruptive of societal processes, is not destructive of property. Creative rioting also differs from revolution in that it tends to be too short-lived, less organized, and less coordinated than required for a full-scale, violent attempt to seize control of society.

33. Similarly, there may be a division of labor within a rioting mob. Some participants

may consciously use rioting as a tactic to promote change, while others simply attempt to improve their personal well-being by acquiring more possessions, and still others try to avenge real or alleged wrongs. The latter two groups are not, strictly speaking, using creative rioting, but by swelling the number of rioters—thereby increasing the duration and intensity of the disorders—they contribute to the overall effect of the creative rioters.

34. *Report on Civil Disorders,* pp. 126–27.

35. Lyford P. Edwards, *The Natural History of Revolution* (Chicago: The University of Chicago Press, 1927), p. 30; and Crane Brinton, *The Anatomy of Revolution* (New York: Norton, 1938), p. 78.

36. *Report on Civil Disorders,* p. 127, n. 130. Henceforth, self-reported rioters and self-reported noninvolved will be referred to, respectively, as rioters and noninvolved.

37. Ibid., p. 175, nn. 131 and 132.

38. For a summary of such literature see James A. Geschwender, "Continuities in Theories of Status Inconsistency and Cognitive Dissonance," *Social Forces* 46 (December 1967): 160–71.

39. *Report on Civil Disorders,* p. 174, n. 126.

40. Ibid., p. 174, n. 124.

41. Ibid., p. 175, n. 129.

42. Ibid., p. 175, nn. 127 and 128.

43. James A. Geschwender, "Negro Education: The False Faith," *Phylon* 29 (Winter 1968): 371–78; and James A. Geschwender, "Social Structure and the Negro Revolt: An Examination of Some Hypotheses," *Social Forces* 43 (December 1964): 248–56 [reprinted in this volume].

44. Geschwender, "Continuities in Theories," pp. 169–71.

45. H. Edward Ransford, "Isolation, Powerlessness, and Violence: A Study of Attitudes and Participation in the Watts Riot," *American Journal of Sociology* 73 (March 1968; 586.

46. Reinhard Bendix and Seymour Martin Lipset, "Karl Marx' Theory of Social Classes," in Reinhard Bendix and Seymour Martin Lipset, eds., *Class, Status and Power* (New York: Free Press, 1953), pp. 26–35.

47. *Report on Civil Disorders,* p. 175, n. 134.

48. Ibid., p. 175, n. 135.

49. Ibid., p. 175, n. 136.

50. Ibid.

51. Ibid., pp. 177–78, nn. 140, 139, 141.

52. Ibid., p. 178, n. 142.

Jules J. Wanderer

This paper is divided into two sections. The first describes an Index of
Riot Severity. The second reports the results of an examination of select
social, economic, and demographic variables to ascertain which among
them is correlated to riot severity as measured by the Index.

AN INDEX OF RIOT SEVERITY

The Index is based upon the analysis of seventy-five riots and civil-criminal disorders reported to have taken place during the summer of 1967.[1]
The analysis employed Guttman scaling techniques, and the derived Index is a Guttman-type scale. Information used in the construction of the
scale was provided by mayors' offices at the request of a U.S. Senate subcommittee.[2] The subcommittee's request for information from cities experiencing major riots and civil-criminal disorders covered the years
1965–67. For each of these years the subcommittee tabulated the following
kinds of information: date of disorder, the city in which it occurred, 1960
population, percentage Negro, number of civilians and law officers killed
and injured, types of criminality (e.g., sniping, vandalism, arson, interference with firemen), the number of arrests, the number of convictions,
police action, estimated financial losses, and a mayor's report of "trigger-
ing incident."

The information selected for the construction of the Index was
based upon the subcommittee's tabulations for 1967, from April 1 to September 8. While an index of riot severity might ideally incorporate information from diverse sources, the Index reported here includes only those
items that could be directly ascertained from official mayors' reports to
the Senate subcommittee.

The final scale includes the following seven items of riot severity:
killing, calling of the National Guard, calling of the state police, sniping,
looting, interference with firemen, and vandalism.[3] The Coefficient of
Reproducibility of this Guttman scale of riot severity for seventy-five riots
and seven items of severity is 92 per cent. Table 1 shows the obtained
scale.

With one exception, the items included in the scale are in the same
form as they appeared in the mayors' reports, that is, indications of the
presence or absence of the event. The exception involves the alteration of
a quantitatively defined variable, number of civilian and police deaths,
so that it could be coded simply as a dichotomy: "no deaths" and
"N-deaths."

From *The American Journal of Sociology* 74 (March 1969): 500–505. Copyright ©
1969 by The University of Chicago; reprinted by permission of the author and
publisher.

TABLE 1. Guttman Scale of Riot Severity

Scale Type	% Cities (N=75)	Items Reported	Scale Errors
8	4	No scale items	2
7	19	"Vandalism"	10
6	13	All of the above + "interference with firemen"	3
5	16	All of the above + "looting"	3
4	13	All of the above + "sniping"	7
3	7	All of the above + "called State Police"	4
2	17	All of the above + "called National Guard"	11
1	11	All of the above + "law officer or civilian killed"	2
Total			$\overline{42}$

Note. — Coefficient = $1 - 42/515 = 92\%$.

Events were selected as items for the scale if they appeared to be logically linked or related to riot severity. To obtain a Guttman scale means, of course, that the items are located in a systematic and cumulative fashion along the unidimensional continuum of severity and that the continuum also locates cities on the severity scale.

Cities are organized into eight scale types, or eight categories ordered on the severity dimension. Table 2 shows the cities that compose each scale type. The reader will note that each riot is treated as a unit.[4] The alternative is to treat each city as a unit, thus eliminating the repetition of those cities with two or more riots. As a consequence of adopting the riot as the unit in developing the Guttman scale, one city is included three times; three cities are included twice each; and one city is included four times.[5]

SOME CORRELATES: A COMPARISON WITH OTHER STUDIES

Explanations of riots have followed from different lines of inquiry. Newspaper reports, personal accounts, and biographical statements have supplied us with a body of popular notions about riots, their causes, courses, and effects. Findings of technical studies have thrown additional light on the characteristics of large numbers of disorders.[6] In these studies, findings usually emerge from a comparison of riot with nonriot (control) cities.[7] In the discussion that follows, however, variables are examined in terms of their relationship to *riot severity,* not in terms of their relationship to the *presence* or *absence* of rioting.

Lieberson and Silverman studied seventy-six events classifiable as Negro-white race riots between 1913 and 1963. They found that when riot

TABLE 2. Cities by Scale Types

Scale type 8:
Louisville, Ky.
West Palm Beach, Fla.
Mount Clemons, Mich.

Scale type 7:
Fresno, Calif.
Kansas City, Mo.
Omaha, Neb.
Montgomery, Ala.
New Britain, Conn.
Houston, Tex.
Sacramento, Calif.
Massillon, Ohio
Rockford, Ill.
Elgin, Ill.
Kalamazoo, Mich.
Albany, N.Y.
Lima, Ohio
Peekskill, N.Y.

Scale type 6:
Hamilton, Ohio
Long Beach, Calif.
Paterson, N.J.
Erie, Pa.
Wyandanch, N.Y.
Hartford, Conn.
Greensboro, N.C.
Erie, Pa.
New York City, N.Y.
Hattiesburg, Miss.

Scale type 5:
Birmingham, Ala.
Cincinnati, Ohio
Buffalo, N.Y.
Dayton, Ohio
Mt. Vernon, N.Y.
Passaic, N.J.
Cincinnati, Ohio
New York City, N.Y.
Washington, D.C.
Syracuse, N.Y.
Minneapolis, Minn.
Toledo, Ohio

Scale type 4:
San Bernardino, Calif.
Houston, Tex.
Peoria, Ill.
Waterbury, Conn.
Riviera Beach, Fla.
Chicago, Ill.
New York City, N.Y.
Englewood, N.J.
Boston, Mass.
New York City, N.Y.

Scale type 3:
New Haven, Conn.
Saginaw, Mich.
Wichita, Kan.
Wilmington, Del.
Flint, Mich.

Scale type 2:
Portland, Ore.
South Bend, Ind.
Providence, R.I.
Tampa, Fla.
Waterloo, Iowa
San Francisco, Calif.
Poughkeepsie, N.Y.
Phoenix, Ariz.
Nashville, Tenn.
Grand Rapids, Mich.
Cambridge, Md.
Tucson, Ariz.
San Francisco, Calif.

Scale type 1:
Milwaukee, Wis.
Rochester, N.Y.
Detroit, Mich.
Pontiac, Mich.
Cincinnati, Ohio
Newark, N.J.
Plainfield, N.J.
Jackson, Miss.

and control cities were compared, (1) percentage increase of Negro population was unrelated to the presence of riots, (2) racial composition did not distinguish between riot and control cities, and (3) housing measured in terms of higher or lower quality did not distinguish between riot and control cities.[8]

Percentage increase of non-whites

Lieberson and Silverman found that percentage increase in Negroes did not differentiate between riot and control cities. They discovered "no sizable difference between riot and control cities in their percentage gains in Negro population during the decades." [9] For each of the cities in the scale reported here,[10] the percentage increase of non-whites in the total population of the riot city in the decade 1950–60 was computed.[11] The Spearman rank correlation coefficient, computed between the *scale types* ranked on severity and mean percentage non-white increase, was .833, significant beyond the .01 level.[12] It seems that while percentage increase of Negroes is unrelated to the presence or absence of a riot, the percentage increase of non-whites is significantly related to riot severity as measured by the Index. Once a riot takes place, the greater the percentage increase of non-whites, the greater the severity of the riot.

Racial composition

Included in each mayor's report was information pertaining to the proportion of the city's population that was Negro. For each scale type the mean percentage of Negroes was computed. The rank order of scale-type mean percentage did not correlate significantly with the Index. A second step involved the elimination of southern cities and again computing scale-type mean percentages. The rank correlation was not significant. It appears that racial composition is neither related to the presence or absence of riots [13] nor to riot severity as measured by the Index.

Housing

Six variables relating to housing were examined to ascertain their relationship to riot severity: (1) percentage living in multi-family dwellings, (2) percentage living in newer than ten-year-old dwellings, (3) percentage in units with substandard plumbing, (4) percentage in housing with more than one person per room, and (6) percentage who owned their own homes.[14] For each scale type, the median percentage was computed for each of the six variables. Of the six variables, only one showed a statistically significant rank correlation between median percentage and riot severity. Measured by the Spearman rank correlation, riot severity and percentage living in newer than ten-year-old dwellings correlated −.86, significant beyond the .01 level. Once a riot occurs, the fewer non-whites in dwellings constructed in the decade 1950–60, the greater the severity of the riot. None of the other five housing variables showed any systematic variation by the Index of Riot Severity.

Economics of housing

Three additional housing variables were examined: (1) median non-white rent, (2) median value of non-white place of living, and (3) median percentage of non-white home owners.[15] For each of the variables, scale-type medians were computed and correlated with riot severity. None showed any relationship to severity.

Density

It is popularly believed that areas of high population density provide arenas for a variety of disruptive behaviors. For each scale type the mean

population density was computed.[16] The Spearman rank correlation coefficient between scale types and mean population density was .18, not
significant at the .05 level. It may be concluded that intensity of riots and
civil-criminal disorders as measured by the Index is not related to population density.

Larceny and assault

It may be thought that cities with traditions of violence and criminality lend themselves to the generation of more severe riots than cities
without such a tradition. One measure of criminal tradition is indicated
by the aggravated assault rate and the larceny rate of each city.[17] The
mean aggravated assault rate for each scale type was computed and
ranked. The rank correlation between riot intensity and mean aggravated
assault rates as measured by the Spearman rank correlation is negligible.

In the same fashion, the mean larceny rate for each scale type and
riot intensity were correlated. The Spearman rank correlation coefficient
was .24, not significant at the .05 level.

Two measures of criminality are found to be unrelated to the severity
of disorders as measured by the Index.

Police preparation

To what extent are the preparations of the police before the outbreak of disorders related to the subsequent intensity of the disorder?
Eight types of information on police preparations were examined.[18] They
include: (1) presence of in-service training for police, (2) riot training for
police, (3) presence of an auxiliary police force, (4) riot training for the
auxiliary police, (5) mutual aid arrangements with a neighboring law enforcement agency, (6) presence of a special riot unit on the police force,
(7) presence of a special riot plan, and (8) use of dogs to control crowds
of people.

Only two of the above variables showed a tendency to vary with riot
severity, and just one correlated significantly. The correlation between
riot severity and mean percentage of scale-type cities employing dogs was
.56, not significant at the .05 level. The mean percentage of cities in each
scale type that reported having a special riot plan was computed and
correlated with riot severity. The Spearman rank correlation coefficient
was .70, significant beyond the .05 level.[19]

Interpretation of the relationship between the variable police preparation and riot severity poses special difficulties. Previously discussed
variables did not imply direct human involvement in anticipation of riots
and civil-criminal disorders. Consequently a significant correlation between riot intensity and police preparation may be interpreted in different
ways. The correlation may lend support to the assertion that the magnitude of the riot was accurately assessed by the police beforehand and that
their preparations thus corresponded to the severity of the riot. On the
other hand, a contradictory assertion suggests that police preparation is
an example of the self-fulfilling prophecy and is a factor in the escalation
of the riot.

The absence of a statistically significant correlation between police preparation and subsequent riot intensity may also be interpreted in the same fashion. Either the police overprepared, or an accurate assessment of the potential led to preparations that did, in fact, reduce the intensity of the disorders. A final interpretation suggests that adequate police preparation might even have prevented the start of the disorder.

Sniping

Janowitz distinguished between two patterns of riots in American cities, communal and commodity riots.[20] The latter are of recent vintage and characterized by widespread use of rifles and other arms among rioters. It can be seen that in the scale of riot severity reported here, thirty-six scale-type cities reported sniping (see Tables 1 and 2). There are scale errors; in fact, thirty-two cities reported sniping. Thus sniping appears as an event midway along the continuum of severity, occurring in less than 50 per cent of the riots and civil-criminal disorders reported to the Senate subcommittee.

CONCLUSION

It has been shown that while certain variables do not correlate with the presence or absence of riots in American cities, they do correlate with riot severity. Such variables are more influential in determining the severity of a riot, once it has begun, than they are in determining the outbreak of that riot.

The Index—a Guttman-type scale—suggests that the events that constitute riots and civil-criminal disorders are *not* bizarre, non-patterned, or randomly generated.[21] On the contrary, employing the properties of Guttman scales, we may predict the sequence of events for levels of riot severity. The Index was developed from materials describing disorders occurring in 1967. Future riots and civil-criminal disorders may not be similarly constituted. Either the set of events or the sequence of events may be altered by social existential conditions.

NOTES

ACKNOWLEDGEMENT: I wish to acknowledge the assistance of Alfred J. Claassen, Hunter H. Durning, Patricia L. Gotchall, and Sigmund W. Krane, who prepared some of the materials used in the following analysis. Tables 1 and 2 were previously published in "1967 Riots: A Test of the Congruity of Events," *Social Problems* 16, No. 2 (Fall 1968); 193–98.

1. Reported by mayors in *Riots: Civil and Criminal Disorders* (Hearings before the Permanent Subcommittee on Investigation of the Committee on Investigation of the Committee on Government Operations, U.S. Senate, 90th Cong., 1st sess., November 1, 2, 3, and 6, 1967. Part 1. [Washington, D.C., Government Printing Office, 1967]).

2. Of 137 cities contacted, 128 responded with reports for the years 1965–67.

3. These items are ordered from most to least severe, or from least to most frequently reported. One aspect of the scale as shown in Table 1 should be noted. Of the cities, 4 per cent did not report any of the items in the ordered sequence generated by the Guttman scale. Since the item defined as "not responding to any of the items" lacks sufficiently large marginals to be considered "scalable," it might be dropped from the scale. The inclusion of that item, however, does not inflate the Coefficient of Reproducibility; in fact, its inclusion deflates the Coefficient. In order to preserve the substantive character of the sequence of events, the item is included in the scale presented here.

4. This approach has been used widely. See Stanley Lieberson and Arnold R. Silverman, "Precipitants and Conditions of Race Riots," *American Sociological Review* 30 (December 1965); 887–98 [reprinted in this volume]; and Milton Bloombaum, "The Conditions Underlying Race Riots as Portrayed by Multi-dimensional Scalogram Analysis: A Re-analysis of Lieberson and Silverman's Data," *American Sociological Review* 33 (February 1968): 76–91.

5. Cincinnati reported three disorders; Erie, Houston, and San Francisco reported two disorders; and New York City reported four.

6. Recent examples, to name just a few, include Peter M. Green and Ruth H. Cheney, "Urban Planning and Urban Revolt: A Case Study," *Progressive Architecture* (January 1968): 134–56; Anthony Oberschall, "The Los Angeles Riots of August 1965," *Social Problems* 15 (Winter 1968): 322–41 [reprinted in this volume]; Tom Parmenter, "Breakdown of Law and Order," *Trans-action* 4 (September 1967): 13–22, which is but one of a series of papers in the same issue analyzing urban violence; Jerry Cohen and William S. Murphy, *Burn, Baby, Burn* (New York: Dutton, 1966); Morris Janowitz, *Social Control of Escalated Riots* (Chicago: University of Chicago Center for Policy Study, 1968); Lieberson and Silverman, "Precipitants and Conditions of Race Riots"; Bloombaum, "The Conditions Underlying Race Riots"; and Irving Louis Horowitz and Martin Liebowitz, "Social Deviance and Political Marginality: Toward a Redefinition of the Relation between Sociology and Politics," *Social Problems* 15 (Winter 1968): 280–96.

7. Lieberson and Silverman, "Precipitants and Conditions of Race Riots," and Bloombaum, "The Conditions Underlying Race Riots."

8. These are only three of the variables that were examined by Lieberson and Silverman.

9. Lieberson and Silverman, "Precipitating Conditions . . . ," p. 893.

10. Southern cities were omitted from the calculations.

11. Source of information is *United States Bureau of Census: County and City Data Book, 1967* (Washington, D.C.: Government Printing Office, 1967), pp. 464–572.

12. A description of Spearman rank correlation may be found in Sidney Siegel, *Nonparametric Statistics* (New York: McGraw-Hill, 1956), pp. 202–11.

13. As reported in Lieberson and Silverman, "Precipitating Condition . . . ," pp. 893–94.

14. Source of information on non-whites is *United States Bureau of the Census: Census of Housing* (Washington, D.C.: Government Printing Office, 1960), Table 8.

15. Source of information for variables (1) and (2) is *ibid.* Source of information for variable (3) is *United States Bureau of the Census: Census of Population* (Washington, D.C.: Government Printing Office, 1960), Table 78.

16. Source of information is *United States Bureau of Census: County and City Data Book, 1967,* pp. 464–573.

17. Source of information is *Uniform Crime Reports—1966: Crime in the United States* (Washington, D.C.: Government Printing Office, 1967), pp. 170–85.

18. Source of information is *Municipal Yearbook, 1966* (Chicago: International City Managers' Association, 1966), pp. 445–65.

19. After correction for ties.

20. Janowitz, *Social Control of Escalated Riots*, esp. pp. 9–13.

21. For a review and criticism of the tradition which interprets crowd behavior as bizarre and sociologically primitive, see Carl J. Couch, "Collective Behavior: An Examination of Some Stereotypes," *Social Problems* 15 (Winter 1968): 310–22; and Jules J. Wanderer, "1967 Riots: A Test of The Congruity of Events," *Social Problems* (Fall 1968): 193–98.

2. Characteristics of Cities

The characteristics of cities have been examined in order to determine the type of underlying conditions which are likely to produce a riot upon the occurrence of a precipitating event. It is well recognized that the particular precipitating event preceding a disorder cannot be considered as the cause of the riot inasmuch as similar events occur time and time again without producing riots. Two major approaches have been taken to the analysis of cities which have produced riots. The selections included in this section illustrate the two approaches. Stanley Lieberson and Arnold Silverman use a paired comparison approach in which cities experiencing riots are matched with cities similar in size and region which have not experienced riots. They then determine the differences which may have contributed to the outbreak. This procedure controls for city size and for region of the country. It insures that neither these, nor closely associated characteristics, will be ascertained to be likely to contribute to riot causation. Bryan T. Downes uses the technique of analyzing the differences in characteristics between cities experiencing outbreaks of differing degrees of intensity and those experiencing none. No attempt is made to control for city size or region of the country. Therefore the Downes technique enables one to discover the extent to which city size, locale, and closely associated characteristics may be productive of riot propensity.

The two techniques yield different kinds of information. The Downes method enables us to determine the type of city which is riot prone. The Lieberson-Silverman method enables us to determine the differences within cities of this type which set apart those experiencing riots from those having no such experience. This corresponds to the distinction between underlying factors which produce tension and more immediate and precipitous causes of a conflagration. However, the difference in time focus of the two selections prevents such an easy integration of their findings. Lieberson and Silverman studied riots occurring between 1913 and 1963 while Downes studied riots occurring between 1964 and 1968. Thus the differences in results may reflect either differences in method or a change in type of riot beginning about 1964. The latter interpretation is probably more nearly correct, but both interpretations have much to offer and they should be integrated.

The results of the Leiberson-Silverman study tended to contradict many popularly held conceptions. Population growth, proportion of blacks in a population, change in the proportion of blacks, the absolute level of black income, absolute level of black unemployment rates, and quality of black housing were found to be *unrelated* to the likelihood of a city's experiencing a riot. Cities which had riots were more likely to be those in which (1) the black occupational structure was most similar to that of whites, (2) black unemployment rates declined to levels similar to those for whites, (3) black income approached white levels, (4) there were proportionately few black policemen, (5) a low level of black ownership of ghetto business existed, (6) there were few councilmen per thousand population, and (7) "at-large" city elections obtained as opposed to the ward system.

However, Lieberson and Silverman did not distinguish between white-initiated and Negro-initiated violence. It is likely that these are different types of disorders and are associated with different sets of conditions. White-initiated violence results when whites perceive blacks as a threat (e.g., when income of the blacks improves relative to that of whites or when gaps in occupational status and/or unemployment rates diminish). Black-initiated violence is most likely to occur when blacks feel powerless to control their own institutions (e.g., when there is a low rate of ownership of ghetto businesses or a low proportion of black policemen) or unable to achieve redress of grievances (e.g., when the city has a political structure inaccessible to minorities because of at-large elections and relatively small numbers of councilmen).

Downes found that racial disorders were more likely to occur, and were more serious, in densely populated cities, large cities which are losing population or are growing very slowly, cities with high death rates, cities with a high and growing proportion of nonwhites, cities with low levels of education and income, high levels of unemployment, poor housing, a low proportion of owner-occupied housing, a lower proportion of persons in white collar occupations, partisan elections, large councils, councilmen with long terms in office, low rates of voter registration but high proportion of registered voters actually voting, a tendency to vote Democratic, high rates of city expenditures, and high rates of civic debt.

If we accept the proposition that the Downes technique produces information on the cause of underlying tensions and the Lieberson-Silverman technique informs us regarding factors associated with precipitous causes of riots, then we may attempt to integrate the findings of both studies.

One possible implication of the conjunction of these findings is that ghetto disorders are more likely to occur in large, older, overcrowded cities which have great need for city services, a large proportion of dilapidated housing, a poor population, a high proportion of blacks, and a tax problem. Within such cities, disorders are most likely when whites perceive a threat from black advances or when blacks feel that they have little access to legitimate channels for the redress of legitimate grievances. On the other hand, the two studies may jointly tell us that 1964 was a turning point and that the nature of racial violence, and the type of city most prone to experience it, were different before and after that date. We are not presently in a position to choose between these two possibilities or to decide if a combination of these two explanations is most appropriate.

The Wanderer selection (earlier in Part IV) further may tell us which cities will have the most severe disorders among those experiencing disorders. It may be significant that the proportion of nonwhites is unrelated to riot severity, but that change in this proportion is related, as is proportion of nonwhites in older homes. Of interest, but of undetermined significance, is the tendency for cities with riot plans to experience more severe riots than those without such plans.

THE PRECIPITANTS AND UNDERLYING CONDITIONS OF RACE RIOTS

Stanley Lieberson / Arnold R. Silverman

Using the *New York Times Index* for the period between 1913 and 1963, we found 72 different events that might be properly classified as Negro-white race riots. Descriptions of riots in various editions of the *Negro Yearbook* supplemented some of the *Times* reports and also provided reports of four additional riots. In several instances, magazines and local newspapers were used for further information. Finally, we employed the sociological descriptions available for some race riots. Reliance on journalistic accounts for our basic sample of riots means the study is vulnerable to any selectivity in the riots actually reported in the newspaper. Our analysis of the immediate precipitants of race riots is similarly limited by the brevity of some of the descriptive accounts as well as by possible distortions in reporting.[1] For the underlying community conditions of riots, we relied largely on census data. . . .

A COMPARATIVE ANALYSIS

Since the type of event that precipitates riots is far more common than actual riots, we ask whether this form of collective violence is due to underlying conditions that keep at least one segment of the population from accepting the normal institutional response to a provocative incident. From this perspective, precipitants are a necessary but not sufficient cause of riots.

A rather wide-ranging array of interpretations have been advanced after the occurrence of riots in particular communities. Such factors as rapidly expanding Negro population, economic hardships, police brutality, job ceilings, Negro competition with whites, slums, unsympathetic city officials, contagion, communist elements, agitators, warm weather, unruly elements, and others have figured in popular and semi-popular interpretations of race riots. Although case studies of race riots are extremely valuable where they provide an accurate description of events before and during a riot, obviously it is impossible to determine which factors are critical on the basis of one city's experience.

When we move from the presentation of *plausible* reasons to a systematic empirical test of the actual importance of various attributes in increasing the chances of riots, we encounter serious difficulties. Not only do we have a plethora of independent variables, but their actual significance is very difficult to test. Quantitative data on many of these characteristics are scarce, and in any case it is difficult to know how much causal significance to attribute anyway. For example, a riot may occur in a city

From the *American Sociological Review* 30 (December 1965): 887–98; reprinted as abridged by permission of the authors and The American Sociological Association.

containing a Negro slum area. The cruel truth is that housing conditions for Negroes are inferior in virtually every city in the U.S. To infer a causal link, one must determine not whether Negro slums exist in the riot city, but whether that city is worse in this respect than others where no riots occurred. Similarly, in any large city unemployed whites and Negroes might respond to an opportunity for a racial riot. Again the question is whether an unusually large number of such people live in one community compared with another.

Our requirements for quantitative data covering at least part of a 50-year span limit the causal hypotheses we can test. For the most part we have relied on U.S. censuses of the past six decades for data bearing on some of the propositions encountered in case studies and popular interpretations of race riots. This part of our study, therefore, necessarily has a certain *ad hoc* quality.

Method

To examine the influence of variables others have suggested as underlying causes of race riots, we used a paired-comparison analysis. Each city experiencing a riot was compared with a city as similar as possible in size and region which had no riot in the ten years preceding or following the riot date.[2] Preference was given to the city in the same state closest in population size, with the provision that it have at least half but no more than twice the population of the riot city. Where no such city existed we selected the city closest in size in the same subregion or region.[3] We compared the very largest cities, such as New York, Chicago, and Los Angeles, with other leading centers in the nation closest in population, regardless of region.

Using the nonparametric sign test, we evaluated the extent to which riot cities differ from their control cities in the direction hypothesized. When a given city experienced more than one riot, it was included as many times as the number of riots. Because census data by size of place and decade were not always available, our "N" in most cases is considerably less than the 76 riots discussed earlier. For convenience in presentation, we have divided the hypotheses into four major categories: population growth and composition; work situation; housing; and government.

DEMOGRAPHIC FACTORS

The rapid influx of Negroes and sometimes whites into cities is certainly one of the most frequently cited reasons for the occurrence of race riots. Although large-scale migration is not usually viewed as a sufficient cause for a riot, it is commonly considered important because rapid influx disrupts the on-going social order and creates various problems in the Negro community. For 66 riots we could determine the growth of the Negro and white populations between the census years preceding and following the race riot, for each riot city and for a comparable community selected at the beginning of the decade. We thus have data for 66 pairs of cities, each pair consisting of a riot city and a control city.

In about half the cases, percentage increases in both total and white population were smaller in the riot cities than in the non-riot cities. Moreover, in 56 per cent of the comparisons the control cities experienced greater percentage increases in Negro population than the riot cities did. Our results clearly fail to support the contention that rapid population change accompanies riots. For the years between 1917 and 1921—a period marked by both Negro migration and numerous riots—we found no sizable difference between riot and control cities in their percentage gains in Negro population during the decades. Also contrary to expectation are the differences in racial composition of riot and control cities. Again for 66 pairs, we find that in exactly half the comparisons, the proportion of Negroes is smaller in the riot city than in its control city.

Since this comparative approach is used with succeeding hypotheses, we should consider briefly the implications of these findings. First, we draw no conclusions about whether Negro population growth in riot cities differs from its growth elsewhere in the U.S. Riot cities have experienced more rapid growth than the remainder of the nation simply because Negro population movement has been largely from rural to urban areas. Similarly, since our method is designed to compare riot cities only with other cities similar in size and region, we make no inferences about differences between riot cities and all other U.S. cities. What we do conclude is that riot cities do not differ from non-riot cities of the same size and region in their rates of population increase, and therefore that increases in population fail to explain the occurrence of outbreaks in one city rather than another.[4]

WORK SITUATION

Traditional occupations

The occupational world of Negroes is far more restricted than that of whites. In particular, certain occupational pursuits have been more or less "traditional" for urban Negroes. These are generally lower in both status and income. Accordingly, wherever possible we determined the proportion of Negro men in the labor force who are employed either as laborers or in domestic and service occupations. Needless to say, we were forced to use some rather crude measures as well as broad categories which undoubtedly include some occupations outside the "traditional" rubric. A serious difficulty is created by contradictory hypotheses that depend on which group appears to be the aggressor. On the one hand, we might expect greater antagonism on the part of Negroes in cities where they are relatively restricted in occupational opportunities, i.e., where most Negroes are in traditional pursuits. On the other hand, we might well expect that where Negroes fare relatively well in their efforts to break through the job restrictions, whites' hostility might be greater and hence riots more likely to ensue.

For 43 riots we were able to determine the Negro occupational distribution in both the riot and control city during the closest census period.

In 65 per cent of these paired comparisons (N = 28), the percentage of Negro men holding traditional occupations is lower in the riot city.[5] This suggests that riots are due to the relative threat to whites where Negroes are less concentrated in their traditional pursuits. If such were the case, then we might expect the white and Negro percentages in these occupations to be more alike in the riot city than in the control city. This is precisely what we find: in 30 of the 43 paired comparisons, the *difference* between whites and Negroes, in proportions engaged in laboring, domestic, and service occupations, is smaller in the riot city.[6] The encroachment of Negroes in the white occupational world evidently tends to increase the chances of a riot, although we must also consider the possibility that Negro militancy increases as Negroes move out of their traditional niche.

Store owners

A more specific occupational factor sometimes associated with riots —particularly ghetto riots—is the low frequency of store ownership in Negro areas and the consequent resentment of white store owners in these areas. We are unable to get at these data directly. If we assume, however, that virtually all Negro store owners are located in the ghetto, then we can simply examine the percentage of employed Negro men who are self-employed in various facets of retail trade, such as store, restaurant, or tavern owners. Although differences between riot and control cities tend to be slight, nevertheless in 24 of 30 riots, the percentage of Negroes who are store owners is larger in the nonriot city.[7] Results might be even stronger had it been possible to subcategorize riots. For instance, the absence of Negro store owners would presumably contribute to Negroes' rioting but would contribute relatively little to white assaults.

Unemployment

As was the case for traditional occupations, unemployment presents contradictory possibilities, so that we might well expect riots when either Negroes or whites have relatively high unemployment rates. Our analysis is even cruder here, since unemployment is far more volatile from year to year, and we are able to use data only for the closest census year.[8] First, the white unemployment rate appears to have no influence on the likelihood of a riot. In 12 comparisons white unemployment rates were higher in the city experiencing the riot, and in 13 cases, higher in the control city. For Negro unemployment, results tend to run counter to what we might expect. Negro unemployment is higher in the control than in the riot city in 15 out of 25 comparisons. And Negro-white *differences* are lower in the riot than in the control city in 15 out of 25 comparisons.[9]

These results do not confirm our expectations: high white unemployment apparently does not increase the chances of a riot, nor is high Negro unemployment associated with riots in the direction expected. On an aggregate basis, the number of riots during the Great Depression of the thirties was not unusually large. In view of the weakness of the data—particularly the fact that we do not have unemployment rates for the specific year in which the riots take place—all we can conclude is that we have failed to confirm the hypothesis, not that we have disproved it.

Income

Since the influence of income on riots may reflect either group's position, our problem is similar to that discussed in connection with Negro occupational composition. Median income data are available for only 12 riots and their controls. In six comparisons Negro income is higher in the control city and in the other six it is higher in the riot city. In 11 of the 12 cases, however, white income in the riot city is lower than in the control.[10] The *difference* between Negro and white income was larger in the city without a riot in ten of the 12 cases.[11] The small number precludes analysis of these findings in greater detail, but we can observe that riots tend to occur in cities where white income is lower than that of whites in comparable areas. The lower white income also means that Negro-white differences tend to be smaller in these cities than in the control areas. Thus, the results, though extremely limited in time and place, do not support the notion that race riots are a consequence either of low Negro income or of relatively large Negro-white discrepancies in income.

HOUSING

Ghetto riots in particular are often attributed to the poor housing conditions of Negroes, but our data fail to disclose any tendency whatsoever for housing to be of lower quality in cities that have experienced riots. For 20 paired comparisons we could determine which city had a larger percentage of Negro families in sub-standard housing (using the census categories of "dilapidated" in 1950 and 1960 and "needing major repairs" in 1940). In ten cases the non-riot city had poorer Negro housing than the riot city. Although obviously not all riots could be considered ghetto riots, surely we should find some tendency for Negroes in cities experiencing riots to have poorer dwellings than they do in cities without riots, if it were true that poorer housing quality increases the likelihood of a race riot. Very likely, Negro housing is poor in so many locales that it cannot distinguish cities experiencing riots from those that do not.

GOVERNMENT

Police

Local government is one of the most important institutions to consider in an analysis of race riots. Municipal policies, particularly with respect to police, can greatly influence the chances of a race riot. Earlier, we observed that many of the precipitating incidents involve white police behavior toward Negroes, and adequate police training and tactics often prevent incipient riots from developing.[12] Moreover, police activities reflect the policies, sympathies, and attitudes of the local municipal government.

One often-cited factor in race riots is the lack of Negro policemen. First, one major complaint on the part of Negroes is that of white police brutality. So far as the police are Negroes, actual brutality will probably not arouse strong racial feelings. Second, police in some riots have encouraged or tolerated white violence toward Negroes, so that we might expect stronger police control where the force is mixed, as well as greater confidence in police protection among Negroes. Finally, since the number of Negro policemen is for the most part controlled by the city administration, the representation of Negroes is an indicator of city policies toward race relations in general.

Data are hard to obtain and for 1950 and 1960 we have been obliged to use census reports for entire metropolitan areas. Also, for some decades policemen are not reported separately from closely related occupations such as sheriffs and marshals. Nevertheless, of 38 pairs of cities, in 24 the city without the riot had more Negro policemen per thousand Negroes than did the matched city that experienced a riot.[13] Although differences between riot and control cities are rather slight, these results do suggest that police force composition influences the likelihood of a riot.

City council

We hypothesize that the manner in which councilmen are elected and the relative size of the city council will influence the occurrence of riots. Our reasoning is based on several assumptions. The election of councilmen at large gives numerically smaller groups a greater handicap in expressing their interests than they encounter in communities where councilmen are elected directly from spatial districts.[14] In cities where the average size of a councilman's constituency is small, we assume that representatives are more responsive to the wishes of the population and therefore that members of the community have a more adequate mechanism for transmitting their interests and concerns. This implies that more diverse interests will be expressed in the city's governing body.

Our hypothesis is that the more direct the relation between voter and government, the less likely are riots to occur. A more responsive government makes riots less likely because it provides regular institutional channels for expressing grievances. Small districts provide more responsive government than large districts, and large districts, more than elections at large. In comparisons between a city with a city-wide election system and one where councilmen are elected both at large and by district, we classified the latter situation as the less likely to lead to riots. Where both cities have the same form of election, we computed the mean population per councilman. (Comparisons involving Deep South cities were based on the white population only.) Thus, we gave form of election priority over size of constituency in our causal hypothesis.

In 14 of 22 pairs, population per councilman was larger in the city experiencing the riot than in the control city, or elections at large were used in the riot city and direct election of representatives in the control city.[15] Considering our inability to take into account the degree of gerrymandering in cities with direct representation, these results offer an encouraging degree of support for our hypothesis.

DISCUSSION

Our analysis of the precipitating and underlying conditions of race riots suggests several generalizations about their evolution. First, precipitating incidents often involve highly charged offenses committed by members of one group against the other, such as attacks on women, police brutality and interference, murder, and assault. In recent years, violation of segregation taboos by Negroes as well as white resistance have been increasingly frequent precipitants. Riots are generalized responses in which there is categorical assault on persons and property by virtue of their racial membership. Such violence is not restricted and may even exclude the specific antagonists responsible for the precipitating event.

The diffuse response generated by the precipitating event, as well as the fact that often the alleged offenses are of the sort normally dealt with by appropriate communal institutions, suggests that additional factors channel the inflammatory act into a riot. Since there are usually a number of factors that could have contributed to a riot in any given community, we used a comparative approach to determine why riots occur in some cities and not in others of comparable size and location.

Going beyond our data and trying to place our findings in a broad framework, we suggest that riots are more likely to occur when social institutions function inadequately, or when grievances are not resolved, or cannot be resolved under the existing institutional arangements. Populations are predisposed or prone to riot; they are not simply neutral aggregates transformed into a violent mob by the agitation or charisma of individuals. Indeed, the immediate precipitant simply ignites prior community tensions revolving about basic institutional difficulties. The failure of functionaries to perform the roles expected by one or both of the racial groups, cross-pressures, or the absence of an institution capable of handling a community problem involving inter-racial relations will create the conditions under which riots are most likely. Many riots are precipitated by offenses that arouse considerable interest and concern. When members of the victimized race are dubious about the intention or capacity of relevant functionaries to achieve justice or a "fair" solution, then the normal social controls are greatly weakened by the lack of faith in the community's institutions.

Our evidence supports the proposition that the functioning of local community government is important in determining whether a riot will follow a precipitating incident. Prompt police action can prevent riots from developing; their inaction or actual encouragement can increase the chances of a race riot. Riot cities not only employ fewer Negro policemen, but they are also communities whose electoral systems tend to be less sensitive to the demands of the electorate. Local government illustrates the possibility that riots occur when a community institution is malfunctioning, from the perspective of one or both racial segments.

Our finding that Negroes are less likely to be store owners in riot cities illustrates the problem arising when no social institution exists for handling the difficulties faced by a racial group. Small merchants require credit, skill, and sophistication in operating and locating their stores, ability to obtain leases, and so on. To our knowledge no widely operating social institution is designed to achieve these goals for the disadvantaged Negro. Similarly, our finding that riots are more likely where Negroes are closer to whites in their proportions in "traditional" Negro occupations, and where Negro-white income differences are smaller, suggests that a conflict of interests between the races is inherent in the economic world.

Our use of significance tests requires further comment. Many of the relationships are in the direction predicted but fail to meet the normal standards for significance. Several extenuating circumstances help account for this. First, many of our hypotheses refer to specific types of riots: for example, some riots are clearly "white riots"; others, equally clearly, are Negro; and many are both, in the sense that extensive attacks are directed at both groups. Were the data in an ideal form, we could separate the ghetto riots, the white assaults, and the interracial warfare into separate categories, and then apply our hypotheses to specific subsets of riots. Because our sample is small and the accounts of many riots are very scanty, we are prepared to accept these weaker associations as at least consistent with our approach to the underlying conditions of race riots.

Several implications of our results are relevant to riots elsewhere. Racial and ethnic incidents in other parts of the world are also frequently precipitated by physical violence. Dahlke's description of the Kishinew pogrom in Russia ascribes considerable importance as a precipitant to the widespread legend that Jews annually kill Christian children, as a part of their religious rites.[16] The extensive riots in Ceylon in 1958 included a number of highly provocative rumors of inter-ethnic violations. For example, "a Sinhalese baby had been snatched from its mother's arms and immersed in a barrel of boiling tar." [17] The Durban riots of 1949 were precipitated by an incident in which an African youth was knocked over by an Indian trader.[18]

A number of other riots, however, are precipitated by violations of symbols rather than persons or taboos. The burning of an American flag by Negroes triggered a race riot in the United States. Our impression is that this type of precipitant is more common in some other parts of the world. Riots in Kashmir, West Bengal, and East Pakistan in late 1963 and early 1964, for example, were precipitated by the theft of a hair of the prophet Mohammed from a Mosque in Kashmir.[19] One of the precipitants of the Chinese-Thai riots of 1945, the Yaorawat Incident, was the Chinese tendency to fly Chinese flags without also flying the Thai flag of the nation.[20] Jews tore down the czar's crown from the town hall and damaged portraits of various rulers prior to Kiev's pogrom in 1905.[21]

Our results also suggest that race riots are frequently misunderstood.

We have encountered a number of accounts in the popular literature attributing riots to communist influence, hoodlums, or rabble-rousers. Although lower-class youths and young adults are undoubtedly active during riots, potential participants of this type are probably available in almost any community. What interests us is the community failure to see the riot in terms of institutional malfunctioning or a racial difficulty which is not met—and perhaps cannot be—by existing social institutions. Many riots in other parts of the world revolve about national political institutions such that a disadvantaged segment is unable to obtain recognition of its interests and concerns through normal political channels. While this type of riot is not common in the U.S., the same basic conditions exist when either whites or Negroes are unable to use existing institutions to satisfy their needs and interests.

NOTES

ACKNOWLEDGEMENT: The comments of Alma and Karl Taeuber, and David Heise are gratefully acknowledged.

1. See, for example, Raoul Naroll, *Data Quality Control—A New Research Technique* (New York: Free Press, 1962).

2. For the most recent riots we could not apply the ten-year limit into the future in selecting control cities, but such cities were included in our analysis.

3. See U.S. Bureau of the Census, *U.S. Census of Population: 1960. Selected Area Reports, Standard Metropolitan Statistical Areas* (Washington, D.C.: U.S. Government Printing Office, 1963), pp. xvi–xvii.

4. See Robin Williams, Jr., in collaboration with John P. Dean and Edward A. Suchman, *Strangers Next Door* (Englewood Cliffs, N.J.: Prentice-Hall, 1964), pp. 135–37. In a study based on a nationwide sample of cities, they find the general level of race conflict and tension no higher in cities with rapid population growth and high mobility than in those with relatively stable populations. In short, our method gets at the question of why riots occur in the particular cities they do, rather than in comparable urban centers.

5. Using a two-tailed test, $p = .0672$.

6. $p = .0073$, single-tailed test.

7. These differences are significant at the .10 level.

8. Although data are available for other years, to our knowledge none can be obtained by race for specific cities.

9. $p = .212$, single-tailed test.

10. $p < .01$, single-tailed test.

11. $p = .038$, two-tailed test.

12. Joseph D. Lohman, *The Police and Minority Groups* (Chicago: Chicago Partk District, 1947), pp. 80–93; Noel J. Smelser, *Theory of Collective Behavior* (New York: Free Press, 1963), pp. 261–68.

13. $p = .07$, single-tailed test.

14. James Q. Wilson, *Negro Politics* (Glencoe, Ill.: Free Press, 1960), pp. 25–33.

15. Though p is not significant (.143), the relationship is in the predicted direction.

16. H. Otto Dahlke, "Race and Minority Riots—A Study in the Typology of Violence," *Social Forces* 30 (1952); 421.

17. Tarzie Vittachi, *Emergency '58: The Story of the Ceylon Race Riots* (London: Andre Deutsch, 1958), p. 48.

18. Anthony H. Richmond, *The Colour Problem,* rev. ed. (Harmondsworth, Middlesex: Pelican Books, 1961), p. 123.

19. *New York Times,* January 16, 1964, p. 17; January 19, p. 6; January 20, p. 6; January 24, p. 2; January 26, p. 15.

20. G. William Skinner, *Chinese Society in Thailand: An Analytical History* (Ithaca, N.Y.: Cornell University Press, 1957), p. 279.

21. From the diary of Shulgin, in *Source Book for History 2.1,* Vol. 2, "History of Western Civilization" (Brooklyn, N.Y.: Brooklyn College, Department of History, 1949), Ch. 31.

SOCIAL AND POLITICAL CHARACTERISTICS
OF RIOT CITIES: A COMPARATIVE STUDY

Bryan T. Downes

Like other conflicts which our society has experienced, racial conflict has all too frequently given rise to incidents of violence. Beatings, shootings, lynching, pogroms, riots, and even rebellions have been an integral part of the historical development of race relations and black protest, occurring with varying frequency and intensity since slavery was first introduced into this country in the 1600's.[1]

The majority of these outbursts of racial violence are examples of that which Smelser labels collective behavior: the mobilization of individuals to act on the basis of belief which redefines social action.[2]

One type of collective behavior which has been occurring with greater frequency in urban areas are the hostile outbursts which have become an integral part of the current black protest movement. Smelser defines a hostile outburst as simply the mobilization of individuals for action under a hostile belief.[3] In the last four years a large number of urban blacks have been mobilized for action on the basis of such beliefs. According to Smelser, these individuals are bent upon attacking someone, such as police and white merchants, who they consider responsible for a "disturbing state of affairs." [4]

It is not surprising that in its current phase black protest is characterized by violence. Many blacks have become impatient with the pace of integration; this is nowhere more apparent than in the case of younger black inhabitants of our nation's urban ghettos. Their "dream" of integration, social justice, and equality has been deferred too long, and since 1964 it has "exploded" in the form of over 225 hostile outbursts—incidents which involve rock throwing, fighting, looting, burning, and

From the *Social Science Quarterly* 49 (December 1968): 504–20; reprinted by permission.

killing.[5] Before turning to the central concern of this article, which is to analyze some of the characteristics of cities experiencing racial violence since 1964, let us briefly examine the nature of current outbursts.

HOSTILE OUTBURSTS, 1964–1968

Today's hostile outbursts differ quite markedly from earlier outbreaks of collective racial violence. For example, in early pogroms, or "southern-style riots," whites attacked and killed Negroes they thought were responsible for "disturbing states of affairs," sometimes burning their homes, with blacks offering little or no resistance. On the other hand, in the race riots which occurred in many northern cities in 1919, 1935, and 1943, large numbers of both blacks and whites engaged in collective violence against each other. In these race riots, which occurred in cities such as Washington, D. C., New York, and Detroit, blacks actively defended themselves and even initiated violence against whites.

The hostile outbursts which we are witnessing today have taken still a different form.[6] In these incidents, blacks have been the primary participants, directing their hostility against police and merchants who they consider responsible for a great deal of racial injustice. Because police are representatives of the dominant white society in the ghetto (as are merchants to a lesser degree), they become symbols of a far greater source of dissatisfaction for many blacks. Although most of the hostile outbursts which we examined were spontaneous and therefore displayed only a primitive organization, some of the most recent incidents occurring this past summer began to take on a greater degree of organization. For example, the outburst which occurred in Cleveland was set off by a systematic ambush of white policemen by black militants.

Not all behavior of participants in these hostile outbursts, however, is instrumental in achieving specific objectives. Many participate simply because such involvement is intrinsically satisfying or satisfying because it allows them to give expression to a state of mind. Although recent hostile outbursts do not carry "the war" to the enemy's ("whitey's") territory, they are directed against rather specific enemies. Furthermore, although many outbursts are precipitated by specific incidents which involve police, these outbursts are also linked to a variety of grievances which exist in the minds of urban ghetto-dwellers.[7]

Data on hostile outbursts

Our data on hostile outbursts has been drawn primarily from a *Congressional Quarterly* special report, entitled, *Urban Problems and Civil Disorders,* and from the *New York Times.*[8] An initial examination of "civil disorders" listings in the *Congressional Quarterly* publication, compiled by the Legislative Reference Service of the Library of Congress, provided us with a brief description of 113 hostile outbursts which occurred from January 1, 1964, to January 1, 1968. In order to check on the accuracy of these listings, however, we consulted the *New York Times*

Index for the same period and found 61 additional incidents. Further information on all incidents was then gathered directly from the *New York Times* as were data on outbursts which occurred during the first five months of 1968.

Reliance on journalistic accounts for our basic universe of incidents meant that the study was vulnerable to any selectivity in the hostile outbursts actually reported in the newspapers. For example, following the recent assassination of Martin Luther King, Jr., the *New York Times* published a report prepared by the United Press International giving the 110 cities which experienced varying degrees of violence during the week following Dr. King's death.[9] Of the 110 cities listed, we could find adequate information on only 60 of these in the *New York Times.* This may say something about the accuracy of the report as well as point up a critical problem which we faced. It also means that we have definitely under-reported smaller incidents simply because of a lack of available data.[10]

Another problem encountered was the amount and accuracy of the information reported; this varied considerably from incident to incident, with the greatest amount of accurate information being provided on more violent outbursts. Outside the *Congressional Quarterly* publication and the *New York Times,* however, we generally found a paucity of data except on the most violent incidents.[11] Our data, therefore, should be looked upon as *approximate* and subject to some change as more complete information becomes available.

The nature of hostile outbursts

Everyone has read that large numbers of blacks were mobilized for action in the most recent outbreak of hostile outbursts. However, studies indicate that only a small percentage of the total Negro population in any given city actually become involved in these outbursts.[12] Although in the most violent incidents the percentage may go as high as 15 per cent, this still represents a relatively small proportion of the Negro population. Furthermore, studies have shown those individuals most likely to participate in hostile outbursts tend to be younger Negroes, roughly between the ages of 15 and 24 years, who were born in the North. These younger Negroes are, by and large, as well educated and are earning about as much money as nonparticipants, although there seems to be somewhat more unemployment (or underemployment) among their ranks.[13]

During the period of January 1, 1964, to May 31, 1968, 239 hostile outbursts occurred. Our data on the number of persons involved in these outbursts are not accurate because: (1) we could find no information on 112 (47 per cent) of the 239 outbursts, and (2) the data which we did find on the remaining 127 were not very useful. For example, many reports in the *New York Times* simply indicated that 100's, etc., had participated. As we have already noted, social scientists, who studied cities in which hostile outbursts took place, indicate that in the most violent incidents—

such as those which occurred in Watts, Newark, and Detroit—about 15 per cent of the Negro population in the outburst area became involved.

On the basis of the information we did have, we estimate that about 150,000 persons actively participated in the 239 outbursts, although this figure could probably go as high as 250,000. This still represents a small percentage of the 21.5 million Negroes in the United States in 1968 and only about 10 per cent of the 15 million who reside in our metropolitan areas. The news media, particularly television, have been largely responsible for creating the impression that greater numbers of Negroes participate in hostile outbursts, for they tend to devote most of their coverage to only the most violent outbursts. We did, however, find that the number of paricipants varies considerably from incident to incident, with the greatest number generally participating in more violent outbursts.

The individuals who were involved in the 239 outbursts wrought tremendous havoc upon certain areas in many of our largest cities. Not only have millions of dollars been lost due to arson and looting, and further millions expended by government to restore order, many individuals were killed and thousands seriously wounded. During the 523 days of hostilities which occurred over the 53 month period, for example, 49,607 persons were arrested, 7,942 were wounded, and 191 were killed. Although these latter figures appear quite high, they are considerably less than the number reported wounded or killed in many early pogroms and race riots or those maimed and killed by firearms in any given year in this country.[14] These figures are low because most outbursts never reached a point where blacks invaded white territory or systematically killed police who were attempting to control them.[15]

Instead, Negroes involved in these outbursts directed their attention primarily to the destruction of property and looting and were only marginally concerned with physically assaulting or killing whites. The amount of property damage and economic loss due to rock throwing, burning, and looting was very high; in 1965, 1966, and 1967, it was estimated that there were $210.6 million in property damages and $504.2 million in economic losses; and these appear to be very conservative estimates.[16]

The preceding information is broken down by yearly totals in Table 1. These data indicate there generally has been an increase in all totals since 1964, except in 1966 when the numbers arrested, wounded, and killed decreased. However, all totals went up quite markedly in 1967. Our information for 1968 is incomplete, and thus it is hard to draw any conclusions at this time. Nevertheless, the number of incidents occurring in July and August approached the number which took place in 1967; therefore, the upward trend in these figures will continue in 1968.[17] One interesting figure in Table 1 is the drastic upswing in the number of persons arrested in 1968. Police are reacting much more quickly and effectively in their attempts to control incidents of collective violence. A more effective policy adopted increasingly by police is to use maximum force in the initial stage of an outburst. This does give rise to a greater number of arrests but less overall violence and property damage. The police used this

TABLE 1. Yearly Breakdown of Information on Hostile Outbursts

Data on Hostile Outbursts	*Totals for Period 1964 – May 31, 1968*					
	1964	1965	1966	1967	1968	*Total*
Number of cities having outbursts	16	20	44	71	64	215[a]
Number of outbursts	16	23	53	82	65	239[b]
Total number of days of hostility	42	31	92	236	122	523
Total number arrested	2,000	10,245	2,216	16,471	18,675	49,607
Total number wounded	580	1,206	467	3,348	2,341	7,942
Total number killed	9	43	9	85	46	191

[a]Because many of the same cities have incidents each year, this figure is high.
[b]Smaller (less violent) incidents are under-reported.

technique very effectively in Washington, D.C. early this summer when an outburst broke out following the conclusion of the Poor People's Campaign.

Almost all incidents occurring each year were of relatively short duration, lasting only one or two days. Also, most outbursts, on which we had data, involved less than 500 persons. Similarly, in 30 per cent of the 239 outbursts no arrests were reported and in an additional 46 per cent a maximum of 50 arrests were made by law enforcement personnel. In over 46 per cent of the incidents no individuals were reported wounded and in 77 per cent no deaths occurred. These percentages do not necessarily remain stable when one examines the number arrested, wounded, and killed each year. In addition, many of these figures have shown some increases since 1964.

If one views hostile outbursts as occurring in a series of stages, it appears that most incidents which have occurred since 1964 never move beyond the first or primarily symbolic looting stage, where destruction rather than plunder appears to be the intent of the participants.[18] Approximately 75 per cent of the outbursts never progressed beyond this initial stage of window breaking, car burning, and the occasional tossing of fire bombs.

An additional 20 per cent of the outbursts progress to a second stage where looting of goods as well as greater destruction of property (equipment and facilities) takes place. In this stage white and even black merchants dealing in consumer goods become the objects of attack. The racial dimension, while never absent, may become secondary to the economic factor in motivating the behavior of looters.

Finally, only about five per cent of the outbursts progress to a third stage in which there is a full redefinition of certain property rights.[19] At this point plundering becomes the normative, the socially supported thing to do. For example, as one social scientist has observed, "the carnival spirit particularly commented upon in the Newark and Detroit outbursts does not represent anarchy. It is, instead, an overt manifestation of widespread localized social support for the new definition of the situation." [20] At this stage, participation of blacks is at its height as is the level of violence. Property damage and economic loss among both whites and blacks is widespread and complete due to arson and looting. When an outburst reaches this stage, any attempt at control usually results in large numbers of blacks being arrested, wounded, and killed.

TYPES OF CITIES EXPERIENCING HOSTILE OUTBURSTS

Now that we have briefly examined the nature of hostile outbursts which have occurred since 1964, we can turn to the central concern of this article. Is there anything distinctive about the environmental context in cities in which hostile outbursts have occurred during the last 53 months? What conditions in these cities are associated with the occurrence of incidents of racial violence?

Lieberson and Silverman, in their earlier analysis of conditions thought to underlie 76 Negro-white "race riots" occurring in the United States from 1913 through 1963, found that population growth, proportion Negro, Negro-white unemployment rates, Negro income, and proportion of Negroes living in substandard housing were substantially the same in matched cities in which racial violence did occur as in cities where such violence did not occur.[21] Although some additional conditions were found to be associated with the occurrence of riots, they were only weakly associated.[22]

The Lieberson and Silverman study provides perhaps the first systematic attempt to assess selected conditions thought to underlie racial violence. But the results, although based on incomplete data, generally failed to provide empirical support for many commonly held beliefs regarding the occurrence of earlier riots.

Bloombaum, in his re-analysis of the Lieberson and Silverman data, also found that no single factor discriminated between riot and control cities.[23] However, he did find the job effect of the nine conditions examined did discriminate between riot cities and their controls much better than any one factor could do.

Our examination of the characteristics of cities experiencing racial violence begins where Lieberson and Silverman ended their study. Although we are using a very different method of analysis, as indicated below, we are concerned with investigating the contextual conditions found in cities which have and have not experienced hostile outbursts. Because of this difference in methodology, however, it is difficult to compare our findings with those of Lieberson and Silverman. Where they could make no inferences about differences between riot cities and all other American cities, and could only conclude that riot cities do not differ from nonriot cities of the same *size and region,* we can systematically undertake the former but not the latter type of comparison.[24]

Method

In order to begin in a preliminary manner to answer the questions posed initially in this section, data in the 1960 Census and the 1963 *Municipal Yearbook* [25] were used. (Professor Robert Alford of the University of Wisconsin collected information from these two sources and was kind enough to let us use his data in our analysis. However, he collected data only on cities of 25,000 or more persons at the time of the 1960 census.) In 1960, there were 676 cities which had 25,000 or more persons; of the 676, 129 (19 per cent) had experienced one or more hostile outbursts since 1964. Furthermore, in these 129 cities, 190 incidents of collective racial violence occurred, with an additional 49 incidents taking place in cities under 25,000 persons.

Our analysis began by dividing cities over 25,000 persons into two groups, those which had no hostile outbursts and those which had, and by running this dichotomous variable against the Alford census data. We next ranked each city according to the intensity of violence of its most hostile outburst and made a second series of computer runs. Since this *preliminary analysis* yielded so much information, we will present only those results which provide a balanced *descriptive characterization* of cities in which hostile outbursts took place and which allow us to examine some of the environmental conditions thought to underlie racial violence in the United States.

The analysis

Most outbursts of collective racial violence are sparked by a very specific incident which channels generalized hostile beliefs into specific hopes, fears, and antagonisms. The data in Table 2 give some indication of the type of precipitants of hostile outbursts which have occurred since 1913. Noting the very different precipitant(s) which have touched off recent outbursts, one finds in the case of many current incidents, it seems the killing, arrest, interference, assault, or search of Negro men and women by police has either confirmed or justified existing generalized fears and hatreds about police in the ghetto and/or signalized a "failure" on the part of the police which demanded explanation and assignment of responsibility. The data also indicate how easily recent outbursts were precipitated; over 30 per cent of these incidents were either spontaneous or set off by the death of Martin Luther King, Jr. What are the conditions in a community which increase the probability that a precipitating incident will lead to an outburst? What are the conditions which give rise to strain and encourage the spread of hostile beliefs which ultimately results in generalized aggression?

TABLE 2. Immediate Precipitants of Hostile Outbursts,
1913-1963 and 1964-1968

Immediate Precipitants	*1913-1963[a]* *(N=76)* Per cent	*1964-May 31,* *1968[b]* *(N=239)* Per cent
Rape, murder, attack, or hold-up of		
white women by Negro men	13	0
Killings, arrest, interference, assault, or		
search of Negro men (and women)		
by police	20	27
Other inter-racial murder or shooting	15	4
Inter-racial rock throwing or fight, no		
mention of lethal weapons	21	10
Civil liberties, public facilities, segregation,		
political events, housing	18	10
Negro strikebreakers, upgrading, or other		
job based conflicts	7	1
Burning of an American flag by Negroes	1	0
Inflammatory speeches by civil rights or		
black power leaders	0	2
Spontaneous (no immediate apparent		
precipitant)	0	10
Other (death of civil rights leader, building	0	26
blown up, vandals, ambulance failure to		
respond quickly to Negro heart attack		
victim, Halloween prank)	0	26
No information available	5	10

[a]Source, 1913-1963 data: Stanley Lieberson and Arnold R. Silverman, "The
Precipitants and Underlying Conditions of Race Riots," *American Sociological
Review* 30 (December 1965): p. 889.
[b]Source, 1964-1968 data: *New York Times.*

Population characteristics

Our data support the argument that hostile outbursts are more likely
to occur in densely populated areas where people are forced to live in
very close proximity to each other. Hostile outbursts are more likely to
occur, also, in larger municipalities which have lost population or gained
very little since 1950. In addition, these same densely populated, large
cities have higher percentages of deaths per 1,000 persons. On the other
hand, cities which have not experienced such outbursts tend to be somewhat smaller, less densely populated, faster growing communities with
somewhat lower death rates. The gamma coefficients in Table 6 give some
indication of the strength of the relationship between intensity of violence in a hostile outburst and the above population data.

Lieberson and Silverman found very little difference in their study
between the proportion of blacks in riot and control cities. They also
found no sizable differences between riot and control cities in their percentage gains in Negro population during the period 1913-1963.[26] On the
other hand, we found that cities which experienced hostile outbursts since
1964 had, on the whole, a much higher proportion of nonwhites (primarily
Negroes) in their populations than cities which experienced no incidents

TABLE 3. Population Characteristics of Cities Experiencing Hostile Outbursts

Population Characteristics of Cities of 25,000 or More Persons, 1960	No Hostile Outburst[a] (N=547) Per cent	Hostile Outburst[a] (N=129) Per cent	Total[a] (N=676) Per cent
1960 population:			
25,000 – 99,999	89	45	81
100,000 – 199,999	7	22	10
200,000 – 499,999	3	19	6
500,000 – 1,000,000 or more	1	14	3
Population growth or decline, 1950 – 1960:			
Declined (0 – 29%)	14	37	19
Increased (0 – 44%)	50	46	50
Increased (45% or more)	29	16	26
Not ascertainable	7	0	5
Population per square mile:			
3,999 or less	45	29	42
4,000 – 4,999 or more	18	12	17
5,000 – 7,000 or more	37	59	41
Deaths per 1,000, 1959:			
7 or less	30	10	26
8 – 9	23	27	24
10 or more	40	63	44
Not ascertainable	7	0	6
Per cent nonwhite:			
4.9% or less	61	12	52
5.0 – 14.9%	21	33	24
15% or more	18	55	24
Change in per cent nonwhite, 1950 – 1960:			
Decreased by 1.0% or more	34	22	32
Increased 0.0 – 0.9%	35	3	29
Increased 1.0% or more	27	75	36
Not ascertainable	4	0	3

[a]If some columns do not add up to 100% it is due to rounding error or missing data.

of racial violence. The nonwhite populations in these cities have also increased, some quite drastically, since 1950. Thus it would appear that the rapid influx of nonwhites may be an important condition underlying hostile outbursts, primarily because such an influx may disrupt the ongoing social order and create or accentuate existing problems in the black community.

Education, income, and employment

As one might expect, there tends to be an inverse relationship between the occurrence of hostile outbursts in a city and the level of education of its inhabitants. Incidents of collective violence are much more likely to take place in cities in which the educational attainment of its citizenry is quite low, with the most violent incidents occurring in those municipalities whose populations have the lowest level of educational attainment (see Table 4).

Also not unexpectedly, we found that in cities which had hostile outbursts, the median income of families tends to be somewhat lower

TABLE 4. Population, Housing, and Economic Characteristics
of Cities Experiencing Hostile Outbursts

Population, Housing, and Economic Characteristics of Cities of 25,000 or More Persons, 1960	No Hostile Outburst[a] (N=547) Per cent	Hostile Outburst[a] (N=129) Per cent	Total[a] (N=676) Per cent
Per cent persons 25 years and over who have completed 4 years of high school or more:			
43% or less	44	65	48
44 – 51%	25	21	24
52 – 99%	31	14	28
Median family income:			
$0000 – 5399	22	31	24
$5400 – 6749	51	58	52
$6750 and over	27	12	24
Per cent of labor force unemployed:			
0 – 3%	32	17	30
4%	24	18	22
5% or more	44	65	48
Per cent housing units sound with plumbing facilities:			
74.9% or less	20	33	22
75.0 – 87.9%	49	57	51
88.0% or more	31	10	27
Per cent occupied housing units owner occupied:			
49.9% or less	16	40	21
50.0 – 66.9%	51	52	51
67.0% or more	33	8	28
Metropolitan status:			
Central employing	15	57	23
Suburban dormitory	23	3	19
Independent balanced	13	4	11
Independent employing	14	9	13
Other	35	27	34
Economic base:			
Manufacturing	34	33	34
Diversified manufacturing	14	29	17
Diversified retail	21	24	21
Retail trade	19	8	17
Other	12	6	11
Per cent employed in white collar occupations:			
0 – 44%	47	59	50
45 – 99%	53	41	50

[a]If some columns do not add up to 100% it is due to rounding error or missing data.

than in cities which experienced no outbursts, with the most hostile incidents occurring in cities which had the lowest median family incomes. Thus, hostile outbursts also appear to be a consequence of generally low educational and income levels in a city (which, in turn, may be a function of the per cent nonwhite).

Unemployment was also much higher in cities which had hostile outbursts, with the most violent incidents occurring in communities with the highest unemployment rates. We know that unemployment tends to be almost twice as high among the black inhabitants in urban ghettos; therefore, this finding generally supports the expectation hostile outbursts are more likely to occur in a city when either Negroes or whites have relatively high unemployment rates.

The Lieberson and Silverman study failed to find any tendency whatsoever for housing to be of lower quality in cities which had experienced riots when they were compared with cities of the same size and region.[27] Our analysis indicates housing units tend to be less sound in cities which had outbursts, with more intensely violent incidents taking place in cities with the lowest percentages of sound housing units. Thus racial violence may also be attributable to poor housing conditions, particularly among blacks, in a city.

Furthermore, in cities in which hostile outbursts did take place, the percentage of housing units which were owner occupied was quite low, particularly when compared to cities which had no outbursts. In almost half of these cities, 50 per cent or less of the housing units were owner occupied. As one might expect, cities which had more violent outbursts also tended to have the least number of dwelling units which were owner occupied.

Metropolitan status and economic base

Of those cities which experienced hostile outbursts, 57 per cent were classified as central employing (see Table 4). As the intensity of violence increased in these cities, so did the number of cities falling into that category—including some 90 per cent of the 10 cities having the highest level of violence. On the other hand, only 15 per cent of the cities which experienced no outbursts fell into the central employing category. Communities which had no incidents were likely to be classified as suburban dormitory (23 per cent), independent employing (14 per cent), or independent balanced (13 per cent). Thus, it would appear that most incidents of racial violence, particularly those which are most destructive, are taking place within the largest central cities.

In terms of their economic bases, cities in which hostile outbursts took place were likely to have manufacturing or diversified manufacturing economies; however, more violent outbursts occurred in diversified manufacturing communities. Cities which experienced no outbursts were just as likely to be manufacturing centers, but less likely to have diversified manufacturing economies. Persons in cities which had outbursts were, therefore, somewhat less likely to be employed in white-collar occupations; this was particularly true in municipalities having more violent outbursts. Although we are unable to substantiate the following observation, we might expect greater antagonism on the part of Negroes toward whites in cities where Negroes are relatively restricted in occupational opportunities—that is, where most blacks are restricted to traditional pursuits because of lack of requisite skills or job opportunities.

Governmental structure

Lieberson and Silverman argue the more direct the relationship between the voter and government, the less likely hostile outbursts will occur. "A more responsive government makes riots less likely because it provides regular institutional channels for expressing grievances." [28] On the basis of this sort of reasoning, we would expect hostile outbursts to occur in cities with the council-manager form of government, in which councilmen are elected to small councils (at large) on a nonpartisan basis. The assumption underlying this observation is that councilmen elected at large to small councils on a nonpartisan ballot will be less responsive to special interests and groups within the population.

Our findings offer very little support for this particular interpretation of municipal political structure. A closer examination of the actual functioning of many of these local governments, however, probably would indicate that they are relatively unresponsive or unable to respond to the demands of black Americans. Cities in which hostile outbursts took place tend to be just as likely to have either the mayor-council or council-manager forms of government, while communities which had no incidents were somewhat more likely to have the council-manager plan. The most violent outbursts, however, occurred in cities which had the mayor-council form.

In addition, cities which experienced incidents of violent collective behavior were somewhat less likely to have nonpartisan elections for municipal offices, but were more likely to have larger councils in which councilmen served for longer terms. These relationships were simply more pronounced in cities which had more violent outbursts. On the other hand, communities which had no hostile outbursts were somewhat more likely to have nonpartisan elections, smaller councils, and councilmen whose terms of office were shorter.

With regard to voting behavior among people in communities which had hostile outbursts, we found that in 1960, individuals in these cities were less likely to register to vote. Those who did register, however, were more likely to turn out at the polls and to vote overwhelmingly for the Democratic party's presidential candidate. In cities which experienced no outbursts, inhabitants were more likely to register, but less likely to vote; although they did cast their ballots for the Democratic presidential candidate. These same relationships were simply accentuated when voter registration, per cent voting, and party receiving the greatest plurality in the presidential election were examined in communities in which more intensely violent outbursts took place.

City expenditures

In cities which experienced hostile outbursts, local government expenditures were generally quite high. For example, in such cities both per capita general expenditure and per capita expenditure for sanitation were higher than in cities in which no outbursts occurred (see Table 5). These

TABLE 5. Political Structure and Expenditure Characteristics of Cities Experiencing Hostile Outbursts

Political Structure and Expenditure Characteristics of Cities of 25,000 or More Persons, 1963	No Hostile Outburst[a] (N=547) Per cent	Hostile Outburst[a] (N=129) Per cent	Total[a] (N=676) Per cent
Form of government:			
Mayor-council	37	45	38
Commission	11	12	11
City Manager	52	42	50
Type of election:			
Nonpartisan	73	62	71
Partisan	26	36	28
Term of office:			
Less than four years	45	36	43
Four years or more	55	64	57
Number of Councilmen:			
Less than 5	51	28	38
5 – 9	42	45	43
10 or more	17	27	19
Per capita general expenditure:			
$00 – 48	25	12	23
$49 – 66	22	15	20
$67 – 98	20	28	22
$99	32	46	34
Per capita sanitation expenditure:			
$00 – 08	50	34	47
$09 – 13	23	32	25
$14 – 99	24	33	26
Not ascertainable	3	0	2
Per capita debt outstanding end of year, in $10 units:			
$00 – 12	49	37	47
$13 – 20	23	25	24
$21 – 99	25	38	27
Not ascertainable	3	0	2

[a]If some columns do not add up to 100% it is due to rounding error or missing data.

expenditures were also highest in cities in which more violent incidents took place. The outstanding debt of local government was also higher in communities in which outbursts occurred. Again, this was particularly true of cities experiencing more violent outbursts.

Demands placed upon city services by the type of population living in cities which have experienced hostile outbursts are very high. These are the cities, however, which can least afford to pay for the expansion of basic services—let alone the establishment of new ones—because of their steadily deteriorating tax base. Such municipalities are in a particularly difficult position and are being forced to rely on new sources of revenue, such as the city income tax, and to look to other levels of government for financial assistance.

CONCLUSION

The information presented on cities in the United States with 25,000 or more persons clearly indicates that the environmental context one finds in cities in which hostile outbursts took place tends to be quite different from that found in communities in which no incidents occurred. Cities experiencing hostile outbursts have a very distinctive set of social, economic, and even political structural characteristics. Hostile outbursts are not randomly distributed among our universe of municipalities; this in itself is a significant finding, given the number of cities in which one or more outbursts have taken place. In addition, the data show that contextual differences tend to be further accentuated in those cities in which more violent outbursts occurred (see Table 6). By solving the major problems confronting our largest cities, the data indicate we would also be taking a giant step toward solving many of the problems of the black people who live in them, thus removing some of the environmental con-

TABLE 6. Conditions Found to be Associated
with the Intensity of Hostile Outbursts[a]

Social, Economic, and Political Characteristics of Cities with 25,000 or more Persons	Intensity of Violence of Hostile Outburst (gamma coefficients)
Population, 1960	.75
Population change, 1950–1960	–.39
Population per sq. mile, 1960	.43
Deaths per 1,000, 1959	.36
Per cent nonwhite, 1960	.70
Change in per cent nonwhite, 1950–1960	.65
Median age, 1960	.31
Per cent persons 25 years old and over who have completed four years of high school or more, 1960	–.41
Median family income, 1960	–.14
Per cent of labor force unemployed, 1960	.30
Per cent housing units sound with plumbing facilities, 1960	–.26
Per cent occupied housing units owner occupied, 1960	–.47
Employment residence ratio, 1960	.37
Manufacturing ratio, 1960	.12
Per cent employed in white collar occupations, 1960	–.15
Form of government, 1963	–.21
Type of election, 1963	.21
Number of individuals on council, 1963	.32
Term of office, 1963	.17
Per capita general government expenditure, 1963	.41
Per capita expenditure on sanitation, 1963	.29
Per capita debt outstanding end of year in $10 units, 1963	.31

[a]In measuring the intensity of violence of a hostile outburst, we made use of the following ordinal scale:
1. Low intensity (rock and bottle throwing, window breaking, fighting);
2. Medium intensity (the above plus some looting and arson);
3. High intensity (the above plus much looting and arson, reports of sniping);
4. Very high intensity (the above plus widespread looting and arson, sniping).

ditions underlying hostile outbursts. For as the Kerner Commission has observed: [29]

> Social and economic conditions in the riot cities constituted a clear pattern of severe disadvantage for Negroes compared with whites, whether the Negroes lived in the area where the riot took place or outside it. Negroes had completed fewer years of education and fewer had attended high school. Negroes were twice as likely to be unemployed and three times as likely to be in unskilled and service jobs. Negroes averaged 70 per cent of the income earned by whites and were more than twice as likely to be living in poverty. Although housing cost Negroes relatively more, they had worse housing—three times as likely to be overcrowded and substandard. When compared to white suburbs, the relative disadvantage is even more pronounced.

Thus many of the general characteristics of the population in cities experiencing hostile outbursts are simply accentuated among blacks living in the urban ghettos or the largest, least rapidly growing, most densely populated central cities.

We are well aware that none of the conditions examined individually cause a hostile outburst to occur. These factors are highly intercorrelated and are probably largely a function of the size and age of a community. Taken together, however, such a set of conditions may provide the basis for an outbreak of racial violence in any given city. Indeed, one might hypothesize that collective racial violence is likely to occur in a municipality when a certain *threshold* in some of these conditions is reached—that is, when environmental conditions within a particular city reach a particularly "explosive" point. This implies that hostile outbursts occur largely because a set of contextual conditions become such that strains arise which further the spread of hostile beliefs among individuals in the black community. When these generalized hostile beliefs are channeled into specific fears, antagonisms, and hopes by a precipitating factor, blacks are ready to be mobilized for participation in a hostile outburst.

Some will continue to argue that in this analysis we have simply confirmed the obvious; however, because social scientists have not had adequate data on (1) the number and character of current hostile outbursts, and (2) the number and types of cities in which such outbursts have been occurring, a number of erroneous conclusions about these outbursts have been drawn. For instance, some have argued that causes of hostile outbursts are not related to social, economic, or political differences between cities; our analysis, while only preliminary, raises doubts about the validity of such a statement. Furthermore, as Tomlinson has observed: [30]

> What produces riots is the shared agreement by most Negro Americans that their lot in life is unacceptable coupled with the view by a significant minority that riots are a legitimate and productive mode of protest. What is unacceptable about Negro life does not vary much from city to city, and the differences in Negro life from city to city are *irrelevant*.

The unifying feature is the consensus that Negroes have been misused by whites and this perception exists in every city in America. . . . urban riots in the North will continue until the well of available cities runs dry. They will continue because the mood of many Negroes in the urban North demands them, because there is a quasi-political ideology which justifies them and because there is *no presently effective deterrent or antidote*. (Emphasis added.)

Some of these comments are probably quite correct. What Tomlinson does not emphasize is that many of the conditions (which give rise to the psychological state of mind he discusses and which may affect, quite dramatically, the course of any given hostile outburst) are rooted in the context of cities in which Negroes live. For example, conditions such as overcrowding, inadequate housing, unemployment, low income, lack of education, poor schools, high death rates, and unresponsive political institutions are not only responsible for maintaining the self-perpetuating cycle of poverty within which many Negroes find themselves, but also for the development of the attitudes Tomlinson discusses. Perhaps the ultimate determinants of hostile outbursts are psychological in nature; however, this is an empirical question. But we should also be concerned with asking why blacks hold such attitudes; we should be asking why they are acting on the basis of these hostile beliefs. This is particularly important when developing deterrents and antidotes, for the attitudes and behavior of Negroes are shaped to a considerable degree by conditions in the environment within which they live, work, and play.

NOTES

ACKNOWLEDGEMENT: Portions of this article have been drawn from "The Black Protest Movement and Urban Violence," a paper presented at the 1968 annual meeting of the American Political Science Association, Washington, D.C., September 2–7, 1968. The author gratefully acknowledges the support of the department of political science at Michigan State University and the assistance of Stephen W. Burks in the preparation and analysis of the data presented in this article. It should be stressed that this analysis represents a *preliminary examination* of the information we have collected. In the future we plan to undertake a more sophisticated statistical analysis of some of these data.

1. For an examination of early racial violence, see Arthur I. Waskow, *From Race Riot to Sit-In, 1919 and the 1960's* (Garden City, N.Y.: Doubleday, 1966).

2. Neil J. Smelser, *Theory of Collective Behavior* (New York: Free Press, 1962), p. 8.

3. Ibid., p. 226. See also Smelser's discussion of the determinants of hostile outbursts in Ch. 8.

4. Ibid., pp. 224–25.

5. The changes which many blacks expected would occur after the 1954 Supreme Court school desegregation decision have simply not been forthcoming. This refers to the lines in a poem by Langston Hughes entitled, "Harlem," in *Selected Poems of Langston Hughes* (New York: Knopf, 1959), p. 268.

6. See the materials in, Louis H. Masotti, ed., "Urban Violence and Disorder," *American Behavioral Scientist* 11 (March-April 1968).

7. Some of these points are raised in: James Q. Wilson, "Why Are We Having A

Wave of Violence," *The New York Magazine,* May 19, 1968, pp. 23–24, 116–20. However, Professor Wilson and I differ quite markedly in our interpretations of the behavior of participants in hostile outbursts.

8. *Urban Problems and Civil Disorder* (Washington, D.C.: Congressional Quarterly Service, Special Report No. 36, September 8, 1967).

9. *New York Times,* April 10, 1968. The news media generally tend to over-report smaller, less violent, incidents.

10. Although we culled all available sources, there simply were not very much data available on the hostile outbursts which had occurred since 1964. The Lemberg Center for the Study of Violence at Brandeis University has recently begun to coordinate systematically the efforts of various researchers in this area.

11. For instance see, The National Advisory Commission on Civil Disorders, *Report of the National Advisory Commission on Civil Disorders* (Washington, D.C.: U.S. Government Printing Office, March 1, 1968); Governor's Select Commission on Civil Disorder State of New Jersey, *Report for Action* (Trenton: Governor's Office, February 1968); Mayor's Development Team, *Report to Mayor Jerome P. Cavanagh* (Detroit, Mich.: Mayor's Office, October 1967); and publications of the Los Angeles Riot Study undertaken by the Institute of Government and Public Affairs, University of California at Los Angeles.

12. T. M. Tomlinson, "The Development of a Riot Ideology among Urban Negroes," *American Behavioral Scientist* 11 (March-April 1968): 27–31. See also the recent supplement to the *Report of the National Advisory Commission on Civil Disorders.* While the averages are about the same for participants and nonparticipants, the distributions differ. Persons from both the very low and very high educational and income levels are under-represented among the participants.

13. For example, see *A Survey of Attitudes of Detroit Negroes After the Riot of 1967* (Detroit: Detroit Urban League, 1957); and Kurt Lang and Gladys E. Lang, "Racial Disturbances as Collective Protest," *American Behavioral Scientist* 11 (March-April 1968): 11–13 [reprinted in this volume].

14. For example, a recent Associated Press survey reported that 149 persons had been killed by firearms in the United States during the week of June 16 to June 23, 1968. This included 80 homicides, 58 suicides, and 11 accidental shootings. In 1966, the Federal Bureau of Investigation indicated that an average of 125 Americans were killed *each week* during that year by firearms.

15. In the last several months, blacks have precipitated a number of hostile outbursts by systematically ambushing and attempting to kill police. This is very different from the anomic pattern of most post-1964 incidents.

16. These estimates were prepared by the Permanent Subcommittee on Investigations of the Committee on Governmental Operations of the U.S. Senate, the so-called McClellan Committee.

17. Our initial tabulation indicates that some 45 hostile outbursts have occurred during June, July, and August. With the exception of incidents occurring in Cleveland, Ohio; Miami and St. Petersburg, Florida; Little Rock, Arkansas; and Grand Rapids, Michigan; most of these outbursts were quite minor.

18. See the discussion of these stages in E. L. Quarantelli and Russell R. Dynes, "Looting in Civil Disorders: An Index of Social Change," *American Behavioral Scientist* 11 (March-April 1968): 8–9. These percentages are the same as those reported in the Kerner Report for the 164 "disorders" reported occurring during the first nine months of 1967.

19. See the discussion in E. L. Quarantelli and Russell R. Dynes, "What Looting in Civil Disturbances Really Means," *Trans-action* 5 (May 1968): 9–14.

20. Quarantelli and Dynes, "Looting and Civil Disorders," p. 9.

21. Stanley Lieberson and Arnold R. Silverman, "The Precipitants and Underlying Conditions of Race Riots," *American Sociological Review* 30 (December 1965):

887–98 [reprinted in this volume]. They define "riots" as involving an assault on persons and property simply because they are part of a given subgroup of the community. In terms of our conceptualization, riots are simply one type of hostile outburst.

22. For a summary of these conditions, see Milton Bloombaum, "The Conditions Underlying Race Riots as Portrayed by Multidimensional Scalogram Analysis: A Reanalysis of Lieberson and Silverman's Data," *American Sociological Review* 33 (February 1968); 77.

23. Ibid., pp. 76–91.

24. In their analysis, Lieberson and Silverman made use of *paired comparisons;* that is, each city experiencing a riot was compared with a city as similar as possible in *size* and *region* which had no riot in the ten years preceding or following the riot date. One of the real problems which plagues such studies is the problem of selecting "appropriate" control cities.

25. *The Municipal Yearbook, 1963* (Chicago: International City Manager's Association, 1963).

26. Lieberson and Silverman, "The Precipitants," pp. 893–94.

27. Ibid., p. 895.

28. Ibid., p. 896.

29. "County Official's Guide to the Kerner Report," *American County Government* 33 (June 1968); 16. As our data indicate, then, cities experiencing hostile outbursts tend to exhibit many overt signs of social and economic decay. For a more detailed discussion of these factors, see Kenneth B. Clark, *Dark Ghetto, Dilemmas of Social Power* (New York: Harper & Row, 1965). Professor Clark also discusses some of the psychological implications of environmental decay.

30. Tomlinson, "A Development of a Riot Ideology," p. 29.

3. Participants

Knowing the nature of riots and the type of city in which they are likely to occur does not tell us everything we need to know. The explanation of riot participation is basically a different process from the explanation of the causes of riots. The two problems call for different types of data and different types of theories. The explanation of riot occurrences calls for a type of structural analysis while the explanation of riot participation calls for a social-psychological orientation. The previous selections have been concerned mostly with the former problem. The selections in this section address themselves to the latter.

Th study of riot participants is very difficult. The best method would be participant-observation. But this approach has its shortcomings. To be able to carry it out well, one must be fortunate enough to be on the scene at the inception of the disorder or close enough at the outbreak to get to the scene before the riot ends. Even if one is this fortunate, the technique presents certain dangers of a legal and physical nature. Barring the unlikely participant-observation study, we must rely either upon the analysis of arrestees, as in the Geschwender and Singer selection, or upon the analysis of self-reported riot participants, as in the Caplan and Paige study of the same Detroit insurrection.[1]

Both techniques have their weaknesses. It is never the case that all riot participants are arrested, nor is it ever likely to be the case that all arrestees are participants. Thus, one is always dealing with impure samples. Similarly, one is likely to be dealing with impure samples when one uses the self-report technique, for there are fear motivations that may lead participants to deny participation, just as there are ideological motivations which might lead non-participants to claim participation in order to swell the reported levels of participation. Probably the wise course to follow is to seek convergences in findings between studies using the two methods.

In an article not included in this volume, David Boesel analyzes the role of youths in the riots.[2] Studies have consistently found that youths are over-represented among riot participants. Boesel demonstrates that conditions encourage the development of higher levels of self-esteem and black militancy among youths. This greater degree of black pride is combined with higher levels of economic deprivation despite a closing of the educational gap *vis-à-vis* whites. The combination of these factors is sufficient to account for a greater likelihood of revolt among black youths than among older blacks. Of course, every urban insurrection found large sprinklings of mature, middle-aged, and older participants as well as youths, but the youths played a key role, as Boesel illustrates with this natural history:

> The development of particular riots after 1964 tended to recapitulate the development of the riots as a whole. Typically the disorder would begin with a confrontation of the sort that became widespread in the early sixties. As the confrontation grew, an elaborate contest would develop between the youths and the police, the object of the police being to maintain order, and that of the youths, to disrupt it. If the young blacks met with success, the police would find it impossible to control the streets. . . . It is at this point, the youths having broken open the situation, that the riot would begin to draw in other segments of the community. . . .[3]

The selection written by Benjamin D. Singer and myself has implications both for the analysis of riot participants and for the analysis of riot growth and development, which will be discussed later in Part IV. Earlier research consistently has produced data which show the riot participant to be better educated but to have lower occupational income and employment status than the nonparticipant.[4] Strangely enough, these data have been used to buttress the conclusion that riot participants are not motivated by deprivation, but are, on the contrary, relatively well off. It may be that the higher level of educational accomplishments has led to this conclusion. Other forms of deprivation are discounted as a function of the youth of the participants, on the assumption that these deprivations will be eliminated as a result of the ageing process and career progress. This selection demonstrates that the riot participant is less well educated than his nonparticipating riot-zone counterpart when age is controlled. He is also more deprived. He has lower occupational status, lower income, and has been unemployed for more weeks in the year preceding the riot. He also has lower occupational status and lower income when education is controlled, and lower income when occupation is controlled. Data presented in another article enabled us to rule out the career progress thesis.[5] We found that the degree to which the riot participants were more deprived than nonparticipants increases when age is controlled. It is precisely at the older age categories that the greatest level of relative deprivation occurs. It is perhaps the case that younger rioters may be motivated for many reasons, but the older rioter appears to be motivated primarily by deprivation. This selection also provides a valuable analysis of the roles that social isolation and ideology play as "filters" between grievance and riot participation on alternative causes of riot participation of nonaggrieved persons.

The selection by Raymond J. Murphy and James M. Watson provides an empirical test of the rising-aspiration hypothesis for the explanation of riot participation. The authors discovered a relationship between aspirations and discontent among low status persons, but they found no relationship between aspirations per se and riot participation and support. However, the combination of high aspirations and discontent did produce increases in both riot participation and support. Thus, the findings in this selection appear to reject the thesis that deprivation in and of itself produces riot participation or support. They suggest that it is only when deprivation is combined with high aspirations that it produces a significant propensity to support, or participate in, riots. This tends to buttress the hypothesis that riots are carried on by persons discontented with the present and seeking a better future.

NOTES

1. Nathan S. Caplan and Jeffery M. Paige, "A Study of Ghetto Rioters," *Scientific American* 219 (August 1968): 15–21.
2. David Boesel, "The Liberal Society, Black Youths, and the Ghetto Riots," *Psychiatry* 33 (May 1970): 265–81.
3. Ibid., p. 273.
4. See, for example, James A. Geschwender and Benjamin D. Singer, "Deprivation and the Detroit Riot," *Social Problems* 17 (Spring 1970): 457–463.
5. Ibid., pp. 461–62.

THE DETROIT INSURRECTION:
GRIEVANCE AND FACILITATING CONDITIONS

James A. Geschwender / Benjamin D. Singer

The present paper takes as its starting point the assumption that ghetto disorders are simply one phase of an ongoing, developing black revolt. With this as a starting point, we may attempt to ascertain the grievances which underlay the insurrections and the conditions which facilitate individual participation. Geschwender has suggested elsewhere that status inconsistency may be one source of the tension that underlies ghetto uprisings [1] and that relative deprivation is the key to understanding why anger and rebelliousness result from status inconsistency.[2] This earlier analysis suffers from the defect of being based upon medians or distributions of variables taken singly without simultaneous measures taken from the same individuals on several variables. The present study will attempt to overcome this problem by utilizing survey data from the Detroit Riot Study.

A number of sources suggest that social isolation produces a predisposition to participate in collective behavior or collective protest.[3] We feel that it is more profitable to view social isolation as a facilitating condition rather than as a predisposing characteristic. Social isolation creates a psychological state which frees one from many of the inhibiting forces and community norms that would tend to restrain one from participating in collective protest activities. The present paper attempts to test the hypotheses that relative deprivation functions as a grievance which motivates participation in ghetto uprisings and that social isolation and perception of violence as legitimate and potentially effective tactics function as facilitating conditions which increase the likelihood of such participation. We shall also attempt to ascertain the mode of communications which contributes to riot development after the occurrence of a precipitating incident.

METHODOLOGY

The hypotheses will be tested with data collected from a sample of 499 black males arrested during the Detroit disorder of 1967 [4] and a sample of 499 black males from the Detroit community. The second sample consisted of male, black neighbors of the persons included in the first sample. The second group was interviewed two to three weeks after the first sample of Negro males. The relative deprivation hypothesis may be tested on the basis that blacks compare themselves with other blacks with whom they exist in close residential propinquity.

An original contribution.

RELATIVE DEPRIVATION

It is difficult to state unambiguously the relative levels of education of the community and arrestee samples due to the fact that the arrestee sample is younger. The arrestee sample simultaneously has a higher median number of years of schooling completed (11.7 to 10.8), a lower proportion of high school graduates (37.1 percent to 43.8 percent), and is less well educated in every age bracket.[5] Relative occupational status is also ambiguous. The arrestee sample is less concentrated in both white-collar (10.1 percent to 15.5 percent) and unskilled and service occupations (51.1 percent to 53.7 percent) but more concentrated in semi-skilled and skilled occupations (38.7 percent to 30.8 percent).[6] The arrestee sample clearly has lower incomes, is significantly more likely to have been unemployed in the year preceding the disorder, and, if unemployed, is significantly more likely to have been unemployed for two months or longer.[7]

The interrelationship of education, occupation, and income is more meaningful than any of these variables taken separately. Table 1 presents these data; the arrestee sample has a smaller proportion of persons with white-collar occupations at every level of education beyond elementary school. It also has a lower proportion of persons earning over $100 a week at every occupational level and at every educational level. None of the Gammas measuring the strength of the relationship between education and occupation, occupation and income, and education and income are significant for the arrestee sample. Only the Gammas measuring the relationship between education and occupation and education and income are significant for the community sample. Both of these are of a low order of magnitude indicating minimal to moderate relationships.

This means that for the members of the community sample increases in education do make for *some* increase in both occupational achievement and in weekly earnings, although there is no significant relationship between the latter two factors. The arrestee sample does not even have this low level of assurance that educational gains lead to better jobs or higher incomes, nor that better jobs produce higher incomes.

The arrestee sample is clearly more deprived, both absolutely and relative to qualifications, than the community sample. They are less well educated on an age-controlled basis, are less likely to hold white-collar jobs, and have lower incomes. They are also less able to translate their educational achievements into better jobs or higher incomes. Neither group is very successful in translating their occupational achievements into higher incomes but the arrestee sample is less so. They are truly the most deprived segment of a deprived class.

SOCIAL ISOLATION

Table 2 presents data on length of residence in Detroit, marital status, residential status, and organizational memberships of the two samples.

TABLE 1. Interrelationship of Education, Occupation, and Income by Sample

		Arrestee		Community	
	N	Percent white collar	N	Percent white collar	Chi Square[a]
Education:					
0-8 years	50	6.0	80	1.2	1.01
9-11 years	191	7.9	100	9.0	0.01
12 years	133	12.0	135	17.0	0.98
13 and over	19	26.3	44	54.5	<u>3.20</u>
Gamma[b]		0.09		0.22	
Z^c		0.79		<u>2.79</u>	

	N	Percent over $100	N	Percent over $100	Chi Square[a]
Occupation:					
White Collar	37	48.6	48	72.9	<u>4.26</u>
Skilled and Semi-skilled	148	72.3	106	77.4	0.59
Unskilled and Service	196	53.6	181	79.0	<u>25.93</u>
Gamma[b]		0.168		0.113	
Z^c		1.60		0.98	

	N	Percent over $100	N	Percent over $100	Chi Square[a]
Education:					
0-8 years	53	50.9	83	56.6	0.22
9-11 years	198	57.1	99	75.8	<u>9.13</u>
12 years	138	63.8	129	82.2	<u>10.46</u>
13 and over	20	80.0	41	87.8	0.18
Gamma[b]		0.13		0.33	
Z^c		1.36		<u>3.43</u>	

[a]Underlining indicates statistical significance.
[b]Computed using four educational, three occupational, and six income categories.
[c]Computed as in the case of Tan to measure statistical significance of Gamma; underlining indicates significant at .05 or beyond.

These four characteristics are taken as indicators of the degree of social isolation of the two samples.

Members of the arrestee sample are significantly more likely to be recent immigrants to Detroit (although they are more likely to be Michigan born), are significantly less likely to be married, are significantly more likely to live alone, and are significantly less likely to belong to voluntary associations. Each of these differences remains when age is controlled. With the exception of marital and residential status, each of the variables is independent of the others.[8] In fact, a significantly higher proportion of

TABLE 2.   Social Isolation by Sample

Variable	Arrestees Percent	Comments Percent	Chi Square
Length of Residence[a]			
1 year	8.8	3.5	
1 – 9 years	20.2	12.1	
10 – 19 years	33.7	23.6	
20 years & over	37.3	60.8	
Total	100.0	100.0	
N	466	462	22.79[b]
Marital Status			
Married	38.6	60.2	
Single, separated, divorced, widowed	61.4	39.8	
Total	100.0	100.0	
N	497	493	45.39
Place of Residence			
Alone	20.3	15.0	
Other	79.7	85.1	
Total	100.0	100.1	
N	492	475	4.44
Organizational Memberships			
None	83.2	29.7	
One or More	16.8	70.3	
Total	100.0	100.0	
N	400	499	20.58
Number Variables Isolated on all 4[c]	4.6	1.1	
3 or more	25.9	14.5	
2 or more	67.3	39.9	
1 or more	95.8	82.0	
N	456	434	46.92[d]

[a]Dichotomized between under 10 years and 10 years and over.
[b]Limited to respondents who gave information on all four variables.
[c]Dichotomized between those isolated on two or more variables and those isolated on one or less.
[d]Underlining indicates significant at .05 level or beyond.

the married members of the arrestee sample live alone (13.6 percent to 3.2 percent).[9] The arrestee sample is simultaneously isolated on significantly more variables than is the community sample. Age controls do not eliminate this difference even though there is less of a difference between those under 25 than there is between those over 25.[10]

IDEOLOGICAL FACTORS

Both level of grievance and social isolation contribute to propensity to participate in riot activities. However, these disposing factors do not operate in a vacuum. We must also consider the role of ideology. Over the course of a number of years, the mass media had provided a platform through which a number of militants had presented the view that riots were a legitimate tactic to be used in bringing about social change. They also presented descriptions of past riot responses on the part of the local, state, and federal governments as well as responses by private organizations that may have provided confirmation for the belief that riots do bring about some social change. Evidence that such a riot ideology was in fact emerging among American blacks may be found in national surveys which ascertained that 2 percent of American blacks in 1964 and 40 percent in 1969 felt that riots helped the Negro cause.[11]

Further evidence is provided by the Sears and Tomlinson study of black Los Angeles curfew area residents.[12] They found that 38 percent of the respondents referred to the disorders as revolt, revolution, or insurrection, 56 percent thought that the disorders had a purpose or goal, 62 percent thought it was Negro protest, 38 percent thought that it helped the Negro cause, 58 percent thought that the main effects would be favorable, and 64 percent thought that the targets attacked deserved it. In addition, 84 percent thought that the riots made whites more aware of Negro problems, 51 percent felt that whites were made more sympathetic to Negro problems, and 24 percent felt that the riots decreased the gap between the races.

We do not have comparable data from Detroit. However, we do have some indication of a differential development of riot ideology between the members of our arrestee and community samples.[13] The arrestee sample reported having seen more riots (other than Detroit) on television. They also reported having seen different things. Fifty percent of the statements of the arrestee sample and 30 percent of statements of the community sample reported acts of violence, while 20 percent of the arrestee sample and 6 percent of the community sample reported acts of police brutality. Not only did the arrestee sample see different things but they felt differently about what they saw. More of the arrestee sample (26 percent as compared to 13 percent) reported feeling anger at whites or police or satisfaction with aggression against whites.

COMMUNICATION AND THE SPREAD OF THE RIOT

Only 27 percent of the arrestees discovered the existence of the riot through direct experience.[14] The rest were first informed, and thus attracted to participation, through some medium of communications. The most prominent additional source of information was interpersonal communications, which accounted for about 47 percent of the sample, while mass media sources only accounted for about 25 percent. There is some reason to believe that mass media sources may have been the initial source of information that spread to the general population of arrestees, for a little over half of those who heard about the riot from mass media sources or over the phone relayed the information to another person while only 37 percent of those who heard through direct interpersonal channels and 28 percent who found out through direct personal experience told another person.[15]

The content of the message which was most likely to attract persons to the scene of the disorder was simply information as to the existence and location of a riot.[16] This would suggest that persons were not attracted by the nature and characteristic of the precipitating incident; rather, they had a high degree of predisposition to participate in an insurrection. They may have been primed and waiting for the day that Detroit would have its explosion. It seems probable that the combination of grievances, riot ideology, and social isolation accounts for this preprimed condition.

It is likely that the crowd which formed during the raid on the blind pig was heterogeneous. It probably included both persons with more and persons with less severe grievances, both persons who are more integrated into the community and those who are more isolated from it, and persons with a high degree of riot ideology and persons with a low degree of riot ideology. Figure 1 shows how the cross-classification of these

FIGURE 1. Types of Potential Crowd Members

Grievance Level	Level of Riot Ideology	Socially Isolated	Socially Integrated
High	High	A	B
	Low	C	D
Low	High	E	F
	Low	G	H

variables, each dichotomized, produces eight types of potential crowd members.

Types *A, B, C,* and *D* would be more prone to participate in the insurrection than would types *E, F, G,* and *H* as a result of their possession of higher levels of grievances. The possession of a highly elaborated riot ideology would predispose types *A, B, E,* and *F* toward participation, while the lack of such ideology would predispose types *C, D, G,* and *H* against participation. Types *A, C, E,* and *G* would be most free to participate because of their high degree of social isolation, while types *B, D, F,* and *H* would be less free because of their high degree of social integration.

The three-way cross classification of these variables yields the prediction that type *A* persons (high in grievances, high in riot ideology, socially isolated) would be the most likely to respond to the precipitating incident by active participation in the initial outbreak. This is a direct result of the fact that they share all three disposing characteristics. A slightly lower probability of participation in the insurrection at its very outset would be associated with types *B* (high in grievances, high in riot ideology, socially integrated), *C* (high in grievances, low in riot ideology, socially isolated), and *E* (low in grievances, high in riot ideology, socially isolated). This results from the fact that types *B, C,* and *E* possess two of the three disposing characteristics. While these types are less likely to be the initial participants than are type *A* persons, they will have a high degree of likelihood of being drawn in by the force of emerging norms. A minimal probability of initial participation and a low degree of likelihood of being attracted by emergent norms will be found among those possessing only one disposing characteristic: types D (high in grievances, low in ideology, socially integrated), F (low in grievances, high in riot ideology, socially integrated), and G (low in grievances, low in riot ideology, socially isolated). Type H persons (low in grievances, low in riot ideology, socially integrated) possess none of the disposing characteristics. They would almost certainly not participate initially, not be drawn in by the force of emergent norms, and might even become counter-rioters.

Once the insurrection was under way the ranks of the participants were swelled by recruits who had not been on the scene at the time of the precipitating incident. Blacks not on the initial scene can be classified into the same eight types, and the same arguments apply to them as well. It seems that type A persons would be the ones most likely to be drawn into the insurrection. But no insurrection of any duration is likely to be carried on entirely by type A persons. The communication process and the force of emergent norms would induce others to participate. It would seem that these additional recruits are most likely to come from among types B, C, and E, with a negligible likelihood of recruits being drawn from among types D, F, and G. It would probably take a full-blown revolution to attract the participation of types D, F, and G. Types D and H (the socially integrated with low grievance levels and low levels of riot ideology) are the least likely to ever participate in ghetto uprisings.

NOTES

1. James A. Geschwender, "Civil Rights Protest and the Riots: A Disappearing Distinction," reprinted in this volume, Part IV, Section 1.

2. James A. Geschwender. "Social Structure and the Negro Revolt: An Examination of Some Hypotheses," reprinted in this volume, Part II, Section 1.

3. Eric Hoffer, *The True Believer* (New York: The New American Library, 1951); Leo Lowenthal and Norbert Gutterman, *Prophets of Deceit* (New York: Harper & Row, 1949); William Kornhauser, *The Politics of Mass Society* (Glencoe: The Free Press, 1959), pp. 182–223; Seymour Martin Lipset, *Political Man* (Garden City, N.Y.: Doubleday, 1960), pp. 94–130; Ralph H. Turner and Lewis M. Killian, *Collective Behavior* (Englewood Cliffs, N.J.: Prentice-Hall, 1957), pp. 409–53; H. Edward Ransford, "Isolation, Powerlessness and Violence: A Study of Attitudes and Participation in the Watts Riot," reprinted in this volume, Part IV, Section 4.

4. For a description of the sample and interviewing, see Benjamin D. Singer, "Mass Media and Communication Processes as Factors in the Detroit Riot of 1967," *Public Opinion Quarterly* 34 (Summer 1970): 236–45.

5. James A. Geschwender, Benjamin D. Singer, and Judith Harrington, "Status Inconsistency, Relative Deprivation, and the Detroit Riot." Paper delivered before the 1969 meetings of the American Sociological Association, Tables 1 and 2.

6. Ibid., Table 3.

7. Ibid., Tables 4 and 5.

8. James A. Geschwender, Benjamin D. Singer, and Richard W. Osborn, "Social Isolation and Riot Participation" (Paper delivered before the 1969 meetings of the American Sociological Association), p. 7.

9. Ibid., Table 4.

10. Ibid., Table 8.

11. Singer, "Mass Media and Communication Processes."

12. David O. Sears and T. M. Tomlinson, "Riot Ideology in Los Angeles: A Study of Negro Attitudes," *Social Science Quarterly* 49 (December 1968): 485–503. [Reprinted in this volume.]

13. Benjamin D. Singer, Richard W. Osborn, and James A. Geschwender, *Black Rioters: A Study of Social Factors and Communication in The Detroit Riot* (Lexington, Mass.: D. C. Heath, 1970).

14. Singer, "Mass Media and Communication Processes."

15. Ibid.

16. Ibid.

LEVEL OF ASPIRATION, DISCONTENT, AND
SUPPORT FOR VIOLENCE: A TEST OF
THE EXPECTATION HYPOTHESIS

Raymond J. Murphy / James M. Watson

INTRODUCTION

Although ultimately historians may decide that the decade of the 1960s represents man's conquest of space and the triumph of science and technology, for many others it will be remembered as a period of social violence symbolized by political assassination and ghetto rioting. Perhaps the supreme irony of this, visible even to the most myopic among us, is that we have more knowledge, and willingness to use it, in matters of space than we do in the more mundane but more pressing matter of achieving peace and understanding in society. Nowhere is our collective ignorance so exposed and nowhere so critical as in an understanding of the dynamics of violence. Assumptions of order and stability, so cherished by generations of sociologists, have been severely challenged by the events of the 1960s. Both commonsense understandings and more sophisticated theoretical explanations often fail to account for participation in violence. For example, the findings of numerous investigations by social scientists, riot commissions, and reporters of the major urban ghetto riots indicate that:

1. Rioters are not predominantly down-and-out "riff-raff" who have little or no stake in the community and therefore little to lose by attacking the system. Evidence indicates that participation and support for riots is far more widespread than expected and that those who have made some achievements are far more likely to be committed to this kind of disorder than are those who have failed. It would thus appear that the

An original contribution.

"absolute deprivation" theory of revolt cannot be supported by evidence from Watts, Newark, Detroit, and other urban centers experiencing riots in the sixties.[1]

2. There is little evidence that rioters are drawn from the ranks of those who have recently migrated to the urban scene from rural areas or small towns. Plausible as this notion may seem, with its implications of alienation and culture shock dear to the heart of the sociologist, and with its suggestions of "outsiders" and "freeloaders" dear to the beliefs of mayors and police chiefs, the data fail to reveal differences in participation by length of time in the urban center.

3. Finally, there is little evidence to date that rioters represent some kind of national (or international) conspiracy devoted to disrupting or destroying the American society. This notion beloved by arch conservatives and some black militants fails to account for the magnitude of support or the variety of motivations evidenced by riot participants in the many studies conducted in the last ten years.

Without doubt, that theoretical approach with the greatest currency which purports to explain the participants of the urban riots of the sixties is an orientation variously called the "expectation theory" or the "theory of the revolution of rising expectations." [2] A version of the relative deprivation notion, this approach suggests that the supporters of violence are those who have accepted the cultural definitions of success in the society, made some gains in achieving these goals, but perceive that the gap between their aspirations and achievements can not be closed because of structural and institutional restrictions. The sense of frustration which results from the comparison between what one wants and has been invited to expect and what one currently enjoys leads to militancy and violence. As Gurr puts it:

> . . . the greater the extent of discrepancy that men see between what they seek and want seems (to them) to be attainable, the greater their anger and consequent disposition to aggression. . . . It is . . . one of the keys to the supposed paradox that dissatisfied people often (but by no means always) revolt just when things begin to get better: a little improvement accompanied by promises that much improvement is to come raises expectations, and if much improvement does *not* come when expected, perceptions of capabilities may drop, sometimes abruptly and sharply.[3]

The specific application of this notion to participation and support for riots is illustrated in a quotation from Bowen and Masotti:

> From the viewpoint of social peace, according to this hypothesis, it is neither the wholly downtrodden—who have no aspirations—nor the very well off—who can satisfy theirs—who represent a threat. It is the man in the middle who is dangerous. . . . The reason why Black Americans riot is because there has been just enough improvement in their condition to generate hopes, expectations, or aspirations beyond the capacities of the system to meet them.[4]

Thus, according to this perspective, those persons who have managed to make some gains in the system but who have higher aspirations which they perceive to be thwarted should be the most prone to support violence and, should the occasion arise, be participants in riots. This paper represents an attempt to explore this hypothesis.

METHODOLOGY

Sample

The data for the present investigation were derived from a probability sample of the black residents of a 46 square mile area of South Central Los Angeles designated by Acting Governor Glenn Anderson as a curfew zone in the aftermath of the August 1965 riot. The curfew area included 128 census tracts of which 119 were sampled and whose total population exceeded 300,000. The area sampled covers a wide range of socioeconomic categories. The sampling frame was provided by the U.S. Census Bureau. Lengthy interviews were conducted beginning immediately after the riot by local black residents especially trained for this research project. Four hundred sixty-eight usable interviews were obtained.[5]

Measures

In order to measure the gap between aspirations and achievement we chose occupation as the most salient aspirational dimension. Numerous investigators have argued that occupation level serves as an index of economic and social status position in the society. Accordingly, data on present occupational level and aspired-to occupational level were coded in terms of the Bogue Socioeconomic Index.[6] This scale was employed rather than the usual Census occupational lists inasmuch as it permits a much more detailed analysis of status differences in blue-collar occupations and it takes into consideration income and educational attainment characteristics associated with occupations. Scores are treated as points along a continuous scale with quasi-equal intervals. The index score of present occupation was subtracted from the index score of that occupation the respondent indicated he aspired to. This procedure resulted in an array of discrepancy scores ranging from 0 to 129. The mean discrepancy score for the entire sample was 32.19.

A moment's reflection will suggest that if we were to use the discrepancy scores per se as our measure of level of aspiration we would introduce an artifact that would make meaningful comparisons impossible. Those already in higher status level occupations cannot, by virtue of the technique, have as great a discrepancy between their present positions and those they aspire to. Accordingly, we divided the sample into eight equal size categories on the basis of index scores of present occupation. For each of these categories, the mean discrepancy score was calculated. As expected, the mean discrepancy scores for those in low status occupations were far greater than for those in higher status occupations. For each occupational status category, we dichotomized respondents on the basis of their discrepancy scores being above or below the mean score for their category. We then combined all of the lows and the highs from each of the eight categories. Thus for the purpose of this paper, persons designated as having low occupational aspirations are those whose discrepancy score is below the mean of those comprising their own present occupational level. Similarly, those we have called persons with high occupational aspirations are individuals having discrepancy scores above the mean of those in their present occupational level. In effect, therefore, we are discussing persons with *relatively* low and high aspirations, rather than measuring all respondents on a scale of absolute aspiration levels.

FINDINGS

Level of aspiration and ghetto aggravation

A major assumption of the expectation theory of riot supporters and participants is that persons with high aspirations will evidence greater frustration and dissatisfaction with their life situation than will those with low aspirations.[7] Presumably it is because of this heightened unhappiness that those with high aspirations are hypothesized to be more militant and prone to support and participate in violence. High aspirations alone are not sufficient grounds for predicting support for violence. The desire for achievement must be accompanied by frustration at the pace of change or by perceptions of structural obstacles making achievement difficult or impossible.

In our study of the Watts riot we included a number of questions dealing with three major areas of ghetto discontent: the behavior of the police, the existence of various forms of discrimination, and the practices of merchants. We found that those respondents who perceived problems in each of these areas were significantly more likely to report that they participated in and supported the riot than were those who evidenced little concern over police, discrimination, or merchants.[8]

We regard these three areas as representing the major sources of ghetto frustration and thus relevant to a test of the expectation hypothesis. First we must demonstrate that there is a relationship between level of aspiration and perception of structurally induced frustration. If this relationship is evidenced we then should proceed to determine whether those with high aspirations sensing frustration are more active or supportive of violence than those with lower aspirations who do not perceive these problems. In this section we seek to determine the relationship between aspirations and perception of discontents.

Each of the three types of discontent represents cumulative scores based on a number of questions dealing with specific complaints of various forms of discriminatory behavior. The Police Malpractice Index is made up of six types of police behavior ranging from the use of insulting language to beating up persons in custody. The Discrimination Index is based on eight items having to do with unfair or unequal treatment in employment, housing, welfare practices, and so on. The Consumer Discontent Index is made up of six items dealing with overcharging, poor quality of goods, unfair credit practices, and so on. For each of these indices respondents were asked whether they had personally experienced prejudicial behavior or had heard of or knew about such occurrences, or whether they felt that such practices did not exist. The scoring on each index reflected the respondent's degree of personal involvement with the problem. A person labeled high on any one of these indices is one who indicated personal involvement with the situation. A low score represents little or no involvement with the problem.[9]

Table 1 shows the relationship between level of occupational aspiration and ghetto discontent. It shows that the predicted relationship

TABLE 1. The Relationship Between Leval of Occupational
Aspiration and Three Types of Ghetto Discontent (In Percent)

Types of Ghetto Discontent	Level of Occupational Aspiration	
	Low	High
Police Malpractice		
Low	41	25
Medium	38	47
High	21	28
Total	100	100
(N)	(211)	(133)
Discrimination		
Low	42	25
Medium	37	49
High	21	26
Total	100	100
(N)	(194)	(125)
Consumer Discontent		
Low	56	48
Medium	25	27
High	19	25
Total	100	100
(N)	(192)	(128)

holds, particularly for police malpractice and discrimination. Those with a high level of aspiration tend to be more aware of, and to have experienced more, prejudicial behavior. The same relationship holds on the Consumer Discontent Index, but the relationship is weaker. It will be noted that differences are greater for the low than for the high group. That is to say, those with a high level of aspiration are significantly less likely to deny having experienced structural mistreatment than are those whose occupational aspirations are low.

A further specification of the expectation theory involves occupational level. According to the theory, those who have already experienced some achievement will be more likely to be frustrated by obstacles than will those who have not made progress. Unfortunately, we do not have any direct measures in our study of the extent to which persons feel that

TABLE 2. The Relationship Between Level of Occupational Aspiration
and Perception of Police Malpractice Controlled for
Occupational Level (In Percent)

	Occupational Level			
	Low		High	
Police Malpractice	low occ. asp.	high occ. asp.	low occ. asp.	high occ. asp.
Low	51	30	30	19
Medium	33	44	44	51
High	16	26	26	30
Total	100	100	100	100
(N)	(106)	(80)	(105)	(53)

they have made substantial occupational gains. It seems logical to assume,
however, that those in our sample in higher occupational statuses will
sense a greater feeling of achievement than those in lower status occupations. Accordingly, we have used level of present occupation as an indicator of achievement. Two occupational levels are distinguished. The
lower occupational status consists of persons in semi-skilled and unskilled
occupations, while the higher consists of persons above the "job ceiling"
—skilled, white-collar, managerial, and professional work. Tables 2–4
present the relationship between occupational aspirations and our measures of ghetto discontent for each occupational stratum.

TABLE 3. The Relationship Between Level of Occupational
Aspiration and Perception of Discrimination Controlled
for Occupational Level (in Percent)

	Occupational Level			
	Low		High	
Discrimination	low occ. asp	high occ. asp	low occ. asp	high occ. asp
Low	51	26	33	22
Medium	29	51	46	45
High	20	23	21	33
Total	100	100	100	100
(N)	(100)	(76)	(94)	(49)

It will be noted in all three tables that the original relationship
between aspiration and discontent is increased in magnitude for those in
the lower occupational stratum. However, this relationship all but disappears for those in the higher stratum. Yet overall the highest magnitude
of discontent for police malpractice and discrimination occurs among
those in the higher occupational stratum. In the case of consumer discontent, those in the lower occupations evidence the greatest dissatisfaction.
These findings suggest a specification in the expectation theory. Although

it is true, with regard to police malpractice and discrimination, as the theory would suggest, that those in the higher occupations who also have higher aspirations are the most sensitive to institutionally induced frustrations, aspiration level makes the most difference with respect to discontent among those in low status occupations. Apparently, having achieved enough to be in a relatively high status occupation is sufficiently powerful to override differences in anticipated future advances. It may well be that the indignities of the police and continued experience of discrimination serve to symbolize for the economically successful the fact that occupational gains cannot be translated into the kind of social acceptance thought to be appropriate to one's position. For this reason, such ghetto frustration is salient to both low and high aspirers among the successful. Among those in the lower stratum there appear to be two distinct types: those with low aspirations, who are the least sensitive to police practices and discrimination; and those with high aspirations, who are nearly as aware of injustices as persons in the high occupations. The former group appears to be the kind of apathetic withdrawn products of the system which Marx labeled the "lumpenproletariat." They seem to have lost ambition and concern. The latter desire advancement and acutely perceive the indignities of their environment.

Turning to Table 4, we see that the pattern is different with respect to consumer discontent. This time the group which seems to stand out

TABLE 4. The Relationship Between Level of Occupational Aspiration and Consumer Discontent Controlled for Occupational Level (in percent)

| | Occupational Level | | | |
| | Low | | High | |
Consumer Discontent	low occ. asp.	high occ. asp.	low occ. asp.	high occ. asp.
Low	57	44	56	53
Medium	28	28	20	25
High	15	28	24	22
Total	100	100	100	100
(N)	(99)	(79)	(93)	(49)

with respect to sensitivity to mistreatment is the low status occupation high aspirers. Those in low occupations with low aspirations are similar to both low and high aspirers in the high status occupations in showing less concern about the practices of merchants. One explanation for this may be that among those in the higher status occupations exploitative practices by merchants can be more easily avoided, and where they do exist are more an annoyance than a threat to status. Thus their response is similar to those who make up our "apathetic" low status group. For those in the lower occupations who have high hopes for achievement, however, the exploitation by merchants can be viewed as a serious economic obstacle to success.

Aspiration and riot support

We have already argued that the expectation theory does not imply that high aspirations alone are sufficient to lead to militancy and support for violence. Nevertheless, it seems worthwhile to examine this relationship for our data.

Our measures of support for the riot include first, responses to a question which asked if the respondent had participated in any way in the riot itself. Those who indicated that they were involved in the activities of the riot we have labeled as actives, those not participating as inactives. The second measure of riot support is the individual's cumulative score on a scale of riot favorability. The scale is made up of three items which dealt with the respondent's attitudes about the kinds of people involved in the riot, what he liked or disliked about the riot, and how he personally felt about what had happened.[10]

Table 5 shows the relationship between level of aspiration and our

TABLE 5. The Relationship Between Level of Occupational Aspiration and Riot Participation and Support (In Percent)

Participation and Support	Level of Occupational Aspiration	
	Low	High
Self-Reported Riot Activity		
Not Active	78	77
Active	22	23
Total	100	100
(N)	(211)	(139)
Favorability toward Riot		
Low	56	44
Medium	24	32
High	20	24
Total	100	100
(N)	(193)	(119)

two measures of riot support. It reveals little association between aspirations and activity or favorability, although there is a slight tendency for those who have high aspirations to report higher favorability to the riot.

Again we introduce the dimension of occupational status into our examination of relationships and, as can be seen in Tables 6 and 7, there is still little relationship between level of aspiration and riot support.

These results are in keeping with the expectation theory as we have outlined it and suggest that it is only when high aspirations are combined with high levels of discontent that support for violence can be anticipated.

Aspiration, discontent, and riot support

We will now proceed to test this proposition. The results are shown in Tables 8 and 9. If the theory is correct we would expect to find the

TABLE 6. The Relationship Between Level of Occupational Aspiration and Self-Reported Riot Activity, Controlled for Occupational Level (In Percent)

| | Occupational Level | | | |
| | Low | | High | |
Self-Reported Riot Activity	low occ. asp.	high occ. asp.	low occ. asp.	high occ. asp.
Not Active	83	75	73	80
Active	17	25	27	20
Total	100	100	100	100
(N)	(108)	(83)	(103)	(56)

TABLE 7. The Relationship Between Level of Occupational Aspiration and Riot Favorability, Controlled for Occupational Level (In Percent)

| | Occupational Level | | | |
| | Low | | High | |
Riot Favorability	low occ. asp.	high occ. asp.	low occ. asp.	high occ. asp.
Low	56	47	56	41
Medium	25	30	22	35
High	19	23	22	24
Total	100	100	100	100
(N)	(103)	(73)	(90)	(46)

TABLE 8. Percent Reporting Themselves Active in Riot, by Level of Aspiration Controlling for Occupational Level and Measures of Discontent

| | Low Occupation | | High Occupation | |
Discontent	Low asp.	High asp.	Low asp.	High asp.
Police Malpractice				
Low	$11_{(65)}$	$23_{(31)}$	$21_{(48)}$	$18_{(17)}$
High	$26_{(39)}$	$28_{(46)}$	$33_{(54)}$	$24_{(34)}$
Discrimination				
Low	$17_{(71)}$	$26_{(39)}$	$27_{(55)}$	$18_{(22)}$
High	$14_{(28)}$	$29_{(34)}$	$27_{(37)}$	$28_{(25)}$
Consumer Discontent				
Low	$9_{(65)}$	$24_{(42)}$	$23_{(62)}$	$15_{(34)}$
High	$24_{(38)}$	$25_{(28)}$	$24_{(25)}$	$22_{(18)}$

TABLE 9.   Percent Favorable Toward Riot, by Level of Aspiration Controlling for Occupational Level and Measures of Discontent

	Low Occupation		High Occupation	
Discontent	Low asp.	High asp.	Low asp.	High asp.
Police Malpractice				
Low	32(62)	41(29)	34(41)	63(16)
High	56(36)	62(39)	53(49)	65(26)
Discrimination				
Low	34(68)	36(36)	31(49)	40(15)
High	68(25)	67(27)	58(31)	68(22)
Consumer Discontent				
Low	40(63)	39(36)	39(56)	50(24)
High	49(35)	63(24)	39(23)	72(18)

greatest magnitude of difference in activity and favorability between those who have low aspirations and low perceptions of discontent on the one hand, and those with high levels of aspiration and high awareness of discontent on the other. In Table 9 we see that this pattern obtains for both occupational status levels. For example, 32 percent of those in the low occupation group with low aspirations and low perceptions of police malpractice favored the riot, while 62 percent of those in the same stratum with high aspirations and high discontent were favorable toward the riot. Similarly, among those in the high occupational stratum, persons with low aspirations and less concern with police behavior are less favorable toward the riot (34 percent) than those with high aspirations and high awareness of police malpractice (65 percent). The same strong relationship holds in both occupational groups for each of the three measures of discontent. Thus the predictions of the expectation theory are supported in the case of riot favorability.

When we turn to the matter of activity in the riot, however (Table 8), we note that the pattern of expected relationships holds only for those in the low occupational status group. Among persons in this stratum the relationship is strong for each of the measures of discontent. That is to say, those persons who are low in aspiration and discontent are less likely to report being active in the riot than those who are high on both dimensions. Among those in the high occupational stratum however, there is little difference in reported activity between those low or high in aspirations and discontent.

We have presented these diagonal comparisons in these two tables because in our judgment they constitute the most direct test of the expectation hypothesis. Another way of looking at the data is to attempt to determine the relative importance in differentiating support and activity of each of the two components of the expectation theory. That is, how important is perception of discontent on the one hand, and level of aspiration, on the other, to favorability and activity for each occupational stratum? Looking at the table on favorability, we note that among those in the lower occupational stratum discontent is a better discriminator of riot support than is level of aspiration, with the exception of consumer discontent where the relationship is additive. Among those in the higher occupational level both factors seem to be important and additive. For the high group, therefore, level of aspiration is more important than it was for the lower group in predicting favorability. This seems particularly important in the case of consumer discontent.

Turning to the table on activity, among the low occupational group differences in police malpractice and consumer discontent appear to be important for those with low aspirations. In the case of discrimination, differences in aspiration level account for all of the variation in activity. Among those in the higher occupations there appears to be no consistent pattern of relationship between activity and either level of aspiration or extent of discontent. It is of interest to note that the highest percentage of activity in the entire table is reported by those in the higher group who report having experienced police malpractice but who have low aspirations.

Thus the data give considerable support to the expectation theory of violence, particularly in the matter of riot favorability. In the case of activity, however, the findings are less clear. The expected pattern obtained for those in the lower occupational group, but not for those in the higher occupations. In all cases the differences are smaller for activity than for favorability.

DISCUSSION

Our findings reported in this paper suggest several lines of comment worthy of brief consideration. In the first case, our data seem clearly to suggest that the "riff-raff" or absolute deprivation hypothesis for violence cannot be supported. That group with the lowest participation or support for the riot consists of those in low status occupations with low aspirations and low perception of discontent. These "down-and-outers," while they may have the least to lose by violence, are the most apathetic and withdrawn of the groups we have compared. Those who supported or participated in the riot are clearly those *with* a stake in the community.

Secondly, we find that among those in low status occupations, the extent of perceived discontent, by itself, is strongly related to support for violence. Among those in high status occupations, however, it is the combination of high aspirations and discontent that seems to provide the best indicator of riot support. One reason for this may be that discontent, by itself, fails to capture the element of striving so often reported by students of middle-class persons. For the less advantaged the obstacles created by discrimination are that much greater, and are thus important motivating factors in support for violence. Thus the theory of expectations must take into account the differing relative significance of discontent and level of aspiration for those in differing status levels in the community.

Third, we have shown that level of aspiration and perceived discontent are more closely related to riot favorability than to riot participation. One reason for this may be that data on participation are more likely to be disguised and subject to a number of errors of measurement. Furthermore, even granting the validity of the data, we need further to specify the type of activity persons have engaged in. The relationships to aspirations and discontent may be quite different for those engaged in looting compared to those engaged in arson or assault. Undoubtedly many of those who become active in riots do so for reasons of geographical proximity rather than ideology. For a number of persons, involvement does not mean endorsement. What we need to know is how and for whom support gets translated into action and what relationship this transformation bears to aspirations and frustration.

Fourth, in this paper, we have considered only one dimension of aspiration—occupational. Without denying the importance of this dimension, it is obvious that for black people in the society, obtaining quality education, better housing, personal dignity, and wider participation as equals in the society are of equal or perhaps greater importance. Before we can conclude that the expectation theory is relevant to violence, we must examine these wider areas of aspiration. It is entirely possible that the calculus of aspiration and discontent works differently for different areas of aspiration. The saliency of the theory may thus depend on the type and definition of aspiration we specify.

Finally, we must examine the experiences and feelings of ghetto residents with white persons before we can fully comprehend the significance of aspirations as a factor in violence. One of the conceits of the white world is that black people desire to inherit and participate fully in a social system created by them. This proposition needs further examination. We must look at the role of white contact, social distance, and racial feelings as they affect the level of aspirations and discontent before we can begin to pass judgment on the adequacy or relevance of "the revolution of expectations" to violence.

NOTES

1. Discussions of the nature of riot participation may be found in Nathan S. Caplan and Jeffery M. Paige, "A Study of Ghetto Rioters," *Scientific American* 219, No. 2 (August 1968); 15–21; *Report of the National Advisory Commission on Civil Disorders* (New York: Bantam Books, 1968), Ch. 2, "Patterns of Disorders," pp. 109–201; Robert M. Fogelson and Robert B. Hill, "Who Riots? A Study of Participation in the 1967 Riots," in *Supplemental Studies for the National Advisory Commission on Civil Disorders* (Washington, D.C.: U.S. Government Printing Office, 1968), pp. 221–48; Raymond J. Murphy and James M. Watson, *The Structure of Discontent* (Institute of Government and Public Affairs, University of California, Los Angeles, 1967).

2. A general discussion of this and similar theoretical formulations may be found in Don R. Bowen and Louis H. Masotti, *Riots and Rebellion: Civil Violence in the Urban Community* (Beverly Hills, Calif.: Sage Publications, 1968), esp. Part. I, "Theoretical Approaches to the Study of Civil Strife," pp. 11–31.

3. Ted Gurr, "Urban Disorder Perspectives from the Comparative Study of Civil Strife," in Bowen and Masotti, *Riots and Rebellion,* p. 53.

4. Don R. Bowen and Louis H. Masotti, "Theoretical Approaches," in Bowen and Masotti, *Riot and Rebellion*, p. 24.

5. A detailed description of the sample and its selection may be found in T. M. Tomlinson and Diana L. TenHouten, *Los Angeles Riot Study Method: Negro Reaction Survey* (Institute of Government and Public Affairs, University of California, Los Angeles, 1967).

6. Donald J. Bogue, *Skid Row in American Cities* (Chicago: Community and Family Study Center, University of Chicago, 1963), pp. 516–21. The logic and rationale for the Index are found on pp. 315–20.

7. For a discussion of the relationship between systemic frustration, aspirations, and violence see Ivo K. Feierabend, Rosalind L. Feierabend, and Betty A. Nesvold, "Social Change and Political Violence: Cross-National Patterns," in Hugh Davis Graham and Ted Robert Gurr, eds., *The History of Violence in America* (New York: Bantam Books, 1969), pp. 632–87.

8. Murphy and Watson, *The Structures of Discontent*, pp. 43–50.

9. A detailed description of these measures of discontent may be found in ibid., pp. 45–49.

10. Ibid., pp. 32–33 contains a discussion of these measures and their properties.

4. Attitudes Toward Riots

Riot participants comprise a minority of the black community—a sizeable minority ranging to as much as 35 percent,[1] but still a minority. Any proper assessment of the meaning of riots to black Americans and to the nation as a whole requires knowledge of the attitudes and perceptions of the members of the black community. It makes a major difference whether the riots are perceived by blacks as the reprehensible and irresponsible behavior of a negligible minority or as a justifiable attack on the system by a large cadre of freedom fighters. It is also important to know the social sources of variation in these perceptions within the black community. Both the Sears and Tomlinson and the Ransford selections within this section explore these problems in separate studies of Los Angeles after the Watts riot.

In the selection by David O. Sears and T. M. Tomlinson about one-third of the curfew zone black residents and half of the arrestee sample had generally favorable feelings about the riot. Approximately two out of every five in each sample labeled the disorders as revolt. Anywhere from half to three-fourths of the two samples said the disorders had a purpose, were protest, and attacked targets which deserved to be attacked. In short, we find that blacks generally held favorable views of the disorders, ranging from mild to strong support as one shifted the focus from one to another of the specific details. But there always remained a high degree of black support and a general feeling that the riots did more good than harm.

The selection by H. Edward Ransford attempts to determine which types of persons within the black community would be most willing to use violence. His data generally indicated that persons isolated from whites, persons with strong feelings of powerlessness, and persons high in racial dissatisfactions were all more willing to use violence. Racial dissatisfactions and feelings of powerlessness interact to reinforce and strengthen each other. Racial isolation increases the propensity to violence of those persons exhibiting feelings of powerlessness and/or racial dissatisfaction, but not for persons who lack either of these two attitudes. These findings take on additional meaning in conjunction with the Geschwender-Singer selection included earlier in Part IV. It may be the case that social isolation should not be viewed as an independent cause of riots, but only as a filter operating between grievance and/or ideology on the one hand, and participation on the other.

NOTES

1. Robert M. Fogelson and Robert B. Hill, "Who Riots? A Study of Participation in the 1967 Riots," in *Supplemental Studies for the National Advisory Commission on Civil Disorders* (Washington, D.C.: U.S. Government Printing Office, 1968), pp. 229–33.

RIOT IDEOLOGY IN LOS ANGELES: A STUDY OF NEGRO ATTITUDES

David O. Sears / T. M. Tomlinson

Each summer from 1964 through 1967 saw urban Negroes in America involved in a series of violent riots. Among the most critical consequences of the riots were the decisions made by the white population about the social changes required to prevent further rioting. These decisions rested in part on the whites' assumptions about the nature and extent of the Negro community's involvement in the riots. Matters of simple fact such as how many people took part in the riots, whether the rest of the Negro community repudiated the rioters, and whether it viewed the riots as representing some form of collective protest against injustice and poverty, were initially quite unclear. Yet whites quickly made their own assumptions about such matters, and these strongly influenced their stance toward the riots and the entire racial problem.

There appear to be three widely held myths about the Negro community's response to riots. The first is that the riots are participated in and viewed favorably by only a tiny segment of the Negro community. The figure often cited by news media and political spokesmen (both black and white) is between 2 and 5 percent of the Negro population. Since riot supporters are thought to be so few in number, a further assumption is that they come from such commonly condemned fringe groups as Communists, hoodlums, and Black Muslims.[1]

The second myth is that most Negroes see the riots as purposeless, meaningless, senseless outbursts of criminality. Many white public officials certainly professed to see nothing in the riots but blind hostility and malicious mischief, drunkenness, and material greed. Perhaps because they held this view so strongly themselves, they tended to assume that Negroes shared it as well.

The third myth is that Negroes generally believe that no benefit will result from the riots. Negroes are supposed to view them with horror, seeing the physical destruction wrought in black ghettos, as well as the destruction of the good will patiently accumulated during early days of campaigning for civil rights. According to this myth, Negroes foresee "white backlash" and cities laid waste, rather than betterment in their life situations, as the main effect of the riots.

The response of the Negro community to the riots is a crucial consideration in determining how the society as a whole should respond to them. If these three myths are correct, perhaps the customary mechanisms for dealing with individual criminal behavior are not only morally justified but also the most practicable means for handling riots. If these myths are incorrect, if Negroes support the riots, see them as expressing meaningful goals, and expect them to better the conditions of their lives,

From *Social Science Quarterly* 49 (December 1968): 485–503; reprinted and abridged by permission of the authors and the publisher.

then the responses traditionally used for dealing with criminals would be inappropriate. They would be impractical, ineffective, and likely to exacerbate an already difficult situation. Instead it would be essential to devise policies which took into account the fact that the riot highlighted a problem pervading the whole Negro community, rather than one limited to a few deviant individuals.

It is apparent that many Americans, black and white alike, have already rejected these myths. Others, however, retain them—those in positions of authority as well as those in the broader white community. Moreover, systematic data on them have not been widely available. Since these myths have had and will continue to have great influence in determining the white population's response to urban problems, it is vital that their validity be subjected to close empirical test. The primary purpose of this article is to present some convincing evidence of their inaccuracy, at least in the important case of the Los Angeles Negro community's response to the Watts riots.

METHOD [2]

The data on which this article is based were obtained from interviews conducted with three samples of respondents in Los Angeles County in late 1965 and early 1966. The most important was a representative sample of Negroes living in the large area (46.5 square miles) of South-Central Los Angeles sealed off by a curfew imposed during the rioting. This sample, numbering 586 respondents, will be referred to below as the "Negro curfew zone" sample. The curfew zone contains about three-fourths of the more than 450,000 Negroes living in Los Angeles County, and is over 80 per cent Negro.[3] Hence it represents the major concentration of Negroes in the Los Angeles area. The sampling was done by randomly choosing names from the 1960 census lists, then over-sampling poverty-level census tracts by a cluster-sampling procedure to compensate for the underrepresentation of low-income respondents due to residential transience. Another 124 Negro respondents, all arrested in the riot, were contacted principally through lawyers providing free legal aid. This "arrestee" sample was not representative but provided a useful reference point. Both Negro samples were interviewed by black interviewers living in the curfew zone. Though the interviews were long (averaging about two hours), interest was high and the refusal rate low. Checks were run on the possible biases introduced by the interviewers' own views and these do not give unusual reason for concern. The same interview schedule was used for all Negro respondents; it was structured, and included both open-ended and closed-ended items.

The third sample included 586 white respondents from six communities in Los Angeles County, half of which were racially integrated and half nonintegrated, with high, medium, and low socioeconomic levels. This sample is thus not wholly representative of the county, over-representing high SES and racially integrated areas, thus probably underestimating racial hostilities. Some, but not all, of the items on the Negro interview schedule were also used with white respondents. The main emphasis in this article is upon Negro opinion, so the white sample is not referred to except when explicitly indicated.

THE THREE MYTHS

Data relevant to the first myth—that only a small fraction of the Negro community participated in the riot of August, 1965, and that nearly everyone else was antagonistic to it—show that it was clearly erroneous on both counts.

The authors' best estimate is that approximately 15 per cent of the Negroes in the area participated in the riot. This was the proportion of curfew zone respondents who stated that they had been "very" or "somewhat" active in the riot and that they had seen crowds of people, and stores being burned and looted. The self-report of active participation, whether wholly accurate or not, indicates, at least, that numerous Los Angeles Negroes (22 per cent of the sample) were willing to identify themselves with the riot.[4]

Furthermore, the Negro community as a whole was not overwhelmingly antagonistic to the riot. This point may be demonstrated in two ways. First, respondents were asked to estimate the proportion of "people in the area" (referring generally to the curfew zone) who had supported or opposed the riot. The mean estimate was that 34 per cent had "supported" the riot, and that 56 per cent had been "against it."

Second, each respondent was asked his own feeling about the riot in a series of open-ended questions. He was asked directly how he felt about the riot, how he felt about the events of the riot, and how he felt about the people who were involved. Answers to these questions yielded three measures of feeling or affect toward the riot.[5] A little under one-third of the Negro curfew zone sample expressed approval of the riot on each of these three measures, and about half disapproved of the riot, as shown in Table 1. This finding closely resembled the respondents' own estimates of public opinion in the area, as cited above.

Clearly, then, support for the riot was far more extensive than the public has been led to believe, numbering about a third of the area's adult residents, though a majority did disapprove of it. Even while disapproving, however, Negro respondents were markedly more lenient toward the riot's supporters than they were toward the destruction of life and property that occurred. Table 1 shows that 42 per cent disapproved of the participants, while 67 per cent disapproved of the events of the riot.

The riot as a protest

The second myth—that the riot was a meaningless, haphazard expression of disregard for law and order—was not commonly held among Negroes in Los Angeles. Many viewed the riot in revolutionary or in-

TABLE 1. Evaluation of Riot and Rioters[a]

	Overall Feeling about Riot	Feeling about Events	Feeling about Participants
Negro curfew zone (N = 586)			
Very or somewhat favorable	27%	29%	30%
Ambivalent or neutral	16	1	19
Strongly or moderately unfavorable	50	67	42
Don't know, no answer	7	3	8
Total	100%	100%	99%
Arrestee sample (N = 124)			
Very or somewhat favorable	52%	50%	57%
Ambivalent or neutral	10	4	12
Strongly or moderately unfavorable	32	45	23
Don't know, no answer	6	1	7
Total	100%	100%	99%

[a]The specific questions were as follows:
For column 1, "Now that it is over, how do you feel about what happened?"
For column 2, "What did you like about what was going on?" and "What did you dislike about what was going on?"
For column 3, "What kinds of people supported it?" and "What kinds of people were against it?"
These questions were not asked of the white sample.

surrectional terms; most thought it had a purpose and that the purpose was, in part at least, a Negro protest.

Official utterances and the mass media, almost without exception, had described the events as being a "riot." Each respondent was asked what term he would use to describe the events. Table 2 shows that, given this free choice, over a third of the Negro sample selected "revolt," "insurrection," "rebellion," "uprising," "revenge," or other revolutionary term, thus flying in the face of the conventional definition. Other items given in Table 2 posed the question of a meaningful protest more directly, and show that a majority of the Negro community did indeed see the riot in these terms. Substantial majorities felt that it did have a purpose, that it was a Negro protest, and that those outsiders attacked in the riot deserved what they got.

Anticipating favorable effects

The third myth—that Negroes viewed the riot with alarm for the future—also was not subscribed to in Los Angeles. Most (58 per cent) foresaw predominantly beneficial effects, and only a minority (26 per cent) anticipated predominantly unfavorable effects. Similarly, more thought it would "help" the Negro cause than thought it would "hurt" it. These data are given in Table 3.

Thus, a large minority of the Negroes in the curfew zone, about one-third, were favorable to the rioting, and the others' disapproval focused more upon the events than upon the participants. Over half saw the riot as a purposeful protest, many even speaking of it in revolutionary terms. Favorable effects were much more widely anticipated

TABLE 2.   The Riot as Protest

	Whites	Negroes (curfew zone)	Arrestees
What word or term would you use in talking about it?			
Riot	58%	46%	44%
Revolt, revolution, insurrection	13	38	45
Other (disaster, tragedy, mess, disgrace, etc.)	27	8	10
Don't know, no answer	2	8	2
Total	100%	100%	101%
Why were targets attacked?[a]			
Deserved attack	--	64%	75%
Ambivalent, don't know	--	17	21
Did not deserve attack	--	14	0
No answer	--	5	4
Total		100%	100%
Did it have a purpose or goal?			
Yes	33%	56%	56%
Don't know, other	4	11	13
No	62	28	29
No answer	--	5	2
Total	99%	100%	100%
Was it a Negro protest?			
Yes	54%	62%	66%
Don't know, other	3	12	15
No	42	23	16
No answer	--	2	3
Total	99%	99%	100%

[a]This question was not asked of white respondents.

TABLE 3.   Expected Effects of the Riot

	Whites	Negroes (Curfew Zone)	Arrestees
What will the main effects be?[a]			
Very or somewhat favorable	--	58%	57%
Neutral, ambivalent, don't know	--	12	14
Very or somewhat unfavorable	--	26	27
No answer	--	3	2
Total		99%	100%
Do you think it helped or hurt the Negro's cause?			
Helped	19%	38%	54%
No difference, don't know	5	30	33
Hurt	75	24	9
No answers, other	1	8	4
Total	100%	100%	100%

[a]This question was not asked of white respondents.

than unfavorable effects. This evidence indicates that the three myths cited above were invalid for the Los Angeles Negro community. It did not wholeheartedly reject and condemn its 1965 riot.

Participants' attitudes

Negroes clearly had more sympathy for the participants than for the events of the riot. In fact, the participants and the community as a whole had rather similar attitudes about the riot. The arrestees were considerably more favorable toward the riot than was the community as a whole (see Table 1), but the community was equally optimistic about the effects of the riot, and as willing to interpret it as a purposeful protest (see Tables 2 and 3). Data presented elsewhere compare participants and nonparticipants within the Negro curfew zone sample, and yield almost exactly the same picture. Most participants tended to approve of the riot, while more nonparticipants disapproved than approved it. However, in both groups a majority expressed optimism about the effects of the riot, and interpreted it as a meaningful protest. In fact participants and nonparticipants hardly differed at all in the latter two respects.[6] This similarity of feeling between the participants (whether arrested or not) and the Negro community as a whole suggests both that the participants were not particularly unusual or deviant in their thinking, and that members of the community were not wholly willing to condemn nor to symbolically ostracize the rioters.

White attitudes

The picture is quite different with respect to whites. As might now be expected, their attitudes toward the riot were considerably less favorable. Table 2 shows that whites thought it was nothing more meaningful than a "riot." Though most did feel it was a Negro protest, the consensus of opinion was that it was a purposeless, meaningless outburst. Table 3 shows that whites felt it definitely had "hurt" the Negro cause. Thus the cleavage in opinion that developed in Los Angeles after the riot was not so much between rioters and the law-abiding people of both races as between whites and blacks.

Other riots, other communities

This is not the place to attempt a complete review of Negro opinion in other communities, or about other riots, but a brief discussion will indicate that results obtained here were similar to those obtained elsewhere in this nation.

Items directly analogous to those here evaluating riots and rioters have not been widely used. A *Fortune Magazine* national survey in 1967 did find that only 14 per cent felt the "violence and rioting that has already occurred" was "essentially good," while 58 per cent felt it was "essentially bad." [7] Similarly, a 1967 Harris national survey found that 10 per cent felt "most Negroes support riots" and 75 per cent felt that "only a minority" supports them.[8] These results indicate disapproval of riots by a substantial majority of Negroes. Yet the same Harris poll reveals that 62 per cent felt looters should not be shot, and 27 per cent felt they should be (in contrast to the 62 per cent of whites who felt shooting was appropriate for looters).[9] Clearly there are substantial limits on the strength of Negro disapproval and condemnation of Negro rioters.

Optimism about the effects of riots has also been characteristic. In several studies, Negroes have been asked whether riots "help" or "hurt" their cause, and the preferred answer has generally been that they "help." This was the result of a 1966 Harris national survey, a 1966 Harris survey of Negro leadership, and surveys of the Negro populations of Los Angeles (1966) and Oakland (1967).[10] The two exceptions have been a 1966 survey in Houston, a Southern city, where a slight plurality felt that riots "hurt," and the 1967 Harris survey (presumably national), which reported that only 12 per cent felt they would help—a result that is grossly out of line with all other surveys and thus difficult to interpret.

THE RIOT IDEOLOGY OF THE NEGRO COMMUNITY

Ambivalent evaluations of the riot, the feeling that it was meaningful, and optimism about its effect represent the simple elements around which a more complex belief system about the riot developed within the Negro community. This centered on a view of the riot as an instrument of Negro protest against real grievances. The substance of this view may be examined through the content of the protest and the grievances. First, let us consider in more detail the question of general community sympathy for the rioters.

Riot events and participants: the community's sympathetic defense

Evaluations of the riot events and riot participants, shown in Table 1, gave the impression that the events of the riot were condemned more heartily than the rioters. Does the content of the respondents' attitudes support this impression?

The actual events of the riot were almost universally condemned. When asked "What did you like about what was going on?" 63 per cent of the Negroes sampled replied, "Nothing." The others gave widely dispersed responses. Crimes against property (such as burning and looting) and crimes against persons (such as killing and shooting) were cited about equally often as disliked aspects of the riot, as shown in Table 4. However, while the events of the riot were generally disliked and disapproved, they were not flatly repudiated. About 75 per cent couched their disapproval in terms suggesting sorrow and remorse (e.g., "regretful," "a sad thing," "a shame," "glad it's over") while only 25 per cent responded in a fashion suggesting repudiation of the riot (e.g., "disgusted,"

TABLE 4. What Did You Dislike About the Riot?[a]

	Negroes (curfew zone)	Arrestees
Crimes against property (burning, destruction, looting)	47%	26%
Crimes against persons	43	70
Negro attacks on white	(1)	(0)
Police shooting, killing, brutality	(14)	(32)
Killing, bloodshed, violence, shooting in general	(28)	(38)
Practical inconveniences	9	5
Negroes breaking law	1	0
Total	100%	101%

[a]Not asked of white respondents.

"disgrace," "unnecessary," "senseless"). Since disapproval of the riot did not necessarily include total dissociation from and repudiation of it, it is perhaps not surprising that the rioters and riot supporters were less harshly criticized than the event they created.

Indeed, the Negro community's description of the riot supporters, on the one hand, and the authorities on the other, reveal considerably more sympathy for those fomenting the riot than for those who tried to stop it. The descriptions of who had supported the riot, shown in Table 5, indicate that such sympathetic and understanding descriptions as "people who suffer" or "people wanting freedom" outnumbered such unsympathetic and repudiating responses as "hoodlums" or "Communists." The predominant conception of a riot supporter was not of a criminal, or of a disreputable or despicable person, but evidently of a

TABLE 5. What Kinds of People Supported the Riot?[a]

	Negroes (Curfew Zone)	Arrestees
Sympathetic descriptions	45%	59%
Everyone	(10)	(15)
Good people (people wanting freedom, sympathetic people, etc.)	(5)	(8)
Deprived, mistreated (unemployed people who suffer, have-nots, poor people)	(30)	(36)
Unsympathetic descriptions	34	16
Anti-social (hoodlums, corrupt)	(12)	(10)
Political (Communists, Muslims)	(2)	(0)
Irresponsible (teenagers, fools, uneducated, thrill seekers)	(20)	(6)
Other	21	25
Estranged people (hopeless people, old people)	(5)	(9)
Middle class (business people)	(1)	(1)
Don't know, no answer	(15)	(15)
Total	100%	100%

[a]Not asked of white respondents.

TABLE 6. Did the Authorities Handle It Well or Badly?

	Whites	Negroes (Curfew Zone)	Arrestees
Well	66%	28%	15%
Badly	32	65	77
Should have stopped it sooner	(26)	(27)	(14)
They made it worse, were			
intransigent	(6)	(33)	(56)
Other	(0)	(5)	(7)
Don't know, no answer, other	2	8	9
Total	100	101%	101%

person not so very dissimilar from the respondent himself, though perhaps somewhat down on his luck.

In contrast, much antagonism was expressed toward the authorities' role in the riot. Only 28 per cent thought the authorities had handled the riot "well," and 65 per cent felt they had handled it "badly." The further breakdown of these responses is shown in Table 6; Negroes who thought the authorities had done badly were split between those who felt they should have put an end to the riot earlier, and those who felt the authorities had exacerbated the situation. Many Negro respondents did not like what had happened then, but their disposition was to defend and justify the actions of Negro rioters, and to criticize the actions of the white authorities.

Explanations of the causes of the riot also demonstrated a sympathetic defense of the rioters, as shown in Table 7. The dominant tendency was to blame the riot on legitimate grievances, such as discrimination, poverty, or police mistreatment (38 per cent), or on long-standing hostility and other pent-up emotions (26 per cent). Relatively few attributed the riot mainly to the incident that precipitated it, the fracas with the Frye family, or blamed any of the obvious candidates for a scapegoat, such as the Communists or gang members.

The contrast with opinions expressed by white residents of Los Angeles was a vivid one. By attributing the riot to grievances and to years of frustration, the Negro respondents suggested that the people who supported the riot had legitimate reasons for doing so. Whites, on the other hand, praised the work of the authorities, or even criticized them for not being more punitive with the rioters (Table 6). Whites were much more inclined to attribute the riot to agitators, Communists, criminals, the weather, or simply to write it off as arising from the Frye incident (Table 7). The Negro community as a whole was much closer to the explicit sympathy for the rioters expressed by the arrestees. Both gave relatively sympathetic descriptions of the rioters (Table 5), harshly criticized the authorities (Table 6), and attributed the riot to legitimate grievances rather than to chance or whimsical or illegal and un-American factors (Table 7).

This contrast between black sympathy for the rioters and white condemnation of them, as reflected in explanations for the riot, has also

TABLE 7.   What Caused the Riot?

	Whites	Negroes (curfew zone)	Arrestees
Specific grievances:	20%	38%	51%
Discrimination, mistreatment by whites	(5)	(7)	(4)
Poverty, economic deprivation, inadequate services	(11)	(10)	(5)
Police mistreatment	(4)	(21)	(42)
Pent-up hostility, desire for revenge, fed-up	14	26	34
Frye incident	18	11	8
Undesirable groups:	29	9	2
Communists, Muslims, civil rights groups, organized groups, KKK, agitators	(16)	(3)	(0)
Criminals, looters	(8)	(2)	(0)
Foolish people, teenagers, Southerners	(5)	(4)	(2)
Spontaneous explosion, accident, weather	10	0	0
Don't know, no answer	10	17	6
Total	101%	101%	101%

been obtained in several more recent surveys made in other areas. For example, in Harris's 1967 survey, Negroes were about twice as likely as whites to attribute recent riots to grievances over jobs, education, housing, police, and inequality. Whites were more likely than Negroes to blame outside agitation, lack of firmness by government authorities, the desire to loot, or a desire for violence.[11] Negroes thought the riots were spontaneous; a vast majority of the whites thought they had been organized.[12] Negroes thought the looted stores had been charging exorbitant prices; whites thought they had not.[13] Among whites, 62 per cent felt looters should be shot; among Negroes, only 27 per cent felt that action was justifiable.[14] In other post-riot surveys, Negroes in Detroit and in Watts have generally explained the rioting in terms of a response to grievances about housing, jobs, the police, and poverty.[15] The most impressive difference of opinion about the rioters, then, is not between the law-abiders and the law-breakers in the Negro community, but between blacks and whites. . . .

PREFERRED MECHANISMS OF GRIEVANCE REDRESS

A riot ideology appears to have developed among Negroes in the curfew zone, in part justifying the Los Angeles riot as an instrument of protest. To what extent did rioting thus become thought of as a legitimate and effective mechanism of grievance redress for the future? Not widely, ap-

TABLE 8.   What Must Negroes Do to Get What They Want?

	Negroes (Curfew Zone)	Arrestees
Conventional approaches:	56%	51%
Get more education	(27)	(15)
Work hard, strive and succeed	(23)	(32)
Get jobs, acquire wealth	(2)	(2)
Change stereotyped qualities	(4)	(2)
Political action:	19	15
Vote more, follow their leaders, etc.	(6)	(6)
Protest, make needs known	(13)	(9)
Violent action	3	10
Increase morale:	7	12
Remove self-hatred	(1)	(0)
Increase racial solidarity	(6)	(12)
Change whites, change both races	1	0
Other	5	7
Don't know, no answer	9	5
Total	100%	100%

parently. Answers to the open-ended question "What must Negroes do to get what they want?" reveal a preponderantly conventional approach to equal rights, as shown in Table 8. Over half of the Negro respondents see some form of conventional middle-class behavior as the road to success (e.g., more education and hard work). Another 19 per cent see more efficient and active political participation as the answer, while only 3 per cent contend that violence is necessary for equal rights. So the majority of Negroes in Los Angeles, even after a riot they perceived as likely to have beneficial effects, still opted for moderate grievance redress procedures and for traditional methods of personal advancement.

The question still remains how strong this preference for conventional mechanisms actually is, and whether or not the riot affected it. A sizable number of respondents expressed interest in demonstrations and nonviolent protest. Only a few (6 per cent) had participated in pre-riot civil rights activity, but 37 per cent said after the riot that they were willing to participate in demonstrations. Thirteen per cent said the riot had made them more willing to do so; so perhaps the riot made some Negroes more militant and unified.

It is hard to determine from the data whether it also increased their attraction to violence. However, when asked the most effective method to use in protest, given the alternatives of negotiation and nonviolent protest, 12 per cent selected violent protest (of the arrestees, 22 per cent did so). And 34 per cent thought there would be a recurrence of rioting in Los Angeles. Another 37 per cent felt they could not predict whether or not there would be another riot, thereby reflecting a lack of confidence in the durability of civic peace. While these data do not suggest that a majority of Negroes in Los Angeles advocate violence, the minority that does is rather sizable, and the expectation of further violence on the part of many others is an ominous sign; prophecies of that kind have a way of becoming self-fulfilling.[16]

CONCLUSIONS

This paper has been primarily concerned with the reaction of the Los Angeles Negro population to the Watts Riots of 1965. The principal findings follow:

1. It is not correct that all but a small minority strongly disapproved of the riots, felt they were a meaningless and random outburst of violence, and felt deeply pessimistic about the probable effects of the riots on the welfare of Negroes. Actually, a large minority (about one-third) approved of the rioting, most Negro residents of the riot area felt it had been a meaningful protest, and most were optimistic about its effects on their life situation.

2. A widespread "riot ideology" appears to have developed in the Negro community following the riot, with the following elements. The events of the riot were deplored, and the wish was expressed that the authorities had stopped it earlier. Yet the authorities tended to be criticized and the rioters defended. The causes of the riot were described in terms of genuine grievances with those who were attacked; e.g., a history of friction, discrimination, and economic exploitation with local merchants and police. The purpose of the riot was seen as being, on the one hand, to call the attention of the whites to Negro problems, and on the other, to express resentment against malefactors. The riot was expected to bring help to the Negro population from whites, though major improvement in interracial personal relationships was not expected. This "riot ideology" seemed to justify and defend the riot, but violence was not often advocated for the future.[17]

3. The major cleavage that developed after the riot was between the white and black populations of Los Angeles, not between lawbreakers and lawabiders within the black population. Whites were much readier to condemn the riot, to see only purposeless violence in it, and to foresee a gloomy future for race relations. Whites were likely to ascribe the riot to agitators and criminal impulse, and less likely to attribute it to genuine grievances. These divisions of opinion along racial lines seem to be characteristic of the ways in which the two racial groups have responded across the country to recent race riots.[18]

Perhaps the most important fact of all is that so many Negroes felt disposed to justify and ennoble the riot after it was all over. It was not viewed as an alien disruption of their peaceful lives, but as an expression of protest by the Negro community as a whole, against an oppressive majority. Here perhaps lies one of the tragedies of the riot. While it was, in the eyes of many Negroes, an outburst against an oppressive social system, the response of whites to the call for attention and help was hoped to be favorable. Perhaps this was an analogy taken from the white response to the Southern civil rights battles of the preceding decade.

However, relatively little help has in fact been forthcoming, and it is not clear that whites expect to give very much. Awareness of the problem seems obviously to have increased, but the retaliatory aspect of the "message" of the riot seems as salient to whites as the plea for help.

NOTES

ACKNOWLEDGEMENT: This study was conducted under a contract between the Office of Economic Opportunity and the Institute for Government and Public Affairs at UCLA, while both authors were members of the Department of Psychology, UCLA. The Coordinator of the research was Nathan E. Cohen. We owe a profound debt of gratitude to the many persons who worked on the Los Angeles Riot Study, with special thanks to Diana TenHouten and John B. McConahay. We also wish to express our appreciation to Esther Spachner for editorial help and to Peter Orleans for his comments on an earlier draft of this paper.

1. See the attributions of the Watts riot to "young hoodlums," "the criminal element," and black nationalists by the mayor and police chief of Los Angeles, in the *New York Times,* August 13, 1965, p. 26; August 14, 1965, p. 8; September 14, 1965, p. 22.

2. For more complete accounts of the methods, see T. M. Tomlinson and Diana L. TenHouten, "Method: Negro Reaction Survey," and Richard T. Morris and Vincent Jeffries, "The White Reaction Study," *Los Angeles Riot Study* (Los Angeles: Institute of Government and Public Affairs, University of California, 1967). See also R. T. Morris and V. Jeffries, "Violence Next Door," *Social Forces* 46 (March 1968): 352–58.

3. See U.S. Bureau of the Census, *U.S. Census of Population: 1960,* Vol. 1: *Characteristics of the Population,* Part 6: California (Washington, D.C.: U.S. Government Printing Office, 1963). Also David O. Sears and John B. McConahay, "Riot Participation," *Los Angeles Riot Study.*

4. For a detailed consideration of these data, see Sears and McConahay, ibid. Rates of participation in the Newark and Detroit riots of 1967 appear to have been similarly high, according to data published in *The Report of the National Advisory Commission on Civil Disorders* (New York: Bantam Books, 1968), p. 172.

5. For a detailed description of the coding procedure, see Tomlinson and TenHouten, "Method: Negro Reaction Survey." The coding reliabilities were all over .95.

6. See David O. Sears and John B. McConahay, "The Politics of Discontent: Blocked Mechanisms of Grievance Redress and the Psychology of the New Urban Black Man," *Los Angeles Riot Study.*

7. Roger Beardwood, "The New Negro Mood," *Fortune* 77 (January 1968): 146.

8. See Hazel Erskine, "The Polls: Demonstrations and Race Riots," *Public Opinion Quarterly* 31 (Winter 1967): 655–77, for many of the results of these polls. This finding is given on p. 671.

9. Ibid., p. 674.

10. See W. Brink and Louis Harris, *Black and White* (New York: Simon & Schuster, 1966), pp. 264–65; *Federal Role in Urban Affairs,* Hearings before the Subcommittee on Executive Reorganization of the Committee on Government Operations, U.S. 89th Congress, 2nd Session, Senate, Part 6, p. 1387; William McCord and John Howard, "Negro Opinions in Three Riot Cities," *American Behavioral Scientist* 11 (March-April 1968): 26.

11. McCord and Howard, ibid.; Erskine, "The Polls," p. 662.

12. Erskine, "The Polls," p. 666.

13. Ibid., p. 665.

14. Ibid., p. 674.

15. Detroit Urban League, "A Survey of Attitudes of Detroit Negroes after the Riot of 1967," Detroit, 1967. See also *Federal Role in Urban Affairs*, p. 1387. The vivid contrast between whites and Negroes also appears in a Brandeis University survey: Lemberg Center for the Study of Violence, "A Survey of Racial Attitudes in Six Northern Cities: Preliminary Findings," Waltham, Mass., 1967, pp. 15–16 (mimeographed).

16. Particularly ominous, as might be expected, were the attitudes of the more militant respondents. Subdividing the curfew zone sample in terms of relative militance reveals considerably greater support for riots and higher endorsement of violence among the militants than among the more conservative respondents. For a detailed account of these data, see T. M. Tomlinson, "Ideological Foundations for Negro Action: A Comparative Analysis of Militant and Non-Militant Views of the Los Angeles Riot," *Los Angeles Riot Study*. See also T. M. Tomlinson, "The Development of a Riot Ideology Among Urban Negroes," *American Behavioral Scientist* 11 (March-April 1968): 27–31.

Findings from other surveys on the level of endorsement of violence are not strictly comparable, because of different question wording. The range of estimates is substantial. In 1964, Kraft surveys in Harlem, Chicago, and Baltimore found 5 per cent saying violence was necessary, but one in Watts after the riot found that 14 per cent thought it was. See *Federal Role in Urban Affairs*, p. 1399. A complex question used by Harris in national surveys in 1963 and 1966 found 22 per cent and 21 per cent, respectively, thinking violence was needed. See Brink and Harris, *Black and White*, p. 260. After the Detroit riot of 1967, an Urban League survey found 24 per cent feeling there was more to gain than lose with violence (see Detroit Urban League, "A Survey of Attitudes"). And the 1967 *Fortune* survey found 35 per cent saying that riots and violence are necessary (see Beardwood, "The New Negro Mood," p. 148). Whether these represent secular changes or merely differently worded questions is unclear.

17. There is considerable justification for speaking of this pattern of beliefs in terms of an "ideology," based on the pattern of interrelationships between various of them. Approval of the riot, optimism about its effects, and perceiving the riot as a meaningful protest were all strongly correlated with one another.

18. This observation of racial differences might seem to set a new record for banality in social science. The impressive finding here is not that whites and Negroes disagree, but that disagreement penetrates so deeply into each group, well beyond those that normally concern themselves with public affairs. It could be, for example, that relatively few people care very much about riots, and that most people of both races reject them as they reject criminal behavior in general. That is not the case, however.

Isolation, Powerlessness, and Violence: A Study of Attitudes and Participation in the Watts Riot

H. Edward Ransford

Since the summer of 1965, it is no longer possible to describe the Negroes' drive for new rights as a completely non-violent protest. Urban ghettos have burst at the seams. Angry shouts from the most frustrated and deprived segments of the Negro community now demand that we recognize violence as an important facet of the Negro revolution.

In attempts to understand the increase in violence, much has been said about unemployment, police brutality, poor schools, and inadequate housing as contributing factors.[1] However, there are few sociological studies concerning the characteristics of the participants or potential participants in racial violence.[2] Little can be said about which minority individuals are likely to view violence as a justifiable means of correcting racial injustices. It is the purpose of this paper to identify such individuals —specifically, to identify those Negroes who were willing to use violence as a method during a period shortly after the Watts riot.

A THEORETICAL PERSPECTIVE

Studies dealing with political extremism and radical protest have often described the participants in such action as being isolated or weakly tied to the institutions of the community.[3] Kerr and Siegel demonstrated this relationship with their finding that wildcat strikes are more common among isolated occupational groups, such as mining, maritime, and lumbering.[4] These isolated groups are believed to have a weak commitment to public pressures and the democratic norms of the community. Thus, when grievances are felt intensely and the bonds to the institutions of the community are weak, there is likely to be an explosion of discontent (the strike) rather than use of negotiation or other normative channels of expression.

More recently, mass society theory has articulated this relationship between isolation and extremism.[5] The mass society approach sees current structural processes—such as the decline in kinship, the increase in mobility, and the rise of huge bureaucracies—as detaching many individuals from sources of control, meaning, and personal satisfaction. Those who are most isolated from centers of power are believed to be more vulnerable to authoritarian outlooks and more available for volatile mass movements. Indeed, Kornhauser instructs us that the whole political stability of a society is somewhat dependent upon its citizens being tied meaning-

From *The American Journal of Sociology* 73 (March 1968): 581–91. Copyright © 1967 by the University of Chicago; reprinted by permission of the author and publisher.

fully to the institutions of the community.[6] He suggests that participation in secondary organizations—such as unions and business groups—serve to mediate between the individual and the nation, tying the individual to the democratic norms of the society.

The relationship between structural isolation and extremism is further accentuated by the personal alienation of the individual. Isolated people are far more likely than non-isolated people to feel cut off from the larger society and to feel an inability to control events in the society.[7] This subjective alienation may heighten the individual's readiness to engage in extreme behavior. For example, Horton and Thompson find that perceived powerlessness is related to protest voting.[8] Those with feelings of political powerlessness were more likely to be dissatisfied with their position in society and to hold resentful attitudes toward community leaders. The study suggests that the discontent of the powerless group was converted to action through the vote—a vote of "no" on a local bond issue being a form of negativism in which the individual strikes out at community powers. This interpretation of alienation as a force for protest is consistent with the original Marxian view of the concept in which alienation leads to a radical attack upon the existing social structure.[9]

In summary, there are two related approaches commonly used to explain participation in extreme political behavior. The first deals with the degree to which the individual is structurally isolated or tied to community institutions. The second approach deals with the individual's awareness and evaluation of his isolated condition—for example, his feeling of a lack of control over critical matters or his feeling of discontent due to a marginal position in society. Following this orientation, this research employs the concept of racial isolation, perceived powerlessness, and racial dissatisfaction as theoretical tools for explaining the participation of Negroes in violence.

STUDY DESIGN AND HYPOTHESES

In the following discussion, the three independent variables of this study (isolation, powerlessness, and dissatisfaction) are discussed separately and jointly, as predictors of violence participation.

RACIAL ISOLATION

Ralph Ellison has referred to the Negro in this country as the "invisible man." [10] Although this is a descriptive characterization, sociological studies have attempted to conceptualize more precisely the isolation of the American Negro. For example, those studying attitudes of prejudice often view racial isolation as a lack of free and easy contact on an intimate and equal status basis.[11] Though the interracial contact may be frequent, it often involves such wide status differentials that it does not facilitate candid communication, nor is it likely to give the minority person a feeling that he has some stake in the system. In this paper, intimate white contact is viewed as a mediating set of relationships that binds the ethnic individual to majority-group values—essentially conservative values that favor working through democratic channels rather than violently attacking the social system. Accordingly, it is reasoned that Negroes who are more racially isolated (by low degrees of intimate contact with whites) will have fewer channels of communication to air their grievances and will feel little commitment to the leaders and institutions of the community. This group, which is blocked from meaningful white communication, should be more willing to use violent protest than the groups with greater involvement in white society.

POWERLESSNESS AND RACIAL DISSATISFACTION

In contrast to structural isolation, powerlessness and racial dissatisfaction are the subjective components of our theoretical scheme. A feeling of powerlessness is one form of alienation. It is defined in this research as a low expectancy of control over events.[12] This attitude is seen as an appropriate variable for Negroes living in segregated ghettos; that is, groups which are blocked from full participation in the society are more likely to feel powerless in that society. Powerlessness is also a variable that seems to have a logical relationship to violent protest. Briefly, it is reasoned that Negroes who feel powerless to change their position or to control crucial decisions that affect them will be more willing to use violent means to get their rights than those who feel some control or efficacy within the social system. For the Negro facing extreme discrimination barriers, an attitude of powerlessness is simply a comment on the society, namely, a belief that all channels for social redress are closed.

Our second attitude measure, racial dissatisfaction, is defined as the degree to which the individual feels that he is being treated badly because of his race. It is a kind of racial alienation in the sense that the individual perceives his position in society to be illegitimate, due to racial discrimination. The Watts violence represented an extreme expression of frustration and discontent. We would expect those highly dissatisfied with their treatment as Negroes to be the participants in such violence. Thus, the "highs" in racial dissatisfaction should be more willing to use violence than the "lows" in this attitude. In comparing our two forms of subjective alienation (powerlessness and racial dissatisfaction), it is important to note that, although we expect some correlation between the two attitudes (a certain amount of resentment and dissatisfaction should accompany the feeling of powerlessness), we propose to show that they make an independent contribution to violence.

UNIFICATION OF PREDICTIVE VARIABLES

We believe that the fullest understanding of violence can be brought to bear by use of a social-psychological design in which the structural variable (racial isolation) is joined with the subjective attitudes of the individual (powerlessness and dissatisfaction).

In this design, we attempt to specify the conditions under which isolation has its strongest effect upon violence. It is reasoned that racial isolation should be most important for determining participation in violence (*a*) when individuals feel powerless to shape their destiny under existing conditions or (*b*) when individuals are highly dissatisfied with their racial treatment. Each of the attitudes is seen as a connecting bridge of logic between racial isolation and violence.

For the first case (that of powerlessness), we are stating that a weak attachment to the majority group and its norms should lead to a radical break from law and order when individuals perceive they cannot effect events important to them; that is, they cannot change their racial position through activity within institutional channels. Violence, in this instance, becomes an alternative pathway of expression and gain. Conversely, racial isolation should have much less effect upon violence when persons feel some control in the system.

For the second case (racial dissatisfaction), we believe isolation should have a far greater effect upon violence when dissatisfaction over racial treatment is intense. Isolation from the society then becomes critical to violence in the sense that the dissatisfied person feels little commitment to the legal order and is more likely to use extreme methods as an outlet for his grievances. Statistically speaking, we expect an interaction effect between isolation and powerlessness, and between isolation and dissatisfaction, in the prediction of violence.[13]

METHODS

Our hypotheses call for measures of intimate white contact, perceived powerlessness, and perceived racial dissatisfaction as independent variables, and willingness to use violence as a dependent variable. The measurement of these variables, and also the sampling techniques, are discussed at this time.

SOCIAL CONTACT

The type of social contact to be measured had to be of an intimate and equal status nature, a kind of contact that would facilitate easy communication between the races. First, each Negro respondent was asked if he had current contact with white people in a series of situations: on the job, in his neighborhood, in organizations to which he belongs, and in other situations (such as shopping). After this general survey of white contacts, the respondent was asked, "Have you ever done anything social with these white people, like going to the movies together or visiting in each other's homes?" [14] The responses formed a simple dichotomous variable: "high" contact scores for those who had done something social (61 per cent of the sample) and "low" contact scores for those who had had little or no social contact (39 per cent).[15]

POWERLESSNESS

Following the conceptualization of Melvin Seeman, powerlessness is defined as a low expectancy of control over events.[16] Twelve forced-choice items were used to tap this attitude.[17] The majority of items dealt with expectations of control over the political system. The following is an example:

> ———The world is run by the few people in power, and there is not much the little guy can do about it.
> ———The average citizen can have an influence on government decisions.

After testing the scale items for reliability,[18] the distribution of scores was dichotomized at the median.

RACIAL DISSATISFACTION

The attitude of racial dissatisfaction is defined as the degree to which the individual feels he is being treated badly because of his race. A five-item scale was developed to measure this attitude. The questions ask the Negro respondent to compare his treatment (in such areas as housing, work, and general treatment in the community) with various reference groups, such as the southern Negro or the white. Each of the five questions allows a reply on one of three levels: no dissatisfaction, mild dissatisfaction, and intense dissatisfaction. Typical of the items is the following: "If you compare your opportunities and the treatment you get from whites in Los Angeles with Negroes living in the South, would you say you are much better off———a little better off———or treated about the same as the southern Negro———?" After a reliability check of the items, replies to the dissatisfaction measure were dichotomized into high and low groups.[19] The cut was made conceptually, rather than at the median, yielding 99 "highs" and 213 "lows" in dissatisfaction.[20]

VIOLENCE WILLINGNESS

The dependent variable of the study is willingness to use violence. Violence is defined in the context of the Watts riot as the willingness to use direct aggression against the groups that are believed to be discriminating, such as the police and white merchants. The question used to capture this outlook is, "Would you be willing to use violence to get Negro rights?" With data gathered so shortly after the Watts violence, it was felt that the question would be clearly understood by respondents.[21] At the time of data collection, bulidings were still smoldering; violence in the form of looting, burning, and destruction was not a remote possibility, but a tangible reality. The violence-prone group numbered eighty-three.

A second measure of violence asked the person if he had ever used violent methods to get Negro rights.[22] Only sixteen respondents of the 312 reported (or admitted) that they had participated in actual violence. As a result of this very small number the item is used as an indicator of trends but is not employed as a basic dependent variable of the study.

SAMPLE

The sample was composed of 312 Negro males who were heads of the household and between the ages of eighteen and sixty-five. The subjects responded to an interview schedule administered by Negro interviewers. They were chosen by random methods and were interviewed in their own homes or apartments. Both employed and unemployed respondents were included in the sample, although the former were emphasized in the sampling procedure (269 employed in contrast to 43 unemployed). The sample was drawn from three major areas of Los Angeles: a relatively middle-class and integrated area (known as the "Crenshaw" district) and the predominantly lower-class and highly segregated communities of "South Central" and "Watts." The sample could be classified as "disproportional stratified" because the proportion of subjects drawn from each of the three areas does not correspond to the actual distribution of Negroes in Los Angeles. For example, it was decided that an approximate fifty-fifty split between middle- and lower-class respondents would be desirable for later analysis. This meant, however, that Crenshaw (middle-class) Negroes were considerably overrepresented, since their characteristics are not typical of the Los Angeles Negro community as a whole, and the majority of Los Angeles Negroes do not reside in this, or any similar, area.

RESULTS

We have predicted a greater willingness to use violent methods for three groups: the isolated, the powerless, and the dissatisfied. The data presented in Table 1 confirm these expectations. For all three cases, the per-

TABLE 1. Percentage Willing to Use Violence, by Social Contact, Powerlessness, and Racial Dissatisfaction

Variables	Not Willing (%)	Willing (%)	Total (%)
Social contact: [2]			
High	83	17	100 ($N = 192$)
Low	56	44	100 ($N = 110$)
Powerlessness: [b]			
High	59	41	100 ($N = 145$)
Low	84	16	100 ($N = 160$)
Racial dissatisfaction: [c]			
High	52	48	100 ($N = 98$)
Low	83	17	100 ($N = 212$)

[a] $\chi^1 = 24.93, P < .001$.
[b] $\chi^2 = 22.59, P < .001$.
[c] $\chi^2 = 30.88, P < .001$.

Note. — In this table and the tables that follow, there are often less than 312 cases due to missing data for one or more variables.

centage differences are statistically significant at better than the .001 level.

The empirical evidence supports our contention that Negroes who are more disengaged from the society, in the structural (isolation) and subjective (powerlessness and racial dissatisfaction) senses, are more likely to view violence as necessary for racial justice than those more firmly tied to the society.

It is one thing to establish a relationship based on action willingness and quite another thing to study actual behavior. Unfortunately, only sixteen of the 312 respondents (5 per cent) admitted participation in violent action for Negro rights. This small number did, however, provide some basis for testing our hypotheses. Of the sixteen who participated in violent action, eleven were isolates while only five had social contact. More impressive is the fact that fifteen of the sixteen "violents" scored high in powerlessness, and thirteen of the sixteen felt high degrees of dissatisfaction. Even with a small number, these are definite relationships, encouraging an interpretation that those who are willing to use violence and those who reported actual violent behavior display the same tendency toward powerlessness, racial dissatisfaction, and isolation.

The next task is to explore the interrelationships among our predictive variables. For example, we have argued that powerlessness has a specific meaning to violence (a low expectancy of changing conditions within the institutional framework) that should be more than a generalized disaffection; that is, we expected our measures of powerlessness and racial dissatisfaction to have somewhat unique effects upon violence.

The data indicated an interaction effect (interaction $\chi^2 = 7.85$; $P < .01$)[23] between the two attitudes. The feeling of powerlessness is a more relevant determiner of violence for the highly dissatisfied or angry Negro. Similarly, racial dissatisfaction is far more important to violence for those who feel powerless. In sum, the data suggest that the powerless Negro is likely to use violence when his feelings of powerlessness are accompanied by intense dissatisfaction with his position. It can be noted, however, that, even among those who were relatively satisfied with racial conditions, powerlessness had some effect upon violence (a 13 per cent difference, $\chi^2 = 5.41$; $P = .02$). Presumably, a low expectancy of exerting control has a somewhat unique effect upon violence.

As a second way of noting an interrelationship between our predictive variables, we turn to the more crucial test of the isolation-extremism perspective in which the effect of racial isolation upon violence is controlled by powerlessness and dissatisfaction.[24] It will be recalled that we expected the isolated people (with a lower commitment to democratic norms and organized channels) to be more violence-prone when these isolated individuals perceive they cannot shape their destiny within the institutional framework (high powerlessness) or when they perceive differential treatment as Negroes and, as a result, are dissatisfied. It is under these subjective states of mind that a weak attachment to the majority group would seem to be most important to extremism. Table 2, addressed to these predictions, shows our hypotheses to be strongly supported in both cases.

Among the powerless and the dissatisfied, racial isolation has a strong

TABLE 2.   Percentage Willing to Use Violence, by Social Contact Controlling for Powerlessness and Racial Dissatisfaction

	Percentage Willing to Use Violence			
	Low powerlessness (%)	High powerlessness (%)	Low dissatisfaction (%)	High dissatisfaction (%)
Low contact	23 (N = 31)	53 (N = 78)	23 (N = 47)	59 (N = 63)
High contact	13 (N = 123)	26 (N = 66)	15 (N = 158)	26 (N = 34)
χ^2	$P < .20$	$P < .01$	$P < .20$	$P < .01$

Note. – The interaction χ^2 between powerlessness and contact: $P < .05$. The interaction χ^2 between dissatisfaction and contact: $P < .01$.

effect upon violence commitment. Conversely, the data show that isolation is much less relevant to violence for those with feelings of control in the system and for the more satisfied (in both cases, significant only at the .20 level).[25]

The fact that isolation (as a cause of violence) produces such a small percentage difference for the less alienated subjects calls for a further word of discussion. Apparently, isolation is not only a stronger predictor of violence for the people who feel powerless and dissatisfied, but is *only* a clear and significant determiner of violence for these subjectively alienated persons. For the relatively satisfied and control-oriented groups, the fact of being isolated is not very important in determining violence. This would suggest that a weak normative bond to the majority group (isolation) is not in itself sufficient to explain the participation of the oppressed minority person in violence and that it is the interaction between isolation and feelings of powerlessness (or racial dissatisfaction) that is crucial for predicting violence.

A final attempt at unification involves the cumulative effect of all three of our predictive variables upon violence. Since it was noted that each of the three predictive variables has some effect upon violence (either independently or for specific subgroups), it seemed logical that the combined effect of the three would produce a high violence propensity. Conceptually, a combination of these variables could be seen as ideal

TABLE 3.   Percentage Willing to Use Violence, by the Combined Effect of Social Contact, Powerlessness, and Racial Dissatisfaction

	Not Willing (%)	Willing (%)	Total (%)
Ideal-type alienated (low contact, high powerlessness, and high dissatisfaction)	35	65	100 (N = 51)
Middles in alienation	76	24	100 (N = 147)
Ideal-type non-alienated (high contact, low powerlessness, and low dissatisfaction)	88	12	100 (N = 107)

Note. $- \chi^2 = 49.37; P < .001$ (2 d.f.).

types of the alienated and non-alienated Negro. Accordingly, Table 3 arranges the data into these ideal-type combinations.

The group at the top of the table represents the one most detached from society—individuals who are isolated and high in attitudes of power-lessness and dissatisfaction. The group at the bottom of the table is the most involved in the society; these people have intimate white contact, feelings of control, and greater satisfaction with racial conditions. The middle group is made up of those with different combinations of high and low detachment. Note the dramatic difference in willingness to use violence between the "ideal-type" alienated group (65 per cent willing) and the group most bound to society (only 12 per cent willing). The "middles" in alienation display a score in violence between these extremes.

SPURIOUSNESS

It is possible that the relationship between our predictive variables and violence is due to an intercorrelation with other relevant variables. For example, social class should be related both to violence and to our isola-tion-alienation measures. In addition, we could expect a greater propensity toward violence in geographical areas where an extreme breakdown of legal controls occurred, such as the South Central and Watts areas (in contrast to the Crenshaw area, where no rioting took place). In such segregated ghettos, violence may have been defined by the inhabitants as a legitimate expression, given their intolerable living conditions, a group definition that could override any effects of isolation or alienation upon violence. In short, it seems essential to control our isolation-alienation variables by an index of social class and by ghetto area.[26]

Because of the rather small violent group, it is necessary to examine our predictive variables separately in this analysis of controls. Table 4 presents the original relationship between each of the independent vari-ables and violence, controlled by two areas of residence: the South Central-Watts area, at the heart of the curfew zone (where violence occurred), and the Crenshaw area, on the periphery (or outside) of the curfew zone (where violent action was rare). In addition, Table 4 includes a control for education, as a measure of social class.[27]

When the ghetto residence of the respondent is held constant, it appears that our independent variables are important in their own right. Education (social class), however, proved to be a more powerful control variable. Among the college educated, only isolation persists as a pre-dictor of violence; powerlessness and racial dissatisfaction virtually drop out. Yet each variable has a very strong effect upon violence among the high school (lower-class) group. In other words, we do not have an in-stance of spuriousness, where predictive variables are explained away in both partials, but another set of interaction effects—attitudes of powerless-ness and dissatisfaction are predictors of violence only among lower-class respondents. These results may be interpreted in several ways. Persons higher in the class structure may have a considerable amount to lose, in terms of occupational prestige and acceptance in white society, by en-

TABLE 4. Percentage Willing to Use Violence by Contact, Powerlessness, and Racial Dissatisfaction, Controlling for Two Geographical Areas and Education

Independent Variables	Neighborhood		Education	
	South Central-Watts	Crenshaw	Low (high school or less)	High (some college)
Low contact	53^b (N = 62)	33^b (N = 45)	52^b (N = 77)	24^a (N = 33)
High contact	27_b (N = 83)	10 (N = 109)	26_b (N = 86)	10 (N = 105)
Low powerlessness	22^b (N = 73)	11^a (N = 88)	19^b (N = 67)	14 (N = 93)
High powerlessness	55_b (N = 77)	25_b (N = 68)	51_b (N = 100)	18 (N = 45)
Low dissatisfaction	26^b (N = 81)	12^b (N = 130)	22^b (N = 96)	12 (N = 114)
High dissatisfaction	53 (N = 68)	39 (N = 28)	59 (N = 73)	17 (N = 24)

$^a p < .05.$ $^b p < .01.$

Note.—Interaction χ^2 between contact and neighborhood: P is not significant. Interaction χ^2 between powerlessness and neighborhood: $P < .02$. Interaction χ^2 between dissatisfaction and neighborhood: P is not significant: Interaction χ^2 between contact and education: P is not significant. Interaction χ^2 between powerlessness and education: $P < .02$. Interaction χ^2 between dissatisfaction and education: $.05 < P < .10$.

dorsing extreme methods. The college educated (middle class) may be unwilling to risk their position, regardless of feelings of powerlessness and dissatisfaction. These results may further indicate that middle-class norms favoring diplomacy and the use of democratic channels (as opposed to direct aggression) are overriding any tendency toward violence.[28] An extension of this interpretation is that middle-class Negroes may be activists, but non-violent activists, in the civil rights movement. Thus, class norms may be contouring resentment into more organized forms of protest.

CONCLUSIONS

In an attempt to locate the Negro participant in violence, we find that isolated Negroes and Negroes with intense feelings of powerlessness and dissatisfaction are more prone to violent action than those who are less alienated. In addition, isolation has its strongest effect upon violence when individuals feel powerless to control events in the society or when racial dissatisfaction is intensely felt. For those with higher expectations of control or with greater satisfaction regarding racial treatment isolation has a much smaller and non-significant effect (though in the predicted direction) upon violence. That is, a weak tie with the majority group, per se, appeared insufficient to explain wide-scale participation in extreme action. This study indicates that it is the interaction between a weak bond and a feeling of powerlessness (or dissatisfaction) that is crucial to violent participation.

Viewed another way, the combined or tandem effect of all three predictive variables produces an important profile of the most violence-prone individuals. Negroes who are isolated, who feel powerless, and who voice a strong disaffection because of discrimination appear to be an extremely volatile group, with 65 per cent of this stratum willing to use violence (as contrasted to only 12 per cent of the "combined lows" in alienation).

Ghetto area and education were introduced as controls. Each independent variable (taken separately) retained some significant effect upon violence in two geographical areas (dealing with proximity to the Watts violence) and among the less educated respondents. Powerlessness and dissatisfaction, however, had no effect upon violence among the college educated. Several interpretations of this finding were explored.

Applying our findings to the context of the Negro revolt of the last fifteen years, we note an important distinction between the non-violent civil rights activists and the violence-prone group introduced in this study. Suggestive (but non-conclusive) evidence indicates that the participants in organized civil rights protests are more likely to be middle class in origin, to hold considerable optimism for equal rights, and to have greater communication with the majority—this represents a group with "rising expectations" for full equality.[29] In contrast, this study located a very different population—one whose members are intensely dissatisfied, feel powerless to change their position, and have minimum commitment to the larger society. These Negroes have lost faith in the leaders and institutions of the community and presumably have little hope for improvement through organized protest. For them, violence is a means of communicating with white society; anger can be expressed, control exerted—if only for a brief period.

NOTES

ACKNOWLEDGEMENT: I am greatly indebted to Melvin Seeman and Robert Hagedorn for helpful comments and advice on earlier drafts of this paper. This is a revised version of a paper presented at the annual meetings of the Pacific Sociological Association, Long Beach, Calif., April 1967.

1. See, e.g., "Violence in the City—an End or a Beginning?" (report of the Governor's Commission on the Los Angeles Riots, December 2, 1965 [commonly known as the "McCone Commission Report"]).

2. One of the very few studies of the potential participants in race violence was conducted by Kenneth B. Clark, shortly after the Harlem riot of 1943 (see Clark, "Group Violence: A Preliminary Study of the Attitudinal Pattern of Its Acceptance and Rejection: A Study of the 1943 Harlem Riot," *Journal of Social Psychology* 19 [1944]: 319–37; see also Alfred McClung Lee and Norman D. Humphrey, *Race Riot* [New York: Dryden Press, 1943], pp. 80–87).

3. See, e.g., William Kornhauser, *The Politics of Mass Society* (Glencoe, Ill.: Free Press, 1959), pp. 183–223; Seymour Martin Lipset, *Political Man: The Social Bases of Politics* (New York: Doubleday, 1960), pp. 94–130; and Clark Kerr and Abraham Siegel, "The Interindustry Propensity to Strike—an International Comparison," in Arthur Kornhauser, Robert Dubin, Arthur M. Ross, ed., *Industrial Conflict* (New York: McGraw-Hill, 1954), pp. 189–212.

4. Kerr and Siegel, "The Interindustrial Propensity to Strike."

5. W. Kornhauser, *The Politics of Mass Society;* and Leon Bramson, *The Political Context of Sociology* (Princeton, N.J.: Princeton University Press, 1961), p. 72.

6. W. Kornhauser, *The Politics of Mass Society.*

7. E.g., Neal and Seeman found that isolated workers (non-participants in unions) were more likely to feel powerless to effect outcomes in the society than the participants in unions (Arthur G. Neal and Melvin Seeman, "Organizations and Powerlessness: A Test of the Mediation Hypothesis," *American Sociological Review* 29 [1964]: 216–26).

8. John E. Horton and Wayne E. Thompson, "Powerlessness and Political Negativism: A Study of Defeated Local Referendums," *American Journal of Sociology* 67 (1962): 485–93. For another report on the same study, see Wayne E. Thompson and John E. Horton, "Political Alienation as a Force in Political Action," *Social Forces* 38 (1960): 190–95.

9. Erich Fromm, "Alienation under Capitalism," in Eric and Mary Josephson, eds., *Man Alone* (New York: Dell, 1962), pp. 56–73.

10. Ralph Ellison, *Invisible Man* (New York: Random House, 1952).

11. Many studies have brought forth the finding that equal status contact between majority and minority members is associated with tolerance and favorable attitudes. For the most recent evidence of the equal status proposition, see Robin Williams, *Strangers Next Door* (Englewood Cliffs, N.J.: Prentice-Hall, 1964). For an earlier study, see Morton Deutsch and Mary E. Collins, *Interracial Housing* (Minneapolis: University of Minnesota Press, 1951).

12. This definition of subjective powerlessness is taken from the conceptualization proposed by Melvin Seeman, "On the Meaning of Alienation," *American Sociological Review* 24 (1959): 783–91.

13. In contrast to the mass society perspective, in which structural isolation is viewed as a cause of subjective alienation, we are viewing the two as imperfectly correlated. For example, many Negroes with contact (non-isolates) may still feel powerless due to racial discrimination barriers. We are thus stressing the partial independence of objective and subjective alienation and feel it necessary to consider both variables for the best prediction of violence.

14. This question was taken from Williams, *Strangers Next Door*, p. 185.

15. As a further indication that this measure was tapping a more intimate form of interracial contact, it can be noted that 88 per cent of those reporting social contact with whites claimed at least one "good friend" ("to whom you can say what you really think") or "close friend" ("to whom you can talk over confidential matters"). Only 10 per cent of those lacking social contact claimed such friendships with white people.

16. Seeman, "On the Meaning of Alienation."

17. The powerlessness scale was developed by Shephard Liverant, Jullian B. Rotter, and Melvin Seeman (see Jullian B. Rotter, "Generalized Expectancies for Internal vs. External Control of Reinforcements," *Psychological Monographs* 80, no. 1 [Whole No. 609], 1966): 1–28.

18. Using the Kuder-Richardson test for reliability, a coefficient of .77 was obtained for the twelve items.

19. Kuder-Richardson coefficient of .84.

20. With a cut at the median, a good many people ($N = 59$) who were mildly dissatisfied on all five items would have been placed in the "high" category. It was decided that a more accurate description of the "high" category would require the person to express maximum dissatisfaction on at least one of the five items and mild dissatisfaction on the other four.

21. As an indication that the question was interpreted in the context of participation in violence of the Watts variety, it can be noted that our question was correlated with approval of the Watts riot ($\phi = .62$).

22. The question, "Have you ever participated in violent action for Negro rights?" was purposely worded in general terms to avoid accusing the respondent of illegal behavior during the Watts violence. However, racial violence in the United States was somewhat rare at that time, so it is likely that most of the sixteen respondents were referring to participation in the Watts violence.

23. The χ^2 interaction test is somewhat analogous to the interaction test in the analysis of variance. A total χ^2 is first computed from the two partial tables in which all three variables are operating. Second, χ^2 values are obtained by cross-tabulating each possible pair of variables (e.g., χ^2AB, χ^2AC, and χ^2BC). These three separate χ^2 values are then summed and subtracted from the total χ^2. The residual, or what is left after subtraction, is the interaction χ^2. It can be viewed as the joint or special effect that comes when predictive variables are operating simultaneously. For a further description of this measure, see Philip H. DuBois and David Gold, "Some Requirements and Suggestions for Quantitative Methods in Behavioral Science Research," in Norman F. Washburne, ed., *Decisions, Values and Groups* (New York: Pergamon Press, 1962), II, 42–65.

24. The independent variables are moderately intercorrelated. For isolation and powerlessness, the ϕ correlation is .36, $P < .001$; for isolation and dissatisfaction, the ϕ is .40, $P < .001$; for powerlessness and dissatisfaction, the ϕ is .33, $P < .001$.

25. The .05 level is considered significant in this analysis.

26. Age was also considered as a control variable but was dropped when it was discovered that age was not correlated with violence or the independent variables. The r's ranged from .04 to .09.

27. For this sample, education was believed to be superior to other indexes of class. It is an index that is freer (than either occupation or income) from the societal restrictions and discrimination that Negroes face. Also, it was discovered that Negro occupations in the more deprived ghetto areas were not comparable to the same occupations listed in standardized scales, such as the North-Hatt or Bogue scales.

28. For a discussion of class norms, see Lipset, *Political Man*.

29. See Ruth Searles and J. Allen Williams, Jr., "Negro College Students' Participation in Sit-ins," *Social Forces* 40 (1962): 215–20; H. Edward Ransford, "Negro Participation in Civil Rights Activity and Violence" (unpublished Ph.D. dissertation, University of California, Los Angeles, 1966); and Pearl M. Gore and Jullian B. Rotter, "A Personality Correlate of Social Action," *Journal of Personality* 37 (1963): 58–64.

5. Context and Developmental Process

This section is designed to focus on the process of development of the ghetto riots both from a historical and from a contemporary point of view. As is the case throughout this book, there is overlap between this and other sections. Several selections already have discussed rioting as part of the evolving tactics within the black revolt; for example, the Geschwender-Singer selection discussed the types of communications between cities that increase the likelihood of the occurrence of ghetto uprisings as well as the types of intra-city communications that contribute to the growth and development of a riot, once underway. The two following selections should be read in combination with those presented earlier.

August Meier and Elliott Rudwick place black violence in an historical context. One might receive the impression, from my discussions of the evolution of tactics which produced the ghetto riots, that black violence appeared on the scene for the first time in 1964. This is not the case. The authors demonstrate that black retaliatory violence can be traced at least as far back as 1917. The "new style" of riot in which blacks destroy white property can be traced back as far as 1935. What distinguishes the events of 1964–1968 from these earlier eruptions is not their nature but their frequency and social definition. It is only in the later period that we find open discussions and advocacy of ghetto uprisings as necessary vehicles of social change. It is only in the later period that we find such a wave of cities experiencing ghetto insurrections within a short time span. Both of these new factors probably result from progress in the area of communications. The mass media have presented the speeches of black militants, have reported the events of insurrections, and have provided evidence of white ameliorative responses. All of these have provided the suggestion of a tactic and the proof that the tactic works. Thus what was a rare occurrence becomes a commonplace within a few decades.

The selection by Louis C. Goldberg uses a much narrower sweep in examining the development of ghetto disorders. There is a demonstrated need to classify riots properly before attempting to analyze them. The distinction between a major and a satellite riot is extremely important. For example, if we examine the events in a city which experiences a satellite riot in search of a precipitating incident, we may never find one. The precipitating incident is simply an insurrection in a nearby major city. Local strains and tensions are still relevant but the riots have different etiological syndromes and different career patterns. Once again we can see the importance of the mass media in the development of the rebellion. Goldberg also makes a significant contribution in underlining the major significance of grievances in producing riot targets, as opposed to the much lesser role in motivating riot participation played by the objectives *for* which one riots. This distinction is undoubtedly more important at the inception of the riot than at its later stages. Riots tend to become politicized as they progress, and objectives tend to either supplement or totally supplant grievances.

Black violence in the 20th century:
A study in rhetoric and retaliation

August Meier / Elliott Rudwick

For most Americans, the increasingly overt talk of retaliatory violence among Negro militants, and the outbreaks in the urban ghettos over recent summers, signify something new and different in the history of Negro protest. Actually, retaliatory violence has never been entirely absent from Negro thinking. Moreover, advocacy of retaliatory violence, and actual instances of it, have tended to increase during periods of heightened Negro protest activity.

Thus the past decade of rising Negro militance has been no stranger to the advocacy of retaliatory violence. For example, as far back as 1959, Robert F. Williams, at the time president of the Monroe, North Carolina, branch of the NAACP, came to public attention when the Union County Superior Court acquitted two white men of brutal assaults on two Negro women, but sentenced a mentally retarded Negro to imprisonment as a result of an argument he had with a white woman. Williams angrily told a reporter, "We cannot take these people who do us injustice to the court, and it becomes necessary to punish them ourselves. If it's necessary to stop lynching with lynching, then we must be willing to resort to that method." The NAACP dismissed Williams as branch president, but he remained a leader of Monroe's working-class Negroes, who for several years had been using guns to protect their homes from white Klansmen. In 1961, falsely charged with kidnaping a white couple, he fled from the country. Williams became the most famous of that group of militants existing at the fringe of the civil-rights movement, who in their complete alienation from American society articulated a revolutionary synthesis of nationalism and Marxism.[1] From his place of exile in Havana, Cuba, Williams undertook the publication of a monthly newsletter, *The Crusader*. In a typical issue, he declared:

> Our only logical and successful answer is to meet organized and massive violence with massive and organized violence. . . . The weapons of defense employed by Afro-American freedom fighters must consist of a poor man's arsenal. . . . Molotov cocktails, lye, or acid bombs [made by injecting lye or acid in the metal end of light bulbs] can be used extensively. During the night hours such weapons, thrown from roof tops, will make the streets impossible for racist cops to patrol. . . . Yes, a minority war of self-defense can succeed.[2]

Subsequently Williams was named chairman in exile of an organization known as the Revolutionary Action Movement (RAM),[3] a tiny group of

From Chapter Nine of *Violence in America: Historical and Comparative Perspectives,* A Report to the National Commission on the Causes and Prevention of Violence, June 1969, edited by Hugh Davis Graham and Ted Robert Gurr; reprinted by permission of authors.

college-educated people in a few major northern cities, some of whose members have been recently charged with plotting the murder of Roy Wilkins and Whitney Young.

Williams, RAM, and the better known Black Muslims [4] were on the fringes of the Negro protest, of the early 1960's. More recently violence and the propaganda for violence have moved closer to the center of the race relations stage. Well over 200 riots have occurred since the summer of 1964. The incendiary statements of the Rap Browns and the Stokeley Carmichaels became familiar TV and newspaper fare for millions of white Americans. The Oakland, California, Black Panthers and other local groups espousing a nationalist and revolutionary rhetoric thrived and received national publicity. As has been often pointed out, there is no evidence that the race riots of the 1960's have any direct relations to the preachings of Williams, of these various groups, even of the SNCC advocates of armed rebellion and guerrilla warfare. Yet both the statements of these ideologists, and the spontaneous actions of the masses, have much in common. For both are the product of the frustrations resulting from the growing disparity between the Negroes' status in American society and the rapidly rising expectations induced by the civil-rights revolution and its earlier successes.

Historically, this doctrine of retaliatory violence has taken various forms. Some have advocated self-defense against a specific attack. Others have called for revolutionary violence. There are also those who hopefully predicted a general race war in which Negroes would emerge victorious. Though seldom articulated for white ears, and only rarely appearing in print, thoughts of violent retaliation against whites have been quite common. For example, Ralph Bunche, in preparing a memorandum for Gunnar Myrdal's *American Dilemma* in 1940, noted that "there are Negroes, too, who, fed up with frustration of their life, here, see no hope and express an angry desire 'to shoot their way out of it.' I have on many occasions heard Negroes exclaim, 'Just give us machine guns and we'll blow the lid off the whole damn business.' " [5]

In surveying the history of race relations during the 20th century, it is evident that there have been two major periods of upsurge both in overt discussion by Negro intellectuals concerning the desirability of violent retaliation against white oppressors, and also in dramatic incidents of actual social violence committed by ordinary Negro citizens. One was the period during and immediately after the First World War. The second has been the period of the current civil rights revolution.

W. E. B. Du Bois, the noted protest leader and a founder of the NAACP, occasionally advocated retaliatory violence, and somewhat more often predicted intense racial warfare in which Negroes would be the victors. In 1916, inspired by the Irish Rebellion, in an editorial in the NAACP's official organ, *The Crisis,* he admonished Negro youth to stop spouting platitudes of accommodation and remember that no people ever achieved their liberation without an armed struggle. He said that "war is hell, but there are things worse than hell, as every Negro knows." [6] Amid the violence and repression that Negroes experienced in the postwar world, Du Bois declared that the holocaust of World War I was "nothing to compare with that fight for freedom which black and brown and yellow men must and will make unless their oppression and humiliation and insult at the hands of the White World cease." [7]

Other intellectuals reflected this restless mood. The postwar years were the era of the militant, race-conscious New Negro of the urban North, an intellectual type who rejected the gradualism and conciliation of his ancestors. The tone of the New Negro was recorded by Claude McKay, who in 1921 wrote his well-known poem, "If We Must Die": "If we must die/let it not be like hogs; hunted and penned in an accursed spot!/ . . . If we must die; oh, let us nobly die/dying but fighting back." A. Philip Randolph, editor of the militant Socialist monthly, *The Messenger,* organizer of the Brotherhood of Sleeping Car Porters, and later leader of the March on Washington Movements of 1941 and 1963, also advocated physical resistance to white mobs. He observed that "Anglo-Saxon jurisprudence recognizes the law of self-defense. . . . The black man has no rights which will be respected unless the black man enforces that respect. . . ." We are consequently urging Negroes and other oppressed groups concerned with lynching or mob violence to act upon the recognized and accepted law of self-defense." [8]

The legality of retaliatory violent self-defense was asserted not only by A. Philip Randolph, but also by the NAACP, which Randolph regarded as a moderate, if not futile organization, wedded to the interest of the Negro middle class. In 1925, half a dozen years after *The Messenger* article, the NAACP secured the acquittal of Dr. Ossian Sweet and his family. The Sweets were Detroit Negroes who had moved into a white neighborhood, and fired on a stone-throwing mob in front of their home, killing one white man and wounding another.[9] More than a quarter of a century later, at the time of the Robert Williams episode, the NAACP in clarifying its position, reiterated the stand that "The NAACP has never condoned mob violence but it firmly supports the right of Negroes individually and collectively to defend their person, their homes, and their property from attack. This position has always been the policy of the NAACP." [10] The views of intellectuals like Du Bois, McKay, and Randolph during World War I and the early postwar years paralleled instances of Negro retaliatory violence which actually triggered some of the major race riots of the period.

The East St. Louis riot of 1917, the bloodiest in the 20th century, was precipitated in July when Negroes, having been waylaid and beaten repeatedly by white gangs, shot into a police car and killed two white detectives. On the darkened street a Negro mob of 50 to 100 evidently mistook the Ford squad car for the Ford automobile containing white "joyriders" who had shot up Negro homes earlier in the evening. The following morning the riot began.[11]

In Houston, several weeks later, about 100 Negro soldiers broke into an Army ammunition storage room and marched on the city's police station. The troops, mostly Northerners, were avenging an incident which occurred earlier in the day, when a white policeman used force in arresting a Negro woman and then beat up a Negro soldier attempting to intervene. A Negro provost guard was pistol whipped and shot at for asking the policeman about the wounded soldier. Even before these events, the Negro soldiers nursed a hatred for Houston policemen, who had attempted to enforce streetcar segregation, frequently used the term "nigger," and officiously patrolled the Negro ghetto. The Houston riot was not only unusual because it involved Negro soldiers, but also because white persons constituted most of the fatalities.[12]

By 1919 there was evidence that the Negro masses were prepared to fight back in many parts of the country, even in the Deep South. In an unpublished report to the NAACP Board of Directors, a staff member, traveling in Tennessee and Mississippi during early 1919, noted that "bloody conflicts impended in a number of southern cities." Perry Howard, the leading colored attorney in Jackson, and R. R. Church, the wealthy Memphis politician, both reported that Negroes were armed and prepared to defend themselves from mob violence. Howard detailed an incident in which armed Negroes had prevented a white policeman from arresting a Negro who had become involved in a fight with two white soldiers after they had slapped a colored girl. In Memphis, R. R. Church, fearing armed conflict, privately advised the city's mayor that "the Negroes would not make trouble unless they were attacked, but in that event they were prepared to defend themselves." [13]

The Chicago race riot of 1919 grew out of Negro resentment of exclusion from a bathing beach dominated by whites. One Sunday, while Negroes and whites scuffled on the beach, a colored teenager drowned after being attacked in the swimming area. That attack was the most recent of a long series of assaults against Negroes. A white policeman not only refused to arrest a white man allegedly involved in the drowning, but actually attempted to arrest one of the two complaining Negroes. The officer was mobbed and soon the rioting was underway.[14]

The Elaine, Arkansas, riot of 1919 was precipitated when two white law officers shot into a Negro church, and the Negroes returned the fire, causing one death. The white planters in the area, already angered because Negro cottonpickers were seeking to unionize and obtain an increase in their share-cropping wages, embarked upon a massive Negro hunt to put the black peons "in their place." [15]

The Tulsa riot of 1921 originated when a crowd of armed Negroes assembled before the courthouse to protest the possible lynching of a Negro who had just been arrested for allegedly attacking a white girl. The Negroes shot at white police and civilians who attempted to disperse them.[16]

In each of these conflagrations, the typical pattern was initial Negro retaliation to white acts of persecution and violence, and white perception of this resistance as an organized, premeditated conspiracy to "take over," thus unleashing the massive armed power of white mobs and police. In the Southern communities, Negro resistance tended to collapse early in the riots. After the church incident in the rural Elaine area, most Negroes passively accepted the planters' armed attacks on their homes. At Tulsa, Negroes retreated from the courthouse to the ghetto, and throughout the night held off by gunfire the assaults of white mobs. But after daybreak, many Negroes fled or surrendered before the white onslaught burned down much of the ghetto.[17] One exception to this pattern was the Washington riot of 1919, where it appears that Negroes did not retaliate until the third and last day of the riot.[18]

Negro resistance generally lasted longer in Northern riots than in Southern ones, but even in East St. Louis and Chicago the death toll told the story: in East St. Louis, 9 whites and at least 39 Negroes were killed. In Chicago, 15 whites and 23 Negroes lost their lives. Negroes attacked a small number of whites found in the ghetto or on its fringes. Negro fatalities mainly occurred when victims were trapped in white-dominated downtown areas or residential sections. Negroes were also attacked on the edges of their neighborhood in a boundary zone separating a colored residential district from a lower class white area.[19] In the face of overwhelming white numerical superiority, many armed Negroes fled from their homes, leaving guns and ammunition behind. In East St. Louis, for example, there was a constant rattle of small explosions when fire enveloped a small colored residential district. Perhaps psychological factors contributed to the terrified inactivity of some Negroes. Despite the wish to meet fire with fire, over the years they had become so demoralized by white supremacy and race discrimination that effective armed defense could exist only in the realm of psychological fantasy.

During World War II, the most important race riot erupted in 1943 in Detroit, where nine whites and 25 Negroes were killed. In many respects the riot exhibited a pattern similar to East St. Louis and Chicago. The precipitating incident involved an attack on whites at the Belle Isle Amusement Park by several Negro teenagers who, a few days earlier, had been ejected from the white-controlled Eastwood Park. In the mounting tension at Belle Isle, many fights between Negroes and whites broke out, and the violence spread to the Negro ghetto where patrons at a night club were urged to "take care of a bunch of whites who killed a colored woman and her baby at Belle Isle." Although there had been no fatalities at the park, the night club emptied and revengeful Negroes stoned passing cars driven by whites. They began smashing windows on the ghetto's main business street, where the mob's major attention was directed to destroying and looting white-owned businesses.[20]

It was this symbolic destruction of "whitey" through his property that gave the Detroit holocaust the characteristic of what we may call the "new-style" race riot. It may be noted that in all the riots discussed above, there were direct clashes between Negroes and whites, and the major part of the violence was perpetrated by the white mobs. The riot pattern since the summer of 1964, however, has involved Negro aggression mainly against white-owned property, not white people. This "new-style" riot first appeared in Harlem in 1935 and 1943.[21] The modern riot does not involve white mobs at all, and policemen or guardsmen constitute most of the relatively small number of casualties.

One can identify perhaps two major factors responsible for this contrast between the old-style and the new-style riot. One is the relatively marked shift in the climate of race relations in this country over the past generation. On the one hand, whites have become, on the whole, more sensitive to the Negro's plight, more receptive toward Negro demands, and less punitive in their response to Negro aggression. The black masses, on the other hand, have raised their expectations markedly and, disillusioned by the relatively slow pace of social change which has left the underprivileged urban Negro of the North scarcely, if at all, better off than he was 10 to 15 years ago, have become more restless and militant than before.

In the second place, there is an ecological factor. From South to North, the migration of the World War I period was a mere drop in the bucket compared to what it later became. The migration to the North in each of the decades since 1940 has been equal to or greater than the migration of the whole 30-year period, 1910 to 1940. At the same time, owing to the Supreme Court's outlawing of the restrictive covenant in 1948, and the tearing down of the older slums through urban renewal, the Negro population has been dispersed over a wider area, thus accentuating the trend toward the development of vast ghettos. Indeed, compared to the enormous ghettos of today, the Negro residential areas of the World War I period were mere enclaves. Today, of course, Negroes are close to becoming a majority in several of the major American cities.

The character of American race riots has been markedly affected by these demographic changes. Even if white mobs were to form, they would be unable to attack and burn down the Negro residential areas; even in the 19th- and early-20th-century riots, white mobs did not usually dare to invade the larger Negro sections, and destroyed only the smaller areas of Negro concentration. Nor, since the Negroes are such a large share of the population of the central city areas, would white mobs today be in a position to chase, beat, and kill isolated Negroes on downtown streets. More important, from the Negroes' point of view, the large-scale ghettos provide a relatively safe place for the destruction and looting of white-owned property; it is impossible for local police forces to guard business property in the farflung ghettos; even state police and federal troops find themselves in hostile territory where it is difficult to chase down rioters beyond the principal thoroughfares.

It is notable that during the 20th century, both the overt discussion of the advisability of violent retaliation on the part of Negroes, and also actual incidents of violence were prominent in the years during and after World War I, and again during the 1960's. While there have been significant differences between the outbreaks characteristic of each era, there have been also important similarities, In both periods retaliatory violence accompanied a heightened militancy among American Negroes—a militancy described as the "New Negro" in the years after World War I, and described in the sixties, with the phrase, "the Negro Revolt." In neither case was retaliatory violence the major tactic, or the central thrust, but in both periods it was a significant subordinate theme. However, in both periods a major factor leading Negroes to advocate or adopt such a tactic was the gap between Negro aspiration and objective status. The rapid escalation of the aspirations of the Negro masses who shared Martin Luther King's "dream" and identify vicariously with the success of the civil-rights revolution, while their own economic, housing, and educational opportunities have not improved, is a phenomenon of such frequent comment that it requires no elaboration here.

A comparable situation occurred during and shortly after the First World War. The agitation of the recently founded NAACP, whose membership doubled in 1918–19, the propaganda of fighting a war to make the world safe for democracy, and especially the great Negro migration to the Northern cities which Southern peasants and workers viewed as a promised land, all created new hopes for the fulfillment of age-old dreams, while Negro soldiers who had served in France returned with new expectations. But the Negro's new hopes collided with increasing white hostility. Northern Negroes assigned to southern army camps met indignities unknown at home. They rioted at Houston and came so close to rioting in Spartanburg, South Carolina, that the army hastily shipped them overseas. In the northern cities like East St. Louis and Chicago, Negroes found not a promised land, but overcrowded ghettos and hostile white workers who feared Negro competition for their jobs. The Ku Klux Klan was revived beginning in 1915, and grew rapidly in the North and South after the war ended. By 1919 economic opportunities plummeted as factories converted to peacetime operations. For a while Negroes resisted, protested, fought back, in the South as well as the North; but the superior might of the whites proved overpowering and the Southern Negroes retreated into old paths of accommodation where they generally remained until the momentous events of the past decade.

There has been no systematic research on Negro advocacy of violence prior to the First World War, but the available evidence supports the thesis that increased overt expression of this tendency accompanies peaks in other kinds of protest activity. For example, it appears likely that Negro resistance to white rioters was minimal in the riots at the turn of the century—at Wilmington, North Carolina, in 1898, and at New Orleans, Akron, and New York in 1900 [22]—which took place in a period when the sentiment of accommodation to white supremacy, epitomized by Booker T. Washington, was in the ascendency.

Again, during the ante-bellum period, one can cite two noted cases of incendiary statements urging Negroes to revolt—*David Walker's Appeal* of 1829, and Rev. Henry Highland Garnet's suppressed *Address to the Slaves of the United States of America,* delivered at the national Negro convention of 1843.[23] Both coincided with periods of rising militant protest activity on the part of the northern free Negroes. *Walker's Appeal* appeared on the eve of the beginning of the Negro convention movement, and at the time of intensified Negro opposition to the expatriation plans of the American Colonization Society.[24] Garnet's speech was made at a time when free Negro leaders were disturbed at the prejudiced attitudes of white abolitionists who refused to concern themselves with obtaining rights for the free people of color, or to allow Negroes to participate in the inner circles of the leadership of the antislavery societies. Consequently they had revived the Negro national convention movement which had been inactive since 1836. (Garnet's speech was also in part a product of disillusionment with the lack of actual progress being made by the antislavery societies toward achieving abolition.)

We lack any careful analysis of race riots during the 19th century. Some certainly were pogrom-like affairs, in which the Negroes were so thoroughly terrorized from the beginning that they failed to fight back. (Perhaps the Draft Riots, and some of the Reconstruction riots as in Mississippi in 1876 were of this sort.) Yet other riots were characterized by some degree of Negro retaliatory violence, such as the Snow Hill riot in Providence, in 1831, and the Cincinnati riots of 1841. Both appear to have been, like the Chicago and East St. Louis riots, the climaxes to a series of interracial altercations. In the Providence riot, a mob of about 100 white sailors and citizens advanced on a small Negro section; a Negro shot a sailor dead, and within a half hour a large mob descended upon the neighborhood, damaging many houses.[25] In the Cincinnati riot, a pitched battle was fought on the streets; the blacks had enough guns and ammunition to fire into the mob such a volley that it was twice repulsed. Only when the mob secured an iron six-pounder and hauled it to the place of combat and fired on the Negroes were the latter forced to retreat, permitting the rioters to hold sway for 2 days without interference from the authorities.[26] A careful study of interracial violence during Reconstruction will undoubtedly produce evidence of comparable situations. These riots occurred at a time of high Negro expectations and self-assertiveness, and seem to have been characterized by a significant amount of fighting back on the part of Negroes.

One period of marked and rising Negro militance, however, was not accompanied by a significant increase in manifestations of Negro retaliatory violence. This was the one following the Second World War. Indeed, the Second World War itself witnessed far less Negro violence than did the First World War. The reason for this would appear to be that the 1940's and early 1950's were years of gradually improving Negro status, and a period in which the expectations of the masses did not greatly outrun the actual improvements being made. In fact, from 1941 until the mid-1950's the relative position of the Negro workers, as compared to the white wage earners, was generally improving and it was not until the recession of 1954–55, for example, that the Black Muslims, with their rhetoric of race hatred and retaliatory violence, began to expand rapidly.

It would appear that both in the World War I period, and today— and indeed during the ante-bellum era and at other times when manifestations of violence came to the fore—there has been a strong element of fantasy in Negro discussion and efforts concerning violent retaliation. Robert Williams talked of Molotov cocktails and snarling up traffic as devices for a largely poverty-stricken ethnic minority to engineer a revolution. The Black Muslims talk of violence, but the talk seems to function as a psychological safety valve; by preaching separation, they in effect accommodate to the American social order and place racial warfare off in the future when Allah in his time will destroy the whites and usher in an era of black domination. Similarly, in view of population statistics and power distribution in American society, Du Bois and others who have spoken of the inevitability of racial warfare and Negro victory in such a struggle were engaging in wishful prophesies. And Negroes have been nothing if not realistic. The patterns of Negro behavior in riots demonstrate this. In earlier times, as already indicated, those who bought guns in anticipation of the day when self-defense would be necessary usually did not retaliate. And Negro attacks on whites occurred mainly in the early stages of the riots before the full extent of anger and power and sadism of the white mobs became evident.

Negroes of the World War I era resisted white insults and attacks only as long as they had hopes of being successful in the resistance. It should be emphasized that one of the remarkable things about the riots since 1964, in spite of their having been marked by particular resentment at police brutality, is the fact that Negro destruction was aimed at white-owned property, not white lives, even after National Guardsmen and policemen killed scores of Negroes. And in those cases where retaliatory violence has been attempted, Negroes have retreated in the face of massive white armed force. Economically impoverished Negroes press as far as they realistically can; and one reason for the explosions of recent years has been the awareness that whites are to some degree in retreat, that white mobs in the North no longer organize to attack, and that to a large degree the frustrated Negroes in slums like Watts, Detroit, Washington, or Newark, can get away with acts of destruction.

It is impossible of course to make any foolproof predictions for the future. Yet, judging by past experience and present conditions, it is our view that, despite all the rhetoric of engineering a social revolution through armed rebellion and guerrilla warfare, of planned invasions of downtown business districts and white suburbs, the kind of violence we are likely to witness will, at most, continue to be the sort of outbreaks against the property of white businessmen such as those we have witnessed in recent years. The advocacy and use of violence as a deliberate program for solving the problems of racial discrimination remains thus far, at least, in the realm of fantasy; and there it is likely to remain.

NOTES

1. For accounts, see Julian Mayfield, "Challenge to Negro Leadership," *Commentary* 31 (April 1961): 297–305; "The Robert F. Williams Case," *Crisis* 66 (June-July-August-September 1959): 325–29; 409–10; Robert F. Williams, *Negroes With Guns* (New York: Marzani & Munsell, 1962).

2. *Crusader* 5 (May-June 1964): 5–6.

3. See the RAM publication *Black America* (Summer-Fall 1965); *Crusader* (March 1965).

4. C. Eric Lincoln, *The Black Muslims in America* (Boston: Beacon Press, 1961), p. 205.

5. Ralph Bunche, "Conceptions and Ideologies of the Negro Problem," memorandum prepared for the Carnegie-Myrdal Study of the Negro in America, 1940, p. 161.

6. *Crisis* 12 (August 1916): 166–67; 13 (December 1916): 63.

7. W. E. B. Du Bois, *Darkwater* (New York, 1920), p. 49.

8. A. Philip Randolph, "How To Stop Lynching," *Messenger* 3 (April 1919): 8–9.

9. Walter White, "The Sweet Trial," *Crisis* 31 (January 1926): 125–29.

10. "The Robert F. Williams Case," *Crisis* 66 (June-July 1959): 327.

11. Elliott M. Rudwick, *Race Riot at East St. Louis* (Cleveland and New York: Meredian Books, 1968), pp. 38–39.

12. Edgar A. Schuler, "The Houston Race Riot, 1917," *Journal of Negro History* 29 (October 1944): 300–38.

13. *NAACP Board Minutes*, Secretary's Report for June 1919.

14. *The Negro in Chicago* (Chicago, 1922), pp. 4–5.

15. *Crisis* 19 (December 1919): 56–62.

16. Allen Grimshaw, "A Study in Social Violence: Urban Race Riots in the U.S.," Doctoral dissertation, University of Pennsylvania, 1959, pp. 42–47.

17. Ibid.

18. Constance M. Green, *Washington, Capital City, 1879–1950* (Princeton: Princeton University Press, 1962), pp. 266–67; John Hope Franklin, *From Slavery to Freedom* (New York: Knopf, 1947), p. 473; *New York Times*, July 20–22, 1919.

19. Rudwick, *Race Riot at East St. Louis*, pp. 226–27; *Negro in Chicago*, pp. 5–10.

20. Alfred McClung Lee and Norman D. Humphrey, *Race Riot* (New York, 1943), pp. 26–30.

21. Roi Ottley, *New World A-Coming* (Boston: Beacon Press, 1943), pp. 151–52; Harold Orlansky, *The Harlem Riot: A Study in Mass Frustration* (New York, 1943), pp. 5–6, 14–15; *New York Age*, March 30, 1935, and August 7, 1943.

22. In the New York riot, however, the precipitating incident was a physical altercation between a white policeman and a Negro; see Gilbert Osofsky, *Harlem: The Making of a Ghetto* (New York: Harper & Row, 1966), pp. 46–52.

23. Herbert Aptheker, *A Documentary History of the Negro People in the United States* (New York: Citadel, 1951), pp. 93–97, 226–33.

24. Founded in 1817 by a group of prominent white Americans, the American Colonization Society officially encouraged colonization as a means of furthering the cause of antislavery. Most Negroes, even most of those who themselves at one time or another advocated emigration to Africa or the Caribbean as the only solution for the Negro's hopeless situation in the United States, denounced the society as a cloak for those attempting to protest slavery by deporting free Negroes.

25. Irving H. Bartlett, "The Free Negro in Providence, Rhode Island," *Negro History Bulletin* 14 (December 1950): 54.

26. Carter G. Woodson, "The Negroes of Cincinnati Prior to the Civil War," *Journal of Negro History* 1 (January 1916): 13–15.

GHETTO RIOTS AND OTHERS: THE FACES OF CIVIL DISORDER IN 1967

Louis C. Goldberg

1. INTRODUCTION

Civil disorders in American cities in 1967 were not all of the same kind. The term "riot" has been too loosely applied to denote disturbances, often quite varied, which occurred last summer and in the previous three years. It has been used to refer to anything from a group of excited teenagers breaking windows after a dance, to a general social upheaval. All were civil disturbances; but only a few warranted the label "riot."

It is misleading also to think of the civil disturbances simply as "Negro riots." To do so suggests that the immediate responsibility for the course of the disturbances and the extent of damage lies solely with the Negro participants. It is necessary, of course, to underscore the reality of violent and aggressive mass actions involving looting, burning, and defiance of local authority within Negro areas; and the initiative of Negro rioters in events. But the threats to civil order and innocent life and property did not come only from the Negro side. In some cities, the behavior of various official control agents—police, national guardsmen, and the courts—in fact constituted official lawlessness: abuses of power in the name of law and order. For the largest disorders especially, the concept of a "tandem riot"—a riot by Negroes against public authorities, followed by a riot of control agents against Negroes—is appropriate.

In other cities, "Negro riots" were more imagined than real. For such disorders, we must distinguish between *actual* collective violence by Negroes, and the *perception* of a riot by white authorities. There is much evidence that in several cities white anticipation of Negro violence led to heavy-handed uses of official force that provoked violence which might not have otherwise occurred.

The news media, for their part, sometimes contributed to building expectations of community violence by over-dramatizing disturbances and helping to create an emotional climate in which even minor incidents were seen as major riots.

2. PROMINENT FEATURES OF DISORDERS: CLASSIFYING THE "RIOTS"

A sample of 23 disturbances which occurred last summer shows clearly that the particular combination of circumstances in each city was to some extent unique. But at the same time certain characteristics of different

From Vol. 5 (1968), pp. 116–28 of the *Journal of Peace Research*, International Peace Research Institute, Oslo; published by Universitetsforlaget, Oslo, Norway; reprinted and abridged by permission of the author and publisher.

disturbances were so similar that we may *group the disorders, particularly the largest ones, on the basis of their most prominent features.*

2.1. General upheavals

Over a period of time a disturbance may develop into an upheaval which draws in thousands or tens of thousands of participants from a Negro ghetto, exhausts the resources of local police, severely taxes the capacities of city institutions, and involves an extraordinarily wide range of lawless activities on the part of both Negroes and control authorities. After the disorder has ended, an area often looks as if it has been through a state of civil warfare. Such was the case in Detroit and Newark, 1967, and in Los Angeles, 1965. These disorders were so massive, events so much beyond the control of either civil authorities or Negro community leadership, the points of street confrontation between police and Negroes so numerous and widespread, that it is difficult to characterize the whole complex of actions over the course of a disturbance in simple terms.

In all three cases, however, a similar pattern of development stands out: the violence in each went through two distinct phases. *In the first, widespread and aggressive action by ghetto Negroes overwhelmed local police forces, leaving them virtually powerless to enforce order in the streets. In the second, reinforced control authorities engaged in harsh retaliatory actions to reassert dominance.*

PHASE 1: NEGRO REBELLION

In this phase *collective* violence was initiated by Negroes. In Detroit and Newark, as well as in Watts, aggressive action by Negroes escalated spontaneously from an initial confrontation with police into a highly generalized rebellion against white authority and white-owned property in the ghetto. In the face of an expanding rebellion, local police lacked the resources to act with the even-handed decisiveness necessary to bring the violence under control; their efforts inflamed rather than quieted Negro participants.

As the ability of police to enforce control of the streets diminished, more and more segments of the Negro community—older people, women, children—joined the young men who had been in the forefront. At the peak of this phase there was a euphoric realization among Negro rioters that they had nullified police control over their territory. Overwhelmed, the police floundered helpless and frustrated.

PHASE 2: CONTROL FORCE RETALIATION

Under the strain of widespread rioting, police order had begun to dissolve; many officers became subject to the same principles of crowd behavior that motivated Negro rioters. Deep-rooted racial prejudices surfaced. The desire to vent hostility, to re-establish dominance, and to avenge police honor became compelling motives. Rumors and racist attitudes fed into each other as determinants of police behavior with the breakdown of routine arrest procedure, police communication systems, and police leadership control of their men on the street.

Once reinforcements arrived in the form of state police and National Guard units, the second phase of disorder was inaugurated. With police discipline severely weakened, many lawless acts initiated by lower-echelon police officers coincided with the reassertion of police dominance over Negro rioters. Many National Guardsmen, ill-disciplined and afraid, showed little restraint in using weapons in areas in which they were strangers. This period was characterized by a marked tendency among control authorities to treat all Negroes categorically as enemies. The presence of massive official force, or its withdrawal, or the exhaustion of Negro rioters and control authorities alike, would finally bring the violence to an end.

PATTERNS OF ESCALATION

Detroit: Phase 1. These two phases of disorder in Los Angeles, Detroit, and Newark—in part the product of a high level of community polarization prior to the upheaval—directly emerged as a result of reciprocating hostile actions by police and Negro activists.

In Detroit, the first phase had 5 escalation points, each occurring within 12 hours from the start of the disturbance.[1] The initial event was a police raid on a blind pig [2] that mobilized a crowd. The second escalation point occurred shortly after the police left the scene, looting beginning as [an] agitator, emerging from the crowd which had grown angry, broke the first window. This was followed by several hours in which the police, returning to the area undermanned, made no visible effort to stop the looting going on under their eyes. Police inaction encouraged a massive expansion in community participation. Then, a sudden and ineffective crackdown—a sweep of the streets by a tough elite riot squad armed with bayonets—outraged the community while simultaneously demonstrating police impotence as the dispersal tactic failed. Shortly thereafter, firebombing, with Negro youths at the forefront, greatly accelerated. The riot had become totally out of control.

Newark: Phase 1. The steps in the development of the Newark rebellion —which preceded and gave impetus to the one in Detroit—differed somewhat from the first phase of the Detroit upheaval but paralleled it in basic process. As in Detroit, a police incident initiated the chain of events. Here, the first step was the arrest and beating of a Negro cab driver which initially mobilized a large and angry crowd of Negroes in front of the police station. While the police in Detroit were permissive in the face of the initial stage of looting, those in Newark were both indecisive and punitive toward the increasingly hostile and aggressive crowd that literally began to lay siege to the police station. A cycle occurred in which the bombardment of the station with bricks, bottles, and Molotov cocktails by some members of the crowd would be followed by a rush of the police toward the crowd, a backoff of the crowd, a police withdrawal to the station, and a reassembly of the crowd to begin the process again. Each time this occurred the crowd's contempt for the police and its own sense of power grew.

As the police sweep in Detroit was followed by firebombing, so in Newark a period of minor looting followed a police charge which nullified efforts by civil rights leaders to organize a march away from the station. Police action subsequently alienated a major source of grapevine information in the ghetto. Twenty-five cabdrivers who had transported some people down to city hall to conduct a non-violent protest and picket became extremely indignant to find their double-parked cars being ticketed and towed away.

The difference between Newark and Detroit at this point, however, was that the possibility existed to save the situation through a political solution between the Italian city administration and Negro militant leaders. Such a solution did not materialize.

Then on the second evening, escalation began again. Events moved almost directly into a period in which rioting was out of control, completing the process that was truncated the evening before. The stopping of a picket line in front of the police station to announce a concession considered trivial by the crowd catalyzed Negro youth into stone throwing at the station. The police in turn charged the crowd. Discipline cracked. Even Negro newspaper reporters, and in one instance a Negro policeman, were beaten by white policemen caught up in an anti-black frenzy. White police in Detroit were permissive toward looters in the first stage, those in Newark had already lost control on the second evening when the looting started in earnest. The absence of police in many areas and the widespread looting in turn produced pressures for participation that proved irresistible for many ordinarily law-abiding people.

Detroit: Phase II. With the introduction of state police and National Guard, and removal of constraints on use of weapons, the character of the riots began to change.

In Detroit the removal of restraint on the use of weapons by control authorities caused violence to escalate on both sides. For the control forces frequent gunfire, and some firing of weapons by some Negroes led to pervasive rumors of massive Negro sniping activity. Fear combined with motives for revenge led many troopers to see themselves as embattled soldiers in a war situation against an enemy people, and they acted accordingly. Lack of command discipline in the general confusion led to situations in which guardsmen became lost, made mistakes, or violated standing orders (e.g., even after federal troops arrived and the commanding general instructed guardsmen to unload their weapons, 90% of the guardsmen did not).

A similar situation occurred for the police. With the top leadership of the police department having lost control over lower echelon officers by midweek, the latter being fatigued from over-work and the arrest procedure system having fallen apart, many policemen engaged in vengeful action. It was not until regular army troops arrived, official violence brought under control, and all parties reduced to a state of exhaustion that the disorders finally ceased.

Newark: Phase II. In Newark, the statements of the governor telling Negroes they were forced to choose between "the jungle" and "law and order" became interpreted by some policemen as a license for summary justice. Police retaliation was further spurred by the killing of one officer: acts of ritual revenge were even carried out in his name. As in Detroit, rumors of snipers, lack of coordination between police and guard forces, and motives of retaliation produced massive onslaughts of gunfire directed at Negro occupied or owned buildings. With a growing retaliatory mood among Negro youth, violence did not end until the governor ordered the guard units withdrawn from the Negro areas.

2.2.   Riots as political confrontations

Newark and Detroit are extreme examples of massive disorder in the summer of 1967. A few disturbances showed many of the characteristics of these general upheavals but developed over time in a distinctly political direction. As in the general upheaval, the level of disorder in the streets was quite large. *But in these disorders explicit political confrontation* [3] *between Negro leadership and civil authorities was at least as important a feature of the riot as violent street confrontation between Negro masses and the police.* This was true in such cities as Cincinnati and Plainfield.

On the first night of disorder in Plainfield, for example, a local Negro politician tried to steer the youth toward a meeting with the mayor to talk about their grievances. The meeting was held, but was unsatisfactory, the youth leadership representatives walking out twice, a minor riot occurring after the second walkout. On the next day, a meeting they were having in a park to formulate grievances and reduce them to writing was broken up by the police. Shortly thereafter violence rapidly escalated as a policeman was killed by a mob after he shot a youth, and the youths, fearing retaliation from the police, stole 46 carbines from a gun factory. Later, one of their representatives—a young man who has since become an important political figure in the community—attempted to use the possession of the guns as a bargaining tool, offering to exchange them in return for a sign of good faith from the authorities. An agreement was reached and Negro-initiated violence ceased, although the guns were not in fact returned. During a two-day period when police were kept out of the area of disturbance, the youths in effect took responsibility for keeping order. In the aftermath, the activities of the youth militants have involved the use of pressure group tactics in council meetings, their first victory being the defeat of an anti-loitering amendment.

Unlike the general upheaval, events in Plainfield, although violent, were not entirely out of the control of community leaders. In Detroit, where there may have been tens or hundreds of bands of rioters at work, any kind of coherence or control over events was impossible. In Newark, the possibility for a political solution was quickly foreclosed by the severe political polarization between the mayor and the middle-class Negro militants, and the lack of control of the latter over the young. But in Plainfield, the existence of a leadership group among the youth who were rioting, and their willingness to negotiate, made possible a political compromise of sorts.

Indeed, a politicized focus and coherence to events occurred wherever rioters were sufficiently organized to "select" their own leadership for negotiation, or where there were leaders within the general community who would act and be accepted as "spokesmen." In such cases, militancy around the conference table would match, and often substitute for, militancy in the streets.

2.3. The riot as expressive rampage

While many of the larger disorders had pronounced instrumental and political components, there is also a type in which a quality of expressive rampaging on the part of the Negro participants was predominant. All of the ghetto riots involved the spontaneous gathering of an angry crowd in the first phase. But in this third type, the behavior of rioters gained little focus or direction over time. The clearest image is a wandering street mob, angry, drunken, milling about, lacking leadership or direction, engaged in breaking windows, or random acts of vandalism.

The riot in Dayton in 1966, which preceded two smaller disturbances during the summer of 1967, was of this type. From the start those engaged in the disturbance were a "bar crowd" of petty hustlers and drunks, marginal elements in the community. Efforts by the mayor to reach a "political solution" to the riot by negotiating with a militant civil rights leader on the scene was ineffective, because the rioting crowd was organized around drinking and chaotic emotional expression. Efforts to organize the crowd into a meeting to express grievance and negotiate failed totally. The disorder was finally suppressed by heavy arrests once local police were buttressed with National Guard forces.

2.4. The riot as fulfillment of anticipations

While the largest disorders generally began with an aggressive ghetto riot followed by a tough police response, there is another category of disturbance in which the flow of events proceeded in the opposite direction. *The first acts of collective aggression came not from Negroes but from control forces—subsequent Negro responses tending to be defensive, protective, or retaliatory.* In such cities as Cambridge, Maryland; Jersey City and Elizabeth, New Jersey, anticipations of Negro lawlessness, rather than actual lawlessness itself, led to periods of disturbance.

These were initiated by precipitous "riot control tactics" or "shows of force" by white authorities. Compared with cities that did have massive ghetto rioting, such disturbances remained fairly minor, although their actual proportions were often greatly exaggerated at the time they occurred.

In Cambridge, Maryland, the presence and speech of H. Rapp Brown had a great effect in stimulating local authorities to acts of disorder against the Negro community. His mere presence evoked images in the minds of white leadership that there was an organized conspiracy afoot to lead Cambridge's Negroes in a rampaging pillage of the town's white business district. His inflammatory speech, although failing to galvanize Negro youth to start breaking things up, did produce a wave of hysteria in the Negro police officers who heard it. These reported that a riot was underway—thus confirming the worst fears of local white officials. At one point, after an injury to an officer, the local police chief wanted to go shooting into the area, and only restraints by state authorities prevented bloodshed. Later on, the white volunteer fire department refused to go into the Negro area to put out a small fire that finally spread into a blaze consuming a block of Negro businesses. This non-action stemmed in part from a fear of a preplanned plot to "trap" fire department equipment in the Negro area, thus leaving the downtown area to be burned and plundered.

In a few disorders, white anticipatory action overlapped with an expressive rampage by Negro youth. In Milwaukee, the first evening of disorder began with window breaking and looting by youths on a "hell-raising" spree after a dance. But the authorities had been waiting for some time in anticipation for a try at containing a riot. The response of officials was to call for the mobilization of 4800 Guardsmen, 200 state police, and 800 policemen.

In a few cities *joint expectations* held by *both* Negroes and whites that a "riot was coming" had something of a self-fulfilling character. However, in the absence of truly intense community polarization, the disturbances possessed a staged or simulated quality. The participants seemed to be going through the motions of a riot more than carrying out serious conflict. Lacking was the quality of vengeance and retribution which pervades so much of the behavior on all sides during a riot out of control.

Staged conflict in this sense occurred in New Brunswick, where youths put on a riot in the main street. An effective political response by the lady mayor brought a quick end to the disorder. The second night of rioting in Tucson was "staged" in another sense. Following queries by a newspaper reporter as to where and when they were going to riot that evening, youths put on a minor riot for the benefit of the press.

2.5. The riots that didn't happen: "mini-riots" and others

In most of the events in which anticipations of violence played an important role, the level of disorder on the Negro side was so minimal as to suggest calling these disturbances "Negro riots that didn't happen." There were also some low-level disturbances—"mini-riots" is an apt term—that reflected in germinal or aborted form dimensions more fully developed in the largest disorders.

The Atlanta and Tampa disturbances showed many characteristics in common with certain northern disorders. In Atlanta as in Newark and Detroit, a crowd formed in a community gathering place in a high density area. The scene in this instance was a neighborhood shopping center where police-related incidents had occurred the two previous nights. Stokeley Carmichael, present to urge the crowd to take to the streets, found an audience willing to take matters into its own hands. But (1) the police immediately moved in with major force and were extremely effective; (2) the mayor quickly responded to the political aspect of the event by beginning visible construction the next day on long-delayed projects demanded by area residents; and (3) a newly-formed Negro Youth Corps helped keep the rest of the summer cool.

In a Northern city like Dayton, there was a significant potential in its two 1967 disturbances for a major Negro riot. The first disturbance followed a meeting protesting the cut of a grassroots poverty program. H. Rapp Brown was the featured out-of-town visitor at the meeting. He excited youth who were already looking for an excuse to riot.

The second followed a bitter meeting protesting the release of a vice squad officer after a controversial killing of a middle-class Negro professional. An initially decisive police response and the "cooling effect" of the Dayton White Hats in both cases rapidly attenuated the escalation potential in the disturbance.

Finally, in the category of "riots which did not occur" is the traditional race riot which has often marked American history. The potential nevertheless was there. In Cincinnati, New Haven, Newark, and Cambridge, whites were attracted to the scene, ready to take up the banner against Negroes and to defend white property. In such cities, effective police practice prevented white outsiders from coming into Negro areas, thus aborting the race riot process. In Cambridge, where there has been a continuing danger of racial confrontation for several years, the state National Guard acted in its customary role as a buffer against violence.

3. PROCESSES IN DEVELOPING DISORDERS

3.1. Urban upheavals and satellite riots:
the propagation of violence

As a nationwide phenomenon, the propagation of violence across the land follows the close link between major ghetto upheavals, or reports thereof, and "satellite" disorders in which authority over-reaction occurs. The former has clearly acted as a trigger to the latter. In the wake of a disturbance the size of Newark or Detroit, rumors of small incidents in a local area become magnified as the beginning of a riot. On the white side, a climate of anxiety is produced by stories of planned violence, and fears of outside agitators and conspirators.

After the Detroit upheaval, eight other Michigan cities reported disorders. After the Newark riot, fourteen cities in the surrounding area had some sort of disturbance. *In at least two-thirds of fifteen cities studied in which disorders occurred shortly after major riots, the immediate precipitant of disorder seems to have been a police action prompted by ghetto violence elsewhere.*

THE PROPAGATION OF DISORDER
IN THE NEW JERSEY CHAIN

To illustrate the propagation effect, let us examine some of the cities in the chain of disturbances that occurred in New Jersey in the aftermath of the Newark riot. In Englewood, police outnumbered participants three to one. In Jersey City, 400 armed police occupied the Negro area several days before the disorder occurred. In most cases, relations became strained as the appearance of armed police patrols increased the likelihood of confrontation with Negro residents. The most frequent citizen demands were for police withdrawal and/or a less visible show of arms. In six of the seven New Jersey "satellite" cities, removal of police from the ghetto signalled an end to violence. Rumors of violence often become self-fulfilling prophecies when credited and responded to with a visible show of force and fear.

Errors in judgment produced by a climate of fear in the white community were typified in many New Jersey cities. One prominent example was officials reacting to rumors that Stokeley Carmichael was bringing carloads of Negro militants into the community, although Carmichael was in London at the time. Planning for disorder by New Jersey police departments, even before the Newark upheaval occurred, showed similar elements of irrationality in the face of uncertainty.

On June 5, 1967, the police chiefs of at least 75 New Jersey communities met in Jersey City. They discussed rumors of planned violence by various militant groups who reportedly intended to kill Jersey City police officers in their homes and foment disorder in other New Jersey communities. Jersey City, Newark, and Elizabeth were said to have "Triple A" ratings for violence over the summer. Plans to coordinate control efforts were established, and the chiefs were informed of the procedures for calling in the state police and National Guard.

Thus, a month and a half before Newark erupted, there were rumors of planned violence, and counter-plans were designed. Riot control training was held in a number of communities. In one instance, Negro residents became alarmed when tear gas used in a practice exercise drifted into the Negro section of town. Whether the rumors of planned violence were solid or merely a product of the preconceptions of city officials is difficult to say. But these rumors existing prior to the Newark riot were confirmed in the minds of officials in other New Jersey cities when Newark erupted, subsequently becoming the basis for "riot control" responses.

Another force in the proliferation of disturbances in the vicinity of the big city riots is the network of kinship and friendship relations between Negroes in major cities and outlying areas. For some it was literally true that "the brothers" in Newark or Detroit were "getting some of the action." Many people in Grand Rapids, for example, have relatives in Detroit. Reports that some of these relatives were killed in the Detroit riot increased tension and the potential for violence in that city.

The intensity of the flow of personal information from the Newark and Detroit ghettos to outlying areas at the peaks of the riots is indicated by the high number of out-of-town phone calls from the areas of greatest disturbance. These equalled top loads for a Mother's Day weekend, one of the periods in the year when telephone lines across the country become overloaded.

3.2.   The media and the propagation of disorder

The majority of people in outlying areas and across the country do not, of course, learn about a riot through immediate personal information. TV can bring people hundreds or thousands of miles distant directly to the scene of a major disorder. *The effect can often be that of the crowd acting at long distance.* This was a typical feature of the non-violent demonstrations of the civil rights movement at its peak. TV pictures of mob violence in the South would spark spontaneous sympathy demonstrations all across the North. And, in many instances, local civil rights movements would indigenously evolve from there.

In the case of the recent disorders, the "crowd at long distance" generated the impression that there was in fact a conspiracy some place for New Jersey to go up all at once. Actually, outbreaks of civil violence were quite spontaneous and unplanned—information from the media lowering the threshold for disorder all across an area.

One definite effect of the media seems to be the determination in time and place that latent tensions will surface into disorder. The potential for major riots in Plainfield and Detroit led by militant Negro youth had been there for some time. It was the Newark riot that dramatically changed "the mood" in Detroit and helped galvanize Negro youths to aggressive action in Plainfield. They might have "blown" anyway, if not at that time, then perhaps at a later date. On the other hand, these cities went through crisis periods before in which a major disorder could have exploded, but did not. Perhaps if Newark had not occurred or if information about it had been totally suppressed, other cities might have weathered the storm—at least temporarily. Progress through institutional channels might have kept one step ahead of the chaos breathing on its heels.

3.3. "Outside agitators" and the spread of disorder

A discussion of the mass media effects in propagating disorder naturally leads into an examination of the actual influence over events of such nationally known, "headline-making" Negro radical "leaders" as Stokeley Carmichael and H. Rapp Brown. Their role in spreading disorder is by no means simple.

A cursory overview of the points where the distribution of disorder around the country crosses the distribution of appearances of Stokeley Carmichael or H. Rapp Brown would indicate that most disturbances occurred without their presence to help things along. Of 23 disturbances in our sample, in only 6 were either Carmichael or Brown around the scene at the time. And in only three of these were their appearance and rhetoric immediately linked with the immediate precipitants of disorder. In the other cities they arrived at the scene after action was already underway. In Cincinnati, for example, Brown's major role was presenting a list of some 20 demands from a nationalist group to a representative from the Human Relations Commission on the fourth day of the disturbance.

Thus the number of specific situations with which the presence of a national firebrand could be associated with disorder were very few. *And considering the large number of communities where Brown and Carmichael appeared which did not have riots, their "riot batting-average," if indeed their purpose was to provoke a disorder on the spot, was extremely low.* Nevertheless, Carmichael and Brown do have influence over some events, which stems from the particular way they "lead" people. Their leadership is symbolic rather than organizational. They cannot "command" others to riot—at least at this time—by coming in from out of town and passing down "orders" from the top. But as a symbolic focus for hopes and fears they can generate the emotional predisposition which might encourage disorder.

In this respect, a good deal depends on the mood of their audience when they arrive on the scene. In Atlanta, Carmichael's speech to a crowd suggesting that they force the police to work until they "drop in their tracks" brought a tumultuous response. In Dayton the youth were "looking for an excuse to riot" before Brown arrived. However, in Jersey City, Negro youth quickly fled a meeting at which Brown was speaking when a rumor spread that the police were coming. Brown reportedly left town muttering "the people here aren't ready."

White authorities, as the Cambridge and New Jersey cases illustrate, have often been emotional "followers" of the "leadership" of Brown and Carmichael, in the sense that fears of the influence or presence of the latter generated precipitous actions.

It should be stressed too that the influence process between audience and agitators is a two-way street. In Detroit it was an unknown local man who took upon himself the role of the agitator. But in so doing, he was responding as well to the mood of the crowd and a situation which "commanded" agitation. And while Brown and Carmichael have a utilitarian interest in seeing violence directed against white society's control of Negroes until equality is produced, most of the evidence indicates that crowds use them as much as they use crowds.

Like headliners and public men everywhere, they become tools of community groups in developing motivation and commitment in followers, creating resources, and getting actions going. Thus far, they have been the focal point for a great deal of emotional energies on the part of both Negroes and whites. It is easier, for example, for whites to see riots as caused by H. Rapp Brown and Stokeley Carmichael, with whom they are familiar, than by the conditions of local Negro communities, with which they are not. Negroes, for their part—especially the young—experience great jubilation in hearing a speaker "tell it like it is" and frighten whites in the process.

Whatever their role at a specific local disorder, however, the major source of influence of leaders like Brown and Carmichael over events is that the media provides them with a national audience. Brown and Carmichael have argued that violence is necessary—violence is occurring around the country—both are reported side by side on TV and in the press. Such a recurrent linking of spokesmen for disorder and actual violence produces cause and effect associations difficult to dispel. Brown and Carmichael become seen as having the extraordinary and dangerous power to spell-bind Negroes into rioting.

While such a conclusion greatly exaggerates their power, we must not underestimate the real importance of their posturing as revolutionaries in the creation of an emotional climate around the country which is conducive to violence. But here too they are not alone. The news media, the political authorities, the reports of the occurrence of actual riots are also central elements in creating a "riot climate."

It would, perhaps, be more appropriate to consider the development of a major ghetto riot, and the appearance of symbolic leaders arguing that violence is legitimate, as but different reflections of the processes of polarization going on throughout the society. It is the role of "spokesmen for rebellion" created by the fact that ghetto rebellions are occurring which is significant, and not Brown or Carmichael specifically. Previously that role was singularly filled by Malcolm X; now new men are moving to fill the gap, rushing to keep up with events more than they are guiding them.

The real source of Brown and Carmichael's influence thus far has been the failure of the white community to make their role irrelevant. Lacking recognition from the white community in other respects, without a place in society for themselves, young Negroes learn quickly that whites are afraid of Brown and Carmichael. *When whites fear your power to cause riots they take you seriously: that is the lesson of events. In this respect whites "load the dice." The role of the militant demagogue and activist is rewarded again and again.*

3.4. Initial conditions in the spread of disorder

"Loading the dice" occurs within disturbances. At any phase, the events that have gone before shape the events that follow. This begins before actual violence erupts. If aspirations have been raised but community issues and conflicts continually find ghetto Negroes on the losing end, if a high degree of community polarization has developed, if racial solidarity and militancy within the ghetto has been growing, if there is a large pool of aggressive and ambitious youth available for confrontation, it may be as difficult to contain a disturbance in its first phase as to contain an atomic chain reaction once the critical point has been reached.

This was the case in Detroit where events happened extremely fast, telescoping in a matter of hours community involvement processes that took three days to develop in Watts. In other cities where a truly explosive potential did not exist, it was very likely that a disorder would have died out of its own accord through normal processes of communal restraint without formal authority controls (e.g., mothers scold sons for rampaging, the youth not being serious about rioting, etc.).

Initial features of a disorder, where it was located, the time of day, who was involved, the weather, etc., also were important in determining the direction an incipient disturbance was to move. Rain stopped some incipient riots. Whether the people who initially became riotous were marginal elements of the Negro community or whether they were stable residents was an important consideration. Disorders that pulled in ambitious, achievement-oriented people were more violent.[4] Disorders that began near housing developments, shopping centers, or other places where ordinary people in the community gathered always had an extremely dangerous potential.

GRIEVANCES IN THE RIOT PROCESS

Like the question concerning the role of Negro leadership in events, the question of the role of grievances, or the grievance process in disorders, is complicated. A popular model of riot causes sees a high level of unacted grievances, producing community tensions, which in turn produce riots. This theory is popularly held by people with programs or ideas they would like to sell that would ameliorate tensions by reducing grievances.

But there were cities in which the grievance level, in an absolute sense, was very high during the summer of 1967 which did not experience aggressive Negro riots. There were others in which the grievance level was much lower which did have aggressive ghetto rioting.

The importance of grievances in an event seems to be determined less by the *level of grievance* than the *kind* of grievance involved. People do not riot *for* better schools, but they will riot *against* the police and government as outside oppressors. Concerns for territory, domination, and hate of "double standards" (social injustice) run like a common thread through most of the largest disorders.

> *Item:*   In Plainfield, the "double-standard" issue of a policeman failing to make an arrest Negro youth thought he should have was the immediate precipitant.

> *Item:*   In Cincinnati, the issue of "double-standards" in the courts generated a sense of rage as a Negro was sentenced for murder and a white man for manslaughter within the same month. The first act of direct action was the stopping of delivery trucks by youths objecting to whites getting most of the jobs in Negro areas.

> *Item:*   In Detroit, the failure of a white newspaper to carry news of a Negro Vietnam veteran's murder at the hands of a white mob created bitterness as the local Negro newspaper reported the incident, including the miscarriage of the murdered man's pregnant wife, in full detail. A few weeks later and a short distance from where the murdered man lived a police raid in an after-hours club where a party for some Negro servicemen was in progress found an agitator haranguing an angry crowd that the police wouldn't do what they were doing in a white area.

> *Item:*   In Los Angeles in 1965, plaintive appeals of a Negro youth that he was not going to let the police take him to jail, aroused a tug-of-war between local community residents and white police which was the first incident in the Los Angeles riot.

> *Item:*   In Newark, a massive urban renewal project which would displace thousands of Negroes became the source of a bitter political struggle between the Italian political leadership and Negro militants, and was considered an important "cause" of the riot. Later, the belief of neighborhood residents that the police had not only beaten a taxi-cab driver but had

beaten him before they got him to the police station catalyzed a mood of rebellion and community solidarity.

Grievances of one Negro group against another can also be considered as having a role in precipitating and shaping several disorders.

Item: Leadership competition between the Negro militants opposed to the mayor of Newark and the group of conservative Negro leaders who supported him in part prevented an effective counter-riot response to the developing Newark crisis.

Item: In Cincinnati, the first outbreak of violence followed a speech by a Negro conservative at a protest rally which supported an anti-loitering law and angered Negro youths.

Item: In Dayton's June 1967 disturbance, an intense controversy between militants and conservatives over the funding of an anti-poverty program found a militant leader threatening a riot which shortly occurred.

Item: In Cambridge, white fear began to mount as two newly-forming Negro groups, one conservative, one militant, began to compete for the leadership role left vacant since Gloria Richardson had left town.

Item: In Grand Rapids, entrenched vice elements in the Negro community, who were being threatened by the rising influence of poverty workers in the community, attempted to use the disorder to buttress their declining domination.

Item: In Detroit, a developing indigenous community organization leadership of a very militant character was threatening established middle-class leaders who were well-incorporated into the Detroit political system. The latter were willing to go along with a policy of extreme repression the first day of the disturbance. Since the riot, they have been outraged at the willingness of city leadership to meet directly with lower-class representatives, and have fought increases in power for the militant groups.

Finally, the *grievance process*—the effectiveness of the response of authorities to Negro grievances whatever these are—can be a crucial source of grievance itself. The substantive grievances (police practices, neighborhood services, schools, housing, etc.) serve as indicators for measuring exactly how much and in what manner white authorities care about Negroes. They become tests of commitment.

In this respect, "liberal" or "moderate" cities are far more vulnerable to incidence of disorders than racially "conservative" ones. Examination of the 23 disorders in our sample indicates that those cities characterized by a general liberalizing, more "humanitarian" trend in elite attitudes—i.e., public recognition of the legitimacy of Negro complaints—are more likely to have the largest and most violent disorders. This is not surprising. Prolonged aggressive action by Negroes in racially conservative cities is less likely, because whites promise little, and what they do promise is immediate and extreme use of violent force to quell any disturbance at the outset, regardless of the merits of Negro complaints. In these cities, Negroes are continually reminded of "their place," and if some do not accept this definition they may be persuaded to refrain from violent protest anyhow.

The "tokenistic" pattern of race relations in more moderate or racially liberalizing cities encourages Negro demands for equalities, lifts the fear of extreme force (policemen increasingly attack the civil libertarian and community-relations emphasis of liberal government on the grounds that "law-enforcement is being handcuffed"), yet generally fails to work great immediate changes in the conditions of ghetto life. Individual members of the group have greater mobility and opportunity than ever before, but many still lag behind, their increased desires for advancement unfulfilled. The dilemma of liberalizing governments is that lifting the more overt forms of repression and promises of equalities encourages a more rapid rate of change in the psychology of Negroes than anything else. In such circumstances where old dominance relations are being undermined or are uncertain, grievances can be expected to escalate as Negroes test out white commitments in more and more areas. Growing "black consciousness" and sense of community increases the desire for action against obstacles that cramp ghetto Negroes in daily life, at the same time that white reaction to Negro "pushiness" invokes a sense of betrayal.

This seems extremely crucial for developing a mood of rebellion. Prior to the disorder there, Newark would have been considered a city undergoing racial liberalization. A Negro-Italian political coalition had put the mayor into office, and there had been many promises to the Negro community. Compared with other Northern cities, the level of political access of Negroes in Newark might have been considered fairly high. But a split had developed in the coalition with the Italian political leadership, and Negro community elites engaged in bitter, emotionally charged disputes over police practices, a plan to tear down Negro-occupied areas to construct a medical complex, appointments to the board of education, and other issues. The Negroes saw broken promises, and an attempt by the Italians to establish their political hegemony at Negro expense. By the second evening of disorder in Newark, people were far beyond the stage where they would be willing to accept a token concession at the price of mitigating their righteous vengeance which had been so long in developing. Once that mood was there, a sudden concession itself triggered disorder as Negroes so to speak threw the concession of a Negro police captain back into the faces of the authorities with the attitude "keep it, you can't buy us that cheaply *now*."

3.5. The competitive process in developing disorders

Negotiations at such points fail because many people want combat more than peace. During a disorder itself, a competitive sense among Negro youths may become a powerful impetus to keeping the violence going. In Newark, some youths did not want to stop the riot because the score in deaths stood "25–2" with the police and guardsmen leading.

THE GAME OF RIOT: EMASCULATING THE POLICE

Within various groups on the street, people were quite conscious of the heroism and daring exhibited by young men. For Negro youth, challenging the police with taunts and dares involved a dangerous and dramatic competition. Their goal was to disrupt police order, to make the police "lose their cool," to produce situations in which police worked until they "dropped in their tracks." Much of the behavior of the youth during a riot can be accounted for by this motivation: *they are interested not in killing policemen, but in humiliating them.* As Negroes have been rendered powerless for so long, as the police have continually disrupted the activities of the ghetto, the disorder becomes the grand opportunity to turn the tables.

In this respect, the riots also serve the functions of "ritual ceremonies" in which manhood is demonstrated. Many acts of confrontation (e.g., laying bare the chest and taunting police to shoot), which have a great intensity and seriousness about them are also dramatic posturing—open and public proof to both oneself and the police that things have changed. The test has dangers, but afterwards one can never go back to what he was before.

This form of street confrontation with the police, it should be noted, is not new. If we include the Southern non-violent movement, it has been going on for 6 years. In the South during 1962–1965 militant civil rights activists, many of whom were of Northern background, became experts in the technique of disorganizing Southern police through non-violent demonstrations.

Negro youth in the North are now the aggressors. Instead of "non-violent" demonstrations, breaking white property, setting fires, and racial taunting have become major aspects of the techniques of breaking up the police.

Much Negro youth "crime" has always had this quality of testing by "street games" with authorities. Confronting police and courts in efforts to construct a self-definition in which one does have some kind of place in society—if only a criminal one—does have a functional basis. Those who have served time return to their old associations with a new status as someone who is really tough and knows the ropes.

What is distinctive now is that this same process feeds into community confrontation. Traditional street testing behavior by Negro youth is channeling into the disruption of city institutions. The massiveness of the disruption in a riot stems from the fact that a great number of youth are getting their badges of manhood all at once. Previously this occurred through the orderly and recurrent process of one-by-one confrontation which white institutions easily handled in the past.

CROSS-CITY COMPETITION

Evidence in our data indicate that cross-city competition among youth: "who holds the record, now?" becomes a salient force once control by police is lost. Cities that have already had major upheavals acquire symbolic value and become standards for comparison in other disturb-ances. For some participants there is a quite explicit desire to outdo New York, or Watts, etc. A Negro girl in Newark asked a reporter, "Was the Harlem riot worse than this?" and assured that it was not, she cried, "That's good, that's great!"

Distinctive features of several major disturbances during the sum-mer of 1967 can in part be attributed to the excitement generated among young Negroes that they were either doing something in a riot that had not been done before, or that they were doing it better than ever. Negro youths in Newark were quite proud that they were the "first" to ever lay siege to a police station. As the governor passed by in a National Guard tank, there were heated street side discussions on "How do you get into a tank with a Molotov cocktail?"

There is no reason to preclude the possibility of disruptive acts more consequential than any that have yet occurred. The "first" tank to be fire bombed, the "first" power station to be blown up, are but logical extension of the present pattern of disorder. "We're number one!" after all is an old American tradition.

NOTES

ACKNOWLEDGEMENT: This paper is based primarily on data published in *The Report of The National Advisory Commission on Civil Disorders* (New York: Bantam Books, 1968). The ideas for this particular analysis were formulated while I worked as a member of the social science research group of the commission. The group was directed by Dr. Robert Shellow and included David Boesel and myself as full-time analysts; Dr. Elliot Liebow, Dr. Gary Marx, and Dr. Derek Roemer as part-time analysts; and Drs. Neil Smelser, Nathan Kaplan, Ralph Turner, Kurt Lang, and David Sears as consultants. Nothing included here should be construed as the official view of either the social science group or the entire commission.

I should, however, like to express my debt to the entire staff of the commission, particularly the field teams who collected the data. Further, I should particularly like to thank my friend and partner David Boesel, who in certain respects must share equal responsibility for the ideas in this paper, for his encouragement and criticism. I also owe an idea to Professor Ralph Turner, and another to Betsy Jameson of Antioch College. Professor James S. Coleman of Johns Hopkins University was kind enough to express ambivalence toward an earlier version of this paper. While I would argue that objective evidence compels a harsher attitude toward civil and police authority stupidities in describing events than he would, I want to thank him for encouraging me to moderate the tone of the analysis.

1. This brief analytical summary is not designed to capture the richness and con-crete details of the events. The reader is encouraged to refer to the excellent nar-rative or the Detroit, Newark, and other disorders provided in *The Report of the National Advisory Commission on Civil Disorders*, pp. 35–108.

2. A "blind pig" is a slang term for private social clubs that serve as after-hours drinking and gambling spots.

3. The use of the term "political" here is not meant to imply either (1) conspiracy, (2) prior organization to achieve specific political objectives through the use of violence (e.g., intimidating election opponents or forcing a city administration to grant a specific concession), or (3) a precipitant which was markedly "political." Nor is calling some disturbances "political riots" meant to imply that the general

upheavals in Newark and Detroit lacked a powerful political component. A high level of political grievance on the part of Negroes, and the lack of significant responses by civil authorities contributed greatly to events in Newark and Detroit. But it would not do justice to the many non-political aspects of generalized chaos in those cities to refer to their disorders as simply political riots. However, in cities like Plainfield and Cincinnati, the actions of Negro participants became directly focused at civil authorities. In turn, the responses of civil authorities to demands —particularly the demand for recognition—dramatically affected the level of aggressive action by Negro rioters.

4. As in other areas of community life, the quality of a riot is affected by the level of energy and competency people bring with them. Those who participate in riots (see pp. 174–78 in the *Report of the National Advisory Commission on Civil Disorders*), as compared with those who do not, tend to be younger, better educated, more politically aware, more achievement oriented, more acculturated to the values of an industrialized urban society, and more dissatisfied with their place within it. Across cities, there is some evidence that the quality and character of Negro mass actions (political focus, degree of organization, volatility) is affected by differences in the level of unincorporated youthful talent.

part V

SEPARATISM

The shift from the nonviolent protest of the civil rights movement through "black power" to ghetto uprisings can be seen as a direct line of evolution over time. However, not all blacks have been involved in this mainstream of protest and attempts at change. Many have been looking on from the sidelines. Others have been involved, but only in tangential developments. One of the major tangents shooting off from the main line has attracted considerable support. This is the move for black separatism, which has taken both religious and secular forms.

There are at least two major varieties of separatist movements. I shall call these tactical separatism and ultimate separatism. Tactical separatism refers to the drive for separation in order to achieve control over one's destiny. The drive for black control of the ghetto, community control of schools, and black industry are but three examples of this. I treat this type of separatism under the concept of "black power," as each of these tactics represents an attempt at greater black self-determination, an attempt by the ghetto dwellers to drive out the colonialists and achieve independence.

Ultimate separatism refers to the separatist groups who are striving for separatism as an end in itself rather than separatism as a means of achieving power. Here the focus is primarily upon identity. It is believed to be intrinsically more desirable for blacks to restrict their interaction to blacks regardless of power relationships.

At a higher level of abstraction, it may be argued, ultimate separatism and tactical separatism tend to merge. Nevertheless, because of their differences at the level of conscious motivations and expressed objectives, I shall treat them as distinct. Indeed, the identity changes brought about by ultimate separatism may be a necessary precondition for a concern with, and striving for, "black power." Helen Icken Safa expresses it this way:

> . . . separatism and assimilation need not be antagonistic trends; they are stages in a process through which most groups must pass to achieve a place for themselves in a pluralistic society. . . . The ultimate goal is thus likely to

be assimilation—depending on the response of the white community. But black separatism may be a necessary prelude for assimilation and integration to take place on an egalitarian basis.[1]

James H. Laue describes an organization which espouses ultimate separatism. The Nation of Islam includes within its tenets the beliefs that black men are divine and white men are devils created by an evil scientist. Who could wish to integrate with devils now or ever? Separatism becomes a logical and moral necessity. The Nation of Islam was one of the first post-World War II movements to be avowedly separatist. As such, it attracted a lot of attention from blacks and whites, and many lower-class blacks joined it. Others, from both the lower and middle classes, sympathized with it but remained outside the fold. We do not know how large it became, but we do know that it was large enough to be considered a threat by the white establishment. This establishment reacted by attempting to paint the Nation of Islam as a racist hate group and by employing police harassment. Some Muslims defended themselves against this harassment, with violent clashes resulting. Eventually the movement split and other separatist organizations emerged.

John R. Howard provides us with some clues as to why splits occurred within the Muslims and why other separatist organizations are able to appeal to blacks who are not willing to join the Nation of Islam. The selection describes the socialization of a Muslim. The life of a Muslim is one of sacrifice. It entails giving up many creature comforts—some of which have been traditionally part of a ghetto life style. Muslim life demands a high level of morality. One must forgo pork, alcohol, tobacco, and extramarital sex. These are only a few of the more superficial changes. Patterns of dress and cooking must be changed. For those willing to pay the price to become a Muslim, there are considerable rewards. These rewards come from a sense of dignity and pride, from a sense of morality, and from a sense of living a proper life. There are also material rewards and rewards deriving from a sense of community. However, many blacks cannot or will not pay the high price of membership. Others cannot accept the religious teachings, so that, although they are drawn to ideas of nationalism and separatism, they cannot join the Nation of Islam. These persons, along with the defectors, make up much of the membership of other black nationalist and separatist organizations.

NOTES

1. Helen Icken Safa, "The Case for Negro Separatism: The Crisis of Identity in the Negro Community," *Urban Affairs Quarterly* 4 (September 1968): 59–60.

A CONTEMPORARY REVITALIZATION MOVEMENT IN AMERICAN RACE RELATIONS: THE "BLACK MUSLIMS"

James H. Laue

Rarely do empirical cases seem so made-to-order for a particular sociological theory as does the Black Muslim movement for Anthony Wallace's formulation of the "revitalization movement." [1]

The "Lost-Found Nation of Islam in North America" is a mushrooming sect of Negro Americans led by some of the country's angriest young men. A politico-religious organization preaching black nationalism and claiming "hundreds of thousands" of members throughout the United States, the Muslim movement is productively viewed in Wallace's revitalization terminology as "a deliberate, organized, conscious effort by members of a society to construct a more satisfying culture." There is no question that Negro Americans have been trying to do this since slave times; the black Muslims stand out as a contemporary and highly organized example of this effort.

Although black nationalist groups have been a force in United States racial patterns for most of the twentieth century—particularly in the northern ghettos—interest in the Muslims is only now beginning to grow among American social critics, popular pulp writers, and social scientists. The first scholarly work on the movement was C. Eric Lincoln's *The Black Muslims in America,* published in 1961.[2] Then in 1962, E. U. Essien-Udom's *Black Nationalism: A Search for an Identity in America* appeared.[3]

While Lincoln and Essien-Udom give considerable attention to the historical and psychological dimensions of the movement, the specifically sociological implications are yet to be explored. In this paper, then, Wallace's theory is juxtaposed with what we know about the Muslims in hopes of clarifying the theory and operationalizing it as a guide for sociological research on the Movement.

A NOTE ON METHOD: I AM A "GRAY"

Since I am a "gray" (or "grayboy"—the hip Negro's terminology for the white man, signifying status as a mutation from the pure black), I cannot get into Muslim temple meetings. It is hardly necessary to say that this is a decided research disadvantage! Research on the movement in the past three years has taken me into a number of temple-type situations, however; one of the chief sources of information presented in this paper has been participation in a number of informal discussion groups with several young Muslim members.

From *Social Forces* 42 (March 1964): 315–24; reprinted by permission of the author and publisher.

Combined with this participant observation have been documentary research on Muslim publications,[4] analysis of various semi-popular articles and television programs, and attendance at public meetings regarding the movement. On two occasions I have seen the Muslims' musical tragi-comedy, *Orgena* ("A Negro" spelled backwards), finding in the two performances differences which are presented later in this analysis. The most productive forms of research, finally, have been interviews and dialogue with leaders and students of the movement,[5] among them Minister Malcolm X, heir apparent to the top position in the movement.

THE THEORY OF REVITALIZATION MOVEMENTS: ". . . A MORE SATISFYING CULTURE"

Wallace's definition of a revitalization movement as a "deliberate, organized, conscious effort by members of a society to construct a more satisfying culture" implies an organismic analogy and the corollary principles of stress and homeostasis. Society is seen as an organic system which is constantly exposed to stress induced in its component subsystems. The total system maintains itself by providing mechanisms sufficient to handle this stress.

Wallace finds each member equipped with what he calls a "mazeway"—a mental image of self, society, nature, and culture through which values operate in maintaining social order. "Whenever an individual who is under . . . chronic stress receives repeated information which indicates that his mazeway does not lead to action which reduces the level of stress, he must choose between maintaining his present mazeway and tolerating the stress, or changing the mazeway in an attempt to reduce the stress. . . . It may also be necessary to make changes in the 'real' system in order to bring mazeway and 'reality' into congruence. The effort to work a change in mazeway and 'real' system together so as to permit more effective stress reduction is the effort at revitalization; and the collaboration of a number of persons in such an effort is called a revitalization movement."

Wallace sees six types of movements reported in the literature which can be classified under the revitalization rubric:

Nativistic—emphasis on elimination of alien persons, customs, and values.
Revivalistic—emphasis on re-institutionalization of customs and values thought to have been in the mazeway of previous generations.
Cargo Cults—importation of alien values, customs, and material into the mazeway via a ship's cargo.
Vitalistic—importation of foreign elements, but ships and cargo are not the necessary mechanisms.
Millenarian—an apocalyptic world transformation engineered by the supernatural.
Messianic—participation of a divine saviour in human flesh in the mazeway transformation.

The most prominent historical cases to which Wallace points are the origins of Christianity and Islam, and the Ghost Dance and the Peyote cult of American Indian tribes.

Revitalization movements move through five ideal-typical stages in what Wallace calls the "processual structure":

I. Steady State—Chronic stress within the system varies within tolerable limits as culturally recognized techniques for satisfying needs operate efficiently.

II. Period of Increased Individual Stress—"Individual members of a population . . . experience increasingly severe stress as a result of the decreasing efficiency of certain stress-reduction techniques." The population may, according to Wallace, be " 'primitive' or 'civilized,' either a whole society or a class, caste, religious, occupational, accultural, or other definable social group." Some of the elements responsible for lowering efficiency of stress-reduction mechanisms may be changes in the physical environment, military defeat, socio-economic stress, political subordination, acculturational pressures, and epidemics.

III. Period of Cultural Distortion—Individual maladjustments combine to produce internal cultural distortion. "The elements are not harmoniously related but are mutually inconsistent and interfering." Stress reproduces itself and anxiety rises as the incongruities of mazeway are perceived. Life is no longer meaningful.

IV. Period of Revitalization—Total cultures or subsystems on the way to disaster are frequently rescued—or, at least delayed—by the revitalization movement. The theory specifies six functional problems at this point: mazeway reformulation, communication, organization, adaptation, cultural transformation, and routinization.

V. New Steady State—A new *Gestalt* is in operation, both for the members of the revitalized group and the host and/or neighboring cultures. Wallace's formulation here clearly implies that the movement has been institutionalized.

THE MUSLIM MOVEMENT TODAY: "THOSE WHO KNOW AREN'T SAYING"

The Muslim movement, according to the most accurate guesses, encompasses less than 100,000 members (some estimates run as low as 5,000) organized in some 80 "Temples of Islam" throughout the country. Muslim leaders do not release exact membership figures—and their refusal to do so adds to the aura of uncertainty about Muslim strength which gives the movement so much leverage in the American racial situation today. "Only Allah knows," smiles Malcolm X, who, like most Muslims, has rejected his "Christian name" and substituted the symbol of an unknown quantity. "Those who know aren't saying, and those who say don't know!"

But the sociological significance of the movement has less to do with numbers than with mood—the militant mood and new sense of urgent activism growing in Negro Americans at all class levels in the last decade. For while the number of fully participating members is uncertain, there is no uncertainty about the way hundreds of thousands of Negroes respond to the Muslims' stark and straightforward articulation of "the problem" and its causes—white evil and intransigence. There is no question that Negroes have been ready to hear this for a long time.

Leadership

There is no doubt that Malcolm X is the Muslims' driving organizational force. But the movement is formally centered around the Messenger, the Prophet of Allah—the Honorable Elijah Muhammad. The Messenger, a Georgia-born, light-skinned man in his middle sixties, is the ideal-typical shaman; he is believed to have had a mystical association with God himself, and "believes in and follows Allah 100 percent." [6]

Membership

Membership is predominantly male and lower class. Selected men belong to the Fruit of Islam, a "secret army" [7] which acts as a security force at temple meetings and speeches by the leaders. The FOI is rigorously trained in military tactics and strategy and, while it will not initiate aggression, it responds with force to any encroachments on its honor. One FOI member was killed and many injured in a recent struggle with police who attempted to break up a temple service in Los Angeles. The FOI is thus symbolic of the Muslim prescription to "act like a MAN!"—and by such an orientation the leaders are working to restore the Negro male emasculated by American discrimination to the head of a partriarchal family structure.

Historical development

The Muslims are one of a long line of black nationalist groups which have made the scene (in the words of the Brothers) in America in the last half-century. A number of these groups work the streets of Harlem and other northern ghettos today; the Muslims are the largest. The most important forerunners of today's Muslim movement were the Moorish Science Temple movement of Noble Drew Ali and the Universal Negro Improvement Association of Marcus Garvey—a "Back to Africa" group.[8] Both hit their peak in the World War I era, and have small followings today.

Today's Muslims stem most directly from the work of Wallace D. Fard, who appeared in Detroit in 1930 as the incarnation of Allah.[9] Elijah Poole, who had recently moved to Detroit, ". . . came under the spell of Fard, who, he recalls gratefully, took him 'out of the gutter . . . and in three-and-a-half years taught [him] the knowledge of Islam.'" [10] Re-named "Elijah Muhammad" by Fard, the enthusiastic migrant established a mosque in Chicago in 1932, where he later sheltered Fard from the police. When Fard disappeared in 1934 (there were rumors that Muhammad had induced Fard to offer himself as a human sacrifice [11]), Muhammad was the logical successor. Under his guidance, the movement grew slowly and maintained a position among the many sects competing for the marginal, disgruntled Negro. Malcolm X was converted while in prison in 1947 (many Muslim members are former convicts, addicts, and social derelicts), and his organizational ability and quick wit have been central to the movement's phenomenal growth in the last few years.

Values: the religious-historical identity

The Muslims claim to be a branch of orthodox Islam, accepting most of the Koran and ". . . only the parts of the Bible which are divine." [12] The Genesis story of the creation is true—for the white man only—and the Muslims have the date placed somewhere around 6,000 years ago. But the black man was created 66 trillion years ago, and the white man is only here as the result of an albino mutation produced by an evil black scientist who succeeded in breeding out the pure black strain.

Muhammad preaches black nationalism (which is often interpreted as black supremacy) and black union against the white world. "The white man has robbed you of your name, your language, your culture, and your religion," Muslims are told. Through this treacherous stripping of the "so-called American Negro" of his heritage, the white man has succeeded in subjugating the black man—whose *real* language is Arabic, whose *real* religion is Islam and whose *original* homeland is the Nile valley in Northern Africa. "The white man was still living in caves in Europe and eating meat raw while our forefathers lived in luxury in flourishing civilizations on the banks of the Nile," continues the Messenger.

Values: the secular program

The Muslims say they want several states of their own to set up a separate black nation. If the United States does not repent for its treatment of this nation-within-a-nation, Allah will strike down the oppressor. The Armageddon date was originally set for 1914, but Allah granted a 70-year extension.[13]

I am convinced from a number of conversations with Muslim leaders, however, that what they *really* want is access to the vices and virtues enjoyed by white Americans. The Muslims' Puritanical ethical prescriptions place them in the mainstream of the dominant American middle class value system. Members are enjoined to run their businesses like the white man, protect their women, abstain from alcohol and tobacco, and give generously to the "church" (many Muslims donate one-third of their livelihood to the temple). And nowhere is the neat, well-mannered, humble model of an American family attending church better exemplified than in the Muslim family going to three or four temple meetings per week. Significantly, the demanding discipline of the Muslims has made them more successful than any other civic, religious, or governmental agencies in social rehabilitation of Negro convicts, prostitutes, addicts, alcoholics, disorganized families, and slum homes. But also significantly, the wave of press attention to the movement has chosen to play down these achievements.

Muslim women are placed on a pedestal (and are the subject of a song popular in the movement, "Black Gold") while the white man is blamed for the long history of miscegenation under slavery and segregation. Many women in the movement enroll in the Muslims Girls Training and General Civilization Class, where they are ". . . taught how to sew, cook, keep house, rear their children, care for their husbands, and how to behave at home and abroad." [14]

Ritual behavior

Temple meetings are quite subdued compared to many lower-class Negro religious gatherings. Members are searched before entering the mosque, and are not admitted if they have alcohol on their breath. Some altar settings present the star and crest of Islam opposite a silhouetted lynching scene backed by the American flag and the cross, with a sign asking, "Which Will You Choose?" Sermons are customarily long. In addition to temple attendance, most orthodox followers bathe and pray five times a day.

Aesthetic expression

Minister Louis X of Boston, a former calypso singer, is the artist of the movement; *Orgena* is his product. The show has played in most of the large Eastern cities, including return engagements in New York and Boston. It depicts the glorious ancient culture of the black man, his enslavement by white colonializers and slavetraders, and the trial of the white man—who finally confesses that he is the devil, and is dragged off stage under the death sentence. The play is punctuated by several of Minister Louis' songs, including "A White Man's Heaven is a Black Man's Hell," which presents Muslim theology attractively backed by a calypso beat. A recording of "White Man's Heaven" is now in national circulation by the movement, and acts as a potent recruiting force.

THE MUSLIMS AS A REVITALIZATION MOVEMENT: THE SHAPING OF A SUBSTITUTE IDENTITY

The Muslim movement is one of several alternative avenues of expression for the angry, sensitive, disillusioned Negro in America today. He is thoroughly Americanized at the value level, but frustrated at the personality level because of lack of institutionalized channels of cultural achievement. While the closed-system nature of the dominant white culture in the nineteenth century dictated clowning, self-hate, and neuroticism as adjustive techniques, the more aggressive channels of protest safely available today include enhanced striving, in-group aggression, prejudice against out-groups, and militancy.[15] The particular cluster of mechanisms demonstrated in the Muslim movement involves all of these, plus denial of membership—substitution of identity as a "Muslim" for identity as a "Negro."

The psychological stances represented by these reactions are all part of the Black Muslims' unique mazeway. They have been translated into a coherent movement, which exhibits elements of five of the six types of revitalization movements Wallace suggests:

The *nativistic* phase of the movement emphasizes elimination of the white slave-master and his evil system, to be replaced by an all-black nation-within-a-nation—in which contact with the white's alien customs and values is neither desirable nor possible.

Consequently, in *revivalistic* fashion the Muslims hope to institute the patterns of ancient Islamic society as they idealize it—an example of the Golden Age approach of every people who have ever suffered cultural disorganization.

From our perspective on the "outside," we can also call the Muslim movement a *vitalistic* effort, stressing importation of foreign elements. But it is clear that the Muslims do not accept this "importation" terminology, for the germ of the core-values they espouse is inherent in every black man, they say; he is phylogenetically a Muslim, and automatically superior to his white counterpart.

The *millenarian* emphasis of the movement is very strong. Minister Malcolm and the Messenger state time and again that Allah will engineer a Babylon-type demise of the white man if he does not repent in time.

And, while Fard was the official incarnation and Muhammad only a shamanistic prophet, Muslim leaders know that many members do not make the distinction, and indeed view the Messenger as a *messianic* figure actually participating in the divine.

Viewing sociological theory as an organizing, economizing, and operationalizing endeavor, we may now specify the points of congruence and variation between Wallace's outline of the "processual structure" and the historical development of the movement:

I. Steady state

While the terminology of "steady state" and "new steady state" which Wallace uses may be a necessary theoretical distinction, it implies too much of a revolutionary character for the revitalization movement, and suggests an almost qualitative split between steady state$_1$, the flux phase, and steady state$_2$. For societies and their subgroups are *never* in a state which can be differentiated as "steady" when compared to another given state. Groups and ideologies dance in and out of power and influence, forming a dynamic matrix whose continuity is violated if we arbitrarily slice out chunks surrounding certain "movements." Social changes in the "movement" form should not be conceptualized as mutations of a former order (which the *"new* steady state" terminology implies), but rather as logical maturations with discernible etiological bases. We would do better to label these periods simply "stage one" and "stage two"—with the intervening processes seen as mediating developments leading to the new stage of systemic equilibrium.

Viewed in this light, it is appropriate to specify some of the dynamic social patterns which bred and nurtured the Muslims. Most obvious is Negroes' irrepressible dissatisfaction with their disproportionate share of the benefits from the expanding American economy—benefits which are paraded before all citizens every day via the mass media. Equally important is the failure of the old philosophical and religious systems to provide meaningful rationalizations for Negroes' non-attainment of deeply internalized democratic goals. The tight white opportunity structure becomes intolerable when a minority member is able to objectify his position and see what he is being denied. And finally—but by no means exhaustively—the emergence of African nations is *the* most specific model for American Muslim militancy today. Muslim leaders press for an identification with the African spirit of black revolt but carefully avoid any implication of actually returning to African ways, thus avoiding Garvey's mistake by recognizing that Negro Americans are too thoroughly middle class in their values for any "Back to Africa" approach to succeed.

II. Period of increased individual stress

I am saying, then, that the "breakdown of stress-reducing mechanisms" for Negro Americans has been occurring since the first slave arrived, and that the breakdown has led to protests of varying intensity throughout the years.[16] In the last few years American society has not been able to provide stress-reducers at a rate rapid enough to satisfy its increasingly heterogeneous population structure. The system has not been able to institutionalize deviant channels of adjustment as they have appeared.

Negro Americans have experienced in varying degree the status-deprivation of which we talked in the last section. But, as Wallace rightly points out, the initial consideration of a substitute mode of adjustment often *increases* stress because of lack of feedback about the effectiveness of this alternate stance. The Muslims have avoided this pitfall by some highly successful advertising of the restructured identity they offer. They have worked in prisons and on the streets of Harlem and other large cities, first convincing potential converts of their totally deprived state as "so-called American Negroes," then presenting a totally new identity, ready-made and ready to put on. It is an active, life-consuming identity, not a "pay-your-membership-fee-without-necessary-commitment-to-action" stance, which for years has been the folk-level format of the now threatened and allegedly non-militant NAACP.

III. Period of cultural distortion

Regressive individual responses to deprivation long have been at a level which produces distortion in the Negro subculture. Crime, alcoholism, addiction, prostitution, and family disorganization have made their mark on the Negro American community. Mr. Muhammad's missionaries have capitalized on this cultural distortion, winning many of their converts from the lowest planes of society. "Look at these acts you committed as a Christian, as a so-called Negro," preach the ministers. "Then look at *our* people, who have rejected their slave-master and their slave religion, and have thrown off the vices taught by the blue-eyed devils."

IV. Period of revitalization

The first important functional task in revitalization is *mazeway re-formulation.* Wallace proposes that this reformulation generally depends on a restructuring of elements and subsystems already current in the system—elements which are articulated, combined, and operationalized by the prophet as guides to action. While the Muslims claim to preach a doctrine entirely alien to America, their position becomes a thinly-veiled acceptance and rephrasing of American ideals, as suggested above.

The revitalization period usually originates in ". . . one or several hallucinatory visions by a single individual. A supernatural being appears to the prophet-to-be, explains his own and his society's troubles as being entirely or partly as a result of the violation of certain rules, and promises individual and social revitalization if the injunctions are followed and the rituals exercised." Muhammad *did* receive instructions from a supernatural being (Fard), but as far as we can determine, it was in-the-flesh and not hallucinatory communication.

After "the dream," the prophet moves to *communicate* his insights, fulfilling the second functional requirement of the revitalization process. The two doctrinal motifs hypothesized for this stage are manifested by the Muslims: ". . . that the convert will come under the care and protection of certain supernatural beings" (Allah); and that "both he and his society will benefit materially from an identification with some definable new cultural system" (Islam, of the Black Muslim variety). Disciples readily assume the responsibility for communicating the word; in the Muslim case, followers like Malcolm X and Louis X have become recruitment agents with charisma at least equal to that of the Messenger—although neither of them would (or could) admit it, of course.

Wallace's discussion of the *organizational* phase of the revitalization stage hinges on what Weber calls the problem of succession: the prophet must transfer his charismatic qualities to other individuals and the organization to effect legitimation of his cause. Muhammad is certainly regarded as an unquestionable authority, sanctioned by the supernatural. His movement has already moved out of the cult stage, since the leadership structure is sufficiently developed to ensure its maintenance when Muhammad dies, even though a good deal of conflict may result as the hierarchy adjusts. The disciplinary action of the Fruit of Islam, the unifying force of *Orgena* wherever it is produced, and the organizational ability of Minister Malcolm combine to give the Muslim movement a solid bureaucratic structure that makes Negro rights organizations and lower class religious groups envious.

Perhaps the most important phase of the revitalization process is *adaptation,* and it seems to be the major area of the theory upon which elaboration is necessary. Wallace suggests three aspects of this process: doctrinal modification, political and diplomatic maneuvers, and force.

Muslim doctrine has undergone drastic modification in the last few years as the membership has broadened, but, contrary to the theory, most of the alterations have been engineered by Malcolm X rather than the prophet.[17]

Some of the major doctrinal modifications which may be seen in the Muslims' sect-to-church drive are:

1. The black supremacy doctrine is being softened in an effort to attract Negro intellectuals. A former *Orgena* focus on problems of the Negro in America, for instance, is now tempered with strong emphasis on colonialism in Asia and Africa. In fact, it now is "colonialism" rather than "the white man" which is sentenced to death in *Orgena*.

2. Relationships with other Negro rights groups are improving. Malcolm X has called former NAACP legal head and now Federal judge Thurgood Marshall a "twentieth century Uncle Tom" loudly and often, but the Muslim leader has accepted a number of speaking engagements at local NAACP chapters in the last two years. Too, former vehemence against the sit-ins and Martin Luther King, Jr., was absent in a recent television debate which found Minister Malcolm consciously trying to tone down his criticism for a national audience.[18] And following the Los Angeles police slaying of a member in 1962, the Muslims readily cooperated in a protest rally with the NAACP, the Congress of Racial Equality, and local Negro ministers—indicating a new level of synthesis not possible only a few years earlier when the Muslims had reached neither their current level of national prominence nor their desire for a broader-based "church" status.

3. Muslims are re-emphasizing the religious character of the movement in response to charges that the Islamic orientation is merely a gimmick and cloak for political motives. Minister Malcolm's Harvard Law School Forum speech in 1961 focused around the Muslims as a *religious* movement—a radical change from an address at Boston University a year earlier. At the same time, the Muslims are not condemning Christianity with their former gusto—at least publicly—as exemplified in open debates and the most recent performances of *Orgena*.[19]

In discussing force as an adaptive technique, Wallace suggests that as organized hostility develops, emphasis in the movement frequently shifts from cultivation of the ideal to combat against the unbeliever. I find this ingroup ideal vs. outgroup combat syndrome more cyclical than lineal, however. For a time, the main task of the Fruit of Islam was ". . . guarding the Black Nation against 'trouble with unbelievers, especially with the police.' " [20] In 1960 and 1961, with the environment perceived as less hostile, the emphasis had moved back to ingroup solidarity and uplift, including policing errant members and performing as a drill team at performances of *Orgena*. But more recently, in response to increased extra-systemic challenge from prison wardens and police as the movement seeks to expand, the FOI has redirected its efforts and training toward outside forces.[21]

The Muslim movement today is clearly in the "adaptive" phase of revitalization, and promises to remain there for several years. The proposed phase of *cultural transformation*—acceptance of the movement as a legitimate mode of social adjustment by a controlling portion of the host population—may come rapidly if the Muslims continue to adapt their doctrines in true third party style.

Routinization—the tragedy that befalls all revolutions—occurs on both integrative (internal) and adaptive (external) planes, although the theory stresses only the integrative aspects of this process. For Wallace, routinization takes place only after the desired transformation has occurred. Perhaps the gravest immediate challenge to rapid rationalization will occur when the ailing Muhammad dies, for a power struggle between Malcolm X and others is certain unless the Messenger makes a definite pronouncement regarding his legitimate successor.[22]

V. New steady state

After my earlier strong objections to the nondynamic implications of "steady state terminology" and analysis of the Muslims as professional discontents, we may conclude that the Nation of Islam cannot logically reach anything resembling a "new steady state"; it would go out of existence first.

There is one more aspect of the theory which deserves clarification —Wallace's qualification that the revitalization terminology is best applicable to a movement which is completely successful. His position here indicates that his data and interpretations derive necessarily from "dead" movements—a characteristic of postdicting which sociology has found hard to overcome. This approach would thus limit analysis considerably, since many powerful and socially disruptive movements do not reach even the adaptive phase. The Muslim movement, on the other hand, is one of a number of researchable in-process movements that offer a dynamic context in which theory can be checked as it is built.

The success or failure of a revitalization movement depends largely on the relative "realism" of the doctrines, according to Wallace. I think that this formulation must be modified to include the *degree to which the leaders make known their doctrinal positions to power elements of the host population.* Many movements fail, says Wallace, because wildly unrealistic predictions which do not come true result in mazeway disintegration of the members. The Muslims have learned this lesson well: they purposely keep predictions and interpretations vague to save themselves embarrassing re-fencing later. More and more in the last years, Malcolm X has been hedging on questions concerning relations with other groups, black supremacy, the battle of Armageddon, and Muslim action plans for the future. He is ever-ready with "Only Allah knows," to counter a prying or threatening question regarding the nature and destiny of the movement.[23]

PROSPECTS FOR FUTURE RESEARCH: "PRETTY SOON, MAN"

The Muslim movement is becoming increasingly aware of its public face —and particularly its image with intellectuals. In the next few years, then, the movement should be more and more amenable to social scientific research. The chief requirement for the social scientist who wishes to successfully execute such research, of course, is the proper skin color! Even these barriers may be loosening, however, for recently when I half-jokingly asked Malcolm X, "When are you going to let me in to a temple meeting?" he half-seriously replied, "Pretty soon, man. Maybe pretty soon."

Now that the facts concerning the etiology of the movement are surfacing, a major longitudinal research study charting the sect's drive toward institutionalization is called for. Here, for instance, the Weberian may find a twentieth-century case of an underdeveloped nation-within-a-nation (the Negro subculture in American society) already exhibiting the religiously sanctioned asceticism to which Weber attached such great importance as motivator and justifier of this-worldly economic activity.

Intensive comparative studies are also needed. As one hypothetical framework for this kind of research, we can view the Muslim movement as analogous in origin and development to the Peyote cult. Antecedents of both Peyotists and the Muslims were aggressive and uncompromising in their orientation to the host population.[24] Indian Ghost Dances at the turn of the century were harsh and unrelenting ritual rejections of the encroaching white culture; earlier black nationalist groups like the Garvey and Moorish Science movements were soon doomed to obscurity by their failure to adapt even marginally to the host population. Just as the emergence of the Peyote cult offered a more readily syncretic alternative for frustrated and hostile Indian Americans, so the Lost-Found Nation of Islam presents today a workable and sufficiently flexible identity for an ever-expanding group of militantly disenchanted Negro Americans.

NOTES

1. A. F. C. Wallace, "Revitalization Movements," *American Anthropologist* 58 (April 1956): 264–81. The few direct quotations concerning Wallace's theory which appear in this paper are taken from these pages.

2. Boston: Beacon Press.

3. Chicago: University of Chicago Press.

4. The most important source of current information is a tabloid called *Muhammad Speaks,* formerly issued in Harlem and now published in Chicago. The magazine has moved from an emphasis on white brutality to its current format offering general information (cooking tips, for instance) as well.

5. I am especially indebted to W. Haywood Burns and William Strickland, formerly of Harvard College, who have contributed many of the insights presented in this paper. Several conversations with Mr. Lincoln and Mr. Essien-Udom have lent additional material and interpretation. And Ministers Malcolm X of New York, Louis X and Rodney X of Boston, Jeremiah X of Atlanta and Brother·John Ali of Chicago have given many hours of conversation to expand my understanding of the Nation of Islam.

6. Malcolm X, speech at Harvard Law School, Cambridge, Mass., March 24, 1961.

7. C. Eric Lincoln, *The Black Muslims in America* (Boston: Beacon Press, 1961), p. 199.

8. For a discussion of the Muslims' antecedents and other current black nationalist groups, see Lincoln, *The Black Muslims in America,* chapter 3, and Essien-Udom, *Black Nationalism,* chapters II and III.

9. See E. D. Beynon. "The Voodoo Cult among Negro Migrants in Detroit," *American Journal of Sociology* 43 (May 1938): 894–907.

10. Lincoln, *The Black Muslims in America,* p. 181. This account is also symbolic of the conversion experiences of most members in the movement today.

11. Ibid., p. 182.

12. Malcolm X, speech at Boston University School of Theology, Boston, Mass., May 24, 1960.

13. No one knows whether George Orwell (*1984*) had the same vision!

14. Lincoln, *The Black Muslims in America,* p. 128.

15. Gordon W. Allport analyzes these and other "traits due to victimization" in *The Nature of Prejudice* (Garden City, N. Y.: Doubleday, 1958), chapter 19.

16. This point is documented in a number of sources, including James H. Laue, "Race Relations Revolutions: The Sit-In Movement" (mimeographed, 1961) and Louis Lomax, *The Negro Revolt* (New York: Harper & Row, 1962).

17. While Muhammad continues to make crude anti-white statements (many of which find their way into the media), Minister Malcolm spends much of his time with Negro and white intellectuals trying to take Muhammad's foot out of the movement's mouth.

18. "Open Mind," presented on educational television, WGBH-TV, Boston, Mass., April 30, 1961.

19. It should be made clear that while the Muslims have a powerful ethico-political program, they must be viewed sociologically as primarily a religious endeavor—a system of beliefs and rituals about ultimate problems (the nature and purpose of existence, death, meaning, right ethical norms, etc.) organized in and for a community of believers. Their this-worldly asceticism is, in fact, quite similar to that of the American Puritans of the eighteenth century.

20. Lincoln, *The Black Muslims in America,* p. 200.

21. For an interesting discussion of this cycle, see Essien-Udom, *Black Nationalism,* chapter XI.

22. While this manuscript was in press, Malcolm X was censured by Muhammad for intemperate public remarks about the death of President Kennedy. Some observers saw the action as a suspension, designed to remove Minister Malcolm from competition with Muhammad's sons for leadership after the Prophet dies. But Mr. Lincoln, following a conversation with Malcolm X in January, 1964, said the incident was "a more or less routine display of hierarchical power," and that "similar sanctions are applied continuously in the temples at a less public level." Minister Malcolm was, in fact, on his way to an important meeting with Muhammad at the time—one month after the censure.

23. Malcolm X exercises this unbeatable theological one-upsmanship in interpretation of past events, too. He linked, for instance, the crash of a Belgian airliner in 1961 with the same-day announcement of the assassination of Congo leader Patrice Lumumba, and suggested that the 1962 crash killing 120 Georgia cultural leaders was also part of Allah's plan for retribution against the white world. With very little tongue-in-cheek I suggest that Malcolm X's connection of these events has unwittingly offered a Muslim formulation of a new F-item. Note the similarity of these linkages with item 10 of the original F-scale, which was designed to test for "superstition and stereotype": "It is more than a remarkable coincidence that Japan had an earthquake on Pearl Harbor Day, December 7, 1944." Adorno, et al., *The Authoritarian Personality* (New York: Harper & Row, 1950), p. 235.

24. See Bernard Barber, "A Socio-Cultural Interpretation of the Peyote Cult," *American Anthropologist* 47 (October-December 1941): 673–75.

THE MAKING OF A BLACK MUSLIM

John R. Howard

You were black enough to get in here. You had the courage to stay. Now be man enough to follow the honorable Elijah Muhammad. You have tried the devil's way. Now try the way of the Messenger.

Minister William X,
in a West Coast Black Muslim mosque

The Lost-Found Nation of Islam in the Wilderness of North America, commonly known as the Black Muslim movement, claims a small but fanatically devoted membership among the Negroes of our major cities. The way of the "Messenger" is rigorous for those who follow it. The man or woman who becomes a Muslim accepts not only an ideology but an all-encompassing code that amounts to a way of life.

A good Muslim does a full day's work on an empty stomach. When he finally has his one meal of the day in the evening, it can include no pork, nor can he have a drink before or a cigarette after; strict dietary rules are standard procedure, and liquor and smoking are forbidden under any circumstances. His recreation is likely to consist of reading the Koran or participating in a demanding round of temple-centered activities, running public meetings or aggressively proselytizing on the streets by selling the Muslim newspaper, *Muhammad Speaks.*

Despite allegations of Muslim violence (adverse publicity from the slaying of Malcolm X supports the erroneous notion that Muslims preach violence), the member's life is basically ascetic. Why then in a non-ascetic, hedonistically-oriented society do people become Muslims? What is the life of a Muslim like? These are questions I asked in research among West Coast members. Specifically, I wanted to know:

What perspective on life makes membership in such an organization attractive?

Under what conditions does the potential recruit develop those perspectives?

How does he happen to come to the door of the temple for his first meeting?

The Black Muslims are a deviant organization even within the Negro community; the parents or friends of many members strongly objected to their joining. So how does the recruit handle pressures that might erode his allegiance to the organization and its beliefs?

Presenting my questions as an effort to "learn the truth" about the organization, I was able to conduct depth interviews with 19 West Coast

From *Trans-action* 4 (December 1966): 15–21. Copyright © by *Trans-action* Magazine, New Brunswick, New Jersey; reprinted by permission of the author and publisher.

recruits, following them through the process of their commitment to the Nation of Islam.

Two main points of appeal emerged—black nationalism and an emphasis on self-help. Some recruits were attracted primarily by the first, and some by the second. The 14 interviewees who joined the organization for its aggressive black nationalism will be called "Muslim militants." The remaining five, who were attracted more by its emphasis on hard work and rigid personal morality, may be aptly termed "Protestant Ethic Muslims."

MUSLIM MILITANTS: BEATING THE DEVIL

Of the 14 Muslim militants, some came from the South, some from border states, and some from the North. All lived in California at the time of the interviews; some migrated to the state as adults, others were brought out by their families as children. They varied in age from 24 to 46, and in education from a few years of grade school to four years of college. Regardless of these substantial differences in background, there were certain broad similarities among them.

At some point, each one had experiences that led away from the institutionally-bound ties and commitments that lend stability to most people's lives. Nine had been engaged in semi-legal or criminal activities. Two had been in the military, not as a career but as a way of postponing the decision of what to do for a living. None had a stable marital history. All of them were acutely aware of being outsiders by the standards of the larger society—and all had come to focus on race bias as the factor which denied them more conventional alternatives.

Leroy X came to California in his late teens, just before World War II:

> I grew up in Kansas City, Missouri, and Missouri was a segregated state. Negroes in Kansas City were always restricted to the menial jobs. I came out here in 1940 and tried to get a job as a waiter. I was a trained waiter, but they weren't hiring any Negroes as waiters in any of the downtown hotels or restaurants. The best I could do was busboy, and they fired me from that when they found out I wasn't Filipino.

Leroy X was drafted, and after a short but stormy career was given a discharge as being psychologically unfit.

> I tried to get a job, but I couldn't so I started stealing. There was nothing else to do—I couldn't live on air. The peckerwoods didn't seem to give a damn whether I lived or died. They wouldn't hire me and didn't seem to worry how I was going to stay alive. I started stealing.
>
> I could get you anything you wanted—a car, drugs, women, jewelry. Crime is a business like any other. I started off stealing myself. I wound up filling orders and getting rid of stuff. I did that for fifteen years. In between I did a little time. I did time for things I never thought of doing and went free for things I really did.
>
> In my business you had no friends, only associates, and not very close

ones at that. . . . I had plenty of money. I could get anything I wanted without working for it. It wasn't enough, though.

Bernard X grew up in New York City:

> As a kid . . . you always have dreams—fantasies—of yourself doing something later—being a big name singer or something that makes you outstanding. But you never draw the connection between where you are and how you're going to get there. I had to—I can't say exactly when, 13, 14, 15, 16. I saw I was nowhere and had no way of getting anywhere.
>
> Race feeling is always with you. You always know about The Man but I don't think it is real, really real, until you have to deal with it in terms of what you are going to do with your own life. That's when you feel it. If you just disliked him before—you begin to hate him when you see him blocking you in your life. I think then a sense of inevitability hits you and you see you're not going to make it out—up—away—anywhere—and you see The Man's part in the whole thing, that's when you begin to think thoughts about him.

Frederick 2X became involved fairly early in a criminal subculture. His father obtained a "poor man's divorce" by deserting the family. His mother had children by other men. Only a tenuous sense of belonging to a family existed. He was picked up by the police for various offenses several times before reaching his teens. The police patrolling his neighborhood eventually restricted him to a two-block area. There was, of course, no legal basis for this, but he was manhandled if seen outside that area by any policeman who knew him. He graduated in his late teens from "pot" to "shooting shit" and eventually spent time in Lexington.

William 2X, formerly a shoeshine boy, related the development of his perspective this way:

> You know how they always talk about us running after white women. There have always been a lot of [white] servicemen in this town—half of them would get around to asking me to get a woman for them. Some of them right out, some of them backing into it, laughing and joking and letting me know how much they were my friend, building up to asking me where they could find some woman. After a while I began to get them for them. I ran women—both black and white. . . . What I hated was they wanted me to do something for them [find women] and hated me for doing it. They figure "any nigger must know where to find it. . . ."

THINGS BEGIN TO ADD UP

Amos X grew up in an all-Negro town in Oklahoma and attended a Negro college. Because of this, he had almost no contact with whites during his formative years.

> One of my aunts lived in Tulsa. I went to see her once when I was in college. I walked up to the front door of the house where she worked.

> She really got excited and told me if I came to see her anymore to come around to the back. But that didn't mean much to me at the time. It is only in looking back on it that all these things begin to add up.

After graduating from college, Amos joined the Marines. There he began to "see how the [the whites] really felt" about him; by the end of his tour, he had concluded that "the white man is the greatest liar, the greatest cheat, the greatest hypocrite on earth." Alienated and disillusioned, he turned to professional gambling. Then, in an attempt at a more conventional way of life, he married and took a job teaching school.

> I taught English. Now I'm no expert in the slave masters' language, but I knew the way those kids talked after being in school eight and nine years was ridiculous. They said things like "mens" for "men." I drilled them and pretty soon some of them at least in class began to sound like they had been inside a school. Now the principal taught a senior class in English and his kids talked as bad as mine. When I began to straighten out his kids also he felt I was criticizing him. . . . That little black man was afraid of the [white] superintendent and all those teachers were afraid. They had a little more than other so-called Negroes and didn't give a damn about those black children they were teaching. Those were the wages of honesty. It's one thing to want to do an honest job and another thing to be able to. . . .

With the collapse of his career as a public school teacher and the break-up of his marriage, Amos went to California, where he was introduced to the Muslim movement.

> I first heard about them [the Muslims] in 1961. There was a debate here between a Muslim and a Christian minister. The Muslims said all the things about Christianity which I had been thinking but which I had never heard anyone say before. He tore the minister up.

Finding an organization that aggressively rejected the white man and the white man's religion, Amos found his own point of view crystallized. He joined without hesitation.

Norman Maghid first heard of the Muslims while he was in prison.

> I ran into one of the Brothers selling the paper about two weeks after I got out and asked him about the meetings. Whether a guy could just go and walk in. He told me about the meetings so I made it around on a Wednesday evening. I wasn't even bugged when they searched me. When they asked me about taking out my letter [joining the organization] I took one out. They seemed to know what they were talking about. I never believed in non-violence and love my enemies, especially when my enemies don't love me.

Muhammad Soule Kabah, born into a family of debt-ridden Texas sharecroppers, was recruited into the Nation of Islam after moving to California.

I read a series of articles in the Los Angeles *Herald Dispatch,* an exchange between Minister Henry and a Christian minister. It confirmed what my grandfather had told me about my African heritage, that I had nothing to be ashamed of, that there were six thousand books on mathematics in the Library of the University of Timbucktoo while Europeans were still wearing skins. Also my father had taught me never to kow-tow to whites. My own father had fallen away. My parents didn't want me to join the Nation. They said they taught hate. That's funny isn't it? The white man can blow up a church and kill four children and the black man worries that an organization which tells you not to just take it is teaching hate.

PROTESTANT ETHIC MUSLIMS: UP BY BLACK BOOTSTRAPS

The Protestant Ethic Muslims all came from backgrounds with a strong tradition of Negro self-help. In two cases, the recruit's parents had been followers of Marcus Garvey; another recruit explicitly endorsed the beliefs of Booker T. Washington; and the remaining two, coming from upwardly mobile families, were firm in the belief that Negroes could achieve higher status if they were willing to work for it.

When asked what had appealed to him about the Muslims, Norman X replied:

> They thought that black people should do something for themselves. I was running this small place [a photography shop] and trying to get by. I've stuck with this place even when it was paying me barely enough to eat. Things always improve and I don't have to go to the white man for anything.

Ernestine X stressed similar reasons for joining the Muslims.

> You learned to stand up straight and do something for yourself. You learn to be a lady at all times—to keep your house clean—to teach your children good manners. There is not a girl in the M-G-T who does not know how to cook and sew. The children are very respectful; they speak only when they are spoken to. There is no such thing as letting your children talk back to you the way some people believe. The one thing they feel is the Negroes' downfall is men and sex for the women, and women and sex for the men, and they frown on sex completely unless you are married.

Despite their middle-class attitudes in many areas, Protestant Ethic Muslims denounced moderate, traditional civil rights organizations such as the NAACP just as vigorously as the militant Muslims did. Norman X said that he had once belonged to the NAACP but had dropped out.

> They spent most of their time planning the annual brotherhood dinner. Besides it was mostly whites—whites and the colored doctors and lawyers who wanted to be white. As far as most Negroes were concerned they might as well not have existed.

Lindsey X, who had owned and run his own upholstery shop for more than 30 years, viewed the conventional black bourgeoisie with equal resentment.

> I never belonged to the NAACP. What they wanted never seemed real to me. I think Negroes should create jobs for themselves rather than going begging for them. That's why I never supported CORE.

In this respect Norman and Lindsey were in full accord with the more militant Amos X, who asserted:

> They [the NAACP and CORE] help just one class of people. . . . Let something happen to a doctor and they are right there; but if something happens to Old Mose on the corner, you can't find them.

The interviews made it clear that most of the Protestant Ethic Muslims had joined the Nation because, at some point, they began to feel the need of organizational support for their personal systems of value. For Norman and Lindsey, it was an attempt to stop what they considered their own backsliding after coming to California. Both mentioned drinking to excess and indulging in what they regarded as a profligate way of life. Guilt feelings apparently led them to seek Muslim support in returning to more enterprising habits.

COMMITMENT TO DEVIANCE

The Nation of Islam is a deviant organization. As such it is subject to public scorn and ridicule. Thus it faces the problem of consolidating the recruit's allegiance in an environment where substantial pressures operate to erode this allegiance. How does it deal with this problem?

The structural characteristics of the Nation tend to insulate the member from the hostility of the larger society and thus contribute to the organization's survival. To begin with, the ritual of joining the organization itself stresses commitment without questions.

At the end of the general address at a temple meeting, the minister asks those nonmembers present who are "interested in learning more about Islam" to step to the back of the temple. There they are given three blank sheets of ordinary stationery and a form letter addressed to Elijah Muhammad in Chicago.

> Dear Savior Allah, Our Deliverer:
> I have attended the Teachings of Islam, two or three times, as taught by one of your ministers. I believe in it. I bear witness that there is no God but Thee. And, that Muhammad is Thy Servant and Apostle. I desire to reclaim my Own. Please give me my Original name. My slave name is as follows:

The applicant is instructed to copy this letter verbatim on each of the three sheets of paper, giving his own name and address unabbreviated at the bottom. If he fails to copy the letter perfectly, he must repeat the whole task. No explanation is given for any of these requirements.

Formal acceptance of his letter makes the new member a Muslim, but in name only. Real commitment to the Nation of Islam comes gradually—for example, the personal commitment expressed when a chain smoker gives up cigarettes in accordance with the Muslim rules even though he knows that he could smoke unobserved. "It's not that easy to do these things," Stanley X said of the various forms of abstinence practiced by Muslims. "It takes will and discipline and time, . . . but you're a much better person after you do." Calvin X told of periodic backsliding in the beginning, but added, "Once I got into the thing deep, then I stuck with it."

This commitment and the new regimen that goes with it have been credited with effecting dramatic personality changes in many members, freeing alcoholics from the bottle and drug addicts from the needle. It can be argued, however, that the organization does not change the member's fundamental orientation. To put it somewhat differently, given needs and impulses can be expressed in a variety of ways; thus, a man may give vent to his sadism by beating up strangers in an alley or by joining the police force and beating them up in the back room of the station.

"Getting into the thing deep" for a Muslim usually comes in three stages:

> Participation in organizational activities—selling the Muslim newspaper, dining at the Muslim restaurant, attending and helping run Muslim meetings.
>
> Isolation from non-Muslim social contacts—drifting away from former friends and associates because of divergent attitudes or simply because of the time consumed in Muslim activities.
>
> Assimilation of the ideology—marking full commitment, when a Muslim has so absorbed the organization's doctrines that he automatically uses them to guide his own behavior and to interpret what happens in the world around him.

The fact that the organization can provide a full social life furthers isolation from non-Muslims. Participation is not wholly a matter of drudgery, of tramping the streets to sell the paper and studying the ideology. The organization presents programs of entertainment for its members and the public. For example, in two West Coast cities a Negro theatrical troupe called the Touring Artists put on two plays, "Jubilee Day" and "Don't You Want to Be Free." Although there was a high element of humor in both plays, the basic themes—white brutality and hypocrisy and the necessity of developing Negro self-respect and courage —were consonant with the organization's perspective. Thus the organization makes it possible for a member to satisfy his need for diversion without going outside to do so. At the same time, it continually reaches him with its message through the didactic element in such entertainment.

Carl X's experiences were typical of the recruit's growing commitment to the Nation. When asked what his friends had thought when he
first joined, he replied: "They thought I was crazy. They said, 'Man,
how can you believe all that stuff?'" He then commented that he no
longer saw much of them, and added:

> When you start going to the temple four or five times a week and selling
> the newspaper you do not have time for people who are not doing these
> things. We drifted—the friends I had—we drifted apart. . . . All the
> friends I have now are in the Nation. Another Brother and I get together
> regularly and read the Koran and other books, then ask each other ques-
> tions on them like, "What is Allah's greatest weapon? The truth. What
> is the devil's greatest weapon? The truth. The devil keeps it hidden from
> men. Allah reveals it to man." We read and talk about the things we read
> and try to sharpen our thinking. I couldn't do that with my old friends.

Spelled out, the "stuff" that Carl X had come to believe, the official
Muslim ideology, is this:

> The so-called Negro, the American black man, is lost in ignorance. He is
> unaware of his own past history and the future role which history has
> destined him to play.
> Elijah Muhammad has come as the Messenger of Allah to awaken the
> American black man.
> The American black man finds himself now in a lowly state, but that was
> not always his condition.
> The Original Man, the first men to populate the earth, were non-white.
> They enjoyed a high level of culture and reached high peaks of achieve-
> ment.
> A little over 6,000 years ago a black scientist named Yakub, after con-
> siderable work, produced a mutant, a new race, the white race.
> This new race was inferior mentally, physically, and morally to the black
> race. Their very whiteness, the very mark of their difference from the
> black race, was an indication of their physical degeneracy and moral
> depravity.
> Allah, in anger at Yakub's work, ordained that the white race should rule
> for a fixed amount of time and that the black man should suffer and by
> his suffering gain a greater appreciation of his own spiritual worth by
> comparing himself to the whites.
> The time of white dominance is drawing near its end. It is foreordained
> that this race shall perish, and with its destruction the havoc, terror, and
> brutality which it has spread throughout the world shall disappear.
> The major task facing the Nation of Islam is to awaken the American
> black man to his destiny, to acquaint him with the course of history.
> The Nation of Islam in pursuing this task must battle against false
> prophets, in particular those who call for integration. Integration is a
> plot of the white race to forestall its own doom. The black bourgeoisie,
> bought off by a few paltry favors and attempting to ingratiate themselves
> with the whites, seek to spread this pernicious doctrine among so-called
> Negroes.

The Nation of Islam must encourage the American black man to begin now to assume his proper role by wresting economic control from the whites. The American black man must gain control over his own economic fortunes by going into business for himself and becoming economically strong.

The Nation of Islam must encourage the so-called Negro to give up those habits which have been spread among them by the whites as part of the effort to keep them weak, diseased, and demoralized. The so-called Negro must give up such white-fostered dissolute habits as drinking, smoking, and eating improper foods. The so-called Negro must prepare himself in mind and body for the task of wresting control from the whites.

The Nation of Islam must encourage the so-called Negro to seek now his own land within the continental United States. This is due him and frees him from the pernicious influence of the whites.

THE PROBLEM OF DEFECTION

Commitment to the Nation can diminish as well as grow. Four of the members I interviewed later defected. Why?

These four cases can be explained in terms of a weak point in the structure of the Nation. The organization has no effective mechanisms for handling grievances among the rank and file. Its logic accounts for this, Muslim doctrine assumes that there is a single, ultimate system of truth. Elijah Muhammad and, by delegation, his ministers are in possession of this truth. Thus only Elijah Muhammad himself can say whether a minister is doing an adequate job. The result is the implicit view that there is nothing to be adjudicated between the hierarchy and its rank and file.

Grievances arise, however. The four defectors were, for various reasons, all dissatisfied with Minister Gerard X. Since there were no formal mechanisms within the organization for expressing their dissatisfaction, the only solution was to withdraw.

For most members, however, the pattern is one of steadily growing involvement. And once the ideology is fully absorbed, there is virtually no such thing as dispute or counter-evidence. If a civil rights bill is not passed, this proves the viciousness of whites in refusing to recognize Negro rights. If the same bill *is* passed, it merely proves the duplicity of whites in trying to hide their viciousness.

The ideology also provides a coherent theory of causation, provided one is willing to accept its basic assumptions. Norman X interpreted his victory over his wife in a court case as a sign of Allah's favor. Morris X used it to account for the day-to-day fortunes of his associates.

> Minister X had some trouble. He was sick for a long time. He almost died. I think Allah was punishing him. He didn't run the temple right. Now the Brothers make mistakes. Everyone does—but Minister X used to abuse them at the meetings. It was more a personal thing. He had a little power and it went to his head. Allah struck him down and I think he learned a little humility.

When a man reasons in this fashion, he has become a fully committed member of the Nation of Islam. His life revolves around temple-centered activities, his friends are all fellow Muslims, and he sees his own world—usually the world of an urban slum dweller—through the framework of a very powerful myth. He is still doing penance for the sins of Yakub, but the millennium is at hand. He has only to prepare.

The Nation of Islam does not in any real sense convert members. Rather it attracts Negroes who have already, through their own experiences in white America, developed a perspective congruent with that of the Muslim movement. The recruit comes to the door of the temple with the essence of his ideas already formed. The Black Muslims only give this disaffection a voice.

part VI

THE
BLACK REVOLT:
RETROSPECT
AND PROSPECTS

This book has included a mass of information on the black revolt, as defined herein. This material has been presented in the form of reprinted articles and papers by social scientists. By and large this material has stood alone, except for brief introductory sections providing limited summaries and discussions of the material included in the selections. Thus the material largely stands unintegrated. This concluding chapter will attempt an integration of this material, and other selections not reprinted, into a meaningful whole.

ORIGINS OF SOCIAL MOVEMENTS

It takes more than dissatisfaction with the present to ignite a social movement.[1] Dissatisfaction must be combined with a vision of a better state of affairs that is seen as both desirable and possible of attainment. Thus the formula producing social movements is dissatisfaction plus hope plus faith: dissatisfaction with the present, hope for a better future, and faith in one's ability to bring about that future.

But even the combination of all three factors does not ensure the production of a social movement. An individual may be dissatisfied with his present job, may hope to achieve a better paying and more desirable job, and may have faith in his ability to achieve this desired job. Such attempts to improve one's lot through individual mobility are not part of a social movement. The dissatisfaction must be shared by members of a collectivity. The collectivity must possess a shared sense of hope and faith. Attempts to change the present situation must be collective and must utilize methods outside traditional, legitimate means of redressing grievances. If traditional means of redressing grievances were available to the members of the collectivity, there would be no need for the social movement. Social movements challenge vested interests. Thus they arouse opposition. The need to overcome this opposition leads to the development of organization, leadership, strategy, and tactics. Social movements will vary in terms of the collective interests represented and the degree of alteration in the social order sought. These lead to variations in the style of a social movement. An analysis of any given social movement must take all of these factors into account.

THE BLACK REVOLT: PRESOCIAL MOVEMENT

It is reasonable to assume that blacks have always been dissatisfied with their lot in America. This is evident from the continuing incidents of presocial-movement black protest discussed in the introduction. Many factors combined to prevent this early discontent from leading to the development of a social movement. Slaves were scattered in relatively small numbers among many different plantations.[2] This had two consequences: it both limited the amount of effective communications that could take place and prevented the development of any effective organization among slaves. The slave owners were organized and had a preponderance of force and laws on their side, which prevented the slaves from developing any real sense of power. The slave revolts that did occur were crushed and the participants were severely punished. Many runaway slaves were recaptured, returned to their owner, and made public examples. All of this combined to produce a sense of fatalism among slaves and served to forestall any revolution.

Abolition may have served to produce a new sense of hope. But it is unlikely that it produced any sense of power, as abolition was largely brought about by whites. The growth and early successes of the Southern Populist movement may have contributed to the development of an incipient sense of power, but the ease with which the populists were crushed would have destroyed this.

Little happened in America between the crushing of the populists and World War I that would give blacks either hope or faith. World War I changed much of this.[3] Many whites and some blacks went into the army. Industry geared up to a war economy. Jobs were opened to blacks that had never been open before. Some black soldiers got to Europe, where they saw societies that were more open in their treatment of blacks than was ever believed possible in America. The accounts of these soldiers were printed in black newspapers throughout the country. Blacks began to develop an image of a better America in which they would have many more opportunities and much greater acceptance. Then the war came to an end. White soldiers returned to resume their old jobs and industry cut back to peacetime levels. With the resulting surplus of workers, white America felt that uppity blacks had to be put back into their proper place. The nation was rocked by a wave of race riots aimed at doing precisely this. The black hopes which had been raised by the war were now dashed.

It is little wonder that many blacks came to feel that America was no place for them. Prior to the war Marcus Garvey had been attempting with little success to gain adherents for his Universal Negro Improvement Association.[4] He now found fertile ground for recruiting among blacks whose hopes for moving into American society had been raised and then dashed to the ground. If America would not let them in, then maybe the solution was to get out. Emigration to Africa became an attractive possibility. Some estimates state that Garvey's supporters came to number over a million. Even this movement proved to be too much of a threat for White America, and Garvey was tried and convicted of fraud under rather questionable circumstances. He was jailed and then deported to the West Indies (his place of birth). The Garvey movement was crushed, giving blacks further evidence of their powerless position.

The next significant event affecting black aspirations was World War II.[5] This produced an effect similar to but more intense than that of World War I. This time the war placed America in more dire straits. It became more vulnerable to internal pressures. Black demands combined with such tactics as A. Philip Randolph's March on Washington produced such results as the Fair Employment Practices Act. Jobs opened up. Eventually the armed forces were integrated. These limited successes provided an example of the fact that organization could produce power. Although situational factors had been more responsible for the success than had the degree of black power, nevertheless the accomplishments served to weaken the image of white invulnerability. The end of the war again brought a slowing of the economy and a restriction of opportunities for blacks. This time cold war tensions prevented as sharp a reduction in the armed forces and in defense spending. The resulting restrictions on black opportunity were not as sharp or as suddenly imposed as they had been after the First World War. The resultant black reaction was also less intense. The separatist Nation of Islam grew, but less rapidly than had the Universal Negro Improvement Association.[6] Efforts on behalf of greater civil rights continued, primarily through the legalistic tactics of the NAACP, until December 1, 1955.

THE CIVIL RIGHTS MOVEMENT

My article reprinted in Part II ("Social Structure and the Negro Revolt") attempted to analyze those economic changes from 1940 to 1960 which helped to produce the civil rights movement. The level of black dissatisfaction which had always been present was intensified by feelings of relative deprivation resulting from more rapid progress of whites than of blacks. Hope for a better life was produced by the improvement in absolute terms experienced by black Americans. Faith in the possibility and probability of change was encouraged by court victories (e.g., the 1954 and 1955 Supreme Court decisions on school desegregation). This latter point suggests one weakness of this essay as originally written. It placed too much emphasis upon economic changes, which are important but do not provide a total explanation. Other changes taking place in American society, such as the school desegregation decisions, helped to create hope and faith on the part of blacks.

Another major change had taken place since the days of slavery. Blacks were no longer scattered in small groups on plantations. They now tended to be concentrated in urban areas.[7] What is even more to the point, they tended to be concentrated in segregated sections of these urban centers. Black college students tended to be concentrated in black universities. Thus communications could flow easily among large numbers of blacks. They could be carried by the black press from urban area to urban area. It was quite easy for blacks with similar grievances to share these among themselves. A sense of collective deprivation could easily emerge. A common definition of the situation emerged combining a sense of deprivation with feelings of hope and faith. A common enemy came to be defined. The Montgomery bus boycott provided a symbol of successful action against that enemy and the mid-fifties witnessed the birth of the civil rights movement as a mass black social movement.[8]

These changes, of course, did not provide the same level of hope for all blacks; to claim that they did would be to indulge in a considerable overstate-ment of the actual situation. The changes largely foreshadowed an America in which there would be a great increase in opportunities for *qualified* blacks. Qualified means educated. The openings that were envisaged were openings primarily for blacks with access to education. Thus they were openings primarily for middle-class blacks. It is only to be expected that much of the civil rights movement of the fifties was a movement by, and on behalf of, middle-class blacks and black college students.

The sense of fatalism and powerlessness on the part of lower-class blacks was hard to overcome. Combined with a feeling that any gains brought about by the civil rights movement would mean little to them or their children as long as they lacked access to the universities, these feelings of fatalism and power-lessness were reinforced with a repugnance directed at the nonviolent tactics of the civil rights movement.[9] Everything in American culture combines to provide a definition of masculinity which includes self-defense and protection of one's women as part of being a man. The lower-class black male experiences so many emasculating situations that it is difficult for him to voluntarily place himself in circumstances that would further emasculate him. What kind of man could stand idly by and allow his women to be attacked and beaten by a white mob? Who could be a man and not retaliate? Thus, for the most part, the lower-class black was an onlooker to the early days of the civil rights movement.

Research in the early sixties found not only that lower-class persons did not participate in the movement, but also that college students of lower-class origin did not participate to the extent of those with more prestigious origins. Orbell found the movement in 1962 to be still dominated by college students from middle-class backgrounds, but he found an increased participation rate among those with lower-class origins.[10] In 1964 Orum and Orum found that class differences among student participants had largely disappeared.[11] It is likely that this represents developments that were taking place within the move-ment as a whole. The earlier successes of the movement may have contributed greatly to the development of hope and faith among college students with lower-class origins. This would account for their increased participation rates. One should note, however, that these new participants may have had lower-class origins but they were still in college and would presumably be in a posi-tion to take advantage of any gains achieved. Lower-class nonstudents would not be in such a position and did not participate in the black revolt at this time.

It is interesting to speculate on the relationship between changes in the social origins of the participants and changes in civil rights tactics. It may be the case that the influx of participants with lower-class origins led to a shift to the more militant tactics of confrontation. These students were probably more impatient with the slow gains made by tactics involving less in the way of di-rect action. On the other hand, it may be the case that the shift to the more militant tactics made the civil rights movement more palatable to this group. Either way, the shift in tactics is evident and is probably related in some fashion to the shift in participants. As the civil rights movement aged, its tactics became increasingly militant and decreasingly respectable. Any success of the civil rights movement further stimulates its growth by providing evidence of white vulnera-bility. Blacks thus develop an increased sense of their own power, increased hope and faith. At the same time they become aware of the minimal level of change wrought by their success. They become more dissatisfied. Limited improvement produces more dissatisfaction with lack of real change or with the slow pace of change. Thus every gain produces an escalation of demands. The new demands cannot always be achieved by the old tactics—at least not fast enough or fully enough. An escalation of demands produces an escalation of tactics. Both are accompanied by an expansion of the base of participants. All of this leads to an increase in white fear and hostility.[12] More fear and hostility means more resistance. The increase in resistance makes a further escalation in tactics inevitable. Social movements grow and feed upon their own successes.

The alteration in tactics and the changed characteristics of participants go hand and glove with changes in leadership.[13] Prior to the civil rights movement black communities were characterized by a type of accommodating leadership. These black leaders were persons who had learned to adjust themselves to the realities of white domination. They could work the white power structure in order to achieve some benefits for blacks. To do this they had to go to whites with hat in hand; they could not appear to be a threat to the white power structure. This is a type of role behavior which is well suited to a particular set of circumstances and is effective in that context. However, the personality demands are such that it would be unlikely that a successful accommodating leader could so alter himself as to be able to serve as a successful confrontation leader. Thus the civil rights movement brought about a major sh'ft in black leadership. Similarly, many blacks could play the role of a confrontation leader with a movement using respectable nonviolent tactics but could not do so with a movement using less respectable ones. The leadership continued to change as the movement evolved. Again, it is clear, one can only lead if one is going the same direction as one's followers. This type of change in leadership was accompanied by similar changes in organizations at the forefront of the movement. Organizations seldom died out completely, but some came to command less attention as others moved to the front of the battle.

The newer organizations specialize in the more dramatic, direct action tactics.[14] Many of their members express disdain for the conservative "Toms" who populate the older, more established civil rights organizations. Many go so far as to write the older organizations entirely out of the civil rights movement. Yet there is a real symbiosis which develops between the new and the old. McWorter and Crain's findings should be as applicable to organizations as they are to individual leaders.[15] Competition between organizatinos tends to radicalize all organizations.

SNCC, CORE, and SCLC began taking the headlines away from the NAACP. With the headlines, went memberships, membership fees, donations of white liberals, and $150-a-plate dinners. The NAACP was rapidly losing funds —funds that were necessary to carry on its own legal battles. In fact, the same actions that were diverting funds away from the NAACP to the militant organizations were increasing the NAACP court costs. The newer organizations spent all their money on direct action and bail bonds. Attorney's fees had to be covered by either the American Civil Liberties Union or the NAACP. The NAACP needed to recapture the headlines and to attempt to get back the money that was being diverted to other organizations. Not coincidentally, the NAACP Youth Council was formed and engaged in direct action. They did gain back some of the headlines and some of the contributions, but the NAACP never again returned to its formerly recognized place at the head of the civil rights movement.

The early accomplishments of the civil rights movement were responsible for the raising of hopes among blacks. They were also responsible for the creating of the belief among blacks that they could collectively harness enough power to force further changes. The combination of these feelings led to a critical reexamination of gains made to date, which produced discontent with the limited and overly slow progress. Thus the accomplishments were directly responsible for drawing more persons—especially more lower-class persons—into the movement, for the escalation of tactics, and the development of new organization. However, these were not the only results, for the entire process had a major impact on the course of white resistance.

Many whites were upset by the arrogance of blacks questioning the *status quo.* They became even more upset by the fact that blacks did not request changes—they demanded them. Court suits and legalistic tactics were reprehensible and should be punished. Direct action was absolutely intolerable and must be crushed, here, now, and for all time. Black direct action tactics and black successes touched off violent white resistance.[16] Violence on the part of whites attracted the sympathy of white liberals and loosened their pocketbooks. It also further motivated both whites and blacks to place their bodies on the line. But perhaps most important, white violence produced anger on the part of blacks who could not, and would not, remain nonviolent. This anger had many diverse consequences. Indeed, violent white resistance may be directly responsible for the emergence of black defense organizations, the black power movement, separatism, and ghetto uprisings. Let us examine these one at a time.

BLACK DEFENSE ORGANIZATIONS

The most obvious connection can be drawn between white violence and black defense organizations.[17] Many blacks initially found nonviolent demonstrators to be amusing in a sardonic way; they saw the activists as fools who would risk getting their heads busted for the right to go to a movie or to get into a restaurant that they couldn't afford anyway. These observers didn't like the beatings and jailings handed out to the demonstrators, but they tended to feel that they were to be expected: "They asked for it." But white violence escalated just as black militance and civil rights tactics escalated.[18] Beatings were supplemented by murders, bombings, and burnings. The national press reported a few of the more spectacular cases or those involving white victims. But by and large, the scores and eventually hundreds of black deaths were known to blacks but went largely ignored by the media and by whites. This produced a potent reaction among all blacks. Intense anger was only a part of it. Any view of whites as moral beings who could be reasoned with was totally destroyed. The worst images of whites were confirmed. It became evident that whites would stop at nothing—not even at the murder of little children, white women, and religious leaders—to perpetuate their system of exploitation.

Nonviolence is a tactic that works when one deals with persons with consciences. If consciences are lacking, nonviolence is an invitation to slaughter. Evidence was ample that the local police could not be relied upon for protection from violent whites. Observation had shown that the FBI worked hand-in-glove with local "law enforcement" agencies. The FBI was not a source of security or protection. The only people concerned with protecting black activists were black people. Some blacks remained committed to nonviolence and attempted to demonstrate to the nation and the world the evils of the system and the need for interference. Others either had never been committed to nonviolence or had lost that commitment. They formed organizations for the defense of blacks. They armed themselves and protected activists, black churches, black homes, and the total black communities. This is another example of the division of labor that took place within the black revolt. The legalistic and the direct action people in the civil rights movement reinforced one another. One provided pressure, the other a respectable group with whom whites could negotiate. The black defense groups provided protection for both of them and helped them remain alive long enough to carry on the struggle.

BLACK POWER

White violence also contributed greatly to the "black power" submovement within the larger black revolt. White violence was not the sole contributor to the movement's growth, but it provided much of the initial publicity. When James Meredith began his nonviolent march through Mississippi he had only a handful of supporters with him.[19] Just as dogs, cattle prods, and firehoses in the past had given an impetus to the black revolt, a bullet fired by a white did the same at this point in time. Meredith was shot. Instead of a handful of people marching, there were hundreds. The march was taken up by nonviolent blacks such as Rev. Martin Luther King, Jr. But the march was also taken up by Stokely Carmichael. He delivered speeches en route, attracting many young people. The nation was treated to the scene of many young blacks marching and chanting or shouting out "black power, black power, black power." A slogan had arrived and a new variant of the social movement which we call the black revolt was launched.

At its most general level, the black power movement is very simple. It is based upon a reasonable analysis of the structure of society.[20] The basic unit of analysis for understanding any society is power. The distribution of power determines all else. He who controls the decision-making apparatus controls the distribution of rewards. The exploited position of blacks in American society is a simple result of their lack of power. Alteration of that lowly position requires a redistribution of power. The black power movement is simply the seeking, by whatever means possible, of such a redistribution of power.

The black power movement will use whatever tactics will lead to a redistribution of power. Violent revolution is not one of these tactics. Twelve percent of the population cannot successfully rise up against 88 percent when that 88 percent controls the army, the police, and the bulk of all weapons. Political weapons, economic weapons, and disruptive tactics may be used to make the costs of retention of advantages greater than the value of such advantages. When the cost becomes too great, some of the advantages will be given up.

There is a more sophisticated version of this ideology based upon a closer analysis of American society, which reveals that it is not whites who hold power but a small portion of the white community. Most whites are also victims, although not to the same extent as blacks. This version of the black power ideology makes possible an alliance between blacks and poor whites.[21] This alliance can then move against the white establishment. The decade of the sixties produced only the merest beginnings of such an alliance, as most poor whites were not yet ready.[22] It is possible that blacks constitute a revolutionary vanguard which eventually will be joined by whites in a socialist revolution.

The sophisticated version of the black power ideology is inevitably socialist, for it sees the major problem as one of exploitation. Black capitalism is not the answer. To overthrow the yoke of white exploitation and simply have white exploiters replaced by black exploiters is not progress. Capitalism is exploitative by its very nature. Any battle against exploitation must be a battle against capitalism. This battle must come eventually, but it is not necessary in the early days of the movement. Thus, the early days of the black power movement can concentrate on building a power base. One essential feature of this power base is black economic self-sufficiency. Thus, community control of the ghetto, black enterprise, and, paradoxically, even black capitalism can characterize the early days of a movement that will eventually oppose all capitalism. This early drive for control of the ghetto economy and for economic self-sufficiency must be accompanied by agitation among poor whites to set the stage for an ultimate interracial socialist movement. It is from this agitation that we find developing organizations like the Friends of the Black Panthers and the White Panthers.[23] It is these organizations that provide a home for the white radicals expelled from SNCC and CORE.

In many ways, black separatism is a parallel movement to black power.[24] Ultimate separatist organizations such as the Nation of Islam get their impetus from observations of the civil rights movement. White resistance, white violence, and limited token gains provide evidence that blacks will never be fully admitted into American society. If one can't get in, why try? Why not withdraw entirely? Why not set up an independent black nation? This line of reasoning has much appeal for many blacks, and numerous separatist organizations came into being. It is extremely difficult to ascertain how many of their members and supporters are committed to separatism as the ultimate solution and how many see separatism as a temporary stopping point on the way to eventual integration on the basis of full equality. It is clear that many supporters see separatism as a temporary tactic that will eventually lead to integration. Meaningful integration requires full equality and a prerequisite of full equality is equality of power. It may be the case that the only possible road to equality of power detours by way of separatism. Thus many persons and groups advocating separatism are really integrationists attempting to create the power base necessary for meaningful integration. The difference between the movement for integration through black power and much of the movement for black separatism is more apparent than real.

GHETTO INSURRECTIONS

The predominant form that the black revolt took between 1964 and 1968 was the ghetto insurrection. Other forms continued throughout this period. Persons and organizations continued to attempt to bring about change through traditional nonviolent civil rights tactics. Organizations and individuals continued to advocate and work for black power. Separatism remained a strong influence and new separatist groups came into prominence. Nevertheless, nothing in the movement commanded as much attention as the ghetto revolts.

The urban riots bear a more peripheral relation to the black revolt than any of the previously discussed submovements. They were not the result of conscious planning.[25] Nor were they deliberately instigated. This does not exclude them from the total social movement; as was indicated earlier, all social movements have both organized and unorganized segments. All that is required is that both the organized and the unorganized segments of the movement respond to the same set of external stimuli and strive for roughly the same set of objectives. By these criteria the participants in ghetto disorders qualify for inclusion within the black revolt.

The ghetto revolts were stimulated by a combination of the nonviolent civil rights movement, national events, and conditions unique to particular local situations. There is little question that residents of northern ghettos followed the civil rights movement with great interest. They were heartened by the actions and accomplishments of the movement. Hopes were raised by governmental response. Federal court orders desegregated the busses in Montgomery. The Supreme Court ordered that schools be desegregated. The federal government passed the civil rights acts of 1964 and 1965 ordering the desegregation of public facilities, ensuring voting rights, and indicating an attempt to reduce job discrimination. Many blacks began to feel that possibly a better life could be had in America after all; it could be brought about through collective action.

Other things were noted as well. White resistance to change was often violent. Ten years after the school desegregation decision less than 10 percent of the southern black children were attending desegregated schools and in the North school segregation actually was increasing.[26] The civil rights act brought token compliance. A handful of federal registrars went into a few southern counties to implement the voting rights act. Change was limited and tokenistic. Even these limited gains did not affect the ghetto dwellers. Jobs were still scarce. Discrimination in employment and housing continued. Schools were still overcrowded, as were, in fact, the ghettos themselves. Life in the ghettos was as intolerable as ever. In reality, it was more intolerable than ever because hope had intruded and driven out fatalism. The war on poverty was introduced amid great fanfare. It promised much and delivered nothing. Police brutality continued unabated.

It is little wonder that ghetto after ghetto exploded. Nor is it any surprise that the ghettos that exploded were located in cities in which there did not appear to be any avenues for the legitimate redress of grievances.[27] Ward systems had been eliminated in order to reduce graft and corruption in politics. With them went any hope that blacks had for effective political representation in cities. Politicians had no need to pay much attention to blacks. Office holders were no longer elected by neighborhoods but in at-large elections. Thus they became primarily concerned with the more numerous white voters. Where black politicians were elected they were elected by machine politics and were more responsive to the machine than to blacks. Chicago is a perfect example of this.[28]

Hopes had been raised, progress was nonexistent, and legitimate avenues for the redress of grievance were closed. Violent insurrection was the inevitable result. The incidents which precipitated specific ghetto revolts often involved the police. This is not unexpected. One of the major grievances in the ghetto has always been the widespread existence of police brutality. This is also one of the areas in which clear proof existed that there were no legitimate avenues open for the resolution of grievances. The suggestion that police review boards be set up was almost always rejected. Time and time again policemen would shoot blacks only to have the shooting ruled justifiable. Upon occasion, it may have been justifiable—but not with the consistency with which it was ruled to be so. Appeals regarding other acts of brutality were either ignored or resulted in wrist slapping. The officer involved often received a minor reprimand which left the police free to further harass the person registering the complaint. If it is impossible to go to the authorities with complaints against the police, then it is necessary to react directly and personally. The recognition of this fact often touched off major riots.[29]

With the exception of clashes between blacks and police or other representatives of authority, the ghetto revolts produced very little violence directed against whites.[30] However, much violence was directed against white-owned property. Black-owned businesses were often left untouched while white-owned stores were looted and burned, although black businessmen who had the reputation of acting like white capitalists often found their stores looted and burned. Where white businessmen had the reputation of extending credit and treating their customers with respect, their stores were left untouched.[31] There was clear evidence that burning and looting were not self-serving activities, but rather were punishment of oppressors.

Riot participants were generally the young, the socially isolated, and the deprived members of the black community.[32] The major motivation for participation appears to be deprivation. Blacks felt themselves to be unjustly deprived of many aspects of the good life to which they felt entitled. They were angry at being so deprived. Concentrated in overcrowded ghettos where the discontent and anger could become social, they generated a sense of solidarity by the communication of their discontent. A form of ethnic class consciousness emerged. When the first insurrection occurred it was reported on television and in newspapers and magazines. When the government responded with money and private industry responded with jobs, this also was reported. Proof was made readily available that riots were not irrational. They didn't change much in the community, but they changed a hell of a lot more than peaceful complaints ever had. Black communities became aware of this. Every time one community rose up in rebellion and made some gains, other communities took note. Respect for rioting as a tactic increased and the likelihood that an insurrection would occur in any given community increased.

Whites have not always been as aware as blacks of the possible utility of rioting as a tactic. An example illustrating this occurred during the television coverage of the 1968 Democratic convention. A speaker on camera was speaking against violence, insisting that grievances could be aired peacefully, and that nothing could be gained by using violent means. David Brinkley cut in to announce an impending commercial. The sponsor was an oil company. The commercial showed a gas station that the oil company had set up in Watts for the purpose of training some of the local people in running service stations. After they served apprenticeships there, the oil company said that it helped place them in similar jobs and tried to get them franchises. The announcer referred to the civic conscience of the oil company, but he didn't mention the fact that if there had been no riot in Watts, there would have been no filling station. When the commercial ended, the camera came back to the convention where the same speaker was still explaining that no one could gain anything from violence!

Riots reached their peak of violence in 1967. They continued to occur in large numbers in 1968 but on a reduced level of intensity compared to those of Detroit and Newark. The explanation for this is rather simple. The riots themselves were often a result of the awareness that this form of behavior brought about concrete results. The gradual cessation of riots was brought about by a reconsideration of this relationship.[33] Many blacks, especially the militant youths, reevaluated the equation. They balanced the gains against the price paid and decided the price was too high. The number of black lives lost in Newark and Detroit was too high a price to pay for the resultant gains.

This thesis should not be misinterpreted as suggesting that the riots were planned or deliberately instigated. They were not. They began as spontaneous responses to precipitating incidents. Many persons had developed a degree of riot awareness and riot readiness. When they observed a potential precipitating incident they responded in a manner which ensured that some sort of riot would follow. Subsequent events determined whether the riot remained small or became a major insurrection. The events that transformed many of these events into major insurrections were responses on the part of militant individuals. Persons who have an ideological commitment to revolution will seize upon any available weapons. It is likely that they would be able to recognize a situation which had the potential of becoming a major insurrection and help it along.

Although none of the riots were deliberately instigated, leadership and organization developed while they were in progress.[34] This leadership helped to direct activities and suggest targets. The militant leadership which emerged helped to sustain the disorders over time and to give them their overtly political character. However, once militants became convinced that riots were counterproductive, they changed the nature of their contribution. As soon as militants decided that the minimal gains were not worth the cost in black lives, they devoted their energies to attempting to cool out potentially riotous situations. This did not prevent outbreaks of violence, but it did help to prevent the violence from growing and spreading into major insurrections.

THE DECADE OF THE SEVENTIES

The black revolt continued to evolve as the sixties ended and the seventies began. The nonviolent civil rights movement continued, but not at the pace that was observed between the mid-fifties and the mid-sixties. The strivings for black power increased and the movement toward separatism continued unabated. Ghetto insurrections disappeared almost entirely. They were replaced by another form of violence. Shoot-outs between black militants and the police became increasingly frequent.[35] There is no evidence that blacks ever ambushed the police or attempted to assassinate any officers, although there is much evidence that police believed that black militants were out to ambush them. Various militant groups have accused the police of attempting to murder their members.

In particular, the Black Panthers claim the existence of a nationwide plot to exterminate them.[36] Again, there is no evidence of such a plot. A charitable view of the evidence would lead one to conclude that some of the Panther deaths have been the result of trigger-happy police officers who shot and killed with no conceivable justification. A less charitable view would lead to the conclusion that several Panthers have been murdered by police officers. But there is probably no nationwide plot organized by the CIA or the federal government to exterminate the Black Panthers. Policemen everywhere view the Panthers as a threat to their personal safety and to the nation's security. They would not feel unhappy at the death of any Panther, and they are secure in the knowledge that they would never be prosecuted for shooting a Panther regardless of degree of suspiciousness of the circumstances (e.g., Chicago).[37] This is bound to create a "shoot-first-ask-questions-later" attitude.

Panthers know police feel this way. They also believe that police are out to murder them. They believe in self-defense. It is not unlikely that Panthers might start defending themselves even before the police start shooting. Police feel the same way about other black militants who return the feelings with interest. There is little question that the seventies will continue to see shoot-outs between black militants and police. Many more militants will die. Some policemen will die. It is possible that some policemen will be ambushed. A full-scale revolution is unlikely. Total genocide is also unlikely. Increasing amounts of direct, personal violence are not unlikely.

NOTES

1. This entire discussion is based upon the definition and analysis of social movement provided by Kurt Lang and Gladys Engel Lang, *Collective Dynamics* (New York: Thomas Y. Crowell, 1963), pp. 489–542.
2. The relatively small number of slaves per plantation was only one factor limiting slave rebellions. For a discussion of others, see Stanley M. Elkins, *Slavery* (Chicago: University of Chicago Press, 1959), pp. 81–139. Of course, many slave revolts did occur despite these conditions. See Herbert Aptheker, *American Negro Slave Revolts* (New York: Columbia University Press, 1945).
3. For a discussion of the impact of World War I upon black aspirations see Gunnar Mrydal, *An American Dilemma* (New York: Harper & Row, 1944), pp. 744–45.
4. Ibid., pp. 746–49.
5. For an account of black protest in World War II see Herbert Garfinkle, *When Negroes March* (Glencoe: The Free Press, 1959), pp. 31–34.
6. A good description of the growth of the "Nation" is provided by E. U. Essien-Udom, *Black Nationalism* (New York: Dell Publishing Co., 1962), pp. 76–94.
7. Blacks are more urban than whites; cf., Louis E. Lomax, *The Negro Revolt* (New York: New American Library, 1962), p. 80. For a discussion of segregation in urban areas see Karl E. Tauber and Alma F. Tauber, *Negroes in Cities* (New York: Atheneum, 1965).
8. Lomax, *Negro Revolt*, pp. 92–111, 133–43.
9. This repugnance is directed at the refusal to defend oneself, not at the action aimed at bringing about change. Marx found a lower level of conventional militancy among low status persons. See Gary T. Marx, *Protest and Prejudice* (New York: Harper & Row, 1967), pp. 55–65.

10. See selection in Part II, Section 5.
11. See selection in Part II, Section 5.
12. See William Brink and Louis Harris, *Black and White* (New York: Simon & Schuster, 1966), pp. 100–16, 220–21.
13. See Part II, Section 3.
14. See Kenneth B. Clark, "The Civil Rights Movement: Momentum and Organization," Part II, Section 2.
15. Part II, Section 3.
16. See John Hope Franklin and Isidore Starr, eds., *The Negro in 20th Century America* (New York: Random House, 1967), pp. 185–258.
17. See Harold A. Nelson, "The Defenders," Part II, Section 2.
18. Consult the files of *The New York Times* from 1960 to 1964.
19. See Joyce Ladner, "What 'Black Power' Means to Negroes in Mississippi," Part III.
20. See Raymond S. Franklin, "The Political Economy of Black Power," and Robert Blauner, "Internal Colonialism and Ghetto Revolt," Part III.
21. This alliance is predicted in Norbert Wiley, "America's Unique Class Politics: The Interplay of the Labor, Credit and Commodity Markets," *American Sociological Review* 32 (August 1967): 529–41.
22. To date most of the white support for the black revolt has come from middle-class backgrounds. See Inge Powell Bell, *CORE and the Strategy of Non-Violence* (New York: Random House, 1968), pp. 65–70. However, the Wallace vote in the 1968 Presidential election indicates that the working class may be quite a distance from such an alliance. See Seymour M. Lipset and Earl Raab, "The Wallace Whitelash," *Trans-Action* 7 (December 1969): 23–35.
23. It is interesting in terms of the "police repression" thesis that John Sinclair of the Detroit group of White Panthers was arrested, convicted and sentenced to the rather heavy term of ten years for possessing marijuana. See *The Detroit News*, July 29, 1969.
24. See Helen Icken Safa, "The Case for Negro Separatism," *Urban Affairs Quarterly* 4 (September 1968): 45–63.
25. *Report of the National Advisory Commission on Civil Disorders* (New York: Bantam, 1968), pp. 201–2.
26. Thomas F. Pettigrew, "The Negro and Education: Problems and Proposals," in Irwin Katz and Patricia Gurin, eds., *Race and the Social Sciences* (New York: Basic Books, 1969), p. 50.
27. See Part IV, Section 2.
28. Harold M. Baron, "Black Powerlessness in Chicago," *Trans-Action* 6 (November 1968): 27–33.
29. The role of the police in precipitating incidents of ghetto disorders was discussed in the selections by Lang and Lang, and by Downes in Part IV.
30. See August Meier and Elliott Rudwick, "Black Violence in the Twentieth Century," Part IV, Section 5.
31. See Bayard Rustin, "The Watts 'Manifesto' and the McCone Report," *Commentary* 41 (March 1966): 29–35.
32. See Part IV, Section 3.
33. See Robert Blauner, "Internal Colonialism and Ghetto Revolt," Part III.
34. See James A. Geschwender, "Civil Rights Protest and Riots," Part IV, Section 1.
35. See Terry Ann Knopf, "Sniping—A New Pattern of Violence?" *Trans-Action* 47 (July-August 1969): 22–29.
36. See Christopher Chandler, "The Black Panther Killings in Chicago," *New Republic*, January 10, 1970, pp. 21–24.
37. Ibid.

Name Index

NOTE: *126 S* refers to author's selection, beginning on p. 126.

Subject Index